THE ORIGIN AND GROWTH

OF THE

ENGLISH CONSTITUTION

An Historical Treatise

IN WHICH IS DRAWN OUT, BY THE LIGHT OF THE MOST RECENT
RESEARCHES, THE GRADUAL DEVELOPMENT OF THE ENGLISH
CONSTITUTIONAL SYSTEM, AND THE GROWTH OUT OF
THAT SYSTEM OF THE FEDERAL REPUBLIC
OF THE UNITED STATES

By HANNIS TAYLOR, LL. D.

LATE MINISTER PLENIPOTENTIARY OF THE UNITED STATES TO SPAIN

IN TWO PARTS

PART II.

THE AFTER-GROWTH OF THE CONSTITUTION

"Tum Lælius, nunc fit illud Catonis certius, nec temporis unius, nec hominis esse constitutionem Reipublicæ." — CICERO.

"The new building has been raised upon the old groundwork; the institutions of one age have always been modelled and formed from those of the preceding, and their lineal descent has never been interrupted or disturbed." — PALGRAVE.

"And thus it comes to pass that Magna Carta, the Acts of the Long Parliament, the Declaration of Right, the Declaration of Independence, and the Constitution of 1787 constitute the record of an evolution." — BRANTLY.

"The Government of the United States is not the result of special creation, but of evolution." — FISKE.

BOSTON AND NEW YORK
HOUGHTON MIFFLIN COMPANY
LONDON: SAMPSON LOW, MARSTON & COMPANY (LIMITED)
The Riverside Press, Cambridge

ANALYTICAL TABLE OF CONTENTS.

BOOK IV.

THE YORK AND TUDOR MONARCHY.

CHAPTER I.

THE FOUNDERS, — EDWARD IV. AND HENRY VII.

CHAPTER II.

HENRY VIII. AND THE BREAK WITH ROME.

CHAPTER III.

EDWARD VI. AND THE ENGLISH REFORMATION.

CHAPTER IV.

MARY AND THE CATHOLIC REACTION.

CHAPTER V.

ELIZABETH AND THE FINAL SETTLEMENT.

BOOK V.

THE STUARTS AND THE PURITAN REVOLUTION OF 1640.

CHAPTER I.

JAMES I. AND THE CONSTITUTIONAL CONFLICT.

CHAPTER II.

CHARLES I. AND THE CONSTITUTIONAL CONFLICT.

CHAPTER III.

THE GREAT CIVIL WAR.

CHAPTER IV.

THE COMMONWEALTH AND PROTECTORATE.

BOOK VI.

THE RESTORATION AND THE REVOLUTION OF 1688.

CHAPTER I.

CHARLES II. AND THE RESTORED CONSTITUTION.

CHAPTER II.

JAMES II. AND THE ATTEMPT AT REACTION.

CHAPTER III.

WILLIAM AND MARY AND THE REVOLUTION-SETTLEMENT.

BOOK VII.

GROWTH OF THE MODERN MINISTERIAL SYSTEM.

CHAPTER I.

ITS PROGRESS DURING THE REIGNS OF GEORGE I. AND GEORGE II.

CHAPTER II.

CHAPTER III.

ITS PROGRESS DURING THE REIGNS OF WILLIAM IV. AND VICTORIA.

BOOK IV.

THE YORK AND TUDOR MONARCHY.

———•———

CHAPTER I.

THE FOUNDERS, — EDWARD IV. AND HENRY VII.

1. In the preceding volume the attempt was made to draw out, as one unbroken story, that marvellous process of change and of growth through which the English constitutional system passed during the period intervening between the Teutonic conquest and settlement of Britain and the end of the fifteenth century. The first step consisted of a somewhat careful examination of the primitive Teutonic system of local self-governing communities as originally established in Britain, — the next of the process through which those communities became bound up in the seven or eight larger aggregates generally known as the heptarchic kingdoms, finally united, after a prolonged and bitter internal struggle for supremacy, under the permanent sway of the royal house of Wessex. The Old-English Commonwealth which thus finally emerged as the product of a gradual process of aggregation was strongest in the cohesion and permanence of its local machinery, and weakest in the higher ranges of power, in its central or national organization. The national unity which grew up through the premature and imperfect concentration of powers around a single throne was continually strained and weakened by the counterforce of the provincial spirit, — a spirit which, at the critical moment, disabled the right arm of Harold and opened the way for the Norman Conquest. When the Norman came, he brought with him the cohesive force which in the insular system had been wanting. He reorganized the central powers of the state, and, upon the Old-English system of local self-gov-

Summary of the Contents of vol. i.

Old-English Commonwealth;

Norman Conquest;

erning communities as a substructure, he built up a system of
central administration as a superstructure, and out of the fusion
between the two has grown the modern constitution.   This

process of
fusion;

process of fusion involved no less than the adjustment of the
compact and despotic system embodied in the Norman *curia
regis* to the tenacious though less closely organized system
of Old-English local freedom embodied in the township, the
hundred, and the shire.   The Norman administrative system
was simply an incorporation of the new kingship to which the
Conquest had given birth, — a kingship which strove to concentrate all the great powers of the state in the person of the
sovereign, who acted ordinarily through his continual council,
from which emanated all the more important acts of government, whether administrative, legislative, judicial, fiscal, or
political.   The story has been told of how the grinding weight
of the feudal monarchy as thus organized was wantonly applied,
during the Norman and early Angevin reigns, to the oppression of all classes and conditions of men ; and how, under the
heel of the common oppression, the united nation, composed
both of English and Norman elements, finally awoke to a sense
of its oneness.   In the spirit of resistance thus aroused, the

struggle for
the char-
ters;

struggle for the charters had its birth, — a struggle in which
the contending forces were the new kingship, on the one hand,
and the nation marshalled in the ranks of the three estates,
on the other.   The history of the struggle was then continued down to the great day at Runnymede, when the monarchy and the three estates entered into a treaty or compact
which, without attempting to wipe out the permanent effects
of the Conquest as embodied in the system of central administration to which it had given birth, undertook to define how far
such system should be permitted to abridge the immemorial
freedom in the time to come.   The fact was then emphasized

treaty of
Runny-
mede;

that the great treaty of Runnymede marked the beginning, not
the end of a conflict ; that it embodied not a final statement of
concessions to the nation from the crown, but rather a definite
programme of reform, in which the nation resolved to perse-
vere until it should be finally accepted by the crown as an
irrevocable basis of government.   The full fruit of the treaty
of Runnymede was never finally secured to the nation until,
under the lines which it defined, a representative national

assembly, with power to supervise and control the entire
system of political administration, was organized out of the
ranks of the three estates, on the one hand, and a permanent
system of law courts, with power to control nearly the entire
system of legal administration, was organized out of the continual council, on the other.   The charters declared the rights   growth of
of the nation as against the crown ; the law courts and the   the law
                                                                   courts and
parliament ultimately secured their enforcement.   While the   the parlia-
                                                                   ment.
growth of the law courts gradually drew into fixed tribunals
the adjudication of the mass of judicial business which had
been originally dispatched by the king in council, the growth
of parliament gradually drew to the national assembly the virtual control of the legislative, taxative, fiscal, and political
business of the kingdom.   By this double process of subtraction was vastly reduced, during the three centuries that followed the Conquest, the sum of governmental power originally
vested in the monarchy as organized under the Norman and
early Angevin kings.

The completion of the Norman Conquest finally established   The rule or
throughout the realm the supremacy of the central govern-   supremacy
                                                            of law
ment ; the growth out of that government of a system of law
courts which everywhere enforced a uniform rule of law against
all classes and conditions of men finally established the principle generally known as the rule or supremacy of law, which
has ever been the special characteristic of the English constitutional system.   Henry II. really initiated the "rule of law,"[1]
when he instituted the policy which for the first time reduced
all classes of men to a state of legal equality under a uniform
judicial system.   This principle of the supremacy of law has
been so expanded as to embrace every officer of the crown,
from the prime minister down to a petty constable or tax col-
lector, all of whom are liable for damages in their personal
capacity for official acts done in excess of lawful authority,[2] —
a liability which cannot be diminished by the plea of obedience
to the commands of the sovereign.[3]   In the weighty words of

---

[1] See Stubbs, *Select Charters*, p. 21, and also *Const. Hist.*, vol. i. p. 284.

[2] As to the application of the princi-ple in particular cases, see *Mostyn* v. *Fabregas*, Cowp. 161 ; *Musgrave* v. *Pulido*, 5 App. Cas. 102 ; *Governor Wall's Case*, 28 St. Tr. 51 ; *Entick* v. *Carring-*ton, 19 St. Tr. 1030 ; *Phillips* v. *Eyre*, L. R. 42 B. 225 ; Dicey, *The Laws of the Const.*, pp. 173-190.

[3] The subordination of the sovereign himself to the law is well expressed in the old saw of the Courts, " La ley est le plus haute inheritance, que le roy

Lieber : " The guarantee of the supremacy of the law leads to a principle which, so far as I know, it has never been attempted to transplant from the soil inhabited by Anglican people, and which, nevertheless, has been, in our system of liberty, the natural production of a thorough government of law as contra-distinguished to a government of functionaries." [1] The presence of this principle, which renders every man, whatever his rank or office, subject to the ordinary law of the land as administered in the ordinary tribunals, has ever made impossible in the English legal system anything corresponding to the "administrative law" (*droit administratif* [2]) or to the "administrative tribunals" (*tribunaux administratifs*), of France, where the servants of the state have been to a great extent protected from the ordinary law of the land by being subject for their official acts only to a system of official law administered by official bodies. While the growth of the law courts and the centralization of justice thus finally established the rule or supremacy of law in England, the growth of the estate system finally established the sovereignty of parliament. These two overshadowing principles, — the supremacy of law and the sovereignty of parliament, — which dominate the English constitution, and which upon a superficial view appear to be antagonistic, really stand to each other in a very different relation. As Mr. Dicey has well expressed it : " The sovereignty of parliament, as contrasted with other forms of sovereign power, favors the supremacy of the law, whilst the predominance of rigid legality throughout our institutions evokes the exercise, and thus increases the authority, of parliamentary sovereignty." [3]

In the first chapter [4] devoted to the growth of parliament,

and the sovereignty of parliament, the dominant principles of the English constitution.

---

ad; car par la ley il même et toutes ses sujets sont rulés, et si la ley ne fuit, nul roi, et nul inheritance sera." — *Year-Books*, 19 Henry VI. See Gneist, *Englische Verwaltungsrecht*, vol. i. p. 454.

[1] *Civil Liberty and Self-Government*, p. 91.

[2] As to the character of that system of law, see Aucoc, *Conférences sur l'administration et le droit administratif* (3d ed.) ; Vivien, *Études Administratives* ; Bœuf, *Droit Administratif* (4th ed.). For a contrast of the rule of law

with *droit administratif*, see Dicey, *The Law of the Const.*, ch. xii., in which the repugnance of the latter to all English ideas is fully explained. Tocqueville was quick to recognize the absence of anything answering to *droit administratif* in the Constitution of the United States. See *Œuvres Complètes*, vii. p. 66.

[3] *Law of the Const.*, p. 334. See ch. xiii., entitled " Relation between parliamentary sovereignty and the rule of law."

[4] Vol. i. pp. 428–514.

the process was drawn out in some detail through which the When parliamentary sovereignty reached its full growth. assembly of estates during the fourteenth century — after drawing to itself the exclusive right to authorize taxation and legislation, to supervise and control the royal administration, and to impeach and punish ministers guilty of misconduct — reached the limit of its growth, when, in the presence of a great emergency, it not only deposed the ruling sovereign, but elected in his stead another member of the royal house whom it deemed more competent to govern. When, through the exercise of this ultimate power, parliament transferred the crown to the house of Lancaster, its sovereignty had reached its full growth. During the period of Lancastrian rule, no new powers are added; nothing, in fact, transpires during that period more important than the settlement of the forms of parliamentary procedure, and the assertion and definition of privileges which belong to parliament as a whole, or to the respective houses of which it is composed, or to its individual members.[1]

Foremost among the sovereign attributes which parliament Exclusive right of parliament to authorize taxation: thus drew to itself during the first period of its ascendency stands the exclusive right to authorize taxation, including both direct taxes and the customs revenue. In order that the difficult history of this all-important right may be kept steadily in view, an outline will be drawn of its development during the four centuries which intervene between the coming of William the Norman and the accession of the house of Tudor.[2] The fact has already been emphasized that William, as a national king, rigorously exacted, under the authority of the old system, every kind of revenue, ordinary and extraordinary, that had ever belonged to any of his English predecessors. In the early days of the Old-English commonwealth, taxation as now Old-English taxes understood did not exist ; the revenues out of which were maintained the royal state and dignity, the king derived from his private estates in land, from the use of the royal demesne, from certain dues in the nature of rents from the holders of folkland, from fines levied in the law courts to the king's use, from tolls, markets, and ports, from heriots assessed upon the estates of the king's special dependents, and from escheats

---

[1] Vol. i. pp. 518–535.
[2] In order to make this outline at all complete, I have been forced to repeat much that has been said already.

and forfeitures.[1] Not until the period of the last Danish invasion did it become necessary for the king and the witan to
impose a general tax for the public service, — the tax known
as the Danegeld, which was levied not only for the purpose of
buying off the invaders but also for the raising of fleets.[2]
With the imposition of the Danegeld, which was a land-tax
imposed upon the hide as a unit of assessment, the history of
English taxation really begins. It seems to be clear that after
the Conquest the Danegeld or land-tax assumed the form of
ordinary revenue, and was collected by the sheriffs as a part
of the ferm or farm of the shire.[3] In the case of the towns, to
which the reckoning by hides could not be applied, the Danegeld or hidage was probably compounded for, and such composition represents no doubt the later talliage.[4] In the ninth
year of Henry II. the Danegeld as such finally disappeared
from the Rolls, but only to reappear as aid or hidage, and in
the reign of Richard I. as carucage.[5] Under all these names
— whether as Danegeld, aid, or hidage, carcucage, or, in the
case of the towns, talliage — the Old-English land-tax, originally imposed by Æthelred on the hide, can be surely distinguished.

supple-
mented by
the new feu-
dal taxes;
The sum of fiscal rights which thus accrued to William as
a national king was greatly augmented in the reigns of his
successors by the feudal incidents which resulted from the
position of the king as supreme landlord. The conclusion is
now established that the development of military tenures in
England was gradual, and that the transition from the military
system by the thegn's service to the new system by knight-
service was also gradual. While William did not directly
introduce military tenures as afterwards understood, the effect
of his vast confiscations and regrants was to firmly establish
the principle that the king was the supreme landlord, and
that all lands were held by grant mediately or immediately of
him.[6] As soon, then, as the idea gained ground that the military
service due from the landowner was due to the king, not as

---

[1] Vol. i. p. 182.

[2] Vol. i. pp. 186, 187.

[3] See Dowell, *Hist. of Taxation*, vol.
i. ch. v., " Danegeld and carucage."

[4] Vol. i. pp. 293, 297. " The cities
and towns not within the scope of the
hidage paid by way of auxilium or

aid ; and these auxilia, at first irregu-
larly charged, changed in time to contributions corresponding to the Danegeld." — Dowell, *Hist. of Taxation*, vol.
i. p. 49.

[5] Vol. i. pp. 293, 294.

[6] Vol. i. pp. 232–239.

head of the state, but as lord, the conception of feudal tenure became complete. The new military service which thus arose out of the development of tenures brought about a departure from the old custom which imposed the equipment of one fully armed man upon every five hides of land. Finally the older system based upon the hide was gradually super-seded by a new division of the land into knights' fees, and by the fixing of the knight's fee to a particular amount of land. Under the new arrangement, which was certainly not completed before the reign of Henry II., the specific obligation was im-posed upon each knight's fee to furnish a fully armed horseman to serve at his own expense for forty days in the year.[1] This duty of military service was the substantive duty due from the tenant in chivalry to his lord; the lord's right to aids, reliefs, wardships, marriages, alienations, and escheats were mere incidents. Such was the general character of the revenue which accrued to the Norman kings as feudal lords, as an addition or supplement to the taxes and dues which came to them by virtue of the ancient constitution. In the fourth year of Henry II. a serious change was made in the feudal revenue by the institution of scutage or shield-money, a pecuniary compensation in lieu of military service. Those tenants of the crown who did not desire to go to the war against Toulouse were allowed to pay two marks on the knight's fee.[2]

The following summary may now be made: at this point in Henry's reign — leaving the receipts from the customs out of view — *all taxation fell upon the land*, and consisted (1) of the ancient customary dues, and the tax on the hide, survivals of the Old-English system, and (2) of the feudal incidents, and the scutage, or tax on the knight's fee, — products of the new system of military tenures. The two great burdens on land which thus stand prominently forth are the ancient tax on the hide, — whether known as aid, hidage, carucage, or, in case of the town, talliage, — and the new feudal tax on the knight's fee known as scutage. And here the vitally important fact must be kept steadily in view that the knight's fee superseded the hide as the unit of assessment only so far as the barons and knights were concerned. The two taxes affected two dis-tinct classes of landowners: the scutage was the tax assessed

hidage and scutage — the great land-taxes

---

[1] Vol. i. pp. 294–296.   [2] Vol. i. pp. 283, 284.

upon the lands of the tenants in chivalry; the hidage or carucage upon the lands of the freeholders.[1]   The tax last named,
when applied to the towns, bore the name of talliage. On great
occasions, under the general name of *auxilium,* both taxes
were sometimes raised at once; but as a general rule a year
in which a scutage was imposed upon the military tenants was
not marked by hidage, carucage, or talliage upon the freeholders.

gradually
superseded
by taxes
upon
personal
property;

   The process must next be drawn out through which the two
historically distinct land-taxes just described were gradually
superseded by a novel system of taxation based exclusively
upon personal property, — a new and tempting source of revenue which the growth of national prosperity consequent upon
Henry II.'s policy of order and reform rapidly brought into
existence.   The new method of taxation begins with the imposition by Henry in 1188 of the famous Saladin tithe of a tenth
of rent and movables on all except crusaders.[2]   The system
thus based upon the grant of fractional parts of movables,
which varied in the earlier grants from a fortieth [3] to a fourth,
continued in use about a century and a half, during which time
the ancient land-tax on the hide, whether known as hidage,
carucage, or talliage, and the new feudal tax on the knight's
fee known as scutage, and all other forms of direct taxation,
were gradually superseded by it.[4]   In 1224 carucage, the name
under which the ancient land-tax appeared in the reign of
Richard I., was granted for the last time;[5] in the records of
fines imposed for a failure to serve in the war against the Scots
in 1322 are found the last vestiges of scutage;[6] while after
the memorable events of 1332 talliage became obsolete.[7]   In
applying the new system to the taxation of movables, it finally

fifteenths
and tenths;

became the custom to grant a fifteenth from the counties outside demesne, and a tenth from cities, towns, and demesne.
Such was the form of the grant made in 1332, whose rigid enforcement gave rise to such complaints that in the grant of
another fifteenth and tenth in the next year power was given
to the commissioners to treat with all bound to pay the tax,

[1] Vol. i. p. 297.
[2] Vol. i. p. 298.
[3] The fortieth of 1232 produced
16,475 *l.* o *s.* 9 *d.*   See Stubbs, *Const.
Hist.*, vol. ii. p. 549.

[4] See Dowell, *History of Taxation,*
vol i. pp. 59–74, 85–126.
[5] Matt. Paris, *Hist. Mag.*, p. 322.
[6] See Dowell, vol. i. pp. 47, 48.
[7] Vol. i. pp. 487, 488, 490, 491.

and to settle upon a sum to be paid as a composition for the fifteenth and tenth, the tax payers in each township being required to assess and collect the amount agreed upon from the various contributors.[1]   After this memorable composition of 1334 a fifteenth and a tenth became a mere fiscal expression for the sum then agreed upon, which amounted to between £38,000 and £39,000.[2]   In that way, when a fifteenth and tenth was granted every county knew the amount to be raised for the fifteenth, and every city and borough the amount to be raised for the tenth.   When less than the whole sum was required, half a fifteenth and tenth was granted; and when a greater sum was required, it was granted under the name of two fifteenths and tenths, or as the case might be.   The new system as adjusted upon the basis of 1334 for a long time held its own against all attempts to supersede it by fresh devices.[3] A new departure was attempted when in 1377 the first poll tax was levied, which was succeeded by another in a graduated form in 1379, and by still another in 1380, the famous tax whose enforcement culminated in the Peasant revolt of the following year.[4]   So unsatisfactory did these expedients prove in practice that there was an immediate return to the old form of a fifteenth and tenth, which was continued down to the accession of the house of Tudor and long after that event.   So fixed did the idea become that taxes should be imposed in a stated sum, divisible among the various districts upon the basis of the composition of 1334, that the tax-payers came to regard it almost as a constitutional right to contribute in that manner.

The exclusive right of parliament to authorize the imposition of the direct taxes whose histories have now been briefly summarized was the final product of the idea that the tax-payer had the right to be consulted in some form before he was taxed.[5]   That idea was rapidly gaining ground at the beginning of the thirteenth century, the period during which was completely established throughout Europe the arrangement generally known as the estate system, which consisted of the

Marginal notes: memorable composition of 1334; unsuccessful attempt to levy poll taxes; right of tax-payer to assent to taxation;

[1] Vol. i. p. 491.
[2] Dowell, *History of Taxation*, vol. i. p. 87.
[3] "Upon the basis of this settlement of the fifteenth and tenth in 1334, direct taxation mainly proceeded from this date until it became the practice to add to the grant of fifteenths and tenths a general subsidy on land and goods." — Ibid., p. 87.
[4] Vol. i. p. 508.
[5] Ibid., p. 482.

division of a nation into the three classes or orders generally

its connection with the growth of national assemblies;

known as clergy, baronage, and commons.[1] The outcome of that system was that type of a national assembly in which each class or order appeared in person, or by representatives authorized to speak for those by whom they were sent. Not until late in the reign of Edward I. (1295) was such a central or national assembly finally built up in England with power to

separate negotiations with each estate as to taxation;

represent every class of tax-payers.[2] During the two centuries which intervene between the completion of the Conquest and that great event, the crown, in the absence of any better means, was compelled to negotiate separately with each of the three estates for its special contribution. The idea that the tax-payer had the right to be consulted before he was taxed reached no doubt its lowest point during the Norman reigns, from whose dim fiscal annals it is hard to determine whether taxes were imposed by mere edict of the sovereign, or with

tax-payer's right dimly recognized during Norman period;

the counsel and consent of the great feudal council composed of the lay and spiritual baronage. The theory that the nation was in some form consulted, even during the Norman period, is strengthened by two records which belong to the reign of Henry I. : in the one, the king describes "the aid which my barons gave me;" in the other, — the charter ordering the restoration of the local courts, — he speaks of summoning the county courts whenever his royal necessities should require it.[3] From these documents two important conclusions may be drawn : first, that whatever consultation took place with the baronage as to taxation occurred in the great council; second, that whatever consultation took place with the rest of the nation as incorporated in shires and towns took place in the

conflict with the baronage results in

county courts. The first serious dispute as to taxation which arose between the crown and the baronage grew out of the frequent demands which the former made upon the latter for the payment of scutage, after that moneyed compensation in lieu of military service was established by Henry II. at the rate of two marks on the knight's fee. During the reigns of Richard I. and John the demands for scutages became more and more frequent until, in the reign of the latter, they became almost

---

[1] As to the rise of the three estates, see vol. i. pp. 337–357.

[2] Ibid., pp. 466–469.

[3] Ibid., pp. 482, 483.

annual, and some of them at the increased rate of two and a
half marks.[1]   Under the pressure of such demands it was that
the baronage in their great struggle with John in 1215 exacted
from him articles 12 and 14 of the Great Charter, which pro- articles 12
vided that no scutage or aid, except the three regular feudal and 14 of
the Great
aids, should be imposed but by the common counsel of the Charter,
and finally
nation, and that such common counsel could only be taken in
in a national council duly summoned under writs regularly
issued.[2]   The fact that these vital clauses were invariably
omitted from all subsequent issues of the Great Charter tends
to show that the declaration of the baronage was premature,
— that for such an absolute assertion of the right of self-taxation the tax-payers themselves were hardly prepared.   Not
until eighty years after the issuance of the Great Charter did
the nation finally win, through the *Confirmatio Cartarum,* a the *Con-*
permanent constitutional guarantee that taxes should never be *firmatio*
Cartarum;
imposed by the unaided force of the royal authority.[3]

The grants made by the lay and spiritual baronage in the separate ne-
great council were absolutely binding only on themselves. gotiations
with clergy
Before contributions could be drawn from the inferior clergy, and com-
mons;
separate negotiations had first to be conducted with the arch-
deacons of each diocese representing the spiritual estate ; and
in like manner with the representatives of the commons in the
county courts.[4]   The agents intrusted by the Conqueror with
the collection of the taxes due from the local communities to
the crown were the sheriffs, who twice in each year accounted
to the Exchequer for the several kinds of revenue due from
their respective shires.   But as local disputes continually arose fiscal visits
out of that method of collection, it became necessary to send of justices
from the
detachments of officers from the Exchequer to settle its busi- Exchequer;
ness in each shire.   As early as the reign of Henry I. such
officers were frequently sent through the country to assess
the revenue, and in the reign of Henry II. this custom was
enforced with systematic regularity.[5]   These exchequer officers, while dealing with the shire communities, sat in the
county courts, and there debated "with the landowners the
number of hides for which they owe Danegeld, or the number

---

[1] As to the pressure of taxation under
Richard and John, see vol. i. pp. 358–
363, 374.
[2] Ibid., p. 387.

[3] Ibid., pp. 418–423.
[4] Ibid., p. 483.
[5] Ibid., pp. 316–319.

of knights' fees from which aids and reliefs are due; they likewise assess the towns, which are now becoming important contributors to the revenue." [1] The county courts which thus met the itinerant justices from the Exchequer were not only popular but representative assemblies, county parliaments in which the reeve and four men appeared as representatives from every township, and twelve burghers as representatives from each borough in the shire. [2] Into both the fiscal and judicial work of the shire election and representation entered as familiar principles, and both were constantly applied to the work of assessing and collecting the revenue. [3] There can be no doubt that representatives were first summoned from the shires to the great council as a mere matter of fiscal expediency. Instead of sending officers of the Exchequer down into the shires to there negotiate separately as to the amount each would give, it was found more convenient for each shire court to send representatives to the national council, armed with power to express its corporate assent to whatever tax the general voice might there impose. The transition was an easy and natural one. When John in 1213 summoned for the first time "the four discreet men" from each county to appear in the great council, he simply applied to national purposes a system of representation that had existed from the earliest times. "The four men and the reeve had from time immemorial represented the township in the shire-moot; now the four men and the sheriff represent the shire-moot in the national council." [4] The same general causes which brought about the appearance in parliament of the elected knights also brought about, at a somewhat later day, the appearance of the elected representatives from the borough communities. To Earl Simon's famous parliament of 1265 were summoned not only the two discreet knights from the shires, but also, for the first time in English history, two representatives from the cities and towns. Not, however, until the meeting of the model parliament of Edward I. in 1295 were the representatives from the boroughs recognized as an integral part of

(marginal notes)
election and representation in the shire courts;

representation in the national council a fiscal expedient;

first the shires;

then the towns represented.

Earl Simon's parliament of 1265;

Edward I.'s model parliament of 1295;

---

[1] *Select Charters*, p. 18. "The earlier method by which the king treated with the several local communities through his officers or through their own magistrates had been generally adopted until the reign of John." — Ibid., p. 460.

[2] Vol. i. p. 320.

[3] Ibid., p. 484.

[4] *Select Charters*, p. 287.

parliament; from that time their representation has been continuous, or nearly so.[1] In the parliament of 1295 the three estates appeared in person or by representatives : the lay and spiritual baronage represented themselves, the inferior clergy and the commons, each as an estate of the realm, appeared through their chosen representatives. Two years after the national assembly was thus constituted, the long struggle of the nation for the right to tax itself was closed at the end of the "Barons' War" by the *Confirmatio Cartarum*, wherein Edward I. was made to promise the clergy, the barons, and "all the commonalty of the land, that for no business, from henceforth will we take such manner of aids, tasks, nor prizes, but by the common assent of the realm, and for the common profit thereof, saving the ancient aids and prizes due and accustomed." Under that saving clause the crown attempted for a time to talliage the cities and towns upon the royal demesnes, without parliamentary authority; but after 1332 that effort was abandoned.[2] Thus before the close of the reign of Edward III. the exclusive right of parliament to authorize every form of direct taxation was fully and finally established, not only in principle but in practice. In that reign it was that even the right of each estate to assent separately in parliament to the quota of the general contribution to be borne by it passed out of view.[3] The financial proceedings which took place in the parliament of Edward I. in 1282–83 marked "the point of final transition from the system of local to that of central assent to taxation;"[4] the giving up by the estates in the reign of Edward III. of the right of separate assent in parliament finally transformed the older feudal taxes resting upon the theory of personal consent into the new national taxes resting upon the fact of general consent.[5]

While the principle was thus becoming settled that the crown could impose no kind of direct taxes — not even talliage upon ancient demesnes — without parliamentary author-

right of the nation to tax itself settled by Confirmatio Cartarum;

transitions from local to central assent, and from feudal to national taxation;

the customs revenue;

---

[1] Vol. i. pp. 465–469.
[2] Ibid., pp. 423, 487, 488.
[3] Ibid., p. 490.
[4] *Select Charters*, p. 460.
[5] "The time for merely granting special privileges by charter and for relying on occasional contributions from particular groups of tenants was now over, and the day had come when the strangely various elements of English population were at last organized into a body politic, and could thus simultaneously share in the advantages and in the burdens of government." — Cunningham, *Hist. of English Industry and Commerce*, vol. i. p. 242.

ity, the royal right to impose indirect taxes became subject to the same limitation. Although the historical origin of the customs is very obscure, their beginnings may be traced with reasonable certainty to the ancient right of the Old-English kings to impose a tax or toll directly upon each ship upon its entry into the harbor, as the equivalent from the merchant for the right to bring his goods into the realm and to trade under the king's protection.[1] It is likely that the duties on imports are thus older than those on exports, which did not become important until wool, skins, and leather became subjects of exportation. Whatever may have been the origin of the customs, it is clear that prior to the date of the Great Charter the levy of tolls at the ports had become customary at fixed amounts or rates.[2] To secure the foreign merchant against all additional exactions imposed by the king's officers, article 41 of the Great Charter, after denouncing the same as evil or unjust tolls, provided that merchants entering and leaving the realm should pay only the ancient and just customs.[3] The next memorable effort to limit the customs occurred in the reign of Edward I. after the export tax on wool and leather, the principal products of the kingdom, had become an important item in the royal revenue. After these tempting commodities had been for a long time subject to all kinds of irregular seizures and exactions, the export tax upon them was definitely settled upon a legal basis by the parliament of 1275, which gave to Edward a custom of half a mark on each sack of wool, three hundred woolfells, and a mark on the last of leather. As Edward's reign drew to a close, he departed from the settlement thus made by exacting from the merchants in 1294 an additional toll on wool, woolfells, and leather; and by the seizure of all the wool in their hands in 1297, in order to enforce a toll of 40 s. the sack. This last exaction led to the provision in the *Confirmatio Cartarum* which, after denouncing the new demand of 40 s. the sack on wool, provided that the royal right of taxing wool should not be exercised "without their common assent and good will; saving to us and our

its probable origin;

article 41 of the Great Charter;

---

[1] Vol. i. p. 299. As to the character of the evidence touching the existence of a customs revenue during the century and a half which follows the Conquest, see Hubert Hall, *A History of the Custom-Revenue of England*, pp. 56–59.

[2] Dowell, *History of Taxation*, p. 76.

[3] "Sine omnibus malis toltis, per antiquas et rectas consuetudines."

heirs the custom of wools, skins, and leather granted before by the commonalty aforesaid." A return was thus made to the tolls as fixed by the parliament of 1275, which were known henceforth as the great and ancient custom — *magna et antiqua custuma.*[1] In 1302 Edward made a final assault upon the foreign merchants by offering to commute his pris- age on wine (the right to take from each English or foreign wine ship one cask out of every ten) for a fixed duty or rate, provided they would agree to certain additional duties on wool and other goods. In view of certain advantages promised for their trade the foreign merchants accepted the offer and con- ceded the further duties, which came to be known as the new or small custom — *nova* or *parva custuma* — as opposed to the *magna et antiqua custuma* of 1275.[2] In the commuta- tion then made of prisage at the rate 2 *s.* the tun on wine we find the origin of butlerage or tonnage; in the tax of 3 *d.* on the pound value of all goods and merchandise not enumerated, exported and imported by the foreign merchants, we find the origin of poundage. When the attempt was made to induce the native merchants to assent to the new arrangement they refused,[3] and continued to pay prisage. "Such was the origin of (1) the ancient or great customs on wool, woolfells, and leather ; (2) the new or small customs payable, in addition to the ancient or great customs, by the foreign merchants; (3) prisage on wine imported by denizens; (4) butlerage or ton- nage on wine, payable in lieu of prisage by the foreign mer- chants ; and (5) the poundage on goods inwards and outwards, payable by the foreign merchants."[4] Early in the reign of Edward II. the new customs on wine and merchandise were declared illegal by the Ordainers, and their collection was sus- pended in 1311 ; but after the king's victory in 1322 they were promptly reëstablished. In the year which followed the acces- sion of Edward III. the customs, as reëstablished in 1322, were confirmed, and from that time they became a part of the per- manent revenue of the crown, and as such they received the sanction of parliament in the Statute of Staples, enacted in 1353.[5] To the permanent and ordinary revenue thus composed

Margin notes: great and ancient cus- tom of 1275; new or small cus- tom of 1302; origin of tonnage and poundage; summary; after 1322 the customs a part of the perma- nent rev- enue;

---

[1] Vol. i. p. 489.
[2] Ibid.
[3] To the colloquium held at York forty-two towns sent representatives.

[4] Dowell, *Hist. of Taxation*, vol. i. p. 81.
[5] Vol. i. p. 490.

of the "ancient customs" and of the "new or small customs" were added, during the reign of Edward III., three distinct and *additional subsidies;* separate kinds of customs revenue in the form of extraordinary subsidies granted by parliament to the king for the time being, as opposed to the crown in perpetuity. They consisted (1) of export duties on wool, skins, and leather, with a complementary duty on exported cloth; (2) of tonnage, an import duty on the tun of wine; and (3) of poundage, an ad valorem duty on goods *custom and subsidy regularly levied after the 23d of Edward III.;* not specially enumerated, exported, or imported.[1] "From the twenty-third year of Edward III. the custom and subsidy, levied as it was henceforth with scarcely any intermission, amounted on an average to some 33 per cent. in the case of denizens, and 40 per cent. in that of aliens, upon the gross value of the commodity."[2] When the new sources of customs *subsidies granted for life to Richard II., Henry V., and Henry VI.* revenue known as the subsidies were granted in 1397 to Richard II. for life, it was with the express proviso that the grant "should not be made a precedent in the time of his successors."[3] While in obedience to that principle no life grant of the subsidies was made to Henry IV., such grants were made to Henry V. in 1415,[4] and to Henry VI. in 1453.[5] Thus before the fall of the house of Lancaster parliament had definitely secured, in addition to its other sovereign attributes, the exclusive control of every form of direct or indirect taxation. With its powers and privileges thus organized and consolidated, it did appear as if in the assembly of estates the English nation had at last found a defender strong enough and constant enough to maintain its liberties against the monarchy in all the years of struggle and of change that were yet to come. And yet the fact remains that the parliamentary system, whose too rapid growth had resulted in a premature development, gave way when it was subjected for the first time to the crucial test in the storm and stress of civil war.

The fall of the house of Lancaster synchronizes with the collapse of the parliamentary system. While the parliament

---

[1] See Dowell, *Hist. of Taxation*, vol. i. p. 165.

[2] Hubert Hall, *Hist. of the Custom-Revenue*, p. 74.

[3] *Par. Rolls*, iii. 114, 368. In a prior renewal in 1381 a week was permitted to intervene, "lest the king by continual possession of the said subsidy might claim it of right and custom." — Ibid., 104.

[4] Ibid., v. 64.

[5] Ibid., v. 228, 229. Like grants were made to Richard III., to the Tudor sovereigns, and to James I. See Dowell, *Hist. of Taxation*, vol. i. pp. 172–177, 182.

did not then cease to exist, its authority, during a long period **Collapse of the immature parliamentary system;** of time, suffered a very serious diminution. With the accession of the house of York began that prolonged period of reaction which reached its highest point under the house of Tudor, during whose sway the monarchy, released from the fetters with which the patriots and statesmen of the thirteenth and fourteenth centuries had hedged it about, resumed in substance if not in form the exercise of that system of royal autocracy it had wielded before the charters were won. The emancipation of the monarchy from the restraints which the **emancipation of the monarchy by Edward IV.;** growth of the law courts and the parliament had put upon it was the work of Edward IV., the prime object of whose policy it was to restore to the crown all of the despotic powers originally wielded by the king in council. The short reign of Richard III., so far as constitutional history is concerned, is a mere episode. The real successor of Edward IV., in a constitutional sense, is Henry VII. The despotic policy which Edward founded was continued by Henry and his successors, by whom it was systematized and enforced as a permanent system of government. The tide of reaction which thus set **overthrow of parliamentary institutions on the continent;** in in England was but a part of a general tendency that characterized the politics of the sixteenth century. With the close of the Middle Ages every effort which had been made in the direction of representative government upon the continent of Europe was brought to an end. Then it was that the free constitutions of Castile and Aragon were overthrown by Charles V. and Philip II.; then it was that the States-General of France met for the last time (1614) before their final meeting (1789) upon the eve of the French Revolution. Such were the results of the formation in the French and Castilian monarchies of great military establishments — indispensable perhaps to their safety and dignity — without any new safeguards in favor of liberty.[1] With the accession of the house of York the English **character of the struggle in England;** national assembly fairly began that prolonged struggle with the growing despotism of the monarchical system which upon the Continent proved strong enough either to sweep away or to reduce to empty forms all parliamentary institutions for nearly

---

[1] Upon this whole subject, see Robertson's *Charles V.*, vol. iii. p. 434; Watson's *Philip II.*, vol. iii. p. 223; Prescott's *Philip II.*, first chapter of book vi.; *Sismondi*, vol. xiii. p. 342; Macaulay, *Hist. Eng.*, vol. i. pp. 46–48; Freeman, *Growth of the Eng. Const.*, p. 139.

two centuries.[1] In England, whose insular position obviated the
necessity for standing armies,[2] the monarchy, armed only with
moral force, never attempted to end the existence of the parliament.[3] The new system of absolutism reëstablished by the
house of York and perpetuated by that of Tudor did not aim
at the abolition of the older forms of legal and constitutional
life by which the monarchy had been fettered for more than a
century; it simply strove to extinguish forever the vital spirit
which in the better days had made them actual restraints upon
the royal authority.

Outline of
the policy
of Edward
IV.;

In the brief review heretofore made of the reign of Edward
IV.[4] the fact was emphasized that the causes which at his
accession led to the reëstablishment of the monarchy, and to
the suspension of the system of parliamentary life by which it
had been for so long a time held in bondage, must be found in
the processes of dissolution and decay which by that time had
not only undermined the corporate vitality of each of the three
estates, but had also dissolved that spirit of union and inter-
dependence which in the earlier days had bound them to each
other.   At the end of the civil war, the one political force that
seems to have survived, the one force that stood out above the
turbulence of the times with power to guarantee order, and
to insure protection to all classes and conditions of men, was
embodied in the royal authority.   To permanently emancipate
that authority from the control of the parliament, and at the
same time to so systematize and incorporate its powers as to
make it the one dominant and irresistible force in the state,
was the prime object of Edward's policy.   Without abolishing

---

[1] "In the fourth period, on the Continent, all efforts towards a representative system have failed or almost
entirely disappeared ; pure monarchy
prevails. . . . This epoch lasts from the
sixteenth century to the French Revolution." — Guizot, *Hist. Rep. Govt.*, p.
258. See also p. 15.

[2] Although Henry VII. at his accession appointed a body of fifty men,
known as yeomen of the guard, as a
necessary appendage to royalty (Hall,
p. 3), no such thing as a standing army
existed until the time of the Commonwealth, and not until after the French
Revolution and the Peninsular War did
the nation finally become reconciled to
its existence.

[3] Such a thing was threatened, however, by Charles I.; and Carleton,
speaking in the king's behalf, told the
house in 1626 : " In all Christian kingdoms you know that parliaments were
in use anciently until the monarchs began to know their own strength : and,
seeing the turbulent spirit of their parliaments, at length they by little and
little began to stand upon their prerogatives, and at last overthrew the
parliaments throughout Christendom,
except here only with us." He concluded by saying, " This is a misery beyond expression, and that which yet we
are free from."

[4] See vol. i. pp. 562–583.

the parliamentary system, without changing the outward form the royal authority becomes the dominant force in the state; of the system of legal administration, the York and Tudor monarchy was content to overawe both, to manipulate both, and to render both subservient to the despotic powers of the council in which the royal will was omnipotent. The vital its vital organ, the council; organ of the monarchy was the council, and the mainspring of the council was "the idea of an extraordinary dictatorial power residing in the king, which in any state crisis could thrust aside the self-imposed barriers, laws, and judicial constitution, and find a remedy by extraordinary measures, jurisdiction, and ordinances."[1] In that way the history of the council became the history of the monarchy. Although he subsequently hereditary right; sought recognition at the hands of parliament, Edward was careful at the outset of his reign to base his claim to the throne solely on the self-sustaining theory of hereditary right, —a right which he claimed the Lancastrian parliaments had no power either to break or set aside. Thus secured against dangers growing out of a purely parliamentary title, he was also careful to resort to every expedient to protect the monarchy against that most dangerous of all the restraining measures to which the parliamentary system had given birth, — the power of the estates to coerce the crown through the withholding of supplies. The most potent safeguard which Edward erected Edward's financial policy; against that danger was embodied in a policy of peace that remained almost unbroken during a period of a hundred and fifty years. While his exchequer was thus saved from the drain of war on the one hand, his coffers were filled on the other by sweeping bills of attainder, and by a grant of tonnage and poundage for life.[2] To these resources were added the proceeds of that most obnoxious form of royal taxation known as benevolences, the profits which the king derived from his ventures as a private trader, the fruits of numberless petty exactions drawn from the revival of dormant claims of the crown, and fines exacted for the breach of forgotten tenures.[3] Thus rendered independent of grants from the estates, the crown

---

[1] Gneist, *The Eng. Const.*, p. 452 (Ashworth's trans.).

[2] This grant was made after the battle of Hexham, *Par. Rolls*, v. 508.

[3] The enforcement of so many claims upon the part of the crown led to an increase in the number of its law offi- cers. Prior to the accession of Edward IV. the only law officer of the crown was the king's attorney. In Edward's first year Richard Fowler was made solicitor to the king, and in his eleventh William Hussey was appointed attorney-general in England, — the first to

infrequent
meetings of
parliament;
soon began to ignore the long established right of the nation to express its will, at least once a year, through a national council. During the quarter of a century of Yorkist rule the nation was but seven times called upon to elect a new parliament. While Edward was thus emancipating the monarchy from the financial restraints which the growth of the parliamentary system had put upon it, he was careful to impart a fresh force to the judicial powers of the council which the growth of the law courts, and the rise of the equitable jurisdiction of the chancellor, had contracted without exhausting.

the council
becomes an
engine of
tyranny.
During the reign of Henry VI. the turbulent local magnates, with their liveried retainers at their backs, had so far disturbed and overawed the local administration of justice that it became necessary to authorize the council by statute (31 Hen. VI. c. 2) to draw before it all persons and all causes that could not be dealt with in the ordinary tribunals. The honest effort thus made to strengthen the hands of the council, in order to make it the defender of order against anarchy, was followed in the reign of Edward IV. by a deliberate attempt to convert the council into an irresponsible engine of tyranny. Although a break in its records deprives us of the memorials of its daily transactions from 1460 to 1520,[1] it may be safely assumed from such facts as are accessible that from the accession of Edward IV. began that systematic and inquisitorial supervision upon the part of the council of all matters, great and small, public and private, which never ceased until the meeting of the Long Parliament.

Henry VII.
2. By his victory at Bosworth Henry VII., scarcely thirty years old, was brought face to face with the double task of founding a dynasty and of maturing and expanding the new monarchical system which Edward IV. had inaugurated. The difficulties which the undertaking involved can hardly be over-estimated. By the fate of a single battle an attainted exile and adventurer was suddenly transformed into a king with a claim to the crown too vague and shadowy for precise definition. Lord Bacon, in his famous history of Henry's reign, tells

---

bear that title. The words of his patent, which is still extant, are still inserted in the patent of the attorney-general: "Cum potestate deputanti clericos ac officiarios sub se in qualibet curiâ de

recordo." See Reeves, *Hist. of Eng. Law*, vol. iv. p. 151; Campbell, *Lives of the Chief Justices*, vol. i. p. 159.
[1] See Dicey, *The Privy Council*, p. 76.

us that "There were fallen to his lot, and concurrent in his his three-fold claim of title; person, three several titles to the imperial crown. The first, the title of the Lady Elizabeth, with whom, by precedent pact with the party that brought him in, he was to marry. The second, the ancient and long disputed title, both by plea and arms, of the house of Lancaster, to which he was inheritor in his own person. The third, the title of the sword of conquest, for that he came in by victory of battle, and that the king in possession was slain in the field." [1] Each one of these theories of right was, however, subject to a serious embarrassment. To base his claim to the crown upon his contemplated marriage with Elizabeth was to make to the hated and vanquished house of York the most humiliating of all acknowledgments. If he claimed as the heir of the house of Lancaster, the fact stood out that the legitimate male line of that house was extinct, — that its claim survived only in the bastard branch represented by the Beauforts, whose right to the succession had been cut off, impliedly if not expressly, by an act of parliament. And even with the house of Beaufort, Henry could only claim connection through one of its female descendants. [2] If he claimed by conquest, the danger was that the nation would be alarmed by the intimation that a general dispossession of the conquered might follow. [3] In the midst of such embarrassments Henry assumed the crown, and as soon as his his declaration of title in parliament; coronation was over, he summoned a parliament, to which he boldly announced, when the commons presented their speaker, that "he had come to the throne by just title of inheritance, and by the sure judgment of God, who had given him victory over his enemy in the field." To allay such apprehensions as the last statement would naturally excite, he added that all might "enjoy his rights and hereditaments, with the exception of such persons as in the present parliament should be punished for their offences against his royal majesty." [4] At this

---

[1] "Hist. of the Reign of Henry VII.," Bacon's *Works*, vol. i. p. 315.

[2] As to Henry's pedigree, see vol. i. p. 584.

[3] So great was the apprehension on that account that at a later day, while the bill for the settlement of the succession was pending before the lords, the chancellor assembled the judges in order to ascertain from them whether, if the bill were passed, it would have the effect "of resuming all the franchises and liberties of all manner of persons," as in the event of the acquisition of the crown by conquest. The judges replied that it would not. *Year-Book*, Term Hil. 1 Hen. VII. 25.

[4] *Rot. Parl.*, vi. 268. See also Lingard, vol. iii. p. 298.

stage of the proceedings a serious question arose, which led to
the declaration of an important principle of constitutional law.
In the preceding reign not only had Henry been attainted, but
more than half of the peers now summoned, as well as a large
number of those who composed the lower house. The suggestion was made that the attainder of the king could not be
reversed in the usual manner because while he was under the
ban he could not lawfully exercise any of the functions of roy-

the descent of the crown held to remove all effects of attainder; alty. In order to remove this difficulty from the path of legislation, the judges were assembled by Hussey, Chief Justice,
who induced them to agree that "the descent of the crown
of itself takes away all defects and disabilities arising from
attainder, and therefore that the act of attainder must be considered as already virtually reversed." [1] But when the proposition was made that the attainders of the members should be
treated as a nullity on the ground that Richard III., who had
assented to the act, was a usurper, the Chief Justice cautiously

attainders of subjects to be removed only by act of parliament; answered "that it would be of dangerous example to suffer
those who ought to observe a law to question the title of the
sovereign under whom the law had been enacted, and that the
attainted peers and commoners ought not to take their seats
in either house till their attainder had been reversed by a new
act of parliament assented to by the king who now is." [2]
When all legal incapacities were removed,[3] and parliament was

declaration of parliament as to Henry VII.'s title; brought face to face with the questions involved in Henry's
claims to the crown, they silently ignored both of his sugges-
tions as to inheritance and conquest, and simply declared that
"the inheritance of the crown should be, rest, and remain, and
abide in the most royal person of the then sovereign lord, king
Henry VII., and the heirs of his body lawfully coming perpetually with the grace of God so to endure, and in none other." [4]
In other words, the estates refused to recognize in the new
aspirant, who claimed to represent the house of Lancaster,

---

[1] *Year-Book*, Term Mich. 1 Hen. VII.
5. "But nevertheless, for honour's
sake, it was ordained by parliament,
that all records, wherein there was any
memory or mention of the king's attainder, should be defaced, cancelled, and
taken off the file." — "Hist. of Henry
VII.," Bacon's *Works*, vol. i. p. 318.

[2] As to the whole transaction, see

Hussey's life in Campbell's *Lives of the
Chief Justices*, vol. i. p. 162.

[3] *Rot. Parl.*, vi. pp. 273, 278, 280–287.

[4] Ibid., vi. p. 270; 1 Hen. VII. c. 1.
Of this act. Hallam (*Const. Hist.*, vol.
i. p. 8) says: "Words studiously ambiguous, which, while they avoid the assertion of an hereditary right that the
public voice repelled, were meant to
create a parliamentary title."

any higher title to the crown than that under which that house
had originally come into possession of it, namely a parliamentary title.   Not until Henry had thus received alone the highest sanction that the nation could give, was he willing to
hearken to the request of the commons to "take to wife and commons
urge his
consort the princess Elizabeth," [1] who was not mentioned in marriage
the act of settlement, and whose coronation he delayed for with Eliza-
beth of
nearly two years.   But neither the solemn sanction of parlia- York;
ment nor his marriage with the heiress of the house of York
gave to the new king peaceful possession of the royal authority.   During a period of nearly thirteen years Henry was
harassed in turn by two pretenders, the histories of whose
exploits constitute a striking illustration of the folly and cre-
dulity of mankind.   Not until the executions in the fall of
1499 of Perkin Warbeck and of Edward Plantagenet, earl of
Warwick, were the last dangers removed which could menace
the peace of the realm and the title of the house of Tudor.
During the latter part of this period of revolt, rebellion, and
uncertainty a natural sense of apprehension brought about
the enactment of a statute which is generally regarded as one
of the most important of the reign.   The act of 11 Henry Act (11
VII. c. 1 provides that "no person attending upon the king Hen. VII.
c. 1) for the
and sovereign lord of this land *for the time being*, and doing security of
the subject
him true and faithful service, shall be convicted of high trea- under a
son by act of parliament or other process of law, nor suffer king *de*
facto.
any forfeiture or punishment; but that every act made con-
trary to this statute shall be void and of no effect." [2]   It is
strange that an act so wisely designed to strengthen Henry's
hold upon the crown should have been characterized by Bacon
as "rather just than legal; and more magnanimous than
provident."

3. The last mentioned act for the security of the subject The court
of star
under a king *de facto* is surpassed in importance only by the chamber:
famous statute, enacted at a much earlier day, to which is
usually traced that abnormal development of the criminal

---

[1] *Rot. Parl.*, vi. p. 278.   The separate
Statute Rolls, which end with 9 Hen.
VII., are merged, after 12 Hen. VII.,
in the *Rotuli Parliamentorum*.   After
4 Hen. VII. the records of statutes are
exclusively in the English language.
[2] As to the inability of this act to

bind future parliaments, Bacon says:
"For a supreme and absolute power
cannot conclude itself, neither can that
which is in nature revocable be made
fixed." — "Hist. of Henry VII.," Bacon's *Works*, vol. i. p. 256.

jurisdiction of the council generally known as the court of star chamber. The fact has been heretofore emphasized that the undefined judicial powers of the king in council were not exhausted by the growth out of that body of the great courts

original jurisdiction of the king in council; of law and equity.[1] "The judicial supremacy of the king is not limited or fettered by the new rule, . . . the old nucleus of light remains unimpaired." [2] After the organization of the four great courts at Westminster the council still retained a residuary jurisdiction, both civil and criminal, original and

the council as a court in the days of Henry III.; appellate. "It seems," says Sir Francis Palgrave, "that in the reign of Henry III. the Council was considered as a court of peers within the terms of Magna Carta ; and before which, as a court of original jurisdiction, the rights of tenants holding *in capite*, or by barony, were to be discussed or decided ; and it unquestionably exercised a direct jurisdiction over all other of the king's subjects." [3] The tendency of this unlimited and undefined jurisdiction of the council, which Bacon says "subsisted by the ancient common laws of the realm," [4] was to encroach upon the inferior tribunals, and such encroachment

jurisdiction of the council first narrowed, then widened by statute; led to the enactment of a series of restraining statutes, which extend from the reign of Edward I. to that of Henry IV. With the reign of Henry VI. a new legislative policy begins, whose aim was not to narrow the criminal jurisdiction of the council, but to give to it wider expansion. When, in the latter part of that reign, the ordinary administration of law gave way under the strain which the turbulence of the times put upon it, parliament authorized the council to draw before it all persons and all causes that could not be dealt with in the ordinary tribunals.[5] When the turbulence, the lawlessness, the uncertainty, which existed at the beginning of Henry VII.'s reign are taken into account ; when the fact is remembered that the evils of livery and maintenance were still in full vigor to hinder the local administration of existing laws, it is not hard to understand why the extraordinary criminal jurisdiction of the council, which Edward IV. had abused, should have been again invoked, as in the days of Henry VI., in the interest of order against anarchy. That such was the motive of the

[1] See vol. i. pp. 249–252.
[2] Stubbs, *Const. Hist.*, vol. i. p. 603.
[3] *Essay on the Original Authority of the King's Council*, p. 34.

[4] "Hist. of Henry VII.," Bacon's *Works*, vol. i. p. 332.
[5] See vol. i. p. 580, and p. 516, note 2.

famous act of 3 Henry VII. c. 1, is clearly revealed by its
terms : "The king our said sovereign lord remembering how
by unlawful maintenance, giving of liveries, signs, and tokens,
and retainders by indentures, promises, oaths, writings, or
otherwise embraceries of his subjects, untrue demeanings of
sheriffs in making of panels and other untrue returns, by
taking of money by juries, by great riots and unlawful assemblies, the policy and good rule of this realm is almost sub-
dued, and for the not punishing of these inconveniences, and
by reason of the premises, little or nothing can be found by
inquiry [*i. e.,* by jury trial]. . . . Therefore it is ordained for
reformation of the premises by authority of said parliament,
that the chancellor and treasurer of England for the time
being, and keeper of the king's privy seal, or two of them,
calling to them a bishop and a temporal lord of the king's
most honorable council, and the two chief justices of the king's
bench and common pleas for the time being, . . . have authority to call before them by writ or by privy seal the said mis-
doers, and them and other by their discretion, by whom the
truth may be known, to examine, and such as they find therein
defective to punish them after their demerits." In the midst
of all the doubt and difficulty which learned refinement has
thrown around the meaning and purport of this act, it is safest
to assume that it was not intended to create a new tribunal, or
even to vest in the council a fresh jurisdiction.[1] The soundest
of the modern critics agree in the conclusion that it was only
intended to invigorate and emphasize by parliamentary sanction the ancient prerogative criminal jurisdiction of the crown,
which, as early as the reign of Edward III., we hear of the
"chancellor, treasurer, justices, and others" exercising in the
"*chambre des estoiles*" at Westminster. The intention of Henry's statute must have been simply to revivify and define this
ancient jurisdiction, and at the same time to commit its exercise as a special duty to a committee of the council composed

*Act of 3
Hen. VII.
c. 1, reviv-
ing and
defining
the crim-
inal juris-
diction of
the council;*

*such juris-
diction
vested in a
special com-
mittee;*

[1] For the older literature touching
the history of the star chamber, see
Hudson's "Treatise on the Star Cham-
ber," in *Collectanea Juridica,* vol. ii. ;
Sir Thomas Smith, *Commonwealth of
Eng.,* bk. iii. cap. 1 ; "Hist. of Henry
VII.," Bacon's *Works,* vol. i. p. 334 ;
Hale's *Jurisdiction of the House of
Lords,* c. v. For the modern literature
on the subject, see Reeves' *Hist. Eng.
Law,* vol. iv. pp. 205-212 ; Palgrave's
"Essay on the Original Authority of
the King's Council," Hallam's *Const.
Hist.,* vol. i. pp. 48-56 ; Sir J. F. Ste-
phen, *Hist. of the Crim. Law of Eng.,*
vol. i. pp. 166-184 ; Dicey, *The Privy
Council,* pp. 94-115 ; Gneist, *Hist. of the
Eng. Const.,* pp. 504-513.

Lord Bacon's views as to the same;

of those specially named in the act.[1] Of the special tribunal thus organized Lord Bacon writes : "And as the chancery had the pretorian power for equity, so the star chamber had the censorian power for offences under the degree of capital. This court of star chamber is composed of good elements, for it consisteth of four kinds of persons, councillors, peers, prelates, and chief judges. It discerneth also principally by four kinds of causes, forces, frauds, crimes various of stellionate, and the inchoation, or middle acts towards crimes capital or heinous, not actually committed or perpetrated."[2] As the elastic jurisdiction of the chancellor grew and widened in civil matters so as to meet the ever expanding wants of litigants, so the extraordinary jurisdiction of the council in criminal matters so widened as to meet the endless demands of despotic authority.[3] This tendency to expansion finally brought about two important departures from the condition in which we find the criminal jurisdiction of the council after its invigoration by the act to which special reference has

powers of the special committee fall back to the general body of the council;

been made. The powers of the special committee or court which was organized under the act of 3 Henry VII. c. 1, and which maintained a separate existence for about fifty years, fell back towards the close of the reign of Henry VIII. to the general body of the council. The act of 31 Henry VIII., which gave to the royal proclamations the force of law, provided that offenders against them might be punished by the ordinary members of the council, together with certain bishops and judges, "in the star chamber or elsewhere." While the "censorian" powers of the special committee were thus falling back to the main body of the council itself, those powers were themselves expanding far beyond the statutory limits which

such powers expand far beyond the limits of the act of 3 Hen. VII. c. 1;

had been originally assigned them. When it became convenient for the Tudor despotism to extend the criminal jurisdiction of the council over offences not named in the act of 3 Henry VII. c. 1, cognizance of them was simply assumed, and those who presumed to contend that the jurisdiction was

---

[1] "This was held to be not so much a novelty as a parliamentary recognition of an ancient authority inherent in the privy council." — Moberly, *The Early Tudors*, p. 71.

[2] "Hist. of Henry VII.," Bacon's *Works*, vol. i. p. 333.

[3] "The king only announces that, owing to the necessities of the times, he intends to exercise his criminal jurisdiction, and delegates for this purpose a small number of privy councillors, with the assistance of two judges." — Gneist, *Eng. Const.*, p. 505.

limited by the act were not only ignored, but sharply reprimanded.[1]   Thus it appears that the court of star chamber as the court in
finally organized was nothing more nor less than the whole its final
form the
council sitting judicially; and its jurisdiction as then exercised whole coun-
was practically unlimited. "It is now no question of what cil sitting
judicially;
it had a right to do, but of what it did."[2]   In its procedure outline of
it disregarded the common law, it dispensed with trial by its pro-
cedure.
jury, it accepted report in lieu of the testimony of witnesses,
it employed torture, and it could pronounce any judgment
short of that of death.[3]   Such an institution, although it may
have been well employed in the early Tudor days for the suppression of anarchy and the maintenance of order, finally
proved itself to be equally efficient as an engine of tyranny,
which forced alike the peasant and the noble, the law courts
and the parliament, to crouch at the feet of its supreme and
irresistible authority.[4]

4. While under the York and early Tudor monarchy the Henry VII.
council was being abnormally developed into the vital organ and parlia-
ment:
of the state,[5] its natural antagonist, the parliament, whose
place it had to a great extent usurped, was languishing under
causes of disintegration and decay to which its constitution
had yielded in the last days of the Lancastrian kings.   As causes
heretofore explained, the restriction of the suffrage had checked which led to
its decline
the growing strength of the house of commons, while the prior to his
accession;
decay of the feudal organization of the baronage and the
weakness of the prelacy broke that of the house of lords.   To

---

[1] "Lord Chancellor Egerton would often tell that in his time, when he was a student, Mr. Serjeant Lovelace put his hand to a demurrer in this court for that the matter of the bill contained other matters than were mentioned in the statute 3 Hen. 7, and Mr. Plowden, that great lawyer, put his hand thereto first, whereupon Mr. Lovelace easily followed. But the cause being moved in court, Mr. Lovelace being a young man, was called to answer the error of his ancient Mr. Plowden, who very discreetly made his excuse at the bar that Mr. Plowden's hand was first unto it, and that he supposed he might in anything follow St. Augustine. And although it were then overruled, yet Mr. Serjeant Richardson, thirty years after, fell again upon the same rock, and was sharply rebuked for the same."

— Hudson, *Collectanea Juridica*, vol. ii. p. 80.

[2] Dicey, *The Privy Council*, p. 105.

[3] For an outline of its procedure, see Ibid., pp. 100–116. Hudson's essay in the *Collectanea Juridica* describes in detail the powers and procedure of the court as it appeared in the days of James I. While its decrees seem to have been lost, the pleadings in the star chamber are in the Record Office.

[4] "The Council stands forth, as at the same moment, powerless and powerful. In its dealings with the crown it is utterly weak, for it has lost every element of independence. In its dealings with the people it is irresistibly strong, for it combines every element of authority." — Dicey, *The Privy Council*, p. 117.

[5] See vol. i. pp. 562–576.

the history of the combined action of these causes, which
made possible the emancipation of the monarchy at the accession of Edward IV., we must look for a full explanation of the
almost entire suspension of parliamentary life which charac-
terizes the politics of the sixteenth century, rather than to the
incomplete and inaccurate statement which attributes such
suspension to the assumptions that the older nobility had been
to a great extent cut off in the Wars of the Roses, and that
the commons had not yet grown sufficiently strong and self-
reliant to act alone. The truth is that the decline of the
baronage, which began in the days of the Edwards, progressed
so rapidly under the Lancasters that, after the battle of Agin-
court, the number of temporal peers touched its lowest point,
— from that time to the accession of the Tudors they numbered but fifty-two. Only two of the great baronial houses —
Beaufort and Tiptoft — became extinct for the want of heirs
during the civil war, and the reason why only twenty-seven
lay peers met Henry VII. in his first parliament is explained
by the fact that he failed to summon twenty-five more upon
whose fidelity he could not rely.[1] The decay of the baronage,
which had been gradually brought about by the wreck of feudalism, the extinction of the greater families, and the breaking
up of great estates, Henry showed no disposition to check or
repair.[2] His coronation was attended with only three creations,
and the new nobility which grew up under him and his successors was composed of new men, creatures of royal favor, who
assumed the rôle rather of courtiers than of parliamentary
barons. Such of the older nobles as the Percies, the Nevilles,
and the Howards were held in check by the advancement of
men like Morton, Fox, Wolsey, Cromwell, Cecil, Bacon, and
Walsingham. As Bacon himself has told us : " Henry VII.
kept a strait hand on his nobility, and chose rather to advance
clergymen and lawyers, which were more obsequious to him,
but had less interest in the people," [3] — a policy which was

*only two of
the great
baronial
houses
became
extinct
in the
civil war;*

*Henry
made no
effort to
check the
decline
of the
baronage;*

*dependent
character of
the new
nobility;*

[1] See Green, *Hist. of the Eng. People*,
vol. ii. pp. 13–15 ; Moberly, *The Early
Tudors*, p. 27.

[2] " The aggregate number of the
newly created peerages, as well as of
those advanced in rank, is given as
follows : under Henry VII., twenty ;
under Henry VIII., sixty-six ; under
Edward VI., twenty-two ; under Mary,
nine ; and under Elizabeth, twenty-

nine. The Tudors restricted their creations, with scarcely an exception, to
the old knightly families. Only once
did the aggregate of the temporal peers
under the Tudors reach the number of
sixty." — Gneist, *Hist. of the Eng.
Const.*, p. 473.

[3] " Hist. of Henry VII.," Bacon's
Works, vol. i. p. 383.

pursued both by Henry VIII. and Elizabeth. The policy of Henry VII. towards the parliament as a whole was simply a repetition of that of Edward IV. Like Edward, Henry was willing to summon parliament only on rare and critical occasions, when it was necessary to draw strength from its authority or revenue from its bounty. Like Edward, Henry looked to parliament for a recognition of his title, for a grant of tonnage and poundage for life, and for bills of attainder from which he could enrich himself from the spoils of his enemies. Strengthened by such a beginning, it seemed to be the prime object of his policy to render himself independent of parliament, by reducing to the smallest possible limit his expenditures, on the one hand, and by increasing his revenues, on the other, by the enforcement of all kinds of obsolete feudal forfeitures and amercements, and by a revival of that odious form of royal taxation known as benevolences.[1] The exchequer was greatly enriched at one time from the source last named through the enforcement of an argument called "Morton's fork," invented by the archbishop of that name, who maintained that those who lived handsomely should give liberally because their wealth was manifest, and that those who lived plainly should be even more liberal because it was certain that economy had made them opulent. More odious even than these forced contributions were the fines and other obsolete feudal exactions which the king, in imitation of Edward IV., mercilessly enforced through two infamous agents, Empson and Dudley, who practiced all kinds of oppressions and illegalities, and who robbed every class in order to enrich the king, and who robbed the king in order to enrich themselves. Such a financial policy, although it deeply stained Henry's memory, brought to him the independence of parliament which he designed to secure. During the twenty-four years of his rule he summoned parliament only seven times, and nearly all of these meetings

Marginal notes:
Henry's parliamentary policy a repetition of that of Edward IV.;

his financial policy;

benevolences;

Morton's fork;

revival of obsolete feudal exactions, Empson and Dudley;

parliament summoned only seven times during the reign;

---

[1] In 1490 and in 1497, when general subsidies (one of a novel character) were levied upon the nation, serious insurrections occurred; the first in the north, and the last in Cornwall, which was suppressed only after great bloodshed. See Lingard, vol. iii. pp. 314, 324. In order to remove the irritation thus produced by the pressure of general taxation, Henry seems to have resorted, with the aid of "Morton's fork," to the system of benevolences under which the burden of taxation fell mainly upon the wealthier classes. Benevolences were abolished in the parliament of Richard III., but Richard himself had ignored the statute the moment that invasion was threatened. Vol. i. p. 588. Upon the whole subject, see Dowell, *Hist. of Taxation*, vol. i. pp. 127-129, 200.

were called in the first half of the reign.   During his last
thirteen years, parliament was summoned only once.[1]   At his

the king's
hoard.

death the king's hoarded treasure is said to have amounted to
nearly two millions of pounds.

Henry's
legislation;

5. A careful review of the legislation of Henry VII. will
hardly sustain the eulogy of Lord Bacon, who has pronounced
him to be "the best lawgiver to this nation since Edward I."
Henry's laws seemed to have been designed, not so much as
Bacon says, "out of providence for the future, to make the
estate of his people still more and more happy, after the man-

its leading
purpose to
provide im-
mediate
remedies
for pressing
evils ;

ner of the legislators in ancient and heroical times," as from
a desire to provide immediate remedies for the lawlessness
and disorder which remained as the natural legacy of the civil
war.   To restore peace, order, and confidence to the realm,
by strengthening the royal authority, and by providing new
expedients for the enforcement of existing laws, seems to have

his two
great stat-
utes,— the
one to
secure the
subject
under a
king *de*
facto ; the
other to
strengthen
the criminal
jurisdic-
tion of the
council ;

been the leading motive of Henry's legislation.   To quiet the
minds of such as might doubt the stability of his title, he enacted the statute for the protection of the subject who served
a king *de facto ;* to crush the expiring system of livery and
maintenance, as well as the riots and disorders which disturbed
the local administration of justice, he enacted the statute which
so greatly invigorated the criminal jurisdiction of the council as exercised in the star chamber.   With the same general
design were passed the acts which provided for the punishment of vagrants, and of those who attempted to enrich themselves by the stealing of women of fortune.[2]   In this connec-

the act in-
creasing the
authority of
justices of
the peace ;

tion may be noted the act (3 Hen. VII. c. 3) which gave
authority to justices of the peace to take bail of felons under
conditions which finally led to their being charged with the
duty of making preliminary investigations in all criminal cases.[3]
The most notable act of the reign touching private right is

Statute of
Fines ;

the act of 4 Hen. VII. c. 24, known as the Statute of Fines,
which Henry was at one time supposed to have enacted with
the subtle design of completing the ruin of the aristocracy by
enlarging their power to alienate their entailed estates.   This
misconception of motive, which seems to have been borrowed

[1] The last parliament called was that
of 1504.

[2] See Reeves' *Hist. Eng. Law*, vol.
iv. pp. 181, 202.

[3] See Gneist, *Hist. of the Eng. Const.*,
p. 466; Stephen, *Hist. of the Crim.
Law of Eng.*, vol. i. pp. 236, 237.

from Bacon by Hume, has now given way before the fact that
the act in question was a mere transcript of another to the
same effect passed in the reign of Richard III. The modern
view is that the act last named was reënacted in Henry's reign
not to give to the tenant in tail a greater power to alienate his
estate, but by establishing a short term of prescription to put
a check upon the large number of suits for the possession of
land which sprang up after the civil war.[1]

No reference to Henry's legislation, however brief, should
omit the fact that, in the hope of developing English shipping, he enacted a navigation law,[2] which provided that traders
with Gascony should import their wine and woad only in English vessels manned by English seamen, when such could be
obtained. To the legislation of Edward I. can be traced the
beginnings of that system of national regulation designed for
the protection of native as opposed to foreign interests, which
appears as a definitely organized scheme of public economy in
the time of Elizabeth.[3] This protective system which was
gradually developed in the interests of industry, agriculture,
commerce, and manufactures was first extended to English
shipping by the navigation act of Richard II., which provided
that " to increase the navy of England which is now greatly
diminished, it is assented and accorded, that none of the king's
liege people do from henceforth ship any merchandise in going
out or coming within the realm of England, in any port, but
only in ships of the king's liegance." [4] The navigation policy
thus inaugurated by Richard, and neglected by the kings of
the house of Lancaster,[5] was not revived until the reign of
Edward IV., when an act [6] was passed which seems to have
expired at the end of three years. The next navigation act

*Henry's
navigation
act;*

*protective
policy be-
gins with
the legisla-
tion of Ed-
ward I.;*

*first navi-
gation act
that of
Richard II.;*

---

[1] See Reeves' *Hist. Eng. Law*, vol.
iii. pp. 373, 374, and notes (Finlason
ed.). Reeves' views are restated and
approved by Hallam, *Const. Hist.*, vol.
i. pp. 11–13 and notes.

[2] 1 Hen. VII. c. 8 ; 4 Hen. VII. c. 10.
See " Hist. of Henry VII.," Bacon's
Works, vol. i. p. 336.

[3] It is a pleasure to be able to refer,
in this connection, to the great work
of Cunningham, *Growth of English Industry and Commerce*, vol. i. pp. 243–
246.

[4] 5 Rich. II. i. c. 3. This act was

modified some years later by 6 Rich.
II. i. c. 8 ; 14 Rich. II. c. 6. As to the
original act see Chalmers' *Political
Annals*, p. 251, and also "The Tariff
Controversy in the U. S." *Stanford
Univ. Monographs*, No. 1, p. 9.

[5] Henry IV. failed to enforce the
navigation policy of Richard, and no
navigation acts were passed under
Henry V. or Henry VII. Schanz, *Han-
delspolitik*, vol. i. p. 363; Cunningham,
Industry and Commerce, vol. i. p. 370
and notes.

[6] 3 Edw. IV. c. 1.

was that passed in the first year of Henry VII. Although Henry may have been too parsimonious to lead in the work of discovery,[1] he was too wise not to see that a great change was at hand, a change destined soon to revolutionize the commerce of the world, and to lay the foundations for the great international trade of modern times. That he was infected with the spirit of maritime adventure, which was the leading feature of the age, can hardly be doubted, when we find him in 1496 issuing to the Genoese navigator, John Cabot, long a resident of Bristol,[2] that famous patent,[3] the oldest surviving document connecting the old land with the new, under which was made the first of those discoveries that became the basis of England's title to the soil of the New World.

Henry's patents to the Cabots.

6. Just as the long night of political reaction, which was coextensive with the supremacy of the York and Tudor monarchy, began to settle down like a blight upon the growth of the English constitution, the dawn of the Renaissance began to break upon the life of the English people. While Edward IV. and Henry VII. were fastening upon the island kingdom that system of absolutism which had begun to prevail throughout the continental nations, the main body of the people were beginning to be stirred by the spirit of that new and marvellous era of national awakening generally known as the English Renaissance, — a term which must not be confined to the mere revival of learning, but so expanded as to embrace the whole process of mental and material development which brought to the English people its new conceptions of philosophy and religion, its new understanding of government and law, its reawakened interest in the arts and sciences, its new-born activity in commerce and manufacture, as well as that spirit of discovery and adventure that widened its destiny through conquest and colonization in another hemisphere. During the period in which Edward IV. was overawing the law courts and trampling upon the parliament, the "shining seed-points of light,"

The English Renaissance;

---

[1] In 1488 Bartholomew Columbus came to Henry's court and sought in vain his patronage for his brother Christopher. See *Nar. and Crit. Hist.* (Winsor), vol. ii. p. 102; Peschel, 112.

[2] See vol. i. p. 17 and note 4. In the patents granted to the Cabots it was provided that whatever commerce resulted from their discoveries should be brought to England.

[3] In 1480 two ships set out from Bristol in quest of the island of Brazil. William of Worcester, *Itinerary* (Dallaway), 153. "Such projects seem to have met with much support from the merchants there." — Cunningham, vol. i. p. 421.

out of which the new life was to spring, were being sown amid
the embers of the dying mediævalism.   The reign of mon- the reign of
archy in England, as in the rest of Europe, brought with it monarchy
brought
peace, which gave a marked impetus not only to agriculture with it
peace;
and manufacture, but to foreign commerce.   The shores of the
Mediterranean no longer marked the limits of the maritime
world ; the dominion of the seas had already begun to pass
from the Italian seaports to the nations bordering on the Atlantic seaboard ; the great era of discovery and conquest had
now come, in which English seamen and soldiers were soon
to bear their part.   During the sixteenth century the Cabots, era of dis-
Gilbert, Barlow, Amidas, Drake, and Raleigh braved every covery and
conquest;
hardship and faced every danger in the prosecution of American discovery ; and in the next age their work was crowned
by the brave English hearts who at last overcame the terrors
of the wilderness, and laid the foundations of the great republic beyond the sea.   While the geographical horizon of the
English people was thus being widened by discovery and conquest, its intellectual activities were being stirred by the new
light now streaming across the Alps from the ancient world.
To the Italy of Petrarch we must look for the cradle of the Italian Re-
Renaissance.   Petrarch it was who in the fourteenth century naissance;
taught his countrymen how to study the Latin masters in a
humanistic spirit, and he also pointed out to them the necessity
of recovering a knowledge of Greek, which had become, in the
full sense of the term, a dead language.   Before its capture
by the Turks, enthusiastic scholars had visited Constantinople
"as the sacred city of the new revelation," and after its fall
the Greek scholars who were driven into exile found in the
cities of Italy not only congenial homes, but earnest disciples,
who were ready to break the new revelation to the Latin and
Teutonic world.   In that way Italy became the seat of a vast
intellectual revival ; in her cities the ancient fountains were
unsealed from which the two great streams of classic literature
flowed into France and Spain, into Germany and the Nether-
lands, and finally into England.   The art of printing, which printing;
had been discovered just in time to aid in the distribution of
the new learning throughout the Continental nations, stood
ready to welcome its advent into the island kingdom.   Caxton,
the first English printer, after a prolonged absence in Flan-

ders, returned home about the year 1476, bringing with him a printing-press, with the use of which he had probably become familiar at Bruges. Encouraged by the patronage of Edward IV.,[1] and such of his despotic courtiers as Gloucester, Rivers, and Tiptoft, and sustained by the growing literary spirit of the age, Caxton printed many of the classics, and all of the best specimens of English literature in poetry and prose. At his death in 1492 he left his art established in England upon a firm foundation. Thus, while Edward and Henry were laying deep the foundations of the monarchy, they were also furthering the establishment of a new institution, which was destined to contribute most to its overthrow. Through the agency of the printing-press, books which had been the property of the few became the possession of the many; by its levelling hand the new " seed-points of light " were sown in every household, and the result was a reëxamination of the whole field of knowledge, — a process which shook at last the foundations both of the church and the monarchy.

slow progress of the new learning under Henry VII.;

the fresh advance under Henry VIII.

Great, however, as was the progress made by the New Learning during the reign of Henry VII., under the lead of Grocyn, Colet, More, and Erasmus, the group of scholars of which they were the central lights remained a small one until after the accession of Henry VIII. Then it was that the circle widened; then it was that the "new order" began in earnest; then it was that England, thus ushered into the new era, definitely entered upon a career of intellectual development abreast with the foremost of the continental nations.

[1] During Edward's reign the statutes and year-books were first printed. The great text-books of Littleton on the common law and Lyndwode on the ecclesiastical law were also published. Reeves' *Hist. of Eng. Law*, vol. iv. pp. 158, 159.

CHAPTER II.

HENRY VIII. AND THE BREAK WITH ROME.

1. DURING the period of transition that intervened between the accession of Edward IV. and the death of Henry VII., the work of reorganizing and consolidating the powers of the monarchy, which had risen triumphant out of the wreck of feudalism and the civil war, went steadily on. The dominant purpose that guided this work of reconstruction was to so endow the monarchy with self-sustaining force as to render it forever free from dependence upon and subserviency to that system of parliamentary sovereignty which had been carried to its highest point in the days of the Lancastrian kings. To transfer the supreme powers of the state from the king in parliament to the king in council,[1] without working any change in the outward form of the constitution, and without destroying any of its vital elements, was the cardinal idea that pervaded the policy which Edward inaugurated and Henry expanded. The details have already been drawn out through which this end was accomplished, by the establishment of a fiscal system which made the crown independent of parliamentary grants, except at long intervals and upon unusual occasions, and by the abnormal expansion of the powers of the council, in which the royal will was omnipotent.[2] Under the new system as thus organized the council became, as in the Norman and early Angevin days, the body from which emanated all the more important acts of government, whether administrative, legislative (by way of ordinance), fiscal, or political.[3] The parliament still survived for purposes of extraordinary deliberation. To the law courts was still committed the

Outline of the conciliar system:

Supreme powers of the state transferred from the king in parliament to the king in council;

from the council emanated all the more important acts of government;

---

[1] Upon that subject, see vol. i. pp. 496, 497.

[2] As Coke has expressed it, "The king's will is the sole constituent of a privy councillor."

[3] "It had at one moment to settle questions of policy; at another to provide funds, by which the administration could be carried on; at another to review minute accounts, to communicate with aliens or merchants, or to interfere for the preservation of the king's peace." — Dicey, *The Privy Council*, p. 50.

ordinary administration of justice.[1]   But the supervision and control of the entire judicial system was subject to the dictatorial and irresistible will of the king in council, to which the judicial constitution could impose no efficient barriers.   "In

some instances the king transferred to the star chamber cases on which the courts were about to pronounce a decision. When this was done, it wanted but one more step for the king, as the phrase went, 'to take the matter into his own hands,' and, if he chose, pardon the offence, generally after the receipt of a large sum of money."[2]   This same kind of interference was also extended to civil suits, and as the records of the coun-

cil show, it was for a time successful.[3]   It was, however, rather as an administrative body than as a law court that the council afforded to the great statesmen of the Tudor age the widest field for their abilities.   Under their guidance the despotic yet vigorous and efficient conciliar system not only brought peace and order out of anarchy at the close of the civil war, but it also guided the country safely through the great social and ecclesiastical crisis incident to the Reformation.   From the accession of Henry VII. to the Revolution of 1640, the history of the council is the history of the monarchy.   During that period of a century and a half not only the law courts, but the parliament, crouched at the feet of its paramount authority.

The strength of the system lay in the power of the crown to pry into all matters, great and small, and to crush any individual, however great, who might dare to oppose a royal mandate ; its weakness lay in the absence of a standing military force, in its powerlessness in the presence of an armed people. More than once during the reign of Henry VII. this weakness had revealed itself when, under the pressure of general taxation, large bodies of men had risen in organized rebellion.[4]   Against this danger, however, the princes of the house of Tudor seemed

---

[1] "As in the fourteenth century it is again the deliberative body with which the king administers the whole of the business of the realm, so far as it does not devolve upon — (i.) The central and lower courts in the ordinary course of justice ; (ii.) The Exchequer and the several administrative departments in the ordinary course of administration; (iii.) The Parliament for extraordinary deliberation." — Gneist, *Hist. of the Eng. Const.*, p. 500.

[2] Dicey, *The Privy Council*, p. 112.
[3] See *Proceedings of Privy Council*, vii. 58, 214, 276. "Nevertheless, for some reason which does not seem to be entirely explained, it paid less and less attention to civil suits, until under Charles I. an attempt was made to revise the jurisdiction in civil causes." — Dicey, *The Privy Council*, p. 115.
[4] See above, p. 29.

to have been guarded by an intuitive insight into the national character.   They never failed to yield at the opportune moment to the serious and menacing demands of a people who, stirred by the spirit of the New Learning, and absorbed by the hope of sudden wealth which the discovery of a new world and a growing commerce had excited, were less eager for political agitation than for the security and peace which in that age they seemed willing to enjoy even under the shadow of despotic authority.   Such was the strength and such the weakness of the political system which Henry VII. carefully matured, and transmitted intact to his youthful and gifted successor.   Under such a system, in which the royal will was the central and driving force, the personal characteristics of the sovereign often became upon critical occasions vitally important links in the chain of causation through which momentous political changes were brought about.   In that way, and only in that way, does the constitutional history of England become involved, during a critical period, with the characteristics and vicissitudes of Henry VIII.

Tudors knew how to yield at the opportune moment;

the royal will the driving force of the conciliar system.

2. While Henry VII. was laying deep the foundations of the house of Tudor, he was not unmindful of the support to be drawn from judicious marriage alliances.   "Lest the spectre of indefeasible right should stand once more in arms upon the tomb of the House of York," [1] he had reluctantly wedded the heiress Elizabeth.   In order to seal with peace the immemorial strife which for nearly two centuries had been going on with the restless kingdom upon his northern border, he arranged in 1503, after a protracted negotiation, the marriage of his eldest daughter Margaret with James IV. of Scotland, [2] —a marriage which ultimately placed the house of Stuart upon the throne of England. [3]   The nature of the union between the two kingdoms which was destined to grow out of this alli-

Marriage alliances arranged by Henry VII.:

marriage of James IV. of Scotland with Margaret, 1503;

---

[1] Hallam, *Const. Hist.*, vol. i. p. 9.   [2] *Lel. Coll.*, iv. 265–300; Hall, 56.
[3] Henry VII.

I. James IV., King of Scots = Margaret = 2. Douglas, Earl of Angus.

James V. = Mary of Guise.   Margaret Douglas = Matthew Stuart, Earl of Lennox.

Mary Queen of Scots = Henry Stuart, Lord Darnley.

James I. of England, VI. of Scotland.

ance, Henry clearly foresaw at the time it was contracted. When one of his council expressed the fear that in failure of the male line, the English crown might some day become an appendage to that of Scotland, he replied, "No, Scotland will become an appendage to the English; for the smaller must follow the larger kingdom."

marriage of Arthur with Catherine of Aragon, 1501;

Some years before the celebration of the Scottish marriage, Henry had betrothed his eldest son, Arthur, Prince of Wales, to Catherine, the fourth daughter of Ferdinand, king of Castile and Aragon,[1] with whom he was desirous for political reasons of entering into closer relations. When Arthur arrived at the age of fourteen, the canonical age of puberty, his marriage with Catherine was celebrated with great pomp at St. Paul's in the fall of 1501.[2] The hopes built upon this union were

Arthur's death and the betrothal of his widow to his brother Henry;

suddenly blasted, however, by the death of Arthur, who seems to have been a weakling, in the fifth month after his marriage. But as a pending contest with France for the possession of southern Italy made the alliance with England more precious than ever to Ferdinand, he was quick to propose the transfer of the youthful widow to Arthur's brother, Henry, who was six years her junior. A serious obstacle to such a union arose out

canonical difficulties;

of the biblical prohibition of marriage with a brother's widow, —an obstacle which many theologians contended could not be removed even by a papal dispensation. On the other hand, it was claimed that the law containing the prohibition was a positive and not a natural law, and as such subject to exception by dispensation;[3] and further, that as the first marriage had never been actually consummated,[4] a dispensation was clearly

the dispensation;

permissible. After delay and hesitation Julius the Second reluctantly granted the dispensation,[5] which was as reluctantly

---

[1] As to the treaties on this subject made in 1492 and 1496, see *Fœdera*, xii. 658-666.

[2] At the door of the cathedral Arthur endowed the bride with one third of his property. *Fœdera*, xii. 780.

[3] A very clear abstract of the biblical argument as developed afterwards in the divorce proceedings may be found in Lingard, *Hist. Eng.*, vol. iv. p. 5, and Note B. at the end of the volume. The king's party, who claimed that the dispensation granted was null, rested their argument upon the prohibition against marrying a brother's widow

contained in *Lev.* xviii. 16, xx. 21. The queen's party, on the other hand, relied upon *Deut.* xxv. 5, to prove that the rule was subject to exceptions when the first marriage had been unproductive of issue.

[4] Such was always Catherine's contention. Polyd., 619.

[5] "It was for some time delayed; and the papal agent was instructed to inform Ferdinand that a marriage which was at variance *a jure et laudabilibus moribus* could not be permitted *nisi maturo consilio et necessitatis causâ.* Minute of a brief of Julius the Second,

accepted by a portion of the English council. Under these circumstances Henry, who was at the time no more than twelve years old, was contracted to Catherine ; [1] and on the day before he completed his fourteenth year, the time fixed for the celebration of the marriage, he was required to enter a secret protest against the legal validity of what had been done in his name during his nonage. [2] Ferdinand was then given to understand that the marriage would in due time take place. In that anomalous and trying position Catherine was detained at the English court, as a queen upon the chess-board of European politics, until the death of her father-in-law in April, 1509.

the secret protest.

3. The accession of the bold and vigorous youth, who assumed in his eighteenth year the royal authority which a fortunate adventurer had seized and consolidated, was hailed as the beginning of a new era. The popular affection which the cold and suspicious father had alienated years before his death instinctively returned to the son, who at the beginning of his reign united with manly beauty and skill in arms a generosity of temper and a nobleness of political aims from which, as his bitterest enemy admitted in later years, " all excellent things might have been hoped." [3] In the mental and moral make-up of the new king seemed to be epitomized all of the characteristic traits of the vigorous versatile age that had just begun. Thoroughly imbued with the spirit of the New Learning, he had manifested even as a boy a capacity for scholarship which had excited the wonder of Erasmus ; [4] in theology his reading was wide and profound ; as a writer of letters [5] and state papers he became the rival of his greatest ministers ; of the art of shipbuilding he acquired a thoroughly practical understand-

Accession and early measures of Henry VIII. :

his characteristics ;

---

dated March 13, 1504, Rolls House MS." — Froude, *Hist. Eng.*, vol. i. p. 117, note 1.

[1] *Fœdera*, xiii. 81, 83, 89, 114.

[2] Henry's protestation, and the dispensation for his marriage with Catherine, may both be found in Burnet's *Hist. Reformation*, vol. ii. (*Collectanea*, vi.). The bull for Henry's marriage with Catherine admits that she had been legally married to Prince Arthur, and that *carnali copula forsan consummavissetis.*

[3] Such was the testimony of Cardinal Pole . . . " *indoles, ex qua præclara*

omnia sperari possent. — *Apologia Reg. Poli.*, p. 86.

[4] " He loved the purity of the Latin tongue, which made him be so kind to Erasmus, that was the great restorer of it, and to Polydore Virgil." — Burnet, *Hist. Reformation*, vol. i. p. 8.

[5] The correspondence of Henry VIII. as published (1830–52) by the Record Commissioners fills eleven quarto volumes. By the publication of state papers much new light has been shed upon Henry's merits as an administrator.

ing ; while in the wrestling match and tourney the mightiest
went down before him.   In obedience to that impulse which
never failed to make him seek the love of his people, Henry's
first act was to bring to justice Empson and Dudley, the finan-

punishment
of Empson
and Dud-
ley ; cial ministers of his father, who had been the instruments of a
policy of extortion which had enriched the crown by the mer-
ciless enforcement of its dormant claims through the revival
of the expiring system of feudal fines and forfeitures.[1] In
order to exclude these objects of popular hatred from the
general pardon which followed the accession, they were cited
before the privy council, where articles were presented against
them in which they were charged with the financial oppressions of which they were really guilty.   Shortly afterwards
they were indicted upon an unsupported and improbable
charge of high treason, upon which they were convicted and
executed.[2]

marriage of
Henry and
Catherine,
June, 1509;   The next grave business upon which the council, still composed of the dead king's trusted advisers, was called upon to
act grew out of the promise made by Henry to the Spanish
ambassador to submit the question of his marriage with Catherine to their immediate consideration.[3]   The time had now
come for England to enter the arena of continental politics ;
the cautious policy of isolation which Henry VII. had been so
careful to maintain was no longer possible ; the rising great-
ness of France had now become an unanswerable argument in
favor of a Spanish alliance.   When the old objection to the

objections
to the mar-
riage re-
vived ; king's marriage with Catherine was revived, the answer was
renewed that the union with Arthur had never been consum-
mated, that the papal dispensation was therefore of undoubted
validity.   Catherine, who always contended that she came to
Henry's bed a virgin, dressed in white and wore her hair loose,
after the manner of a maiden,[4] at the nuptials which were celebrated in June.   In his first parliament, which met in the following January, the king was granted tonnage and poundage

---

[1] Bacon (*Hist. Henry VII.*, p. 217)
tells us how they " turned law and justice into wormwood and rapine."   A
fine epitome of the expedients which
they employed to extort money may be
found in Lingard, *Hist. Eng.*, vol. iii.
p. 338.
[2] They both suffered on Tower-hill

in 1510, but the heirs of both were
restored in blood in 1512.
[3] *Apologia Reg. Poli.*, pp. 83, 84.
[4] Sanford, 480. As to the evidence
of Catherine's virginity upon which the
validity of the dispensation for her marriage with Henry was supposed to
largely depend, see Lingard, *Hist. Eng.*,
vol. iii. p. 343, note 2, 5th ed.

for life ;[1] Empson and Dudley were attainted ;[2] and an act was passed which mitigated to a great extent such evils as their harsh and inequitable procedure had inflicted.[3]

From the time of Henry's marriage with Catherine the influence of Ferdinand became dominant in the English council chamber ; and the king of Aragon was not slow to draw his ardent son-in-law, who was thirsting for glory and conquest upon the fields of France, into the Holy League,[4] which had been formed in October, 1511, between Ferdinand, the pope, and the Republic of Venice for the avowed purpose of freeing Italy from French domination. Henry's hopes were fed by the prospect of recovering the French provinces which had been lost by his ancestors, and when the campaign opened in 1512 it was with an open assertion upon his part of the old claims upon "our heritage of France." This new departure from the traditional policy of peace brought with it the inevitable consequence. Two demands for money were made in quick succession upon parliament, which were promptly met. The parliament in 1511 granted two tenths and two fifteenths, while in 1513 the clergy granted two tenths, and the laity a tenth, a fifteenth, and a poll tax, towards the prosecution of the war.[5] In order to provide a sum which the poll tax failed to produce, there was granted to the king in the next year a general subsidy of 6 *d.* in the pound, and if his needs should require it, a second of the same amount. This grant is memorable as marking the time from which it became the custom to grant in the same act with tenths and fifteenths, *and as a supplement thereto*, a general subsidy, an income and a property tax, which continued to be used down to the Civil War.[6]

Henry's first parliament, January, 1510, — tonnage and poundage for life;

he enters the Holy League and breaks the policy of peace;

two demands for money in quick succession in the parliaments of 1511 and 1513;

the general subsidy of 1514 marks a point in the history of taxation;

---

[1] 1 Hen. VIII. c. 20. With the proviso, however, that "these grants be not taken in example to the kings of England in time to come." See as to such grants, above, p. 16.

[2] They had been already convicted by juries, but had been respited.

[3] 1 Hen. VIII. c. 3. The official Journals of the House of Lords (printed with a general index, and a special calendar from 1 Hen. VIII. to 30th August, 1642) begin with 1 Hen. VIII. The Journals of the House of Commons begin with 1 Edward VI.

[4] *Fœdera*, xiii. 306.

[5] *Lords' Journal*, i. p. 25. As to the rates after which the poll tax was fixed, see *Rolls*, xxvi., xxvii.

[6] "In form the Tudor subsidy was a personal tax charged upon two distinct classes of tax-payers : 1, persons possessed of movables ; and 2, persons possessed of land." — Dowell, *Hist. of Taxation and Taxes in England*, vol. iii. p. 71. See also Ibid., vol. i. p. 130. Persons charged in respect to movables were not charged in respect of profit from land, and *vice versa*, — "none are to be doubly charged." — Ibid., vol. iii. p. 71. "A subsidy was an income tax of 4 *s.* in the pound upon the annual value of land worth 20 *s.* a year, and a

During the campaign of 1513–14, not long after Henry's hopes
had been lifted by an important victory in France and by a
greater in Scotland,[1] he was suddenly robbed of the fruits of
success by the desertion of his allies, who ended the coalition
by a sudden and unexpected peace with Louis XII. While
the results of the war thus abruptly closed freed the papacy,
broke the prestige of France, and lifted England from an
humble to a high place in European politics, the cost to the
island kingdom was enormous. Not only were the accumu-
lated treasures of Henry VII. and the liberal subsidies granted
by parliament exhausted, but trade was greatly disturbed by
the heavy pressure of taxation, and by the disorganization of
labor. Against the dangers and demoralization thus brought
about by the fresh outbreak of the spirit of conquest, a protest arose from the men of the New Learning, which was
pointed by the solemn denunciations of Colet and by the bitter satires of Erasmus, — the first of whom declared that "an
unjust peace is better than the justest war," while the latter denounced all wars of ambition as sacrilegious madness.[2]
Nothing could have been farther removed from these novel
and humane aspirations to which the New Learning had given
birth than the worldly and ambitious spirit of the rising favorite, who was destined soon to strive, through diplomacy and
war, to win for himself the chair of St. Peter, and for his master the imperial crown.

results of the heavy pressure of taxation;

protest of the New Learning against the spirit of conquest.

Wolsey, 1515–29.

4. Amongst the new men who had lately grown into royal
favor was Thomas Wolsey, the son of a wealthy townsman of
Ipswich, and an ecclesiastic, who before the end of the last
reign had become one of the royal chaplains. By the Bishop
of Winchester, a leading member of the council, he had been

property-tax of 2 s. 8 d. in the pound
upon the actual value of all personal
property worth 3 l. and upwards. Personal property was, therefore, much
more heavily burdened than real property. The tenths and fifteenths were
levied upon the counties and boroughs
at a fixed rate, settled by a valuation
made in the reign of Edward III. Each
county or borough was responsible for
a certain sum, which was levied by persons appointed by its representatives in
the house of Commons. The subsidies were levied by Commissioners appointed by the Chancellor from amongst

the inhabitants of the county or borough." — Gardiner, *Hist. Eng.*, vol. i.
p. 297 and note 1.

[1] The victory won by the Earl of
Surrey at Flodden.

[2] "It was the first time in modern
history that religion had formally dis-
associated itself from the ambition of
princes and the horrors of war, or that
the new spirit of criticism had ventured
not only to question but to deny what
had till then seemed the primary truths
of political order." — Green, *Hist. Eng.
People*, vol. iii. p. 94.

taken into the service of the crown, and soon after the beginning of the present reign we find him exercising the office
of royal almoner, which drew him near to the king's person.[1]
During the late war, as the active organizer of the forces in
the campaign of 1513, Wolsey had rendered such services as
secured his elevation in that year to the see of Tournay.[2]
Honors then fell thick and fast upon him. In 1514 he was his rapid promotion in the church ;
made bishop of Lincoln, and before the end of that year he
was translated to the archbishopric of York. In 1515 Henry
obtained from Rome his elevation to the office of cardinal,[3]
and in December of that year, upon the retirement of Warham,
he received the seals as chancellor.[4] In that office, although receives the seals as chancellor in 1515 ;
unacquainted with the details of legal procedure, it was ad-
mitted even by his enemies that his decrees were characterized by the greatest equity and good judgment. So popular
was his administration, by reason of his capacity for expedition
and justice, that his court became overcrowded with business,
and four subordinate courts had to be established for its relief, origin of the office of master of the rolls ;
of which that presided over by the master of the rolls [5] still
survives. It was, however, in the wider field of continental
politics that the new minister, now supreme in the council,
was to find a domain worthy of his ambition. Taking up the
thread of diplomacy where the end of the late war had left it,
Wolsey's first design was to turn Henry's resentment of Ferdinand's desertion of him to a good account by making it the
means of freeing England from Spanish domination, as the
results of the war had freed her from the menace of French
ascendency. By the death of Louis XII. in 1515 the destinies
of France had passed into the stronger hands of Francis I.,
while by the death of Ferdinand in the next year his grandson, Charles of Austria, had been able to add all Spain to his

[1] It is from Polydore Virgil (663),
who had been imprisoned by Wolsey,
that we learn of the orgies which took
place at his house when he happened
to be visited by his royal master.
[2] *Fœdera*, xiii. 584.
[3] Raynald, xx. 192.
[4] *Fœdera*, xiii. 530.
[5] See Lingard, *Hist. Eng.*, vol. iii. p.
370, 5th ed. "The earliest mention of
him as master of the rolls is in 11 Hen.
VII. c. 18. . . . In the course of time,
from causes which are not very easy to
trace, his original functions as keeper
of the records passed away from him
and he gradually assumed a jurisdiction
in the Court of Chancery second only
to that of the lord chancellor himself.
. . . By 1 & 2 Vict. c. 94, the custody
of the records was restored to him, and
he is chairman of the State Papers and
Historical Manuscripts Commission."
— *Enc. Brit.*, vol. xx. p. 628, 9th ed.

already vast yet widely scattered dominions.   Out of the rivalry between these nearly evenly balanced powers arose

Wolsey's diplomacy makes England a leading factor in European politics ;

Wolsey's opportunity to lift England to a position of the first importance by making her alliance with either the controlling factor in European politics.   By the year 1518 the success of this policy seemed to be assured, and as a crowning reward Henry procured from the pope in July of that year the cardi-

appointed legate *a latere*;

nal's appointment as legate *a latere*, a station in which his jurisdiction extended over all bishops, suspended all special privileges and exemptions, while his court took the place of that of Rome as the final court for ecclesiastical appeals.   In a word, the legatine commission conferred upon the cardinal, so far as England was concerned, nearly all of the prerogatives of the supreme pontiff himself.[1]   As the chief of both the home and foreign administration, as president of the council,

concentrates in his hands the control of both secular and ecclesiastical business;

as chancellor, and as legate, Wolsey now concentrated in his hands the power to direct and control the entire secular and ecclesiastical business of the kingdom.   In this abnormal con- centration of power in a single hand can be traced not merely a desire upon the part of the crown to exalt a subject, whose fortunes could be blasted by a frown, but rather the con- summation of the new system of personal government which rested upon the notion that the supreme powers of the state were all vested in the council as the mere agent of the royal will.   Under the system as thus organized and directed by Wolsey the country enjoyed eight years of peace without a parliament.[2]

French and Spanish war of 1521 ;

Not until the beginning of the great French and Spanish war of 1521 was England again forced from her position of neutrality into open participation in a struggle in which Henry hoped, through a fresh alliance with pope and emperor, to accomplish at last the re-conquest of his French inheritance. Although years had passed by since the estates had been assembled, the first attempt to raise money for the war was made in the form of a fresh application of the old system of

forced loans of 1522 ;

forced loans or benevolences.   In March, 1522, commissioners were sent into the shires to make assessments, and in the mar- itime counties to array all men between the ages of sixteen

---

[1] See *Fœdera*, xiii. 734, xiv. 18.   [2] There was no parliament from 1515 to 1523.

and sixty upon the pretext of an apprehended invasion.[1] As a temporary expedient, a loan of £20,000 was exacted of the merchants of London, while the wealthiest citizens were cited to appear before the cardinal as royal commissioner, where they were required to give the true values of their estates, which were received "upon their honesties."[2] When all of these oppressive expedients had failed to produce a sum sufficient to supply the great quota of troops which Henry had promised for the war, a parliament was finally summoned to meet in April, 1523, out of whose subsidies all of the unwilling lenders hoped for indemnity. The unprecedented demand of £800,000, which the king was compelled to make, Wolsey undertook to present in person, backed by all the prestige and power of the conciliar system. At the head of the representative branch of the parliament, the ancient foe of that system, now stood an historic figure, who embodied all that remained of the free spirit of the past.

parliament of 1523.

Near the close of the preceding reign, a young lawyer by the name of Thomas More, the son of an eminent barrister, had attracted public attention by daring to oppose in the parliament of 1504 an unreasonable demand for money in a speech which resulted in the reduction of a proposed subsidy

Sir Thomas More as popular leader;

---

[1] Stowe, 316; *Fœdera*, xiii. 770.

[2] Holinshed, iii. 680; Hall, 101, 102, 105; Herbert, 121, 122. Each person was required to contribute a ratable portion according to his admission, upon the royal promise of repayment out of the next subsidy. The promises or "privy seals," as they were called, were in form as follows : "We Henry VIII. by the grace of God, king of England and of France, Defender of Faith, and Lord of Ireland, promise by these presents truly to content and repay unto our trusty and well-beloved subject   the sum of   which he has lovingly advanced unto us by way of loan, for defence of our realm, and maintenance of our wars against France and Scotland." — Instructions to the Commissioners in contemporary MS. in the possession of Mr. Hallam. See *Const. Hist.*, vol. i. p. 19. When in 1526 another attempt was made to collect a forced loan through royal commissioners who demanded a sixth from the laity and a fourth from the clergy, such forcible resistance was made in several shires that the king was compelled to give up the attempt, and to declare that he would take nothing from the people but by way of an amiable grant or benevolence (Holinshed, iii. 709 ; Hall, 696, 700), which was nothing less than a forced loan without a definite promise of repayment. Such promises when made by Henry VIII. were of little value. In 1529 (21 Hen. VIII. c. 24) and in 1544 (25 Hen. VIII. c. 12) he called upon parliament to release him from all such promises by statute. In 1528 he demanded an "amiable grannte" or benevolence, and in 1545 still another. The practice of collecting benevolences and the cognate exaction known as forced loans was then continued during the reigns of Elizabeth, James, and Charles I., until it was put an end to by the Petition of Right, which provided "that no man hereafter be compelled to make or yield any gift, loan, benevolence, tax, or such-like charge, without common consent by act of parliament."

of three fifteenths to £30,000.[1] As the king refused to forgive this audacious act, the offender found it expedient for a time to seek safety in seclusion.   From that seclusion he emerged, *as a light of the New Learning;* after the beginning of the present reign, as one of the bright lights of the New Learning, whose daring spirit of inquiry he undertook to extend beyond the domain of mere educational and religious reform into that of social and political speculation.   Drawn by his wit and wisdom into the service of the court, he was sent more than once upon diplomatic missions *as a diplomat;* to the Low Countries.   While thus employed by a despotism which he despised, More embodied in a work, published in 1516,[2] his protest against the whole scheme of social and political oppression which Wolsey had just begun to organize into a vast and comprehensive system.   The conceit upon *the "Utopia," its scope and character;* which the "Utopia" is founded is that, upon one of his diplomatic missions, More had met by chance a sailor, who had been a companion of Amerigo Vespucci in his voyages to the New World, from whom he learned of the kingdom of "Nowhere."[3]   In this vague intellectual vision of a higher and better social and political life, in this "ultra-Platonic fancy, bred of the Platonism of the Renaissance,"[4] we find beneath the idealism of the dreamer, not only a statement of all the grave social, religious, and political questions involved in the life about him, but also a series of philosophical speculations as to their solution, far in advance of the age in which the writer lived.   In nothing is this prescience more manifest than *religious toleration;* in his premature announcement of the principle of religious toleration, embodied in the statement that in Utopia every man could hold whatsoever religious opinion he would, and propagate the same by argument, but without offence to the *aspirations for the improvement of the laboring classes;* religion of others.[5]   It was, however, to the cause of the laboring poor — bowed down like beasts of burden under a system of social tyranny whose evils had been intensified by a scheme

---

[1] The leading contemporary authority is the life by his son-in-law, William Roper, to which is added an appendix of letters. Chiswick, 1817. The very best recent contribution is the Life by W. H. Hutton, a rising scholar of St. John's College, Oxford.

[2] *Utopia*, originally printed in Latin, 1516. Translated into English by Robinson, and edited by Edward Arber,

1869. All references will be to the Arber ed.

[3] "Thence the Portuguese Hythlodaye wanders to the island of 'Nowhere,' which to More's mind was 'beyond the line equinoctial' between Brazil and India." — Arber, Int. p. iv.

[4] Pollock, *Hist. of the Science of Politics*, p. 22.

[5] Arber ed., p. 145.

of erroneous legislation which extended from the earlier Statutes of Laborers to the statute (6 Hen. VIII. c. 3) by which
parliament had last attempted to fix the rate of wages [1] — that
the sensitive mind of More addressed itself with the greatest
zeal and sympathy.   This whole system of oppression he de-
nounces as nothing but a conspiracy of the rich against the
poor, a conspiracy through which the rich are ever striving to
pare away something further from the daily wages of the poor
by private fraud and even by public law, so that the wrong
already existing is made yet greater by means of the law of
the state.[2]   In the realm of " Nowhere" no such conditions

---

[1] The important and continuous history of the Statutes of Laborers may
be summarized as follows : The foundations of the system for the regulation of the wages of labor were laid by
23 Edw. III. (1349) and 25 Edw. III.
(1357); the first of which, passed to
prevent a rise in wages as a consequence of the Black Death, provided
that all laborers should be forced to
serve for the rate which prevailed before the plague began, while the second
rendered the first measure more stringent by denying to the laborer the right
to quit his parish in search of better
employment.   Then followed a long
series of statutes confirming, amending, extending, and modifying the original acts with the double purpose of
regulating wages and preventing and
punishing as conspiracies all combinations to raise them.   Chief among the
series are the following: 12 Rich. II.
cc. 3, 4, 5, 6, 7, 8, 9, 10 (1388); 7 Hen.
IV. c. 17 (1405); 2 Hen. V. c. 4 (1414);
6 Hen. VI. c. 3 (1427); 6 Hen. VIII.
c. 3 (1514); 2 & 3 Edw. VI. c. 15 (1548);
and 5 Eliz. c. 4 (1562). The comprehensive statute last named, which remained in force during a long period
of time, was supplemented during the
eighteenth century by a set of acts regulating particular trades and prohibiting combinations in respect to wages
payable in such trades.   Among these
may be mentioned, 7 Geo. I. st. 1, c. 13
(as to journeymen tailors) ; 12 Geo. I.
c. 34 (as to woollen manufacturers) ;
22 Geo. II. c. 27 (as to the hat trade);
17 Geo. III. c. 55 (as to silk weavers);
and 36 Geo. III. c. 111 (as to the paper
trade).   These special regulations widened in 1799 into a general act, 39
Geo. III. c. 81, which provided for a
suppression of all combinations of work-
men for the purpose of raising wages.
That act, after remaining in force one
year, was superseded by 40 Geo. III. c.
60, which, while it encouraged the reference of labor disputes to arbitration,
perpetuated the prohibitions against
combinations down to 1824.   In that
year was passed 5 Geo. IV. c. 95, which,
after repealing all prior laws as to combinations, put the whole subject upon
a new basis by treating labor as a commodity to be bought and sold according to the ordinary rules of trade. After
remaining in force only one year, that
act, which was charged with encourag-
ing all kinds of combinations, was superseded by 6 Geo. IV. c. 129, an act of
the same general character, but with
more stringent provisions against combinations.   During the next fifty years
the courts carried what was claimed
to be the old common law doctrine,
that trade unions or combinations in
restraint of trade were criminal conspiracies, to such an extent that in
1871 a contrary principle was declared
by statute (34 & 35 Vict. c. 31).   In
order to render that act more effective was passed the "Conspiracy and
Protection of Property Act" of 1875
(38 & 39 Vict. c. 86), which provided
that no agreement by two or more in
furtherance or contemplation of a trade
dispute should be considered as an in-
dictable conspiracy unless the act agreed
upon would be criminal if committed by
one person only.   Upon the whole subject, see Reeves' *Hist. Eng. Law*, vol.
iii. (Finlason ed.), pp. 128, 365, 413;
vol. iv. p. 344; Sir J. F. Stephen's *Hist.
of the Criminal Law*, vol. iii. pp. 203,
204.

[2] Arber ed., p. 159.

as these exist, because there the whole aim of legislation is to nurture and develop the laboring classes as the true foundation of society, by providing for their physical, moral, and intellectual welfare. There the cottages of the poor are light and cleanly, there the period of daily toil is reduced to nine hours, there a system of public education is provided by law for all.[1] And here should be noted the comment which the writer makes upon the injustice of punishing too severely men who have been badly taught in their youth, and whose morals have been corrupted from childhood.[2] An appeal is made for a readjustment of punishment upon the basis of a just relation between the penalty and the offence. Reformation is declared to be the end of all punishment, "nothing else but the destruction of vices and the saving of men."[3] Amid these humane aspirations for the improvement of the intellectual, moral, and physical condition of the laboring classes, the larger question involving the maintenance of political liberty against the growing despotism of the monarchy is by no means lost sight of. Regardless of the danger which such a dissent from the prevailing king worship involved, the suggestion is boldly made that a king should be removed who is even suspected of a design to enslave his people.[4] Then follows an outline of the process through which a people may be enslaved by a straining of the law in favor of the royal authority. Where such a tendency exists there will never be wanting some pretence for deciding in the king's favor; as that equity is on his side; or the strict letter of the law, or some forced interpretation of it.[5] While the equal administration of justice is undermined by the growth of such false principles, the notion that the English is an absolute instead of a limited monarch is fostered by the maxim that the king can do no wrong, however much he may wish to do it; that not only the property but the persons of his subjects are his own; and that a man has a right to no more than the king's goodness thinks fit not to take from him.[6] When disentangled from much that is fanci-

reformation declared to be the end of all punishment;

when a king should be deposed;

straining the law in favor of the crown;

---

[1] Arber ed., pp. 78, 83, 104.
[2] Ibid., p. 44.
[3] Ibid., p. 50.
[4] "The princes office continueth all his life tyme, oneles he be depofed or put downe for fufpition of tirannie." — Ibid., p. 81.

[5] Ibid., p. 60.
[6] Ibid., pp. 60, 61. "Furthermore that a kynge, though he would, can do nothinge vniuftlye. For all that men haue, yea alfo the men them felfes be all his," etc.

ful, such is the essence of the social, religious, and political More, on account of his popular influence, made speaker in 1523.
creed of the great thinker, who, on account of his popular
sympathies and consequent influence with the commons, was
elected at the instance of the crown to preside as speaker in
the approaching parliament.

The opposition which Wolsey encountered when he came Wolsey makes an unprecedented demand for money;
in person to the commons, "with all his pillar and pole-axe
bearers," to present his terrible demand for a sum which could
be raised only by the imposition of a property-tax of twenty
per cent., shows that something of the old spirit still lingered.
The commons listened to him in silence ; and when the speaker
was called upon for a reply, his response was that according to More's response for the commons;
the ancient liberties of the house, they were not bound to make
answer, and that as speaker he could make no reply until
he received their instructions.[1] After a long contention the
matter was settled by a vote which granted much less than
had been asked, payable in four years in instalments.[2] Then
followed an extraordinary demand[3] upon the clergy, whom
the cardinal, by virtue of his legatine authority, attempted to
assemble in a national synod. This assault upon their consti- clergy assert their right to grant money only in convocation;
tutional right to grant money only in convocation the clergy
resisted, and not until after a four months' struggle did the
matter end in a compromise.[4] The bulk of the great sums
thus extorted from clergy and laity was expended in another
expedition to France and in aid of the allies in Italy, without
materially advancing the ambitious schemes of either king or
cardinal. The struggle was nevertheless continued, with a
pressing need for money as the inevitable consequence, until
1526, when matters reached a crisis. Then it was that the the forced loan of 1526;
cardinal, unwilling to meet a fresh rebuff from the hands of
parliament, attempted to enforce another loan of a sixth from
the laity and a fourth from the clergy, through royal commissioners. In the teeth of a stern popular opposition, which
brought the country to the verge of such a peasants' war as
was then raging in Germany, the demand was unconditionally

---

[1] See More's *Life of Sir T. More*, p. 51 ; Roper's, p. 11.
[2] Hall, *Par. Hist.*, vol. i. p. 488 ; Dowell, *Hist. of Taxation*, vol. i. p. 131.

[3] Amounting to fifty per cent. on the yearly income of their benefices.
[4] Wilkins, *Conc.*, iii. 701 ; Strype, vol. i. p. 49. The fifty per cent. demanded was voted payable at ten per cent. each year for five years.

withdrawn.[1] With this failure to raise more money really
ended the Austrian alliance, through which the king had
striven to realize his dream of French conquest, and the cardinal his hope of a papal election. From that time may be
dated the downward turn in Wolsey's fortunes.

downward turn in Wolsey's fortunes.

Two years before the election of Charles V. to the imperial crown, a startling event occurred within his dominions
which affected the whole after-history of the Christian world.
The movement set on foot by Luther, who in 1517 fixed
certain propositions against a church gate at Wittenberg,
rapidly grew and widened, until it broke the mediæval conception of an indivisible Christendom [2] by disuniting the Teutonic
nations from communion with the See of Rome. The ultimate outcome of this movement has been a widely extended
system of Christian theology, which rests upon the right of
private judgment as opposed to the dogma of an infallible
church.[3] Although in its broader and more general aspects
the religious movement known as the Reformation may be thus
considered as an indivisible whole, the fact remains that in
each country in which it has prevailed it has assumed a special
and peculiar form, which can only be clearly defined in the light
of its local history. In no one of the Teutonic nations did
the protest of Luther find a fainter echo than in the English
kingdom. From the court and the higher classes it received
no response at all.[4] So outraged was the king by Luther's
contumacy, which the emperor had been slow to punish, that
he felt called upon as a Christian prince and as a trained theo-
logian to enter the lists against him ; and in July, 1521, he
published in reply to Luther's " Babylonian Captivity of the
Church " an " Assertion of the Seven Sacraments," [5] a performance for which he was rewarded by Leo with the newly
coined title of " Defender of the Faith." [6] The replies of Sir

Luther and the Refor-mation ;

in each country in which it prevails it has a special and local history ;

Luther and Henry VIII. ;

[1] Hall, 696, 700 ; Holinshed, vol. iii.
p. 709. In Kent the commissioners
were resisted and put to flight, while
in Suffolk four thousand men took up
arms. The next benevolence was the
"amiable grannte" of 1528. Dowell,
vol. i. p. 201.

[2] As to the mediæval theory which
regarded the Roman Empire and the
Catholic Church as two aspects merely
of a single and indivisible Christian
monarchy, see vol. i. pp. 369–371.

[3] No one has stated this with more
force than Buckle, *Hist. of Civilization*,
vol. i.

[4] "In Germany all classes shared the
common feeling ; in England it was almost confined to the lowest."—Froude,
Hist. Eng., vol. i. p. 506.

[5] This work, printed by Pynson in
1521, did not attempt new lines of
thought ; it adhered strictly to received
tradition.

[6] This new title, granted to the king

Thomas More and Bishop Fisher to Luther's gross response to the king's assault show how completely the men of the New Learning stood apart from the reformer, whose temper had nothing in common with the tolerant spirit of the Renaissance. It was first in the ranks of the common people that the new movement found a home, upon whose hearth it kindled into flame the smouldering embers of the ancient Lollardry which, in spite of the continued persecutions evidenced by the bishop's registers, had never entirely died out. The vague spirit of restlessness and discontent with the doctrines and practices of the mediæval church which Lollardry had left behind it, after it had ceased to be an organized and concerted movement, was quickened and intensified in 1526 by the importation into England of Tyndale's [1] translation of the New Testament, made and printed in Lutheran strongholds, at Luther's instance and solicitation. By the aid of "The association of Christian Brethren," Tyndale's work, which came over as a part of the new movement, was circulated, together with Lutheran pamphlets and reprints of the tracts of Wycliffe, amongst the trading and laboring classes, from whose hands it passed first to Cambridge, then to Oxford,[2] where the New Learning had prepared the way for religious speculation. Absorbed as Wolsey was in foreign politics, careless as he was of all purely religious matters, he certainly made some effort to reform the clergy, and to suppress at the outset the growing Lutheranism. As early as 1521 he directed all bishops "to take order that any books, written or printed, of Martin Luther's heresies and errors should be brought in to the bishop of each diocese." [3] In 1523, at the instigation of Fox, the bishop of Hereford, he commanded a visitation of both the professed and secular clergy in response to a general complaint against their manners.[4] Two years after that time he obtained permission from Rome for the suppression of a number of smaller monasteries, whose endowments, mingled with large gifts from his own

Marginal notes: Luther and the New Learning; Lutheranism and Lollardry; Tyndale's translation and Wycliffe tracts appear together; Wolsey's attempt to reform the clergy;

personally, and not to his successors, was retained after the separation, and in 1543 it was annexed to the crown by 35 Hen. VIII. 3. The bull granting the title to Henry has a gold seal, according to custom. See Lingard, vol. v. p. 461, note 1.

[1] "The smouldering embers needed but a breath to fan them into flame, and the breath came from William Tyndale."—Green, *Hist. of the Eng. People*, vol. ii. p. 126.

[2] For details, see the *Reform. of the Church of Eng.*, Blount, pp. 525–527.

[3] Strype, *Memorials*, i. 56.

[4] Ibid., i. App. 19.

he sup-
presses
some
smaller
monasteries
and founds
Christ
Church;

purse, were devoted to the establishment at Oxford of the new college,[1] reëstablished by his master after his fall as Christ Church.   Into his new foundation the cardinal introduced not only great scholars from foreign universities, but also several students of special promise from Cambridge, an institution which he had sheltered from a visitation proposed by the bishops in 1523, "for trying who were the fautors of heresy

Cambridge
first re-
ceives the
Lutheran
literature;

there."[2]   Around the little group thus drawn from Cambridge — which, on account of its nearness to the seaports on the eastern coast, had been the first to receive the Lutheran literature — gathered the larger circle of Oxford brethren, whose attempt at an organized movement drove Wolsey to his first really vigorous and decided effort at suppression by means of persecution.   By his direction the books of the brethren were

in 1528
Oxford
purged of
heresy.

seized, several of their number imprisoned, and the rest dispersed.   And so before the end of the year 1528 Oxford was purged of heresy.[3]

Wolsey and
the divorce:

Whilst the cardinal was thus plagued in the midst of great affairs by the uncongenial work of persecution, a matter began to be mooted, touching the peace of the royal household, which was destined to involve him in far more serious perplexities. In spite of the difficulties which had attended their union, dictated at the outset by political convenience,[4] the marriage of Henry with Catherine had produced many years of peaceful association, broken so far as we know on the king's part

no male
heir, and
Mary's
legitimacy
assailed;

by only one or two infidelities.[5]   But what it had not produced was a male heir to succeed Henry in the royal office. Although three boys had been born, they had died almost instantly,[6] leaving as the only living fruit of the marriage a sickly girl, whose legitimacy had lately been questioned upon a

[1] For details, see Burnet's *Hist. of Reform.*, vol. i. p. 17.   For the papal bull, and the king's license to act upon it, see *Fœdera*, vol. vi. part ii. pp. 8, 17.

[2] His refusal to interfere when his legatine authority was invoked for that purpose was made the basis of one of the charges in the indictment against him seven years afterwards.

[3] A full and graphic account of the whole matter may be found in Froude, vol. i. pp. 522–547.

[4] See above, pp. 38, 39.

[5] The most notable of the king's mistresses were Elizabeth, daughter of Sir John Blount, and Mary, an elder sister of Anne Boleyn.   Lingard says that "the reluctance of Burnet to acknowledge Mary as one of the king's mistresses must yield to the repeated assertions of Pole, in his private letter to Henry, written in 1535." — Pol. f. lxxvi., lxxvii., *Hist. Eng.*, vol. iv. p. 45, note 2.

[6] Such misfortunes had occurred in 1511, 1513, and 1514.

critical occasion by reason of the original obstacles to a union [1] upon which the king now claimed to fear that heaven had set a curse. Catherine had already reached an age which precluded the hope of further issue; and besides the fact remained — in spite of the feudal rule which did not deny the descent of the crown in the female line — that no queen regnant had ever sat upon the throne of England. Such circumstances as these may well have excited in the king's mind a genuine solicitude as to who should succeed him "in this Imperial dignity." What has overshadowed and belittled the reasons which might have justified Henry, upon patriotic grounds, in seeking a divorce, was the impetuous yet characteristic zeal with which he sought it, with the open purpose of hastening his union with a young woman of his court, who for a time goaded his passion by a stiff and obstinate refusal to bow to his will. It is not clear when the king's resolve to obtain a divorce first crystallized into a definite purpose; [2] but certainly not before 1527 did the matter pass as a problem of state into the hands of Wolsey as the highest representative of the only power which, according to then existing theories, was competent to solve it. At an earlier stage of this work the attempt was made to emphasize the fact that it is impossible to grasp the full and true significance of many transactions which occurred between the Christian nations and the Roman See, during the existence of the mediæval empire, without some insight into the structure of that fabric which rested upon the magnificent notion of a vast Christian monarchy whose sway was absolutely universal. The chiefs of this comprehensive society were the Roman emperor and the Roman pontiff, — the one standing at its head in its temporal character as an empire, the other standing at its head in its spiritual character as a church. [3] Under this system the Roman pontiff naturally assumed the office of supreme judge of appeals in all causes which arose in the ecclesiastical courts of the Christian

real grounds for a divorce belittled by unworthy motives;

position of the pope as final judge in such matters, under the theory of the mediæval empire;

---

[1] During the negotiations for the marriage of Mary to the son of the king of France (1526-27), the bishop of Tarbes questioned the validity of the dispensation granted for Henry's marriage with Catherine. — Lord Herbert, pp. 80, 81. The treaty for the marriage was, however, concluded. For a full discussion of the transaction with the bishop of Tarbes, see Lingard, vol. iv. p. 584, Note F., Appendix.

[2] "The earliest intimation which I find of an intended divorce was in June, 1527, at which time Wolsey was privately consulting the bishops. *State Papers*, vol. i. p. 189." — Froude, vol. i. p. 115, note 2.

[3] See vol. i. pp. 367-371.

nations under the canon law.[1]   In a matrimonial cause involving the validity of a royal marriage, where the result might affect the legitimacy of the issue, and in that way the peace of a nation, it was a matter of the last importance to have all questions passed upon by the one authority whose judgment was entitled, in theory at least, to universal acceptance.   Instead of submitting the question of the divorce to the pope in the first instance, Wolsey made an abortive attempt to solve it by virtue of his legatine authority.   In May, 1527, he opened his court as legate, and, in a collusive action, cited Henry to appear and answer to the charge of cohabiting with his brother's widow.   As Catherine refused to admit the facts involved in the accusation, and as her appeal would have at once removed the case to the papal court, the matter was suddenly dropped,[2] for in that very month Rome had been surprised and sacked by the imperial forces.   The results of the victory of Pavia in 1525 had placed the pope at the emperor's mercy, — the last blow had left him a prisoner in the Castle of St. Angelo.[3]   And yet, in spite of the attitude in which Clement now stood to Catherine's all-powerful nephew, who never once wavered in his devotion to her cause, Wolsey concurred with the king in the reference of the whole matter to Rome, where they hoped to secure a successful conclusion.[4]   The details of the complicated negotiations which followed are more or less familiar to all readers of English history.   If the case could have been adjudged upon its real merits, free from political pressure, the chances all are that Henry would have failed by reason of the fact that the weight of unbiassed opinion among the theologians and canonists seems to have been decidedly against him.[5]   But involved as the cause was with political

[Marginal notes:]
Wolsey first attempts to hear the case as legate;

then refers it to Rome, and guarantees successful issue;

---

[1] The canon law of the Middle Ages was "a system, claiming to regulate the most important concerns of practical life, administered by courts which, though belonging to different nations, were under the control of one central authority." — Hunter's art. on Canon Law, *Enc. Brit.*, vol. v. p. 21, 9th ed. See also vol. i. of this work, p. 348.

[2] See Green, *Hist. of the Eng. People*, vol. ii. p. 134.

[3] Pallavicino, pp. 242–246.

[4] Knight and Cassalis, representatives of king and legate, united in a series of formal demands, the leading ones of which were that the pope would empower Wolsey or some other to hear the divorce, or that he would so use his dispensing power as to enable Henry to marry a wife who could bear him children.   See Knight to Henry, *State Papers*, vol. vii. pp. 2, 3; Wolsey to Cassalis, Ibid., vol. xii. p. 26; Burnet's *Hist. Reform.* (*Collectanea*), vol. ii. pp. vii.–xi.

[5] For the history of the appeal to the universities, see Burnet, vol. i. pp. 64–71; Lingard, vol. iv. pp. 84–86, and notes.

motives, at a turning-point in European history, it was impos- conflicting
sible that it should have been severed from the extraneous motives which there
forces which dictated everything which actually occurred. As embar-rassed its
a devoted son of the church, and as her valiant defender, considera-
if was natural that Clement should have been eager to hold tion;
Henry at a time when his resentment threatened to sever
England from the Roman communion.   On the other hand,
apart from the emperor's hold upon the papal dominions in
Italy, the defection in France and the spread of protestantism
in North Germany admonished the pope that a final break
with Charles might lose to him a far wider dominion.   In
the midst of such conflicting motives and interests, Clement
sought security in a temporizing policy of delay, so designed
that no definite result could be reached in favor of either
party.   As a part of that policy, he issued in the summer of appoint-ment of
1528 a legatine commission to cardinals Wolsey and Cam- Campeggio
peggio for the trial of the case in England.[1]   Campeggio, who and failure of his mis-
loitered on the way, did not arrive within the realm until Octo- sion;
ber ; and not until May, 1529, did the two legates open their
court in the great hall of the Blackfriars in order to summon
the king and queen to appear before them on the 18th of June,
at which time Catherine protested against the judges and appealed to a higher jurisdiction.[2]   During that very month the
destruction of the last remnant of the French army resulted
in an open alliance between Charles and Clement, upon which
soon followed the revocation of the legatine commission and
the removal of the cause to Rome.[3]   The failure of Wolsey's Wolsey's
efforts resulted at once in his overthrow,[4] an event which overthrow; last of the
marks the termination of the rule of the great ecclesiastics great eccle-siastical
who, since the accession of Henry VII., had dominated at the statesmen;
council board.   When at a little later day the cardinal was
actually stripped of his office, the vast powers which had been

---

[1] See Burnet, vol. i. pp. 38, 39, and
vol. ii. (*Collectanea*) p. xv.
[2] See Cavendish, pp. 423–428. As
to the speeches attributed to Catherine
and Henry, which Burnet has treated
as fictitious, see Lingard, vol. iv. p. 71,
note 3. Notwithstanding the queen's
appeal, she was pronounced contuma-
cious, and the trial was continued in her
absence until the 23d of July, when the
whole matter was adjourned in order

that it might be laid before the pontiff.
[3] See Burnet, vol. i. p. 57, and vol. ii.
(*Collectanea*) p. 38.
[4] In October, 1529, the attorney-general filed two bills against him, charging
him with having violated as legate the
Statute of Præmunire (16th of Rich.
II).   He pleaded guilty and threw himself upon the king's mercy. Cavendish,
p. 250.

distribu-
tion of his
powers ;

concentrated in his hands were distributed. The seals were given to Sir Thomas More, while the real direction of affairs passed into the hands of the dukes of Suffolk and Norfolk, — to the former as president of the council, to the latter, the

his portrait
of Henry
VIII.

uncle of Anne Boleyn, as lord treasurer. As Wolsey lay dying, he drew a pathetic picture of the infinite ruthlessness and selfishness which twenty years of despotic power had developed in the breast of a master whom he had served before God and country, when he said to Kyngston: "He is a prince of most royal courage; rather than miss any part of his will, he will endanger one half of his kingdom; and I do assure you, I have often kneeled before him, sometimes for three hours together, to persuade him from his appetite, and could not prevail."[1] It was this uncontrollable and stubborn temper, this unbending courage and unreasoning appetite, which became under the manipulation of Cromwell, during the ten years which followed Wolsey's fall, the mainspring of a system of despotism which has no parallel in English history.

Cromwell,
1529-40 :

5. About the time the cardinal obtained from Rome permission to suppress the smaller monasteries, whose revenues he diverted to his foundations at Ipswich and Oxford, he took into his service a middle-aged man of business, of whose history prior to that event we know little that is clear and defi-

his early
life ;

nite. It is reasonably certain, however, that about the year 1490 Thomas Cromwell was born near Putney, the son of an iron-worker, and that his earlier years were passed in roving adventure.[2] He must still have been in his teens when he made his way to Italy, where, according to the popular story, he enlisted in the wars as a common soldier, and where he imbibed in the most unscrupulous school the world ever saw those views of Italian statecraft which were destined to mould his after-history.[3] It was in the land of the Borgias and the Medici that Wolsey's successor became the disciple of

disciple of
Machia-
velli ;

Machiavelli, whose "Prince" he dared to commend as a political guide-book to Reginald Pole while he was still in Wolsey's

[1] Cavendish, pp. 513-535.
[2] See sketch by T. McK. Wood, in *Enc. Brit.*, vol. vi. 9th ed.
[3] For an account of his travels in Italy, see Foxe, vol. v. p. 392. As to the historic value of Foxe's strange story, see Froude (vol. i. pp. 583-585),

who says that "a cloud rests over the youth and early manhood of Thomas Cromwell, through which, only at intervals, we catch glimpses of authentic facts; and these few fragments seem rather to belong to a romance than to the actual life of a man."

service.[1]   After his career as a soldier had ended, Cromwell turned his hand to commercial pursuits, and as early as 1512 we find him back in England practising as a scrivener, a combination of attorney and money-lender.   In 1523 he appears as an active and influential member of the parliament which met in that year, and two years later we find him engaged in the unpopular task of suppressing the lesser monasteries, a work which he executed with a ruthless severity that involved him in the hate then gathering around his master.   But when the end came, when that master had been convicted in the king's bench, plundered of his fortune,[2] and deserted by the crowd that had fed upon his bounty, Cromwell alone was faithful in his adversity.   As an intermediary he undertook to buy off the hostility of the courtiers who had fallen heir to Wolsey's possessions by procuring from him confirmations of their grants ; as a fearless friend he defeated in the parliament of 1529[3] a bill, driven through the lords but rejected in the commons, designed to fix upon the cardinal the crime of high treason.[4]   In the course of this business it was that Cromwell, whose fidelity had attracted attention, found access to the king in order to negotiate for Wolsey's pensions.   By his "witty demeanor" he so impressed himself upon his sovereign that he was soon able to obtain a private audience, in which he disclosed a daring policy, which he said would at once free Henry from all the difficulties by which he was surrounded.   The substance of his suggestion was that the king should solve the problem of the divorce by disavowing the papal supremacy, and by declaring himself the head of the church in England,[5] a position which would leave him free to apply for relief to his own ecclesiastical tribunals.   In order to attain the end in view it was suggested that the clergy — the only order in the

member of the parliament of 1523;

his fidelity to Wolsey, who had employed him in the suppression of monasteries;

after Wolsey's fall he suggests to the king a new line of policy;

[1] Pole, pp. 133–136.
[2] Legrand, vol. iii. pp. 377, 379 ; *Fœdera*, vol. iv. p. 375.
[3] After an interval of about six years, the seven years' parliament met in November, 1529.
[4] Cavendish, p. 463; Lingard, vol. iv. p. 536, and note 2.
[5] Pole (*Apologia*, pp. 121–123) gives the account of what occurred upon the authority of Cromwell and others who were present. Cromwell is reported to have said to Henry in conclusion :

"Vindices ergo quod est proprium Regii nominis, ut sis caput in tuo regno, et solum caput."   This occurred on the day following that on which Cromwell left Wolsey, after saying to Cavendish (453) that he would go to the court "where I will either make or mar." In Baily's *Life of Bishop Fisher*, p. 89, the suggestion as to the new form of the king's title is attributed to Cranmer. See Blount, *Reform. of the Church of Eng.*, vol. i. p. 204, note 6.

state at all able to hinder the new project — should not only be shorn of their wealth and power, but driven also to relinquish the false position involved in their double allegiance. As Machiavelli had dreamed of a regenerated Italy under a tyrant who had crushed out all other tyrannies, so Cromwell dreamed of a regenerated England, in which the crown should

outline of that policy in its broader aspects. rise supreme upon the wreck of every rival authority.[1] When viewed in its broader aspect, Cromwell's bold and original design meant no less, so far as England was concerned, than a final repudiation of the mediæval conception of a vast Christian commonwealth, whose sway was supposed to be universal, and whose law, flowing from a supreme source, was supposed to bind every nation, and the substitution in its stead of the new Lutheran notion of national religion, under which each state or kingdom possessed the right to determine for itself the form of belief which should prevail within its own boundaries, free from all external interference whatsoever.[2] More than two centuries before, a like tendency to resist and modify the papal overlordship had manifested itself in the island kingdom, and an impetus had been given to it by both the crown and the parliament.

Review of the prior relations between the English Church and papacy : At an earlier stage of this work the attempt was made to show how that perfect oneness which existed in England between the church and state before the Conquest was rudely broken after that event by William's new ecclesiastical policy, which brought about the severance of the temporal and spiritual jurisdictions, and the drawing of the English Church, whose character had always been distinctly national, from its position of independence and isolation into closer relations with the rest of Western Christendom, and into greater dependence upon the See of Rome.[3] The inevitable result of that policy — despite William's efforts to preserve the subordination of the church to the state, despite the struggles waged against the papacy by Henry I. and Henry II. on the questions of investitures and clerical immunities from civil jurisdiction [4] — was a steady advance in favor of the privileges of both church and

---

[1] See Green, *Hist. of the Eng. People*, vol. ii. pp. 151, 152.

[2] " Despairing, in the end, of a 'true general council,' they had simultaneously arrived at the conclusion that it was the paramount duty of ' every prince to redress his own realm.' " — Hardwick's *Hist. of the Articles*, p. 52.

[3] Vol. i. pp. 258–264.

[4] Ibid., pp. 286–289.

papacy, which reached their highest point when John surrendered his kingdom as a fief to Innocent III.[1] Not until the reign of Edward I. was the political and ecclesiastical supremacy of the pope, as admitted by John and Henry III., challenged by the crown with the aid of the parliament. The successful repudiation by the latter of the political or feudal supremacy asserted by Boniface VIII.[2] was followed by a series of statutes designed to protect the internal administration of the church from foreign interference. As heretofore explained, the greatest of these statutes were: that known as *De asportatis religiosorum* (35 Edw. I.), designed to prevent alien priors from drawing tribute from English religious houses; the Statute of Provisors (25 Edw. III. st. 4), which, after declaring that the elections of bishops and others should be free as in time past, denied to the pope the right to make nominations to benefices within the kingdom, with severe penalties upon all "provisors" who should obtain them from him by purchase or otherwise; the statute (27 Edw. III. st. 1) which forbade, under severe penalities, any person to withdraw any cause from the cognizance of the king's court by means of a citation to the court of Rome; and lastly the famous Statute of Præmunire (16 Rich. II. c. 5), in which it was provided that all who shall obtain from the court of Rome, or elsewhere, any sentence of excommunication, ecclesiastical process, or any other thing touching the rights of the crown, or bring the same within the realm, shall be put out of the king's protection, shall be subject to forfeiture and to be attainted, and shall also be subjected to process to "be made against them by *præmunire facias*, in manner as it is ordained in other Statutes of Provisors against those which do sue in the court of another in derogation of the regality of our lord the king."[3] While the parliament was thus engaged in asserting the rights of the crown against the claims of the papacy occurred the great religious rebellion in the ranks of the common people which, taking color and form from the teachings of Wycliffe, seriously threatened for a time not only the spiritual influence of the church, but the vast possessions by which it had been enriched.[4] But the time had not yet come for final and definitive action; the

[marginal notes:] resistance of the feudal supremacy of Boniface VIII.; Statute *De asportatis;* Statute of Provisors; Statute of Præmunire; Lollardry;

---

[1] Vol. i. p. 373.
[2] Ibid., p. 569.
[3] Ibid., pp. 570, 571.
[4] Ibid., pp. 538, 571, 572.

conservative sense of the nation recoiled from the socialistic
tendencies by which the Lollard movement was discredited;
and so the premature ecclesiastical agitation of the fourteenth
century, after a brief period of success, passed into history as
religious revolt of the four- teenth cen- tury a mere prologue to that of the sixteenth.. a mere prologue to the drama to be enacted upon a grander
scale in the sixteenth.   When the real drama begins, the first
act opens with the revival of the then obsolete Statute of
Præmunire (16 Rich. II. c. 5), under which Wolsey was indicted in October, 1529, and upon his own confession convicted
of having obtained bulls from Rome, which he had made public, and under which he had exercised his legatine authority in
derogation of the jurisdiction of the royal tribunals.[1]

The bold and far-reaching policy which Cromwell was now
pressing upon Henry involved, however, far more than the
mere revival and enforcement of statutes in restraint of the
papal power which, since the accession of the house of Lan-
Cromwell aimed not at the restraint but entire abolition of the papal power; caster, had been passing into desuetude; the disciple of Machiavelli aimed at no less than the transformation of the church
into a mere department of state, and the transfer to the crown
of the entire papal jurisdiction.   In the presence of such a
proposal even Henry faltered.   He had no personal sympathy
whatever with the new movement which was threatening to
wreck the spiritual unity of the mediæval empire, and he had
no mind to break with the papacy until he had exhausted every
means possible to prevent a disputed succession by obtaining
a divorce from the only tribunal whose decree could command
anything like general acceptance.   And yet the impression
made upon the king by Cromwell was so great that he was at
sworn of the privy council; once sworn of the privy council,[2] and after a short period of
waiting, during which every effort to move Clement failed, he

---

[1] The act under which Wolsey was
indicted was broad in its language, and
prohibited the exercise of any kind of
jurisdiction encroaching upon the royal
authority. This general policy, as above
explained, was embodied in a series of
acts beginning with that of Edward I.
35 Edw. I.; 25 Edw. III. st. 4; st. 5,
c. 22; 27 Edw. III. st. 1; 13 Rich. II.
st. 2, c. 2; 16 Rich. II. c. 5; 9 Hen.
IV. c. 8.   Although no express mention was made of legates in the act
under which Wolsey was charged, the
claim was that he had incurred the

penalty of a *præmunire* by acting as
legate *a latere*. He could have pleaded
the king's license, but did not.   Cavendish, p. 276.   A clear statement of the
merits of the case is contained in Amos,
Reformation Parliament, pp. 59, 60. If
the license had been pleaded, the sufficiency of the plea would have involved
a discussion of the dispensing power,
which had been held to extend, in the
reign of Henry VII., to the penalties
of every act *malum prohibitum*, but not
malum in se.

[2] Pole, *Apologia*, pp. 122, 123.

was permitted, as a last resort, to put in force his entire policy. In that way, the divorce became the mainspring of the revolution that grew out of the revived contest with Rome, which religious reaction and civil war had suspended for more than a century, — a revolution which, in the absence of the motive involved in the divorce, Henry would no doubt have opposed with the full force of the royal authority. The record of the proceedings of the great parliament, through whose enactments the legal and political separation of the Church of England from the papacy was finally brought about, puts beyond all question the fact that so long as the hope of a successful issue at Rome remained, Henry's efforts were confined to a series of tentative measures in restraint of papal and clerical privileges, designed rather as methods of coercion than as the means of separation.[1] Not until Henry's policy of menace and coercion had failed were Cromwell's decisive measures permitted to begin. The fact that the parliament was now seized upon by the crown as its tool in the final struggle with Rome indicates a radical departure from the system which had prevailed since the accession of Edward IV. If Edward, Henry VII., and Wolsey had looked upon the assembly of estates as a menace to the conciliar system, Henry VIII. now felt sure enough of its subserviency [2] to submit to it during the remainder of his reign every measure, ecclesiastical, judicial, or political, which could draw moral weight from its sanction or legal force from its authority.

the divorce becomes the mainspring of separation;

Henry's policy of menace and coercion;

the parliament made the tool of the crown.

Although, with the exception of a single session, the government had been carried on for fourteen years without a parliament, that summoned for 1529 was continued by prorogation from year to year until April, 1536.[3] Through the acts of this parliament it was that the papal overlordship was finally overthrown, the royal supremacy fully established, and the clergy reduced to a state of abject submission at the feet of the monarchy. Only by a consecutive examination, in

Outline of the work of the Reformation Parliament of 1529:

[1] The whole story can be traced with more or less distinctness by the aid of the preambles of the statutes, which during this reign "are prolix, diffuse, and redundant, beyond all former example, as if, apparently, to guard the enacting clauses from misrepresentation of motives rather than misinterpreta- tion of texts." — *Reformation Parliament*, Amos, p. 9.

[2] See the able summary upon this subject in *Reformation Parliament*, Amos, pp. 1–9.

[3] The parliament met on the 3d of November, 1529, and was dissolved on April 14, 1536.

the light of the contemporary history, of the legislative work
which took place during the seven sessions of this memorable
parliament, is it possible to mark the undulations of a policy
which advanced or retreated as the conduct of the great controversy involved in the divorce required that the king should
bear towards the papacy an attitude of menace or conciliation.
From the letters of the French ambassador[1] we learn of the
eager spirit of expectancy which pervaded all London as the
members gathered there for their momentous work early in

its first ses-
sion began
in Novem-
ber with an
an attack
upon the
clergy;

November. In view of the fact that the unpopularity of the
divorce was so great that Anne Boleyn hardly dared to stir
abroad,[2] it is not strange that an effort should have been made
to attract popular sympathy to the king's cause by an assault
upon the clergy with which the session opened, and which

detailed ac-
cusation
against
them;

consisted of a detailed accusation against them, in the form of
a petition from the commons to the king, in which were summarized all grievances and abuses that could then be charged
upon the administrators of the Anglican Church. The petition — after stating that "the discord, variance, and debate"
which had lately arisen was attributable no more to the "new
fantastical and erroneous opinions grown by occasion of frantic
and seditious books compiled, imprinted, published, and made,
in the English tongue, than to the extreme and uncharitable
behavior and dealings of divers ordinaries" — proceeds to enu-
merate the legislation of the clergy in convocation without
the assent of king or people, the oppressive and expensive procedure of the spiritual courts, the excessive number of holy
days, and the abuses of ecclesiastical patronage, as the subjects
which called most urgently for remedial legislation.[3] After
referring back to the parliament such subjects as in his judgment required immediate attention, the king submitted the

the bishops
called upon
to answer;

petition itself to the bishops, with the requirement that they
should make a prompt answer to the charges preferred against
them. After some delay they responded in a lengthy document, answering the accusations *seriatim*, which the king,
with a slighting remark, referred to the commons.[4] A few

---

[1] Letters of the Bishop of Bayonne, Legrand, vol. iii. pp. 368, 378, etc.

[2] See Green, *Hist. Eng. People*, vol. ii. p. 147.

[3] A full statement of the petition,

with the reply of the bishops thereto, taken from the MS. in the Rolls House, is printed in Froude's *Hist. Eng.*, vol. i. pp. 208–241.

[4] "The king's conduct and observa-

days later he said to a delegation from the houses that "we thought that the clergy of our realm had been our subjects wholly, but now, we have well perceived that they be but half our subjects ; yea, and scarce our subjects, for all the prelates, at their consecration, take an oath to the pope clean contrary to the oath they make to us, so they seem to be his subjects and not ours."[1]   From this deliverance it is plain that the king had hearkened to the suggestion of Cromwell as to the danger involved in the clergy's dual allegiance.   Putting aside the larger questions touching the legislative independence of the clergy in convocation and the jurisdiction of the church courts, the parliament confined itself during the six weeks of the session to enactments for the discipline of the clergy, and for the reduction within fixed limits of certain clerical fees and exactions.   As far back as the reign of Edward III. the extortion of discretionary fees upon the granting of probates and administrations had become such an abuse that an effort was then made to provide a remedy by a statute,[2] which was supplemented by another[3] of a temporary character in the reign of Henry V.   As that too had proved ineffectual, a third and more positive act was now passed to remedy the evil.[4]   At the same time the mortuary fees,[5] or "corse presents" of the parochial clergy, were reduced and regulated by an act which forbade their collection when the effects were small, and which limited their amount within reasonable bounds when the estate was large.[6]   This was followed by a statute passed for the discipline of the clergy which forbade them to cultivate more land than was necessary for the support of their own households, to buy or sell merchandise for gain, or to keep tanneries or breweries.[7]   This act also made residence imperative, and

clergy's dual allegiance ;

acts for their discipline, and for the reduction of probate and administration fees ;

mortuary fees or "corse presents ;"

act as to clerical trading, residence, and pluralities ;

---

tions with regard to it showed that he favored, and, perhaps, had originated, the bold and novel inquiry." — Amos, p. 232.

[1] Hall, quoted by Amos, *Reformation Parliament*, p. 233.

[2] 31 Edw. III. st. 1 c. 4.

[3] 3 Hen. V. c. 8.   See Reeves' *Hist. Eng. Law*, vol. iii. p. 230.   The first statute attributes the abuses complained of to the "ministers or bishops and other ordinaries;" in the second "the ordinaries" are said to have promised a reformation.   "The term *Ordinary* is generally synonymous with Bishop;

but it includes every ecclesiastical judge who has the regular *ordinary* jurisdiction independent of another.   *Co. Litt.*, p. 344." — Amos, p. 234, note 1.

[4] 21 Hen. VIII. c. 5.

[5] As to the distinction between burial-fees and mortuaries, see note to the case of *Andrews v. Cawthorne*, Willes, p. 536.

[6] 21 Hen. VIII. c. 5 ; Reeves, vol. iii. p. 233.

[7] 21 Hen. VIII. c. 13.   As to the subjects to which it related, this act "contained the principal enactments in force before the reign of Victoria." — Amos, p. 236.

forbade all pluralities in respect to benefices above the yearly value of eight pounds. Through the proviso annexed to these clauses which gave to the crown, under certain limitations, the right to sell dispensations as to pluralities and non-residence,[1] — declared to be illegal when issued by papal or episcopal authority, — the king had his first foretaste of the new ecclesiastical power that was soon to come. By such legislation as the foregoing for the redress of ecclesiastical exactions and abuses, which were certainly flagrant, Henry was able not only to win popular favor, but also "to let the pope see what he could do if he went on to offend him, and how willingly his parliament would concur with him, if it went to extremes."[2] A very striking illustration of this perfect oneness existing between the king and the parliament occurred before the end of the session, when by its action he was released from all his

king released from his debts.

debts, and from all suits that might arise therein.[3] When the session ended in December, the effort to bend the pope to his will, which Henry had been attempting to advance by legislation hostile to the clergy, he transferred once more to the field of diplomacy.

Wiltshire's mission to the emperor;

In January, 1530, the earl of Wiltshire, the father of Anne Boleyn, attended by a council of divines, was sent on a mission to the emperor, who was at that time sojourning with the pope at Bologna, where the delegation arrived in March.[4] This mission was the outcome of the new policy of Norfolk, who hoped to win the emperor to the king's cause by an abandonment of Wolsey's French policy, which it was claimed had driven him into a hostile attitude.[5] But the effort failed; the emperor, putting aside all of the blandishments held out to him, remained faithful to the cause of his aunt, and the pope would do nothing without him.[6] And so ended the first and last communication between Henry and Charles V. upon the

---

[1] Upon the subject of pluralities and non-residence, see Reeves, vol. iii. pp. 234–237; Amos, pp. 237–243.

[2] Burnet's *Hist. Reform.*, vol. i. p. 62.

[3] This act, not printed with the other statutes, is contained in Burnet, vol. ii. (*Collectanea*) p. xxxviii. For a full exposition of the scope and purpose of this iniquitous act, see Amos, pp. 66–70.

[4] For the instructions to the ambassadors, see the transcripts for the N. Rymer, p. 168.

[5] See Green, *Hist. of the Eng. People*, vol. ii. p. 149.

[6] For details, see letters written 27th and 28th March from Bologna by the bishop of Tarbes. Legrand, vol. iii. pp. 401, 454.

subject of the divorce.   One of the divines who attended the attended by Cranmer, who had suggested the submission of the question of the divorce to the learned; earl on his unfruitful mission was Thomas Cranmer, then a lecturer on theology at Cambridge,[1] who, it is said, had suggested to the king two years before[2] the submission of the questions involved in the divorce to the learned canonists and universities throughout Christendom.   It was claimed that, if a decided preponderance of opinion could thus be drawn out in the king's favor, it would certainly influence the pope; and if not, that such an expression could be made the basis of an appeal to a general council.   So favorably was the suggestion received that Cranmer was at once instructed to devote himself exclusively to the study of the subject, upon which he wrote a treatise[3] that he was called upon to defend at Oxford he writes a treatise upon the subject; and Cambridge.[4]   Immediately thereafter he was sent to Bologna, where "the matter of the divorce was to be disputed and ventilated."   That effort having failed, Cranmer's scheme his scheme put into practical operation; was put into practical operation by the submission of the all-important question to home and foreign universities, and by the dispatch of English agents to Germany, Italy, and France, armed with all the grosser means of persuasion which power and money could command.   When all the details of this scandalous transaction[5] have been carefully examined, it is hard to doubt, despite the fact that half, or nearly half, of the expressions obtained were adverse to the papal position, that the real preponderance of unbiassed opinion was decidedly the other way.   Only by a stern exercise of the royal authority was it possible to extort favorable responses from Oxford and Cambridge; without like pressure from Francis, even Henry's bribery would have failed at Paris; while in Protestant Germany, where little was to be hoped for the bitter enemy of Luther, every institution was pronounced against him.   So

---

[1] Cranmer, born in 1489, was now about forty years of age.

[2] The account which says that the suggestion was made by Cranmer in 1529 rests upon the authority of Morice's narrative, printed in Nichol's *Narratives of the Reformation*, p. 240. It is almost certain, however, that the suggestion was first made in 1527 by the letter of Wakefield (Knight's *Life of Erasmus*, App. p. xxviii), or by the assembly of bishops convened in that year by Wolsey, in which "the mat-

ter of the king's case (was) debated, reasoned, argued, and consulted of from day to day," as we are told by Cavendish.

[3] The book was written in the house of the earl of Wiltshire, Anne's father.

[4] Nichol's *Narratives of the Reformation*, p. 242.

[5] The whole story has been told by Burnet, vol. i. pp. 64–69; by Lingard, vol. iv. pp. 548–552; and by Froude, vol. i. pp. 263–285.

coercion and bribery fail to produce a consensus of opinion.

complete was the failure to unite the voices of the learned throughout Christendom in the king's favor that no attempt was made to lay before the pontiff[1] the great mass of literature which resulted from Cranmer's grand inquest; it was laid instead before the second session of the parliament, which met in January, 1531.[2]

Henry draws nearer to Cromwell's policy; fresh assault upon the clergy in second session, January, 1530-31;

Angered and disheartened by the failure of Norfolk's bungling diplomacy, by Cranmer's fruitless appeal to the learned, and by the fresh refusal of the pope to permit him to settle the question of the divorce in his own courts,[3] Henry was now ready to renew his assaults upon the clergy, and to draw nearer, as a last resort, to Cromwell's policy. Upon Wolsey's conviction a year before under the Statute of Præmunire, it had been held, through a legal fiction of the judges, that the entire clergy of the realm had become involved in his guilt by their recognition of his legatine authority; and the attorney-general had been directed to file an information against them in the king's bench as his "fautors and abettors."[4] Startled by this novel method of attack, the convocation of Canterbury, which was hastily assembled, offered the king a hundred thousand pounds for a full pardon. To this offer the response was made that it could not be accepted unless in the preamble to the grant the king should be acknowledged "to be the protector and only supreme head of the church and clergy of England."

convocation forced to admit the king's headship of the church with a qualification;

After an earnest remonstrance, the difference was settled by a compromise suggested by Warham, which qualified the admission by the saving clause, "as far as the law of Christ will allow, the supreme head."[5] The convocation of York adopted the same language in a grant which gave to the king nearly one fifth of the sum granted by the southern convocation.[6] When the bill for the pardon of the clergy was

---

[1] Such was the original intention. See Legrand, vol. iii. p. 443.

[2] On the 30th of March Sir Thomas More read to the Commons the decisions of the various universities. Hall, p. 780; Burnet, vol. i. p. 80.

[3] January 5, 1531, a bull was issued by the pope and published in Flanders forbidding any person or court to pronounce a divorce between Henry and Catherine. Legrand, vol. iii. p. 531. "He seems to have done nothing further in the matter during the whole of

the year 1531."—Blount, *Reform. of the Church of Eng.*, vol. i. pp. 178, 179.

[4] As to the whole matter, see Burnet, vol. i. p. 81; Amos, *Reformation Parliament*, p. 51.

[5] With that proviso the grant was first carried by the silent consent of both houses. Wilkins, *Conc.*, vol. ii. pp. 725, 742. Subsequently, express assent was demanded and granted. Blount, *Reform. of the Church of Eng.*, vol. i. pp. 207-209.

[6] "The statute for pardoning the

presented for parliamentary sanction, the ever cautious com- cautious policy of the commons;
mons, fearing that with the king's love of the letter of the law
the subtle theory upon which the church had been impaled
might be extended to the whole nation, refused their assent
until a general pardon should be granted to the laity as well.
After some negotiation, the matter was adjusted by the passage of a bill for the pardon of the clergy of the province of
Canterbury,[1] after it had been settled that another should be
passed wherein his majesty, " by the authority of the present parliament, granted to all and singular his temporal and
lay subjects and temporal bodies politic and corporate, and to
every one of them his pardon for offences against the Statutes
of Provisors and Præmunire."[2]   Shortly after adjournment, after ad-journment, lords and part of the commons address the pope in the king's behalf;
the king made a fresh attempt to influence events at Rome
by an address to the pope, signed by the lords temporal and
spiritual, and part of the commons, in which they, after espous-
ing the cause of the king as their own, laid before the pontiff
their version of the judgments which had been pronounced by
the universities in favor of the divorce, with the significant intimation that " extreme remedies are ever harsh of application ;
but he that is sick will by all means be rid of his distemper."[3]
And as a further evidence of the firmness of his resolve, Henry
followed up this covert threat by the banishment of Catherine
in July, 1531, from the royal palace to Ampthill.[4]   Before the Catherine banished to Ampthill;
end of the year still another effort was made to obtain a favor-
able answer from Clement by the dispatch of a fresh embassy
to Rome, headed by the new bishop of Winchester, Stephen
Gardiner, whose rapid rise in royal favor since the fall of Wol- Gardiner's mission to Rome.
sey was now being surely surpassed by the great and growing
influence of Cromwell.   The utter failure of Gardiner's mission[5] left the new favorite free to make a fresh attack in parliament upon papal and clerical privileges through the two

clergy of the province of York was not
passed till the next session (23 Hen.
VIII. c. 19) ; it is similar, in its terms,
to the statute relating to Canterbury,
only the price of the pardon was to
be £18,840, 0 *s*. 10 *d*." — Amos, pp. 57,
58.

[1] 22 Hen. VIII. c. 15.

[2] 22 Hen. VIII. c. 16. The admission
of parliament into a participation with
the king in the exercise of the pardon-

ing power was certainly remarkable.
" The effects of these pardons was to
clench a subsidy that had been tyran-
nically extorted from the clergy." —
Amos, p. 57.

[3] Herbert, p. 331.

[4] " Go where I may," she said, " I
shall still be his lawful wife." — Hall,
p. 200 ; Herbert, p. 354.

[5] See Green, *Hist. of the Eng. People*,
vol. ii. p. 154.

acts [1] which specially distinguish the proceedings of the third session of 1531–32.

The first of these acts, passed to prohibit the citation of persons out of the diocese in which they reside, recites in its preamble that much vexation and oppression had been occasioned by requiring persons to go far away from their homes in order to appear in the court of archives, and in other high archiepiscopal courts, in order to answer in causes of defamation, tithes, and the like, which were more often begun through malice than from any just cause; and in which, if the party did not appear, the spiritual sentence which was pronounced could only be absolved by the payment of court fees together with the charges of the summoner or apparitor by whom the process had been served. It was therefore enacted that, with certain exceptions, no person should be cited outside of the diocese of his residence, while the fee for the summons was reduced from two shillings to three pence.[2] The limitation

thus imposed upon the jurisdiction of the spiritual courts was soon followed by an act forbidding the payment to the pope of the annates,[3] or firstfruits of benefices, which the bishops had been for a long time compelled to pay before they could receive the papal bulls necessary for the confirmation of their elections. It was now enacted that if any bishop should pay such tribute, it should cause a forfeiture of his lands and goods; that if any bishop presented by the king to the pope should be hindered by the withholding of the bulls, he should be

consecrated without them by the archbishop; and that if any archbishop should be so hindered, he should be consecrated by two bishops to be named by the king. In accordance with the prevailing policy of menace and supplication this act was qualified by a proviso, which empowered Henry at his discretion to declare by letters patent, before the beginning of the next session, whether the act should take effect "as an act or statute of this present parliament [4] or not." This assault upon the papal exchequer Cromwell quickly followed up by a fresh assertion of his theory of the ecclesiastical supremacy

---

[1] Another act, the first of the session (23 Hen. VIII. c. 1), taking away the benefit of clergy from the perpetrators of certain crimes, is also worthy of mention.

[2] 23 Hen. VIII. c. 9; Amos, pp. 245 246.

[3] 23 Hen. VIII. c. 20.

[4] Amos, p. 254.

of the crown.   That theory, already admitted by convocation a year before, "so far as the law of Christ will allow," now found expression in an address [1] procured from the commons, in which they were made to complain that the clerical legislatures, without consultation with the other estates, often enacted laws touching temporal matters which, in spite of contrary statutes, were enforced by spiritual penalties.   After a long and painful negotiation Henry demanded, and convocation was forced to make, an act of "Submission," wherein the clergy were made to promise "that we will never from henceforth enact, put in use, promulgate, or execute any new canons, or constitutions provincial, or any new ordinance, provincial or synodal, in our convocation, or synod, in time coming (which convocation is, always hath been, and must be assembled only by your high commandment of writ), only your Highness, by your royal assent shall license us to assemble our convocation, and to make, promulgate, and execute such constitutions and ordinaments as shall be made in the same; and thereto give your royal assent and authority." [2]   The "Submission" was subscribed May 15, 1532, and at the end of 1533 it was embodied in the "Act of Submission," 25 Hen. VIII. c. 19, passed at that time, in which it was provided that all canons ecclesiastical then in force, not in conflict with the laws of the realm or the royal prerogative, should continue to bind until abolished by further legislation.   Thus by this new concordat between church and state it was settled [3] (1) that the old canons of the church, not in conflict with the laws of the realm or the royal supremacy, should remain in force; (2) that convocation should not discuss the enactment of new canons without a license from the crown; (3) that no new canons should have force unless they were ratified by the crown, — an arrangement which has continued until the present time. [4]   The counterblast from Rome to these fresh assaults upon the clergy was a brief issued in November, in which Clement declared both Henry and Anne excommunicate unless

convocation forbidden to legislate without royal license ("Act of Submission," 25 Hen. VIII. c. 19, passed at the end of 1533);

---

[1] This address was presented to the king in March, 1532.   Herbert's *Henry VIII.*, p. 357.

[2] Wilkins, *Conc.*, vol. iii. p. 754.

[3] As to the status of convocation as a legislative body after the Reformation Statutes, see vol. i. p. 344, citing Mr. Gladstone on the Royal Supremacy, p. 31.

[4] As to the canons enacted since the passage of the "Act of Submission," see Blount, *Reform. of the Church of Eng.*, vol. ii. pp. 368–373.

conditional
excommu-
nication of
Henry and
Anne.
they should cease to cohabit within a month ; and in the event
they should attempt to marry, such a marriage was declared
beforehand to be illegal.[1] But the time had now come when
neither papal bulls nor acts of parliament could stay the march
of physical conditions which made it imperative that the marriage of Henry and Anne should be hastened. Although the
date of the marriage was at the time intentionally involved in
confusion, there can hardly be a doubt that it was secretly
celebrated late in January, 1533.[2]

Fourth
session,
February,
1532-33 :
statute
forbidding
appeals to
Rome in
certain
cases ;
Such was the condition of things on the 4th of February,
when the fourth session of the parliament began,[3] in which
was passed the act of forbidding appeals to Rome[4] in all
causes testamentary, of marriage and divorce, oblations, tithes,
and obventions, whether already commenced or hereafter to
be commenced. It was provided that in all such causes,
whether affecting the king or his subjects, the hearing should
be had in the king's courts, temporal or spiritual, and not
the course
of appeal ;
elsewhere ; and furthermore that the course of appeal should
be from the archdeacon to the bishop, and from the bishop to
the archbishop of his province ; and in any cause touching the
king or his successors, the appeal should be to the upper house
of convocation.[5] Such an act had now become a pressing

[1] Burnet, i.; *Records*, ii. 111–119;
Legrand, i. 228–230.

[2] Lingard (vol. v. pp. 2, 3, and notes)
fixes the day as the 25th of January, not
only on the authority of Sanders, but
upon that of a manuscript history of
the divorce published thirty years before
it. Legrand, ii. p. 110. Froude (vol. i.
p. 410, note 2), after setting the date of
the 25th of January in the margin, says,
upon the authority of Cranmer, "and
'somewhere about St. Paul's day,' Anne
Boleyn received the prize for which
she had thirsted seven long years," etc.
Burnet (vol. i. p. 95) says that the marriage took place on the 14th of the
previous November. He states at the
same time, however, that Stowe fixes
it on the 25th of January. Elizabeth
was born on the 7th of the following
September.

[3] It closed April 7, 1533.

[4] 24 Hen. VIII. c. 12.

[5] As to the modification of this act
providing that in all manner of appeals
the appeal should be made " from the
archbishop's court to the king in his
chancery, where a commission shall be
accorded for the determination of the
appeal, and from thence no further," see
Reeves' *Hist. Eng. Law*, vol. iii. p. 241,
note (b), Finlason ed. The modifying
provision is contained in the " Act of
Submission," 25 Hen. VIII. c. 19. The
right of appeal to Rome was revived
in the reign of Mary, but during that
of Elizabeth (1 Eliz. c. 1) the jurisdiction of the crown as settled by the Act
of Appeals was restored, " and though
the court has been changed, the privy
council being substituted for the delegates, the principle of the law has remained untouched to the present day."
— Blount, *Reform. of the Church of
Eng.*, vol. i. p. 261. The Delegates of
Appeal, as the commissioners were
called, were superseded by the Judicial
Committee of the Privy Council by
virtue of 2 & 3 Will. IV. c. 92. By the
" Supreme Court of Judicature Act,
1873 " (36 & 37 Vict. c. 66, sec. 21) the
queen is empowered, by order in coun-

necessity.   A new heir to the throne was on the way, whose legitimacy could not possibly be upheld without a dissolution of the union between Catherine and Henry, and such dissolution could not be accomplished as a finality through the decree of an English ecclesiastical court, until all chance of an appeal to the pope was made impossible.[1]   That end having been accomplished by the act in question, the next step was the selection of a judge upon whom the king could surely rely.   Such a one was easily found in Cranmer, the king's tried advocate, who *Cranmer appointed primate;* upon the death of Warham had been tendered the archbishopric of Canterbury, to which he was consecrated in March.[2] The king's marriage, which, pending the papal confirmation of Cranmer's appointment, had been kept strictly secret, was made public soon thereafter, when the questions involved in *questions involved in divorce submitted to convocation;* the divorce were submitted in a special and peculiar form to convocation, where, after considerable debate, answers favorable to the king were carried by large majorities.[3]   The new archbishop, thus supported by the voice of the clergy, soon exhorted his master to permit him to take cognizance of the divorce, and, for the good of the realm, to hear and determine it.[4]   In May Cranmer rendered his decree, in which it was held *Cranmer's decree,* that the marriage with Catherine was void from the beginning by reason of the fact that the original dispensation of Julius II. was beyond the papal power;[5] and at a little later day another hearing was had, at which the marriage with Anne was confirmed as valid and lawful.[6]   Two months later the *which the pope declared null;* pope annulled the sentence pronounced by Cranmer upon the

---

cil, to refer all ecclesiastical appeals and petitions, now cognizable by the judicial committee, to the new court of appeal constituted by that act. When so acting, such court of appeal shall consist of " such and so many of the judges thereof, and shall be assisted by such assessors, being Archbishops and Bishops of the Church of England," as shall be directed by any general rules to be made by order in council.

[1] The " dates appear to supply a cogent reason why the king should have availed himself of the aid of parliament, in the present session, to corroborate his marriage, and, prospectively, the archbishop's sentence, by a new law of ecclesiastical appeals that might gag the mouth of an appellant

queen." — Amos, *Reformation Parliament,* p. 257.

[2] The necessary bulls were expedited on 21st and 22d February and on the 3d of March, and the consecration took place on the 30th of that month.

[3] See the account in Burnet, vol. i. p. 98, as corrected by Lingard, vol. v. p. 8.

[4] For Cranmer's abject memorial letter (April 11) to the king, see *State Papers,* vol. i. p. 390.

[5] The decree contained in an Inspeximus, *Rot. Parl.,* 25 Reg. 2d part, is printed in Burnet, vol. ii. (*Collectanea*), liv.

[6] On May 29 the second decree was given at Lambeth, and is in the same Inspeximus.

Elizabeth born, September 7, 1533.

ground that the case was then pending before himself;[1] and so matters stood at the birth of the princess Elizabeth,[2] on the 7th of September, 1533.

Fifth session, January 15, 1533-34;

When the fifth session began, on the 15th of January,[3] everything was still involved in a state of painful uncertainty. The long protracted negotiations with Rome were still pending, and no one knew when or how the end would be reached. And yet, in evident anticipation of the final catastrophe, all judicial and financial connection with Rome was now com-

statutes confirming submission of clergy,

pletely broken by two memorable statutes : in the first [4] the surrender which had been made by the clergy a year before of their legislative independence was confirmed, and the partial restriction which had been put upon appeals to Rome in the fourth session was extended to all cases whatsoever ; in the

forbidding all appeals to Rome, and the payment of Peter's pence;

second [5] was contained a prohibition against the payment of Peter's pence, and every other kind of payment made to the pope for dispensations, licenses, faculties, grants, relaxations, and the like usually obtained from that source. This last named statute at the same time provided that certain dispensations, licenses, faculties, and other writings which had been formerly obtained from Rome should thereafter be sought of the archbishop of Canterbury, who might be compelled by the king's writ to grant licenses, faculties, or dispensations.[6]

statute as to annates reënacted with provision authorizing nomination of bishops by *congé d'élire*,

Turning then to the Annates Act,[7] which had finally been confirmed by letters patent, after the refusal of the pope to notice the communication made to him under it, parliament reënacted it [8] with additional clauses, providing that bishops should no longer be presented to the pope for confirmation, but that, on the vacancy of any cathedral church, the king should grant to the dean and chapter, or to the prior and

[1] The brief (July 12) declared that Henry by his disobedience had incurred the penalties of excommunication, which, however, as an act of grace, were suspended until the following September. Bonner to Cromwell, *State Papers*, vol. vii. p. 481.

[2] Hall, p. 805.

[3] It closed on the 30th of March, 1534.

[4] This was the act entitled "An act for the submission of the clergy to the king's majesty" (25 Hen. VIII. c. 19), already referred to as the "Act

of Submission." See above, p. 70, note 1.

[5] 25 Hen. VIII. c. 21, entitled "An act for the exoneration from exactions paid to the See of Rome."

[6] For a commentary upon the act, see Reeves' *Hist. Eng. Law*, vol. iii. pp. 244–246 and notes.

[7] See above, p. 68.

[8] 25 Hen. VIII. c. 20. In the first act the pontiff is called "Our holy Father, the Pope ; " in the second, "Bishop of Rome, otherwise called the Pope."

monks, "a license under the great seal "[1] to elect the person named in the letters missive, which right, if not exercised within twelve days, should be forfeited to the crown. It was further provided that the prelate named or elected, after he had sworn fealty, and after he had been invested and consecrated, should sue his temporalities out of the king's hands, and make corporal oath to the king and to no other.[2] This ancient method of nominating and electing bishops and arch- the method employed to the present day. bishops by *congé d'élire*, under which the real power of appointment was vested in the crown, has continued in force to the present day, although its character has been completely transformed by the growth of the modern constitution, under which the appointing power has passed from the crown to the minister, who represents the will of the people.[3]

In order to remove as far as possible the doubt and uncer- Henry's first succession act; tainty which still surrounded the legitimacy of the princess Elizabeth, there was also passed at this session the first [4] of Henry's statutes for the settlement of the royal succession, which, after adjudging that his marriage with Catherine was null, and that his subsequent marriage with Anne was valid, carefully marked out the order in which the children of Anne should follow him. First, the sons were to succeed, with their heirs; if sons failed them, then "to the eldest issue female, which is the Lady Elizabeth, now Princess . . . and so from issue female to issue female, and to the heirs of their bodies, one after another, by course of inheritance, according to their

---

[1] The license contained no restriction, but it was attended "with a letter missive containing the name of the person which they shall elect and choose."

[2] For commentaries upon this act, see Amos, *Reformation Parliament*, pp. 270–273; Reeves' *Hist. Eng. Law*, vol. iii. p. 242 and note (a). The account given by Amos of the controversy touching the *congé d'élire*, which occurred in the reign of James I., and to which Coke was a party, is specially interesting.

[3] " Practically therefore our English prelate, alone among all the prelates of the world, is now raised to his episcopal throne by the same popular election which raised Ambrose to his epis-

copal chair at Milan." — Green, *Hist. Eng. People*, vol. ii. p. 160. For a few years the *congé d'élire* was abolished as a mere pretence by 1 Edw. VI. c. 2; and the acts both of Henry and of Edward were repealed by 1 Mar. cap. 2; and 1 & 2 Phil. & Mar. c. 8. Then the act of Henry only was revived by 1 Eliz. c. 1. By 1 Jac. I. c. 25, s. 48, the act of Phil. & Mar. was entirely repealed, and three years after it was claimed that Edward's act was thereby revived, but the judges held adversely, saying that elections must still be held.

[4] 25 Hen. VIII. c. 22. Amos, *Reformation Parliament*, devotes a chapter to the special consideration of this act, pp. 12–37.

ages, as the crown of England hath been accustomed and
ought to go, in cases where there be heirs female to the same."
To slander the king's last marriage was declared to be high
treason, if the offence was committed in writing, and misprision of treason, if by words only ; and all subjects of full age
were commanded to swear obedience to the act under penalty

oath to sup-
port the
succession
drafted
under the
act refused
by Fisher
and More;

of misprision of treason.   Under this mandate an oath to support the succession, whose form had not been prescribed, and
whose terms seem to have been more comprehensive than the
provisions of the statute warranted, was drawn and presented
by a commission, and generally taken by all, including the
universities and convocations,[1] with the notable exceptions of
Bishop Fisher and Sir Thomas More,[2] whose refusal was

breach
made final
by papal
decree,
March 15,
1534, con-
firming
Henry's
marriage
with Cath-
erine;

quickly followed by their imprisonment.   Early in April,[3] 1534,
and within a week after the end of the session last referred to,
the news was received in England that on the 23d of March
the long struggle, which had begun six years before with the
application to Rome for a bull annulling the king's marriage
with Catherine, had ended at last in a decree adjudging that
marriage to be legal, and the papal dispensation under which
it had been contracted regular and valid.   And in accordance
with the papal practice it was ordered that, if the king should
within a given time fail to bow to the judgment, he should be
excommunicate, and should forfeit the allegiance of his subjects ; and finally that he should be deposed by the emperor,
who had undertaken the execution of that part of the sentence
even before it was rendered.[4]   To this final thrust from Rome
Henry responded, in the face of the threatened invasion, in a

Henry's
bitter re-
sponse.

royal proclamation ordering the pope's name to be erased from
the prayers, canons, and mass-books of the churches, with the
injunction that it should " be never more (except to his con-

---

[1] Wilkins, *Conc.*, vol. iii. pp. 771, 774, 775.

[2] The form of the substituted oath, which is printed in Blount, vol. i. pp. 417, 418, contained a virtual acknow-ledgment of the king's ecclesiastical supremacy prior to the passage of the Act of Supremacy. Both Fisher and More were willing to swear to the suc-cession as fixed by the statute, but both refused the substituted oath in April, 1534, and were thereupon com-

mitted to the Tower. During the year they were both attainted for misprision of treason for refusing " since the first of May last to take the oath for the establishment of the succession." As to the examination of More, see his *Works*, pp. 1429, 1447.

[3] See Amos, *Reformation Parlia-ment*, p. 279.

[4] Legrand, vol. i. pp. 273–276 ; vol. iii. pp. 630–638 ; *State Papers*, vol. vii. p. 579.

tumely and reproach) remembered, but perpetually suppressed and obscured." [1]

In this temper it was that the parliament, whose sixth session began on the 3d of November, entered upon the task of completing the work of separation, which had been gradually approaching consummation according to the definite and comprehensive plan of Cromwell that now culminated in the Act of Supremacy,[2] whose brief and comprehensive language defies abridgment : "Albeit," runs the act, "the king's majesty justly and rightfully is and ought to be the supreme Head of the Church of England, and is so recognized by the clergy of this realm in their convocation, yet nevertheless, for corroboration and confirmation thereof, and for increase of virtue in Christ's religion within this realm of England, and to repress and extirp all errors, heresies, and other enormities and abuses heretofore used in the same : Be it enacted, by authority of this present Parliament, that the king our Sovereign Lord, his heirs and successors kings of this realm, shall be taken, accepted, and reputed the only supreme head on earth of the Church of England, called *Anglicana Ecclesia*, and shall have and enjoy, annexed and united to the imperial crown of this realm, as well the title and style thereof, as all the honors, dignities, preëminences, jurisdictions, authorities, immunities, profits, and commodities, to the said dignity belonging and appertaining ; and that our said Sovereign Lord, his heirs and successors, kings of this realm, shall have full power and authority to resist, repress, redress, reform, order, correct, restrain, and amend all such errors, heresies, abuses, contempts, and enormities, whatsoever they be, which by any manner of spiritual authority or jurisdiction ought or may lawfully be reformed — most to the pleasure of Almighty God, the increase of virtue in Christ's religion, and for the conservation of the peace, unity, and tranquillity of this realm — any usage, custom,

Sixth session, November, 1534, completes the work of separation:

Act of Supremacy;

---

[1] Royal Proclamation, June, 1534.

[2] 26 Hen. VIII. c. 1. The title indorsed on the original act is " The King's Grace to be authorized Supreme Head ; " that on the Statute Roll is " An Act concerning the King's Highness to be Supreme Head of the Church of England, and to have authority to reform and redress all errors, heresies, and abuses in the same." See Amos, p. 280. As to the theory which maintains that this act was merely *declaratory*, " that no new thing was introduced when the king was declared to be Supreme Head," see Blount, *Reform. of the Church of Eng.*, vol. i. p. 230, note 9 ; Dixon, *Hist. of the Church of Eng.*, vol. ii. p. 182.

foreign laws, foreign authority, prescription, or any other thing
or things to the contrary thereof notwithstanding." The fact
above all others which this parliamentary assertion of the royal
supremacy was intended to establish was that, by the final
secession of England from the great Christian commonwealth
of which the pope was the spiritual head, the dual allegiance
existing under that system was completely extinguished; that

all alle-
giance now
due to
Henry as
king and
pontiff:

every kind of allegiance, spiritual as well as temporal, was now
concentrated in the head of the state as king and pontiff. In
order to pave the way for the recognition of this far-reaching
change, it was considered necessary to compel every subject
to swear to his belief in the reality of the king's new pretensions in the succession oath,[1] the refusal of which was de-

statute to
remedy de-
fects in the
succession
oath;

clared to be treason. To remedy the defects in that oath, and
to make it adequate to the end in view by putting its authority
beyond all question, a special act was now passed,[2] declaring
that the oath which the commissioners had drawn should be,
with certain verbal alterations, accepted as the oath which
parliament had intended, and that every subject should be

the new
oath, and
penalties
for its
refusal;

compelled to take it under the penalties which the succession
act provided.[3] In addition to that, another act[4] was passed
making the denial of supremacy treason, wherein it was declared to be treason to wish or will any harm to the king or
queen, "or to deprive them or any of them of the dignity, title,
or name of their royal estates," or to pronounce the king to be
"heretic, schismatic, tyrant, infidel, or usurper." Under this
act it was held not to be necessary that positive guilt should
be shown; it was only necessary that a man should refuse to
give satisfactory answers to such questions[5] as should be put
to him, in order to incur the guilt of treason. To enforce the
new system of despotism thus built up, to enable the crown
the more efficiently to execute the great mass of duties which

---

[1] See above, p. 74, note 2.

[2] 26 Hen. VIII. c. 2.

[3] This retroactive statute was intended to legalize the substituted oath
refused by Fisher and More, which was
again tendered them before a special
commission in June, 1535, and again
refused by them. Amos, *Reformation
Parliament*, p. 12, says, "An auxiliary
act was passed in the next year of the
reign for establishing the identity, in

point of *law*, of the oath required by
the previous act with another oath
differing from it in point of *fact*."

[4] 26 Hen. VIII. c. 13. Under the
color of this statute More, Bishop
Fisher, the Carthusians, and many
others less famous were convicted.

[5] See Lingard, vol. v. pp. 40, 41;
Amos, pp. 144–148. As to More's
warning to Fisher on this point, see
State Papers, vol. i. p. 434.

the ecclesiastical supremacy had cast upon it, Henry's first step was to appoint Cromwell, the architect of the new order, its chief administrator with the title of vicar-general,[1] thus reproducing by the concentration of the supreme ecclesiastical jurisdiction in the hands of a subject, who as first minister already wielded the supreme civil jurisdiction, substantially the same condition of things that had existed in the days of Wolsey. When thus armed with supreme power, Cromwell never for a moment faltered in the perilous task of pressing his policy to its ultimate conclusion. In order to emphasize the fact that the king was really pontiff, an act[2] was passed, in which it was provided that the firstfruits and tenths of the annual income of all ecclesiastical benefices, which had but lately been taken away from Clement as against all right and conscience, should be "united and knit to the king's imperial crown forever." After the passage of another act,[3] which provided for the appointment of twenty-six suffragan bishops, the parliament adjourned, not to meet again for more than a year.

During that interval it was that the new vicar-general addressed himself to the task of illustrating, through the sacrifice of many noble victims, the fact that the royal supremacy which had been admitted by convocation and ratified by parliament was no barren theory, but a terrible reality. By the Act of Supremacy, the king had been declared head of the church with "the title and style thereof;" by the penal act which followed as a corollary thereto, it was declared that any attempt to deprive him "of the dignity, title, or name" of his royal estate should constitute high treason;[4] under the special act

Cromwell appointed vicar-general;

firstfruits and tenths taken from the pope and given to the king;

statute creating twenty-six new bishoprics.

The new machinery of persecution,

---

[1] He was appointed "the royal vice-gerent, vicar-general, and principal commissary, with all the spiritual authority belonging to the king as head of the church, for the due administration of justice in all cases touching the ecclesiastical jurisdiction, and the godly reformation and redress of all errors, heresies, and abuses in the said church." — St. 31 Hen. VIII. c. 10; Wilkins, *Conc.*, vol. iii. p. 784. The ecclesiastical courts were permitted, however, to retain their jurisdiction, each judge making an addition to his style of *auctoritate serenissimæ regiæ majestatis in hâc parte legitime fulcitus.* See Amos, p. 283, and note 2.

[2] 26 Hen. VIII. c. 3.

[3] 26 Hen. VIII. c. 14. This act was passed as a supplement to the act of 25 Hen. VIII. c. 20, which had failed to provide for the appointment and consecration of suffragan bishops such as had been "accustomed to be had" for the assistance of diocesan bishops. See Blount, vol. i. p. 267, note 6, where all the details are given.

[4] The crime of treason, which is as old as English law, is briefly described by Glanvill (lib. xiv. ch. 1), who says, "Cum quis itaque de morte regis, vel de seditione regni, vel exercitus infamatur aut certus accusator apparet aut non." Then follows the definition of

providing the amended oath, it was possible to call upon any one to declare his belief in the validity of the new title, and a failure to do so was sufficient evidence of guilt. And yet even in the presence of this terrible machinery there were steadfast hearts that did not falter; there were a faithful few who were ready to refuse the oath and to die for their devotion to the ancient order, — "gallant men, whose high forms, in the sunset of the old faith, stand transfigured on the horizon, tinged with the light of its dying glory." [1] Foremost among this band of English martyrs, who dared to maintain that matters of religious belief stood even above the omnipotence of parliament, — were the Charterhouse monks of London, who are admitted on every hand to have been the noblest and purest of all churchmen. When, in April, 1535, the tidings reached Cromwell that these dreamers of the cloister, who

first applied to the Carthusians;

Bracton (2 Brac. 258), who (so says Sir H. Twiss), "as regards the jurisprudence of the crime of high treason, adopts the whole doctrine of the Roman law as to what constitutes the *crimen læsæ majestatis*." The earlier judicial decisions (see Hale, 79) reveal the fact that there was great latitude of construction, with a strong tendency upon the part of the judges to declare as treason many cases which could not justly be considered as such. To remedy that evil was passed, in 1352, the great Statute of Treason (25 Edw. III. st. 5, c. 2), which, when viewed broadly, declared it to be treason (1) to form and display by any overt act an intention to kill the king; (2) to levy war against the king; (3) or to adhere to the king's enemies. The act then declared that as many cases of treason may arise which "cannot be imagined or declared at the present time," the judges shall not declare such new cases to be treason until the king and parliament shall first determine whether or no they should be so considered. The first material addition made to Edward's act was embodied in the statute of 11 Hen. VII. c. 1 (see above, p. 23), which provided in substance that the followers of a king *de facto* should not be exposed to the penalties of treason after the king *de jure* had established himself. Such was the condition of the law at the accession of

Henry VIII., during whose reign nine acts were passed creating new treasons. Four of these were designed to uphold the new assumptions of the king as against the pope (26 Hen. VIII. c. 13 (1534,) 28 Hen. VIII. c. 10 (1536), 31 Hen. VIII. c. 8 (1539), and 35 Hen. VIII. c. 3 (1543)); and five were designed to protect the succession as affected by the king's various marriages (25 Hen. VIII. c. 22 (1534), 28 Hen. VIII. c. 7 (1536), 32 Hen. VIII. c. 25 (1540), 33 Hen. VIII. c. 21 (1542), and 35 Hen. VIII. c. 1 (1543)). The new treasons thus created by Henry were all repealed by 1 Edw. VI. c. 12, which provided that nothing should be held to be treason except offences against the statute of 25 Edw. III., and such as were created by that act. Upon the whole subject, see Sir James F. Stephen, *Hist. of the Crim. Law of Eng.*, vol. ii. pp. 241–297; Reeves' *Hist. of Eng. Law*, vol. ii. pp. 317, 415; Foster's *Crown Law*.

[1] Froude, vol. ii. p. 236. This generous outburst stands in strange contrast with the author's prior declaration that the new treason act under which these gallant men were convicted "was necessary to stop the tongues of the noisy mutinous monks, to show them once for all that these high matters were no subjects for trifling." — Ibid., p. 221.

had already taken the succession oath, were unwilling to subscribe to the royal supremacy, they were at once singled out
as victims fit for the sacrifice.[1]   The terrible rapidity and
thoroughness of the process through which the London Carthusians were seized and dashed to pieces by the new legal
machinery was the highest possible tribute to its efficiency.[2]
Turning then for still nobler victims, Cromwell found in the   then to
Tower the famous two who had already been attainted of mis-   Fisher and
prision of treason [3] for their refusal to take the succession oath,   More;
in a bill imposing the penalty of forfeiture and perpetual imprisonment.   The legal proceedings through which the bishop
of Rochester and Sir Thomas More were brought to the block
were but a repetition of what had been gone through with in
the case of the Carthusians.   After their final refusal to take
the substituted oath recognizing the king's ecclesiastical supremacy, indictments drawn under the new treason act were
presented against both in substantially the same form.[4]   In   form of the
that against Fisher he was charged with having attempted   indict-
to deprive the king of "the dignity, title, and name of his   ments;
royal estate," etc., by uttering the words, "the kyng oure
sovereign lord is not supreme hedd yn erthe of the cherche
of Englande." [5]   So loud and deep were the execrations, both   outcry
at home and abroad, which followed the executions of these   which fol-
steadfast men that Henry was forced to attempt an explana-   lowed their
tion of his conduct.   Even his ally of France held up his   executions;
hands in horror; and when the cardinal of Tournon described
in the conclave at Rome Fisher's death upon the scaffold,
his audience was moved to tears.[6]   The response then made   the bull of
was a bull of deposition, in which the Roman rhetoricians   deposition.

---

[1] Chauncey's *Historia . . . Marty-
rum*, cap. 9.   See also Pole's *Defensio
Eccles. Unit.*, fol. lxxxiv.

[2] As to these trials and executions,
see *Baga de Secretis;* Appendix to the
Third Report of the Deputy Keeper
of the Public Records; Strype's *Memorials*, vol. i. p. 305; Froude, vol. ii. pp.
236–255.

[3] *Stat. of Realm*, vol. iv. pp. 527, 528.

[4] The indictments against Fisher,
More, and the Charterhouse monks
were drawn in substantially the same
form, only that against More was more
elaborate.   It is printed in full in Amos

(Appendix I.), who gives an excellent
account of the legal aspects of the trials,
pp. 140–152.   Translations of the indictments are given by the Record
Commissioners.

[5] The extract from which this is
taken is contained in *Archæologia*, vol.
xxv. p. 94.   Lingard (vol. v. p. 41)
quotes this extract with the remark
(note 2) that it has been erroneously
asserted that Fisher was not convicted
for a denial of the supremacy.

[6] Cassalis to Cromwell, *State Papers*, vol. vii. pp. 620, 621; Froude,
vol. ii. p. 279.

spared no anathema which could add color to the papal condemnation.[1]

The decline of the later monasticism which set in early in the fourteenth century was emphasized in England before its close by the outcry of Wycliffe, who denounced the existence of the religious houses as intolerable, — an assault which was soon followed by a petition from the commons to Henry IV.

for the secularization of church property,[2] and by the confiscation by the crown in the reign of Henry V. of the possessions of alien priors, whereby "priories were suppressed to the number of more than a hundred houses." [3] After the storm which thus threatened without breaking began that long period of reaction in the church's favor, during which each of the rival roses sought in turn to secure its support by permitting all legislation hostile to the papacy to fall into abeyance; while the clergy, secure in the enjoyment of their special privileges and immunities, were left free to uphold the cause of orthodoxy by the unrestrained enforcement of the statutes against heresy. Not until after the accession of the house of Tudor were the English ecclesiastics aroused from their long repose

by the application which Cardinal Morton, then archbishop of Canterbury, made in 1489 to Innocent VIII. for a commission[4] authorizing him to make a general inquiry throughout the realm into the conduct of the regular clergy. The inquiry thus instituted, which was feebly executed and limited in extent, was followed by another, still more languid and limited,

set on foot by Warham in 1511.[5] Twelve years later Wolsey instituted a movement which seems to have contemplated a

---

[1] Upon the death of Clement in September, 1534, Cardinal Farnese (Paul III.), who had been on Henry's side, was elected to succeed him. By Paul the bull of interdict and deposition was prepared in August, 1535 (*Bullar. Rom.*, vol. i. p. 704, ed. 1673), but it was not issued until three years thereafter. The bull and the suspension are both printed in Burnet (*Collectanea*), lxxiii. *et seq.*

[2] Vol. i. pp. 571–573.

[3] Stowe's *Chronicle*, p. 345. In the reign of Edward II. the Knights Templars had been dissolved, and by a bull from the pope, dated November 22, 1307, the custody of their lands had

been given to the king until further orders from the Holy See. They were ultimately assigned by the king, with the assent of parliament (17 Edw. II. c. 3), to the brethren of the Hospital of St. John of Jerusalem. As there was no appropriation by the crown in this case, it really has no force as a precedent to justify subsequent confiscations. See Johnstone's *Assurance of Abbey Lands*, p. 40; *Fœdera*, iii. p. 323; Blount, vol. i. p. 291.

[4] Morton's Register, MS. Lambeth Library.

[5] Warham's Register, MS. Lambeth Library. See Froude, vol. ii. pp. 298–348.

general reform of the professed as well as the secular clergy and the suppression of monasteries; but he soon narrowed his designs down to the suppression of certain houses under papal authority for the purpose of endowing his colleges at Ipswich and Oxford.[1] In this work it was that Cromwell and his friend Dr. Leighton, who was associated with him in the cardinal's service, earned the name of being very "dexterous and diligent men." [2] With his appetite thus whetted by his past experience, it was not likely that Cromwell, the prime object of whose policy was the complete subordination of the church to the state, would now fail to strike the final blow by taking away from the monastic bodies the vast wealth with which they were endowed. As the right of visitation [3] over them had been transferred by the Act of Supremacy from the papacy to the crown, commissions [4] were issued at the instance of the vicar-general, who now bore the still more pretentious title of "vicegerent of the king in all his ecclesiastical jurisdiction within the realm," [5] to Drs. Leighton, Legh, and Ap Rice, who, together with certain subordinates, were charged with the making of a general visitation of the religious houses, the universities, and other spiritual corporations. Nothing could have been more commendable than the terms in which the instructions to the commissioners were drawn, and yet the very limited time in which they were to be carried out precludes the idea that they were honestly intended. Although the visitation of the monasteries only began in October, 1535, the report of the commissioners was to be laid before the seventh and last session of the parliament which met on the 4th of the following February. After several weeks of delay, during which the houses disposed of some minor business, the famous report, known as the Black Book of the monasteries,

[margin notes:] Wolsey's attempt in 1523 supplemented by the suppression of lesser monasteries; Cromwell and Leighton employed in the work; right of visitation transferred by the Act of Supremacy from the pope to the king; terms of the commission to Leighton, Legh, and Rice; their report to the seventh and last session, which began in February, 1536;

---

[1] See above, p. 51.

[2] Burnet, vol. i. p. 136.

[3] The first act upon this subject (25 Hen. VIII. c. 21, § 20) was soon followed by the Act of Supremacy (26 Hen. VIII. c. 1).

[4] "Their commissions, if they were passed under the great seal, and enrolled, have been taken out of the rolls; for there are none of them to be found there." — Burnet, vol. i. p. 137. The instructions to the commissioners are printed in Burnet (*Collectanea*), vol. ii. lxix., lxx. The instructions, or "articles of inquiry," consisted of eighty-six questions, and to these were added twenty-six "injunctions," to be left in each house by the visitors. They may still be seen in the British Museum Library, Cotton MSS., *Cleop. E.*, 4 fol. 13, 21.

[5] As to the scope of Cromwell's powers as vicegerent, see above, p. 77, note 1.

was laid on the table of the house of commons.   As the report itself does not exist, and as the journals of the session during which "a great debate"[1] took place are lost, a serious controversy exists not only as to the truth of the report, but also as to what it actually contained.   It seems, however, to be clear from the accounts that remain that while the commissioners admitted that about one third of the houses, including the bulk of the greater abbeys, were fairly conducted, they charged that the conduct of the remaining two thirds was deeply stained both by profligacy and crime.   While it is now impossible to determine the amount of truth which the accusation contained,[2] certain it is that parliament accepted the report as a sufficient basis of its action, which took the form of an act[3] providing that all religious houses, the incomes from whose lands were less than two hundred pounds a year, should be suppressed, and all their property, real and personal, given to the king, his heirs and assigns, "to do and use therewith his or their own wills to the pleasure of Almighty God and the honor and profit of the realm."   Under the authority of this act nearly four hundred out of the one thousand religious houses then existing in England were suppressed and their revenues transferred to the crown.   With this great act of confiscation — if confiscation it can be called[4] — ended the

a great debate on the report;

statute for the suppression of all monasteries with annual incomes of less than two hundred pounds;

---

[1] 27 Hen. VIII. c. 28.

[2] The best summing up in favor of the truth of the report is to be found in Froude, vol. ii. pp. 332, 333.   For a pungent criticism of his conclusion, see Amos, *Statutes of the Reformation Parliament*, pp. 302–305.

[3] 27 Hen. VIII. c. 28.

[4] There can be no question of the constitutional power of the omnipotent parliament, then as now, to annul corporate rights, and to appropriate any kind of property, public or private, lay or ecclesiastical, to any purpose whatsoever.   The only cloud or restraint upon that power is the ethical theory stated by Austin (*Province of Jurisprudence*, lect. vi.), that an act of parliament which violates fundamental rights, though legal and binding, is still unconstitutional.   See also Leslie Stephen, *Science of Ethics*, p. 143. "The founder of all corporations, in the strict and legal sense, is the king alone, for he only can incorporate a

society" (1 *Bl. Com.*, p. 480); and yet the king by virtue of his prerogative possesses no power to alter their charters or to divest them of their franchises without their consent.   *Rex* v. *Pasmore*, 3 T. R. p. 199, and cases cited.   But as against the parliament, corporations, like individuals, have nothing but the ethical theory to fall back upon.   It is claimed that that theory was not violated without excuse in the disendowment of the monasteries because, apart from the peculiar status of corporate property, there were precedents in the dissolution of the Knights Templars in the reign of Edward II., and in the confiscation of the alien priories in that of Henry V. Such an exercise of legislative power was made impossible in the United States by that clause of the constitution (art. 1, sec. 10) which provides that "no State shall pass any law impairing the obligation of contracts." In the famous case of *Dartmouth*

work of the famous parliament of 1529, whose most notable summary of the work of the great parliament of 1529. achievement was the extinguishment of the papal supremacy in England, which consisted in the main (1) of the right to hear appeals in all matters ecclesiastical; (2) of the right to send delegates into the realm, and through them to overrule the domestic synods; (3) of the right to grant licenses and dispensations; (4) of the right to grant investiture to bishops, to confirm their elections, and to dispense the church patronage; (5) and finally of the right to receive the firstfruits, the tenths of English benefices, and the goods of clergymen who died intestate.[1]   In addition to the emancipation of the national church from foreign supervision, by the transfer of the bulk of these rights from the papacy to the crown, this parliament by its various acts deprived the convocations of the independent power of legislation; humiliated the bishops by making them in reality nominees of the king; validated Henry's marriage with Anne and settled the succession upon her descendants; multiplied the royal prerogatives and swelled the royal exchequer by the donation of the vast property of the religious houses, — acts more notable by reason of their revolutionary character and far-reaching importance than all others, save those of the Long Parliament itself.

When the parliament of 1529, whose life had been so prolonged, was dissolved, on the 14th of April, 1536, the country A new parliament meets in June, 1536; little thought that before the end of the month writs would be issued for a general election, in order that another might be assembled as quickly as possible.[2]   The necessity for this

---

College v. *Woodward*, 4 Wheat. 519, it was held by the Supreme Court of the U. S. that the charter granted to the college by the British crown in 1769 was a contract within the meaning of the constitution, and as such the rights granted by it were inviolate by the legislature.   It was also held that although a corporation is established for purposes of general charity, or for education generally, that fact does not, *per se*, make it a public corporation subject to legislative control.   The court also took occasion to say: " Had parliament, immediately after the emanation of this charter, and the execution of those conveyances which followed it, annulled the instrument, so that the living donors would have witnessed the

disappointment of their hopes, the perfidy of the transaction would have been universally acknowledged, . . . but its power is unquestioned."   No better illustration can be found of the doctrine of " vested rights " which has resulted from the American invention of constitutional limitations upon the legislative power.   See vol. i. pp. 47, note 2, 73.

[1] See Hardwick's *Hist. of the Articles*, p. 6.

[2] The lord chancellor told the houses in his opening speech " that when the former parliament was dissolved, the king had no thoughts of summoning a new one so soon."   He then proceeded to tell them of the execution of Anne and the king's marriage with Jane, and

extraordinary and sudden proceeding arose out of certain terrible charges against the chastity of the queen which, during the month of April, were secretly laid before the privy council.

trial and execution of Anne Boleyn;

Before the estates could be assembled on the 8th of June, Anne had been indicted by the grand juries of Middlesex and Kent,[1] convicted of adultery by the peers summoned for her trial before the Lord High Steward,[2] and executed. On the day before the execution the archbishop who had confirmed her marriage with the king declared it null and void,[3] and on

Henry marries Jane Seymour;

the next day thereafter Henry was married to Jane Seymour. The changed condition of things thus brought about made it necessary for parliament to resettle the succession by a fresh

second succession act;

enactment,[4] which, after declaring the king's marriages with Catherine and Anne both void, and the issue of both illegitimate, entailed the crown on his sons by Queen Jane successively and their heirs, with remainder to his sons by any future marriage, and on failure of sons to his daughters in like manner. The act then bestowed upon the king, in default of lawful issue, the extraordinary power, unknown to the constitution, "to dispose, by your letters patent under your great seal, or else by your last will made in writing, and signed with your hand, the imperial crown of this realm, and all other the

---

exhorted them to resettle the succession. See *Lords' Journal*, p. 84; Burnet, vol. i. p. 155.

[1] The two indictments, found on the 10th and 11th of May against Anne, are printed in Amos, *Reformation Parliament*, Appendixes II. and III. See the author's comments as to the practices of grand juries at that time (Appendix IV.), and also as to the connection between the charges and the new treasons created by the first succession act, pp. 25, 26.

[2] As to the jurisdiction and practice of this court, specially when parliament is not sitting, see vol. i. p. 440. "In this tribunal the steward sits as the only judge, while the peers summoned by him — the 'lords triers' — act as a jury." — Ibid. The steward then possessed the power to limit his court to such peers only as he saw fit to summon. As to the proceedings in Anne's case, which was without a precedent, see *Baga de Secretis*, pouches 8 and 9: Appendix II. to the Third Report

of the Deputy Keeper of the Public Records, quoted by Froude, who has given an elaborate account of the whole matter. See vol. ii. pp. 377–391. The four commoners indicted with Anne — Norris, Weston, Smeton, and Brereton — were convicted of adultery with her by a petty jury, May 12. On May 15 Anne and her brother Lord Rochford were tried and convicted before the Lord High Steward, who with the peers summoned by him sat in the Tower.

[3] The divorce was pronounced on the 17th of May by Cranmer, and the proceeding was afterwards confirmed by convocation and parliament. See Wilkins, *Conc.*, vol. iii. p. 803; 28 Hen. VIII. c. 7. Anne was executed on the 19th, and on the next morning Henry married Jane Seymour.

[4] 28 Hen. VIII. c. 7. This was followed by the third succession act (35 Hen. VIII. c. 1), passed after the marriage of Catherine Parr. As to the first succession act, see above, p. 73.

premises thereunto belonging, to such person or persons as shall please your Highness."

From this time onward the king's reign became more and more troubled.   The ghastly domestic tragedy which had ended on the block was soon followed by a great rebellion in the north, which grew out of the disaffection of the country gentlemen and the older nobles, who looked with horror and contempt upon the innovations in the ancient faith which had been brought about by king and commons in the face of their sullen disapproval.   Emboldened by the ruin of the queen, which was generally accepted as an ill omen to the cause with which she had become identified, and aroused by the brutal conduct of the commissioners in the spoliation of the monasteries, which were specially popular in the north, the party of reaction inaugurated the movement, ultimately known as the "Pilgrimage of Grace,"[1] by resisting in arms the visitation which began at Louth in October, 1536.   Although this rising in Lincolnshire collapsed for the want of an organizing hand, Yorkshire soon broke into revolt, where a leader was found in the person of Robert Aske, a country gentleman and lawyer, in whose name an appeal was made to all good Englishmen to make a stand "for the commonwealth; and make your proclamation every man to be true to the king's issue and the noble blood; to preserve the church of God from spoiling, and to be true to the commons and the wealths."   Around Aske, who clearly distinguished the king from his evil councillors in his zeal for the "commonwealth" — the term then used to express the growing political idea of the age — gathered the whole of the northern nobility, who, with thirty thousand men at their backs, demanded that the king should be rid of his base-born councillors (Cromwell and "other villern blood"), that a reunion with Rome should be effected, that Mary's right to the throne should be recognized, that the Statute of Uses[2] should be repealed, that the monasteries should be restored, and that the wrongs done to the church should be righted.   In the midst of this peril Cromwell, who was the real object of attack, stood undaunted.   By diplomacy,

Marginal notes: great rebellion in the north, 1536–37, known as the "Pilgrimage of Grace;" Aske's appeal for the "commonwealth," a term which embodied the growing political idea of the age;

---

[1] The banner of the "Pilgrimage" was borne by monks and marked with the five wounds of Christ.   [2] 27 Hen. VIII. c. 10.

duplicity, and a show of force the rebels were soon dispersed; and when in the spring of 1537 a few fresh outbreaks gave an excuse for the withdrawal of such concessions as had been

the rebel-
lion cruelly
suppressed
by Crom-
well.

made, whole districts were given over to military executions. With his personal enemies among the northern nobles who had led the revolt Cromwell dealt without mercy.[1]

Strife of
the rival
factions at
the council
board;

The struggle in which Henry was thus involved from without with the catholic party, who rejected as a whole the new order of things which the separation from Rome had brought about, was scarcely less perplexing than the strife which grew from within out of the conflicts between the two rival factions who were now struggling at the council board for the control of the new ecclesiastical system, whose theology had not yet

divergent
views of
Anglicans
and Luther-
ans;

received from the state authoritative definition. On the one hand stood the Anglicans, led by Norfolk, Suffolk, Gardiner, and Bonner, with whom were the majority of the bishops and the older nobles, who, while they acquiesced in the separation from Rome, were unalterably opposed to any serious departure from the tenets, the forms, the traditions of the past. On the other hand stood the Lutherans, led by Cranmer, supported by such of the newly created peers as Cromwell and the lords Russell and Southampton, and by such of the newly elected bishops as Shaxton, Barlow, Hilsey, and Fox, who, while they adhered to the doctrine of the real presence, and, in a general sense, to the sacraments, accepted Luther's theory of justification by faith, and rejected with him masses, images, pilgrimages, ceremonies, and clerical celibacy with the zeal of the later Puritans.[2] Between these two hostile factions, who were warring with each other in the new and broad field of theological

Henry's
attempt to
provide a
common
ground
upon which
all parties
could meet;

controversy with the bitterness characteristic of the age, Henry and Cromwell were forced to mediate with the hope of providing some common ground upon which all could dwell together in peace and concord within the fold of the reorganized national church. The first effort in that direction was made when, in

convocation
of 1536;

the convocation which met at St. Paul's in June, 1536, Cromwell, who presided as vicar-general,[3] delivered to the clergy a

---

[1] The history of the rebellion rests upon the accounts contained in Holinshed, Herbert, Stowe, Hall, Speed, State Papers, and Depositions on the Rebellion; Rolls House MS.

[2] "This party after a few years

ceased to exist, developing gradually from the type of Wittenberg to that of Geneva." — Froude, vol. iii. p. 177.

[3] Cromwell first sent Dr. Petre as his deputy. Not until after the convocation had refused to accept him did

message in which they were told that "the king studieth day and night to set a quietness in the church, and he cannot rest until all controversies be fully debated and ended, through the determination of you and his whole parliament." [1] The Ten Articles [2] of religion in which the deliberations of the convocation ended, dictated certainly by the king, if not drawn by his own hand,[3] bear the impress of Lutheran doctrine to an extent which can be explained only in the light of the urgent political motives which then impelled Henry to sink his prejudices and to yield as far as he could to German theological ideas. When in 1530 the German protestants, who had embodied their creed in the Confession of Augsburg which they laid at the feet of Charles V.,[4] were repulsed by a hostile edict, they had gathered for mutual defence in the League of Schmalkald, into which no one could enter who refused to subscribe to the accepted basis of belief. A few years later, the prospect of a close alliance between Charles and the French king forced Henry to seek a union with these Lutheran princes, who offered to take him into their confederacy, provided he would comply with the usual conditions, agree to defend the league as its "Patron and Protector," and subscribe to the Confession of Augsburg.[5] While thus pressed by this diplomatic motive, as well as by the desire to make peace with the Lutheran party within his own realm, Henry put forth, through the agency of convocation, the first authoritative statement of the new doctrines of the Anglican Church in the form of the Ten Articles of 1536, upon at least five of which the impress of the Augsburg Confession is plain and palpable. In the next year these articles were expanded through the work of a notable commission into the larger statement known as the "Institution of a Christian Man," which was published as a concise yet complete statement of the doctrines of the Church of England.[6]

Ten Articles of religion the result;

Lutheranism and the League of Schmalkald,

into which Henry strives to enter;

the Ten Articles expanded into the larger statement known as the "Institution of a Christian Man;"

Cromwell appear himself. Wilkins, *Conc.*, vol. iii. p. 803. When parliament met in June, the convocation as usual assembled with it.

[1] Foxe, *Acts and Mon.*, vol. v. pp. 379–384. June 23 the clergy of the Lower House presented a "Protestation" against the growing heresy, consisting of sixty-eight articles, which appear at length in Wilkins, *Conc.*, vol. iii. p. 137, and in Strype, vol. ii. p. 260.

[2] The original copy subscribed by

the clergy on July 10 is in the British Museum MS. *Cleop. E.*, v. 59. The articles, with collations, are printed in Hardwick's *Hist. of the Articles*, Appendix I.

[3] See Hen. VIII. to bishops and clergy, Wilkins, *Conc.*, vol. iii. p. 825; Jenkyn's *Cranmer*, vol. i. p. 15.

[4] See Harwick, pp. 13–30.

[5] See Herbert's *Life of Henry VIII.*, p. 441; Ranke, vol. iii. p. 661.

[6] Archbishop Cranmer issued his

While the English theologians were thus striving to formulate a creed which would prove acceptable at home, the king had sent an embassy abroad to confer with the Lutheran divines with the view of arriving at a common basis of religious belief, and the result was the tentative scheme embodied in certain articles [1] drawn up at Wittenberg early in 1536. But nothing came of the negotiation at the time, and the whole matter was permitted to sleep until 1538, when Henry, again anxious to strengthen his hands by an alliance with the "princes of the Augsburg Confession," sent a confidential agent to them with the request that they would send over Melancthon and other divines for the purpose of a conference. In response to this request a German embassy, the chief of which was Burckhardt, was sent to England to confer with a commission with Cranmer at its head, and after actually agreeing upon Thirteen Articles,[2] the conference of the joint body progressed favorably until the sacraments were reached, when a hopeless disagreement ended rather abruptly the last real effort ever made to unite the Lutherans in one common doctrine with the Church of England.[3] Thus disappointed of his hope of a German alliance, and of his plan of satisfying the Lutheran party within his own realm, Henry, whose catholic instincts had been shocked by the assaults which that small yet aggressive faction were now making upon the shrines, the reliquaries, the ceremonies of the older faith, resolved to hush,

[margin notes:]
certain articles drawn up at Wittenberg in 1536;

Thirteen Articles of 1538.

---

mandate under the king's order that it should be read on Sundays and holy days, and that preaching should conform thereto, September 10, 1537. Wilkins, *Conc.*, vol. iii. p. 827. In May, 1543, a revised edition of the "Institution" was published under the title of "A Necessary Doctrine and Erudition for any Christian Man," with a preface or letters patent from the king. For a full history of both books, see Blount, *Reform. of the Church of Eng.*, vol. i. pp. 444–469.

[1] An account of these articles is given by Seckendorf, *Comment. de Lutheran.*, lib. iii. § xxxix. "These Articles are said to exist both in Latin and German. Melancthon, *Opp.*, iii. 104, note 2." — Hardwick's *Hist. of the Articles*, p. 55, note 2.

[2] These articles were found by Dr.

Jenkyns among the papers of Cranmer, and are printed in his *Cranmer*, vol. iv. p. 273. They are also printed in Hardwick, Appendix II., where the passages, which are almost identical with the Augsburg Confession, are included between [ ], and where "the passages or phrases which have reappeared in the Edwardine Articles are denoted by *Italics*."

[3] See Strype's *Eccl. Mem.*, i. chaps. xxxii. and xxxiv., with documents in Appendix; and also Blount, *Reform. of the Church of Eng.*, vol. i. p. 471. The final statement made by the German divines of their views as to the sacrament, the marriage of the priesthood, etc., and Henry's reply thereto are printed in Burnet, Addenda to Part I. (*Collectanea*, pp. 138 and 140).

once for all, religious dissension by a more stern and reactionary policy, for the definition and enforcement of which was
called the parliament which met in London in April, 1539.

The popular branch of the preceding parliament, which had Parliament of 1539 called to hush religious discord;
been hastily assembled in 1536, was filled by creatures of the
court, some of whom were returned under circumstances of
the grossest pressure.[1]   From the history of the election of
1539 it is clear that the crown did not fail to make every
effort to again secure the same advantage, the attainment of
which was in due time certified by Cromwell to the king in a
letter in which he said that "your Grace had never more tract-
able parliament."[2]   After the speech from the throne had speech from the throne;
been read, announcing to the houses that they had been called
together to close the religious quarrels by which the kingdom
was distracted, the lords were invited to appoint a committee
to consider the nature of the evil and to report a remedy.[3]
A long pause then followed, during which the parliament,
while awaiting the report of the committee on religion, passed
three memorable statutes, two of which embodied the ex-
tremest effort which the estates could possibly make for the
exaltation of the royal authority.   Upon the complaint of the
king that his proclamations were not duly observed, and that statute giv-ing king's proclama-tions the force of law;
offenders against them could not be punished as law-break-
ers,[4] an act[5] was passed in which the parliament so far abdicated its functions as to declare that royal proclamations,
issued with the consent of the council, should have the same
force as its own enactments, and that pains and penalties
might be inflicted upon all who violated them, provided the
same were duly defined beforehand in each proclamation.   A
further limitation was also imposed to the effect that the king

[1] For details, see Froude, vol. iii.
pp. 189–193 and notes, special reference being made to the account of the
Canterbury election.
[2] Cromwell to Henry VIII., *State
Papers*, vol. i. p. 693.
[3] The committee was composed of
Cromwell, the two archbishops, and
ten bishops. *Lords' Journal*, 31 Hen.
VIII.   Six questions were submitted
to the committee by the king (the six
articles in an interrogative form) which
are stated in the preamble of the act.
The committee failed to agree, and the

questions were, on the 16th of May,
put into the hands of the house of
lords.   On June 2 the six questions
were submitted to convocation, and
were all answered in the affirmative.
Wilkins, *Conc.*, vol. iii. pp. 845, 848.
As to the synod of the whole church
(York holding its session with the
convocation of Canterbury) assembled
at the time, see 31 Hen. VIII. c. 14.
[4] The reasons are set forth at length
in the preamble.
[5] 31 Hen. VIII. c. 8.

should not by virtue of his new powers set aside either existing statutes or the customary law.[1] The unprecedented grant of legislative power thus made to the crown was soon followed by an act [2] confirming the surrender of all the religious houses which had dissolved themselves since the act of 1536, and empowering the king to extend its provisions to all others that "might be hereafter dissolved, suppressed, surrendered, or had or might by any other means come into the hands of the king." Thus at a blow fell the six hundred greater monasteries which had survived the first assault, and with their fall disappeared from the house of lords the twenty-six abbots and the two priors who then sat as lords of parliament by virtue of their baronial status,[3] which ended with the destruction of their houses. The fruit of the spoliation of the monasteries was so great that the king promised never again to call upon his people for subsidies.[4] In addition to this promise the hope was held out that from its fresh resources the crown would create twenty-one new bishoprics, and convert a large proportion of the religious houses into chapters of deans and prebendaries, which were to be attached both to the old and new sees. In order to facilitate that pious purpose, an act [5] was passed authorizing the crown to make such creations and endowments by letters patent. The number of new bishoprics dwindled down, however, to six,[6] while only seven [7] religious houses were actually converted. And yet apart from the ex-

Margin notes: suppression of the greater monasteries; disappearance of the parliamentary abbots; creation of new bishoprics;

---

[1] As to the prior history of "Delegated Legislation," see Amos, *Reformation Parliament*, pp. 64, 65.

[2] 13 Hen. VIII. c. 13.

[3] See vol. i. p. 355. After witnessing without opposing the bill offered in May, 1539, for their destruction, the abbots sat for the last time in the upper house on the 28th of June, the last day of the session, the act not having passed until that day. After their retirement the spiritual peerage was reduced to the archbishops and bishops, who, in the next parliament, numbered only twenty-one spiritual as against forty-one temporal peers. To the twenty-one old bishoprics were added the six new ones whose creation grew out of the appropriation by the state of the monastic property as explained below. Thus was the spiritual peerage reduced from a majority to a minority.

[4] Blount (*Reform. of the Church of Eng.*, vol. i. p. 371), after a careful computation, concludes that "the property which the king confiscated amounted in value (taking estates, money, plate, and jewels) to at least fifty millions of pounds (£50,000,000), this being probably much below the real state of the case."

[5] 31 Hen. VIII. c. 9.

[6] Oxford, Peterborough, Bristol, Gloucester, Chester, and Westminster, the last named suppressed in 1550.

[7] Canterbury, Durham, Winchester, Ely, Carlisle, Norwich, and Worcester. "These thirteen cathedrals are therefore called those of the 'New Foundation.'" — Blount, vol. i. p. 371, note 7.

penditures made upon the fortification of the coast,[1] and upon the building of the new navy which was soon to give England fresh strength at sea, the crown derived but little permanent benefit from its vast acquisitions of church property.   The bulk of the abbey lands were either lavished as gifts upon court favorites, or sold at low prices, not so much to the older nobility as to the new men who had come into power under Wolsey and Cromwell, or else to the great merchants and manufacturers who were swelling the ranks of the territorial aristocracy.[2]   By the very nature of their acquisitions the new proprietors were irrevocably pledged against the restoration of the papal authority, while by the numberless transfers thus brought about land became as it had never been before the subject of sale and purchase, to facilitate which were soon passed a series of important statutes.[3]   While measures of such moment were swiftly passing through parliament without hindrance or debate, the king was being wearied by the failure of the lords' committee to report such an act as would complete the chief business for the settlement of which the parliament had been called together.   In order to end the complication into which the matter finally drifted, the king resolved to cut the knot by dictating to parliament, as he had dictated to convocation under similar circumstances in 1536, the articles of religion which he intended should receive the sanction of the state.[4]   The result was the Statute of the Six Articles,[5] in which it was declared : 1. That in the sacrament of the altar is really present, under the form of bread and wine, the natural

how the abbey lands were disposed of;

sale and transfer of land facilitated by statute;

Henry dictates the Statute of the Six Articles, which closes the doctrinal legislation of his reign;

---

[1] Dowell, *Hist. of Taxation*, vol. i. p. 137.

[2] As to the fate of the monastic property, see Froude, vol. iii. p. 206; Blount, vol. i. pp. 372–379, who comments upon the social results of the dissolution.

[3] "In the very next year after the act passed for the dissolution of the greater monasteries, there were enacted the statutes of wills, of limitations, of fines, for conveyances of titles, for lessees of tenants in tail, for executions upon lands, for partitions, for disseizins, for grantees of reversions, for collusive recoveries, for arrearages of rent claimable by executors, for buying of titles ; — a goodly array of improvements, which may not seem to have

been fortuitous." — Amos, *Reformation Parliament*, pp. 313, 314.

[4] After the disagreement of the first, two other committees were finally appointed (*Lords' Journal*, 31 Hen. VIII.), who made separate reports. The report adopted by the peers modified, in two particulars, the statute which Henry had drawn.   Froude therefore concludes that "it was not, in its extreme form, the work of the king, nor did it express his own desires." — Vol. iii. p. 208.

[5] 31 Hen. VIII. c. 14, entitled "An Act for Abolishing of Diversity of Opinion in Certain Articles concerning Christian Religion."   It received the royal assent June 24, 1539, and took effect July 12.

body and blood of Christ, which, after consecration, remains but the substance of Christ.   2. That communion in both kinds is not necessary to salvation.   3. That it is not permitted to priests, after their ordination, to marry and have wives. 4. That vows of chastity ought to be observed as perpetual obligations.   5. That private masses ought to be continued for godly consolation and benefit.   6. That auricular confession to a priest must be retained and continued.   The efficacy of this measure, which thus fixed the standard of orthodoxy, Henry had no intention of leaving to pious exhortation merely. In spite of the strenuous opposition of Cranmer [1] and the five bishops, who partly sympathized with the protestant party, the act imposed upon all who should refuse to submit to its terms penalties so severe as to foreshadow the revival of active

penalties for offending against the act.

persecution.   The penalty for denying transubstantiation as defined in the first article was burning, without the chance of abjuring; while for offences against the other five, for the first offence forfeiture of property, for the second, death as a felon. The act declared the marriages of priests and nuns utterly void ; to refuse to go to confession was felony ; to refuse to receive the sacraments was also felony.   By this fierce and bloody measure, under which in London alone five hundred protestants were soon indicted, Latimer and Shaxton imprisoned, and Cranmer seriously endangered,[2] the doctrinal legislation of Henry's reign was brought to a close.

Revival of persecution by the Anglicans ;

Nothing could have been more disappointing than the fresh outbreak of the persecuting spirit which thus so quickly followed Henry's supreme effort to hush religious discord by command of parliament.   Nothing could have been farther removed from the king's pacific designs than the cruel use which the triumphant Anglicans were so quick to make "of the whip with six strings " to lash their Lutheran opponents into fury.   As a man of the New Learning, as a catholic proud of his orthodoxy, the king had no personal sympathy with the protestant party, now struggling into life, no patience with

[1] It seems to be clear, however, that Cranmer's opposition was withdrawn when the bill finally came before the house of lords for a vote. See Hook's *Life of Cranmer, Lives of the Archbishops,* etc., 2d series, vol. ii. p. 46.

[2] Hall, p. 828.   Latimer and Shaxton resigned their sees, either voluntarily or at the king's request. Godwin, *Annals,* p. 70 ; *State Papers,* vol. i. p. 849.   As to the king's intervention in behalf of Cranmer, see Burnet, vol. i. p. 194.

the excesses with which they were insulting the sacred things of the older faith.   And yet there was a deep political motive, in antagonism with the king's personal feelings, which had been continually working in their favor at the council board ever since, by the severance from Rome and the consequent alienation of the catholic nations, England had stood in Europe without an ally, isolated and alone.   If Henry's prejudices made him loath to admit the fact, it was clearly perceived by his great minister that every dictate of prudence and self-interest impelled England to seek at any cost an entrance into the great Teutonic league which the Lutheran princes had formed for the defence of the Reformation.   Guided by Cromwell's counsel, Henry had, as we have heretofore seen, striven again and again to form such an alliance, and it was only when the disagreement as to a common basis of religious belief seemed to be final [1] that he had yielded to the reactionary policy which had ended in the Statute of the Six Articles, and the consequent persecution.   Although Cromwell bent for a moment to the storm by seeming to acquiesce while the persecuting statute was passing through parliament, he was swift to arrest its execution the moment that its enforcement threatened to destroy the only party in the state that did not long for his overthrow.   Nothing could have made the gulf between Cromwell and the Anglicans more impassable than the dexterous manœuvre by which he suddenly checked them in the hour of victory by opening the prison doors of the bishops, by quashing the London indictments, by restraining the magistrates who were proceeding under the commissions, and by extending a general pardon to those who had been imprisoned under the late statute as heretics. [2]   The news of this counter movement was not slow to reach Germany, where it did much to pave the way for the long-sought alliance with the Lutheran princes which Cromwell was making a fresh effort to effect through the marriage of the king, now two years a widower, [3] with Anne, daughter of the duke of Cleves and sister-in-law to the Lutheran Elector of Saxony. [4]   Through this marriage

motives for a Lutheran alliance;

Cromwell reverses the policy of persecution;

the effect in Germany;

[1] See above, p. 88.
[2] Hall, p. 828 *et seq.;* Burnet, vol. i. pp. 194, 195. An important and practical feature of the act consisted of the appointment under its provisions of

commissioners for searching out and trying heretics.
[3] Jane Seymour died October 24, 1537, after having given birth to Edward on the 12th.
[4] Dr. Barnes, one of the English

designs
involved in
the mar-
riage of
Henry with
Anne of
Cleves;

Cromwell hoped not only to form a union between Henry and the princes of North Germany, but also a league with them including France for the overthrow of the emperor,[1] — a far-reaching design which, had it been crowned with success, would no doubt have changed the entire aspect of European politics. The scheme ended, however, in involving Henry in a hateful marriage, and in the humiliation of a fresh divorce,[2] without bringing to him as compensation a single advantage that had been promised him. The Lutheran princes feared a contest with the emperor, while France shrank from an alliance whose happy issue could be fatal only to catholicism, thus leaving Henry to bear alone as before the resentment of

the failure
of Crom-
well's
scheme re-
sults in his
overthrow.

the house of Austria. In the presence of his first great failure the king in his wrath and disappointment now abandoned the faithful minister, who had won for him so many triumphs, to the long-hoarded vengeance of his foes.[3] In the midst of the catastrophe parliament met;[4] and on the 10th of June, 1540, Norfolk tore the ensign of the garter from Cromwell's neck at the council board and arrested him as a traitor.[5] A parliamentary attainder soon followed,[6] and before the end of July "the hammer of the monks," the organizer of the English Terror, had perished on the scaffold.

Henry's
secular
legislation;

6. The absorbing interest which naturally centres in the ecclesiastical legislation of Henry's reign should not be permitted to exclude all consideration of his secular legislation, specially that part of it which facilitated the important changes in the law of real property which happily followed the transfer

---

representatives, carried over the news that the prosecutions under the Six Articles had been terminated, and the elector wrote to the king in a way to indicate that he was satisfied. Strype's *Memorials*, vol. ii. p. 437.

[1] The duke of Norfolk was sent on a mission to France with that view. See Henry's letter to the duke, outlining the plan, *State Papers*, vol. viii. 245 *et seq.*

[2] The marriage with Anne, celebrated in January, 1540, was dissolved in July. See Judgment of Convocation, *State Papers*, vol. i. p. 632.

[3] "In Henry VIII. no free self-devotion, no loftiness of soul, and no real sympathy for any living man can be discerned; they are all in his eyes

nothing but instruments, which he first uses and then breaks." — Ranke, *Engl. Gesch.*, vol. i. p. 224.

[4] On the 12th of April, when Cromwell made an address. *Lords' Journals*, 32 Hen. VIII.

[5] *State Papers*, vol. viii. p. 349. Marillac to the Constable, June 23, 1540: MS. Bibliot. Impér., Paris; Froude, vol. iii. p. 304.

[6] At the king's command Cromwell had addressed an inquiry to the judges, which brought forth the response that if a man should be condemned by parliament for treason without being heard in his defence, his attainder could never be subsequently questioned in a court of law. Coke, *Inst.*, iv. 37. Cromwell was not heard in his defence.

of the vast estates that passed first from the monasteries to the crown, and then from the crown to lay subjects. Land thus became to an extent never known before the subject of bargain and sale, and out of that condition of things grew the necessity for a relaxation of the feudal restrictions which had so long hindered its alienation. The right to direct the descent of land by will, which had matured to a certain extent before the Conquest, was soon extinguished after that event by the growth of feudalism, whose policy it was to prohibit or burden every form of alienation which tended to lessen feudal dues and services.[1] As a protection to the interests of the feudal lords were passed the statutes of mortmain, which embodied the prohibition against the transfer of lands into the dead hands of religious houses.[2] In order to defeat the operation of these statutes, the practice of giving lands by way of use or trust was largely resorted to, whereby the legal title was vested in one person and the beneficial use in another.[3] This method of transfer,[4] very extensively employed during the civil war to facilitate family settlements and to prevent the forfeiture of estates,[5] finally came to be a common and usual form of alienation. By this means the ancient right of devise, which feudalism had for a long time extinguished, was revived by the growth of the power of the chancellor to compel the feoffee to convey to the person named in the will of *cestui que use.*[6] This widely developed system of uses that infected nearly every transaction involving real property not only hindered the enforcement of feudal rights, but it also embarrassed every purchaser who attempted to deal with a subject-matter over which two different persons possessed within certain limits

Marginal notes: relaxation of feudal restraints upon alienation; feudalism extinguished the right of devise; and enacted the statutes of mortmain; origin of uses or trusts; right of devise thus in a measure revived;

---

[1] The early restraints based upon the duty of the ancestor to the heir were succeeded by new restraints based upon the duty of the tenant to his lord. See vol. i. pp. 137, 410–413. The right of devising interests in land by will survived, however, by the force of local customs in certain boroughs and in gavelkind lands. Cases relating to "burgages devisable" occur in the Year Books.

[2] Vol. i. p. 407.

[3] Blackstone, vol. ii. p. 271.

[4] "It appears that the practice of conveying lands to uses prevailed to a great extent as early as the reign of Edward III."— Digby, *Law of Real Property*, p. 316; Reeves' *Hist. Eng. Law*, vol. ii. p. 575.

[5] If a person who had only the use of land (the legal title being in another seized to his use) committed treason or felony, the lands were subject neither to escheat nor forfeiture.

[6] As to the growth of the equitable jurisdiction of the chancellor over uses, see Digby, *Law of Real Property*, pp. 321–326. "The practice of disposing of uses of land by will became prevalent under the protection and encouragement of the chancellors."— Ibid., p. 375.

the power of disposal.   To modify these evils was passed the

famous statute of 27 Hen. VIII. c. 10, entitled "An Act Concerning Uses and Wills," whose primary object was, by joining the possession or seizin to the use, to abolish the distinction between the legal and beneficial ownership, and in that way to make the ostensible tenant also the legal tenant, and liable as such to the feudal lord and to the world.[1]   One of the immediate effects of this statute was to facilitate the trans-

fer of land by giving legal validity to "bargains and sales,"[2] a means of transfer which required no particular ceremony, or open and notorious act, such as livery of seizin.   On the other hand, this statute entirely abolished, as a collusive device, the power to dispose of interests in land by will which the fiction of uses had brought about.   Not until the passage, a few years

statute of
32 Hen.
VIII., re-
establish-
ing the
right of
devise;

later, of the statute of 32 Hen. VIII. c. 1, was the power of devising interests in lands by will — a power which had been exercised in some form ever since uses had been protected and enforced by the chancellor — fixed upon a firm legal foundation. By "The act of wills, wards, and primer seizins, whereby a man may devise two parts of his land,"[3] whose terms are somewhat complicated, every tenant in fee was allowed to devise all his lands held by socage tenure, and two thirds of that held by knight-service, subject to careful provisions for the protection

of the lord in both cases.[4]   Another statute passed at this time, whose ultimate design was to facilitate the transfer of land by fixing a limit within which certain suits concerning it should be brought, was the statute of 32 Hen. VIII. c. 2, known as

the Statute of Limitations.[5]   As restraints upon alienation were passed the statute of 23 Hen. VIII. c. 10, prohibiting all gifts of lands to what were then and since known as super-

---

[1] Efforts had long before been made to protect creditors, the king, and the feudal lords against the effects of feoffments to use by 1 Rich. II. c. 9, 1 Rich. III. c. 1, and by 4 Hen. VII. c. 17.

[2] Digby, *Law of Real Property*, p. 355.   In order to prevent secret conveyances of this character a second act was passed in the same year providing for their enrolment.   As to the subsequent history down to the conveyancing acts of 1881, 1882, see Ibid., pp. 364, 365.

[3] 34 & 35 Hen. VIII. c. 5 was "An

Act for the Explanation of the Statute of Wills."

[4] The law of wills of all property, real and personal, now rests on the provisions of the Wills Act, 7 Will. IV. and 1 Vict. c. 26.   Upon the whole subject, see Digby, *Law of Real Property*, pp. 375–390.

[5] "The principle of this statute had already been established in the statute of non-claim (4 Hen. VII. c. 24)." — Reeves' *Hist. Eng. Law*, vol. iii. p. 310, note a (Finlason ed.).

stitious uses; and the statute of 32 Hen. VIII. c. 31, restrict- statute as to common recoveries, 32 Hen. VIII. c. 3; ing the method of conveyancing known as common recoveries by the proviso that all such recoveries had by the assent of parties against the life-tenant, tenant by the courtesy, and others should be void as to those in reversion of remainder without their consent, unless it was by a good title.[1] From the time of the famous "Taltarum's Case" (12 Edw. IV.), the ficti- tious suits known as common recoveries had been employed as a method of conveying lands, and they continued to be so employed down to 1834, when by the statute of 3 & 4 Will. IV. c. 74, "fines and recoveries were abolished, and tenant their recent abolition. in tail may now, by a deed enrolled in the Chancery Divi- sion of the High Court of Justice, alienate his lands for any estate in fee simple or otherwise, and thus defeat the ex- pectations of his own issue and of all remaindermen and reversioners."[2]

Another important change brought about by the dissolution Dissolution of monas- teries trans- ferred care of poor from church to state; of the religious houses which should be noted here was that which resulted in the transfer of the care of the poor from the church to the state. During the Middle Ages, the relief of the poor which the church assumed finally devolved in the main upon the monasteries, not only because such work was one of the objects of their foundation, but for the further rea- son that there had been appropriated to their use a large por- tion of the tithes, a third of which had always been devoted to the care of the poor.[3] Under this condition of things the state

---

[1] "In this manner, by obviating the abuse of it, did the parliament tacitly acknowledge and ratify the application of a recovery as an assurance of land." — Reeves' *Hist. Eng. Law*, vol. iii. p. 272.

[2] Digby, *Law of Real Property*, p. 252.

[3] "The recognition of the legal obli- gation of tithes dates from the eighth century, both on the continent and in England. In A. D. 779 Charles the Great ordained that every one should pay tithe, and that the proceeds should be disposed of by the bishop; and in A. D. 787 it was made imperative by the legatine councils held in England, which being attended and confirmed by the kings and ealdormen had the au- thority of Witenagemotes. From that time it was enforced by not unfrequent legislation, . . . the cathedral church being . . . the normal recipient, and the bishop the distributor." — Stubbs, *Const. Hist.*, vol. i. p. 228. "In the neighborhood of the cathedrals were gathered together the maimed, the lame, the blind, the homeless, and friendless, to be fed, clothed, and cared for for God's sake." — Kemble, *Saxons in England*, vol. ii. p. 440. It became the custom for the bishop to divide the tithes equally between the church, the clergy, and the poor, and that cus- tom was confirmed by a law of Æthel- red II. As the monasteries became possessed of a large portion of the tithes, the care of the poor specially devolved upon them.

contented itself with the negative duty of enacting statutes
for the punishment of begging and vagrancy.[1] But when the
crown took away from the monasteries the means by which
the care of the poor had been maintained, it was confronted
by a correlative duty which it could not refuse to assume.
The first assumption of this duty was embodied in the statute
of 27 Hen. VIII. c. 25, whereby the incorporated towns, hundreds, parishes, and manors were charged with the duty of
putting to labor all such as were able to work, and of receiving
and supporting all such as were unable, — the means for that
purpose to be collected as alms on Sundays, holidays, and other
festivals, or otherwise among the people.   Such was the beginning of the parochial poor-law system which, after much im-

*begging
and
vagrancy;*

*state first
assumed
the care of
the poor by
statute of
27 Hen.
VIII. c. 25;*

*beginning
of the
parochial
poor-law
system;*

[1] In their inception such statutes
were a mere corollary of the Statutes
of Laborers (see above, p. 47), because
by their terms the laborer who refused to work where he happened to
be, at the wages there offered him,
became as soon as he went away a
vagrant and a criminal. To punish
vagrants for crimes committed while
wandering from place to place, and to
force them back to their usual places
of abode, were passed 1 Rich. II. c. 6
(1377); 2 Rich. II. c. 6 (1378); 7 Rich.
II. c. 5 (1383); 12 Rich. II. (1388);
2 Hen. V. c. 4 (1414); 11 Hen. VII.
c. 2 (1494); 19 Hen. VII. c. 12 (1503);
and 22 Hen. VIII. c. 12, a very severe
act (see abstract in Nicholas' *Hist. of
the Poor Laws*, vol. i. pp. 119–124),
which was amended by 27 Hen. VIII.
c. 25 (1535, 1536). In 1547 all these
acts, upon the ground that they were
not sufficiently severe, were repealed
by the specially cruel statute of 1 Edw.
VI. 2, which at the end of two years
was repealed by 3 & 4 Edw. VI. c.
26, which revived the acts of Hen.
VIII. In 1552 was passed 5 & 6
Edw. VI. c. 2, which confirmed those
acts with a provision for licenses to
beg under certain conditions. In 1555
the system of licensed begging was
elaborated by 2 & 3 Phil. & Mary,
c. 5, which connected with it a provision for weekly collections for the
poor. In 1572 all prior statutes upon
the subject were repealed by 14 Eliz.
c. 5, superseded in 1597 by 39 Eliz. c.
4, which, with an amendment made in
1604 by 1 Jas. I. c. 7, remained in force

for more than a century, to the terror
of all rogues, vagabonds, and sturdy
beggars. Not long after the passage
of Elizabeth's act of 1597 followed
her famous poor law of 1601 (43 Eliz.
c. 2), from which time the legislation
against vagrancy "may be regarded to
a great extent as forming the criminal
aspect of the poor laws," which undertook to provide for the helpless, to
furnish work for the willing and able,
and punishment for the able-bodied
who were unwilling to work. In 1713
Elizabeth's act of 1597, as amended
by James, was reënacted by 12 Anne,
st. 2, c. 23, with a few omissions and
alterations; and in 1737 that act was
so explained by 10 Geo. II. c. 28 as
to extend it to persons acting plays in
certain places, or without license from
the lord chamberlain. In 1740 all such
acts were repealed and reënacted by
13 Geo. II. c. 24, which was merged
four years later into 17 Geo. II. c. 5,
which was amended in 1792 by 32
Geo. III. c. 45, and repealed in 1822
by 3 Geo. IV. c. 40, designed to consolidate the law upon the subject.
Two years later that act was repealed
by 5 Geo. IV. c. 83, now in force,
which so extends the definition of a
rogue and vagabond as to include
many persons of a suspicious class
not actually criminals. Upon the subject of vagrancy and wages, see Amos,
Reformation Parliament, pp. 83, 84,
92–94. As to the vagrancy statutes
considered as a part of the history of
the criminal law, see Sir J. F. Stephen,
vol. iii. pp. 266–275.

provement in the intervening reigns, was finally settled in that of Elizabeth,[1]—a system which grew more and more necessary as the conversion of feudal into free labor swelled the ranks and increased the distress of the laboring classes. Another act made necessary by the transfer of monastic property to lay hands which may be mentioned here is the statute of 32 Hen. VIII. c. 7, whereby a legal remedy was for the first time given to laymen who had estates, or interests in parsonages or vicarages, enabling them to sue for the subtraction of tithes in the church courts.[2]

statute of 32 Hen. VIII. c. 7, authorizing laymen to sue for tithes;

The first statute of bankrupts is that of 34 & 35 Hen. VIII. c. 4, which was intended rather to prevent trade-debtors from fraudulently concealing or disposing of their goods than as a means through which they could be discharged from their debts after an honest surrender. By the statute of amendment and jeofail, 32 Hen. VIII. c. 30, the administration of substantial justice in civil proceedings was greatly promoted; while by the statute of 23 Hen. VIII. c. 1, taking away the benefit of clergy in many cases in which it had been before enjoyed, manifold abuses resulting from that source were removed from the criminal administration.[3]

first statute of bankrupts, 34 & 35 Hen. VIII. c. 4; statute of amendment and jeofail, 32 Hen. VIII. c. 30; benefit of clergy taken away in many cases by 23 Hen. VIII. c. 1.

7. Before Cromwell was hurled by his ungrateful master from the bad eminence to which his genius had exalted both, the revolutionary policy he had undertaken to enforce had reached a perfectly successful consummation. High as the power of the monarchy had been lifted by Wolsey, his pupil had lifted it higher still. Not only had the crown been emancipated from without by the complete abolition of the papal overlordship, but it had also been raised from within above every rival force, temporal or spiritual. When Cromwell's administration began, the one really formidable foe by which it was confronted stood forth in the corporate person of the church, whose immemorial spiritual authority was greatly enhanced, not only by its vast temporal possessions, but by its more or less independent assemblies and tribunals, subject in

The closing years of Henry's reign (1540–47): general results of Cromwell's policy; exaltation of the crown;

---

[1] 43 Eliz. c. 2. The history of that act as the basis of the modern poor-law system will be considered hereafter.

[2] As to the ecclesiastical jurisdiction over tithes, see Reeves' *Hist.* *Eng. Law*, vol. iii. p. 95 *et seq.*, and p. 468.

[3] For a masterly review of that subject, see Sir James F. Stephen, *Hist. of the Crim. Law of Eng.*, vol. i. pp. 469–472.

the last resort to the direction of a foreign head.   That Crom-

humiliation of the church ;
well should have undertaken to prostrate the church at the
feet of the monarchy is not so remarkable as that he should

Cromwell employs the parliament as the tool of the crown ;
have essayed such a task with the aid of the parliament.
From the accession of Edward IV. down to the fall of Wolsey,
the settled policy of the crown had been to discourage parliamentary action, by calling the estates together only on rare
and critical occasions, and by confiding as far as possible the
entire central administration of the state to the privy council.
Under that system the council, in its judicial aspect as the star
chamber, had overawed the entire administration of justice in
the ordinary tribunals by making them subservient to the royal
will, while, in its political aspect as an administrative body, it
had to a serious extent substituted the system of royal benevolences in the place of parliamentary taxation.   Under this
condition of things, which the collapse of the estate system at
the end of the civil war had made possible, there seemed to be

the lords a spiritless body, and the commons made up of royal nominees ;
but little hope of a parliamentary revival.   The fact that the
lords were still a subservient, spiritless body that cowered at
the feet of the king, the fact that the commons were largely
made up of members nominated directly or indirectly by the
privy council, were no doubt the determining causes which
emboldened Cromwell to reverse the royal policy by the constant employment of parliament as the agent through whose
acts the papal supremacy was overthrown and the church
stripped at once of its estates and of its independence.   So

estates called to- gether year after year to sanction the royal policy ;
far from shrinking from an appeal to the estates, it was the
essence of Cromwell's policy to call them together year after
year, and to force upon their attention every possible question
to which he desired to add the forms of legality or the apparent sanction of popular approval.   The review which has just
been made of that unbroken series of parliamentary enactments, beginning with the comparatively mild measures of
1529 and ending at last with the act of the Six Articles, has
shown how completely the revolution which Cromwell carried
on by the authority of the crown was at every step sanctioned
and approved by the national legislature.   When that series
of royal edicts, over which was thus thrown the thin veil of
national assent, are examined as a connected whole, the fact
appears that Cromwell permitted nothing to rob his work of

the merit of completeness. Upon the abnormal aggregation of civil powers which the growth of the conciliar system had already concentrated in the hands of the crown the absolute control of the entire ecclesiastical system was superimposed. From its high place as an estate of the realm the church was reduced to a mere department of state ; its wealth was laid at the feet of the king, while its ministers, from the highest to the lowest, were made to feel that their right to exercise their spiritual functions depended alone upon the royal authority, — an authority which claimed the supreme right not only to prescribe the forms of worship, but also to define through the agency of parliament and convocation principles of belief, and in that way to fix the difficult line which then divided heresy from orthodoxy. During the seven years of Henry's reign that remained after Cromwell's fall, it was not found necessary to add anything to the system he had founded ; it was administered to the end in substantially the same form in which he had left it by the king, whose one desire seems to have been simply to conserve and rest upon the results their joint efforts had accomplished. After Cromwell was gone, the task of upholding the new ecclesiastical system was not lightened by the necessity that existed of forcing upon the two rival religious factions an unqualified acceptance of a theology which demanded at once an admission of the mass and of the royal supremacy. After the return of Norfolk to power, which followed the king's marriage with his niece, Catherine Howard, in the summer of 1540, it seemed for a time as if, under the influence of the older nobles at whose head he stood, and of the more conservative churchmen under the lead of Gardiner, there was a gradual drift back to catholicism. Norfolk's hostility to the new religious movement was undisguised ; and as he looked forward hopefully to a general council as the prelude to a reunion of England with the main body of the Catholic Church, he turned away from Francis and the Lutheran princes in favor of an alliance with the emperor, through whose influence alone such a council could be brought about. And even after the decline of Norfolk's power, by reason of the execution of Catherine Howard in February, 1542, and the king's subsequent marriage with Catherine Parr in July, 1543, Henry still clung to the general line of foreign

an abnormal aggregation of civil and ecclesiastical powers vested in the crown;

the church a mere department of state;

its dogmas and liturgy fixed by royal authority;

rivalry of the religious factions after Cromwell's fall;

Norfolk's return to power after Henry's marriage with Catherine Howard in 1540;

his hostility to the new religious movement undisguised;

Henry mar-
ried Cath-
erine Parr,
July, 1543; policy which the duke had advocated.[1] Not until after the
hostile action towards the Lutheran movement which was
taken in the council opened at Trent, in December, 1545, and
the subsequent effort of the emperor in the following year to
when he
realized
that the
breach with
the papacy
was final; break up the League of Schmalkald, did Henry finally realize
the fact that the breach which the Reformation had made
between the papacy and the Teutonic nations was final and
irrevocable.[2]

In spite, however, of his hopes of a reunited Christendom,
and of his devotion to the dogmas of the ancient faith as embodied in the Six Articles, the king found it impossible, as his
reign drew to a close, to resist the demands of the protestant
party for certain changes in the devotional system of the
church suggested by the continental Reformation. As a part
'translation
of the Bible
and parts of
the service-
books into
English; of the Lutheran movement Tyndale's translation of the Bible,
made at Cologne in 1525, had come over into England,[3] and
that was followed by Coverdale's translation, also published
abroad in 1535. The translation last named is probably that
referred to in the royal license given for placing the first complete edition of the English Bible in churches for the general
reading of lay people, in 1536.[4] In the next year a similar
license was issued, permitting another edition to be used without hindrance by every one in private.[5] To prevent the difficulties which at once arose out of the publication of a great
number of unofficial translations by private persons, there was
'the "Great
Bible" of
1539; issued in 1539 the authorized version known as the "Great
Bible," reprinted in the next year, with a preface by Archbishop
Cranmer.[6] The same general impulse which thus prompted

---

[1] In his review of the prospects of
an Anglo-imperial alliance in the summer of 1542, Froude (vol. iii. p. 507)
says "it was possible that the difficulties of Europe might be settled at last
by Henry's favorite project,—a council under the auspices of himself and
the emperor, where England and Germany might be freely represented."

[2] In the last year of his life Henry
was forced to fall back upon Cromwell's policy, and to offer to form an
alliance with the German princes which
"might be called indeed a very Christian league and confederacy." Henry
VIII. to Bruno, State Papers, vol. xi.

pp. 281, 282. But they had no faith in
him, and his offer was rejected.

[3] See above, p. 51.

[4] Wilkins, Conc., vol. iii. p. 815.

[5] See State Papers, vol. i. p. 561;
Jenkyn's Cranmer, vol. i. p. 199 et seq.
In 1543 a reaction set in, which is
marked by an act passed in that year
"for the advancement of true religion"
(34 Hen. VIII. c. 1), whereby the liberty of reading the Bible was abridged.

[6] "The 'Great Bible' of 1539 (well
known to us still by our Prayer Book
Psalms) continued to be the authorized version of the Church of England
until 1568, when it was superseded by
that made under the direction of Arch-

the translation of the Bible into English at the same time
brought about changes of a similar character in the devotional
system of the church: "This process went slowly on in the
issuing of two primers in 1535 and 1539, the rendering into
English of the Creed, the Lord's Prayer, and the Ten Commandments, the publication of an English Litany for outdoor an English Litany;
processions in 1544,[1] and the adding to this of a collection of
English prayers in 1545." [2] In the last month of that year it
was that Henry, worn out by the hopeless task of hushing a
strife which day by day increased in bitterness, made his last
exhortation to parliament, an exhortation in which he appealed
to the warring religious factions about him to be tolerant with Henry's appeal for religious toleration;
each other, so that "you, by verity, conscience, and charity
between yourselves, may in this point, as you be in divers
others, accounted among the rest of the world as blessed
men." [3] All such vain hopes were, however, destined soon to
be blighted, as Henry's steadily failing health now surely admonished him that the religious truce, which rested alone upon
his personal authority, was soon to be broken by his death.
How to provide for the permanency of his work, how to secure his final arrangements;
the stability of his throne during the bitter strife that was
sure to follow the transfer of the vast powers which he had
concentrated in his own strong hands to those of his infant
successor, were the perplexing problems that vexed the king's
life as it drew to a close. The nearest male relatives of Jane the Sey-mours and the nobles of the "new blood;"
Seymour's son, now nine years old, were her two brothers, the
eldest of whom, Edward Seymour, had been raised to the earldom of Hertford, and had been intrusted with the chief command in the war against Scotland. The part which Hertford
was sure to play in the coming reign, coupled with his well-
known inclination to the new doctrine, naturally made him the
leader of the court faction known as the "new men," a term
of reproach applied by their adversaries to the new nobility
who, without historical connections with the past, had been

---

bishop Parker: which was to be superseded in its turn, after forty years, by
that since used for two centuries and a
half." — Blount, *Reform. of the Church
of Eng.*, vol. i. p. 521.

[1] See as to the Litany, which after
receiving the final sanction of convocation in March, 1543–44, was promul-

gated by the crown on June 11, 1544,
Wilkins, *Conc.*, vol. iii. p. 868.

[2] Green, *Hist. of the Eng. People*,
vol. ii. p. 220.

[3] An account of the speech is given
by Hall, and by Mason in a letter to
Paget, in MS., in the State Paper Office. See Froude, vol. iv. pp. 196–199.

built up from the court by royal favor, and enriched by the crown out of the monastic estates of which the church had been plundered.   To these nobles of the "new blood," such as the Seymours, the Russells, the Wriothesleys, the Cavendishes, the Fitzwilliams, and the Herberts, who were thus raised up as the great temporal lords were stricken down, and who by *irrevocably bound to the cause of the Reformation.* the very method of their creation and enrichment were bound irrevocably to the cause of the Reformation,[1] the small yet resolute party of change were looking for guidance in the movement to be made after Henry's death for the breaking of the yoke of the Six Articles, and for the drawing of the English Church into closer communion with the reformed churches of the continent.

Edward's title to the crown: 8. As to the validity of Edward's title to the crown there could be no possible difficulty.   Since the kingship had ceased *summary of principles regulating the succession —* to be purely elective the two principles which regulated the succession were "that, no act of the legislature intervening, the crown and the royal dignity ought to descend from ancestor to heir in a certain established course of descent ; but that this course of descent is subject to the controul of the legislature." [2]   These principles were the natural outcome of the *elective kingship blended with feudal theory of hereditary right,* process through which the ancient elective kingship gradually became blended with the new feudal theory of hereditary right. The several stages of that process, as heretofore explained, may be summarized as follows : (1) The Old-English kingship, although elective, was associated from the beginning with the hereditary principle by virtue of the rule which limited the election to the members of a single royal house.[3]   Subject to that limitation, the right of election was freely exercised by the witan, whose action conferred the inchoate right to become *civil always followed by ecclesiastical election,* king, a right which was perfected, after the taking of the usual oaths, by the ceremony of unction and coronation,[4] wherein the clergy and assembled people repeated the election in the

---

[1] " Those families indeed, within or without the bounds of the peerage, which are now deemed the most considerable, will be found, with no great number of exceptions, to have first become conspicuous under the Tudor line of kings ; and if we could trace the titles of their estates, to have acquired no small portion of them, mediately or immediately, from monastic or other ecclesiastical foundations." — Hallam, *Const. Hist.*, vol. i. p. 79.

[2] Sir Michael Foster, *Crown Law*, p. 408.

[3] See vol. i. p. 175.

[4] Maskell, *Monumenta Ritualia Ecclesiæ Anglicanæ*, vol. iii. ; Freeman, *Norman Conquest*, vol. iii. pp. 44, 622, 623.   See also *Fœdera*, vol. vii. p. 158.

sanctuary, as a spiritual ratification of the choice which the state had made.[1] The new reign was then dated from the coronation, and during the interval the king's peace was suspended. After the king came to be regarded as the source of all peace and law, both were supposed to die with him and to rise again with his successor.[2] (2) The coming of William and the consequent substitution of a new royal stock worked no immediate change in the outward form of the primitive system.[3] The change which followed that event resulted from the quickening of the feudalizing process, already under way, through which the archaic idea of personal or tribal was gradually transformed into that of territorial kingship, a process wherein the king of the English was ultimately developed into the king of England.[4] Thus under the influence of feudal ideas the theory gained ground that the royal office was an estate that belonged to the king as feudal lord, descendible from ancestor to heir, according to the strict rules of hereditary right which had begun to regulate the descent of land. This doctrine had so far advanced by the time of the accession of Edward I. that the old rule of dating the new reign from the coronation was abandoned. At the funeral of Henry III., which occurred four days after his death, the baronage swore fealty to the absent Edward, and three days thereafter the council declared the new peace in the name of the first English king who had so far reigned before his coronation.[5] This new rule, which was emphasized by the accession of Edward II. the day after his father's death,[6] never ripened, however, until the reign of Edward IV., into the maxim that the king never dies, from

(marginal notes:) king's peace died with him, the Conquest worked no immediate change in the primitive system, transition from personal to territorial kingship, royal office regarded as a descendible estate, Edward reigns before his coronation,

---

[1] "The ceremony was understood as bestowing the divine ratification on the election that had preceded it, and as typifying rather than conveying the spiritual gifts for which prayer was made." — Stubbs, *Const. Hist.*, vol. i. p. 144.

[2] Vol. i. p. 177.

[3] Ibid., p. 231, as to William's election and coronation.

[4] Ibid., p. 130. John was the first who always called himself King of England. On his great seal he was *Rex Angliæ.*

[5] The reigns of all prior kings, including that of Henry III., had dated only from the coronation. Henry II.,

Richard I., and John, who were absent in France at the deaths of their predecessors, did not assume the royal title until after election and coronation. Nicolas, *Chron. of Hist.*, p. 272. In the interval of course the king's peace was suspended. The regnal years of Edward I. were dated from his recognition by the baronage, which occurred four days after his father's death, as above stated.

[6] In the proclamation he was declared to be already king by descent, — "ja roi d'Engleterre par descente de heritage." — *Fœdera*, vol. ii. p. 1. No reference was made to the consent of the magnates.

maxim that the king never dies finally established,

which results the correlative idea that the king's peace can never be suspended.[1] When Richard II. as the heir of his grandfather succeeded to the crown to the exclusion of his

accession of Richard II. under the doctrine of representation,

uncles by virtue of the doctrine of representation, that doctrine, already settled as one of the rules regulating the descent of feudal estates,[2] was for the first time applied to the succession of the crown of England. (3) While the new feudal rule of representative primogeniture was thus becoming a part of the

elections become a mere ceremony,

law of the land, the dual right of election by church and state became a mere ceremony, and then the ceremony itself became obsolete. As such the ecclesiastical election by clergy

ecclesiastical election of Henry VIII.,

and people survived down to the accession of Henry VIII., in the programme of whose coronation, prepared by the king himself, traces of the ancient system still lingered in the declarations that Henry, the "rightfull and undoubted enheritour by the lawes of God and man," was "electe, chosen, and required by all the three estates of this lande to take upon hym the said coronne and royall dignitie." [3] (4) While the ancient forms under which the witan had immemorially regulated the succession of the crown were thus passing away, the reorganized

assembly of estates reasserts right to regulate succession,

national assembly was careful to reassert the substance of the right in a manner so emphatic as to put its existence beyond all question. The right of deposition which had been exercised by the witan before the Conquest was never asserted by the less authoritative feudal councils that gathered around the Norman and early Angevin kings during the two centuries which followed that event. Not until after those feudal councils had been transformed into an assembly of estates, did the representatives of the nation dare to revive that highest of all rights which the witan had occasionally exercised from the earliest times. To Edward I. belongs the honor of having transformed the feudal councils into an assembly of estates, and within thirty years after the meeting of such assembly at

[1] Vol. i. p. 405.
[2] See Reeves' *Hist. Eng. Law*, vol. i. p. 77.
[3] The people were asked: "Woll ye serve at this tyme, and geve your wills and assents to the same consecration, enunction, and coronacion? Whereunto the people shall say with a grete voyce, Ye, Ye, Ye; So be it; Kyng

Henry, Kyng Henry."—Marskell, *Monumenta Ritualia, etc.*, vol. iii. p. 73; Freeman, *Norm. Conq.*, vol. iii. p. 622. This form, devised by Henry VIII. to be used "at every coronation," was not observed at that of Edward VI. See the new order for that occasion printed in Burnet, vol. ii. (*Collectanea*) cxcv.

Westminster, the limit of its sovereign power was reached in the deposition of his son Edward II.,[1] an event which was followed after an interval of seventy-two years by the deposition of Richard II.[2] If upon the deposition of Richard the new feudal rule of representative primogeniture had prevailed, the crown would have passed at once to Edward Mortimer, the ancestor of the house of York. But the parliament saw fit to ignore that rule, and to elect another member of the royal house whom it deemed more competent to govern. The long rule of the house of Lancaster by virtue of the parliamentary[3] title thus acquired gave all possible emphasis to the right of parliament not only to depose the king but to elect his successor. While Edward IV. did all that he could to assert the contrary doctrine of indefeasible hereditary right, upon the assumption that he really succeeded to Richard II., and that the Lancastrian kings were mere usurpers, mere kings *de facto non de jure*,[4] he finally sought a parliamentary recognition of his title; and a like recognition became the only real basis of the right of the house of Tudor. The three memorable acts[5] by which parliament as many times regulated the succession during the reign of Henry VIII., often in open defiance of the rules of hereditary right, removed any doubt that might have remained as to the fact that the crown cannot "descend from ancestor to heir in a certain established course of descent," when there is an "act of the legislature intervening." Under either theory the right of Edward was perfect. He was not only Henry's lawful male heir, but his right to the succession had been expressly recognized not only by the act of 28 Hen. VIII. c. 7, but also by the subsequent act of 35 Hen. VIII. c. 1,[6] which, after affirming his right, put in the entail, next after the lawful issue, male or female, of the king and Prince Edward, first Mary and then Elizabeth, subject to such conditions as the king by letters patent or his last will might appoint.

Marginal notes:

deposition of Edward II. and Richard II.,

parliamentary title of the Lancasters,

Edward IV.'s. assertion of indefeasible right,

parliamentary settlements in reign of Henry VIII.

Statutes recognizing Edward's right.

---

[1] See vol. i. pp. 504, 505.

[2] Ibid., p. 513.

[3] Ibid., p. 536. The succession was four times regulated by parliament during the reign of Henry IV. For the history of these acts — specially as to the act of 1406 establishing Salic succession — see Bailey, *The Succession to the Crown*, pp. 32–36.

[4] Vol. i. p. 577. See also Bailey, p. 59.

[5] 25 Hen. VIII. c. 22; 28 Hen. VIII. c. 7; 35 Hen. VIII. c. 1. See above, pp. 73, 84. For a detailed history of the acts, see Sir Michael Foster's *Crown Law*, p. 406 *et seq.*

[6] That was Henry's third and last succession act. As to the first, see above, p. 73; as to the second, p. 84.

Under the power thus given to the king to make further dispositions by will he simply supplemented the arrangement which parliament had made by the provision that, on the failure of issue of his three children, the crown should pass to the heirs of his younger sister Mary, duchess of Suffolk, to the detriment of the descendants of his elder sister Margaret of Scotland.[1]   Having thus arranged every detail touching the

succession, Henry next named the sixteen executors who were to constitute the council of regency during the minority, a council whose members were drawn in such equal proportions from the ranks of conservatives and reformers as to warrant the hope that the influence of the one would stand as a check upon that of the other.   How ineffectual such an arrangement was to prove in practice was quickly demonstrated the moment that the long truce, which only the king's irresistible personal

force had made possible, was broken by his death, which occurred on the 28th of January, 1547.

[1] *Fœdera*, vol. xv. pp. 114–117. As to the vexed questions involved in the alterations of the will and in its valid execution, see Lingard, vol. v. p. 212 *et seq.*, and notes; Hallam, *Const. Hist.*, vol. i. p. 289 *et seq.*; Blount, *Reform. of the Church of Eng.*, vol. ii. p. 6; Bailey, *Succession to Eng. Crown*, pp. 156–164.

CHAPTER III.

EDWARD VI. AND THE ENGLISH REFORMATION.

1. THE council of regency constituted by the last will of History of regencies from Henry III. to Edward VI.: Henry VIII. was not so much the creation of that instrument as of the act of parliament under whose authority the will was drawn. While the assembly of estates was settling the principle that the new feudal theory of hereditary right was subject to its omnipotent power to suspend that rule of succession at will, it was also careful to assert its power to provide for the administration of the royal office during the absence of an adult king, or for a regency in the event of infancy or mental incapacity. During the Norman reigns, as heretofore pointed Administration of royal authority during absence, infancy, or incapacity of the king; out, the royal authority, during the temporary absence of the king from the realm, devolved officially upon the justiciar as viceroy, or, as he was afterwards called, "*secundus a rege.*"[1] After the justiciar ceased to be viceroy and became the mere head of a law court,[2] it became the rule to vest the royal authority during the king's absence in such a council (*custodes regni*) as was appointed by Henry III. in the year prior to his death, and which governed until the return of Edward I., nearly two years after that event.[3]

The first regency, properly so called, which occurred after first regency after the Conquest constituted at the accession of Henry III. the Conquest, grew out of the accession of Henry III. just after the completion of his tenth year. How at that time the royal authority was vested in the earl-marshal, the elected representative of the baronage, who carried on the government under the title of *rector regis et regni*, has been explained already.[4] Such action upon the part of the baronage was made necessary by the fact that the common law neither con-

---

[1] See vol. i. p. 244.
[2] Vol. i. p. 398.
[3] *Seventh Rept. of Dep. Keeper of the Public Records*, App. II. p. 259; Stubbs, *Const. Hist.*, vol. ii. pp. 103, 104. See also vol. i. of this work, p. 405. After the death of Mary in 1695, a like arrangement was made for carrying on the government during the absence of William III. from the realm, by the appointment of the principal officers of state, with the archbishop of Canterbury, as lords justices.
[4] Vol. i. p. 394.

templated nor provided for a minority, a circumstance which
no doubt arose out of the fact that under the ancient elective
system the king was supposed to be adult and personally competent to govern.[1]

regency
at the
accession of
Edward
III.;

After the deposition of Edward II.[2] and the election of his
son, then in his fourteenth year, parliament was a second time
called upon to constitute a regency, a duty which it discharged
by the appointment of a standing council of four bishops, four
earls, and six barons, who, under the lead of the earl of Lancaster, the king's cousin, were to advise in all matters of government.[3]

proceed-
ings at the
accession of
Richard
II., the first
to succeed
under the
doctrine
of repre-
sentation;

Although Richard II. at the time of his accession was only
eleven years old, no personal regent was appointed. The day
after his grandfather's death, the first king to succeed under
the new doctrine of representation took the great seal from
the hands of its keeper and passed it over to his uncle the
duke of Lancaster, who, four days later, passed it to the bishop
of St. David's, who, by virtue of its possession, under the
subtile legal theory then in vogue, was able to legalize all
acts of government. The lords then limited this arrangement
by the appointment of a council of twelve, without whose concurrence nothing was to be carried into effect, and whose
constitution was from time to time modified by parliament,
which is said to have itself acted as "a great council of regency"
during the earlier years of Richard's reign.[4]

Regencies
during the
reign of
Henry VI.;

We have seen already how parliament, at the accession of
Henry VI., dealt with the fourth minority since the Conquest
by ignoring the directions of the dead king, and by setting up
in their stead an arrangement of its own under which the duke
of Bedford (and in his absence the duke of Gloucester) became
protector and defender of the realm with the aid of a council
of sixteen, afterwards constituted to aid him in carrying on
the government.[5] The prolonged absence of Bedford on the

---

[1] Coke tells us that in contemplation of law the king cannot be a minor, "for when the royall bodie politique of the king doth meete with the
naturall capacity in one person, the
whole bodie shall haue the qualitie of
the royall politique, which is the greater
and more worthy, and wherein is no
minoritie." — *Co. Litt.*, 43.

[2] As to the deposition of Edward,
the first since the Conquest, see vol. i.
p. 505.
[3] *Rot. Parl.*, ii. 52; Knyghton, col.
2556.
[4] *Rot. Parl.*, iii. 386; Hallam, *Middle Ages*, vol. iii. p. 186.
[5] Vol. i. p. 553.

continent cast the protectorate upon Gloucester, who, when in the sixth year of the reign he called upon the lords to define his powers as protector and defender of the realm, was told in a written answer from them that he had no right to his office either by reason of his kinship, or by reason of the late king's will; that "the king that dead is, in his life nor might by his last will nor otherwise alter, change, nor abrogate, without the assent of the three estates, nor commut nor grant to any person governance or rule of this land longer than he lived." He was then told why the title of protector and defender had been given him, "granting you therewith certain power, the which is specified and contained in an act of the said parliament, it to endure as long as it liked the king."[1] As the infancy and imbecility of Henry VI. really rendered his reign a continual minority, its history is made up of a series of struggles between the leading statesmen of the time for control as protector.[2] In the course of the long struggle the duke of York was in 1454 elected by the lords protector and defender of the realm during the king's pleasure; and after the abrupt termination of his first protectorate by the king's recovery, he was again elected protector in 1455 by the lords, — but at the earnest solicitation of the commons, who seem to have exercised a controlling influence upon the proceeding. The duke was chosen the second time to hold the protectorate, not as at first "during the king's pleasure," but "until he should be discharged of it by the lords in parliament."[3]

sole power of the estates to create regencies emphasized;

growing influence of the commons.

The brief and tragic reign of the infant king Edward V. opens with a struggle for the regency between the queen mother and the duke of Gloucester, who, in May, 1483, was declared "protector of king and kingdom" by an irregular assembly of magnates and citizens.[4] By this time the following principles of constitutional law seem to have been distinctly recognized: (1) That to parliament as a whole belonged the exclusive right to constitute a regency, wherever the king from infancy or mental incapacity was personally incapable of performing his functions; (2) that the king did not possess the power to constitute, "by his last will nor otherwise," a regency during the minority of his successor, "without the assent of

Regency at the accession of Edward V.;

four principles of constitutional law now distinctly recognized;

---

[1] *Rot. Parl.*, iv. 326.
[2] Vol. i. pp. 552–560.
[3] *Rot. Parl.*, v. 284–290.
[4] Vol. i. p. 583.

the three estates;" (3) that neither the heir presumptive nor any other member of the royal house had the right as such to claim the regency, although they were often chosen by reason of their nearness in blood; (4) that when a regency was to be constituted, it was usual for parliament to vest the royal power either in some magnate individually, as guardian or protector, acting with the advice of a council; or in a council of regency without a dominant head.

provisions made by Henry VIII. for a regency during minority of Edward VI.;

Such were the principles that stood forth as guides and as warnings to Henry VIII., when the time came for him to provide for a regency during the stormy period occupied by the minority of Edward VI. Clearly understanding that no such attempt could be made with any hope of success without the aid of parliament, it was provided in his second succession

provisions of the act of 28 Hen. VIII. c. 7;

act [1] (28 Hen. VIII. c. 7), passed just after his marriage with Jane Seymour, that the heir to the throne if a male and under eighteen, or if a female and under sixteen, should be, if the king approved, until such ages respectively, under the government of his or her mother, and of such other councillors as the king might appoint by letters patent or by his last will. Under

council of regency appointed by will under authority of the act;

the authority of that act it was that Henry provided in his will for a council of regency consisting of the sixteen executors, to whom were committed the government of the realm and the control of Edward's person during the minority, subject to the further provision that the sixteen should consult and advise with another council of twelve, who were also named.[2] It was

act of 28 Hen. VIII. c. 17;

further provided by statute (28 Hen. VIII. c. 17) that any infant coming to the throne should have the power, upon attaining his or her majority, to repeal by letters patent all measures enacted in his or her name during minority. From the terms of that act, coupled with the fact that Henry attempted to select the executors [3] as equally as possible from the ranks of conservatives and reformers, so that neither faction should predominate, it is plain that his purpose was to preserve the results of his work intact, at least until Edward should attain his majority. And yet despite such precautions the whole

[1] See above, p. 84.
[2] More than two centuries then elapsed before the act of Henry VIII., passed in 1536, was followed by the Regency Act of 24 Geo. II. c. 24, passed in 1751.
[3] As to the persons named, see Froude, *Hist. Eng.*, vol. iv. pp. 234, 235.

scheme was at once set aside through the ambitious designs of Edward Seymour, earl of Hertford, uncle of the infant king, who, in defiance of the terms of the will, and without the authority of parliament, converted the carefully balanced regency into a protectorate, with himself as its head. The process through which Hertford accomplished this usurpation was at once bold and ingenious. Assuming at the outset the validity of the will,[1] the executors were assembled in the Tower on the Monday following the king's death, where they swore to maintain it "in every part and article of the same." Then upon the ground that business could not be conveniently dispatched unless some one "should be preferred in name and place before other, to whom, as to the head of the rest, all strangers and others might have access," it was resolved, at the instance of Paget, that Hertford should be given the first place "as protector of all the realms and dominions of the king's majesty, and governor of his most royal person, with the special and express condition, that he shall not do any act but with the advice and consent of the rest of the executors."[2] The convenient revelations of Paget soon followed as to the king's intention to enrich and ennoble the faithful few to whom he had committed the execution of his will, and out of the shower of titles that ensued Hertford emerged as the duke of Somerset, his brother Thomas as Lord Seymour, Lisle and Wriothesley as the earls of Warwick and Southampton, while estates carved from the possessions of the monasteries passed to many more, including Cranmer.[3] The next step involved the removal of the hostile chancellor, the new earl of Southampton, who had the official custody of Henry's will, and who had manifested a purpose to thwart the protector's plans by maintaining the status contemplated by that instrument. Through an illegal act upon the part of Southampton in appointing, shortly after the king's death, the master of the rolls and three civilians as vice-chancellors, with power to hear equity causes and to make decrees therein subject to his approval, it was

usurpation of Seymour;

process by which he established his protectorate;

modification of plan of government provided by the will;

removal of the lord chancellor;

---

[1] As to the grave difficulties upon that subject, see above, p. 108.

[2] Records of the Privy Council, Edward VI., MS. Council Office. The letters to foreign sovereigns announcing Henry's death went out "under the hand and subscription only of the Lord Protector."

[3] Strype, *Eccl. Mem.*, II. i. 123, ed. 1822; Records of the Privy Council, Edward VI., MS.

held by the judges that by affixing the great seal to the commission without the authority of a royal warrant, the chancellor had not only forfeited his office, but had also incurred the danger of fine and imprisonment at the king's pleasure.[1] The result was the removal [2] of Southampton from office and the transfer of the great seal to the more pliable hands of Lord St. John as keeper, who on the 12th of March affixed it to a new patent for the protectorate issued in Edward's name, wherein, after ratifying all that the protector had done, it was provided that until the king should become of age, he might "do anything which a governor of the king's person, or protector of the realm, ought to do." [3]   In this instrument the sixteen executors as such were ignored by being blended with ten others into a new body of twenty-six as the nominees of Edward, a body to which the protector could add at will, and from which he was authorized to "choose, name, appoint, use, and swear of privy council, such and so many as he from time to time shall think convenient."   Thus within six weeks after the king's death the elaborate regency which he had constructed was completely set aside, and in its place substituted the protectorate, by virtue of the document under which Somerset became practically as absolute as Henry himself had been.   The one shadow which rested upon the new commission resulted from the fact that it was countersigned by only seven of the executors, and in the list of those who held back was the ominous name of Dudley, earl of Warwick, better known in history as the duke of Northumberland.

patent issued in Edward's name making Somerset protector with unlimited powers.

Protectorate of Somerset:

2. From March 12, 1547, until October 14, 1549, Somerset was in full possession of the royal authority as protector, an authority which he wielded from the king's death in January until the following November without the aid of parliament or convocation.   During that interval it was that the English Reformation was fairly inaugurated through the joint efforts of Somerset and Cranmer, the former supplying the political authority, the latter the intellectual guidance which directed the English Church along the conservative path through which it approached without reaching the goal already at-

English Reformation inaugurated by Somerset and Cranmer;

---

[1] For a full statement, see Burnet, *Hist. Reform.*, vol. i. p. 300.

[2] This conclusion was reached on the 6th of March.   Privy Council Records, Edward VI., MS.

[3] The letters patent are printed in Burnet's *Collectanea.*

tained by the continental Reformation. The first act of the policy of regarding the church as a mere department of state continued; privy council after Henry's death was intended to indicate to the clergy in no uncertain terms that his policy of regarding the church as a mere department of state was to be continued. On February 1, after the lord chancellor had given up the seals and received them back from Edward's hands, he was directed to make out new patents for the judges, a proceeding new patents for bishops as well as judges; which was soon followed by the making out of new patents for the bishops as well, under the theory announced by the council that the king's death had determined the authority of their spiritual jurisdiction, which they had derived during the preceding reign "by force of instruments under the seal appointed *ad res ecclesiasticas.*"[1] The character and scope of source and extent of episcopal jurisdiction as defined in Cranmer's patent; the jurisdiction which the patents to the bishops undertook to confer was clearly defined in that granted to Archbishop Cranmer, in which the fact was asserted that all kinds of jurisdiction were derived from the king as supreme head of the church, as well the right of the archbishop to ordain in his diocese as his right to hear causes in his ecclesiastical court.[2] The new doctrine thus emphatically asserted, that the crown and not the pope was the source of all ecclesiastical jurisdiction, soon received a fresh application through the order made by the council on May 4 for a general "visitation," right of visitation first transferred from the pope to the crown by 25 Hen. VIII. c. 21, extended; a prerogative which, as we have heretofore pointed out, was first transferred from the pope to the crown by the act of 25 Hen. VIII. c. 21, § 20, which was soon followed by the Act of Supremacy (26 Hen. VIII. c. 1), under whose comprehensive terms the right to visit and reform received a still wider application.[3] The commission now issued for the general visitation, Cranmer's scheme of reform outlined in the instructions now issued for a new visitation; projected but never carried out during Henry's reign, was attended by a mandate from the privy council, which not only suspended the ordinary jurisdiction of the two archbishops and their suffragans during the visitation, but also prohibited the clergy from preaching outside of their own churches with-

---

[1] Privy Council Register. In the reign of Henry VIII. that seal was employed only for letters patent, the bishops still using their own seals for documents issued under their authority. See Blount, *Reform. of the Church of Eng.*, vol. ii. p. 35, and note 3.

[2] Cranmer's commission is entitled *Commissio regia archiæpiscopo Cantuar.*

ad exercendam suam jurisdictionem. Wilkins, *Conc.*, vol. iv. p. 2 ; Burnet's *Collectanea.*

[3] See above, pp. 72, 75. The act of 26 Hen. VIII. c. 1 was repealed by 1 & 2 Phil. & Mary, c. 8, but the part relating to visitations, reënacted by 1 Eliz. c. 1, § 17, has ever since remained in force.

out a royal license.[1]   A Book of Homilies[2] was at the same time put forth as a guide to doctrine, and the commissioners were armed with seventy-four "Articles of Enquiry," and with thirty-seven general injunctions,[3] from whose terms may be gathered a very definite idea of the plan of reform devised by Cranmer as the basis of the new system.   Foremost among the churchmen of the old school who ventured to resist the fresh tide of innovation were Bonner, bishop of London, and Gardiner, bishop of Winchester, both of whom were imprisoned.   While Cranmer was thus advancing the new ecclesiastical movement within the realm, Somerset had crossed the border and had won his great victory at Pinkie Cleugh, from which he returned to London in triumph in September.   With the political influence of the protector thus at its height, the parliament met, on the 4th of November, in which the religious revolution inaugurated by the privy council was to receive the sanction of legislation.

resisted by Bonner and Gardiner, who were imprisoned;

necessary legislation enacted in the parliament which met on November 4, 1547;

In order that the subject of ecclesiastical reform might be discussed without danger, it was first necessary to repeal the bloody Act of the Six Articles, in which Henry had attempted to put forth for the first time a positive statutory definition of the crime of heresy.   An account has heretofore been given of the civil and ecclesiastical law upon that subject prior to the enactment in 1382 of the statute of 5 Richard II. st. 2, c. 5, which was followed in 1400 by 2 Hen. IV. c. 15 (*De hæretico comburendo*), and in 1414 by 2 Hen. V. c. 7, which dealt mainly with the question of procedure.[4]   The statutory system as thus established continued in full force down to 1533, when Henry VIII. undertook to improve it by the enactment of 25 Hen. VIII. c. 14, which, after repealing 2 Hen. IV. c. 15, because it failed to "decline any certain cases of heresy," and because it gave the bishops an unlimited power to put men on trial for heresy on bare suspicion, confirmed and reënacted the statute of 5 Rich. II. c. 5, and 2 Hen. V. c. 7.   The negative definitions of heresy contained

necessity for the repeal of the Six Articles defining heresy;

statutory definitions of heresy prior to that act;

[1] Wilkins, *Conc.*, vol. iv. pp. 10–14; Burnet, *Hist. Reform.*, vol. i. p. 308.
[2] These had been prepared some years before by Cranmer and others for the use of convocation, but never published.
[3] See Strype's *Eccl. Mem.*, II. i. 75–83; Burnet, *Hist. Reform.*, vol. i. p. 309; Blount, *Reform. of the Church of Eng.*, vol. ii. pp. 43–59.
[4] Vol. i. pp. 537–540.

in Henry's act of 1533 were supplemented in 1539 by the positive and emphatic declarations contained in the Act of the Six Articles (31 Hen. VIII. c. 14), whose terms were extended four years later by 34 & 35 Hen. VIII. c. 1. In order to wipe out this whole statutory system for the punishment of heresy was passed the statute of 1 Edw. VI. c. 12, in which not only the Act of the Six Articles, but all "acts of parliament and statutes touching, mentioning, or in any wise concerning religion and opinions" were repealed.[1] Thus was restored "the common law as to heresy," but the law so restored was understood to be the law as settled in Sawtre's case at the beginning of the reign of Henry IV., which authorized the burning of a heretic by the writ *De hæretico comburendo*[2] after a conviction by a provincial council."

all prior statutes upon the subject repealed by 1 Edw. VI. c. 12;

common law as to heresy as settled in Sawtre's case revived.

The mass which the Act of the Six Articles had so resolutely retained was superseded in 1547 by the communion under the authority of an act[3] which, after providing punishment for such as should revile the sacrament, enjoined the receiving of it under both kinds on the laity as well as the clergy, an act which after repeal and revival is still in force. While the Act of Supremacy remained unrepealed until the next reign, the famous treasons act (26 Hen. VIII. c. 13) by which it was supplemented was now wiped out by 1 Edw. VI. c. 12, providing that nothing should be held to be treason except offences against the old treasons act of 25 Edw. III. c. 3, and such as were created by its own terms. In 1552, after the fall of Somerset, some of the abolished treasons were reënacted and some new ones created, subject, however, to the all-important constitutional limitation which provided that no person should henceforth be indicted or attainted for any kind of treason except on his voluntary confession, or upon the testimony of two lawful witnesses with whom the accused should be confronted on the trial.[4] The traditional form of

The mass superseded by the communion;

treasons act of 26 Hen. VIII. c. 13, repealed, and act of 25 Edw. III. c. 3, with a few amendments, restored;

in 1552 provision made for two witnesses in cases of treason;

---

[1] A masterful exposition of the whole subject may be found in Sir J. F. Stephen's *Hist. of the Crim. Law of Eng.*, vol. ii. pp. 438–475.

[2] As to Sawtre's case, see vol. i. p. 537, note 6. For Sir J. F. Stephen's review of that case, see vol. ii. pp. 445–459.

[3] 1 Edw. VI. c. 1. That act confirmed a canon passed by convocation

in December, 1547, providing for communion in both kinds. Strype's *Mem. Cranmer*, ii. 37; Wilkins, *Conc.*, vol. iv. p. 16.

[4] The act of 5 & 6 Edw. VI. c. 2 provided for "two lawful accusers; which said accusers, at the time of the arraignment of the party accused, if they be then living, shall be brought in person before the party so accused

elections of bishops by *congé d'élire* abolished, and their appointment vested in the king;

electing bishops by *congé d'élire* was abolished by an act which completely swept away the ancient fiction by the provision "that from henceforth no *congé d'élire* be granted, nor election of any archbishop or bishop by the dean and chapter made, but that the king may, by his letters patent, at all times when any archbishoprick or bishoprick is void, confer the same to any person whom the king shall think meet." [1]   By the same

act giving royal proclamations the force of law repealed;

act [2] which abolished the new treasons created during the reign of Henry VIII. was repealed the act that had given to his proclamations the force of law.   In painful contrast with the liberal spirit of such legislation as this stands the vagrancy

cruel vagrancy act of 1 Edw. VI. c. 2.

act of 1 Edw. VI. c. 2, which, after repealing the prior statutes upon that subject as not sufficiently severe, substituted a new set of penalties against unfortunates of that class that culminated in the provision that if the vagrant should run away from the temporary bondage to which he was first consigned, he should be adjudged a slave for life, branded with the letter S, and hanged if he should run away a second time. [3]

Origin and fate of the chantry lands;

Apart from the estates of the monasteries, and despite the statutes of mortmain, gifts of land had for a long time been made to the use of parish churches, chapels, guilds, fraternities, companies, or brotherhoods, erected for devotion, or by common assent, without incorporation.   The perpetuity of such grants was secured by the conveyance of lands to per-

primary objects of such donations;

sons in trust, and the primary object of the trust was to maintain the saying of masses for the benefit of the souls of the donors or their relations ; or the trust was created primarily for the benefit of a church chapel, hospital, school, college, or other charitable, religious, or educational institution with the obligation of obits or prayers for the souls of the donors or others superadded as an incidental object. [4]   In order to prevent the

and avow and maintain that that they have to say against the said party to prove him guilty of the treason or offences contained in the bill of indictment laid against the party arraigned." As to the subsequent disregard of the act, see Foster, *Crown Law*, pp. 232–251.

[1] 1 Edw. VI. c. 2.

[2] 1 Edw. VI. c. 12.   Despite the statute, however, the practice of issu-

ing proclamations continued for a long time thereafter.   See below, p. 179.

[3] The best history of the vagrancy statutes may be found in Sir J. F. Stephen's *Hist. of the Crim. Law*, vol. iii. pp. 266–275.

[4] Reeves' *Hist. of English Law*, vol. iii. pp. 269–271 and notes (Finlason ed.).   An excellent statement of the whole matter is contained in note (b).

making in future of grants of this character, embracing not only "superstitious uses," but also "good and charitable uses" as afterwards defined, was passed the statute of 23 Hen. VIII. c. 10, which declared all such dispositions void. After the confiscation of the monastic property by the acts passed in the 27th and 32d years of Henry's reign, a restrospective act [1] was passed in the 37th of that reign giving the lands granted in trust as above described, and generally known as the chantry lands, to the king. As the execution of that act was prevented by Henry's death, another of the same character was passed in Edward's first parliament,[2] under which commissioners were appointed who soon placed the chantry lands under the control of the privy council. Although this act declared that the property so appropriated was to be applied "to good and godly uses," as in erecting grammar schools, few were in fact established, the bulk of the chantry endowments being dispersed and wasted as the monastic lands had been.[3]

An account has heretofore been given of the opposition of the clergy to the scheme of Edward I., who designed, by means of the *præmunientes* clause contained in the writs addressed to the bishops, to incorporate their representatives as a distinct parliamentary estate. Under the persistent opposition of the clergy themselves, who preferred to vote their aids in their provincial councils and convocations, Edward's plan broke down, and the *præmunientes* clause, though still inserted in the writs, became merely an empty formula.[4] After the loss of power that the clerical assemblies suffered, through the submission which the whole clerical body was forced to make to Henry VIII., they attempted to regain something of their old influence first by petitions to Cranmer that statutes concerning religion and ecclesiastical ordinances should not pass without their sanction, and when such requests were ignored, they asked that they might now be "associated with the commons in the nether house of parliament."[5] No disposition was shown, however, to disturb existing relations, and the im-

Margin notes:
distinction between "superstitious" and "good and charitable uses;"

act of 37 Hen. VIII. c. 4, giving the chantry lands to the king;

act of 1 Edw. VI. c. 14, declaring that such lands should be applied "to good and godly uses."

Unsuccessful attempt of the clergy to gain representation "in the nether house of parliament;"

---

[1] 37 Hen. VIII. c. 4.
[2] 1 Edw. VI. c. 14.
[3] As to the disposition actually made of the chantry lands and their probable value, see *Reform. of the Church of Eng.*, Blount, vol. ii. pp. 60–66.

[4] Vol. i. pp. 480, 481.
[5] Wilkins, *Conc.*, vol. iv. p. 15; Cardwell's *Synodalia*, vol. ii. p. 420; Burnet's *Hist. Reform.*, vol. i. p. 323.

portant work of ecclesiastical reform was continued as before without clerical coöperation in the lower house.

marriage of priests declared to be lawful ;

In the second session of Edward's first parliament, which met in November, 1548, the work of the English Reformation was materially advanced by the enactment of a statute declaring the marriage of priests to be lawful ;[1] and by the adoption of the changes of creed and ritual brought forward by Cranmer in the first Book of Common Prayer, which received the sanction of the state by being annexed as a schedule to

first Act of Uniformity and the Book of Common Prayer ;

the first Act of Uniformity [2] providing that it should go into effect throughout the Church of England on the 9th of July, 1549. Although the details of the making of this famous and melodious compilation are obscure, it seems to be clear that it was built up out of the old Latin service-book of the Church of England under the guiding hand of Cranmer, who, after conference with continental reformers of every school, submitted the completed work to both houses of convocation and the privy council, prior to its submission for parliamentary

question of the communion ;

approval.[3] The supreme question involved was that of the communion, a question that had already been passed upon in the previous session by the act [4] which, without materially changing the catholic dogma, commended the giving of the elements in both kinds to clergy and laity alike. In order to adapt the change thus made to the service of the mass, an " Order of Communion " had been promulgated by the crown,[5] prior to the adoption of the first prayer-book, consisting of a brief service in English which, beginning after the communion of the priest, regulated the administration of the sacrament to

first or "high church" prayer-book of 1549 ;

the laity. In the first or " high church " prayer-book of 1549 the communion service so arranged was retained without material alteration. The devotional changes thus brought about were not to be accepted, however, without a protest from at least a part of the nation. The day after the new liturgy

---

[1] 2 & 3 Edw. VI. c. 21. The act of 5 & 6 Edw. VI. c. 12 was afterwards passed in order to counteract the effects of the preamble of the first act, which seriously reflected upon clerical marriages while it permitted them.

[2] 2 & 3 Edw. VI. c. 1.

[3] " The Book of Common Prayer, thus set forth with the full authority of church and state, may very fairly be called an expurgated and condensed English version of the ancient Missal, Breviary, and Manual, by which the services of the Church of England had been conducted during mediæval times." — Blount, *Reform. of the Church of Eng.*, vol. ii. p. 93.

[4] 1 Edw. VI. c. 1.

[5] By proclamation dated March 8, 1548.

went into effect, the flame of revolt broke out in Devonshire; Cornwall soon followed suit; and the result was an organized movement extending over a considerable district, that culminated in a formal protest put forward by the insurgents consisting of fifteen articles, in which the restoration of catholicism as it had existed at the end of the preceding reign and the abolition of protestantism were distinctly demanded.[1]

While Lord Russell was engaged in stamping out the religious revolt that thus arose in the western counties, a rebellion more serious still began in the east, under the leadership of Robert Ket, a Wymondham tanner, who, pitching his camp near Norwich, marshalled his forces under an Oak of Reformation in order to demand the redress of grievances that were mainly agrarian. The most important social revolution which followed the Conquest was that which resulted from the breaking up of the manorial system, a process wherein the lord of a manor passed from his original position at the head of a cultivating community composed of dependents owing personal services, which were either paid in kind or commuted, to that of a modern landlord receiving rent in money from his tenants, and supplying their places in the cultivation of the demesne lands by paid laborers as occasion required. Prior to the ravages of the Black Death that made its advent into England at the close of 1348, the supply of hired labor, which became more and more necessary as the process of enfranchisement advanced, had been both abundant and cheap.[2] After that event, which swept away perhaps half of the population, hired labor became so scarce that the wealthier craftsmen of the towns as well as the farmers of the country became alarmed at what they considered the extravagant demands of the laboring classes. The counterblast of the landowners to this revolt was the Statute of Laborers, the first passed at the close of 1349, whereby parliament attempted not only to fix arbitrarily the price of labor, but also to drive the peasant class back into the state from which they were fast escaping through enfranchisement by cruel provisions forbidding the laborer, under heavy penalties, to quit his parish in order to ob-

---

[1] The demands of the rebels are printed in Strype's *Cranmer.* Another version to the same effect is given in Holinshed. See also Burnet's *Hist. Reform.*, vol. i. p. 376.
[2] Vol. i. p. 507.

tain better employment.[1] When the villeins refused to accept the starvation wages thus held out to them, the lords fell back upon their demesne rights, which they were quick to enforce through the manorial courts presided over by their own stewards whenever a manumission or exemption could be cancelled upon the ground of informality. The story has been told of how this bitter conflict between capital and labor culminated at last in the Peasant Revolt of 1381, which, in spite of the period of repression that immediately followed it, was so far successful that at the end of a century and a half from the time of the rising, villenage had become a rare if not obsolete institution.[2] Misfortunes that might have fallen upon the landowners through the gradual revolution in the system of labor were averted, however, by a serious change in the method of agriculture which, beginning with the Black Death, went steadily on for a century after that event. The rise that took place in the price of wool made it expedient for the landlords to dispense to a great extent with the services of agricultural laborers by laying down the land in pasture. In that way there began in England during the fifteenth century a steady increase of sheep farming, and such a consequent decrease of corn growing as to cause serious anxiety.[3] Out of the change consequent upon this increase of pasture farming at the expense of tillage, which signified the inclosing of large districts of country and the expulsion of tenants occupying small holdings therein, grew the famous question of "enclosures," — a question embracing not only the eviction of tenants from their holdings, but also the inclosure of the common, waste which in some instances was so curtailed that the peasantry could not obtain pasturage enough to maintain the stock necessary to work their fields. To check the growth of this evil a statute was passed in the reign of Henry VII. (4 Hen. VII. c. 16), followed by 6 Hen. VIII. c. 5, 7 Hen. VIII. c. 1, and 25 Hen.

Marginal notes: conflict between capital and labor culminated in Peasant Revolt of 1381; extinction of villenage; consequent change in the method of agriculture; the question of "enclosures;" statutes passed to check the evils arising from inclosures;

[1] Vol. i. pp. 507, 508.

[2] Ibid., pp. 508–510. In some instances the manorial lords exacted predial services from villeins as late as the reign of Elizabeth, but without any formal change in the law the right was extinguished. See the report of the case of Somerset, a negro slave, in 1771, Howell's *State Trials*, vol. xx. p. 40.

[3] . . . "Of that we shall hear much more in Tudor times, but it is of more immediate importance to notice how a death-blow had now been given to the old manorial system. It was not only that it had become difficult to work it, but that another mode of using the land was proving profitable." — Cunningham, *Growth of English Ind. and Commerce*, vol. i. p. 361.

VIII. c. 13, the last of which, after denouncing the process that was gathering "together into few hands as well great multitude of farms as great plenty of cattle and in especial sheep," provided remedies of a very stringent character.[1] But the effort thus made in 1534 to check the evil was immediately followed by the dissolution of the monasteries,[2] which event is admitted on every hand to have greatly increased it, by the transfer of the abbey lands from the hands of the most indulgent of landlords to those of the courtiers, who were eager to swell their resources by devoting their new possessions to the use that would produce the greatest immediate income. Thus in spite of well-meaning legislation, the oppression of the peasant class consequent upon the advance of inclosures went steadily on, the general distress being greatly increased by a serious rise in prices resulting from a debasement of the coinage which had begun in the reign of Henry VIII.[3] When Somerset was called upon to cope with the evil, his sympathy with the laboring class was manifested in no uncertain terms by the appointment in the summer of 1548 of an Enclosures' Commission, charged with the duty of searching out and reporting the names of the landlords who were violating the tillage statutes.[4] The commissioners presented a report fully explaining the extent of the evil, which was made the basis of the Enclosure Bill rejected in the fall session by the house of lords. The refusal of parliament to act brought the protector face to face in the summer of 1549 with the armed rebellion headed by Ket, who raised the eastern countries in order to demand the prohibition of inclosures and the general redress of grievances from which the peasant class were then suffering.[5] In the presence of this new danger, Somerset, whose

which were greatly increased by the dissolution of the monasteries;

Enclosures' Commission appointed by Somerset in the summer of 1548;

refusal of parliament to grant relief brought on rebellion headed by Ket, who demanded general redress of agrarian grievances;

---

[1] See Cunningham, *Growth of Eng. Ind. and Commerce*, vol. i. pp. 468–472.

[2] "It appears that the suppression of the monasteries in the last reign had tended greatly to increase the appropriation of land to pasture. For in a proclamation of Edward VI., as stated by Strype, it was lamented that the realm was wasted, by bringing arable land into pasture, and letting houses and families decay and waste; so that various villages were entirely destroyed, and one shepherd dwelt where many industrious families dwelt before." — Reeves' *Hist. of Eng. Law*, vol. iii. p. 466, note (a), Finlason ed.

[3] See Froude, *Hist. Eng.*, vol. iv. pp. 350, 488; Cunningham, *Growth of Eng. Ind. and Commerce*, vol. ii. pp. 482, 483.

[4] Instructions of the Protector to the Commissioners of Enclosures, Strype's *Memorials*, vol. iv.

[5] "These pretended nothing of religion, but only to suppress and destroy the gentry, and to raise the commons, and to put new councillors about the

sympathy with the common people was notorious, so far lost
the confidence of the council by his hesitation that they
resolved to act without him.   At this juncture the earl of

*earl of
Warwick
selected by
the land-
owners to
put down
the revolt ;*

Warwick, who was now passing into prominence, became the
chosen leader of the landowning class, known as the gentlemen, and under his generalship the revolt in the eastern counties was put down before the end of August by the aid of
German and Italian mercenaries, who were now for the first
time employed by English rulers for the coercion of English

*Warwick
supplanted
Somerset in
October,
1549.*

subjects.   The prestige of victory thus gained the subtile
and ambitious Warwick was not slow to turn to his personal
advantage.   Drawing to his side the majority of the council,
open opposition was avowed early in October to the protector,
who was declared a traitor on the 7th, and sent to the Tower
on the 13th.[1]   Thus practically ended the protectorate of
Somerset, whose brief period of power marks that stage of
the English Reformation during which took place the memorable revision of the devotional system of the Church of
England.

*Govern-
ment of
Warwick,
duke of
Northum-
berland :*

3. The hope of a reaction in favor of catholicism which the
fall of the protector excited for a moment vanished in the presence of the fact that the same motives that had prompted
Somerset to put himself at the head of the reformers dictated
a like policy to his successor.   Warwick,[2] no less than Somerset, was one of the " new men " whose fortunes had sprung out
of the religious revolution to which all the nobles of the new
blood were irrevocably committed.   It was soon made appar-

*Henry's
executors
regained
authority
under the
lead of
Warwick ;
no change
of policy ;*

ent, therefore, that the recovery of authority by the executors
under the lead of Warwick, who at a later day assumed the
title of duke of Northumberland,[3] was to signify no change of
policy.   The despotic conciliar system which Cromwell had
organized, and which Somerset had enforced by the aid of
foreign mercenaries, was to be administered as before by a
new master, as cautious and decisive as his predecessor had
been imprudent and irresolute.   In the parliament that met in

king." — Burnet, *Hist. Reform.*, vol. i.
p. 376.
[1] *Grey Friars' Chron.*, Camd. Soc.,
p. 14.
[2] Dudley, earl of Warwick, was the
son of the Edward Dudley who, with
Empson, was punished upon the ac-

cession of Henry VIII. for financial
oppressions practised in his father's
reign.   See above, p. 40.
[3] In October, 1551, he took the title,
which had long been extinct by reason
of the attainder of Lord Thomas Percy
in 1537.

November assurance was given to the landowning gentlemen, with whose aid Warwick had put down the agrarian revolt, by the passage of a riot act, which made it felony for persons to the number of twelve or more to assemble for the purpose of abating the rents of farms or the price of provisions, for the destruction of houses or parks, or for the assertion of common rights. When the object of such assembly was to alter the laws, or to kill or imprison a member of the king's council, the offence was made high treason.[1] At Christmas the king issued a circular letter to the bishops, informing them that he would proceed with the reformation,[2] and requiring them to deliver up all the old service-books to be burned or otherwise destroyed, a mandate which was soon followed by an act providing that all persons, clerical or lay, who should persist in keeping such books in their possession should be fined for the first and second offences, and imprisoned at the king's pleasure for the third.[3] And in spite of the conservative opposition of many of the lords, an act was also passed commanding the removal from the parish churches of all paintings and statues except "the monumental figures of kings or nobles who had never been taken for saints."[4] While an attempt to give back to the ecclesiastical courts a portion of their former authority failed,[5] an act was passed repealing the cruel vagrancy act of the previous session, which imposed slavery as a punishment for idleness, and restoring the statutes of Henry VIII. upon that subject,[6] under which laborers who refused to work were punished as vagabonds. Not, however, until the years 1552–53 transpired the two memorable events in the history of the English Reformation which specially distinguish the rule of Northumberland.

Not long after the promulgation of the prayer-book of 1549, a bitter and persevering attack upon it began under the lead of John Hooper, afterwards bishop of Gloucester, who had lived abroad at Strasburg and Zurich, and who was thoroughly imbued with the ideas of the anti-sacerdotalist school

riot act of 3 & 4 Edw. VI. c. 10;

work of reformation continued;

attempt to restore jurisdiction of ecclesiastical courts failed; vagrancy act of Edw. VI. c. 2 repealed.

Bitter attack upon the prayer-book of 1549 led by Hooper; main points of attack;

---

[1] 3 & 4 Edw. VI. c. 10.
[2] See the letter from the council to the bishops, dated December 25, printed in Burnet's *Collectanea*.
[3] Burnet, *Hist. Reform.*, vol. i. p. 395.
[4] 3 & 4 Edw. VI. c. 10.

[5] See Burnet, *Hist. Reform.*, vol. ii. p. 434.
[6] 3 & 4 Edw. VI. c. 16. By 5 & 6 Edw. VI. c. 2 those statutes were confirmed, but licenses to beg upon certain terms were given.

led by Zwingli and Bullinger. The brunt of the attack was
directed against the doctrine of the real presence in the eu-
charist, against the established method of consecrating bishops,
and against the use of all ceremonies and customs that specially
savored of the ancient pomp of the older faith. The agitation
thus begun by Hooper, which received in 1551 the support of
Peter Martyr and Martin Bucer, foreign divines who had become Regius professors of divinity at Oxford and Cambridge,
finally enlisted the sympathy of the young king, who probably
gave the weight of his personal authority to a revision the
history of whose making is not recorded.[1] We only know for
certain that the results of the revision, however made, were
annexed as a schedule to a new Act of Uniformity[2] passed in
April, 1552, which provided that the second or "low church"
prayer-book should take the place of the first or "high
church" on the 1st of the following November. While Cranmer may have been forced by the agitation of Hooper into
modifications which would not otherwise have been made,
there is no reason to doubt that his guiding hand was potent
throughout in the work of devotional reform which had now
reached its consummation. "First had come the primers of
Henry VIII. ; then the Litany was added ; and then the first
Communion-book. The next step was the Prayer-book of 1549;
and now at last the complete Liturgy, which survives after
three hundred years." [3]

second Act of Uniformity and the "low church" prayer-book of 1552;

Liturgy thus completed still survives.

While the archbishop was thus engaged in completing the
revision of the church's devotional system, he was at the same
time advancing the preparation of the famous formularies
known as the Forty-two Articles of 1553 (afterwards reduced
to Thirty-nine), which were designed to end doctrinal controversy and to establish uniformity of opinion by virtue of authoritative definitions upon disputed questions sanctioned by
both church and state. Such formularies had been put forward by the Lutherans in 1530 in the "Confession of Augsburg," by the Calvinists in 1530 and 1536 in the "Confession
of Basle," and by the Church of Rome in the decrees passed
during the years (1546–63) occupied by the sessions of the

The Forty-two Articles of 1553, afterwards reduced to Thirty-nine;

prior formularies put forward by Lutherans, Calvinists, and Roman Catholics;

---

[1] A very good account of the prayer-
book of 1552 may be found in Blount's
Reform. of the Church of Eng., vol. ii.
pp. 94–107.

[2] 5 & 6 Edw. VI. c. 1.

[3] Froude, *Hist. of Eng.*, vol. v. p.
54.

Council of Trent. As heretofore pointed out, this process of definition began in England with the promulgation of the Ten Articles of 1536, which, in their final form as "A Necessary Doctrine of a Christian Man,"[1] had continued as an authoritative standard of belief, so far as the same was not overruled by the more recent teachings of the Homilies, the Ordinal, and the Prayer-book. In order to provide a clearer and more comprehensive set of definitions made necessary by the changes which had taken place since the beginning of Edward's reign, Cranmer was engaged, certainly as early as 1549, upon the new articles, whose history is involved in great doubt and confusion not only as to the method of their composition, but also as to the manner of their promulgation. Out of the uncertainty has arisen the question : "Were the Articles of 1553 submitted to the English convocation? Or were they circulated during the brief remainder of the reign of Edward on the sole authority of the royal council?"[2] An answer to that question may be found in the following summary made by the leading authority upon the subject as a statement of what most probably occurred in the composition and ratification of the Edwardian articles : "An early draft of them appears to have been made by Cranmer as far back as 1549. This document he used on his own authority, or in conjunction with the royal council, in the course of 1550. In the following year, we find the same series of articles, or one suggested by it, in circulation among other prelates, and the substance of it pressed by Hooper on his clergy in the shape of a religious test. On the 2d of May, 1552, the council ask the archbishop whether articles have 'been set forth by any *public authority*,' and this question naturally suggests the thought that some intention then existed of submitting the new formulary to the southern convocation, which had been but recently prorogued (April 16). That such intention was then executed we have no means of proving ; but there is no doubt that, in the interval which elapsed from the inquiry of the council to the autumn of the same year, the Formulary had been passed from hand to hand and made to undergo still further modification. We lose sight of it upon the 24th of November, 1552,

process of definition began in England with the Ten Articles of 1536;

the making and promulgation of the Forty-two Articles;

Hardwick's statement:

---

[1] See above, p. 87 and note 6.   [2] Hardwick's *Hist. of the Articles*, p. 105.

when a copy was remitted to the royal council. In their custody it seems to have continued till the meeting of the southern convocation in the March of 1553. If discussed at this time either in one or both houses, the debate must have been speedily concluded; for on the 1st day of the following month the synod was itself dissolved, and royal orders for the printing of the articles appeared on the 20th of May. They would thus have been 'prepared by the authority of the king and council, agreed to in convocation, and there subscribed by both houses; and so presently promulgated by the king's authority, according to law.'"[1] After the death of Edward the articles passed into an obscurity from which they did not emerge at the accession of Elizabeth. Not until five years after that event were they submitted for revision to the convocation that met in January, 1563, at which time, after certain omissions and additions, the completed work appeared as the famous Thirty-nine Articles, which then became by the joint action of church and state[2] the standard of doctrine of the Church of England; and as such, since the final revison of 1571,[3] they have remained unaltered during the three centuries that have elapsed since that time.

not until 1563 were the Forty-two Articles reduced to Thirty-nine;

the final revision of 1571.

Abortive attempt made to codify the ecclesiastical laws;

ancient canons not in conflict with the Reformation statutes continued in force;

The attempt made in Edward's reign to codify the ecclesiastical laws of the realm, which the religious revolution had left in a state of great confusion, proved abortive. When the church entered into new relations with the state by virtue of "The Submission of the Clergy," which took place in 1532–33, it was agreed (1) that where they did not conflict with the royal supremacy or with the laws of the realm, the ancient canons of the church should remain in full force; (2) that convocation should not discuss the enactment of new canons without a license from the crown; (3) that no new canons should have any force until ratified by the crown.[4] To remove the great uncertainty which naturally existed as to what canons actually remained in force after the passage of the Act of Sub-

---

[1] Hardwick's *Hist. of the Articles*, pp. 111, 112, citing Wake, *State of the Church*, pp. 598–600.

[2] As to their adoption by convocation, see Wilkins, *Conc.*, vol. iv. p. 237; Gibson's *Synod. Anglic.*, p. 145, ed. 1854. They were then submitted to the crown for ratification, according to the Act of Submission, and were so ratified under the great seal. Coke's *Inst.*, vol. iv. p. 74.

[3] As to the nature of the alterations made in 1571, and as to the authenticity of the English and Latin versions, see Hardwick, pp. 154–156.

[4] See above, p. 69.

mission, provision was made, not only in that act but in two others passed during the reign of Henry VIII., for a codification of the canon law.[1] As no action was taken prior to Henry's death, the subject was renewed in the first year of Edward's reign in a petition from the clergy of the lower house of convocation to the archbishop, in which they asked that a commission should be appointed to establish ecclesiastical laws "so that all judges ecclesiastical, proceeding after these laws, may be without danger or peril."[2] In response to that petition was finally passed 3 & 4 Edw. VI. c. 11, providing for the appointment by the king of such a commission as his father had been authorized to appoint. Accordingly in October, 1551, the council ordered the chancellor to issue a commission to thirty-two persons, who were named, which order was superseded a month later by another, limiting the commission to eight. In February, 1552, still another order appears for "a letter to the lord chancellor to make out a commission to the Archbishop of Canterbury and other bishops, learned men, civilians, and lawyers of the realm, for the establishment of the Ecclesiastical Laws, according to the act of parliament made the last session." The dead fruit of this commission, which failed to receive parliamentary sanction, is embalmed in a manuscript volume in Latin,[3] embracing not a codification of the ancient canon law as it remained in force after the Reformation, but a new creation composed in a narrow and inquisitorial spirit, which went so far as to provide among its many severe penalties that of death for obstinate heretics. This still-born production, known to the learned as "The Reformation of the Ecclesiastical Laws," could not be resuscitated by the effort made to that end in 1571.[4] After the utter failure thus made by the crown and the parliament to provide a comprehensive ecclesiastical code, which, like the Prayer-book and the Thirty-nine Articles, might have stood as an enduring monument, convocation contented itself with the enactment from time to time of such canons as the discipline

[margin notes:] unsuccessful attempt to codify made in Henry's reign revived by 3 & 4 Edw. VI. c. 11;

appointment of a commission;

refusal of parliament to approve the results of its labors;

since the failure to make a code convocation has enacted such canons as the discipline of the church required;

---

[1] 27 Hen. VIII. c. 15; 35 Hen. VIII. c. 16.
[2] See Cardwell's *Synodalia*, vol. ii. p. 420; Wilkins, *Conc.*, vol. iv. p. 15.
[3] Harl. MSS., p. 426. This volume was printed by Foxe in 1571, and by Cardwell in 1850, with additions made in the reign of Elizabeth.
[4] See Blount, *Reform. of the Church of Eng.*, vol. ii. pp. 112–115. Upon the whole subject, see also Lingard, vol. v. pp. 347–350.

of the church most urgently required. In that way three[1] sets
of canons were promulgated during the reign of Elizabeth.
But as the sanctions for the enactment of these canons did not
extend beyond the reign of the sovereign by whom they were
granted,[2] it became necessary at the accession of James I. to
deal anew with the whole subject. Availing itself of the opportunity thus offered, convocation in reënacting the canons of
the preceding reign undertook to expand them into something
like a code of church discipline, based of course upon the principles of the Reformation. The one hundred and forty canons
thus compiled remained unaltered down to the year 1865, when
material changes were made in four of them.[3] No change has,
however, taken place in the relations between the crown and
the clerical legislatures as fixed by the concordant of 1532–33.
The canons of 1865, like those of 1603, were enacted by the
convocations, after license first granted by the crown, by
whose authority they were afterwards ratified and confirmed
by letters patent under the great seal, prior to their promulgation, "to be diligently observed, executed, and equally kept
by all our loving subjects[4] of this our kingdom, within the
provinces of Canterbury and York, in all points wherein they
do or may concern every or any of them."

The last year of Edward's reign, marked by the promulgation of the revised Prayer-book and the Forty-two Articles,
found the realm in a state of great administrative disorder.
In spite of the vast sums which had accrued to the crown
through appropriations of ecclesiastical property, the greed of
the courtiers, the growing expenses of the court, and the cost
of military enterprises had produced an oppressive debt and an
empty treasury.[5] Northumberland, treading in the footsteps
of his father, first attempted in the fall of 1552 to supply the

(marginal notes:) canons of Elizabeth; compilation made by convocation in the reign of James I. remained unaltered until 1865. Great administrative disorder at the end of Edward's reign;

---

[1] As to the canons of 1575, 1585, and 1597, see Cardwell's *Synodalia,* vol. i. pp. 133, 139, 147.

[2] Gibson's *Codex,* p. 994.

[3] For details, see Blount, *Reform. of the Church of Eng.,* vol. ii. pp. 368–373.

[4] Lord Hardwicke held that such canons do not bind the laity "*proprio rigore.*" But he said, "There are many provisions contained in these canons which are declaratory of the ancient usage and law of the Church of Eng-land, received and allowed here, and which in that respect, and by virtue of such ancient allowance, will bind the laity." — *Middleton* v. *Croft,* Str. Rep. 1056; 2 Atkyn's Rep. 650.

[5] For a full statement of the finan-cial situation as taken from the *State Papers,* see Froude, *Hist. Eng.,* vol. v. pp. 110–112. "The expenses of the household, which in 1532 were nine-teen thousand pounds, in 1549 were more than a hundred thousand." — Ibid., vol. iv. p. 397.

deficit by the creation of all kinds of commissions to raise money,[1] and when that expedient failed he was driven, in January, 1553, to issue writs for a parliament that met on the 1st of March, memorable by reason of the measures which the council deemed it expedient to employ in order to check the growing spirit of independence by dictating the election of such members to the lower house as would be subservient to its will.   In that way a practice, which had prevailed to a greater or less extent since the days of Henry VII., was emphasized by a flagrant interference with elections by means of circulars sent directly to the sheriffs of counties or to the mayors of towns naming the persons to be chosen, or by royal orders sent to the favored candidates indicating the wish of the crown that they should be elected, or by directions to the electors themselves from individual members of the council.[2] Although the nomination parliament thus assembled granted the subsidy asked after much debate, the spirit of resistance manifested was so marked that it was dissolved on the last day of the month in which it met.   Edward was able to dissolve parliament in person, but immediately thereafter he was removed on account of his rapidly increasing infirmity to Greenwich, and by the 1st of May it was clear that he was slowly dying.   Thus was Northumberland brought face to face with a catastrophe that threatened not only his personal fortunes, but those of the Reformation.   The problem was, how to provide an heir to the throne who would be propitious to both.   The legal difficulties to be overcome were certainly serious.   By Henry's third and last succession act first Mary and then Elizabeth had been put in the entail in default of issue of Edward, with a proviso that the succession should be subject to such further arrangements as the king by his last will might appoint.   Under the power thus given Henry simply supplemented the parliamentary entail by providing that on failure

Marginal notes: parliament met in March, 1553; memorable attempt to influence elections to the lower house; the system of royal nominations; spirit of resistance so great that parliament was dissolved in the month in which it met; Edward's approaching death forces Northumberland to attempt to regulate the succession; the legal difficulties to be overcome; claims of Mary and Elizabeth;

---

[1] During the fall and winter of 1552–53, there were no less than nine such commissions. As to the visitation to glean the last spoils from the churches, see Burnet, *Hist. Reform.*, vol. i. p. 450.

[2] See first draft of a circular in British Museum, Lansdowne MSS., p. 3; letter to a candidate, Sir P. Hoby, Harleian MSS., p. 523; Froude, *Hist. Eng.*, vol. v. pp. 125, 126; Hallam, *Const. Hist.*, vol. i. p. 46, citing Strype, vol. ii. p. 394. When Froude refers to this as the first attempt to make a nomination parliament, he forgets that later on (vol. v p. 432) he admits that the circulars sent out by Mary to influence the elections for the parliament that met in November, 1554, "were copied from a form which had been in use under Henry VII."

of issue of his three children, the crown should pass to the
heirs of his younger sister Mary, duchess of Suffolk, to the
detriment of the heirs of his older sister Margaret of Scotland.[1]   The representative of the Suffolk claim was Frances,
the daughter of Mary, who was herself the mother of three
daughters[2] by her marriage with Grey, Lord Dorset, a zealous
protestant.   Northumberland's complicated conspiracy began
with a marriage[3] between Lady Jane Grey, the eldest daughter of Frances, and his fourth son Guildford Dudley.   Having
thus engrafted a branch of the Suffolk house upon his own
stock, the next step was to remove the three prior claimants
who stood before Jane in the line of succession.   The means
determined upon for the accomplishment of this end was a
will to be made by Edward, without parliamentary authority,
naming Lady Jane as his immediate successor.   This grossly
illegal attempt to set aside the succession as settled by parliament by a king still in his minority was earnestly opposed by
the judges, the law officers of the crown, and the archbishop,
as a desperate measure which would involve all concerned in
it in the guilt of treason.[4]   But boy as he was, and dying as he
was, Edward was immovable.   His zeal for the "religion" was
such that he felt that everything must yield to the necessities
of "his device for the succession," through which he confi-
dently believed he could transmit the crown to a protestant
successor.   On the 21st of June all the formalities incident to
the execution of the will or letters patent[5] were completed,
and on July 6 Edward died.   Although Northumberland was
reluctantly supported at first by the council backed by the
foreign mercenaries and by the extreme protestants, his whole
incoherent and impracticable conspiracy collapsed in the presence of a popular outburst in Mary's favor, which sent him to
the block, and with him the hapless girl whom he had involved
in the toils of his ambition.

Marginal notes: claims of the house of Suffolk; the marriage between Lady Grey and Guildford Dudley; Edward's illegal attempt to set aside all claimants prior to Jane by means of a will; will executed June 21, and Edward died July 6, 1553; failure of Northumberland's conspiracy.

[1] See above, p. 108.   And also Bailey's *Succession to the English Crown*,
pp. 135, 136.

[2] Lady Jane, born in 1537, Lady
Catherine, born in 1539, and Lady
Mary, born in 1545.

[3] Celebrated 25th of May, 1553.

[4] Burnet, *Hist. Reform.*, vol. i. p. 454.

[5] See the copy printed for the Camden Society by Mr. John G. Nichols,
*Letters Patent for the Limitation of
the Crown: Queen Jane and Queen
Mary*, Appendix.   A clear analysis of
the letters, showing Edward's leaning
to male succession, may be found in
Bailey, p. 167.

CHAPTER IV.

MARY AND THE CATHOLIC REACTION.

1. WITH the death of Henry VIII. ended the first stage of the English Reformation, which consisted of the severance from the Roman See, by a political act, of a people impelled by a growing sense of nationality to assume absolute independence, without any departure whatever from the Roman dogma and ritual employed by the national church from the earliest times. While, in response to the touch of self-interest, Henry was prompt to embody in his Act of Supremacy the new Lutheran doctrine[1] of national religion that claimed the right for each people to determine the form of belief which should prevail within its bounds, he as sternly imposed by his Act of the Six Articles the severest penalties upon all who dared to dissent from the teachings of the older faith. Apart from the bitter feeling which the subsequent suppression of the monasteries excited, there can be no doubt that the bulk of the nation went with the king, in his first great act involving the legal and ecclesiastical severance of the realm from the Roman dominion. While the papal party, which rejected as a whole the new order of things brought about by the separation, included in its ranks such lofty spirits as Fisher and More, its numbers were certainly insignificant when compared with the greater mass of Catholic Anglicans and Lutherans who fully accepted the royal supremacy, while they differed sharply as to what should be the future doctrine of the emancipated national church. So far did the bulk of the nation acquiesce in the change which Henry's legislation brought about that when, in the reign of Edward, organized rebellion broke out in the western counties against the introduction of the new service which the prayer-book inaugurated, the demand was for the retention of the mass and for the reëstablishment of catholicism, not

The first, embodying only a legal and ecclesiastical separation from Rome,

was cheerfully accepted by the bulk of the nation,

with the understanding that the ancient dogma and ritual should be retained.

[1] See above, pp. 50, 76.

with the pope as its head, but as the laws of King Henry had left it.[1]

The second stage, embodying a change of dogma and ritual, not accepted at first by the bulk of the nation;

With the death of Edward VI. ended the second stage, embracing the changes of dogma and ritual embodied under the guidance of Cranmer in the Prayer-book and the Forty-two Articles, which, by virtue of the Acts of Uniformity, were made the standards of orthodoxy. That the changes thus brought about by the authority of the privy council under the presidency first of Somerset and then of Northumberland did not at the time receive the assent of the bulk of the nation is a fact which seems to be settled as well by the consensus of historians as by the sudden reaction in which Cranmer's work

the cause greatly prejudiced during the second stage by the greed and recklessness of its leaders;

was for a time overthrown. Certain it is that the period occupied by the second stage of the English Reformation was a period of great want, misery, and administrative disorder, during which the cause was greatly prejudiced by the selfish conduct of the knot of greedy protestant nobles who at Henry's death seized upon the powers of the privy council, by means of which they completed the confiscation of the property of the church in order to enrich themselves, while they permitted the public treasury to become empty, the expenses of the court to increase, the coinage to be debased, and the peasantry to be oppressed by the enforcement of the heartless policy of inclosures which they carried out in the interest of the landlords

the nation finally refused to support the protestant party headed by Northumberland,

by the aid of foreign mercenaries.[2] It is not therefore strange that when the upstart Northumberland, around whom had gathered the hate which such a policy naturally engendered, attempted to consummate his selfish work by a grossly illegal attempt to transfer the crown itself to his own family, the nation should have risen in arms against him ; and that when

even in the interest of Jane Grey;

his puppet queen, protestant as she was, was proclaimed, on the 10th of July, 1553, but " few or none said, God save her." [3]

religious status of Mary;

As to Mary's religious status there could be neither doubt nor question. So firm had been her insistence during her brother's reign upon her right to reject the new service and to cling to the mass that she was brought into sharp collision with both the king and the privy council,[4] who only yielded to her

---

1 See above, p. 121.
2 See above, p. 124.
3 *Grey Friars' Chron.*, p. 79; Holinshed's *Chron.*, p. 1087.

4 *Privy Council Register*, entry of June 16, 1549.

demands under a threat of war from her powerful cousin the emperor.[1] But the fact remained that she was the daughter of a king who had never lost his popularity; that her right to the crown had been sanctioned by an act [2] of parliament; and that her accession would end at least a period of political and religious chaos during which the nation had become thoroughly disheartened. So it was that within the ten days that followed the proclamation of Lady Jane, Northumberland's conspiracy collapsed; and Mary, around whom had gathered an army of thirty thousand men [3] drawn mainly from the eastern counties in which the new religious movement had taken the deepest hold, was proclaimed by order of the council in London on the 19th, and in Cambridge on the next day. On August 3 the queen entered London with Elizabeth by her side amid the acclaim of the populace, and according to custom she proceeded to the Tower, where she found upon the green, awaiting release at her hands, an historic group of state prisoners,[4] among whom were the old duke of Norfolk, and Gardiner, bishop of Winchester, who, after a rigid confinement of five years, now came forth to take the first place at Mary's side as the councillor who was to direct the conservative policy that prevailed down to the Spanish marriage, and the subsequent domination of Philip and Pole.

her right to the crown sanctioned by parliament;

proclaimed by the council in London on the 19th of July, 1553;

visits the Tower and releases Norfolk and Gardiner.

2. Gardiner, an ecclesiastical statesman, trained in the tolerant school of Wolsey, and who became secretary of state after his fall,[5] had taken an active part in the measures that culminated in the repudiation of the papal supremacy, which he denounced at the time in a tract in which he said "that no new thing was introduced when the king was declared to be supreme head." [6] And yet in spite of his well-known advocacy of an independent national church, he was with Norfolk excluded from the list of Henry's executors because they were both known to be unalterably opposed to any further change involving either doctrine or ritual. Upon that ground he was finally sent to the Tower by Somerset, despite the fact that,

Mary's accession: The conservative policy of Gardiner;

his views as to the supremacy;

sent to the Tower by Somerset;

[1] See Cecil's statement of the matter, MS. Germany, bundle 15, State Paper Office, cited by Froude, vol. iv. p. 538.
[2] 35 Hen. VIII. c. 1. See above, p. 107.
[3] Haynes' *State Papers*, p. 157.
[4] Renard to Charles V., Rolls House MSS.
[5] See above, p. 67.
[6] In his book *De Vera Obediencia.* See Brown's *Fasciculus*, vol. ii. p. 806.

while he maintained that there should be no new ecclesiastical legislation during the minority of Edward, he had openly declared in a memorable sermon [1] against the papal and in favor

comes back to power resolved to restore Henry's ecclesiastical system;

of the royal supremacy. Inspired by such principles Gardiner now came back to power, resolved to reëstablish Henry's ecclesiastical system in the identical form in which he had left it. After the restoration of the bishops [2] who had been deposed and imprisoned in the preceding reign, and the execution of justice upon three of the ringleaders of the conspiracy

Mary's first parliament legislated only to that extent;

against the queen,[3] Mary's first parliament, which met on the 5th of October, 1553, addressed itself under Gardiner's guidance to the task of wiping out only so much of Edward's ecclesiastical legislation as would make possible the restoration of the legal conditions as they existed in the last year of Henry VIII. The session opened with the ancient form of the mass, so long omitted, and the first act of the reign

treasons act of 25 Edw. III. restored;

reëstablished the law of treason as defined by 25 Edw. III., by reënacting the repealing section of the act of Edward VI., with the addition of words extending it to misprision of treason.[4]

queen's legitimacy settled and her mother's divorce annulled:

The next act,[5] in order to settle the question of the queen's legitimacy, after declaring the validity of the marriage of her mother with Henry, annulled the sentence of divorce pronounced by Cranmer, as well as all acts of parliament which questioned her legitimacy. Then followed the act [6] repealing

nine statutes of Edward's reign, as to creed and ritual, repealed;

nine statutes passed in Edward's reign, relating to creed and ritual, the marriage of priests, and the election of bishops, which may be enumerated as follows : the two Acts of Uniformity, and that authorizing the Ordinal (2 Edw. VI. 1 ; 5 Edw. VI. 1 ; 3 Edw. VI. 12), the act authorizing the communion in both kinds (1 Edw. VI. 1), the act authorizing the appointment of bishops without election (1 Edw. VI. 2), the act for the limitation of holy days (5 Edw. VI. 3), the act abolishing the old service-books (2 Edw. VI. 10), and the two acts permitting priests to marry (2 Edw. VI. 21 ; 5 Edw. VI.

---

[1] Foxe, vol. vi. pp. 87–93, ed. 1838.

[2] As to the return of Bonner from the Marshalsea, see *Grey Friars' Chron.*, p. 82.

[3] Northumberland, Gates, and Palmer were executed for high treason on August 22.

[4] 1 Mary, c. 1.

[5] 1 Mary, sess. 2, c. 1. Nothing was said in the act as to the papal dispensation, an omission of which Pole afterwards bitterly complained. See Strype's *Cranmer*, vol. iii. pp. 477, 479. *Eccl. Hist.*, Soc. ed.

[6] 1 Mary, sess. 2, c. 2.

12).   By the express terms of the repealing act "all such form of divine service in use at the end of Henry's reign reëstablished by law; divine service and administration of the sacraments as were most commonly used in this realm of England in the last year of the reign of our late sovereign lord, King Henry VIII., shall be, from and after the 20th day of December, 1553, used throughout the whole realm of England, and all other the Queen's Majesty's dominions."   And the same rule was repeated in the next act,[1] which provided for the punishment of all who should molest priests, "celebrating the mass or other such divine service, sacraments, or sacramentals, as was most commonly frequented and used in the last year of the reign of the late sovereign lord, King Henry the Eighth."   While thus conserving and restoring Henry's work, parliament was careful not to repeal the Act of Supremacy, and Mary accordingly Act of Supremacy not repealed, Mary remaining the "Supreme Head" down to April, 1554. retained the title of "Supreme Head" down to April 2, 1554,[2] a date subsequent to the arrangement of her marriage with Philip, an event which marks the beginning of a new policy that culminated in the wiping out of the whole scheme of legislation through which the supremacy of the pope had been repudiated.

There can be no doubt that Mary was resolved from the Mary resolved from the outset to reëstablish the Roman supremacy; outset to do her utmost to restore the realm to full communion with the Roman See, and that she only acquiesced for the moment in the moderate policy of Gardiner until she could sufficiently strengthen her hands by a marriage alliance for the final enterprise.   Motives both religious and political sug- seeks to strengthen her hands by a marriage with Philip; gested that she should seek a husband from her mother's kin, and the emperor was more than willing to offer to her the hand of Philip[3] in extension of the ambitious policy of the house of Austria.   Cardinal Pole, the queen's second cousin Cardinal Pole advocates the alliance; once removed, who had been commissioned as legate[4] the moment that Edward's death was known at Rome, although he was prevented by his attainder from entering the kingdom,

---

[1] 1 Mary, sess. 2, c. 3.
[2] The first parliament was summoned in the name of "Mary . . . Defender of the faith and of the church of England, and also of Ireland, in earth Supreme Head;" a title retained in the first nineteen acts of the reign. On April 2, 1554, the title was changed by an omission of the last clause.

[3] Renard's MSS. iii. fol. 49.
[4] By Julius III., who at the same time sent from Brussels a secret agent, Commendone, through whom Mary communicated to the pope and Pole her desire to reunite her kingdom to the Roman See.   Pallavicino, ii. 397; Quirini's *Collection of Pole's Letters*, vol. iv. p. 111.

soon journeyed as far as Flanders in order the more promptly
to act as the queen's adviser.   In spite of opposition to the
Spanish alliance, which manifested itself in no uncertain terms
at the council [1] board, the queen and the emperor hastened

marriage treaty executed in January, 1554;
it on, and early in January, 1554, the marriage articles that
Charles had proposed in December ripened into a marriage
treaty,[2] which, after the insertion of all possible safeguards
against foreign influence, was finally approved.   Against such

national opposition to the marriage;
a marriage the nation had been resolved from the outset.   The
dread of such an event had given strength to Northumberland's
conspiracy, and in Mary's first parliament the commons, as an

the commons petitioned against it;
assertion of their growing importance, presented a petition to
the queen in which, after suggesting the dangers that would
result from a union with a foreign prince, they earnestly advised her to marry one of her own subjects.[3]   The queen's passionate reply,[4] in keeping with her Tudor blood, so alarmed
the protestant party, who clearly foresaw that a Spanish alliance would not only overthrow their plan of religious reform,
but also expose them to active persecution, that they broke into

the revolt under Wyatt;
open revolt under the lead of Wyatt the moment that the
completion of the marriage treaty was publicly announced.
The outbreak, although premature, assumed such a dangerous
form that the queen was for a time in great peril, and only her
own queenly courage at the critical moment [5] saved her crown

the queen's triumph;
and her life.   But her triumph was complete.   By the 7th of
February the insurrection had failed, and the prisons were
crowded with the fugitive insurgents, who, together with the
surviving leaders of Northumberland's conspiracy, now waited

Lady Jane Grey, Wyatt, and others sent to the block, and Elizabeth to the Tower;
the queen's vengeance, which was sharp and summary.   Lady
Jane Grey, her husband, father, and uncle, were sent to
the block.   Wyatt and his chief adherents soon followed;
while Elizabeth, whose complicity was suspected and who was
sent to the Tower,[6] was saved only by the interposition of the
lords,[7] who demanded that the slaughter should cease.   For

---

[1] Noailles, vol. i. p. 214.

[2] Marriage treaty between Mary and Philip. *Fœdera*, vol. xi.

[3] Burnet, vol. i. p. 479.

[4] Renard's account of Mary's speech has been translated by Froude, vol. v. p. 297.

[5] As to Mary's speech at the Guild-hall, February 1, see Noailles, vol. iii.

pp. 52, 66; Foxe, vol. iii. p. 25; Holinshed, 1096.

[6] As to her arrest, see MS. Mary, Domestic, vol. iii., State Paper Office; Renard to Charles V., February 17, Rolls House MSS.

[7] Renard to Charles V., March 22, Rolls House MSS.

the moment the protestant party, whose leaders fled over sea, protestant party crushed;
was crushed, and Mary was left free to throw off the mask of
moderation, and to enter upon the reactionary policy upon Mary inaugurates a policy of reaction;
which she had resolved from the beginning.   Faithful to her
promise made at the Guildhall in the midst of the rising, that
she would not marry without the consent of parliament, the
houses were called together on the 2d of April, when the marriage articles, as proposed by the emperor and as modified by
the queen's advisers, were submitted for approval.   The gross
means of persuasion [1] which were employed having secured to
a certain extent a compliant house of commons, the marriage a marriage bill passed by parliament;
bill was passed as soon as the parliamentary forms could be
complied with.[2]   Then followed an act made necessary by the
fact that Mary was the first queen regnant who had ever made
good her title to the crown of England.[3]   Some of the protestant preachers had claimed that the rule of a woman was not
only prohibited by the word of God, but that the laws of the
land, made alone for kings, failed to recognize the prerogatives
of queens.   To remove all constitutional difficulties upon that also an act to legalize Mary's position as the first queen regnant;
score, an act [4] was passed providing that "the royal power and
dignities vested in a queen the same as in a king," and that
all statutes applied equally to the sovereign whether male or
female.   After the failure to secure the passage of four bills
presented by the chancellor to regulate the succession, to restore the Six Articles, to reënact the statute *De hæretico comburendo*, and to restore the jurisdiction of the bishops,[5] parliament was dissolved on the 5th of May, and before the end of Philip and Mary married in July, 1554.
July the fateful union between Philip and Mary was celebrated
at Winchester.

3. Philip, while sacrificing himself to a political marriage, The reconciliation with Rome — Philip and Pole:
was no more intent upon restoring England to the Roman
communion than upon binding the realm to his own house as
an effective ally upon whom he could rely for aid in his struggles with France.   Statesman as he was, he clearly foresaw
that the first enterprise could not be attempted with any hope
of success unless he could win from the pope such concessions

[1] Burnet, vol. i. pp. 479, 491.

[2] The marriage bill passed by the 12th of April. 1 Mary, c. ii.

[3] As to Matilda's attempt to secure that position, see vol. i. p. 275.

[4] 1 Mary, sess. 3, c. 1.

[5] The last two bills passed the commons, but were lost in the upper house.

as would assure the holders of the vast estates which had been
torn from the church during the two preceding reigns that, in
the event of a restoration of the papal power, they would not
be disturbed in their possessions. With the view of assuring
the nation upon that vital point, Pole, in his first legatine commission, was authorized to "treat, compound, and dispense"
with the holders of church property as to the rents and profits
which they had received.[1] But as that concession was deemed
inadequate, the pope was assured that however offensive it
might be to his dignity to make a bargain, and to set aside the
canons of the church which positively forbade the alienation
of ecclesiastical possessions, it was absolutely impossible to win
English submission unless he was willing to extend the dispens-

ing power to real as well as personal property. Accordingly,
in a second brief,[2] dated June 28, 1554, the legate was authorized "to give, aliene, and transfer"[3] to their possessors all
real and personal property which had been taken from the
church since the schism. Having thus prepared the legate
to contract in behalf of the pope, it next became necessary for
Philip, who certainly exercised a powerful political influence
from the time of his arrival, to prepare a parliament to con-

tract in behalf of the English nation. There was certainly
interference with the elections to the lower house of the parliament which met on the 12th of November, by means of
circulars accompanying the writs, in which the crown, after
declaring that no "alteration was intended of any man's possessions," directed the sheriffs, mayors, and others to admonish
the voters to choose from among themselves "such as, being
eligible by order of the laws, were of a wise, grave, and catholic sort, such as indeed meant the true honor of God and the

prosperity of the commonwealth."[4] Such were the precautions taken to assure the acquiescence of parliament in the
reëstablishment of the papal supremacy which had now been
abolished for thirty years, a period during which it is said that
forty thousand families had profited from the church's possessions. But the assurance that no restitution would be de-

---

[1] The first paper, dated March 8,
1554, and printed in Burnet's *Collectanea*, is explained in the text, vol. ii. p.
780.

[2] Printed in Burnet's *Collectanea*.

[3] This clause was devised by Gardiner in order to satisfy present possessors. Pallavicino, vol. ii. p. 411.

[4] The royal circular is printed in
Burnet's *Collectanea*.

manded, coupled with the other expedients, proved completely effective. The attainder of Pole having been reversed without difficulty, the legate, after his long exile, entered London by the river on November 24, prepared to coöperate with the assembly of estates in the august ceremony which was to attend the absolution and reconciliation of England with the See of Rome. On the 29th both houses resolved with scarcely a dissenting voice [1] to reacknowledge the supremacy, and they joined in a formal petition [2] to Philip and Mary, praying that they would intercede with the legate for a national absolution, which he duly pronounced the next day. [3] Passing then from form to substance, the new concordat thus entered into between the pope and the nation was carefully embodied in an act which passed the commons on the 4th of January, 1555, entitled " An Act repealing all Articles and Provisions made against the See Apostolick of Rome *since the twentieth year* [4] *of King Henry the Eight*, and for the establishment of all spiritual and ecclesiastical possessions and hereditaments conveyed to the laity." [5] This act, which took the form of a petition to the crown, specially designated the acts made in parliament since the 20th of Henry VIII. in derogation of the papal supremacy, which were to be repealed, as follows: "The act against obtaining dispensations from Rome for pluralities and non-residence (21 Hen. VIII. c. 13); the act that no person shall be cited out of the diocese where he or she dwelleth (23 Hen. VIII. c. 9); the act against appeals to the See of Rome (24 Hen. VIII. c. 12); the act against the payment of annates and firstfruits to the See of Rome (23 Hen. VIII. c. 20 [6]); the act for the submission of the clergy (25 Hen. VIII. c. 19); the act for the election and consecration of bishops (25 Hen. VIII. c. 20); the act against exactions from the See of Rome (25 Hen. VIII. c. 21); the act of the Royal Supremacy (26 Hen. VIII. c. 1); the act for the consecration of suffragan

Marginal notes:
Pole's attainder reversed;

parliament acknowledges the supremacy and receives absolution;

contents of the act embodying the new concordat;

list of the Reformation statutes repealed;

---

[1] As to the two dissenting votes in the commons, see Strype, vol. iii. p. 204; *Ep. Poli.* v. App. 314.

[2] See Foxe, *Acts and Mon.*, vol. vi. p. 571.

[3] Ibid., vol. vi. p. 572, as to the form of absolution used.

[4] "In the second stage the line of retrogression was drawn at 'the twentieth year of King Henry the Eight [April 22, 1528–April 21, 1529], which was the year before the Royal Supremacy had been reasserted and that of the pope abrogated." — Blount, *Reform. of the Church of Eng.*, vol. ii. p. 204.

[5] 1 & 2 Phil. & Mar. c. 8.

[6] Although the act was repealed, the annates were not restored.

bishops (26 Hen. VIII. c. 14); the act for the reform of the canon law (27 Hen. VIII. c. 15); the act against the authority of the pope (28 Hen. VIII. c. 10); the act for the release of those who had obtained dispensations from Rome (28 Hen. VIII. c. 16); the act authorizing the king to appoint bishops by letters patent (31 Hen. VIII. c. 9); the act of pre-contracts and degrees of consanguinity (33 Hen. VIII. c. 38); the act for the king's style (35 Hen. VIII. c. 3); the act permitting the marriage of doctors of the civil law (37 Hen. VIII. c. 17)."

all that remained of Henry's ecclesiastical legislation thus swept away; By the legislation of Mary's first parliament catholic ortho-doxy had been restored; by the sweeping repeal just described all that remained of Henry's ecclesiastical legislation was swept away. Parliament, having thus faithfully performed

precautions taken to secure the holders of church property against the claims of the clergy; its part of the compact, was careful to see that the consid-eration promised to the holders of church property was fully secured. By virtue of the dispensation, which was recited in the statute, the pope had promised that the holders of either church lands or goods should never be molested by any papal decree whatever. But prudence required that the clergy themselves, who had perhaps a better title than the pope, should be made parties to the agreement. To accom-plish that end the clergy were required to state their claims in a petition,[1] and then to relinquish them. In consideration

authority of church courts restored with a proviso which in-volved a relinquish-ment; of that concession, which was fully recited in the act, the legislative powers of the clergy were reëstablished, and the authority of the church courts was restored, subject, how-ever, to the express declaration that "the title of all lands, possessions, and hereditaments in their majesties' realms" was subject to the jurisdiction of "their courts only," and that any

mortmain act sus-pended for twenty years; person who obtained any process from any ecclesiastical court in order to "molest any person or persons, or body politic, for any of the said lands or things above specified, should incur the danger of a præmunire."[2] Although the mortmain act was suspended for twenty years for the benefit of the clergy, the

parliament defends the rights of Elizabeth; terrors of the præmunire were not withdrawn. With the com-pletion of the ecclesiastical legislation the temper of the compli-ant parliament hardened into something like a spirit of resistance.

[1] Burnet, *Hist. Reform.*, vol. i. p. 503. The petition itself is printed in the *Collectanea.*   [2] 1 & 2 Phil. & Mar. c. 8, § 31.

When Mary attempted to remodel the succession so as to destroy the rights of Elizabeth, the houses refused to repeal the two acts[1] upon which her status depended only so far as they affected the papal prerogative, and the only concession that could be won in favor of Philip was a regency bill,[2] which vested in him the guardianship during their minority of any children that the queen might bear him. No such spirit, however, opposed the attempt now successfully made, after two failures in preceding parliaments, to revive the heresy statutes of the years 1381, 1400, and 1414.[3] On the 16th of January, 1555, parliament was dissolved, and during the next month, under the authority of the revived statutes, the fires of Smithfield were lighted, and the bloody drama began.

the regency bill;

revival of the heresy statutes.

4. Out of the condition of things brought about by William's famous ordinance severing the spiritual from the temporal tribunals grew, first, the claim of the clergy to exemption from all temporal jurisdiction, with the right of appeal to Rome; second, the claim upon the part of the new ecclesiastical courts themselves to a jurisdiction that grew and widened with the growth of the canon law,[4] which only in a certain modified form was ever recognized in England.[5] And yet in spite of the resistance offered by the common lawyers to its introduction, the canonical code gained sufficient hold to mould during many centuries the proceedings of the church courts which have left so deep an impress upon English history. So far as the criminal jurisdiction of these courts is concerned, it rested upon the lofty notion that they possessed the inherent

The persecution and its consequences:

clerical exemptions; origin of the church courts and the growth of the canon law;

criminal jurisdiction of the church courts;

---

[1] 28 Hen. VIII. c. 7; 35 Hen. VIII. c. 1.

[2] 1 & 2 Phil. & Mar. c. 10.

[3] 5 Rich. II. 5; 2 Hen. IV. 15; and 2 Hen. V. 7, were revived by 1 & 2 Phil. & Mar. c. 6. The practical effect of the revival of these acts was to do away with the necessity for a writ *De hæretico comburendo* signed by the queen.

[4] Vol. i. pp. 338–342.

[5] "The *Corpus Juris Canonici* includes Gratian, 1151; Gregory IX.'s decretals, 1230; Sixtus decretalium, 1298; the Clementine Constitutions, and Extravagantes Joannis, 1317. The English canon law consisted partly of the ordinary canon law, so far as it was received here, and partly of constitu-

tions enacted at national synods by Cardinals Otho and Othobon, about the years 1220 and 1268, and partly of provincial constitutions, or decrees of convocation, made at different times, from Stephen Langton's days down to the days of Archbishop Chichele, in the reign of Henry V. These, however, had no force except as far as they were recognized and adopted by the king and parliament. Thus limited, they were so vague that it is almost hopeless to say how far the canon law upon any given point was and is in force or not. Blackstone, vol. i. pp. 82, 83." — Sir J. F. Stephen's *Hist. of the Crim. Law of Eng.*, vol. ii. p. 440, note 4.

right to
punish sin
as such
usually
limited in
practice to
heresy,
blasphemy,
and certain
other
offences;
power to punish, without reference to precise rules or definitions, all notorious offences against religion and morals by
virtue of the church's right to punish sin as such.   From the
actual history of their procedure it appears that this broad
power was usually limited (1) to offences directly connected
with religion, such as heresy and blasphemy, neglect of church
services and ceremonies, contempt of the clergy, and neglect
by the clergy of their clerical duties; (2) to all offences against
the marriage relation, of which the church was the special
guardian, such as bigamy, incest, incontinence, abortion, and
the like; and (3) to such offences as perjury, defamation,
witchcraft, breach of faith, and drunkenness, which were pun-

inquisito-
rial pro-
cedure,
ished simply because they were sins.[1]   According to the course
of the canon law, when an accused person was summoned before an ecclesiastical court of his diocese, he was called upon
to answer either an "inquisition," an "accusation," or a "denunciation,"[2] containing the charge against him as presented
by the judge or some third person; and he was then liable to

the *ex officio*
oath;
be subjected to the inquisitorial *ex officio*[3] oath, by which he
could be forced to reveal the inmost secrets of his domestic

enforce-
ment of
clerical
decrees;
life.   In the event of conviction, the court could enforce its
decrees by excommunications of greater or less degree, each
carrying with it civil incapacities; it could also impose pen-
ances, such as carrying a fagot, or some other public humiliation, which, in the event the condemned refused to perform,

imprison-
ment under
the writ
*De excom-
municato
capiendo.*
could be forced upon him by imprisonment under the writ
De excommunicato capiendo issued by the king in chancery.
Such, in general terms, was the broad jurisdiction with which
the church courts were endowed, and such the comparatively

Since the
conversion
English law
has rested
upon the
tacit as-
sumption
of the
truths of
Christian-
ity;
limited assistance rendered them by the state in the enforcement of their decrees, when the crime of heresy became of
sufficient importance to suggest the necessity for more radical
measures for its extirpation.

From the time of the conversion from Woden to Christ of
the Teutonic tribes who settled in Britain, and the quick union
that followed between church and state, all legislation and

---

[1] For the best statement of the whole subject, see Stephen's *Hist. of the Crim. Law of Eng.*, vol. ii. ch. xxv.

[2] See Archdeacon Hale's *Ecclesiastical Precedents*, Preface, lvii–lxi.

[3] When the ecclesiastical courts were revived in 1661, this hated feature of their procedure was omitted.

government has proceeded upon the unexpressed assumption of the truths of Christianity.[1]   In the early days, in the absence of serious speculative controversy, it was only necessary to define heresy in a general way by prohibiting by law any relapse into the old heathenism from which the new nation had emerged.   Such was the character of the heresy laws enacted by the early English kings.[2]   During the three centuries which follow the Conquest a single passage from Bracton,[3] of doubtful import, alone throws light upon the subject, and in the absence of contrary evidence it seems to be safe to conclude that down to the Lollard revolt at the end of the fourteenth century no new means had been provided for the punishment of heresy, apart from the ordinary process of the church courts as already described, for the simple reason that there were too few heretics to justify any unusual precautions.   But by the advent of Lollardry the clergy were thoroughly alarmed into the belief that the time had come for them to ask at the hands of the state additional powers for its suppression.   By that time, what was known on the continent as the canon law had taken on a definite form, and to a certain extent it had been introduced into England ; and the English canonists, who drew their ideas from abroad, began to claim, against the protest of the common lawyers, that after the church courts had pronounced a conviction for heresy the civil power should become their executioner, and inflict death by fire, the penalty imposed by the continental canon law in such cases.[4]   The first effort in that direction was the statute of 5 Rich. II. c. 5, which the clergy obtained in 1381, without the sanction of the commons, and which, after reciting that the preachers of heresy refused to obey the summons of the ordinaries, and despised the censures of the church, provided that

[marginal notes: first heresy statutes aimed against the old heathenism; down to the Lollard revolt ordinary process of the church courts sufficed for the punishment of heresy; continental canon law in cases of heresy imposed death by burning; statute of 5 Rich. II. c. 5;]

[1] " What specifically Christianity is ? and by whom and how questions relating to it are to be determined ? has been the subject of passionate controversy." — Stephen's *Hist. of the Crim. Law of Eng.*, vol. ii. p. 437.

[2] Edward and Guthrum, Thorpe, vol. ii. p. 72 ; Cnut, p. 5 ; Thorpe, vol. i. p. 379.

[3] *De Corona*, vol. ii. p. 300.

[4] The continental canonists drew the idea that heresy should be punished by death from the Theodosian Code, which imposed that penalty upon heretics under certain circumstances.   Bk. xvi. tit. v.   By the third of the Constitutions of Innocent III., generally known as the Canons of the fourth Council of Lateran (1216), it was decreed that convicted heretics should be delivered for punishment to the secular power.   About that time it was that burning was first applied as the proper punishment in Spain.

such persons, on the order of the bishops, should be arrested
and imprisoned by the sheriffs "till they will justify, according
to the law and reason of holy church." Not until 1400 did
the clergy obtain, under circumstances heretofore described,

2 Hen. IV.
c. 15 (*De
hæretico
combu-
rendo*);
the famous statute of 2 Hen. IV. c. 15 (*De hæretico com
burendo*), in which it was provided that the convicted heretic
who refused to abjure, or who after abjuration should relapse,
should be taken by the sheriff or other civil authority and
burned in a public place as an example and terror to others.
Although this first burning statute was not passed until March

Sawtre
burned a
week before
its passage
under the
writ *De
hæretico
combu-
rendo;*
10, the fact remains that a week before one William Sawtre
was burned under a writ *De hæretico comburendo* entered upon
the Parliament Roll, and dated March 2. The writ recites
the fact that Sawtre had been convicted by the archbishop
and bishops in a provincial council, and commands the mayor
and the sheriffs to burn him in a public place. While the
older lawyers upon inadequate authority promulgated the idea,
for a long time accepted, that this writ was as old as the common law itself, a reëxamination of the whole subject has re-

no such
writ ever
issued
before that
time;
sulted in the conclusion that there is no evidence that such a
writ was ever issued prior to Sawtre's case.[1] In 1414 followed
the supplementary statute of 2 Hen. V. c. 7, which relates
mainly to the question of procedure. These three acts of

acts of
1381, 1400,
and 1414,
unaltered
until 1553;
1381, 1400, and 1414 — which first gave to the ecclesiastical
courts the power to arrest and imprison by their own authority, and, in the absence of definitions, made any judgment the
ordinary might render as to what constituted heresy conclusive upon the civil power, and which gave to the ordinary the
power to command the sheriff to burn the condemned without
a writ *De hæretico comburendo* — remained unaltered down to

statute of
25 Hen.
VIII. c. 14;
1533. Then it was that by the statute of 25 Hen. VIII. c. 14,
the statutes of 5 Rich. II. c. 5 and 2 Hen. V. c. 7 were confirmed, while that of 2 Hen. IV. c. 15 was repealed, because it
gave power to the ordinaries to put men on trial for heresy

first posi-
tive stat-
utory de-
finition
of heresy
contained
in the Act
of the Six
Articles;
upon bare suspicion, and because it failed to "decline any certain cases of heresy." The first positive statutory definition
of the crime of heresy came in the following Act of the Six
Articles (31 Hen. VIII. c. 14), which, by reason of the new
machinery it provided for its punishment, made it "in great

[1] Vol. i. pp. 537–540.

measure a secular offence." [1]   Some slight mitigations of the Act of the Six Articles were made by 34 & 35 Hen. VIII. c. 1 ; and so the law stood at the time of his death.   Upon the accession of Edward VI. the whole statutory system for the punishment of heresy was swept away by 1 Edw. VI. c. 12, and what was then understood to be the common law was reinstated, that is to say the right of the ecclesiastical court, after conviction, to ask for the writ *De hæretico comburendo* as granted in Sawtre's case. [2]   In that condition, in which the crown and the bishops had to concur before a burning could take place, the law remained until the old statutes of Richard II., Henry IV., and Henry V. were reënacted by 1 & 2 Phil. & Mar. c. 6, as heretofore explained.

whole statutory system for the punishment of heresy swept away by 1 Edw. VI. c. 12;

revived by 1 & 2 Phil. & Mar. c. 6.

It is now generally admitted on every hand that religious persecution was the natural outcome of the mediæval spirit of intolerance, the common heritage of all religious sects and factions which date from that period.   The idea had its root in the belief that whoever possessed the infallible power to teach should likewise possess the correlative right to extirpate error by physical means.   Down to the Reformation, infallibility was claimed as the exclusive heritage of the Church of Rome.   After that event, under the opposing theory of private judgment, "the papal infallibility was sometimes transferred to the leader of a petty sect ; at other times a dreaming enthusiast would become his own pope, and would consult nothing but the oracle within his own breast." [3]   The theory of the right thus underwent no change ; a new question simply arose as to the functionary or tribunal by whom it could be legitimately exercised.   When Calvin burned Servetus, [4] he simply put into force the new theory of personal as opposed to the older theory of corporate infallibility.   The persecution that took place during Mary's reign constitutes a long and livid chapter

Religious persecution the outcome of mediæval intolerance;

the infallible power to teach supposed to carry with it the right to extirpate error by physical means ;

the right claimed by all sects;

personal as opposed to corporate infallibility;

---

[1] Hale, P. C., p. 403 ; Stephen's *Hist. of the Crim. Law*, vol. ii. p. 438.

[2] See above, p. 146.   Under that condition of things Joan Bocher suffered in May, 1550, and George Van Paar in the next year.   Stephen considers that the executions in both cases were illegal, for the reason that it was a mistake to suppose that the issuance of the writ was justified by Sawtre's case.   *Hist. Crim. Law*, vol. ii. p. 459.

[3] Le Bas.   See Cranmer's *Works*, vol. ii. p. 88.

[4] For the sympathetic views of Bullinger, see his letter of approval written to Calvin, October 15, 1553, *Orig. Lett.*, p. 742.   Cartwright, the great English Calvinist, wrote : "I deny that upon repentance there ought to follow the pardon of death. ... Heretics ought to be put to death now."

in the sad story of catholic and protestant intolerance, which extends from the Lollard revolt down to the reign of James I., when executions for heresy came to an end.[1] The Marian persecution was carried on under old statutes and in the old form, with an additional stimulus in the shape of commissions, by virtue of which certain high public officials were associated with the bishops as "co-assessors,"[2] in order to insure their zeal in the sickening work which was executed with a fanatical ruthlessness never before known.

the Marian persecution carried on under old statutes and in the old form.

The statistics of the persecution, drawn in the main from the narrative of Foxe, reveal the fact that from the execution of John Rogers, who was to "break the ice," on the 4th of February, 1555, down to the end of Mary's reign, about two hundred and seventy-seven persons, men and women, suffered by fire, of whom about two hundred and forty belonged to the laboring classes, while the remainder consisted of seven tradesmen, nine of the village gentry, sixteen priests, and five bishops, — Hooper, Ferrar, Ridley, Latimer, and Cranmer. It further appears that nearly all the victims were taken from the southeast of England, from a district having as its principal centres London and Canterbury, and in which it is reasonable to suppose protestantism was more general than elsewhere.[3] And yet, despite the persecuting zeal which has wreathed Mary's name with a terrible epithet that will live forever, she utterly failed either to satisfy the papacy, or to drive the nation back into the fold of the older faith. In the desperate effort made to attain these ends the queen was ably supported, first by Gardiner, and then by Pole. Although the prior training of the former made him hesitate at first as to the restoration of the papal supremacy,[4] he yielded to pressure as the reign advanced, while from the outset he committed himself by his conduct in parliament to the policy of active persecution.

Statistics of the persecution;

nearly all the victims taken from the southeast of England;

its failure to accomplish the desired end;

Gardiner as a persecutor;

---

[1] The last person burned for heresy in England was Edward Wightman, who suffered at Lichfield, in April, 1612. Fuller's *Ch. Hist.*, vol. iii. pp. 252–255, ed. 1837. The infliction of such punishment was, however, legally possible down to the year 1677, when the writ of *De hæretico comburendo* was taken away by 29 Chas. II. c. 9, which also abolished "all punishment of death in pursuance of any ecclesiastical censures."

[2] See Strype's *Mem. Eccl.*, vol. iii. pt. i. pp. 286–296; Foxe's *Acts and Mon.*, vol. vi. pp. 587, 598, 649; Ibid., vol. vii. pp. 293, 296.

[3] The whole matter is well summed up by Blount, *Reform. of the Church of Eng.*, vol. ii. pp. 220–226.

[4] See above, p. 135.

Not until after Mary's third parliament had passed the great act of reconciliation that swept away the whole legislative fabric which Henry VIII. had built up, and not until after the heresy statutes, at the same time reënacted, had been put into vigorous operation under Gardiner's personal supervision,[1] did his death in November, 1555, leave Pole, after the manner of Wolsey, the supreme counsellor in all matters both of church and state.   The only particular in which Pole fell short of complete success in his effort to reëstablish the condition of things that had existed before the schism began was his failure to restore to the monastic communities the abbey lands which had been so widely distributed, and to the See of Rome the annates[2] and firstfruits which had been annexed to the crown since the 20th of Henry VIII.   As a partial compensation, Mary had of her own motion, and in the face of pressing obligations, given back to the church in March, 1555, all the abbey lands that remained to the crown,[3] while in the parliament which met in the following October an act was passed, not restoring the annates and firstfruits to the pope directly, but providing that they should be devoted under the direction of the legate to church purposes.[4]   Such concessions, which might have satisfied another pontiff, fell far short, however, of the absolute demands soon to be put forth upon the part of the papacy by Caraffa, who, as the uncompromising leader of the church party organized to meet the Reformation with the Inquisition, was elected to the papal throne in May, 1555, as Paul IV.   On the day of the new pope's election arrived in Rome the English ambassadors,[5] who were sent to make formal announcement of the act restoring the papal supremacy ; and on the 12th of July Paul, among his first acts, put forth a sweeping bull reasserting the decision of the canons as to the sacred and inalienable character of church estates, and threatening all who should dare to withhold them with spiritual penalties.[6]   In order to save Pole's work from destruction by

after his death in November, 1555, Pole became supreme in church and state;

failure to restore the abbey lands and first-fruits;

partial restitution made by crown and parliament;

edict of Paul IV. as to the inalienable character of church estates;

---

[1] The heresy statutes were passed in December, 1554, and in the following January Gardiner presided at the trial of Hooper, Rogers, and others. Foxe's *Acts and Mon.*, vol. vi. pp. 587, 598, 649.

[2] As heretofore pointed out, although 23 Hen. VIII. c. 20 was re-

pealed, the annates were not restored. See above, p. 141, note 6.

[3] Burnet, vol. i. p. 514.

[4] 2 & 3 Phil. & Mar. c. iv.   See *Poli. Ep.*, vol. v. pp. 51, 53, 56.

[5] Burnet, vol. i. p. 515.

[6] Ibid., vol. ii. p. 791.   At the time of the schism Henry VIII. had as-

an exception made of England in order to save Pole's work;

excepting England from the general edict, the ambassadors finally succeeded in obtaining from Paul a confirmation of the dispensation of Julius III., the basis of the reconciliation, which was read in the commons on the 23d of the following October.[1] But behind the reluctance with which Paul made this exception in order to uphold a bargain that embodied for

Paul's animosity to Pole;

him less of triumph than humiliation stood an old animosity against the legate, which had grown out of personal rivalries and widely divergent views as to the methods by which Lutheranism should be confronted. As viewed by the violent orthodoxy of Paul, the more liberal theologians, led at that time by Contarini and Pole, were but little better than heretics. This prejudice against Pole and his work, which Paul was induced to stifle for a moment, manifested itself in no uncertain

revoked his legatine commission in the summer of 1557;

terms in the summer of 1557, when he revoked his legatine commission,[2] against the protest of both queen and council, the moment that Philip succeeded in dragging England into war with the pope's ally of France. Mary, with something of the Tudor spirit, resisted the attempt to force a new lega-

Pole accused at Rome of heresy;

tine upon her, while Paul went so far as to subject Pole to a formal accusation at Rome for heresy.[3] To the sorrow thus brought upon the queen by the hostility of the one power for which she had sacrificed everything was added the growing consciousness that the very means that she had so zealously employed to drive the nation back to its spiritual allegiance had not only failed of their purpose, but had converted the broad popularity with which she had ascended the throne into a detestation at once deep and universal. At enmity with the pope, forsaken by Philip, and hated by the nation, the childless queen, who had struggled in vain to make her husband

loyalty of the nation to Elizabeth;

her successor, was doomed to see, as she sank to the grave, the tide of popular enthusiasm rising around Elizabeth, whose right to the throne every parliament had protected against her

sumed the title of King of Ireland, and in that way Mary took the title of Queen of Ireland, and so styled herself in the credentials of her ambassadors. As the pope held that he alone could constitute kingdoms, he felt called upon to remove the difficulty by creating Ireland into a kingdom on the 7th of June. The ambassadors were then received on the 23d.

[1] *Commons Journal*, 2 & 3 Phil. & Mar. See Froude, vol. v. p. 566.

[2] Burnet, vol. i. p. 546, and *Collectanea;* Strype, *Mem. of the Reformation*, vol. vi. p. 476.

[3] *Poli. Ep.*, vol. v. pp. 31–36; Lingard, vol. v. pp. 515–518.

designs, and whom the nation itself had guarded in the midst of every peril as its deliverer. Thus overwhelmed by failure and disappointment, Mary, in the midst of the depression that followed the loss of Calais, died in the morning of the 17th of November, 1558, and a few hours later Cardinal Pole, the zealous counsellor who had toiled in vain by her side, was no more.

both Mary and Pole died on the 17th of November, 1558.

CHAPTER V.

ELIZABETH AND THE FINAL SETTLEMENT.

The last two stages of the English Reformation: the third stage, co-extensive with the reactionary reign of Mary,

I. WITH the death of Mary ended the third stage of the English Reformation, the period of reaction during which the nation — wearied and disheartened by the political and religious chaos, the social and financial distress endured under Edward's selfish and despotic councillors, and alarmed at the prospect of a fresh dynastic struggle — sought peace and order at the feet of the legitimate sovereign even upon terms that involved the surrender of the entire fruit of the religious revolution which Henry had inaugurated, excepting only the ecclesiastical property, whose wide distribution had made it almost a national endowment. The hope of a reconciliation upon such a basis, faint enough at best in view of the general aversion to the papal overlordship and to clerical domination

culminated in her famous persecution;

through the ecclesiastical courts, utterly vanished in the presence of the Marian persecution, which so deepened and intensified the religious strife as to leave the nation more hopelessly divided than ever before into two irreconcilable and warring

the fourth and last stage began with the accession of Elizabeth, who compelled all parties to acquiesce in a state system of religious uniformity;

factions. The fourth and last stage began with the accession of Elizabeth, upon whom devolved the difficult task of formulating and enforcing a political programme through which the nation was finally emancipated from papal and Spanish domination, and all parties and sects compelled to accept or acquiesce in a system of religious uniformity which rested upon parliamentary enactments, and which was enforced with all the despotic authority of the conciliar system. Utterly devoid of the reli-

Elizabeth's political temper;

gious enthusiasm that had in turn driven Edward and Mary in opposite directions, and viewing all theological differences in a purely political light, the new queen came to her task with a mental equipment which harmonized completely with that of the wise and wary counsellor who for forty years stood by her side. Foremost among that class of English statesmen known as "politicals," who accepted the new doctrine that every people possessed not only the right to determine for itself the form of the national belief, but also the right to enforce such belief as a matter of state policy,[1] stood William Cecil, afterwards Lord Burghley, whose one aim was to restore order and unity, and to build up the national power and influence at the sacrifice of every other consideration. It may be true "that the wisdom of Elizabeth was the wisdom of her ministers, and that her chief merit, which circumstances must divide with herself, lay in allowing her policy to be guided by Lord Burghley."[2] Whatever its source, the fact remains that the wisdom that shaped the masterful policy of the crown during Elizabeth's reign was a tentative, political, and yet withal a patriotic wisdom, which, holding the best interests of England steadily in view, chose in the effort to reëstablish the religious unity of the nation that judicious middle course so imperiously dictated by the pressure of circumstances. From the outset every line of action which opened before the queen, who was forced to move on, was beset with serious difficulties. At war with both France and Scotland, England's only ally was Philip, behind whom stood the pope, and more important still the English catholics, who "were in the majority in every county in England, except Middlesex and Kent."[3] To ward off probable dangers which might have resulted from a sudden breach with Spain and the papacy, the celebration of the mass was permitted to go on,[4] a proclamation was issued[5] forbidding any change or innovation until consultation could be had in parliament, while the queen, whose title to the throne grew out of a marriage made in defiance of papal authority, took care to formally notify Paul IV. of her accession. The haughty response of the pontiff,[6] reproaching Elizabeth with her pre-

Cecil's masterful policy;

the judicious middle course;

difficulties confronting Elizabeth and Cecil;

all changes forbidden until the meeting of parliament;

Paul IV. and Elizabeth's title to the throne;

---

[1] See above, p. 58.

[2] Froude, Preface to *Hist. of England.*

[3] "Distresses of the Commonwealth," Domestic MS., Elizabeth, vol. i. "The Protestants were confined chiefly to the great towns and seaports; and those who deprecated doctrinal alteration, either from habit, prudence, or mere instinct of conservatism, still constituted two thirds, perhaps three fourths, of the entire population." — Froude, vol. vi. p. 114, citing "Note on the State of the Realm, in the hand of Sir William Cecil, *Cotton. MSS.*, Calig. B. 10."

[4] The queen was crowned with mass on January 20, 1559, and on the 25th parliament was opened with the old form, except that the communion was administered in both kinds. The queen was to commune as she pleased. Strype's *Annals*, vol. ii. p. 397; Burnet, *Hist. Reform.*, vol. i. p. 565.

[5] On the day of her accession, commanding her subjects "not to attempt, upon any pretence, the breach, alteration, or change of any order or usage presently established within our realm."

[6] Burnet, vol. i. pp. 560, 561. This fact, generally stated in all histories, has been denied by Mr. Tierney, the editor

sumption, reminding her of her illegitimacy, and demanding that her claims to the succession should be submitted to his tribunal, quickly assured her, however, of the fact, already realized, that her very title to the throne was irrevocably bound up with the cause of the Reformation.   Under the force of that conviction her first move had been to so reorganize her

council so reorganized as to put the protestants in the ascendant;

council [1] as to place protestants in the ascendant, in order to secure to herself the support of that able and aggressive minority in the contest which a fresh break with Rome would make inevitable.   The only conclusive response that could be made to the pope's pretensions was the reassertion of the Lutheran doctrine, which Henry had originally put forward, of the exclusive right of the nation not only to decide upon the title to the crown, but also as to the form of religious belief

first parliament met in January, 1559.

which should prevail within its bounds.   For that purpose was called Elizabeth's first parliament, which met on the 25th [2] of January, 1559.

Terms of the final settlement:

2. Although it was not passed until near the end of the session, the first act to go upon the statute-book was that entitled "An act to restore to the crown the ancient jurisdiction over the estate, ecclesiastical and spiritual, and abolishing all foreign powers repugnant to the same." [3]   The contents of that

summary of the act restoring the royal supremacy;

act, wiping out the papal and reëstablishing the royal supremacy, may be summarized as follows : (1) the act of 1 & 2 Phil. & Mar. c. 8, whereby Henry VIII.'s ecclesiastical legislation was swept away, was repealed, and ten of his acts were revived ; [4]

persecuting statutes repealed;

(2) the persecuting statutes of 1381, 1400, and 1414, which Mary had revived, were also repealed ; (3) the ground being thus cleared, the papal supremacy was expressly abolished in

penalties for recognizing the papal supremacy;

sweeping terms, which made its exercise as illegal as it had been under Henry VIII. ; and penalties, in three grades, were imposed upon all who should "by writing, printing, teaching, preaching . . . maintain or defend the authority" abolished by the act ; (4) the provisions then made for the reëstablish-

---

of Dodd's *Church Hist. of Eng.*, vol. iv. Preface, who bases his denial upon the letters in the State Paper Office of Carne, the ambassador at Rome, upon whose authority the transaction is supposed to rest.

[1] Ibid., vol. i. p. 561 ; and for more complete details, Froude, vol. vi. p. 122.

[2] It was summoned for the 23d, but was prorogued until the 25th.

[3] 1 Eliz. c. 1.

[4] 23 Hen. VIII. c. 9 ; 24 Hen. VIII. 12 ; 25 Hen. VIII. cc. 1, 8, 19, 20 ; 26 Hen. VIII. c. 14 ; 28 Hen. VIII. c. 16 ; 32 Hen. VIII. c. 28 ; 37 Hen. VIII. c. 17.

ment of the royal supremacy were of an impersonal character, in order to escape the awkward dilemma which would have resulted from a simple revival of Henry's Act of Supremacy, and the consequent declaration of the queen as the " Supreme Head." [1]   Instead of again transferring the papal prerogatives to the sovereign personally, it was now declared that they should " by the authority of this present parliament be united and annexed to the imperial crown of this realm." [2]   (5) The vast powers thus vested in the crown the sovereign was authorized to exercise through commissioners,[3] who were finally organized into the Court of High Commission, which as a corporate body undertook to discharge the corrective jurisdiction of the crown over " the ecclesiastical state and persons," clerical and lay.   (6) In order to make the new supremacy effective, an oath of allegiance and supremacy was provided, whose refusal disqualified any one from accepting any office under the crown or any benefice in the church, while those who were already in possession of such offices or preferments were upon a refusal of the oath liable to be deprived of them.[4]   The logical sequence of the act reëstablishing the royal supremacy was a new Act of Uniformity, restoring the devotional system as established during the reign of Edward VI.   A tendency in that direction had been manifested from the outset by a proclamation issued in December, 1558, which, while it silenced the pulpits and forbade radical change until there could be consultation in parliament, partially restored the use of the vernacular in divine service ;[5] and by another issued in March, 1559, forbidding irreverent speaking of the sacrament of the altar, and enjoining the reception of the communion in both kinds.[6]   At the same time a royal commission [7] was appointed to secretly draft a new prayer-book for submis-

papal prerogatives now annexed to the crown and not to the sovereign personally ;

origin of the Court of High Commission ;

new oath of allegiance and supremacy ;

new Act of Uniformity ;

preliminary proclamations ;

secret commission to draft a new prayer-book ;

---

[1] As originally introduced in the commons, the bill restored to the queen that title.   See Strype's *Annals*, vol. i. pt. ii. p. 405.

[2] The act declared the sovereign " the only Supreme Governor of this realm, and of all other her Highness' dominions and countries, as well in all spiritual or ecclesiastical things or causes as temporal."

[3] 1 Eliz. c. 1, §§ 17, 18.

[4] 1 Eliz. c. 1, §§ 19–26.

[5] Strype's *Annals*, vol. ii. p. 389 ; Cardwell's *Docum. Ann.*, p. 176.

[6] Lansd. MS., p. 198 ; Blount, *Reform. of the Church of Eng.*, vol. ii. p. 338.

[7] See Burnet, vol. i. p. 562 ; Strype's *Annals*, vol. ii. pp. 392, 397.   In the preliminary consultations it was decided that the revisers should meet " at Sir Thomas Smyth's lodgings in Channon row."

sion to the approaching parliament.   The result was that the commission, after making only two material alterations, recommended the " low church " prayer-book of Edward VI. (1551), which, after submission to the council, was attached as a schedule to the Act of Uniformity passed near the end of the session, and entitled, " An Act for the Uniformity of Common Prayer in the Church, and Administration of the Sacraments." [1] After the enactment of laws declaring that firstfruits and tenths should again be vested in the crown,[2] that all religious houses refounded by Mary should be suppressed and their property given to the state ; [3] that the queen's title to the throne was as good as her father's or brother's had been, and as good as her sister's at any time since the passage of 35th Henry VIII.,[4] upon which Elizabeth's right really rested ; that any attack upon the queen's title by writing should be treason on a first conviction,[5] — parliament was dissolved on the 8th of May.

"low church" prayer-book of 1552 annexed as a schedule to the Act of Uniformity ; after enacting other important legislation;

parliament dissolved in May, 1559.

Defiant spirit of convocation under the presidency of Bonner;

In striking contrast with the compliant spirit of Elizabeth's first parliament, whose composition in the popular branch had no doubt been influenced by Cecil in the protestant interest,[6] stands that of the convocation which sat by its side under the presidency of Bonner,[7] and in which the Marian bishops and clergy, speaking in behalf of the entire " spirituality of England," presented a protest to the lords [8] in which they embodied their convictions in five articles,[9] asserting in an extreme form the cardinal propositions of the older faith.   The unsuccessful yet vigorous opposition thus made at the outset admonished the council that in order to bring the church establishment into harmony with the new system, it should at once undertake the reorganization of the episcopate.   At the queen's

protest of the Marian bishops and clergy against Elizabeth's innovations;

reorganization of the episcopate;

---

[1] 1 Eliz. c. 2.
[2] 1 Eliz. c. 4.
[3] 1 Eliz. c. 24.
[4] 1 Eliz. c. 3.   See Sir Michael Foster's comments upon the peculiar language of this act, *Crown Law*, p. 409.
[5] 1 Eliz. c. 5.   The act of 1 & 2 Phil. & Mar. c. 10, was reënacted and applied to Elizabeth.   Attacks by words were made treason on a second conviction.
[6] As to the lists of court candidates

sent to the sheriffs, see Strype, vol. i. p. 32 ; *Clarendon Papers*, p. 92.
[7] The archbishopric of Canterbury being vacant, the bishop of London presided.
[8] Five new peers of protestant principles had been added to the upper house at the coronation.   Including these, the lay peers numbered sixty-one, of whom eighteen failed to attend Elizabeth's first parliament.
[9] Wilkins, *Conc.*, vol. iv. p. 179; Strype's *Annals*, vol. i. p. 79.

accession seven vacancies already existed in the twenty-seven[1] English bishoprics, and before parliament could meet the number was swelled by death to ten.[2]   At the close of the session but fifteen diocesan bishops remained in the realm, two[3] having fled from their posts in order to find security abroad.   The means of removing those who remained was readily supplied by the Act of Supremacy, which provided that every bishop who should refuse the oath of allegiance should be deprived of his see.   And yet, in spite of that penalty, every one of the fifteen,[4] except Kitchin, bishop of Llandaff,[5] refused the oath when it was offered by the commissioners to whom a general visitation[6] of the church was intrusted in the summer of 1559.   How to fill up the twenty-six vacancies thus existing in such a way as to comply at once with the law of the land and with the requirements of the theory of apostolic succession became a question of serious difficulty.

It was of course all important that the vacant see of Canterbury should be given a new incumbent whose spiritual lineage should be beyond all question, and whose legal title should rest upon the provisions of the revived statute of the 25th of Henry VIII.,[7] which made it necessary that the election of an archbishop should be confirmed and his consecration performed by at least four of the episcopate.[8]   Before the deposition of the Marian bishops had been fully accomplished, a commission was issued by the crown on the 9th of September, 1559, to six bishops,[9] commanding them or four of them to meet, confirm, and consecrate Dr. Parker, who had on the 1st of August been elected by the dean and chapter of Canterbury to the primacy of the kingdom.   This commission, whose action would have removed the difficulty, proved abortive through the refu-

means of removal furnished by the Act of Supremacy;

all the bishops refused the oath, except Kitchin of Llandaff;

how to fill the vacancies a difficult problem;

the vacant see of Canterbury;

failure of the first attempt to consecrate Dr. Parker;

[1] There were besides several suffragans.

[2] The death of Pole left Canterbury vacant, and he was soon followed by the bishops of Bristol and Rochester.

[3] Bishops of Worcester and St. Asaph.

[4] It was assumed that the two bishops abroad would also refuse.

[5] Burnet, vol. i. p. 576.

[6] For the history of the visitation, carried on by the crown under 1 Eliz. c. 1, § 17, and whose main purpose was no doubt the administration of the oath of allegiance, see the imperfect record in Strype's *Annals*, vol. i. p. 245.

[7] 25 Hen. VIII. c. 20, regulating the appointment to bishoprics, was revived by 1 Eliz. c. 1.   See above, p. 154.

[8] See Strype's *Parker* (Parker's letter with notes by Cecil), p. 40.

[9] Tunstall of Durham, Bourn of Bath and Wells, Pole of Peterborough, Kitchin of Llandaff, and Barlow and Scory, bishops of Bath and Chichester, who had been deprived under Queen Mary.

sal of Tunstal, Bourn, and Pole, three of its members, to obey
the royal mandate, by reason of which they were all deprived
before the end of September, thus leaving Kitchin as the only
diocesan bishop in the kingdom.   In the face of such difficulties a second commission, with a sanitary clause [1] which
undertook to cure all defects by virtue of the royal supremacy,
was, on the 6th of December, directed to Kitchin of Llandaff ;
to Scory, formerly of Chichester, now elect of Hereford ; to
Barlow, formerly of Bath, now elect of Chichester ; to Coverdale, formerly of Exeter ; to Bale, bishop of Ossory in Ireland,
and to Hodgkins and Salisbury, suffragan bishops of Bedford and Thetford, commanding them, or any four of them, to
confirm and consecrate the archbishop elect.   Scory, Barlow,
Coverdale, and Hodgkins obeyed the mandate by confirming
his election in Bow Church on the 9th, and by consecrating
him at Lambeth on the 17th, according to the form adopted
near the end of the reign of Edward VI. [2]   Thus installed, the
new archbishop, whose title became the vital link binding the
new to the old episcopate, proceeded, with the assistance of
those who had taken part in his own consecration, to consecrate all the other bishops elect, who were taken either from
among the Calvinistic refugees who had returned from Geneva
and Frankfort, or from those who in the preceding reign had
been conspicuous in the cause of the Reformation. [3]

The spirit of resistance manifested by the Marian bishops
to the inauguration of the new system does not seem to have
extended after their deprivation to the inferior clergy, as only
about a hundred cathedral dignitaries and eighty parochial
priests are said to have been deprived or to have resigned by
reason of the oath which the commissioners tendered. [4]   Before

Marginal notes:

the second commission with the sanitary clause ;

Parker finally consecrated according to a form which existed in the reign of Edward VI. ;

he takes part in the consecration of all the rest.

Spirit of resistance manifested by the bishops did not extend to the inferior clergy.

---

[1] *Fœdera*, vol. xv. p. 549.

[2] Lingard claims that that form
was not then recognized by law. "The
use of the ordinal of Edward VI. had
been abolished by parliament in the
last reign, that of the catholic ordinal
by parliament in the present." — Vol.
vi. p. 17.   He further says, in Appendix, note C, that " on the illegality of
that ordinal, both Parker and Cecil
were agreed," citing Strype's *Parker*,
p. 40.

[3] The Church of England view of
this important transaction is clearly
stated by Blount, *Reform. of the Church*

of Eng., vol. ii. pp. 385–395; the Roman Catholic view by Lingard, vol.
vi. pp. 16–18, and Appendix, note C.
Lingard admits that the famous Nag's
Head story, which pretended that the
consecration of Parker was a mere
burlesque that took place at a tavern
of that name, is a pure "fable."   Copies of the official documents which
prove the consecration at Lambeth beyond all doubt are printed in Bailey's
*Ordinum Sacrorum in Ecclesia Angli-
cana Defenso*, 1870.

[4] Such is the assertion of Burnet,
Strype, Camden, and Heylin, based on

the end of the year 1559 the work was over, and the English
Church, whose clergy were thus severed from their Roman
allegiance, definitely ranged itself on the side of the Reformation, a result which was formally emphasized in the summer
of 1561 by Elizabeth's refusal of the invitation of Pius IV. to
send representatives to the Council of Trent.[1] The changed
conditions thus brought about made it possible for convocation
to make a definite statement of the distinctive principles of
the reorganized national church, such as had been put forward
by Edward VI. in the Forty-two Articles, which, suspended
during Mary's reign, had not yet enjoyed the honor of a revival. In order to supply temporarily the want of such a formulary, Eleven Articles were compiled under the eye of the new
archbishop in 1559 or early in 1560,[2] and published in 1561,
which, although never officially promulgated by the crown,
were considered as binding on the clergy[3] down to the meeting of the memorable convocation, assembled, after an interval
of four years, in January, 1563. In this first convocation of
the church as reorganized by Elizabeth, which sat under the
presidency and intellectual guidance of Parker, who drew his
theological ideas largely from Cranmer,[4] the Forty-two Articles
of 1552–53, after various additions and subtractions, were finally
adopted as the famous Thirty-nine Articles, which in the summer of 1563 were, according to the Act of Submission, ratified by the crown under the great seal and promulgated as a
canon of the Church of England.[5] In the next convocation,
that met in 1571, these articles were reviewed and the royal
ratification given anew; and by an act of parliament passed
in the same year[6] it was provided that they should be sub-

Marginal notes:

English Church definitely allied to the cause of the Reformation; Elizabeth refused to send representatives to the Council of Trent;

the Eleven Articles of 1559-61;

the Thirty-nine Articles adopted in 1563, in a convocation which sat under the presidency of Parker; reviewed in 1571, and made binding upon the clergy by act of parliament;

---

the visitors' report. As to the form
subscribed by those who submitted,
see Strype's *Annals*, vol. i. p. 255.

[1] First Parpalia was sent, and then
Martinengo, as nuncios; but Elizabeth
would permit neither to land in England. "From that time all treaty with
Rome was entirely broken off. Pius
the Fourth proceeded no further."
— Burnet, vol. i. p. 591. See elaborate note upon the subject in the *State
Papers*, Dom. Eliz. 175.

[2] Strype's *Annals*, vol. i. p. 220.

[3] Wilkins, *Conc.*, vol. iv. p. 195 *sqq.*
The articles are printed in Hardwick's

Hist. of the Articles, Appendix IV., and
are explained in the text.

[4] Parker so esteemed Cranmer that
he said he "wolde as moche rejoyce
to wynne" some of his lost writings as
he "wolde to restore an old chancel to
reparation." See Strype's *Cranmer*,
Appendix, No. xc., Parker to Cecil,
August 22, 1563.

[5] For the text of the articles and a
critical history of the making of them,
see Hardwick's *Hist. of the Articles;*
Blount, *Reform. of the Church of Eng.*
vol. ii. pp. 381–385.

[6] 13 Eliz. c. 12.

scribed by the English clergy, who, with more or less satisfaction, have accepted them as a standard of doctrine for over
three hundred years.   Thus it was that Elizabeth, with the
aid of parliament and convocation, finally succeeded in placing
the Anglican state church upon a permanent basis by fusing
her father's external policy of national independence with the
scheme of internal reformation of dogma and ritual formulated
in Edward's reign under the guidance of Cranmer.   Such a
settlement necessarily involved not only the uncompromising
hostility of the Roman Catholic party, who could not accept
the royal in lieu of the papal supremacy, but also that of the
extreme protestants of the anti-sacramental school, generally
known as Puritans, who earnestly protested against the continuance of the episcopal system, the sacrificial character of
the communion, and the retention of certain of the ancient
ceremonies which the new formularies perpetuated.   The result was a bitter and uncompromising warfare against both
of the opposing factions carried on to the end of Elizabeth's
reign through a series of persecuting and disabling statutes,
whose contents will be summarized in the two following sec-
tions.

composite character of Elizabeth's work;

Roman Catholics and extreme protestants both refused to accept the result;

a bitter warfare against both.

3. By the Act of Appeals,[1] enacted by Henry VIII. and
reënacted by Elizabeth,[2] the theory of the identity of church
and state was distinctly embodied in terms which declared
that "both their authorities and jurisdictions do conjoin together, in the due administration of justice, the one to help
the other."   Proceeding upon that basis, the ecclesiastical legislation of Elizabeth assumed that the regulation of religious
worship was a state function to be exercised through parliament, and that all subjects who failed to accept or comply
with the forms thus provided should be punished by the law
of the state.   It was further assumed that to acknowledge the
right of the pope to interfere with such legislation was a step
towards treason, and that to act by his command in opposition
to the law of the land was actual treason.[3]   Upon these principles were framed the acts of Elizabeth designed to punish
the offence of non-conformity to the established church, some

Struggle of Elizabeth with the catholic party:

regulation of religious worship assumed to be a state function;

statutes designed to punish the offence of non-con-formity to the state church;

---

[1] 24 Hen. VIII. c. 12.   See Amos,
Reformation Statutes, pp. 256–262.
[2] 1 Eliz. c. 1.

[3] See Sir J. F. Stephen, *Hist. of the
Crim. Law,* vol. ii. p. 477.

of which were intended to apply generally to both of the resisting factions, while others were designed for special application to Roman Catholics, or to protestant dissenters, in order to
meet special emergencies.   At the outset the worldly and tolerant spirit animating both Elizabeth and Cecil, which demanded
only an outward conformity to the church establishment,
refused to enter the sacred realm of individual opinion.   While
there was a positive refusal upon the part of the state to grant
freedom of public worship, which was then generally considered as incompatible with public order, it was distinctly announced that there was to be no interference with the rights
of conscience.[1]   In this temper it was that Elizabeth at once
put an end to burnings for heresy, and ordered the release of
all who had been imprisoned for religion in the preceding reign.[2]
In the same tolerant spirit the oaths prescribed by the Act of
Supremacy were certainly applied to the ten thousand catholic
priests who then occupied the benefices of the Church of
England, the bulk of whom are said to have simply left the
commissioners' summons unheeded.   While the bishops and
greater dignitaries were dealt with without mercy, only about
two hundred of the inferior clergy actually suffered deprivation.[3]   Upon the part of the English catholics a disposition
was manifested to meet this tolerant policy by outward conformity, which continued until it was suddenly checked in
August, 1562, by a brief from the pope forbidding their attendance at church, and denouncing their joining in the common
prayer as schismatic.[4]   The sharp assault thus made from
Rome upon Elizabeth's hopeful policy was promptly met by
a memorable act[5] passed in the parliament which met in

at first only an outward uniformity demanded, but freedom of public worship denied;

Elizabeth put an end to burning for heresy;

tolerant treatment of the inferior clergy;

tendency of English catholics to outward conformity checked by a papal brief in 1562;

the counter-blast;

---

[1] See Green's *Hist. of the Eng. People*, vol. ii. pp. 297, 298, as to Elizabeth's toleration at the outset.   Hallam tells us, however (vol. i. p. 113 of
his *Const. Hist.*), that "we find instances
of severity towards Catholics, even in
that early period ; and it is evident that
their solemn rites were only performed
by stealth at much hazard."   "Opinion,
it was announced, was to be practically free, but all must go to church,
and the exercise of the Roman Catholic worship was rigidly suppressed." —
S. R. Gardiner's *Hist. Eng.*, vol. i. p. 12.

[2] Strype's *Annals*, vol. i. p. 54;
Blount, *Reform. of the Church of Eng.*,

vol. ii. p. 338.   The power of the High
Commission to punish heresy really extended only to the Anabaptists, or as
we should now say, Unitarians.   See
Stephen, *Hist. of the Crim. Law*, vol.
ii. pp. 460, 461.   As to their actual punishment, see Stowe's *Ann.*, pp. 678, 679,
685, 697 ; Strype's *Ann.*, vol. iii. p. 564;
vol. vi. p. 73.

[3] See above, p. 158.

[4] Green, *Hist. of the Eng. People*,
vol. ii. p. 342.

[5] 5 Eliz. c. 1, and entitled, "for the
assurance of the queen's royal power
over all estates and subjects within
her dominions."

the act of
1563, the
first of the
series for
the oppres-
sion of
Roman
Catholics;

January, 1563, that laid the foundation for a system of legal oppression which English catholics were forced to endure for nearly two hundred and fifty years. This act, which was opposed in the lords in an historic speech from Viscount Montague,[1] after declaring that it was necessary for " correcting the marvellous outrage and licentious boldness of the fautors of the bishop of Rome," and after imposing severe penalties upon all who should maintain his authority within the realm, provided for a commission to be composed of the bishops and other commissioners to be appointed by the crown, who were

contents of
the act;

authorized to tender the oath of supremacy (1) to all members of the house of commons, to all who had ever been admitted to holy orders or to degrees in the universities, to schoolmasters, private tutors, barristers, and attorneys, as well as to all other persons engaged in the execution of the law ; (2) to all who should openly disapprove of the established worship, or who should celebrate or attend any mass said in private. From the terms of this sweeping act, which embraced the entire catholic population, were excepted only the catholic peers, in whom the queen still expressed confidence. The penalty for the first refusal of the oath was forfeiture and perpetual imprisonment ; for a second, death, as in the case of high treason.

moderation
of the
primate in
its enforce-
ment;

The terrible result which a rigid enforcement of this act might have brought about was wisely averted by the moderation of the primate, who privately instructed the bishops to use great caution in tendering the oath, which was never to be offered the second time, so as to make a case of treason, without his previous approval.[2] And yet, in spite of this admonition,

Horne
tendered
the oath to
Bonner;

Horne, bishop of Winchester, persisted in tendering the oath to Bonner, the hated and deprived bishop of London, then in prison in the Marshalsea, whose refusal to take it was duly

legal status
of the new
bishops
questioned
in the
queen's
bench;

certified to the queen's bench, where, under the advice of Plowden, Bonner pleaded not guilty on several grounds, one of which was that the person who had tendered him the oath was not a bishop.[3]   In order to cut short a controversy which

1 Strype's *Annals*, vol. i. pp. 259–273.

2 Strype's *Life of Parker*, pp. 125, 126.

3 " After a long argument in Serjeants' Inn, all the judges agreed that Bonner had a right to an inquiry before a jury as to the matter of fact, whether Horne, at the time when he offered the oath, was or was not a bishop in the eye of the law." — Lingard, vol. vi., Appendix, note C, p. 668.

thus presented the legal status of the new episcopate, the controversy ended by an act passed in 1566.
prosecution was dropped, and an act [1] passed in the parliament
of 1566, "declaring the manner of making bishops and archbishops in this kingdom," employed since the queen's accession, "to be good, perfect, and lawful."

The act of 1563, which suspended a sword over the head The scheme for the deposition of Elizabeth,
of every catholic by a thread that the queen could break at
pleasure, was regarded at Rome as a challenge to which the
papacy should reply by the reassertion of the right, still
claimed by the pontiffs, to depose sovereigns for the commission of heinous crimes against the church through decrees enforceable with the aid of temporal princes.   Upon that theory
was organized a far-reaching scheme, which contemplated the
deposition of Elizabeth through the joint action of the pope, to be car-ried out by the pope, Philip, and the English catholics in favor of Mary Stuart;
Philip of Spain, and the English catholics,[2] and the placing in
her stead upon the throne of Mary Stuart, who, at the queen's
accession, had assumed the arms and title of an English sovereign.   In order to meet as they arose the manifold dangers
to which the several attempts to execute that design gave
birth, the remaining statutes of Elizabeth specially hostile to
catholics were enacted.   The central point in the controversy
was the right to the succession, which the advocates of the in-
defeasible hereditary theory claimed belonged to Mary Stuart, Mary's claim to the succession;
the undoubted heir of Henry VIII.'s eldest sister Margaret,
as against Elizabeth, whom they assumed to be illegitimate.[3]
The claim thus set up against the childless queen was greatly
strengthened by Mary's marriage with Darnley on July 20,
1565, and the birth of a son,[4] who, on July 29, 1567, was sol-
emnly crowned as James VI. of Scotland.   The bright hopes forced to abdicate in favor of her son, James VI. of Scot-land;
which the appearance of an heir naturally excited were dark-
ened, however, by the fact that three days before his coronation Mary had been forced to abdicate in his favor by the
Scotch Calvinists, who, after routing her partisans in battle,
drove her in May, 1568, to cross the border, in order to seek

---

[1] 8 Eliz. c. 1.   The main purpose of
this act was to legalize retrospectively
the Edwardian ordinal used at the
consecration of Parker and his associates.
[2] See the interesting evidence upon
this subject collated by Blount, *Re-*

form. of the Church of Eng., vol. ii. pp.
427-454, where special reference is
made to Denham's and Catena's accounts of the papal plans.
[3] See Bailey, *The Succession to the
English Crown*, p. 174 *et seq.*
[4] July 19, 1566.

a prisoner
in Eliza-
beth's
hands;

protection and succor at the hands of Elizabeth.[1] Mary's imprisonment, which thus began, and which ended only with her
death, instead of removing the dangers to which she had so
long exposed her rival, at once gave rise to fresh designs in
her own behalf, that soon involved the English queen in the
gravest peril with which she had so far been confronted.
With Philip triumphant in the Netherlands, and the Guises
dominant in France, the time had now come for Rome to
strike a decisive blow in Mary's favor, which was to be given

the threat-
ened
Spanish
invasion in
her behalf;

through a Spanish invasion,[2] to be met by a rising of the catholic peers under Norfolk, the head of the nobility, who was to
remove all prejudice against Mary by making her his wife.
But when the time for action came, the irresolute allies failed

failure of
the rising
in the
north which
took place
in Novem-
ber, 1569;

to coöperate. The rising in the northern counties, then chiefly
catholic, which took place in November, 1569, under the leadership of the earls of Westmoreland and Northumberland, unsupported by Philip, was quickly suppressed, and the rebels
punished by ruthless measures which mark the first stage of
actual severity in the reign of Elizabeth. The counterblast

bull of ex-
communi-
cation and
deposition
published
in March,
1570;

from Rome was the publication by Pius V. in March, 1570, of
the famous bull of excommunication and deposition,[3] really
prepared the year before, declaring that the heretic queen had
forfeited all right to the throne, absolving her subjects from
their oaths of allegiance, and forbidding them to obey her upon
pain of excommunication. The response made by parliament
to the attempt against the sovereign, of which the revolt of
the northern earls and the bull of deposition were component

two
statutes
passed for
the queen's
protection:
the first to
prohibit the
publication
of papal
bulls;

parts, was embodied in two statutes enacted within a year after
the bull was published. In the first[4] it was provided that the
penalty of treason should be imposed upon all who should
obtain or put in use any bull or other writing from the bishop
of Rome, or absolve or be absolved by virtue of the same ;
and that the penalties of præmunire should be imposed upon
their aiders and abettors, and upon all who should introduce or
receive pictures, crosses, beads, or other things "hallowed and
consecrated, as it is termed, by the bishop of Rome." In the

---

[1] Keith, pp. 477–483; Anderson, vol.
iv. p. 333.
[2] The aid was expected from the

Spanish army in the Netherlands. *Ep.
Pii V.*, edit. Goban, p. 290.
[3] Printed in Burnet's *Collectanea.*
[4] 13 Eliz. c. 2.

second[1] it was provided (1) that any one should be guilty of treason who claimed the crown during the queen's life, or who should assert that it belonged to any other person than the queen, or who should affirm that the queen was a heretic, schismatic, tyrant, infidel, or usurper, or who should deny the right of parliament to regulate the descent of the crown by statute; (2) that every one should be punished by imprisonment and forfeiture who should by writing or printing affirm that any particular person was the heir to the queen who was not "the natural issue of her body."

During the ten years which followed the enactment of the statutes of 1571, existing laws were enforced with such severity against the catholic population that many were forced to seek refuge beyond sea, while the catholic priesthood, thinned by death and unrecruited by fresh ordinations, threatened to become extinct. In order to supply "a new English clergy," it occurred to William Allen, who had been principal of St. Mary's Hall at Oxford, to establish a college at Douay, in Flanders, where priests could be educated who, after ordination, might return to labor in England. The stream of missionaries thus set in motion from Douay, where the first seminary was founded in 1568,[2] was swelled in 1579 by the founding of an additional seminary at Rome;[3] and about the same time the general of the Jesuits assented to Allen's request that the members of his aggressive order should share the fortunes of the enterprise.[4] To meet this new danger, by which the council seems to have been thoroughly alarmed,[5] an act[6] was passed in the parliament that met in January, 1581, which provided (1) that it should be high treason to withdraw others or to be withdrawn from the established religion; (2) that the saying and hearing of mass should be punished by fines

---

[1] 13 Eliz. c. 1.

[2] In 1576, driven out by a riot, the seminary was removed to Rheims, where it remained until 1593, when it was reëstablished at Douay. There it remained until the French Revolution, when it migrated to Old Hall Green at Ware, in Hertfordshire, and is now known as St. Edmund's College. Blount, *Reform. of the Church of Eng.*, vol. ii. p. 455.

[3] Others were also founded at Madrid, Seville, Paris, Lisbon, and in other continental cities in the following forty years. Butler's *Hist. Mem.*, vol. ii. pp. 172, 440.

[4] Lingard, vol. vi. p. 334.

[5] A proclamation was first issued denouncing as abettors of treason any one who should harbor or fail to reveal the presence of any Jesuit or seminarist in the kingdom. Camden, p. 348; Sanders, p. 384.

[6] 23 Eliz. c. 1, "to retain the queen's majesty's subjects in their due obedience."

heavier than ever before; (3) that all persons over sixteen who should absent themselves from the established church should be fined £20 a month, and in default of payment for three months after judgment should be imprisoned until they should conform; and (4) that in order to prevent the concealment of priests as tutors or schoolmasters in private families, all such should be licensed by the ordinary, and that any one who should teach without a license, or employ a teacher unlicensed

torture and conviction of the Jesuit, Campian;

should suffer a heavy penalty. During the year which followed the passage of that act, Campian, who, together with Persons, had been sent into England as a leader of the Jesuit mission, charged with its reconversion, was, after being forced on the rack [1] to reveal the names of several of his co-religionists who had sheltered him, convicted of high treason under an indictment presented against him and others, charging them with a conspiracy, said to have been formed at Rheims and Rome, for the murder of the queen and for the overthrow of church and state.[2]

association formed for the protection of the queen's life;

A few years after this it was that a voluntary association was formed for the protection of the life of Elizabeth, who was continually alarmed by reports of conspiracies against her formed in the interest of the Queen of Scots.

an act legalizing the association passed in 1584;

In the new parliament which met in November, 1584, the association for the queen's protection was legalized by an act,[4] the first to be passed, in which it was originally proposed that in the event of any attempt to injure the royal person, or in the

[1] As to the earliest authenticated instance of the use of torture in England, see vol. i. p. 582, and note 3. Theoretically, it was never a part of the law of England. Coke says that the rack in the Tower was introduced by the duke of Exeter in the reign of Henry VI. 3 *Inst.*, p. 35. It was extensively used by the Tudors and by James I. and Charles I., not only to obtain evidence in political cases, but also as to ordinary crimes. For the proof see Jardine's *Reading on Torture*, with letters taken from the Council Book and running from November, 1551, to May, 1640. The Tudors evidently assumed that the right to inflict torture was a part of the royal prerogative which could be exercised by special license from the crown. See Gardiner, *Hist. Eng.*, vol. i. pp. 265, 266, and notes; Strype's *Whitgift*, p. 83.

The judges, however, expressed a contrary view when consulted on the subject in the time of Charles I. as to the case of Felton. 3 *State Trials*, pp. 36, 571. As to the gradual introduction of torture on the continent during the fourteenth, fifteenth, and sixteenth centuries, and its connection with the revival of the Roman Law, see Lea, *Superstition and Force*, Philadelphia, 1878, pp. 371–522.

[2] *State Trials*, vol. i. pp. 1049, 1072; Bridgewater, pp. 219, 304. Campian and two other priests were executed in December, 1581.

[3] Camden, p. 411.

[4] 27 Eliz. c. 1, "for the security of the queen's person & continuance of the realm in peace." The second act of this parliament was directed against "Jesuits, seminary priests, & other such like disobedient persons."— 27 Eliz. c.

event of an invasion or rebellion in behalf of any one claiming title to the crown after the queen's death, the person by
whom or in whose behalf such attempt should be made should
forfeit all right to the succession, and should with his or her
confederates be pursued to death by all the queen's subjects.
An amendment [1] was, however, made, which provided that no
person should be pursued to death by the association until
their privity to treason had first been established by a special
commission to be constituted by royal authority. Under the terms of that statute it was that the commission was constituted which in 1586 found Mary guilty of having been privy
to Babington's conspiracy contemplating an invasion of the
realm and the queen's death.[2] And yet even after the removal of the chief danger by the execution of Mary in February, 1587, and after the loyal response made by the English
catholics to Elizabeth's call in the presence of the peril that
arose out of the presence of the Spanish Armada in 1588, they
were subjected down to her death to incessant persecution,
whose hardships were deepened by the passage, in 1593, of an
act [3] which increased the penalties of recusancy by providing
that all persons convicted of non-attendance at church should
not travel more than five miles from particular places of residence; and in the event of an inability to pay the monthly
fine of £20 to which such persons were subject, they were to
abjure the realm or suffer as felons. It has been estimated
that, apart from those who died in prison, about two hundred
catholics suffered death during Elizabeth's reign under the
persecuting statutes just enumerated,[4] either for denying the

under that act as amended was consti- tuted the commission which in 1586 condemned the Queen of Scots;

persecution of catholics continued;

the act of 1593 increasing the penal- ties of recusancy;

result of Elizabeth's persecution compared with that of Mary's.

---

[1] Lingard, vol. vi. p. 374.
[2] For a picturesque account of Mary's trial and execution under the commission, see Froude, vol. xii. pp. 169–255; for a legal review, see Hal- lam, *Const. Hist.*, vol. i. pp. 158–162.
[3] 35 Eliz. c. 2: "An act for restrain- ing popish recusants to some certain places of abode." "The result of this legislation was that at the end of the reign of Elizabeth every Roman Cath- olic priest in England, except the few who might have been ordained in the reign of Queen Mary, was by the very fact of his presence in England guilty of high treason; that to celebrate the mass was an offence in itself punish-

able with fine and imprisonment, and that popish recusants were not only liable to ruinous penalties, but were forbidden to travel above five miles from their registered places of abode." — Sir J. F. Stephen, *Hist. of the Crim. Law of Eng.*, vol. ii. p. 486.
[4] Dodd puts the number at 191, Milner at 204. Quoted by Hallam, *Const. Hist.*, vol. i. p. 163. Lingard says, "Sixty-one clergymen, forty-seven laymen, and two gentlewomen suf- fered capital punishment for some or other of the spiritual felonies and trea- sons which had been lately created." — Vol. vi. p. 525. That was prior to 1590.

royal supremacy, for exercising the functions of the priest-hood, or for becoming reconciled to the See of Rome. Thus it appears that while ecclesiastical persecution by burning was suspended at the queen's accession, the number of deaths re-sulting from what may be called political persecution, carried on under statutes extending the penalties of treason to offences against the state church, closely approximates that which oc-curred under the heresy statutes in the reign of Mary.[1]

Struggle of Elizabeth with the Puritan party : 4. The fact has heretofore been emphasized that the spirit of restlessness and discontent with the doctrines and practices of the mediæval church which Lollardry had left behind it, and which had its root in the idea that each individual should look

The Bible as the only source of inspiration; Tyndale's translation of the New Testament; to the Bible alone as the source of religious truth, was strength-ened and intensified in the ranks of the common people by the importation into England, in 1526, of Tyndale's translation of the New Testament, which had been made in Lutheran strongholds at Luther's instance and solicitation.[2] The prin-ciples of dissent from the ancient ecclesiastical order, which

Lollard ideas live on until the reign of Henry VIII. ; the Lollards had promulgated two centuries before the English Reformation really began, thus lived on until the reign of Henry VIII., when the repudiation of the papal supremacy gave a fresh impulse to the attack long before begun against the whole system of theology which the papacy embodied. The tendency thus manifested by the revived Lollardry to unite itself with the Lutheran movement ceased, however, with

influence of Luther supplanted by that of Calvin; the fall of Cromwell,[3] and with the rise of a new apostle, who about that time became the great intellectual light of the pro-testant world. In 1535 Calvin produced at Basle his "Insti-tutes of the Christian Religion;" in the next year he became the spiritual head of the protestant community which had be-come dominant at Geneva; and from his return to that city in 1541 down to his death in 1564, he reigned as the pontiff of

Calvinistic system of church goverment; protestant opinion. In the new theology which he promul-gated was embodied an elastic and adaptable system of church government, which, ignoring the Lutheran theory of national religion, rested upon the assumption that the reformers as a

---

[1] See above, p. 148.
[2] See above, p. 51.
[3] "From the hour of Cromwell's fall the sympathies of the English reformers had drawn them, not to the Lutheran churches of North Germany, but to the more progressive churches of the Rhineland and the Nether-lands." — Green, *Hist. of the Eng People*, vol. ii. p. 281.

whole, regardless of nationality, constituted a vast Christian commonwealth, subdivided into independent and self-governing churches, in which the source of all power and authority was the sovereign Christian man, elect of God and predestined to eternal life, whose most sacred duty involved the assertion even unto death of his private judgment in all matters of conscience against any form of religious belief that princes or states might attempt to force upon him.   Thus it was that the church as embodied in this new Christian democracy was thrown into hostile relations with the state by virtue of the doctrine which claimed that the religious supremacy of kings should yield to the higher sovereignty of the individual conscience.[1]   While the principles of the new system thus assailed from without the spiritual supremacy of the state, they still more sharply menaced from within the supremacy of the episcopate[2] through the substitution of a new system of church government, in which all power came from below from the church members, in whom was vested the right to elect the lay elders and deacons who, with the existing body of pastors, were to elect new ministers.[3]   The avowed purpose of this school of reform was to substitute in the place of the pomp and power of the ancient ecclesiastical system a simple and "pure" form of doctrine and discipline, a claim out of which probably arose the later name of "Puritan."[4]   The theology of Calvin, which reasserted the right, always maintained by the papacy, of the subject to draw the sword against ungodly princes, soon took vigorous hold in Scotland,[5] where the protestant party led the way in its application by the making of "a covenant" at the close of 1557, in which the members

a common-
wealth of
independ-
ent, self-
governing
churches;
the source
of author-
ity the
sovereign
Christian
man ; his
right of
private
judgment;

the new
Christian
democracy
denied the
religious
supremacy
of kings;

also the
authority
of the
episcopate ;

reformers
declared
their
purpose to
substitute
for the
ancient a
simple and
"pure"
form of
doctrine;

the Scotch
"cove-
nant" of
1557;

---

[1] "Both the Calvinists and the Papists, widely as they differed in other respects, regarded with extreme jealousy all encroachments of the temporal power on the domain of the spiritual power.   Both Calvinists and Papists maintained that subjects might justifiably draw the sword against ungodly rulers. . . . The Church of England meantime condemned both Calvinists and Papists, and loudly boasted that no duty was more constantly or earnestly inculcated by her than that of submission to princes." — Macaulay, *Hist. Eng.*, vol. i. p. 29.

[2] "Affecting to be thought a supe-

rior order to presbyters, and claiming the sole right of ordination and the use of the keys." — Neal's *Hist. of the Puritans*, vol. i. pp. 211, 235–240.

[3] Calvin's *Inst.*

[4] "It first came into use as the designation of an English church party about the year 1564 [Fuller's *Ch. Hist.*, vol. ix. p. 66], but after a few years it got to be used also as inclusive of many who had separated from the Church of England." — Blount, *Reform. of the Church of Eng.*, vol. ii. p. 391, note 1.

[5] For John Knox's views upon this subject, see Strype, p. 119.

Calvinistic
ideas in
England;

the Marian
exiles
sought
refuge at
Zurich and
Geneva.

The inevit-
able conflict
between
Calvinistic
ideas and
the state
church as
reëstab-
lished by
Elizabeth;

the queen's
personal
predilec-
tions;

bound themselves to defy the religion of the state, and to maintain " even unto death " that of the " congregation." [1]   In a less aggressive form the ideas of Calvin took so firm a hold in England during the reign of Edward VI. that upon the accession of Mary, when persecution drove many of the re- formers beyond the sea, they sought a refuge not with the Lutheran churches of North Germany, but with the Calvinistic churches of Zurich and Geneva,[2] whence they returned at the accession of Elizabeth, fired with the zeal which personal con- tact with the leaders of the new movement naturally excited.

Nothing could have been more inevitable than the conflict that ensued between the returning exiles thus pledged to a radical programme which repudiated the religious supremacy of the crown, the episcopacy as a form of church government, together with the ceremonies of the older faith, and that con- servative system of church reform reëstablished by the statutes of Elizabeth, which recognized nearly every principle against which the Calvinists protested.[3]   Not only was the royal su- premacy, the episcopal system, and much of the ancient ritual jealously preserved by law, but the fact was also known that the queen herself, who never would consent to a legal recogni- tion of the right of the clergy to marry,[4] possessed a strong personal predilection for many forms of worship which the ex- treme protestants denounced as the " leavings of idolatry." [5] As the strict enforcement of the Acts of Supremacy prevented for a time the formation of sects outside of the state church, the first opposition to the established system came from within,

[1] Keith, p. 66; Knox, pp. 98–100. The subscribers had the earls of Ar- gyle, Morton, and Glencairn at their head.

[2] As to some of the eminent divines who went at that time, see Burnet, vol. i. p. 471.   See also as to their return from Zurich and Geneva, Ibid., vol. ii. pp. 808, 809.

[3] " In the eye of the Presbyterian clergy, the king and the beggar were of equal importance, and ought to be possessed of only equal influence, as soon as they entered the church doors. Noble as this idea was, it may safely be said that this organized ecclesiasti- cal democracy could not flourish upon English soil." — S. R. Gardiner, *Hist. Eng.*, vol. i. p. 23.

[4] Permission had been given by 2 & 3 Edw. VI. c. 21, and confirmed by 5 & 6 Edw. VI. c. 12.   These acts were repealed by 1 Mary, s. 2, c. 2.   While the marriage of bishops and priests was connived at during Elizabeth's reign, the queen would never consent to dis- turb Mary's act, which was never re- pealed until the first year of James I.   In one diocese it was the custom after Elizabeth's accession to pay the bishop for a license to keep a concu- bine.   Strype's *Parker*, p. 203.   The offspring of all clergymen during that reign were in legal contemplation ille- gitimate.

[5] Elizabeth even went so far as to quiz the Puritans as " brethren in Christ."

from a church party which about the year 1564 was designated as Puritan,[1] a term so extended a few years later as to embrace many who had then separated from the Church of England. In 1565 it was that the first coercive measures were taken against the Puritan sympathizers among the clergy who had for some time, with the connivance of some of the bishops, ventured to deviate from the uniformity established by law by refusing to observe many ceremonies which they deemed either as superfluous or superstitious. To suppress such irregularities, the archbishop in the year last named put forward, without the royal sanction formally given,[2] a set of regulations for the discipline of the clergy called "Advertisements;" and through the authority of the ecclesiastical commission many of the leading Puritan divines who still refused to conform were either deprived of their preferments,[3] or suspended from the ministry under threat of deprivation. Thus it was that the Puritans were driven to the open schism which manifested itself by their withdrawal from the state church, and by the establishment of separate conventicles. In June, 1567, an assembly of that character which had met in Plummer's Hall in London was dispersed, and out of a hundred or more brought before the court of high commission, thirty or more were imprisoned, the first punishment to which protestant dissenters were actually subjected.[4] Five years later, the attack which was confined at first to what the Puritans regarded as obnoxious church ceremonies was expanded by them into an assault upon the bishops, led by Cartwright, a professor of divinity at Cambridge, who boldly advocated an abolition of the episcopal in favor of the presbyterian system.[5] This demand was presented in an "Admonition to the Parliament" published in 1572, the year in which appeared a "Book of Discipline" advocating the same idea, written by Walter Travers,[6] a lecturer at the Temple, with whose master, Hooker, he had a controversy,

first opposition to the state church arose from within from a party called Puritan;

coercive measures taken in 1565 against Puritan clergymen;

those who refused to conform were deprived;

thus driven to open schism;

a separate conventicle suppressed in 1567;

Puritan assault upon the episcopate led by Cartwright;

---

1 Fuller's *Church Hist.*, vol. ix. p. 66.

2 Strype's *Annals*, p. 416; *Life of Parker*, p. 159.

3 Examples were made in that way of Sampson, dean of Christchurch, and Humphrey, professor of divinity and president of Magdalen College, Oxford, while thirty-seven London clergymen, who refused to comply with legal ceremonies, were suspended from

their ministry. Wilkins, *Conc.*, vol. iv. pp. 246, 247.

4 Strype's *Parker*, p. 242; Lingard, vol. vi. p. 247.

5 As to Cartwright's views as expressed in his lectures, see Strype's *Annals*, vol. ii. p. 379; and Brooke's *Memoir of Cartwright*, 1845.

6 With an introduction by Cartwright.

memorable by reason of the fact that from it resulted the
immortal work known as the "Laws of Ecclesiastical Polity,"
in which its author met the narrow dogmatism of the Puritan
by arguments based upon the broad principles of moral and
political science as embodied in the eternal obligations of natural law.   In order to imbue the younger clergy as well as
the laity with the ideas which they now aggressively advocated,
the Puritans organized within the church a set of religious
meetings called "prophesyings,"[1] devoted mainly to polemical
discussions, whose participants were required to subscribe a
confession of faith in which they pledged themselves to a general reform of the established system.[2]   For his refusal[3] to
suppress these "prophesyings" Grindal, who with strong
Puritan tendencies had succeeded Parker as primate in 1575,
was sequestered from his see for five years ; which sequestra-
tion was not removed until a short time before his death, which
took place in 1583.   In that year it was that the new archbishop Whitgift, a leader of the orthodox school, began with
the aid of the court of high commission, permanently established not long after his consecration, that systematic attempt
to punish such of the clergy as were imbued with Puritan
principles which finally resulted in the bitter assault upon the
bishops, embodied in the series of pamphlets published under
the pseudonym of Martin Mar-Prelate.[4]   In order to punish
the authors of these Puritan "libels," as they were called,
resort was had to an act,[5] passed in 1581, originally directed
against the seminary priests, in which it was made a capital
felony to "write, print, or set forth any manner of book, rhyme,
ballad, letter, or writing, containing any false or seditious matter to the defamation of the queen's majesty, or the encour-
aging of insurrection or rebellion within the realm."   By a
forced interpretation of the judges, it was held that the libels
in question came within the terms of the act, because they

[Margin notes:]
Hooker's "Ecclesiastical Polity" an answer to Puritan dogmatism ;

the polemical discussions called "prophesyings ;"

Grindal, who refused to suppress them, sequestered ;

succeeded by Whitgift, who proceeded with the aid of the high commission ;

Martin Mar-Prelate tracts ;

forced interpretation put upon the act of 1581 in order to punish Puritan "libellers ;"

---

[1] For a description of these meetings,
named in imitation of the inspired in-
terpretations of Scripture mentioned in
1 Cor. xiv. 31, see Strype's *Life of
Grindal*, p. 325.

[2] Neal's *Hist. of the Puritans*, vol. i.
p. 277.

[3] The queen sent a circular letter to
the bishops, May 7, 1577, commanding
them to put an end to the "prophe-

syings."   Cardwell's *Doc. Annals*, vol.
i. p. 373.   As to Grindal's spirited refusal to obey, see Strype's *Life*, pp.
219, 230, 272.

[4] The first of these were published
in 1588.   Strype's *Whitgift*, p. 288.
For a full account of the whole series,
see Maskell's *Hist. of the Martin Mar-
Prelate Controversy*, 1845.

[5] 23 Eliz. c. 2.

tended to overturn the constitution of the church and the religious supremacy of the queen ; and upon that general theory it was that convictions were obtained against[1] Udal in 1591, and against Greenwood, Barrow, and Penry, in 1593.   By that time, as a result of the defeat of the Spanish Armada, the state church had been strongly reinforced by the adhesion of a large body of moderate Roman Catholics, who, in the hope of another reaction, had until then withheld their allegiance. Thus strengthened, the queen was able to direct a final blow against each of the extreme factions which stood out against the establishment through two acts passed in the parliament that met in 1593.   The one, entitled "An act for restraining popish recusants to some certain places of abode," has been explained already ;[2] the other, entitled "An act to retain the queen's majesty's subjects in their due obedience,"[3] put protestant non-conformists in the same category with "popish recusants," by providing that any person over sixteen who resisted the queen's supremacy, who refused to go to church or persuaded others not to go to church, or who should go to any unlawful conventicle, should be imprisoned until he conformed.   If he failed to conform for three months, he was to abjure the realm, and, after abjuration, if he did not leave, or returned without a license, he was to be guilty of felony without benefit of clergy.[4]

the state church reinforced by the adhesion of many moderate Roman Catholics;

fresh assault made upon recusants and non-conformists by two acts passed in 1593.

5. The great mass of powers and duties cast upon the crown by Elizabeth's assumption of the royal supremacy in matters of religion was materially increased by the enactment of the persecuting statutes just enumerated, through which she attempted to force with equal severity on "popish recusants" and protestant "non-conformists" an acceptance of her ecclesiastical compromise which rested on parliamentary authority. When her father assumed the supremacy, he, in accordance

Court of high commission in causes ecclesiastical:

---

[1] 1 St. Tr. 1271.   This case has an important connection with the beginnings of the law of libel. " Side by side with prosecutions of this kind under special statutes, there were in progress the prosecutions before the star chamber of which I have already given specimens.   It was upon these that Sir E. Coke founded his report of the case *de famosis libellis*." — Stephen, *Hist. of the Crim. Law*, vol. ii. p. 304, citing Coke's *Reports*, pt. v. fol. 125 ; pt. ix. fol. 59, the earliest authorities of any importance upon the law of libel.

[2] See above, p. 167, note 3.

[3] 35 Eliz. c. 1.

[4] "The law relating to protestant dissenters stood thus till the Civil War, being enforced with various degrees of rigour according to the circumstances of the time." — Stephen, *Hist. of the Crim. Law*, vol. ii. p. 478.

Henry
VIII.
governed
the church
first
through
his vicar-
general;

and then
by means
of royal
proclama-
tions and
commis-
sions,
which
for a time
superseded
synodical
canons;

Elizabeth
authorized
by the
Act of
Supremacy
to govern
through
commis-
sions;

the perma-
nent Court
of High
Commis-
sion
created in
1583;

its jurisdic-
tion as
defined
in the com-
mission;

a statutory
limitation
in cases of
heresy;

with papal ideas, had appointed Cromwell as his legate or vicar-general, and in that way exercised his visitorial and reforming powers down to Cromwell's death,[1] after which time every special assertion of the supremacy was executed through commissions.   The general statement may be made that from the humiliation of the clergy through the Act of Submission (1532–33), the actual government of the church passed from convocation to the crown, which asserted its authority by means of injunctions, proclamations, and royal commissions, that for a time superseded synodical canons.[2]   That system of church government carried on by Henry, Edward, and for a time by Mary,[3] was resumed by Elizabeth under the Act of Supremacy,[4] which, after recognizing her as "the only Supreme Governor, . . . as well in all spiritual or ecclesiastical things or causes as temporal," provided that she and her successors should exercise all ecclesiastical jurisdiction, and specially ecclesiastical criminal jurisdiction, through commissioners appointed from time to time under the great seal.[5]   Under that power five high commissions[6] were issued during the first twenty years of the queen's reign, and then in December, 1583, another followed,[7] creating the permanent body afterwards known as "The Court of High Commission in Causes Ecclesiastical."   By the terms of the instrument last named, the forty-four commissioners appointed by it, twelve being bishops, and three a quorum, were authorized "to inquire from time to time during our pleasure, as well by the oaths of twelve good and lawful men, as also by witnesses and all other ways and means you can devise, of all offences" against the acts of Supremacy and Uniformity, and specially as to "all heretical opinions, seditious books, contempts, conspiracies, false rumors or talks, slanderous words and sayings," and the like.   The power to try cases of heresy was limited, however, by a negative provision[8] or definition, which provided that the commis-

---

[1] See above, p. 77.

[2] "When the danger of the immediate crisis had passed away, the convocations of the church were again allowed to issue canons for its government." — Blount, *Reform. of the Church of Eng.*, vol. ii. p. 351.

[3] She issued a general commission February 8, 1556 (Burnet's *Hist. Reform.*, bk. v. p. 469); and one of a special character, February 16, 1556 (Wilkins, *Conc.*, vol. iv. p. 140).

[4] 1 Eliz. c. 1.

[5] §§ 17, 18.

[6] Neal, *Hist. of the Puritans*, vol. i. p. 330.

[7] The text is published by Neal, vol. i. pp. 330–332.

[8] § 36.

sioners "shall not in any wise have authority or power to order, determine, or adjudge any matter or cause to be heresy, but only such as heretofore have been determined, ordered, or adjudged to be heresy by the authority of the canonical scriptures, or by the first four general councils, or any of them, or by any other general council wherein the same was declared heresy by the express and plain words of the said canonical scriptures, or such as hereafter shall be ordered, judged, or determined to be heresy by parliament, with the assent of the clergy in their convocations." By the terms of the commission the commissioners were authorized to administer the hated *ex officio* oath, — the special weapon of the older ecclesiastical courts, whose jurisdiction remained nominally concurrent,[1] — and to punish offenders "by fine, imprisonment, censures of the church, or by all or any of said ways." The commissioners could not, however, inflict the penalty of death, and for that reason Archbishop Whitgift contended that "they ought not to be compared to the inquisition," when Lord Burleigh expressed his disapproval of their procedure as "too much savoring of the popish inquisition."[2] The court thus organized extended its jurisdiction not only to the enforcement of conformity upon all persons, clerical and lay, and to the punishment of clerical improprieties, but also to the punishment of lay immorality.[3] The enforcement of such vast powers through inquisitorial means naturally excited resistance, and an appeal to the courts of common law to restrain the commissioners within bounds. In the course of the legal contest recorded in Coke's Reports, the general nature of the ecclesiastical law,[4] the right of the commissioners to administer the *ex officio* oath,[5] and the right of the law courts to restrain by prohibition and to deliver by habeas corpus[6] persons illegally imprisoned by the high commission, were learnedly expounded. And yet, in spite of such opposition, the powers

authorized to administer the ex officio oath;

but could not impose the death penalty;

punished not only non-conformity and clerical improprieties, but lay immorality;

the conflict with the courts of common law;

---

[1] "The two jurisdictions were concurrent, but the Court of High Commission had, or at all events used, powers which the inferior courts had never claimed." — Stephen, *Hist. of the Crim. Law*, vol. ii. p. 414.

[2] See Burleigh's letter, Neal, *Hist. of the Puritans*, vol. i. p. 339.

[3] A good general statement may be found in Gardiner, *Hist of Eng.*, vol. i. pp. 34, 35.

[4] See the great case of Cawdrey, with the heading *De jure regis ecclesiastico*, 5 Rep. 1, vol. iii. p. xv, ed. of 1826.

[5] 12 Rep. 19, vol. iii. p. 217; 12 Rep. 26, vol. vi. p. 227.

[6] *Roper's Case*, 12 Rep. 47, vol. vi. p. 258; *Charnley's Case*, 12 Rep. 82, vol. vi. p. 309; *Fullers' Case*, 12 Rep. p. 750.

of the court continued practically unimpaired during the reigns of Elizabeth and James, and down to the 16th of Charles I., when it was abolished by the Long Parliament in an act [1] which declared that it had exercised throughout a jurisdiction never conferred by the statute creating it.

abolished by an act of the Long Parliament.

6. However distinct and potent an entity the high commission may have been during the eighty years of its existence, it must not be forgotten that it was simply an agency of the conciliar system, to whose supervision it was subject. The fact has already been emphasized that, despotic and powerful as was the Tudor system of government, the source of its strength was not in a standing army, but in the moral force of the royal authority, which exercised a supervising and directing power over every branch of the administration through the council, whose functions were to a limited extent legislative as well as judicial and political. [2] In order to render its influence all-pervading, the powers of the council were applied to particular subjects through such agencies as the star chamber, the high commission, the court of requests, — a minor court of equity supposed to have had its origin in an order made in the 13th of Richard II., [3] — the court of the president and council of the north, erected by Henry VIII. after the suppression of the great insurrection of 1536, and which — together with the courts of the president of the council of Wales and the Welsh marches, of the duchy of Lancaster, and of the counties palatine of Chester [4] and Durham — is said to have finally deprived one third of England of the privileges of the common law. [5] By Poyning's Act of 1494 the Irish parliament was brought under the control of the council, and in the same

Constitution of the council in the days of Elizabeth:

Tudor system of government drew its strength from the moral force of the royal authority;

the council the great organ of administration;

its agencies;

Ireland, Jersey, and Guernsey controlled by the council;

---

[1] 16 Chas. I. c. 11, A. D. 1640. The nature of the proceedings of the high commission during the last seven years of its existence can best be understood from its act, Books lately printed under the authority of the Master of the Rolls, in the *Calendar of State Papers*, Domestic series, 1633–1640.

[2] See above, pp. 35–37.

[3] Requiring certain members of the council to hear "particular petitions offered by poor persons and those of the king's household." — Reeves' *Hist. of the Eng. Law*, vol. iii. p. 401, Finlason ed. This court, virtually abolished

by a decision of the court of queen's bench in the reign of Elizabeth, was finally dissolved with others of its class by 16 Car. I. c. 10. See Spence, *Eq. Juris.*, vol. i. p. 351; Palgrave, *Original Authority of the King's Council*, pp. 79, 99.

[4] The best and most recent history of these courts may be found in Sir J. F. Stephen's *Hist. of the Crim. Law*, vol. i. pp. 126–135, 138–144, 166, 167, where the fate of each one is fully detailed.

[5] Hallam, *Const. Hist.*, vol. ii. p. 99.

reign Jersey and Guernsey were made subject to its rule.[1]
On grave occasions the crown, through the council, also appointed temporary courts or commissions for the trial of particular offenders, and among them should be noted the courts-
martial, by whose creation the common law could be suspended courts-martial as agents of the council;
by the law martial, an authority originally exercised by the con-
stable and marshal over troops in actual service, and specially
in foreign service.[2]   This system, which could be legitimately
used only in actual war, or in cases of foreign service, was improperly employed in times of peace;
gradually employed by the crown, and specially by Elizabeth,
in sudden emergencies in times of peace, and often for the
suppression of mere breaches of the peace.[3]   The execution of
the vast and far-reaching powers thus cast upon the council as
the Tudor period advanced necessarily involved changes in its
internal constitution which should be noted here.   With the the council gradually transformed from an independent body into a corps of royal officials;
decline of the influence of the nobles as leaders of the nation,
the council, without any change in its outward form, was gradually transformed from an independent body, which stood as a
bridle upon the royal authority, into a mere corps of officials
subject to the king's will and direction.[4]   While the nobles still
retained their hereditary offices, whose diminishing duties were,
as a rule, performed by deputies, the council was continu-
ally reinforced by commoners, who assumed the more active reinforced by common-ers, who assumed the more active duties;
duties ; and thus it was that, during the reigns of Henry VIII.
and Elizabeth, " England was governed, not through peers of
ancient lineage, but through the Cromwells, the Sadlers, the
Petres, and the Cecils, who constituted the glory of the Tudors' rule." [5]   From the picture of the council contained in
the regulations drawn up by Edward VI. in [6] 1553, it appears

---

[1] Dicey, *The Privy Council*, p. 90.
[2] See *Black Book of Admiralty*, vol.
i. p. 282 *et seq.*, as to " Statutes and Ordinances to be kept in time of Warre ; "
and essay as to the " Laws of War," by
Professor M. Bernard, Oxford Essays
for 1856.   For modern expositions of
the law as it now exists, see *Wright* v.
Fitzgerald, 27 St. Tr. 765 ; *R.* v. *Eyre*,
case and opinion, in Forsyth's *Const.
Law*, p. 551 ; Stephen, *Hist. of the Crim.
Law*, vol. i. pp. 207-216.
[3] For such a commission issued in
July, 1595, to Wyllford, authorizing
him as provost-marshal to proceed by
martial law, see *Fœdera*, vol. xvi. p.

279.   As to the case of Burchell, which
occurred in 1573, see Strype's *Annals*,
vol. ii. p. 288.   In that case the council, with great difficulty, persuaded the
queen to permit the case to take the
usual course.
[4] Vol. i. pp. 542-546.
[5] Dicey, *The Privy Council*, p. 86.
[6] Burnet says that the king prepared
" a regulation of the privy council,
which was divided into so. many committees, and every one of these had
its proper work, and days appointed
for the receiving and dispatching of
all affairs." — *Hist. Reform.*, vol. i.
p. 448.   Under the rules of business

that the forty members of whom it was then composed, twenty-two being commoners, were divided into five commissions or committees, to each of which was assigned a definite class of official duties, whose discharge was governed by minute regulations.   The essence of the arrangement was that everything should be brought under the royal eye by the secretary as the channel of communication between the councillors and the king, who was all in all.   Originally, there was but one secretary without rank or influence, the king's clerk, as he was often called until the reign of Henry III., after which time the dignity of the office gradually increased, until the secretary was invariably made a member of the council, in which he took rank with the barons of the realm.[1]   During the reign of Henry VIII. the increasing pressure of business brought about the appointment of two secretaries, both of whom received a signet for the sealing of all warrants and cabinet letters "both inside and outside, as was customary ;" and before the close of that reign, by the Statute of Precedence (31 Hen. VIII. c. 14), they were made members of the council *ex officio*.   In the reign of Elizabeth, Cecil as secretary stands out as the principal officer of the government, and in 1601 the transition was completed when, for the first time, the title of "our principal secretary of estate"[2] was given to his son.   The process has already been drawn out through which the sworn and paid councillors who devoted themselves regularly to the king's business began to be known during the reign of Henry VI. as the privy council, the private or inner circle of the greater body of nobles, lawyers, and others who were only occasionally summoned.[3]   At a later day, by a similar process, the privy council itself was divided into two classes. In the reign of Henry VIII. the occasional councillors, who acted probably as members of particular commissions, generally of a judicial character, were for the first time designated as "ordinary" councillors, to distinguish them from the privy

Marginal notes:

divided into committees, to each of which special duties were assigned ;

origin and growth of the office of secretary ;

become members of the council *ex officio* ;

Robert Cecil becomes "principal secretary of state ;"

the privy council ;

division of its members into two classes ;

---

prescribed by Henry VIII. in 1526 for the privy council (Nicholas, vol. vii. pp. 5–7), twenty were to compose it, ten only of whom were to be in constant attendance upon the king.

[1] Dicey, *The Privy Council*, pp. 83, 84.

[2] "It needed but one step more for them to pass from mere secretaries into Secretaries of State."—Dicey, p. 84.   As to the origin of that office, see judgment of Camden, C. J., in *Entick* v. *Carrington*, 19 St. Tr. 1030 (case as to general warrants); Nicholas, vol. vi. p. 117 *et seq.*

[3] Vol. i. pp. 546, 547.

councillors proper who constituted the inner circle or working body which directed the royal administration as a whole.[1] In that way can be traced the beginnings of that vitally important division between those members of the privy council who hold the title without performing the duties of the office, and that inner working body which, through a set of tacit understandings, has been transformed into the cabinet of modern times.

the inner or working body transformed into the cabinet of modern times.

Having now defined in general terms the constitution of the council, the character of its agencies, and the wide scope of its powers as they existed during the Tudor period, some reference must be made to the manner in which those powers were applied either directly to the punishment of individuals, or to the supervision and direction of the entire state machinery, from parliament itself down to the local self-governing bodies. And here the fact must be kept steadily in view that the council habitually acted in three distinct capacities : as a legislature ; as a law court ; and as an administrative body.[2] At an earlier stage of this work the statement has been made that, while after the organization of the estate system a strenuous effort was made by the national assembly to draw to itself the exclusive exercise of the legislative and taxative functions originally vested in the king and council, it stopped short of complete victory by leaving in the hands of the king in council an undefined residuum of legislative power, which was for a long time exercised in the making of a class of temporary regulations known as ordinances and proclamations. While the principle was firmly established that the permanent and fundamental law of the land, which was the customary law as amended by parliamentary statutes, could be repealed or amended only by the king acting with the consent of the estates, it was equally well settled that without their consent he could make and unmake a set of tentative and temporary enactments with the advice of the council alone.[3] In order to reinforce these acts of the council Henry VIII., whose policy it was to use parliament as his tool, obtained the famous [4] statute giving to his proclamations the full force of law, — an admission that without parliamentary authority they could not possess such force. After the repeal [5] of Henry's statute by Edward's first

The council supervised the entire state machinery and punished individuals directly;

the council a legislature, law court, and administrative body;

the ordaining power of the king in council;

the law of the land which it could not alter;

parliament gave to the proclamations of Henry VIII. the force of law;

---

[1] Dicey, *The Privy Council*, p. 84.
[2] Vol. i. pp. 543, 544.
[3] Ibid., pp. 496, 497.
[4] 31 Hen. VIII. c. 8.
[5] Edw. VI. c. 12.

proclama-
tions con-
tinued to
be issued
after the
repeal of
31 Hen.
VIII. c. 8;
the ordain-
ing power
as exercised
by Mary
and Eliza-
beth;

parliament, the crown fell back upon the old theory of the ordaining power, by virtue of which several proclamations were issued in Edward's reign, notably that issued in 1549, which provided that all "sowers and tellers abroad of forged tales" should be committed by the justices of the peace to the galleys, where they should row in chains as slaves during the king's pleasure.[1] Under Mary, by whom the practice was continued, a proclamation was issued which declared that any one who should have in his possession certain heretical or treasonable books should be regarded as a rebel and executed by martial law.[2] Throughout the reign of Elizabeth the ordaining power of the queen in council was carried to great lengths in a series of proclamations by which all anabaptists were banished from the realm,[3] the culture of woad and the exportation of corn and other articles prohibited, and severe penalties imposed upon all who should erect houses within three miles of London,[4] or who should kill flesh meat in lent.[5] In 1588, in the presence of the Armada, the limit was reached in a proclamation which provided that any person importing or distributing papal bulls or certain prohibited books should be instantly

the practice
contrasted
with the
legal theory.

seized and punished by martial law.[6] Although such was the practice, the legal theory was "that while a proclamation cannot make a law, it can add force to a law already made; that (to use the words of judges living in the reign of Mary) 'the king may make a proclamation *quoad terrorum populi*, to put them in fear of his displeasure, but not to impose any fine, forfeiture, or imprisonment; for no proclamation can make a new law, but only confirm and ratify an ancient one.'"[7] Regardless, however, of this purely legal view as afterwards expressed, the continual effort of the Tudors was to make the council a real legislative body by claiming for proclamations, always issued with its advice, the full force of law.

[1] Strype, vol. ii. p. 149.
[2] Ibid., vol. iii. p. 459.
[3] Three such proclamations were issued by Elizabeth, Lingard, vol. vi. p. 344.
[4] Camden, p. 476.
[5] Strype's *Annals*, vol. i. p. 235.
[6] Ibid., vol. iii. p. 570. It bears date July 1.
[7] See Dicey, *The Privy Council*, pp. 91, 92. This famous judgment was de- livered by Coke and three other judges (12 Rep. 74) at the request of the council in 1610, as to the illegality of royal proclamations prohibiting new build- ings near London, and the making of starch from wheat. See Hallam, *Const. Hist.*, vol. i. pp. 336, 337. The judg- ment was brought about by the re- monstrances made by the commons upon those subjects.

The council when acting as a law court " held its sittings in
the ' Starred Chamber,' an apartment situated in the outer-
most quadrangle of the palace, next to the bank of the river,
and consequently easily accessible to the suitors, and which
at length was permanently appropriated to the use of the
council." [1] To the history of the origin, jurisdiction, and procedure of the star chamber as already set forth [2] but little need
be added here. From the passage of the statute of 3 Hen.
VII. c. 1 to the meeting of the Long Parliament, the invigorated judicial power of the council was so extended as to embrace all matters, great and small, public and private. As a
court of original jurisdiction, it not only claimed the right to
try by its peculiar procedure every class of crimes from sheep-
stealing up to high treason, but it also interfered with rights
of property by taking jurisdiction of civil suits. In addition to
this, it claimed the right to supply the defects of trial by jury
through the exercise of a vigilant supervision over the ordinary law courts, whose proceedings it undertook to control, —
at one time by withdrawing from them a case upon which they
were about to act, at another by summoning before it for fine
and imprisonment a jury whose verdict had been unsatisfactory. [3]
It is not therefore strange that when the press as an instrument for the expression of public opinion came into prominence during the reign of Henry VIII., the star chamber
should have been quick to assume over it a control which soon
ripened into a repressive system. [4] Among its earlier proceedings in that regard may be noted the case of the printer
Grafton, who was imprisoned, as the records show, for having
published certain " invectives," and for having in his possession " a certain seditious epistle, in the English tongue, by
Melancthon." [5] At the instigation of Whitgift the press was
subjected in 1585 to a regular censorship by ordinances of
the star chamber, which undertook its complete regulation in

---

[1] Palgrave, *Essay on the Original Authority of the King's Council*, p. 38.
[2] See above, pp. 25–27.
[3] Dicey, *The Privy Council*, pp. 112, 113; Stephen, *Hist. of the Crim. Law*, vol. i. pp. 169–173.
[4] The censorship of the press was first assumed in England, as in the rest of Europe, by the church, which suf-

fered nothing to be published without the *imprimatur* of the licenser. After the Reformation this high function passed from the church to the state. As a royal prerogative the crown un-dertook to exercise it through the star chamber.
[5] *Proceedings of the Privy Council*, vol. vii. p. 106.

order to prevent the "enormities and abuses of disorderly persons professing the art of printing and selling books."[1]

printing without a special license prohibited; By the restrictions thus imposed every one was prohibited from printing without a special license,[2] and the whole printing trade was put as a monopoly into the hands of ninety-seven

the monopoly known as the Stationers' Company; London stationers, who as the Stationers' Company constituted a guild empowered to seize all publications put forth by outsiders. Nothing was to be printed that had not received the approval of the bishops, while the guild was authorized to search houses in order to destroy books unlawfully printed, and to bring the offenders before the star chamber, which thus became specially charged with the punishment of press offences.

to the star chamber can be traced the beginnings of the law of libel; And so it is that to this source we must go for the beginnings of the law of libel.[3] Apart, however, from the judicial powers which the council thus exercised in its corporate capacity, each

right of individual councillors to order arrests; individual member claimed the right of his own motion to order the arrest and commitment of any of his fellow-citizens who might be deemed obnoxious.[4] So serious did the grievance become during the reign of Elizabeth that the judges,

the remonstrance made by the judges in 1591 against that right; who were much hindered in their attempts to give relief by habeas corpus, presented a joint remonstrance to some of the council in 1591, in which they asked that "order may be taken that her highness' subjects may not be committed or detained in prison, by commandment of any nobleman or councillor, against the laws of the realm, to the grievous charges and oppression of her majesty's said subjects." And yet while the judges thus opposed the right of arrest when asserted by

admission of the right when exercised by the council as a whole. an individual councillor, they seemed to admit its proper exercise directly by the crown, or by the council as a whole, when they said : "We think that, if any person shall be committed by her majesty's special commandment, or by order from the

[1] See Strype's *Whitgift*, p. 222, and App. 94. For the elaborate order made by the star chamber in July, 1637, for the better regulation of the press, see Rushworth, vol. iii. App. 306.

[2] "Side by side with the restrictions on printing — which appear to have more or less broken down — there grew up a system of licensing which constituted a true censorship."— Dicey, *The Law of the Constitution*, p. 247.

[3] "In all ages libels have been se-

verely punished in this court, but most especially they began to be frequent about 42 & 43 Eliz. when Sir Edward Coke was her attorney-general."— Hudson, pp. 100–104, "Treatise on the Star Chamber," in *Collectanea Juridica*, vol. ii. As to the control exercised over the press from that time down to the Restoration, see Odgers, *Libel and Slander*, pp. 10, 11.

[4] Dicey, *The Privy Council*, p. 116.

council board, or for treason touching her majesty's person, . . . which causes being generally returned into any court, is good cause for the same court to leave the person committed in custody." [1]

As an administrative body, the council exercised a multiplicity of functions, the chief of which related to the management of the finances, the regulation of commerce, including the intercourse with foreign merchants, the supervision of the church, and the preservation of the peace.[2] And when the destiny of England widened through the planting of colonies in the New World by adventurers who derived their right to the soil from charters granted by the crown and not by the parliament, the council was called upon to assume still another vitally important branch of administration. The governing power in the colony was usually vested in a local legislature, limited by the charter, which sat as a subordinate body subject to the control of the king in council, to whom all contested matters passed in the last resort.[3] In the home land the council likewise undertook to supervise, and to a certain extent control, every branch of the political administration, from parliament itself down to the local self-governing bodies. Out of its attempts to interfere with the proceedings of parliament during the reign of Elizabeth grew the memorable struggle between the conciliar and parliamentary systems, which will be made the subject of special treatment. In the same way it will be convenient to consider separately the relations of the council with the system of local administration which, during the Tudor period, entered upon a marked and rapid development.

As an administrative body the council controlled the finances, commerce, the church, and the public peace;

also the affairs of the colonies;

and to a certain extent all branches of political administration at home.

7. Nothing is more difficult for the student of English constitutional history than to grasp with all its complicated details the process through which the local self-governing communities were gradually developed by the growth of the nation from their ancient to their modern form. And yet the

Development of local institutions:

[1] Such is the text of an original MS. in the British Museum (Lansdowne MSS., lviii. 87) adopted by Hallam (*Const. Hist.*, vol. i. pp. 234–236) in preference to the printed text of Anderson's *Reports*, vol. i. p. 297. As to the presentation of a MS. continuing Chief Justice Anderson's resolution in his own handwriting by his heirs to Sir John Eliot at the opening of the third parliament of Charles I., see Gardiner, *Hist. Eng.*, vol. vi. p. 244.

[2] For an elaboration of its jurisdiction over these four subjects, see Dicey, *The Privy Council*, pp. 53–68.

[3] Vol. i. pp. 15–48.

difficulties which surround the inquiry do not exceed its im-

England an
aggregation
of local,
self-govern-
ing com-
munities;
portance. The starting-point of every effort to solve these difficulties should consist of a clear comprehension of the fact that the consolidated kingdom of England is a mere aggrega- tion of shires, local administrative districts divided into hun- dreds, which, in their turn, are subdivided into townships,

the town-
ship became
involved
in several
distinct
relations,
from each
of which it
derived a
new title;
generally known in modern times as parishes.[1] The history of the smallest local subdivision, "the unit of the constitu- tional machinery," is specially difficult and involved by reason of the fact that the township has been called upon to act in several distinct capacities, from each of which is derived a new title. In order to escape the confusion which thus arises, the following facts must be kept steadily in view : (1) that

the village
community
as the tun or
township;
the village community, the unit of organization throughout the Aryan world, which appeared in Britain as the tun or *town- ship*, ordered its village and agricultural life through the action of the town meeting (tun-moot), a body which elected the town officers, provided for the representation of the town in the assemblies of the hundred and shire, and regulated the internal affairs of the township by the making of by-laws ;[2] (2) that the administration of the primitive police system based upon the peace-pledge (*frithborh*), which devolved first upon the family group (*maegth*), and then upon the artificial politi-

the town-
ship as the
tithing;
cal association called the tithing, was finally cast upon the township, when the personal division known as the tithing became territorial. (In that way the police duties, for a time exercised by the tithing as a personal association, passed to the township as a territorial district ; and, except in some of the western counties, even the name of *the tithing* is lost in

the town-
ship as the
manor;
that of the township) ;[3] (3) that as the process of feudalization advanced, the township became dependent upon a superior lord, and as such it was known after the Conquest as *the manor* of the lord, and in that way a large part of the jurisdiction origi-

the mano-
rial court;
nally vested in the tun-moot passed to the manorial court, known as the court-baron, whose criminal side is the manorial

the town-
ship as the
parish;
court-leet ;[4] (4) that with the advent of Christianity the town- ship as the primary political division of the state was, as a rule, adopted by the church as the district which should define the

---

[1] Vol. i. pp. 170-173.   Ibid., pp. 196-198.
[2] Ibid., pp. 101, 102, 143.   [4] Ibid., pp. 144, 210, 253, 266.

jurisdiction of a single priest.   Thus it was that the ancient township, regarded ecclesiastically, came to be known as *the parish*, and the meetings of the members of the parish for church purposes, usually held in the vestry, came to be known as vestry meetings.   In that way the township became so involved with the parish, and the meeting of the township for church purposes became so involved with the meeting of the vestry, that in small parishes the idea and even the name of the township is frequently lost in that of the parish.[1]   And so it came to pass that the territorial district originally known as the township was finally designated in every-day language as the parish ; while the self-governing powers originally vested in the tun-moot passed to the parish vestry, with the exception of such as were absorbed by the manorial courts.   With the decay of the feudal fabric the manorial courts have gradually passed out of view,[2] until such as survive may be regarded as mere archaisms.   On the other hand, the parochial system, vitalized by a scheme of legislation enacted during the Tudor period, which imposed upon the parish important political functions, has survived through their exercise as a fundamental institution of the state.

Some account must therefore be given of the composite machinery of the modern parish,[3] and of the manner in which it has been applied first to church and then to state purposes. In the broad ecclesiastical sense, all inhabitants [4] of the parish, all embraced in the cure of souls, are members of it ; but in a narrower and more practical sense, those only are parishioners who bear their share of the public burdens by the payment of money or by the performance of personal services.[5]   In the ecclesiastical sense, the head of the parish is the parson, and, if he does not own the tithes, the vicar ;[6] and in the same sense,

[margin notes: the parish vestry; the township generally known as the parish; which survives as a fundamental institution of the state. The composite machinery of the parish: who are members of it; the rector as its ecclesiastical head;]

---

[1] Vol. i. pp. 143, 144, and notes.

[2] The business of the courts-leet was transferred to the quarter sessions.

[3] The highest authority upon the whole subject is Toulmin Smith's *The Parish, its Powers and Obligations at Law*, in which the origin of the parish, the scope of its influence, the character of its officers, its capacity to raise rates and taxes, and to apply them to parish purposes are fully set forth.

[4] " The actual common law test of being a parishioner, and being bound, therefore, as well as entitled, to be upon the Roll, is — the being an inhabitant." — Smith, *The Parish*, p. 473.   For a definition of "inhabitancy," see Ibid., note 2, giving the authorities.

[5] In other words, " bearing *lot* and paying *scot*."   " By the common law, all the parishioners who pay *scot* and *lot* have a right to be of the vestry."— *Berry* v. *Banner*, 1 Peake, 161.

[6] In a civil sense he is not an inte-

church-
wardens
as parish
officers;

the assistants of the incumbent are two church-wardens, immemorially elected by the parishioners as "of common right," [1]
and for that reason recognized by the courts as officers of the
parish and not of the patron.[2]   To the parishioners belongs the
right to remove the church-wardens,[3] and to appoint others in
their stead ; [4] and to the church-wardens and not to the incum-

their right
to summon
the vestry
meeting,

bent belongs the right to summon the vestry meeting,[5] over
which the parson presides by courtesy due to his ecclesiastical
headship.   In such meetings, according to the ancient custom
preserved in the courts-leet and in the parliamentary elections,

in which
every per-
son present
has an
equal right
to vote;

all questions are decided by vote, which each person present
has an equal right to cast, and which is taken either by a show
of hands or, in case of doubt, by a division.[6]   The decision of
the majority [7] has the binding force of law expressed in the

origin of
the right
to make
by-laws;

form of by-laws, the right to make which passed from the tun-
moot to the parish vestry as well as to the manorial court-
leet.[8]   By the making of by-laws the parish vestry, according
to Lord Coke, provides for the discharge of its legal duties,
whether "for the reparation of the church, or a highway, or of

right of the
parish to
levy taxes
begins with
the imposi-
tion of the
church rate;

any such thing which is for the general good of the public." [9]
Thus the parish vestry regulated the imposition of the church
rate, through which was collected the sum necessary for maintaining and beautifying the church building after the third

---

gral part of the parish, has no voice in
the election of church-wardens, and has
no right to preside at parish meetings.
As to his true relations to the parish
as a secular institution, see Smith, *The
Parish,* pp. 292, 297, 324, 327.

[1] "If the incumbent chooses one in
any place, it is but by usage." — Cases
temp. Hardwicke, p. 275.   And the
usage must be proven prior to 1603.
Smith, pp. 73–77, 86.

[2] Strange's *Reports,* p. 715.

[3] *Year-Books,* 26 Hen. VIII. fol. 5.

[4] *Year-Books,* 8 Edw. IV. fol. 6.

[5] 1 Mod. Rep. 236.   "The parson
never summons the vestries, that being
the office of the church-wardens." —
Strange's *Reports,* p. 1045.

[6] Smith, *The Parish,* pp. 60–62, 483–
485.   Note the objections of the author to polling.

[7] After due summons "the major
part of them that appear may bind the
parish." — 1 Mod. Rep. 236.

[8] It has often been declared by all
the judges that "those in a *Leet* can
make bye-laws, and their own assent
shall bind them.   And a *Parish* can
make bye-laws, and these shall bind
them."   Toulmin Smith has collated
all the authorities upon this all-important point.   See pp. 47–51, 134, 238,
note, 584–586, 608.   Dr. Gneist (*Const.
Hist.,* p. 529, note 4) contends that
Toulmin Smith errs in "the overesti-
mation of the parochial autonomy.
The right of making their own by-
laws and the right of self-taxation only
existing in England for objects and
purposes, which were entailed upon
the parish by law as a common obligation."   It may be safely said that the
great German jurist errs in the opposite direction.

[9] "And in such case the greater part
shall bind the whole, without any custom." — 5 Rep. 63 a.

part of the tithes originally set apart for that object had been diverted to other purposes. Originally, the church rate was a voluntary contribution,[1] which finally became enforceable by the church courts through the imposition of spiritual penalties with which the temporal tribunals were forbidden to interfere.[2] To obviate difficulties of that character, it became the custom for the church-wardens to impose the church rate as a common burden upon the parish after the consent of the parishioners had been obtained through consultation.[3] Thus it was that while the commons were establishing the right to grant taxes to the state after deliberation in parliament, the parishioners were establishing a similar right to grant contributions to the church after deliberation in their parish assemblies. From the beginning the church rate was a personal one, assessed upon the Christian household according to the extent of its visible profitable property in the parish of whatever character, a burden which was also extended to those living outside of the parish, according to the extent of their landed property within it.[4] Upon this liability to contribute to the parish taxes as evidenced by the parish registers rested the status of the parishioner and his right to vote in the parish assembly.[5] Such was the general character of the parochial constitution at the time the Tudor monarchy laid hands upon it, as the natural instrument to be employed, when, by the dissolution of the monasteries, the care of the poor so long maintained by the church was suddenly cast upon the state.

originally a voluntary contribution;

afterwards imposed by the wardens as a common burden, after consultation;

parochial and parliamentary taxation compared;

the basis of parochial taxation;

upon the liability to contribute, as evidenced by the parish register, rested the status of the parishioner.

[1] It was not a common law obligation, nor a charge on land. Smith, *The Parish*, pp. 582, 586.

[2] Gneist, *Const. Hist.*, p. 518, supported by Watson (*Clergyman's Law*, 1725, p. 642), who says "the cognizance of Rates made for reparation of churches and church yards belongs to the spiritual courts; and protestations have often been denied." Smith, however, denies the jurisdiction, pp. 317, 318, 595, note.

[3] "A church rate is good, not because it is a church rate, but because it is made under a bye-law passed in due form, by an institution of local self-government." — Ibid., p. 586. The first mention of what was afterwards known as the church rate occurs in the *Year-Books* of 44 Edw. III., where it is referred to as a custom in a single parish.

[4] Jeffery's case, 5 Coke's Reports, 66, 67. In that case it was declared that it is "not where a man eats or sleeps or lies, that makes him a parishioner," but where he puts forth effort, — "by that he is resident."

[5] "It is the business of the proper officers to take care that every man occupying within the parish is on the parish books. He is there as a responsible man. Being there, he comes under obligations to contribute to all local rates and other burdens. Being there he is a parishioner, and has a common right to a voice at every meeting of parishioners." — Smith, *The Parish*, pp. 63, 64.

During the Middle Ages the church provided for the poor by means of tithes;

As heretofore pointed out, the church during the Middle Ages derived the means that it devoted to the maintenance of the helpless from tithes which were applied, according to ancient usage, one third to the maintenance of the church building, one third to the clergy, and one third to the poor.[1] While the church thus assumed the positive obligation of providing for the indigent, the state assumed only the negative duty of preventing begging and vagrancy, a duty which was discharged through a series of cruel statutes, already enumerated,[2] which extend from the reign of Edward III. to that of George IV. The general obligation which in early times devolved upon the church as a whole became at a later day the special business of the monasteries, not only by reason of the duty of hospitality and almsgiving,[3] one of the main objects of their foundation, but also because, as impropriators[4] of parochial benefices, they had become possessed of a large portion of the tithes. When, therefore, the church system of poor relief, which the monasteries had dispensed with perhaps a too lavish hand, was abolished by their dissolution, the state was forced to meet an obligation made the more pressing by reason of the transition then setting in from feudal to free labor, which greatly increased the distress of the laboring classes.[5] The first positive assumption of the duty was embodied in 27 Hen. VIII. c. 25,[6] whereby the incorporated towns, hundreds, and parishes were charged with the putting to labor of all such indigent persons as were able to work, and of receiving and supporting all such as were unable, by means to be collected for that purpose as alms on Sundays, holidays, and other festivals, or otherwise from the people. It was further provided that indiscriminate almsgiving should be forbidden, and that "valiant and sturdy beggars" refusing to work should be punished. The duty of making the collections on Sundays was cast primarily upon the church-wardens, who, with two others of the

the state undertook only to punish begging and vagrancy;

care of the poor became the special business of the monasteries;

their dissolution finally cast the duty upon the state;

first assumed by 27 Hen. VIII. c. 25,

which provided only for voluntary contributions;

duty of the church-wardens;

---

[1] See above, p. 97, and note 3.

[2] See above, p. 98, note 1.

[3] See the declarations upon that subject in the Statute of Carlisle, 35 Edw. I.

[4] After the Reformation impropriations of benefices often passed from the crown to favored laymen. Sir H. Spelman (*Of Tythes*, ch. xxix.) says "they are called impropriations, for they are improperly in the hands of laymen."

[5] See above, p. 121.

[6] As to the prior statutes of 11 Hen. VIII. c. 2; 19 Hen. VII. c. 12; and 22 Hen. VIII. c. 12, for the correction of begging and vagrancy, see Reeves' *Hist. Eng. Law*, vol. iii. pp. 134, 258, Finlason ed.

parish,[1] were to provide work for the capable and help for the incapable. By 5 & 6 Edw. VI. c. 2 it was provided that the contributors should be called upon at a particular time to put down in writing how much they would give during the following year, and if any should be obstinate, the clergy were to exhort them. The radical defect in the system thus established was, of course, its voluntary character, to remedy which was passed 5 Eliz. c. 3, empowering justices of the peace to assess an unwilling contributor who had been exhorted in vain, and to coerce him if necessary by imprisonment, a power enlarged and perfected by 14 Eliz. c. 5, which led to the taxation of every parishioner.[2] Then followed 18 Eliz. c. 3,[3] and the far more comprehensive statute of 39 Eliz. c. 3, of which the great act of 43 Eliz. c. 2 is but an amplification in a permanent form. Upon the foundations laid by this last and great act of 1601 the English system of poor relief has rested for nearly three centuries. The three great principles settled by this act were: (1) that every parish was to be primarily responsible for the maintenance of its own poor, and not for the poor of other parishes; persons who could not or would not work were to remain in the parish in which they were born, or in which they had lived for the last three years; (2) that the means for the maintenance of the poor was to be provided by a parochial tax, to be imposed upon the landed property of the parish by parish officers as a general and uniform burden; (3) the administration of the system was to be vested in the church-wardens, and in two, three, or four substantial householders, to be appointed annually by justices of the peace as "overseers" of the poor. It was made the legal duty of the church-wardens and overseers "to raise the necessary sums by the assessment of every inhabitant, incumbent, vicar, and others, and every owner of lands, houses, and tithes,"[4] and out of the poor rate thus collected they were

[marginal notes] 5 & 6 Edw. VI. c. 2; compulsory contributions inaugurated by Elizabeth; the great act of 39 Eliz. c. 3, upon which the English system of poor relief has since rested; a parochial tax imposed as a general and uniform burden; how assessed; how applied;

---

[1] "The persons thus alluded to were chosen by the parish, in vestry assembled, and fulfilled their charge subject to the supervision of the parish."— Smith, *The Parish*, p. 145.

[2] Reeves' *Hist. Eng. Law*, vol. iii. p. 603.

[3] This ordained that a stock should be provided in order to set the poor at work in every city and incorporated town.

[4] "Thus arises a complete fixed tax, which was destined to become the basis of all parochial taxation."— Gneist, *Hist. of the Eng. Const.*, p. 524 (Ashworth trans.). "The creation of the church rate in Elizabeth's law is the fusion of the former attempts into a

(1) to care for the impotent and aged, the lame, the blind, and all other poor persons unable to work, and who had neither parents nor children to maintain them; (2) and to provide work for the able-bodied poor, who were unable to procure it for themselves. In order to carry out the first purpose, they were authorized to build a separate poor-house for the impotent poor of the parish, while to facilitate the second they were to supply a sufficient amount of flax, hemp, and other stuffs in order to afford employment to those willing to work, the unwilling being subject to removal to a work-house or prison. Of the execution of their trust the church-wardens and overseers[1] were required to give an account at the end of each year to two justices of the peace, after the new overseers were appointed. The vitally important feature of the system which has so long endured was the legally established poor rate, which as a burden upon real property has become the basis of all parochial taxation.

poor-houses;

work-houses;

the poor rate the basis of all parochial taxation.

While the organizing hand of the Tudor monarchy was thus fixing upon the parish the statutory duty of caring for the poor, it did not neglect to provide in the same way a more efficient system for maintaining the public highways, for which the parish was already responsible. From the earliest times, as we have heretofore pointed out, a threefold obligation, known as the *trinoda necessitas*,[2] was originally imposed upon all people,[3] regardless of the holding of land, which consisted, in addition to military service for the defence of the state, of services for the building of roads, bridges, and fortresses, — the peace duties of the local militia which came to be known as the *posse comitatus*. With the growth of feudal ideas the performance of these duties, which were at first purely personal, was imposed upon the holding of all land by freemen as a necessary burden.[4] This obligation of keeping the roads and bridges in repair, which was for a long time enforced as the

The parish and the public highways;

the trinoda necessitas, originally a personal obligation,

finally imposed upon the holding of all land by freemen;

---

uniform system." — Ibid., note (c). For a detailed history of the poor rate, see Smith, *The Parish*, pp. 28–31, 144, 145, 451, 576, 597–604.

[1] They were required to meet at least once a month in the parish church on Sunday, in order to consult as to the current work.

[2] Vol. i. p. 133.

[3] *Essays in A. S. Law*, p. 61.

[2] Digby, *Law of Real Property*, p. 22. "Highways, bridges, and military defence constituted the threefold conditions (*trinoda necessitas*) always inseparably attached to the tenure of land, which even religious endowments could not evade." — Smith, *The Parish*, p. 205.

special care of the sheriff's toun and leet,[1] was finally so apportioned that the burden of maintaining the highways devolved alone upon the parish, while the more general duty of building and repairing bridges passed to the county as a whole. In order to clearly define the duty last named was passed the statute [2] of bridges (22 Hen. VIII. c. 5), whereby the burden of contributing to their maintenance was cast upon all householders, whether landowners or not, and upon all real estates, whether their owners lived in the county or not. As all inhabitants, regardless of the holding of land, used the roads, the duty of maintaining them was cast upon all as a common law obligation,[3] enforceable by the old Norman practice of fines and amercements imposed under indictments presentable either in the courts of assize or greater sessions. In order to render more efficient a system that depended in the main upon the power to punish the delinquent parish by indictment was passed, in aid of the common law, the statute of 2 & 3 Phil. & Mar. c. 8, which created the offices of surveyors of highways,[4] whose incumbents were electable by the parish, and whose special duty it was to keep the roads in repair through services which they were authorized to exact in kind from all parishioners, according to a scheme that imposed a certain part of the labor upon every possessor of an acre of land, upon every owner of a team or plough, and upon every other inhabitant able to work who was not in a domestic relation of annual service.[5] And when the labor in kind thus provided did not suffice, the parish could escape an indictment for roads badly kept [6] only by bearing a highway rate assessed as a supplementary tax by the justices of the peace.[7] And so, before the Tudor period ended, the parish, in addition to the

the parishes maintain the roads, the counties the bridges; the statute of bridges (22 Hen. VIII. c. 3);

common law obligation to maintain the roads enforced against the parish by indictment;

surveyors of highways created by 2 & 3 Phil. & Mar. c. 8;

a highway rate assessed by justices of the peace;

---

[1] It was the duty of the constable to see that each landowner fulfilled this condition of his tenure, and to report his failure to the court-leet. Smith, *The Parish*, p. 105, and notes.

[2] This act was simply declaratory of the common law obligation, which required that all bridges should be repaired by the whole county as "of common right." — Coke, 2 Inst. 701. As to the effect of 43 Geo. III. c. 59 upon the liability, see *R. v. Wilts*, 1 Salkeld, 359.

[3] Coke, 2 Inst. 700.

[4] Two persons were to be chosen for one year "as surveyors and orderers."

[5] For a full discussion of the act, see Smith, *The Parish*, pp. 106–108. The act was renewed by 5 Eliz. c. 13, for twenty years, and by 29 Eliz. c. 5 was made perpetual. See also 18 Eliz. c. 10.

[6] Dalton, *Justice*, c. 26.

[7] See Gneist, *Hist. of the Eng. Const.*, pp. 526, note (3), 530, and 643.

church rate in reference to which it had a constitutional right to be consulted, became subject to a poor rate and to a supplementary highway rate.[1]   The former, imposed by the churchwardens and overseers of the poor, was expended under the supervision of the justices of the peace ; the latter, assessed by the justices, was expended under the immediate supervision of the surveyors of highways whom the parish elected.   The most important change which then ensued in the parochial constitution as thus reorganized — a change that made its mark upon the local institutions of the new world — was that through which

the open vestry gradually hardened into a close corporation known as the select vestry.

the powers originally vested in the open vestry, composed of all parishioners, gradually passed to a committee or council of that body which, under the name of a select vestry, hardened into a close corporation that filled all vacancies in its own ranks by coöptation.[2]

Development of the system of county administration ;

As a part of the development which took place during this period in the parochial constitution should be noted here the coincident growth in the system of county administration, to whose supervision and control the parishes were subordinate in almost every particular.   The progressive element in the

justices of the peace ;

county constitution was the office of justice of the peace, whose history has been heretofore reviewed down to the point

in their courts of quarter sessions, try all lesser offences originally punished in the courts-leet ;

at which the justices, fully armed with judicial powers, hold regular courts known as quarter sessions, in which as police magistrates they try, with the aid of juries, all the lesser offences which, in the period following the Conquest, had been presented and tried in the courts-leet.   In that way the criminal and police jurisdiction of the manorial courts, excepting the view of frank-pledge,[3] was, through the rise of justices of the peace, gradually transferred to the quarter sessions which try

all serious offences reserved for the courts of assize ;

"petty larcenies and misdemeanors " only, while trials of all serious offences are reserved for the courts of assize.[4]   The high constables originally appointed at the courts-leet of the hundred or franchise, in default of an election in that way, are

---

[1] "The personal service nominally continued, as to highways, under the name of statute duty, until the present Highway Act was passed in 1835.   It was regularly compounded for, however, on what were called 'composition days.'   *The whole is now commuted to a rate*," and is levied by the highway surveyors, the elected officers of the parish. — Smith, *The Parish*, p. 566, and notes.

[2] Cf. vol. i. p. 37, and notes.

[3] "A manorial right exercised in the courts-leet, where it still exists." — Stubbs, *Const. Hist.*, vol. i. p. 88.

[4] Vol. i. pp. 452–454.

appointed by the justices at their quarter sessions,[1] a practice which has been extended to the appointment of the petty constables as well.[2]   From the right of appointment naturally followed the right of dismissal, and in that way the quarter sessions acquired full control over all local police officers, including even the coroners themselves.[3]   Thus deprived of every important function, the courts-leet withered and became obsolete in the shade of the quarter sessions, just as the ancient county courts, after having their powers transferred to the courts of assize, withered into that theoretical existence which they have preserved to the present day.[4]   The court of quarter sessions must be viewed, however, not simply as a police court, but rather as the supreme administrative body of the county, constituted by the crown for the supervision and direction of the limited system of local self-government which the parishes were permitted to enjoy.   The supervisory power of the quarter sessions — which by 43 Eliz. c. 2, s. 6, was declared to be a general court of appeal for "all persons who feel themselves aggrieved by any action or neglect of the church-wardens or overseers of the poor" — really extended to nearly every branch of the parochial administration.   While the church-wardens as church officers were accountable only to the ecclesiastical parish,[5] as administrators of the poor rate they were directly accountable to the justices of the peace, who appointed the overseers as their colleagues, who examined their accounts, who settled all appeals against the rating, who assessed other parishes in the hundred when any one parish was unable to make the necessary provision;[6] in fine, who supplied all the coercive authority necessary for the enforcement of the poor-law system.   Over the management of highways the justices exercised a similar control through the statutory

the quarter sessions control the local police system; courts-leet become obsolete;

the quarter sessions as the supreme administrative body of the county; made a general court of appeal by 43 Eliz. c. 2, s. 6;

the justices supervise the poor-law system,

and the management of highways.

---

[1] Vol. i. p. 454.

[2] The right of the courts-leet to chose parish constables was taken away in 1842 by 5 & 6 Vict. c. 109, s. 21. As to the ancient mode of appointment by the courts-leet, see Sir Thomas Smith, *The Commonw. of Eng.* (1621), bk. ii. c. 12.

[3] By 1 Hen. VIII. c. 7, the magistrates were authorized to punish the coroners for breach of duty.

[4] Vol. i. pp. 320, 321, and notes. In theory and as matter of law, both the ancient county courts and the courts-leet still exist. "Every man was formerly, and still legally is, bound to attend the court-leet." — Smith, *The Parish*, p. 216.

[5] The church courts had no jurisdiction over the settlement of a church-warden's account. Strange's *Reports*, pp. 974, 1133.

[6] Upon all these points, see Toulmin Smith, *The Parish*, pp. 146, 151, 158, 579.

power to fix the working days for the repair of the roads,[1] and through the imposition of the supplementary highway tax, which, like the bridge rate, was levied upon the same basis as the poor rate. The primary agent, then, of the Tudor admin- istrative system was the invigorated parish, which discharged its functions under the supervision and control of the county government as represented by the quarter sessions of the jus- tices of the peace, who were appointed by the crown, and who could be summarily punished by it, either by dismissal, or through the corrective jurisdiction over the abuses of office as exercised in the star chamber.[2]

Tudors strength- ened the control of central over local admin- istration.

In connection with the system of county administration must also be mentioned the reorganization, which took place during the Tudor period, of the county militia, the national force, whose existence is clear from the earliest times. In the review heretofore made of the military system as it existed after the Conquest, the conclusion was reached that as suc- cessors of the Old-English kings the Norman and Angevin rulers retained the right to summon, under the command of the sheriffs, the ancient constitutional force of the shire, while as feudal lords they gained through the growth of tenures the right to call upon the feudal array to perform the military service due from their lands.[3] To the army thus made up of feudal and national elements were sometimes added mercenary soldiers, whom the Norman kings employed from the begin- ning. As the primary and normal duty of the county militia was that of national defence, the crown was forced to rely mainly upon the feudal array for military service abroad or in the border wars against Wales and Scotland. And yet the very nature of that service implied long campaigns, with which the short-time service due from the feudal array was incompatible. The need thus created for mercenary soldiers, whose services could be controlled as long as they were required, led to the commutation of personal service for the money payment called

Tudors reorganized the militia;

the Norman host composed of both feudal and national elements;

mercenary soldiers sometimes added; primary duty of the militia national defence; feudal array and mili- tary service abroad;

---

[1] See 5 Eliz. c. 13; 29 Eliz. c. 5.

[2] "As the local officials were in all matters made responsible to the ma- gistrates, so also by the subordination of the office of justice of the peace to the central administration, that unity in the administrative system was at- tained, which in the continental states was only technically developed some- what later by the formation of a ' Staatsrath ' and ' Behördensystem ' for the provincial and district govern- ment." — Gneist, *Hist. of the Eng. Const.*, p. 531.

[3] Vol. i. p. 296.

scutage, an anti-feudal device, whereby a fund for the hiring of mercenaries was provided.[1]   In addition to that blow at the feudal array, by the breaking up of the great estates which the process of subinfeudation steadily advanced, the great lords were gradually deprived of their military followings, whose numbers originally depended upon the extent of their territorial possessions.[2]   In spite, however, of both assaults the feudal element was able to nourish and maintain itself as the most powerful military force in the state by an artificial process of adoption, which consisted of the giving of their liveries by the baronial houses not only to the smaller gentry and farmers of the neighborhood, but also to the vagrant or the outlaw who was willing to swell the retinue of the great man and to wear his livery, in consideration of his maintenance and protection.[3]   Through the artificial vassalage which thus grew up the great baronial leaders were surrounded after the French wars began by standing companies of trained and liveried soldiers, who stood to their chief in a relation which substantially reproduced that embodied in the *comitatus*[4] of earlier times. With the feudal array thus reconstituted the crown soon entered into new relations through a series of contracts, which appear in the archives in great numbers from the time of Edward III., and in which the great lords undertook to furnish greater or smaller bands at a daily rate per man which varied according to rank.[5]   Of the superior efficiency of these trained bands in foreign warfare there can be no doubt, but the difficulty was that when such warfare ended, the military households of the baronial chiefs became hotbeds of a lawless spirit of disorder, ever ready to overawe not only the law courts and the parliament, but even to defy the king himself.[6]   By this condition of things was fostered the two rival parties which for so long a time involved the realm in the dynastic struggle carried on under the opposing banners of York and Lancaster. It is not therefore strange that at the close of the War of the Roses, during which the strength of the feudal element was

such service commuted for the money payment called scutage;

how the great lords were deprived of their military followings;

an artificial vassalage created;

livery and maintenance;

the crown contracts with the feudal array as reconstituted;

the new military households become hotbeds of disorder;

the system of liveries extinguished by Henry VII.;

---

[1] Vol. i. p. 284.
[2] Ibid., pp. 412, 413, 566.
[3] Ibid., pp. 566, 567.
[4] Ibid., pp. 110, 111.
[5] Cf. Grose's *Military Antiquities*, vol. i. p. 71 *seq*. As to the extant muster-roll of the English army which besieged

Calais, giving every detail as to the pay of the different classes of soldiers, see Brady, vol. iii. App. No. 92. See also several contracts in *Fœdera*, vol. ix. pp. 227–239.

[6] Vol. i. p. 567.

well-nigh exhausted, the house of Tudor, which rose triumphant as the one dominant force in the state, should have addressed itself as a primary duty to the final extinction of the
system of liveries, by which the peace of the realm and the
authority of the crown had been for so long a time imperilled.[1]
So fully was that end accomplished during the reign of Henry

*by the end
of his reign
the feudal
array
practically
abolished.*

VII. that at the accession of his son the old feudal arrays were
in practice abolished,[2] leaving as the only armed force in the
realm [3] the national militia, whose reorganization thus became
an imperative necessity.

*Henry II.'s
Assize of
Arms
reviving
and
rearming
the county
militia;*

The statement has heretofore been made that the natural
supplement to Henry II.'s assault upon the feudal array
through the institution of scutage was his Assize of Arms,
whereby the old constitutional force of the shire was revived
and rearmed by the imposition of the duty upon every freeman to provide himself with weapons according to his means.[4]
In order to insure the performance of that duty, the itinerant
justices were required to ascertain by the oaths of local jurors
the value of the rents and chattels of all freemen, who were
then enrolled in classes according to the nature of the arms
which the estate of each compelled him to provide.[5]   The lists
were then read in open court, where all were required to swear
that they would provide themselves with the proper arms
within a given time, and that they would be loyal to the king.[6]

*the system
of Watch
and Ward;*

By that time the ancient system for the security of the peace
embodied in the ancient *frithborh* (incorrectly translated by
the Norman lawyers into *frank-pledge*) had become so inadequate that it was necessary to supplement it by a new arrangement known as Watch and Ward, whereby the duty of keeping
watch from sunset to sunrise was imposed, in every city, borough, and township, upon companies whose numbers depended

---

[1] See above, pp. 24, 25.
[2] The feudal array, summoned for
the last time by Charles I. to serve in
his expedition of 1640 against the
Scots, was extinguished by 12 Charles
II. c. 24, abolishing military tenures.
[3] From that statement must be excepted the small body-guard of household troops maintained by Henry VII.
and Henry VIII., a force which never
numbered more than two hundred, and
the garrisons kept at the Tower of

London, Portsmouth, the castle of
Dover, the fort of Tilbury, and before the union, at Berwick and a few
other places on the Scottish border.
Cf. Macaulay, *Hist. Eng.*, vol. i. p.
20; Hallam, *Const. Hist.*, vol. ii. p
131.
[4] Vol. i. pp. 284, 312.
[5] Ibid., p. 298.
[6] For the assize, see Benedictus, vol
i. p. 278; Hoveden, vol. ii. p. 261.

upon that of the inhabitants. This system, whose structure was clearly defined in 1233, was twenty years later strength-ened and perfected through a union with the county militia as reorganized under the Assize of Arms, which was at that time renewed.[1] In order to render the militia more effective for the protection of internal peace, it was ordered that those who were required to provide themselves with arms should be placed under the command of the civil authorities : in the cities and boroughs under the mayor and bailiffs ; in each township under the constable ; the whole being subjected to the higher command of the chief constable of the hundred. All were to join the hue and cry[2] when required, and none except those charged with the preservation of the peace were to bear arms. Then in the reign of Edward I. the whole scheme, both in its police and military aspects, was still further developed by the Statute of Winchester, which "may be re-garded as representing the sum of the series of documents, touching the Assize of Arms and Watch and Ward."[3] By reason of attempts made during the reigns of Edward I. and Edward II. to constrain individuals to furnish equipments at their private cost,[4] and to compel the county force thus bound only to national defence and the preservation of the peace to perform service abroad, a serious opposition arose, which brought about in the first year of Edward III. the enactment of a statute which provided "that no man from henceforth should be charged to arm himself otherwise than he was wont in the time of the king's progenitors ; and that no man be compelled to go out of his shire but when necessity requireth and sudden coming of strange enemies into the realm ; and then it shall be done as hath been used in times past for the defence of the realm."[5] When Edward attempted to evade this statute by reviving the practice of calling upon the counties, boroughs, and townships, as corporate bodies, to furnish him with troops,[6] parliament replied through an

perfected through a union with the county militia,

which was placed under the command of civil officers ;

the hue and cry ;

the scheme as perfected by the Statute of Win-chester ;

1 Edw. III. c. 5 enacted to prevent the employ-ment of the militia abroad ;

---

[1] *Select Charters,* pp. 362, 370, 374.

[2] Cf. Reeves, *Hist. of Eng. Law,* vol. iii. p. 713, and note (a), Finlason ed.

[3] *Select Charters,* p. 469. See, also, p. 410.

[4] For illustrations of these irregular demands, see *Fœdera,* under the reigns of Edward I. and Edward II.

[5] Edw. III. c. 5.

[6] In 10 Edw. III., in addition to a levy of knights, a certain number of horsemen were demanded from the counties, with the option of a payment in lieu of such service at a fixed rate. In the next year men were demanded of the boroughs and townships, at the

act [1] which declared that the county force should never be compelled to go beyond the realm without its mandate. In spite, however, of such precautions, which were repeated in the reign of Henry IV.,[2] forcible recruiting was revived in the reign of Henry VIII. through "commissioners of array," employed by the crown as early as the fourteenth century [3] for the training and organizing of the militia when invasion was apprehended. Henry's commissioners were commanded, as his lieutenants, to compel the counties to furnish the necessary number of men, and in the third of Edward VI. such lieutenants were appointed for the "bringing of the counties into military order." By 4 & 5 Phil. & Mar. c. 2 the liability to bear arms was readjusted in accordance with changes which had taken place in the military system, and penalties were imposed upon all who should fail to report when ordered to muster either by the king, or by any lieutenant acting under his authority. Thus was legally recognized not only the system of forcible recruiting, but also the office of lord lieutenant, who as the military head of the shire took the place of the Old-English earl,[4] and as such overshadowed the sheriff, who henceforward became in practice purely a civil officer. With the ancient national force thus recognized, armed, and officered, the Tudors were able to maintain themselves without the aid of a standing army, the creation of a later time.

8. In the somewhat extended account which has now been given of the constitution of the Tudor monarchy, the effort has been made to emphasize the fact that through the abnormal development of the conciliar system the crown became the one dominant and guiding force, which, without the support of a standing army, was able to direct and control every branch of the state machinery from the star chamber down to the parish vestry. The doctrine that the crown should be controlled by the council, and the council by the parliament,[5] es-

expense of the incompetent and aged. In 16 Edw. III. every man possessing land of a certain value was to furnish an archer to the king.

[1] 25 Edw. III. c. 5.
[2] 4 Hen. IV. c. 13 confirmed 1 Edw. III. c. 5 as well as 25 Edw. III. c. 5.
[3] A commission of 1324 may be found in the *Fœdera*.

[4] Vol. i. pp. 129, 130. By 34 & 35 Vict. c. 86, s. 6 (Army Regulation Act), the authority of the lords lieutenant has been transferred to officers appointed by the crown with the advice of the secretary of war.
[5] Vol. i. p. 543.

tablished through the struggles of the fourteenth and fifteenth centuries, gave way during the sixteenth to the doctrine that the crown could dominate the council and employ the parliament as a tool whenever it was desirable to give to its acts the forms of legality, or the apparent sanction of popular approval.[1] *it dominated both council and parliament;*

Without any change whatever in the outward form of the constitution, the centre of gravity of the state shifted from the parliament to the council, a result which the collapse of the estate system at the end of the civil war made possible. And yet, during this very period it was that the entire system of *centre of gravity of the state shifted from parliament to council;*

local self-government, embodied in the organization of the counties, towns, and parishes, out of which the popular branch of parliament had grown, was quickened into a new life through a reorganization which drew the local communities, as administrative bodies, into a closer organic connection with the central authority than had before existed. Far more important, however, than the mere outward political development which thus took place in the system of local self-government was the *closer organic connection between the systems of central and local administration;*

change which grew from within out of the new conception of political and religious liberty born of the Renaissance and the Reformation. From the former the English people drew a fresh understanding of philosophy, politics, and law, a reawakened interest in the arts and sciences, a new-born activity in *the new conception of liberty born of the Renaissance and the Reformation;*

commerce and manufacture, as well as that spirit of discovery and adventure which widened its destiny in another hemisphere; from the latter it drew that sense of individual responsibility which broke the spell of tradition by asserting the right of private judgment against the dogma of an infallible church. Of the broader and deeper stream of philosophical skepticism, of historical research into the entire past of man which the English Renaissance set in motion, the English Reformation finally became the channel into which, through the greater intensity of the religious impulse, the force of the larger movement was narrowed and concentrated. We have heretofore *relation of the two movements to each other;*

seen how it was that the party of religious reform designated in England by the comprehensive name of " Puritan " generally accepted the bold and definite scheme of theological and political thought which emanated from the dark though powerful mind of Calvin, — a scheme which rested upon the

[1] See above, p. 100.

Calvinistic
conception
of a Chris-
tian com-
monwealth
adopted
by the
Puritans;

resistance
to princes
in all
matters of
conscience.
assumption that the reformers as a whole, regardless of nationality, constituted a vast Christian commonwealth, subdivided into independent and self-governing churches, in which
the source of all power and authority was the individual Christian man, elect of God and predestined to eternal life, whose
most sacred duty involved the assertion even unto death of his
private judgment in all matters of conscience against any form
of religious belief which princes or states might attempt to
force upon him.   Such was the religious theory of a Christian
democracy which, about the middle of the sixteenth century,
"entered into the middle sort of Englishmen, and added to
that force, fibre, and substance which they have never wanted,
an ideal warmth and fervour which they have almost always
wanted." [1]

Rise of
the middle
classes;
Before the close of the Middle Ages there began to arise
upon the wreck of feudal England a new social fabric, generally known as the middle classes, consisting in the main of
the lesser landowners or country gentry, whose rent-rolls often
equalled those of the older nobles whom they had in a measure supplanted, and of the greater merchants of the towns,
who had been able to rapidly advance in wealth and social importance through the material progress which the tranquillity
the back-
bone of
the landed
gentry the
freeholding
knight-
hood;

simply a
distin-
guished
social class
with open
ranks;
of the Tudor rule had made possible.   The backbone of this
landed gentry was the freeholding knighthood, which instead
of becoming in England as upon the Continent an hereditary
order,[2] took its place at the head of the commons simply as a
distinguished social class, whose ranks were ever opening to
those who, with the proper qualifications, either voluntarily
or through coercion, caused themselves to be made knights.[3]
Those who possessed knights' fees, but who had not taken
on the formal dignity of knighthood [4] came to be known as
esquires;
esquires (*scutarii*).   As we have heretofore seen, the early
attempt made to confine the right of representing the shires

[1] Bagehot, *Eng. Const.*, p. 282.

[2] Vol. i. pp. 357, 479.

[3] The exchequer, during the reign
of Henry III., as a financial and military measure, established the practice
of calling upon all vassals, even under-
vassals, to be made knights.   When
knighthood was thus granted, fees were
charged, and when application was not
made, penalties were imposed.   See

Madox, vol. i. p. 510.   This compulsory knighthood, revived by Charles I.
(Clarendon, *Hist. Rebellion*, vol. i. p.
67), was abolished by the Long Parliament.   16 Car. I. c. 20.

[4] These contented themselves with
the maxim, " Sufficiens honor est
homini, qui dignus honor est."   Coke,
1 Inst. 231, 232.

in parliament to the knighthood gave way only when the difficulty of forcing their attendance led to the statute which extended the privilege to such notable esquires and gentlemen of birth as might become knights.[1] This honorary title of esquire, sparingly granted before the Tudor period began, gradually became after that time the common possession of that ever increasing civic class composed of those who, by virtue of wealth, education, and magisterial services, finally came to be known as gentlemen.[2] The most necessary qualification for entrance into the ranks of the gentry as thus widened was the possession of a landed estate, whose acquisition had always been possible by reason of the fact that knights' fee had from the beginning been both divisible and alienable, qualities unintentionally emphasized through the practical effect of the statute of *Quia emptores.*[3] The acquisition of small estates, that thus began with a splitting up of the great feudal possessions, was greatly accelerated by virtue of the series of statutes, enacted immediately after the dissolution of the monasteries, which, through the removal of the more serious feudal restraints upon alienation, made real property in a sense never before known the subject of bargain and sale.[4] At the base of the social fabric which thus arose as feudalism fell into decay still abided the immemorial principle that has always vitalized individual energy and ability in the English nation, by providing a way through which the ranks of every class have ever been open to members from the class beneath it.[5] Through this power of the individual to rise in the social scale it was possible for the laborer in the country by thrift and industry to become a tenant and small proprietor; for the retail trader or artisan of the town to become a freeholder; for the wealthy merchant to buy an estate with the rights of a manor attached, to find his way to municipal offices, commissions of the peace and parliament; while to the exceptional few among the higher gentry, specially distinguished by unusual possessions, position at the bar, or eminent public services, remained the hope of a summons from the crown calling them to a place in the ranks of the peerage itself.

Marginal notes: their right to represent the shires in parliament; a title finally applied to all who were known as gentlemen; possession of land the most necessary qualification; how the acquisition of small estates was facilitated; removal of feudal restraints upon alienation; power of the humblest individual to rise in the social scale; until the peerage itself was reached.

---

[1] Vol. i. p. 475.
[2] Cf. Mackintosh, *Hist.*, vol. i. p. 269.
[3] Vol. i. p. 413, and note 1.
[4] See above, pp. 95, 96.
[5] Vol. i. pp. 132, 133.

Into this ever widening and progressive middle class that dominated the house of commons when Elizabeth's reign began entered the new spirit of liberty, which impelled each sovereign Christian man to question and challenge all claims upon his civil and political obedience, whenever such claims were rejected by the supreme oracle supposed to be enthroned in each individual Christian conscience.   As early as the reign of Edward VI. the coming change began to be felt through the disappearance of that slavish spirit of obedience which had characterized the parliaments of Henry VIII.   To overcome the opposition to its policy that thus arose out of the reviving spirit of independence, the crown was driven to adopt a system for the "management" of the house of commons which consisted not only of its packing with royal nominees[1] through a direct interference with elections, but also of the creation of new boroughs, generally small towns or hamlets of no importance, whose constituencies the crown could dominate.   In that way under Edward VI. were created or restored twenty-two boroughs ;[2] under Mary, fourteen ; while Elizabeth in the same way increased the numbers of the house by the addition of sixty-two members.   And yet, in spite of all such expedients, the Puritan opposition to the Tudor system, that grew stronger and stronger as Elizabeth's reign advanced, not only reasserted successfully many vitally important parliamentary privileges, but also maintained to a marked extent the right of the house to deal with the three great questions touching the succession, the church, and the regulation of trade, which were claimed by the Tudor sovereigns as within the exclusive province of the king in council.

Among the parliamentary privileges belonging either to the house as a whole, or to its individual members, which were thus asserted during the reign of Elizabeth, should be noted here : (1) The right of the house to determine contested elections.   In the first year of Queen Mary's reign the right to look into the returns, previously vested first in the king in council and then in the justices of assize,[3] was assumed by the house, and so widened as to embrace the question involved in

---

[1] See above, p. 131.
[2] While some of these were places of note, at least half of the number, including seven in Cornwall, were of

no kind of importance.   Cf. Hallam, *Const. Hist.*, vol. i. p. 45.
[3] Vol. i. pp. 528, 529.

the validity of the election of Alexander Nowell, a prebendary Nowell's case; of Westminster. The committee charged with the inquiry reported that as Nowell had a voice in the convocation house, he "cannot be a member of this house, and the queen's writ to be directed for another burgess in his place." [1] That assertion of the right of the house to pass upon such questions, without the intervention of the judges, was followed in Elizabeth's reign by the action taken in regard to an irregular election held in the county of Norfolk, in reference to which the committee reported that they had not inquired into the action taken by the lord chancellor, "because they thought it prejudicial to the privilege of the house to have the same determined by others than such as were members thereof." [2]

case of the county of Norfolk;

(2) The right of the house to punish members for violations of its rules of order was emphasized in the reign of Edward VI. by the imprisonment of John Storie, a burgess, who was committed to the Tower until he made a full submission for some offence committed against the king and council; [3] and in the next reign Thomas Copley was given in custody to the sergeant of the house for disrespectful words spoken of her majesty. [4] In the reign of Elizabeth the house, probably for the first time, asserted its right to expel a member in the case of Arthur Hall [5] (1581), whose expulsion was followed a few years later (1585) by that of Dr. Parry. [6] In the next year it was that the house reasserted its right to punish a person not a member by bringing one Bland to its bar and fining him for having spoken contemptuously of it. [7]   (3) The right of the commons to release a member or his servants from custody by the authority of the mace alone, first maintained in the reign of Henry VIII. in the case of Ferrers, [8] was reasserted in that

right of the house to punish its members;

Storie's case;

Copley's case;

right of expulsion — cases of Hall and Parry;

right to punish a person not a member;

right to release by the authority of the mace alone;

---

[1] *Commons' Journals*, 1 Mary, p. 27. Another prebendary (Dr. Tregonwell) was returned at the same time, but being a layman was, on consideration, permitted to retain his seat. See Froude, *Hist. Eng.*, vol. v. p. 283.

[2] As to the final settlement of the whole question, see vol. i. pp. 530, 531.

[3] The proceedings are recorded in the *Commons' Journals* of the first parliament of Edward VI., 21st of January, 20th of February, and 2d of March, 1547–48.

[4] *Commons' Journals*, 5th and 7th of March, 1557–58.

[5] D'Ewes, p. 291; Hatsell, p. 93.

[6] D'Ewes, p. 341.

[7] D'Ewes, p. 366; Hallam, *Const. Hist.*, vol. i. pp. 271–274. As to the modern practice touching the suspension and expulsion of members, see Sir T. Erskine May's *Parl. Practice*, pp. 53, 55, 325.

[8] The commons refused a writ of privilege offered by the lord chancellor, "being of a clear opinion that all commandments and other acts proceeding

of Elizabeth in the cases of Smalley, Fitzherbert, and Neal.[1]
(4) In the reign of Elizabeth was also asserted for the first

right to
punish
bribery at
elections;

time the right of the house to punish bribery at elections by
the fine imposed in 1571 upon the borough of Westbury for
having received a bribe of four pounds from Thomas Long, a
sitting member.[2]   (5) The spirit which thus prompted the

right of the
house to
originate
money bills
assailed
in 1593;
freedom
of speech
defined at a
later day.

house to maintain its lesser privileges did not fail to fully assert itself when its vital and exclusive right to originate money
bills was unsuccessfully assailed in 1593 by the house of lords.[3]
(6) While the right to freedom of speech in parliament, frankly
conceded by Henry VIII., was challenged persistently by Elizabeth, the precedents by which it was finally established belong to a later time, a circumstance that may be explained
by the fact that in all such conflicts the queen, in spite of her
prejudices, generally gave way.[4]

Crown
claimed the
right to
initiate all
legislation
touching
the succes-
sion and
the church;

Whenever the statement is made that the Tudor sovereigns
claimed the right to deal with all questions touching the succession and the church with the advice of the council only, it
must be understood to mean that in reference to such matters
of state the crown claimed the exclusive right to initiate all
necessary legislation, which the parliament was expected to
ratify when called upon to do so.   When, in Elizabeth's reign,
that body attempted to reverse the rule by assuming the initiative, the crown resented its attempt to so legislate as an

right of
parliament
to deliber-
ate upon all
questions
of state
denied;

assault upon the prerogative.   The history of the conflicts thus
brought about clearly illustrates how the earlier right of deliberation as to all matters touching the commonwealth [5] was
narrowed and modified by the Tudor system of government,
of which the council was the embodiment.   From the time of

---

from the nether house were to be done
and executed by their sergeant without writ, only by the show of his
mace, which was his warrant." — Holinshed, vol. i. p. 824; Hatsell, vol. i.
p. 57.   As to the history of the writ of
privilege prior to this case, see vol. i.
pp. 531, 532, where the final settlement
of the parliamentary exemption from
legal arrest and distress is fully explained.

[1] Hatsell, vol. i. p. 107; D'Ewes,
pp. 482, 514, 518, 520. May's *Parl.
Practice*, p. 103, note 1.

[2] *Commons' Journals*, p. 88.

[3] D'Ewes, p. 486.   For the earlier
history of that right, see vol. i. pp. 525,
526.   In 1671 the commons successfully disputed the right of the lords
to amend money-bills, a contention
which the upper house has admitted
since that time.   For a full statement,
see May, *Const. Hist.*, vol. i. pp. 104–
112.

[4] The history of this right down to
and including the reign of Henry VIII.
has heretofore been stated, vol. i. pp.
522–524.   Its later history will be considered hereafter.

[5] Vol. i. pp. 498–502.

Elizabeth's half-promise to her first parliament to marry,[1] the question of the succession grew more and more urgent, until in 1563 it became the subject of serious debate,[2] and in 1566 the cause of a serious conflict between the crown and the commons, in the course of which the queen expressed her displeasure "that the succession question should have been raised in that house without her consent," and the commons their intention not only to debate it fully, but also, if the queen should persist in her refusal to marry, to name a successor against her will.[3] On that occasion the protestant element then dominant in the commons, fearful of the accession of Mary of Scotland, first linked the question of the succession with that of supply,[4] and then called upon the lords to join them in an address, prepared by committees of the two houses, to which the queen replied with a vague promise to marry, coupled with a positive order that the subject should be discussed no further on pain of her displeasure. Aroused by this assault upon the right of deliberation, Paul Wentworth moved to know whether such order "was not against the liberties" of parliament.[5] In the course of the discussion that ensued, Mr. Dalton,[6] who ventured to touch upon the forbidden subject of the Scottish title, was arrested by royal order and examined before the star chamber. In the midst of the crisis thus brought about, in which the question of the succession was lost in that of privilege, Elizabeth was forced to yield by releasing the prisoner, and by relieving "the house of the burden of her commandment."[7] In spite, however, of this apparent concession, the queen was careful, in her reply to the usual demand of freedom of speech made in the next parliament of 1571, to reassert her pretensions by reminding the house that they would "do well to meddle with no matters

commons ventured to discuss the marriage of Elizabeth;

question of the succession linked with that of supply;

Dalton, who ventured to discuss the Scottish title, arrested by royal order;

Elizabeth forced to yield for the moment;

but reasserted her pretensions in 1571;

---

[1] See D'Ewes, p. 46; *Commons' Journals*, p. 54.

[2] The queen had been near death, and the suspense of the nation was becoming intolerable. The pretensions of the different claimants were discussed with a decided bias against the Queen of Scots, whose claims it was said were "barred" by the will of Henry VIII. D'Ewes, pp. 82, 85; Strype, vol. i. p. 258. For speech in favor of Lady Catherine Grey, see Domestic MSS., Elizabeth, vol. xxvii.

[3] Froude has given a graphic account of the occurrence with references to the documents. Vol. vii. pp. 454–468.

[4] D'Ewes, p. 124.

[5] *Commons' Journals*, 8 Eliz.

[6] See Report of his speech, Domestic MSS., Elizabeth, vol. xli.

[7] D'Ewes, p. 117; Domestic MSS., Elizabeth, vol. xli.

of state but such as should be propounded unto them, and to occupy themselves in other matters concerning the common-wealth," [1] a warning which was restated in a more positive form in the answer given to a like request made by the speaker, Sir Edward Coke, at the opening of parliament in

1593 : " Privilege of speech is granted, but you must know what privilege ye have ; not to speak every one what he listeth, or what cometh into his brain to utter ; your privilege is 'aye' or 'no.' " [2]   Regardless of the warning, Peter Wentworth

and Sir Henry Bromley, on the first day of the session, ventured to reopen the question of the succession by the presentation of a petition and bill upon the subject, for which presumption they were promptly taken in hand by the council and imprisoned. [3]

The break with Rome, and the almost entire suspension of the functions of convocation as a legislative body which followed the submission of the clergy, cast upon the king as the supreme head a set of new ecclesiastical duties, as to whose discharge there were no precedents.   In order to definitely settle all such difficulties, Henry VIII. assumed that as the real government of the church belonged to the crown, it was its ex-

clusive right to draft and submit to parliament for its ratification all necessary ecclesiastical legislation.   In that way was proposed and ratified the famous series of statutes enacted by the Reformation Parliament. [4]   That Elizabeth firmly adhered to her father's theory was put beyond all question when in 1571 the commons, who were then entirely under the control of the Puritan element, attempted to assume the initiative in

church affairs by the enactment of a number [5] of bills for the modification of the religious compromise, which at the queen's suggestion had passed into law.   In the course of the conflict that ensued, the speaker was directed to say, after a bill touching church rules and ceremonies had been read a third

---

[1] D'Ewes, p. 141.

[2] *Parl. Hist.*, vol. iv. p. 349.   " Free speech in parliament had been one of the privileges which Henry VIII. had not attempted to interfere with.   Elizabeth could never bring herself to regard it as anything but an intolerable impertinence." — Froude, vol. ix. p. 430.

[3] *Parl. Hist.*, vol. iv. p. 365.

[4] For summary of these acts, see above, p. 83.

[5] " No fewer than seven bills, for a further reformation, were introduced into the lower house." — Lingard, vol. vi. p. 248.

time, that " No bills concerning religion shall be proposed or received into this house, unless the same be first considered by the clergy;" and Mr. Strickland, "a grave and ancient man," who seems to have been the main author of the obnoxious measures, was summoned before the council, reprimanded, and ordered not to appear again in the house, for the reason that the part he had taken was a direct assault upon the royal prerogative.   In the midst, however, of the cry of privilege which at once arose, the queen gave way to the extent of withdrawing her inhibition against Strickland's return to his place in the house.[1]   In 1588 another attempt to initiate ecclesiastical reform was made by Mr. Cope, who introduced a sweeping measure for the abolition of the existing system, which he proposed to supersede by a new form of common prayer contained in a book annexed to his bill.   Under a command from the queen the speaker attempted to stop the reading of the bill, and after discussion of the matter he was forced to deliver up both bill and book to her majesty.   As a counterblast to this assault upon the right of parliament to legislate of its own motion upon all subjects touching the interests of the commonwealth, Peter Wentworth insisted that a series of questions should be read to the house by the speaker, of the following import : "Whether this council was not a place for any member of the same, freely and without control, by bill or speech, to utter any of the griefs of this commonwealth ? Whether there be any council that can make, add, or diminish from the law of the realm, but only this council of parliament ? Whether it be not against the orders of this council to make secret or matter of weight, which is here on hand, known to the prince or any other without consent of the house ? Whether the speaker may overrule the house in any matter or cause in question ?   Whether the prince and state can continue and stand and be maintained, without this council of parliament, except by altering the government of the state ? " For propounding these mighty questions, which outlined the entire attack to be made by parliament in the next age upon the conciliar system, Wentworth and his supporters, including Cope, were committed to the Tower, where they were permitted to remain until the dissolution of parliament, which

Side notes:
Strickland's reprimand;

the queen yielded to the cry of privilege;

fate of Mr. Cope's bill to introduce a new book of common prayer;

the speaker forced to deliver up bill and book;

Wentworth propounded questions as to parliament's unlimited right of deliberation,

for which he and others were imprisoned;

[1] D'Ewes, pp. 156, 175, 176.

took place three weeks thereafter.[1] When in 1593 Morice,
the attorney of the court of wards, attempted to repeat Cope's
experiment by offering a bill for the reform of the practice of
the ecclesiastical courts, he received more serious punishment
through royal orders which not only forbade the speaker to
read his bill, but also consigned him to prison, deprived him
of his office as attorney in the court of wards, and disabled
him from practising as a barrister.[2]

And yet, in spite of the failure of the commons to maintain
its right to initiate such legislation as it deemed necessary for
the reform of the church and for the settlement of the succession, in spite of the rarity of its assemblings and the persistent
assaults made upon its right to freedom of discussion, its privileges steadily grew and its powers widened, until at the close
of Elizabeth's reign it was able to win its first great victory
within a forbidden domain, always considered as the special
province of the king in council. From the earliest times the
crown had asserted a broad and undefined jurisdiction over
commerce and trade,[3] by virtue of which it claimed the right
to coin money, to regulate weights and measures, to make special rules for the government of foreign merchants, to appoint
certain towns as staples possessed of the exclusive right to sell
certain kinds of merchandise, to authorize the holding of fairs
and markets, and to declare what places should be entitled
to the privileges of a port. And in addition to the right to
bestow such special immunities upon particular cities and
towns, the crown also undertook to grant valuable commercial
privileges to individuals and corporations, under patents which
conferred upon the holders the exclusive right to deal in a
multitude of articles, many of them the common necessaries
of life. So great was the abuse that arose out of the grant
of such monopolies to favored individuals,[4] generally courtiers,
during the reign of Elizabeth, that in the parliament of 1571
Mr. Bell called the attention of the house to the subject. But
the startling rebuke promptly administered by the council[5] to

---

[1] D'Ewes, p. 410; *Parl. Hist.*, vol. iv.
p. 316.

[2] D'Ewes, p. 478; *Parl. Hist.*, vol. iv.
p. 396; Townsend, p. 60.

[3] For a general statement, see Dicey,
The Privy Council, pp. 53–62.

[4] It was the leading subject of com-

plaint in and out of parliament. *Secret
Correspondence*, pp. 25, 26.

[5] After his admonition, he returned
to the house " with such an amazed
countenance that it daunted all the
rest." — D'Ewes, p. 159.

the offending member was so efficacious that the question was not again reopened until 1597, when the commons presented it in an address, to which the queen made answer through the lord keeper, expressing the hope that "her dutiful and loving subjects would not take away her prerogative, which is the choicest flower in her garden, and the principal and head pearl in her crown and diadem." [1]   In spite, however, of such an appeal from such a source, the abuse, which had become unbearable, was made the subject of a bill introduced in the commons in 1601, "for the explanation of the common law in certain cases of letters patent," which gave rise to a long and angry debate, whose stern spirit of protest seems to have received a hearty response from the people at large.   So great was the pressure thus brought to bear upon the crown that Elizabeth, with that consummate tact which always taught the Tudors how to yield at the critical moment, sent a message to the house with the promise that as to such patents as were "grievous to her subjects, some should be presently repealed, some superseded, and none put in execution, but such as should first have a trial, according to the law, for the good of the people."   For this concession the house returned an address of thanks, in reply to which the queen assured them that she had never put her pen to any patent, "but upon pretext and semblance made to me, that it was both good and beneficial to the subjects in general, though a private profit to some of my ancient servants who had deserved well." [2]   Despite, however, the loyal and affectionate spirit in which this memorable transaction thus ended, the fact remained that the conciliar system had lost the first battle in that prolonged struggle through which was finally reëstablished the all-important principle that the supreme powers of the state are vested not in the king in council, but in the king in parliament.

the queen's plea for her prerogative made in 1597;

the commons nevertheless attacked the monopolies in 1601;

Elizabeth yielded gracefully,

and received the thanks of the house;

the crown thus lost the first battle in the great struggle now begun.

---

[1] She added a promise " to examine all patents and to abide the touchstone of the law." — D'Ewes, p. 547.

[2] D'Ewes, vol. ii. pp. 644–654; Townsend, pp. 224, 230, 248; *Parl. Hist.*, vol. iv. p. 480.

BOOK V.

THE STUARTS AND THE PURITAN REVOLUTION OF 1640.

CHAPTER I.

JAMES I. AND THE CONSTITUTIONAL CONFLICT.

Title of the house of Stuart;

1. The house of Tudor, whose right to the throne really rested upon a parliamentary title, never deemed it either becoming or expedient to revive the Yorkist theory of indefeasible hereditary right. Henry VIII., while admitting the principle that the "royal dignity ought to descend from ancestor to heir in a certain established course of descent," was careful to emphasize the fact "that this course of descent is subject to the control of the legislature," by the approval of the three famous enactments in which he as often regulated the succession according to his convenience. The last of those acts, after affirming the right of Edward and his heirs, put in the entail next after them first Mary and then Elizabeth, subject to such conditions as Henry by his last will or letters patent might appoint.[1] Under this power to add a further limitation by will, the king simply supplemented the arrangement which parliament had made by the provision that in the event of failure of issue of his three children, the crown should pass to the heirs of his younger sister Mary, who had married the duke of Suffolk, to the detriment of the heirs of his elder sister Margaret, who had married James IV. of Scotland.[2] Elizabeth, after asking a fresh confirmation of her title at the hands of her first parliament,[3] resolutely refused throughout her long reign to disturb in any way the course of descent which he

Tudor theory of the right of succession;

settlement made by Henry VIII.'s statutes and will

undisturbed by Elizabeth;

---

[1] See above, p. 107.
[2] *Fœdera*, vol. xv. pp. 114–117.

[3] 1 Eliz. c. 3. As to the peculiar terms of that act, see above, p. 156.

father had arranged under the authority of the legislature. And yet, at the time of Elizabeth's death there seems to have been no intention upon the part of the nation to carry out that arrangement, despite the fact that descendants of two daughters of Mary, the first duchess of Suffolk, existed, who were ready to receive their mighty inheritance. If it be true that Lord Beauchamp was illegitimate by reason of defects in the private marriage [1] of the earl of Hertford with his mother, Catherine Grey, the child of Mary's eldest daughter, Frances Brandon, certainly no such objection could be raised against the descendants of Mary's youngest daughter, Eleanor,[2] the countess of Cumberland. Why the English people with its strong sense of legality should have been willing, under such circumstances, to quietly set aside both the law and the fact in order to divert the title to the crown from the house of Suffolk to that of Stuart, can be explained only by two assumptions: first, that politically it had become highly convenient that the crowns of the two kingdoms should be united by the accession of James VI. of Scotland; second, that the will of Henry VIII., which deprived him of the succession, and whose execution was of doubtful validity,[3] embodied a novel conception of legality with which the nation was not familiar. While the English people perfectly understood how parliament itself could change the course of descent, it was not prepared to accept the idea that that supreme power could be delegated even to the mightiest of sovereigns. Robert Cecil, who succeeded his father as Elizabeth's chief councillor, had secretly pledged himself to James in obedience to the popular will,[4] and within a few hours after the death of the great queen, the council itself proclaimed his succession in the midst of a general approval, which coolly ignored not only the Suffolk claim, but a dozen more[5] of a less plausible character.

(marginal notes:) representatives of the house of Suffolk; why the crown was diverted from that house to that of Stuart; Cecil pledged himself to James in obedience to the popular will; council ignored all other claims.

---

[1] After an inquiry instituted by Elizabeth into the validity of the marriage before a commission of civilians and privy councillors, Archbishop Parker, in the absence of positive proof apart from their own declarations, declared their cohabitation illegal. For the proceedings and evidence, see Harl. MSS. Hales, who wrote, probably at Bacon's suggestion, in favor of the validity of the marriage, was sent to the Tower. Haynes, p. 413; Strype, p. 410.

[2] Her only daughter married the earl of Derby, from whom the claim again passed to females.

[3] As to the execution of the will, see above, p. 108.

[4] See Bruce, correspondence of James VI. with Sir R. Cecil and others.

[5] It is said that as many as fourteen claimants existed. See Doleman (Per-

2. The title which James thus acquired to the English throne could be grounded only upon the theory of popular election as manifested by universal consent, or upon the antithetical theory of indefeasible hereditary right.   To the latter theory the new king had already given an extreme statement, far in advance of what had been asserted by Edward IV., who claimed only that there was a peculiar human virtue in a particular line of succession which the power of parliament itself could not overthrow.[1]   Some years before his accession to the English throne James had prepared for the instruction of his

son a work known as the " Basilicon Doron,"[2] in which he claimed that the right of kings was not only indefeasible, but divine and absolute over all orders of men within their realms, a theory afterwards expanded into the statement that the rule of succession in the order of primogeniture was a divine institution, which antedated not only the Christian but the Mosaic dispensation.[3]   While James was careful to set forth his claim of indefeasible hereditary right in a pompous proclamation,[4]

he was equally careful to have that claim sustained upon the meeting of parliament in an act which declared that " the imperial crown of the realm of England did, by inherent birthright and lawful and undoubted succession, descend and come to his most excellent majesty, as being lineally, justly, and lawfully next and sole heir of the blood royal of this realm."[5] If the prolonged and bitter struggle waged by James and his predecessors against the turbulent Scotch nobility for the ex-

altation of the crown had created in his mind an extravagant idea of the royal prerogative as applied to the government of the state, his no less bitter conflict with the Scotch kirk as organized by Knox and Melville had convinced him that the royal authority should likewise dominate in the government of the church.   The intense moral enthusiasm excited by Knox

---

sons), *Conference on the Succession.* The bulk of such claimants, however, derived their rights from sovereigns who reigned prior to the accession of the house of Tudor.   Chief among that class was Isabella, the eldest daughter of Philip II. of Spain.   As to her pretensions, see *Conference on the Succession*, p. 151.

[1] See vol. i. p. 577, and note 1.

[2] Mentioned probably for the first time in the advices from Nicolson, ascribed by Thorpe to October, 1598. See *State Papers*, Scotl., vol. lxiii. p. 50.

[3] Such was the system of Sir Robert Filmer, whose doctrines were solemnly adopted by the University of Oxford. See Macaulay, vol. i. pp. 35, 132.

[4] King's MSS., p. 123, fol. 18 b.

[5] 1 Jac. c. 1.

and his followers had found prompt and coherent expression in Scotland through an ecclesiastical system formed strictly upon the Calvinistic model, with kirk sessions, presbyteries, and provincial synods, subject to the supreme control of a general assembly composed of elected delegates. Thus alongside of the Scotch parliament, composed of prelates and nobles whose resolutions were influenced largely by the crown, there grew up a really representative national assembly, that soon learned how to extend its deliberations beyond mere religious to political questions. In 1580 this new Christian democracy, which had arisen without legal sanction, abolished in its general assembly the office of bishop, as having "no sure warrant, authority, or good ground out of the word of God;" and in the next year, by the adoption of a second Book of Discipline, it organized upon a purely Calvinistic basis those presbyterian institutions which, with slight modifications, have survived to the present day.[1] In order to bridle this new national force that threatened to take from the nobles the lands of which they had despoiled the church, and to make the crown a mere instrument for the establishment of the religious system which it embodied, James, in 1584, obtained from the Scotch parliament an act that restored the entire government of the church to the bishops, while it denounced both the legislative and judicial authority which the general assembly had assumed. Although the ministers of the kirk yielded for the moment to the blow thus inflicted, a struggle for the reëstablishment of the presbyterian system soon began, whose pressure finally compelled James to consent in 1592 to an act which repealed the legislation of 1584, formally abolished episcopacy, and fixed the Calvinistic organization of the church upon a legal basis.[2] James was permitted to retain only the right of being present in the general assembly, and of fixing the time and place of its annual meeting. Four years later, when he attempted to question the right of the assembly to meet without his warrant, Melville, who had come to him as one of a deputation from that body, took him by the sleeve, and, after calling him

in 1580 bishops abolished and presbyterian system completed;

in 1584 the work undone by hostile legislation;

in 1592 Calvinistic organization reëstablished on a legal basis;

Melville defined James' relation to the new system;

---

[1] See Green, *Hist. of the Eng. People*, vol. iii. p. 49; Gardiner, *Hist. Eng.*, vol. i. p. 47. Some years before, the bishops had been reduced to the state of "Tulchans," or dummies, whose only function was to hand over the greater part of their revenues to the nobles to whom they owed their sees.

[2] Gardiner, vol. i. p. 50.

"God's silly vassal," told him there were two kings and two kingdoms in Scotland. "There is Christ Jesus the King, and his kingdom the church, whose subject James VI. is, and of whose kingdom not a king, nor a lord, nor a head, but a member. And they whom Christ has called and commanded to watch over his church, and govern his spiritual kingdom, have sufficient power of him and authority so to do, both together and severally; the which no Christian king nor prince should control and discharge, but fortify and assist."[1] In order to put an end to this condition of things, which threatened to subvert the power of the monarch as it had subverted that of the bishops, James resolved to make their cause his own. To restore the episcopate became with him a matter of settled policy; "No bishop, no king" became an axiom in his political philosophy. And at the same time, in order to prevent the collisions which constantly occurred between two national assemblies legislating independently of each other, often upon the same subject-matter, it was deemed wise to devise some scheme through which representatives of the church could be admitted to a share in the deliberations of the parliament. As a concession to that demand, the estates, at the close of 1597, passed an act authorizing such persons to sit in their midst as the king might appoint to the office of bishop or abbot, or to any other prelacy.[2] The settlement thus attempted proved, however, equally unsatisfactory to both parties: to the kirk, because it had demanded the admission not of royal nominees, but of representatives of the clergy chosen by themselves; to the king, because the new bishops whom he finally appointed under the act in the fall of 1600 were not acknowledged by the church as having any spiritual status or jurisdiction.[3] Thus did James fail to put in practice the ideas embodied in his "Basilicon Doron," in which he had only a short time before announced the hope of reëstablishing his authority over the Scotch kirk by the restoration of the bishops as the agents through whom his absolute and divine right could be asserted over every class within the realm. Such was the mental temper and such the political experience of the man who, on the

Marginal notes:
James espoused the cause of the bishops;

in 1597 the estates conceded their right to sit with them;

in the midst of the failure of this attempted settlement James wrote the "Basilicon Doron."

---

[1] J. Melville's *Diary*, pp. 368–371.
[2] *Acts of Parl. Scotl.*, vol. iv. p. 130.
[3] See Nicolson to Cecil, November
15, 1600, *State Papers*, Scotl., vol. lxvi. p. 96; Gardiner, vol. i. p. 77, and note 1.

24th of March, 1603, assumed the task of governing a people with whose political institutions and habits of thought he never became thoroughly familiar.

3. In order to estimate clearly the extent to which James and Charles were able to put in force their personal ideas of government, the fact must be kept steadily in view that the highly centralized system of "government by councils," which the Tudors had organized and employed for more than a century, passed into their hands with all of its organs unimpaired. In the account heretofore given of the growth of that system the statement was made that, owing to the decline which had taken place in the constitution of the national assembly at the end of the civil war, Henry VII. and his successors were able to transfer the centre of gravity of the state from the king in parliament to the king in council. Out of that new condition of things grew the necessity for a subdivision of the labors of the council among a number of committees, to each of which was assigned a definite class of official duties. In that way the council gradually became a body of trained administrators, whose duty it was to direct and supervise the entire state machinery, from the parliament itself down to the local self-governing bodies, and to mark out for punishment, in special cases, all persons, whether in or out of parliament, who undertook to defy or obstruct royal mandates. An enumeration has already been made of the agencies employed by the council as it existed in the days of Elizabeth in order to make its influence all-pervading, chief among which were the inquisitorial high commission and the dreaded star chamber.[1] The motive power, the guiding force of this great central machine, was the king himself, under whose eye everything was supposed to pass, and who was all in all. If such an abnormal centralization of power was necessary in the days of Henry VII. in order to bring peace and law out of the anarchy which the civil war had left behind it, if it was necessary in the days of his son to bear England safely through the crisis of the Reformation, if during those days it gave birth to much administrative organization invaluable to later times, certain it is that the peaceful and prosperous conditions which existed at the accession of the house of Stuart made it imperative that the

Marginal notes:
The conciliar system of the Tudors passed to the Stuarts unimpaired:

scope of conciliar jurisdiction in the Tudor time;

agencies through which the powers of the council were exercised;

the king's personal influence;

---

[1] See above, pp. 176–183.

abnormal powers of the king in council should once more be
beginning
of the
conflict
between
conciliar
and parlia-
mentary
systems;
restored to the king in parliament. With the new life that
entered into the national assembly as Elizabeth's reign drew
to a close came the conviction that the two systems of government were incompatible; that the Tudor system was fast
becoming unequal to the task of governing a nation which
had already entered upon a career of marvellous development.
Although the first move was made, before the end of the
great queen's reign, by the prosperous middle class, who had
long administered the local affairs of the country, and who
were fast becoming independent by reason of wealth acquired
in commerce, manufactures, and daring adventure, the feeling
seems to have been general that no real change of system
should be enforced until after the installation of Elizabeth's
James and
Charles
intensified
it by resist-
ing reforms
demanded
by changed
conditions;
successor. James and Charles, so far from accepting the mission of change and reform which thus naturally arose out of
changed conditions, not only continued the system of government by councils which the Tudors had bequeathed to them,
but attempted to intensify its absolutism both in theory and
practice.[1] What the constitution of the council was in the
days of Elizabeth it remained down to the meeting of the Long
Parliament, and during that period its powers were stretched
to a greater extent than had ever before been known. Between the parliamentary system, animated by the new spirit of
liberty which had entered into the commons, and the system
of government by councils, animated by the new spirit of absolutism derived from James, a conflict was inevitable. That
not until
after two
revolutions
was the
conflict
finally
solved in
favor of
parliament;
conflict was a long and bitter one. Not until after the completion of two revolutions was the English nation able finally to
subject the conciliar system as organized by the Tudors and
enforced by the Stuarts to the parliamentary system as it exists in modern times. The result of the transition was not to
abolish the council, but to so reform, reorganize, and readjust
it in its relations to the parliament as to make the national will
substitution
of the
national
for the
royal will.
instead of the royal will its driving and directing force. The
immediate task before us is to draw out the details of the
constitutional conflict thus inaugurated from the accession of

---

[1] "The Stuarts might have ruled
with more skill. They might have
been the leaders of a reform, instead
of the victims of a revolution. No
policy, however, could have long averted
some alteration in the government."—
Dicey, *The Privy Council*, p. 120.

James I. down to the beginning of the civil war, a period during which its battles were fought out in parliament and in the courts of common law.

4. After confirming Cecil and his fellow councillors in office until his arrival in England, James set out from Edinburgh on April 5, 1603, holding court on the way at Berwick, Newcastle, and York successively. While thus engaged in the northern counties, the new king was brought face to face with the dominant ecclesiastical question then pressing for solution by the presentation of what is called the "Millenary Petition," because it purported to have been signed by one thousand of the clergy of the Church of England, which then numbered about ten thousand.[1] The Puritans who thus came forward to ask a modification of the religious settlement that Elizabeth had made, and to which they were then outwardly conforming, did not demand the abolition of episcopacy and a reorganization of the church upon a presbyterian basis, but only a removal from the prayer-book of some usages which they considered superstitious, the amendment of the Thirty-nine Articles by the addition of nine Calvinistic "assertions," the reformation of the church courts, a more rigorous observation of the Puritan Sabbath, and a provision for the training of a preaching clergy.[2] Despite the fact that the petition, upon which no action was taken for the moment, was met by warm and contemptuous protests from the two universities, the king informed them that he intended to accept the suggestion for the maintenance of a preaching clergy, and urged them to follow his example.[3] Thus encouraged, the Puritan party attempted to strengthen their views during the summer by obtaining signatures to petitions among the laity, an attempt that led to a proclamation forbidding all such demonstrations. In order to settle the pending questions in the forum of debate, the king ordered that a conference[4] should be held in his presence between certain learned advocates of the two parties

James on his way to London was confronted with the religious question;

the "Millenary Petition," its scope and purpose;

James' response to the protest of the universities;

---

[1] It is said to have been signed in fact by only seven hundred and fifty persons. See Fuller's *Ch. Hist.*, vol. iii. p. 172, ed. 1837; Blount, *Reform. of the Church of Eng.*, vol. ii. p. 465; Neal's *Hist. Puritans*, vol. ii. 5th ed. 1733.

[2] For the full text, see Fuller's *Ch.*

Hist., vol. iii. p. 193; Collier's *Ch. Hist.*, vol. vii. p. 271.

[3] Wilkins, *Conc.*, vol. iv. p. 369; *State Papers*, Dom., vol. ii. p. 38.

[4] The king admitted that "time may have brought in some corruptions which may deserve a review and amendment." — Wilkins, *Conc.*, vol. iv. p. 371.

the conference at Hampton Court,

which, after several postponements, finally began at Hampton Court, on January 14, 1604. During the debate, which proceeded with great acrimony, the king seems to have borne himself with reasonable patience until Reynolds, president of an Oxford college, and one of the Puritan champions, in advocating the restoration of "Prophesyings," ventured to suggest that all disputed questions presented by them should be referred to the bishop and his presbyters. At that hated name

in which James declared against the Puritan party within the church;

the king, with Melville's words burning in his ears, fired up as he answered that, "If you aim at a Scottish presbytery, it agreeth as well with monarchy as God with the Devil. Then Jack, and Tom, and Will, and Dick, shall meet, and at their pleasure censure me and my council, and all our proceedings. Then Will will stand up and say, 'It must be thus;' then Dick shall reply, 'Nay, marry, but we will have it thus;' and therefore here I must once more reiterate my former speech and say, *Le Roi s'avisera.*" Thus it was that James declared himself against the adoption of any material part of the Puritan system, while he clearly manifested in his various speeches made during the conference that he was not imbued with that

Bacon's idea of toleration;

broad spirit of toleration with which Bacon had attempted to impress him by the dedication of a treatise, in which the great thinker had earnestly advocated spiritual freedom under the guardianship of law as the true panacea for existing evils.[1] Every important request made by the Puritan clergy was re-

James' intolerant declaration;

fused; and the conference was closed by a declaration from James, who felt that he had vanquished his opponents by his logical prowess, that "If this be all they have to say, I shall make them conform themselves, or I will hurry them out of the land, or else do worse."[2] The one good and practical outcome of the conference, which thus ended angrily between James and the most aggressive element in the realm, resulted from the prompt acceptance by the king of a motion made

the making of the "Authorized Version."

by Reynolds[3] for a revision of the Bible, which gave to the English-speaking world the famous "Authorized Version." The confusion that arose from the fact that there were three versions then in use — the "Great Bible" of Henry VIII.; the

[1] See Bacon's *Letters and Life*, vol. iii. p. 103: "Certain Considerations touching the Better Pacification and Edification of the Church of England."

[2] Gardiner, *Hist. Eng.*, vol. i. p. 157.

[3] Caldwell's *Conf.*, p. 187.

"Bishops' Bible," revised under the direction of Parker; and the "Geneva Bible," prepared in that city by Whittingham and others during the Marian persecution — made it highly desirable that there should be "one uniform translation." And thus after five or six years of systematic labor by the greatest scholars of the time was finally published that version which, for more than two centuries and a half, has charmed all lovers of pure and melodious English prose.[1]

While the Puritans were persuading themselves that James' Calvinistic education would prompt him to lift from their necks the yoke of the Elizabethan church, the catholics were hoping that the unwavering support they had given to his mother's cause would induce him to lighten the pressure of the persecuting statutes under which they were then suffering. And for a time their hopes were greatly encouraged. A week before his coronation, which took place on the 25th of July, the king heard a deputation of the leading catholics, in the presence of the council, and in reply to their petition he assured them that while he could not tolerate their worship, he would remit the fines for recusancy so long as they demeaned themselves as loyal subjects.[2] As a result of the toleration thus extended, it is said that within the nine months which followed Elizabeth's death, one hundred and forty priests landed in England, through whose conversions the number of the catholic population was considerably increased.[3] This condition of things so offended the Puritan party, which was already accusing the king of papistry, that he was compelled to return hastily to the old methods of repression. Measures were at once adopted for the discovery and presentment of recusants; the magistrates were ordered to put the penal laws into immediate execution; and on the 22d of February, 1604, a proclamation was issued ordering the banishment of all priests by March 19, the day fixed for the meeting of James' first parliament.[4]

James and the catholics;

he hears a deputation a week before his coronation;

his tolerant response;

increase in the catholic population;

driven by the Puritans to return to the old methods of repression;

proclamation for the banishment of priests.

5. The stern rebukes which the king thus administered, first to the Puritans at Hampton Court and then to the catholics, were emphasized in his opening speech to the two houses by

---

[1] For a full statement, see Blount, *Reform. of the Church of Eng.*, vol. ii. pp. 472–478.

[2] Jardine's *Gunpowder Plot*, p. 10; Gardiner, *Hist. Eng.*, vol. i. p. 115.

[3] December 13, *Roman Transcripts, R. O.;* Gardiner, *Hist. Eng.*, vol. i. p. 142.

[4] Lingard, *Hist. Eng.*, vol. vii. p. 37.

the declarations that he was averse to the former, not because they differed from him in opinion, but because they were "ever discontented with the present government, and impatient to suffer any superiority, which maketh their sect unable to be suffered in any well-governed commonwealth;" and that the clergy of the latter could not be permitted to remain in the kingdom so long as they held to the doctrine that the pope possessed "an imperial civil power over all kings and emperors."

In reply to the imputation made against them, the Puritans, who are said to have composed three fourths [1] of the house, were quick to remind the king, in the answer made by the speaker to the address, that "new laws could not be instituted, nor imperfect laws reformed, nor inconvenient laws abrogated, by any other power than that of the high court of parliament, that is, by the agreement of the commons, the accord of the lords, and the assent of the sovereign: that to him belonged the right either negatively to frustrate, or affirmatively to ratify, but that he could not institute; every bill must pass the two houses before it could be submitted to his pleasure."

In this angry spirit it was that the commons turned to the consideration of their exclusive right to try contested elections, a question which grew out of the fact that the king had directed, in his proclamation [2] calling upon the constituencies to send up members, that all returns should be made into chancery, where they might be rejected as unlawful, if any "should be found to be made contrary to the proclamation."

The merits of the cases of Goodwin and Fortescue [3] that thus arose have already been set forth at an earlier stage of this work, where

the freedom of members from arrest was also considered, — a privilege again vindicated by this parliament in the case of Sir Thomas Sherley,[4] which brought about the enactment of 1 Jac. 1. c. 13, defining for the first time by statute the rights of the house, the duties of officers, and the rights of creditors in such cases. Having thus maintained its privileges, the house next

[1] See Gardiner's qualification of that statement, vol. i. p. 178.

[2] See *Fœdera*, vol. xvi. p. 561.

[3] See vol. i. pp. 530, 331.

[4] *Commons' Journals, passim*, from March 22 to May 22, vol. i. pp. 149–222. The great case of Ferrers (vol. i. p. 533) occurred in 1542. In 1575 occurred Smalley's case (Hatsell, vol. i. p. 90), which was followed in the same reign by the case of Fitzherbert in 1592, and by that of Neale shortly thereafter. Hatsell, vol. i. p. 107; D'Ewes, pp. 518, 520; May, *Parl. Practice*, pp. 132, 133. Then came Sherley's case in 1604.

addressed itself to the consideration of the feudal survivals known as purveyance and wardship, under the first of which the approach of the king's court carried terror into every district invaded, and under the last of which the lands of the greater landowners were liable at their deaths to undergo a temporary confiscation.[1] In order to cut off once and for all these vexatious abuses, two bills were introduced, which offered to give to the crown as revenue sums larger than those derived either from purveyance or the court of wards. At the same time the Puritan element, smarting under the results of the Hampton Court conference, revived the religious question through a motion made by Sir Francis Hastings, on April 16, for a committee to consider "of the confirmation and reëstablishing of the religion now established within this kingdom, as also of the settling, increasing, and maintaining a learned ministry." In reply to a suggestion from the king that they should first confer with convocation upon that subject, the house distinctly refused, expressing their willingness, however, to confer with the bishops as lords of parliament. The only result of discussion of these tangled questions was to delay all action upon the one subject upon which James had set his heart, the union of England and Scotland, a consummation which he had told the commons would enable him to leave at his death "one worship of God, one kingdom entirely governed, one uniformity of law." [2] In order to advance that object, the king on May 30 called the commons to his presence and rated them sharply upon their proceedings, the result of which was that a bill was hurried through the house on June 2 naming twenty-eight commissioners, who were to confer upon the subject of union with a similar body to be appointed by the Scots, it being understood that parliament should meet in the following year to receive their report.[3] Shortly before this, however, the commons had refused to assent to the proposal that James should immediately assume the title of King of Great Britain, upon the ground that there should first be some agreement as to the terms of the union.[4] In order to bring about a better

Margin notes: purveyance and wardship; Puritan element in the house revived the religious question; house refused to confer with convocation; union of England and Scotland projected; commissioners appointed;

---

[1] See Blackstone, *Com.*, vol. i. p. 262; vol. ii. p. 58. A good historical review of both rights, with a statement of all prior legislation affecting them, may also be found in Gardiner, *Hist. Eng.*, vol. i. pp. 171, 174.

[2] *Commons' Journals*, vol. i. p. 171.

[3] Ibid., vol. i. pp. 230–232.

[4] Gardiner, *Hist. Eng.*, vol. i. p. 177.

understanding with the king, whose plans they were so often

compelled to thwart, and in order to vindicate their motives, the commons prepared a protestation entitled "A Form of Apology and Satisfaction to be delivered to His Majesty," which was read in the house on the 20th of June.   This document is of constitutional importance, from the fact that it set forth at the beginning of the conflict in a conservative and monarchical spirit all the grievances which the nation then called upon the crown to redress, with the assurance that "if Your Majesty shall vouchsafe at your best pleasure and leisure to enter into gracious consideration of our petitions for each of those burdens under which your whole people have long time mourned, hoping for relief by Your Majesty, then may you be assured to be possessed of their hearts forever, and if of their hearts, then of all they can do and have."   Passing over the explanations made of their conduct as to the union with Scotland, and in reference to the bills introduced for the

abolition of purveyance and wardship, the gravamen of the petition is found to consist of the definitions given of parliamentary privilege and of the demands made by the Puritans in the matter of religious reform.   The commons assured the king, firstly, that it was a grave error to suppose that their

privileges were held not of right, but of grace only; they are, they said, "of right and due inheritance no less than our very lands and goods;" secondly, that it was equally erroneous to suppose that they "were no court of record, nor yet a court that can command view of records," not as a courtesy, but as a matter of right; and finally, that the gravest of all mistakes was embodied in the idea that the right to examine the returns of writs for knights and burgesses was without their "compass, and due to chancery."   Such misconceptions, they said, tended "directly and apparently to the utter overthrow of the very fundamental privileges of our house, and therein of the rights and liberties of the whole commons of the realm of England."

Upon the ecclesiastical question, the "Apology," after denying "that the kings of England have any absolute power in themselves either to alter religion, . . . or to make any laws concerning the same, otherwise than in temporal causes by consent of parliament," frankly admits that no man from weakness of conscience "may be exempted after parliament from obedience to laws established." The petitioners then declared that they "have not come in any Puritan or Brownist [1] spirit to introduce their parity, or to work the subversion of the state ecclesiastical as now it stands." In order that "a perpetual uniformity may be enjoined and observed," they asked only that certain ceremonies should be abolished, that certain abuses should be corrected, and "that the land might be furnished with a learned, religious, and godly ministry." [2] Descending, then, from questions of conscience to questions of trade, the commons finally addressed themselves to the task of breaking up the practical monopoly of the commerce of the kingdom as carried on by certain great trading companies whose members were chiefly Londoners. [3] The bill introduced upon that subject, and which fell through in the lords, did not propose to abolish the companies, but, by depriving them of their monopolies, to throw the trade of the kingdom open alike to all. In the mean time the vital question of supply was neglected; no grant was made, upon the ground that a considerable part of the last subsidies had not been levied, it being contrary to precedent to grant a fresh one before the preceding had been fully paid. On the 26th of June, James assured the commons in a letter that he did not desire that they should burden themselves in order to supply his wants, [4] and on the 7th of July he prorogued the first session of his first parliament, after making a bad-tempered speech, in which he told the house that he would depart from the usual custom: "I will not thank where I think no thanks due." [5]

Shortly after the prorogation James assumed the title of King of Great Britain, to which parliament had refused its assent, [6] and proceeded to sharpen the persecution of the Puritan clergy [7] by demanding of them the more rigid conformity prescribed by the canons adopted in the convocation of 1604 at the instigation of Bancroft, who was now promoted, for his

attack upon the monopolies;

the question of supply;

parliament prorogued, July 7.

James assumed the title of King of Great Britain; canons of the convocation of 1604;

[1] A sect which took its name from Robert Browne, a kinsman of Lord Burleigh, whose principles were probably identical with those of the later Independents. See Blount, *Dict. Sects, etc.*

[2] *Parl. Hist.*, vol. i. p. 1020; *State Papers*, Dom., vol. viii. p. 70.

[3] See Macpherson's *Annals of Commerce*, vol. ii. p. 164; Cunningham's *Growth of Eng. Industry and Commerce*, vol. ii. p. 106; Gardiner, *Hist. Eng.*, vol. i. pp. 187–190.

[4] *Commons' Journals*, vol. i. p. 246.

[5] *State Papers*, Dom., vol. viii. p. 93.

[6] Green, *Hist. of the Eng. People*, vol. iii. p. 61.

[7] See Wilkins, *Conc.*, vol. iv. pp. 408, 409.

zeal, to the vacant see of Canterbury. The refusal of the
Puritan clergy to subscribe to the articles touching rights and
ceremonies, which the statutes of Elizabeth had not required,
resulted in the driving of three hundred[1] of them from their
livings in the spring of 1605. Through the enforcement by
the judges of the new act against Jesuits, seminary priests,
and recusants,[2] passed by parliament before the close of the
session, James at the same time drove the catholics to such
despair that a conspiracy for the destruction of king, lords,
and commons, which Catesby had been for a long time con-
cocting, assumed serious proportions, and came very near a successful issue in the fall of the same year. By reason of the
discovery of the Gunpowder Plot, the second session of the
parliament, which met on November 5, was adjourned until
the 21st of January, 1606.[3] The only constitutional conflict
that occurred during this session arose between the houses
themselves out of the peremptory rejection by the lords of a
bill upon the subject of purveyance, sent up to them by the
commons shortly after they had refused their assent to a previous bill upon the same subject,[4] — an occurrence which
probably established for the first time the rule that a bill cannot be twice proposed during the same session. The sympathy
that arose between the crown and the commons out of their
deliverance from a common danger seems to have suspended
for a moment the battle over privilege and prerogative, and
the result was the grant of subsidies and fifteenths[5] sufficient
to pay the debt which Elizabeth had bequeathed to James, it
being understood that the fixed charges of the crown should
be paid out of the permanent and ordinary revenue. A material
element of such revenue was the customs duties, a brief account
of which has already been given down to the accession of the

---

[1] Gardiner, *Hist. Eng.*, vol. i. p. 197, and note 3.

[2] See Challoner's *Missionary Priests*, vol. ii. p. 44; Jardine, *Narrative of the Gunpowder Plot*, p. 44. The best complete statements are to be found in Gardiner, *Hist. Eng.*, vol. i. pp. 234–264; and in Lingard, *Hist. Eng.*, vol. vii. pp. 37–96.

[3] An act (3 Jac. I. c. 1) was then passed, which continued in force for two centuries and a half, making No-

vember 5 a day of thanksgiving for ever.

[4] *Parl. Hist. Journals*, pp. 274, 278 etc.; Hallam, *Const. Hist.*, vol. i. p. 308 and note t.

[5] Three subsidies and six fifteenths and tenths from the laity, and four clerical subsidies. 3 Jac. I. cc. 25, 26 Cf. Dowell, *Hist. of Taxation*, vol. i p. 159. The whole was estimated at £453,000. *Abstract of His Majesty's Revenue*, p. 11.

sovereigns of the house of Tudor, all of whom received life-grants of the subsidies on wool, skins, and leather, tonnage and poundage, likewise made to James I. in the first session of his first parliament.[1]   Near the close of the reign of Henry VIII. a material decrease in the relative value of the port duties set in, in consequence of the general advance in the price of all merchandise.   To prevent the deficiency which thus arose, as well as to enforce the protective or mercantile system against foreign goods, Mary, *by an order in council,* laid an impost upon short cloth, and in 1556 increased by impost the duty on sweet wine to correspond with the increase in the price of wine.   Elizabeth followed the examples set by her sister by the making of a special impost upon wines ; and in October, 1586, a new book of rates was published.[2] Following in the path of his predecessors, James, in order to increase the customs revenue of the crown, which at the beginning of his reign amounted to but £112,400,[3] and for the purpose of protecting Virginian against Spanish tobacco, put a new impost upon that article by virtue of a royal ordinance.[4] This power, to levy new impositions by virtue of the royal authority only, had also been exercised in the reign of Elizabeth by the grant of a monopoly to the "Levant Company," which was authorized to exact 5 *s.* 6 *d.* the hundredweight as customs upon all currants imported by merchants not members of that company.   When, after the issuance of James' proclamation against monopolies, the "Levant Company" surrendered its charter as such, the crown claimed the right to impose directly, in addition to a statutory poundage of 2 *s.* 6 *d.* the hundredweight, the duty upon currants which it had originally delegated.[5]   Of this imposition the merchants complained to parliament, and at the end of the second session now under consideration, the house demanded in the petition of grievances[6] then presented that neither the royal impost on cur-

Marginal notes: life-grants of the customs ; decrease in their relative value in the reign of Henry VIII. ; increased by Mary and Elizabeth through orders in council ; James also imposed a new impost upon Virginian tobacco ; a like impost upon currants exacted through the "Levant Company ;"

[1] See above, p. 16, and note 6.
[2] Cf. Dowell, *Hist. of Taxation,* vol. i. pp. 178–181.
[3] "This was the rate at which it was farmed for seven years, from 1604," etc. — Hall, *A Hist. of the Custom-Revenue,* pt. i. p. 174.
[4] Ibid., pp. 174–177.
[5] The great case of Impositions. Lane's *Reports,* p. 22 ; Howell, *State Trials,* vol. ii. pp. 371–534 ; Hall, *A Hist. of the Custom-Revenue,* part i. pp. 16, 145, 148, 185 ; Gardiner, *Hist. Eng.,* vol. ii. pp. 1–12.
[6] For the text of this petition, see Petyt's *Jus Parliamentarium.* Cf. *Parl. Deb. in 1610,* p. 123.

house
declared
both to be
illegal
without
parliamen-
tary
sanction;

Bate
resisted the
currant
impost
in the
exchequer;

unanimous
judgment
against
him;

its
substance;
rants, nor that laid upon tobacco by James, should be levied, because no such duties could be legally demanded without parliamentary sanction.   In order to put this contention to a legal test, a Levant merchant by the name of Bate resisted the payment of the royal impost on currants, whereupon an information was exhibited against him in the exchequer cham-ber,[1] where it was unanimously decided by the four barons that impositions could be legally levied both upon imports and exports by the unaided force of the royal prerogative.   From the only two opinions which have come down to us, those of Clarke and Fleming, we learn that they, in common with all royalist statesmen of that day, held that, in addition to the king's ordinary or common law power, he possessed an abso-lute authority, which he could exercise whenever he saw fit, *salus populi*.   It was held that, while it was true that the king could not tax any commodity within the realm without the consent of parliament, it was equally certain that he could tax without its consent foreign goods brought into it by means of foreign commerce, for the reason that "commerce and all affairs with foreigners, war and peace, and all treatises what-soever, are made by the absolute power of the king; he there-fore who has power over the cause has power also over the effect.   No exportation or importation can be but at the king's ports.   But the seaports are the king's gates, which he may

Baron
Clarke's
extreme
declaration;
open or shut to whom he pleases."   Baron Clarke even went so far as to hold that Edward III., in assenting to the act for-bidding any new impositions upon wool and leather, wherein the exclusive right of parliament to authorize all forms of direct and indirect taxation was expressly recognized in his day, "did not bind his successors."   Bitterly as these opinions have been condemned by succeeding generations, sharply as they were criticised in the debate which took place in the parliament of 1610, they certainly were not so regarded by all lawyers and statesmen[2] of that day who clearly understood the exchequer

even Coke
admitted
the right of
the crown.
precedents by which they were moulded.   Even Coke, with his passionate devotion to the common law, admitted that the crown had right on its side in this particular case.[3]

---

[1] Michaelmas Term, 4 James I.
[2] Hakewell afterwards declared that while he listened to the judgments, he was satisfied by the arguments sup-porting them.   *State Trials*, vol. ii. p. 404.
[3] *Rep.*, vol. xii. p. 33.

When the third session of parliament began on the 18th of November, 1606, James was able to announce that in the case of Bate the court of exchequer had a few days before rendered a judgment in his favor, a result that seems to have been acquiesced in for the moment, as the house passed without further comment to the consideration of the report which had been made by the commissioners appointed to devise an acceptable basis of union for the two kingdoms. The scheme of union proposed by the commissioners embodied four suggestions: (1) That all hostile laws between the two kingdoms should be repealed; (2) that an arrangement should be made for the mutual extradition of criminals; (3) that freedom of commercial intercourse, with a few exceptions, should be established; (4) that each kingdom should naturalize the natives of the other.[1] Against the proposal for freedom of commercial intercourse a storm of opposition arose from the English traders that found expression in the house of commons, where a stormy debate occurred, during which Fuller denounced the Scots as peddlers rather than merchants. To this Sir Christopher Pigott added in a passionate oration a general denunciation of the whole Scottish nation, whom he characterized as beggars, rebels, and traitors.[2] Aroused by this assault, and angered at the failure of the house to take immediate action against Pigott, the king instructed the council to bring him immediately to justice. To prevent that result, the commons took up the matter themselves, and after resolving that Pigott could not be called in question elsewhere, ordered that he should be expelled from the house and committed to the Tower.[3] Unable to reach any agreement on the commercial question, the house passed to the consideration of the equally difficult problem of naturalization, as to which the commissioners had reported that by the common law of England, the post-nati, as those were called who were born in Scotland after the king's accession, were no more aliens than if they had been born on the soil of England. The ante-nati, those born before the king's accession, were not, they said, denizens, a privilege which could be conferred upon them only by statute. The

Marginal notes:
James announced the result to the third session, which began November 18, 1606;

scheme of union proposed by the commissioners;

stormy debate in the house;

Pigott's expulsion;

the post-nati declared to be denizens;

ante-nati not entitled to that privilege;

---

[1] Cf. Gardiner, *Hist. Eng.*, vol. i. pp. 324–337.

[2] *Commons' Journals*, vol. i. p. 333.

[3] Ibid., p. 335. He was released, however, within a fortnight upon the plea of ill-health.

commission at once proposed two acts, one declaratory and the other remedial, to remove all difficulties by the parliamentary recognition of the rights of both classes.[1] A debate then ensued, during which Fuller sharply assailed the statement **Bacon defended the report;** made as to the legal rights of the post-nati,[2] to which Bacon replied[3] in defence of the report of the commissioners, in whose proceedings he had taken an active part as one of their number. The judges were next consulted, including Coke, who was then chief justice of the common pleas, and with a single **naturalization of the post-nati upheld by the judges;** exception they accepted the theory of the naturalization of the post-nati by force of the common law. But as the commons refused to accept the legal theory as to the status of the post-nati, and as James was unwilling to give up his rights to issue letters of denization to aliens, under which the ante-nati could be clothed with all the rights of naturalization except that of inheriting lands in England, the attempt to settle the question in parliament had to be abandoned. Thus reserving the questions of commercial intercourse and naturalization for future consideration, a bill[4] passed both houses which **all legislation hostile to Scotland repealed conditionally.** attempted only to provide for the repeal of all English legislation directed against Scotland as a hostile country, on condition that a like statute should be passed in the next Scotch parliament, and for the extradition of criminals. Such was the condition of things when the third session was prorogued on the 4th of July, 1607.

Status of the post-nati argued in king's bench and chancery in Colvill's case; Before the end of the year, the king resolved to transfer the contest for the naturalization of the post-nati, which he had lost in parliament, to the courts of law, where, from the known opinion of the judges, he was sure of a victory. With that end in view a piece of land was purchased in the name of Robert Colvill (or Calvin), an infant born in Edinburgh in 1605, in whose behalf two suits were brought, one in the king's bench and the other in chancery, against persons who were supposed to have deprived him of his land. The issue was so made up as to directly present the question whether or no Colvill was an alien, and as such disqualified from holding land in England. The question of law was argued in the exchequer

---

1 Gardiner, *Hist. Eng.*, vol. i. p. 326.
2 *Commons' Journals*, vol. i. p. 334.
3 *Letters and Life*, vol. iii. pp. 90, 218.

4 4 Jac. I. c. 1. The bill also regulated the manner in which Englishmen were to be brought to trial for offences committed in Scotland.

chamber before the chancellor and the twelve judges, all of whom, except two, declared in June, 1608, that Colvill was no alien, that allegiance is the obedience due to the sovereign, and persons born in the allegiance of the king are his natural subjects, regardless of locality. As allegiance was due by both kingdoms to one sovereign, it was held for that reason that internaturalization followed, although each kingdom had its own parliament and its own laws.[1]

judgment in favor of the post-nati, June, 1608;

This early doctrine as to allegiance has since been modified by statute; it is now regulated by 21 & 22 Vict. c. 48. By 7 & 8 Vict. c. 66, the law as to aliens was also greatly relaxed; and by the Naturalization Act, 1870, 33 & 34 Vict. c. 14, provision has been made for the naturalization of aliens, and also for the naturalization of British subjects in foreign states, as well as for their resumption of British nationality. Under the terms of that act both real and personal property may be acquired and held by an alien as by a natural-born British subject, and a title to such property may be acquired through an alien as through a natural-born British subject.[2]

early doctrine of allegiance modified, and law as to aliens relaxed, by recent statutes.

Within a month after his triumph in the case of the post-nati, James was driven by the condition of his exhausted treasury to utilize the decision in Bate's case, in which the judges had declared more than a year before that he had the legal right to impose customs dues upon merchandise in addition to those granted in the Tonnage and Poundage Act. The annual expenditure had now risen to £500,000, while the ordinary revenue hardly exceeded £320,000.[3] Under these trying conditions Salisbury, the new lord treasurer, after conference with the principal merchants, published on July 28, 1608, a new book of rates,[4] or values of goods from the poundage, which was accompanied by a royal order for the collection of new duties "to be forever hereafter paid to the king and his successors, on pain of his displeasure." But all such expedients failed to relieve the king's financial difficulties; after an interval of two years and a half, he was again forced to face the representatives of the nation.

New duties imposed by the crown under Bate's case;

a new book of rates.

---

[1] Calvin's case, *State Trials*, ii. 559, 7 Jac. I. 1608. See also notes of the judgments in *State Papers*, Dom., xxx. 40 and xxxiv. 10. Cf. Denman's Broom's *Const. Law*, 1885, pp. 4–59.

[2] Cf. Excursus III., Thomas' *Leading Cases in Const. Law*, p. 37.

[3] Gardiner, *Hist. Eng.*, vol. ii. p. 12. See also "Comparative View of the Estimated Ordinary Revenue of the Crown," in Appendix at the end of the work.

[4] Cf. Hall's *Hist. of the Custom-Revenue*, pp. 145, 174.

The fourth
session
began Feb-
ruary 9,
1610;
the "Great
Contract;"
To the fourth session which thus began on February 9, 1610, Cecil, in the hope of closing the ever-widening breach between the king and the parliament, submitted a proposal called the "Great Contract," that embodied an offer in general terms to redress all just grievances, provided the house would consent to grant as compensation a sum sufficient to pay the king's debts, and to provide a permanent support of £200,000 a year.   Before it was possible to determine whether or no the house could consent to make so great a concession, it was necessary first to define what the representatives of the

popular party considered as "just grievances;" and second, to ascertain how far the king would yield to the demands to be made for their redress.   From the stirring debates which took place in the house, from the conferences of that body with the lords and with the representatives of the king, and from the Petition of Grievances reported by a committee of the house, it is possible to make the following summary.   Turning first to the subject of impositions, to which the publication of the royal order of July 28, 1608, imposing new duties, had given a fresh interest, the lawyers of the house engaged in a debate that lasted for four days, in the course of which Hakewill,

Whitelocke, and Martin sharply assailed the judgment rendered by the judges in Bate's case, by a masterly review of all the statutes and precedents bearing upon the matter from the time of Edward I.   In reply Bacon and Yelverton said all that could be said in support of the royal contention.[1] Angered that his prerogative should be assailed after its recognition by the judges, James had sent a message more than a month before to the commons, forbidding them to debate his right to levy impositions in general at all.[2]   But relying upon the "ancient, general, and undoubted right of parliament, to debate all matters which do properly concern the subject," the house continued to listen to the opposing views of the constitutional lawyers,

until a compromise was reached, wherein the king agreed to consent to an act prohibiting him from levying impositions for the future,[3] provided he was allowed to retain those already

---

[1] *Parl. Deb. in 1610; State Trials*, vol. ii.   An excellent summary may be found of the whole in Hall's *A Hist. of the Custom-Revenue*, pp. 145–185, and also in Gardiner, vol. ii. pp. 75–82.

[2] Cott. MSS., tit. F. iv. fol. 255; *Commons' Journals*, vol. i. p. 427.

[3] *Parl. Deb. in 1610*, p. 62.   This bill was, however, dropped in the lords

imposed.   Before that conclusion was reached, however, full   purveyance
consideration was given to the old questions involving the king's   and ward-
surrender of the right of purveyance and the emoluments   ship;
which still resulted from feudal tenures, — specially those arising out of wardship and marriage, — when it was ascertained,
after a debate in which Bacon [1] elaborated the feudal branch
of this complicated subject, that the king would make all necessary concessions for an adequate pecuniary compensation.
Next in constitutional importance stood the abuse made of the   abuse of the
ordaining power of the king in council by means of proclama-   ordaining
tions, an abuse of which the commons complained because "there   power;
is a general fear conceived and spread amongst Your Majesty's
people, that proclamations will by degrees grow up and increase
to the strength and nature of laws, . . . and this fear is the
more increased by occasion of certain books lately published,
which ascribe a greater power to proclamations than heretofore
had been conceived to belong to them."   Reference was thus
made to a new law dictionary lately published by Dr. Cowell,   Cowell's
reader in civil law at Cambridge, in which the new notions of   law dic-
the prerogative had led the author to assert that the king "is   tionary;
above the law by his absolute power ; and though for the better
and equal course in making laws he do admit the three estates
into council, yet this in divers learned men's opinion is not of
constraint, but of his own benignity, or by reason of the promise made upon oath at the time of his coronation." [2]   In
order to satisfy the indignation excited by this ridiculous publication, the king issued a proclamation suppressing the book,[3]   suppressed
admitting beforehand "that he was a king by the common law   by procla-
of the land," and that he "had no power to make laws of him-   mation;
self, or to exact any subsidies *de jure* without the consent of
his three estates, and, therefore, he was so far from approving
the opinion, as he did hate those that believed it." [4]   While
James still held on to the right to issue proclamations beyond
the law in cases of emergency, when parliament was not sitting, he agreed to consult the judges and the council upon the

---

[1] *Letters and Life of Bacon*, vol. iv.
p. 163. See also *Parl. Deb. in 1610*,
p. 164.
[2] See the articles entitled " King,"
" Prerogative," " Parliament," " Subsidy."

[3] The proclamation may be found
in the preface to the 1708 ed. of the
Interpreter.
[4] Such was the report made by Salisbury to the lords. *Parl. Deb. in 1610*,
p. 24.

subject, and to cause those already issued to be amended.[1]
To the demand made by the house that he should exempt the
four counties on the Welsh border from the jurisdiction of
the president and council of Wales, a court which was a mere
agency of the conciliar system, the king replied that he could
not solve a question of such difficulty without further inquiry.[2]
If nothing more had remained, an amicable settlement might
have been reached.   But such a result became impossible by
reason of James' refusal to make any concessions whatever to
the demands of the commons upon the subject of ecclesiastical grievances.   To the requests that the deprived ministers
should be allowed to preach upon certain conditions, that the
old grievances of pluralities and non-residence should be removed, that the conflict of jurisdiction, which had arisen out
of the efforts made by the court of king's bench to limit
the powers of the high commission by writs of prohibitions
should be settled against the latter by a restraining statute, —
the house could obtain no satisfactory responses whatever.[3]
Under these discouraging circumstances the parliament was
prorogued on the 23d of July.

Two months after that event the king, in accordance with
his promise to consult the judges as to his power to issue proclamations, summoned Coke, the chief justice of the king's
bench, to appear before the council, where he was asked by
Salisbury, first, whether the king could by proclamation prohibit the building of new houses in London, in order to check
the overgrowth of that city ; second, whether he could in the
same way forbid the manufacture of starch from wheat, in
order to prevent the diminution of the supply for purposes of
food.   After conference with three of his brethren, an opinion
was delivered by the four a few days later, in the presence
of the council, against the king's pretensions, in terms which
have been set forth already.[4]

On the 16th of October, when the fifth and last session
began, the commons took up the task of opposition at the point
at which it had been broken off, and on the 31st the king

the presi-
dent and
council of
Wales ;

James
refused to
redress
ecclesias-
tical griev-
ances ;

parliament
prorogued
23d of July;

judges
called upon
to define
extent of
ordaining
power.

Fifth and
last session
began Oc-
tober 31 ;

----

[1] Gardiner, *Hist. Eng.*, vol. ii. p. 86.
[2] Upon that question, see Mr. Heath's
introduction to the " Argument on the
Jurisdiction of the Marches," in vol.
vii. of Bacon's *Works*.

[3] Such was the nature of the king's
answer read in the lords at the prorogation, in answer to the memorial there
presented on the 21st.
[4] See above, p. 180, and note 7.

informed them that if they did not intend to go on with the " Great Contract," he could find some other way to supply his wants. In vain were the terms of the bargain then debated again and again ; in vain did the king offer to consider the case of the four counties, and to grant the demands of the house as to proclamations and impositions. A vital subject of difference still remained. The king was immovable in his pur- failure to agree upon the terms of the " Great Contract ;" pose neither to permit any modification whatever in the ritual of the state church, nor to suffer any reform in the constitu- tion of the ecclesiastical courts by permitting their jurisdiction to be narrowed, either by an act of parliament, or by the courts of common law.[1] Angered and disheartened by a state of things in which the commons, while denouncing his Scotch favorites, withheld all supply, James adjourned the house ; and shortly thereafter dissolved the parliament on February 9, parliament dissolved in anger February 9, 1611. 1611, after an existence of nearly seven years. As the mem- bers returned to their homes, the ominous news was carried to every borough and to every shire "that the monarchy had broken with the great council of the realm." [2]

During the life of James' first parliament, thus brought to Seeds of the English constitu- tion sown in the New World ; a close, a momentous event occurred in the history of the Eng- lish Constitution, whereby its seeds were sown in the virgin soil of another hemisphere, where they ripened into the group of local self-governing communities out of whose union has arisen the federal republic of the United States. Before the close of the sixteenth century, every attempt at permanent settlement made by Englishmen in America had ended in failure and disappointment,[3] and Raleigh, whose adventurous spirit had planted in 1587 the lost colony [4] in the land to which Elizabeth had given the name of Virginia, was confined by James behind prison bars. But the time had now come for Raleigh's dream to be realized. Under a charter granted by charter of the Virginia Company ; James on April 10, 1606,[5] at the instance of Chief Justice Popham, a company was organized, which sent out three small vessels from the Thames on the 19th of the following Decem-

---

[1] For the proceedings of this session, see *Parl. Deb. in 1610*, pp. 126–145.

[2] Green's *Hist. of the Eng. People*, vol. iii. p. 82.

[3] See vol. i. p. 16.

[4] As to the fate of that colony, see Andrews, *Hist. of the U. S.*, vol. i. p. 30.

[5] Hening, *Statutes of Virginia*, vol. i. p. 57. See also for details, vol. i. pp. 17 and 18, and note to p. 18.

ber, containing the one hundred and five colonists who made the first permanent English settlement upon the soil of the New World.[1] After naming the headlands between which they sailed upon their arrival in the Chesapeake Cape Henry and Cape Charles, in honor of the royal princes, they gave the king's name to the river upon which they built Jamestown. In spite of a bitter struggle for existence, this colony so steadily advanced that from the towns, hundreds, and plantations into which it was subdivided were summoned the twenty-two delegates who, on the 30th of July, 1619, organized in the chancel of the church at Jamestown the first American representative assembly.[2]

the settlement at Jamestown;

first American representative assembly.

6. With the memorable dissolution that took place on the 9th of February, 1611, ended that oneness of aim, that singleness of purpose, which had united the crown and the nation during the storms of the Reformation ; and from that time can also be dated a marked change in the internal mechanism of the conciliar system itself, which became in a sense never before known subject to the king's personal will. Even in the days of Henry VIII., the great statesmen who sat at the council board had stood as a constitutional check upon the arbitrary exercise of the prerogative ; and throughout the reigns of Edward, Mary, and Elizabeth, the same influence had remained as an arbitrating force, ever ready to mediate in the event of a conflict between the royal and the national will. When James accepted Cecil as his chief councillor, he accepted with him the Tudor tradition which he embodied, and so long as he lived, the king was more or less restrained by the guiding hand of his great minister. But when Cecil, the last of the Tudor statesmen, passed away on the 24th of May, 1612, after having failed to reconcile the king and the nation through the execution of the "Great Contract," James was relieved of the yoke of which he had become weary, and he at once took into his own hands the personal direction of affairs by putting the treasury into commission,[3] and by resolving to act as his own secretary of state.[4] While the entire conciliar system was

Marked change in internal mechanism of conciliar system dates from

Cecil's death, May 24, 1612;

---

[1] Smith's *Hist. of Virginia*, 41 ; Purchas, iv. 1683–1733.

[2] See vol. i. p. 21.

[3] The chancellor of the exchequer at the time was no less a person than Sir Julius Cæsar.

[4] As to the king's objections to any candidate for the vacant office sup-

thus passing under the personal control of James, the king
himself was passing under the sway of a court favorite, — a
familiar influence in the royal system of Scotland, which had
not been heard of in England since the days of Gaveston and
De Vere.[1] A year before the death of Cecil, Robert Carr, a
young countryman who had won James' heart by his personal
beauty, was raised to the peerage with the title of Viscount
Rochester, after having been enriched by the grant of a manor
of which the imprisoned Raleigh had been despoiled for his
benefit.[2] In December, 1613, Rochester, the first Scotchman
to obtain a seat in the house of lords,[3] was created earl of
Somerset, a few weeks before his marriage to Frances Howard,
the daughter of the earl of Suffolk, who, in order to consummate her guilty union with the new favorite, had prosecuted a
scandalous proceeding for divorce, which the king himself had
aided and abetted. This upstart, who had no title to distinction save the king's favor, soon became not only James' sole
confidant, but his sole minister, the real chief of state. From
a dispatch of the Spanish ambassador written only a year after
Cecil's death, we learn that "the Viscount Rochester, at the
council table, showeth much temper and modesty, without
seeming to press or sway anything, but afterwards the king
resolveth all business with him alone." [4] Without the slightest
sympathy with the popular party, Somerset had urged James
to dissolve his first parliament, and in the second he voted in
the upper house against a conference of that body with the
commons upon the subject of impositions. But while the
breach between the crown and the parliament was thus being
widened through the influence of a mere adventurer, the king
was fortunate in having at his side the greatest thinker of the
age, whose advancement had no doubt been retarded by Cecil's
jealousy. In the parliament of 1604, Bacon had appeared as
a reconciling statesman, and in that year it was that he was
made a king's counsel; and in 1607 he was made solicitor-
general. When in August, 1613, the death of Fleming made
a vacancy in the chief justiceship of the king's bench, Bacon

appearance of court favorites;

Robert Carr made a peer;

first Scotchman to sit in the upper house;

becomes the real chief of state;

Bacon as a reconciling statesman;

---

ported by parliament, see *Court and
Times*, vol. i. pp. 171, 173, 179.

[1] See vol. i. p. 544.

[2] For a full statement of that transaction, see Gardiner, vol. ii. pp. 42–47.

[3] Ibid., p. 111.

[4] Sarmiento's dispatch sent home
by Digby, September 22, 1613, *State
Papers*, Spain.

found a fresh opportunity for advancement by inducing the king to raise his bitter adversary, Coke, to that position from the more congenial and more lucrative place of chief justice of the common pleas.   The vacancy thus created by Coke's "penal promotion" was filled by Hobart, the attorney-general, into whose office Bacon was at once inducted.   Such was the character of James' legal adviser when, at the close of 1613, he was compelled by the pressure of debts upon him to determine whether or no he could attempt to carry on the government any longer through the mere enforcement of legal rights incident to the prerogative, without the aid of parliament.   Since the last had refused to give him subsidies, every expedient had been employed in the effort to raise revenues. Loans had been made on privy seals; debts due from France and the Dutch had been collected; fines due through the star chamber had been enforced with a fresh severity; lands had been sold which were to have been indissolubly annexed to the crown; and the hereditary title of baronet now created was offered to all reputable knights and esquires possessed of lands worth £1,000 a year, provided they would pay to the exchequer £1,080 for their patents.[1]   Not until after all these expedients had failed to supply even approximately the king's wants, did a majority of the council advise him in February of 1614 to call a parliament.[2]   Some time before, both Bacon and Neville had urged him to that course, and both had ventured to suggest a way in which all differences could be settled between the nation and the king.   Neville, who, in 1612, had drawn up a memorial on the subject, even went so far as to undertake that the house of commons would be liberal in the grant of supplies, if the king would make the required concessions,[3] a circumstance which gave for the moment to him and his associates the title of "undertakers."   A suspicion that some kind of a compact had thus been made with the view of packing the approaching parliament with royal nominees

(marginal notes:) made attorney-general;

expedients for raising revenues;

creation of the title of baronet;

calling of a parliament resolved upon;

the "undertakers;"

---

[1] It was expected that this new order of hereditary knights would number two hundred. See Collins' *Baronetage*, vol. iv. p. 289. Only ninety-three patents, however, were sold in the first six years. *Abstract of the King's Revenue*, pp. 36–38; Somers' *Tracts*, vol. ii. p. 254.

[2] Council to the king, February 16, *State Papers*, Dom., lxxvi. 22.

[3] *State Papers*, Dom., lxxiv. 46; Carte, *Hist.*, vol. iv. p. 17. James afterward denied that he had any bargain with the "undertakers." *Parl. Hist.*, p. 1149.

resulted in the rejection of the government candidates on every hand, and in the return to Westminster of three hundred members, nearly two thirds of the whole house, who were elected for the first time.[1] Among the new men who thus came upon the stage were John Eliot and Thomas Wentworth, destined to bear such mighty parts in the time to come.[2]

James' second parliament, which met on the 5th of April, 1614, at once emphasized the fact that it had inherited the spirit of its predecessor by promptly rejecting as inadequate the unimportant concessions offered in the king's speech, and by announcing that no supply could be granted until a settlement should first be made of the open questions involved in the impositions, the ecclesiastical grievances, and in the monopolies. After the matter of impositions had been reargued for the benefit of the new members, a resolution was reached to ask a conference with the lords, who were to be invited to join the house in a petition to the king upon that all-important subject.[3] The lords, however, declined the conference,[4] and refused to accept the invitation to lead the constitutional resistance to the crown by calling upon the judges to give opinions upon the legal point in which was involved the whole issue. But the judges, led by Coke, prudently declined the responsibility by suggesting that they might be called upon to judge the question judicially.[5] In the course of the debate which took place in the lords the commons were sorely offended by a denunciation pronounced against them by Bishop Neile, who said that men who had taken the oaths of supremacy and allegiance could not in good conscience even discuss the subject of impositions, whose consideration would only lead to disloyal and seditious speeches, to which the peers should not even listen.[6] When the lower house was about to make the false step of appealing to the king for action, they were rescued by a motion for redress to the lords themselves, who, after calling the bishop to account in that particular case, plainly intimated that in future they would not permit a mem-

Marginal notes: Eliot and Wentworth.

James' second parliament met April 5, 1614;

the subject of impositions revived;

judges decline to give opinions upon it extra-judicially;

the question of privilege involved in Neile's case;

---

[1] A list of this parliament, printed from the Kimbolton MS., is in the *Palatine Note-Book*, vol. iii. No. 30.

[2] The statement that Pym sat in this parliament as a member from Calne is now known to be erroneous. He did not appear in that capacity until 1621.

[3] For details, see *Commons' Journals*, vol. i. pp. 481, 486.

[4] *Commons' Journals*, vol. ii. pp. 707, 708; Petyt's *Jus Parliamentarium*, p. 340.

[5] *Lords' Journals*, vol. ii. p. 706.

[6] Ibid., vol. ii. p. 709.

ber of their house to be called in question upon common fame alone.[1]   In that way time passed without action until the 3d of June, when James sent a message to the house, saying that unless they proceed to discuss supply without further delay, he would order a dissolution, a threat which only produced a fresh outburst of abuse of the courtiers and the Scotch favor-

dissolution of "The Addled Parliament."

ites.   Four days later James kept his word by dissolving the houses, after a session of little more than two months, within which time not a single bill received the royal assent, a circumstance out of which arose the nickname of "The Addled Parliament."[2]

James resolved to live without parliaments;

Exasperated by another failure to obtain supplies, the king now resolved to live without parliaments, a resolve in which he persevered for nearly seven years.   During that long interval every resource of the conciliar system was employed to raise by means of the prerogative alone, which Bacon called "the accomplishment and perfection of the common law," sums sufficient to supply the ever-increasing wants of the crown, and to strike down by means of its despotic power every individual who might dare to oppose the royal will.   Such an

revival of all forms of royal taxation;

undertaking necessarily involved the revival of all those illegitimate forms of royal taxation which the parliaments of the fourteenth and fifteenth centuries had branded as unlawful.

a benevolence demanded;

The most obnoxious, perhaps, of all such demands was that known as a benevolence, that arbitrary taxation by the crown of individuals and corporations which had been so positively forbidden by the memorable act of Richard III.   In the month that followed the dissolution the king, to whom the bishops and other great lords had made a genuine offer of a benevolence the moment that parliament refused to supply his wants,[3] directed the council to send out letters to every county and to every borough, in the way of an appeal for a general and voluntary contribution.[4]   In September a second batch of letters followed,[5] and in a few months pressure was applied directly to the tax-payers by the council through the sheriffs and justices of the peace.[6]   In the face of such proceedings the

[1] *Lords' Journals*, vol. ii. p. 713.
[2] *Court and Times*, vol. i. pp. 320, 323.
[3] Ibid., vol. i. p. 325.
[4] This was done against Bacon's advice. *Letters and Life*, vol. v. p. 81.

[5] Council to the sheriffs, September 17, *Council Register*.
[6] Cf. Gardiner, *Hist. Eng.*, vol. ii. pp. 265–267.

people of the counties of Devonshire and Somerset [1] dared to remonstrate against a precedent which they said would injure their posterity, and Oliver St. John, a gentleman of Marlborough, not only refused to subscribe, but wrote a letter in which he denounced the benevolence as contrary to the Great Charter, the act of Richard III., and the coronation oath of the king. As a rebuke for his intemperate language, he was at once committed to the Tower by the council, and in April, 1615, Attorney-General Bacon undertook his prosecution, which resulted in the imposition by the star chamber of a fine of £5,000, and imprisonment during the king's pleasure.[2]   In the course of that proceeding Bacon maintained that the benevolence in question was really a free gift, entirely different from exactions called by that name in former times; and Coke, strange to say, so far agreed with him as to take back his former opinion against the illegality of benevolences demanded by letters under the great seal.[3]

Oliver St. John boldly resisted it;

prosecuted by Bacon and imprisoned;

Coke's opinion.

While the council was thus engaged in the punishment of one who had ventured to resist its peculiar methods of taxation, it was called upon to deal with another, who dared to raise his voice against abuses of an ecclesiastical character. Edmond Peacham, a Somersetshire rector, who had made charges against his bishop and against the officials of the consistory court, was found guilty of libel by the high commission December 19, 1614, and deprived of his orders.[4]   In the course of that proceeding his house was searched, and among his papers was found an unpublished manuscript in the form of a sermon, which embodied an attack not only upon the ministers, but upon the king himself, who was denounced for his refusal to subject the ecclesiastical to the temporal courts.   Coupling these expressions with the fact that their author lived in Somerset, a shire which had taken a leading part in resisting the benevolence, the council took Peacham in hand, and in January, 1615, he was cruelly tortured [5] in the

Prosecution of Peacham;

first convicted of libel in the high commission;

subjected to torture;

---

[1] Like protests came from Warwickshire and Nottinghamshire. *Privy Council Register*, November 2, 14, 16, 30.

[2] *State Trials*, vol. ii. p. 889.

[3] Ibid., Bacon's *Letters and Life*, vol. v. p. 136.   To his last opinion Coke adhered in his reports.   12 Rep. 119.

[4] *State Papers*, lxxviii. 78.

[5] See Bacon's *Letters and Life*, vol. v. p. 91; *State Trials*, vol. ii. p. 871. As Secretary Winwood has expressed it, the old man was put to the rack and examined "before torture, in torture, between torture, and after torture." But he suffered in silence.

hope of extorting from him a revelation as to the existence
of a conspiracy that existed only in the imagination of his
persecutors. When it became apparent that no evidence of a
conspiracy could be obtained, the council resolved to proceed

*and then
prosecuted
for treason;*

against Peacham alone, not for a seditious libel, but for treason
in compassing the king's death, under the terms of the statute
of Edward III. In order to maintain such a prosecution, it
was necessary to overcome the legal difficulties involved in the
suggestions, first, that the writing in question had never been
published; second, that even if it had been, its contents did
not constitute treason. To remove these obstacles James
directed his attorney-general, in accordance with a custom

*judges
consulted
separately
on the law
point
involved;*

which existed at that time,[1] to consult the judges of the king's
bench separately, in the hope of obtaining favorable opinions
upon both points. While the three puisne judges submitted
to this process without difficulty, giving opinions favorable to
the crown, Chief Justice Coke resisted upon the ground that
the judges could be consulted only as a body : "Such particular and auricular taking of opinions," he said, "is not according to the custom of the realm." [2] Overborne on that point,

*Coke's
opinion;*

he finally gave a very unsatisfactory opinion, in which, after
passing over the question of publication, he held that no mere
declaration of the king's unfitness to govern constituted treason, unless it "disabled his title." [3] In spite, however, of that

*Peacham's
conviction.*

declaration in his favor, Peacham was sent to the Taunton
assizes, where he was convicted and sentenced to death. Although the sentence was not carried out, he died in jail about
seven months afterwards.[4]

*James
assailed the
independ-
ence of
the judges;*

It was thus made apparent to James that when matters
were brought to a final test, the one force to which the nation
could appeal against the crown, when parliaments were suspended, was embodied in the courts of common law, whose

*no dismis-
sal for
political
reasons
since
accession of
Elizabeth;*

efficacy depended alone upon the independence of the judges.
While in theory their tenure rested only on the pleasure of
the sovereign, the fact remained that no one of them had been
dismissed for political reasons since the accession of Elizabeth.[5]

---

1 Bacon's *Letters and Life*, vol. v. p.
91, and note 2.

2 Bacon to the king, January 27, *Letters and Life*, vol. v. p. 100.

3 Ibid., vol. vi. p. 92. See also

Spedding's *Letters and Life of Bacon*,
vol. v. p. 114.

4 March, 1616.

5 Gardiner, *Hist. Eng.*, vol. ii. p. 8.
As to the case of Chief Baron Man-

An opportunity to abolish that security, and at the same time to get rid of the troublesome and influential chief justice who relied upon it, was given to James in 1616 by the "Case of Commendams," heard in the exchequer chamber in that year before the twelve judges, wherein the general prerogative of the king to grant a living to be held *in commendam*, that is, along with a bishopric, was argued by counsel in connection with the special points of the case. When, in 1607, Fuller as counsel for two Puritans had disputed the power of the high commission to fine and imprison, he was punished by that court for having slandered the king's authority;[1] and when, in 1613, Whitelocke, a lawyer who had denounced impositions in James' first parliament, gave a private opinion to his client that a commission issued by the king to inquire into the state of the navy was illegal, he was committed to the Fleet, and then censured in the star chamber.[2] Equally regardless of the independence of the judges, the king now directed the attorney-general to write a letter to those who were charged with the decision of the "Case of Commendams," in which they were instructed not to proceed to judgment until after consultation with him.[3] The judges then replied[4] collectively to the king that as the attorney-general's letter was illegal, they had proceeded with the case on the appointed day. When, however, the judges were subjected to censure by the king and council, they all finally gave way but Coke, who maintained that the delay demanded was contrary to law and to their oaths. To the abstract question whether in a like case in future he would consult with the king before rendering judgment, in the event his majesty should consider himself interested, nothing more could be drawn from him than the statement that when such a case should arise, he would do what was fitting for a judge to do.[5] For this noble declaration, Coke, after suspension from office and censure by the council, was dismissed from the chief

[marginal notes: the "Case of Commendams;" independence of the bar assailed by the punishment of Fuller and Whitelocke; in the "Case of Commendams" all the judges yielded to pressure except Coke;]

wood in 1572, see Foss, *Judges*, vol. v. p. 321.

[1] It was afterwards held by the twelve judges that Fuller's contempt was punishable by the common law courts and not the ecclesiastical. 12 Rep. 41.

[2] Whitelocke's *Liber Famelicus*, pp. 33–40, 113–118; June 12, *Council Register*.

[3] Bacon first wrote to Coke alone (April 25); and then, at his suggestion, directly (April 26) to the rest. *Letters and Life*, vol. v. p. 273.

[4] April 27. *State Papers*, lxxxvii. 44, ii.

[5] Carte, vol. iv. p. 35.

dismissed
from the
chief
justiceship
November,
1616.
justiceship in November, 1616.[1] The Tudor system of government still survived, but the policy employed by the Tudors in
its administration was now completely at an end.   Not only
had James destroyed that oneness of aim, that singleness of
purpose, which had united the parliament to the monarchs of
that house, but he had at last overthrown the sacred independence of the judges which they had to a great extent upheld.

Somerset
superseded
by Buck-
ingham,
In the year preceding the dethronement of Coke from the
kingship of the common law, Somerset, who had risen so rapidly
to giddy heights of political power, was suddenly eclipsed by
the rise of a fresh favorite, the son of a Leicestershire knight,
whose personal beauty was as great as his own.   In the fall
of 1614, George Villiers, at the age of twenty-two, first presented himself to James, and so rapid was his rise that, upon
the overthrow of Somerset in the next year, he was able to
take his place as evidence of the fact that the rule of personal
dependents was to become in England, as it had been in Scotland, a matter of settled policy.   Before the close of 1616, Villiers was raised to the peerage as Viscount Villiers ; during
the two following years he was made first earl and then marquis of Buckingham ; in 1619 he was made lord high admiral ;[2]
for whom
the title of
duke was
revived in
1623;
and in 1623 the king revived the title of duke, which had been
in abeyance since the execution of Norfolk, in order to bestow
upon the favorite the highest honor in the gift of an English
sovereign.[3]   To the rising fortunes of Buckingham Bacon
promptly attached himself, and in June, 1616, he became a
privy councillor ;[4] in the next year he was made lord keeper ;[5]
Bacon
made lord
chancellor
in 1618;
and in January, 1618, he became lord chancellor, an honor to
which was soon added a place in the peerage as Lord Veru-
lam.[6]   Such were the two leading statesmen, of strangely
different temper, who were called upon to look into the king's
finances in 1617, when it was found that his debts amounted
to £726,000.[7] Bacon had always counselled economy, and the

[1] Bacon's *Letters and Life*, vol. vi.
p. 94.
[2] January 28. Patent Rolls, 16 Jac.
I. pt. 17.
[3] "Since Norfolk's execution, there
had been no dukes in England." —
Gardiner, *Hist. Eng.*, vol. v. p. 54.
[4] *Council Register*, June 9.
[5] On March 3 Chancellor Brackley

resigned, and on the 7th the great seal
was given to Bacon with the inferior
title of lord keeper.
[6] A name which posterity has ignored. See Spedding's *Letters and
Life of Bacon*, vol. vi. p. 316.
[7] The council to the king, September
27, 1617. *State Papers*, Dom., xciii.
99.

king now consented to a policy of retrenchment, the carrying out of which was committed to Cranfield, who had been appointed[1] surveyor-general of the customs.   While Cranfield reduced expenditures on the one hand, the income was growing upon the other through a rapid increase in English trade.   In that way, without any additional tax upon the consumer, the great customs, which at the king's accession had produced less than £86,000, were now leased for £140,000, the duties on wine having increased from £4,400 to £15,900.[2]   While such accessions gave encouragement for the moment, they became of no consequence when the king was confronted with the prospect of a foreign war, which the drift of affairs upon the Continent soon put before him.

> *Cranfield surveyor-general of the customs, which greatly increase with the growth of trade.*

When, in May, 1561, Queen Elizabeth joined the Lutheran states in their refusal to send delegates to the council of Trent, England, after long hesitation, definitely espoused the cause of the Reformation;[3] and the Elizabethan tradition, that the German protestants should not be abandoned in any fresh struggle with the house of Austria, which Cecil brought to the council board of James, was greatly strengthened when, in 1612, that minister arranged the marriage of the king's daughter Elizabeth with the heir of the Elector Palatine Frederick IV., the leading prince in that Protestant Union which had been formed in 1608 for mutual protection, when the Calvinistic states found themselves begirt on every side but one by catholic opponents.   In 1609 the formation of the Protestant Union was met by the organization of the Catholic League under the leadership of Maximilian, duke of Bavaria, who found it convenient to appeal to Spain as the champion of catholicism, — a quarter from which he received a promise of aid, provided he should be named as director of the league.   After the death of Cecil had made James his own minister, he conceived the idea that by a union with Spain, with which he had made peace shortly after his accession,[4] he could protect the German protestants by controlling the action of the league

> *James' daughter married to the elector palatine; formation of the Protestant Union in 1608 met by organization of Catholic League in 1609; James' attempt to control the league through Spanish influence;*

---

[1] Through Buckingham's influence, in 1615. See Dowell, *Hist. of Taxation*, vol. i. pp. 189–191.

[2] Gardiner, *Hist. Eng.*, vol. iii. p. 196; and to the same effect, Dowell, vol. i. p. 189.

[3] See above, p. 159.

[4] For the terms of the treaty to which James swore in August, 1604, see *Fœdera*, vol. xvi. p. 617.

through Spain's influence with every catholic power. James' interest in that design was greatly strengthened when his friendly disposition was encouraged by a hint from Spain of an alliance[1] between his son and the infanta, in whose great prospective dowry he saw a hope of relief from appeals to parliament. In 1614 James proposed such a marriage to Spain, and in 1617, by the formal opening of negotiations, the nation became alarmed at the prospect of a catholic queen, a catholic heir to the throne, and consequent concessions in favor of their co-religionists within the realm.[2] In 1619 Ferdinand, that member of the house of Austria who had not only proclaimed but carried out the policy of suppressing heresy by force in the countries he ruled, was elected emperor, and thus became the possessor of the whole Austrian heritage in Germany.[3] In the hope of protecting her protestantism against the impending doom, Bohemia, after solemnly decreeing the deposition of Ferdinand, chose the young Elector Palatine Frederick V., the son-in-law of James, as her king.[4] By the new conditions thus created, the value of James' diplomatic scheme for the control of the Catholic League through Spain's influence with the house of Austria was put to a practical test. The result was that in the spring of 1620 Spain threw off the mask by taking an open part with the emperor in military operations which not only sealed the fate of Bohemia, but resulted in the driving of James' son-in-law as a fugitive to North Germany.[5] Aroused by the cry for war that arose upon the reception of the news from the Palatinate, the king finally promised aid to the princes of the union, and in the council, where his resolve was received with enthusiasm, a benevolence was agreed upon for the purpose of carrying on the war.[6] Not, however, until it was ascertained that even the prevailing enthusiasm in the protestant cause was insufficient to make such an illegal method of taxation effective was the calling of parliament resolved upon, a conclusion

proposal of marriage made to Spain in 1614;

James' son-in-law, Frederick V., chosen king of Bohemia;

and in the spring of 1620 he was driven from his dominions;

James resolved on war and demanded a benevolence.

[1] July, 1605.
[2] For the whole story, see Gardiner, *Hist. Eng.*, vol. i. p. 343; vol. ii. pp. 138, 252, 316 *et seq.*
[3] See Bryce, *The Holy Roman Empire*, pp. 323, 324.
[4] Voigt, in Raumer's *Historisches Taschenbuch*, 1853, pp. 134, 220; Gardiner, vol. iii. p. 309.
[5] The decisive struggle took place at Prague, October 29.
[6] Contributions to the Palatinate, *State Papers*, Dom., cxvii. 21, 30, 64; cxix. 14. The actual collections were very small.

which was announced in a proclamation issued on the 6th of November.

7. To his third parliament, which thus met on the 30th[1] of January, 1621, James, after giving a vague assurance that English religion should suffer no detriment through the pending Spanish marriage, appealed for means to aid him in the recovery of the Palatinate, a cause in which, he said, he had already expended all that he could beg or borrow, not a penny having been received from the estates during a period of ten years. Under these circumstances, the houses unanimously agreed to grant two subsidies,[2] not as a sum sufficient for the expenses of the war, but as an earnest of their good intentions. Having thus discharged their religious duty, the popular party in the house, under the leadership of ex-Chief Justice Coke, who had returned to their ranks after an absence of many years, addressed itself with renewed zeal to the redress of national grievances. Despite the promises, first of Elizabeth, then of James, monopolies had continued to multiply until it now became necessary to check the abuses which arose from them by extraordinary means. During the preceding period of one hundred and sixty-two years (1459–1621) there is no record of a parliamentary impeachment either in the rolls of parliament or in the lords' journals.[3] No such proceeding had taken place since Lord Stanley was impeached in 1459 for not sending his troops to the battle of Bloreheath.[4] The long disuse of this great weapon of parliamentary warfare finds its most probable explanation in the fact that the popular branch of parliament was in no position to initiate such aggressive measures during the period of depression which was coëxtensive with the reign of the house of Tudor, whose princes found it far more convenient to execute either justice or vengeance through bills of attainder, or through judgments rendered in the star chamber. However that may be, the fact remains that the next regular impeachment to Lord Stanley's in 1459 was that of Sir Giles Mompesson, who in the parliament of 1621[5] was impeached, together with Sir Francis Mitchell,

Marginal notes: A third parliament met January 30, 1621: two subsidies granted in aid of the war; impeachment revived as a means of punishing monopolists; impeachment of Mompesson, Mitchell, and

---

[1] Postponed from the 16th, the date named in the proclamation.

[2] Equivalent to about £160,000. See *Proceedings and Debates*, vol. i. pp. 48, 50.

[3] Sir J. F. Stephen, *Hist. of the Crim. Law*, vol. i. p. 158.

[4] *Rot. Parl.*, iii. 458.

[5] Since that date fifty-four impeachments have taken place, the last being

for fraud and oppression committed as patentees for the ex-clusive manufacture of gold and silver thread, for the inspec-tion of inns and hostelries, and for the licensing of ale-houses. While no definite articles were presented according to mod-ern forms, an accusation was made by the commons and a judgment rendered by the lords, condemning both to fine, imprisonment, and degradation from the honor of knighthood.[1]

Yelverton; A judgment imposing both fine and imprisonment was also rendered at the same session by the lords against Sir H. Yel-verton, who had become involved in the proceedings against Mompesson and Mitchell, and who had declared that the patent for the manufacture of gold and silver thread was not a mo-

same process ex-tended to ministers — impeach-ment of Bacon. nopoly.[2] Turning then from the prosecution of private persons, the house ventured to revive the old system of impeaching the king's ministers by bringing to the bar of the upper house Lord Chancellor Bacon upon a charge of judicial corruption,[3] a crime which seems to have been shockingly prevalent at that day. The great philosopher, in touching, abject humility, admitted his guilt and renounced all defence. "I do again confess," he said, "there is a great deal of corruption and neglect, for which I am heartily and penitently sorry."[4]

House attempted to act as a court in Floyd's case; While the house was thus legitimately engaged as the grand inquest of the realm in presenting offenders for judgment at the bar of the lords, it was impelled in a moment of passion to usurp a higher judicial function, which it was forced to relin-quish in confusion. It having been reported to the commons that a catholic barrister, named Floyd, then a prisoner in the Fleet, had rejoiced at the news of the battle of Prague, whereby the elector palatine and his wife "were now turned out of doors," he was brought before the house, where, in a paroxysm of a rage, what purported to be a legal judgment of condemna-

that of Lord Melville in 1805. For the list, see note to p. 159, vol. i. of Sir J. F. Stephen's *Hist. of the Crim. Law.*

[1] Sentence was pronounced against Mompesson, who escaped, in his ab-sence. For the sentence against Mitch-ell, who actually suffered punishment, see *Lords' Journals*, vol. iii. pp. 89, 95, 108.

[2] For debate in the lords on his case, see *Journals*, vol. iii. pp. 111, 115; El-sing's *Notes*, p. 71.

[3] In March the charges of bribery were laid before the lords "without prejudice or opinion." — *Commons' Journals*, vol. i. p. 560.

[4] *Lords' Journals*, vol. iii. p. 98. When questioned by a committee as to the genuineness of his signature to his submission, he replied: "My lords, it is my act, my hand, my heart. I beseech your lordships be merciful unto a broken reed."

tion was pronounced against him.[1] Before, however, the cruel sentence could be executed, the king inquired of the house how it was that they could inflict punishment upon any one who, not being one of them, had neither offended against the house, nor against any of its members ; and to this was added a refer- ence to the parliament rolls, where an entry appeared as early as the first year of Henry IV., in which the commons had ad- mitted that they had nothing to do with sentencing offenders.[2] As a settlement of the difficulty, it was finally agreed that the lords should pass judgment upon Floyd,[3] a proceeding which seems to have been really as unconstitutional as that taken by the commons, owing to the fact that the house failed to give the lords jurisdiction of the case by presenting a definite charge against Floyd at its bar. Angered, perhaps, at the assumption of the commons in the case of Floyd, and irri- tated by the contemptuous silence with which they received his appeals for further subsidies, James, on the 28th of May, ordered an adjournment of parliament within a week until the following November.

such judicial power disclaimed in reign of Henry IV.;

adjourned until November.

When the houses came together on the 20th of that month, the popular branch was at once called upon to deal with a question of personal privilege, arising out of accusations made after the adjournment against Sir Edward Coke and Sir Edwin Sandys, two influential members, who had been proceeded against upon charges which upon their face had no connection with their political conduct in the house. That body, however, assuming that such conduct was the real motive for the prose- cutions, ordered Coke's accusers to be taken into custody by the sergeant-at-arms, and sent a committee to inquire of San- dys, who was absent at the opening of the session on account of illness, as to the real cause of his arrest.[4] While the king subsequently denied that the commitment of Sandys had any connection with his public conduct, he added the alarming

Questions of privilege involved in cases of Coke and Sandys;

---

[1] He was sentenced to be pilloried three times, to ride bareback, and then to pay a fine of £1,000. *Commons' Journals*, vol. i. p. 601; *Proceedings and Debates*, vol. i. p. 370.

[2] In 1399 the judicial power, at the suggestion of the commons themselves, had been declared to reside in the lords alone. *Rot. Parl.*, vol. iii. p. 427.

[3] *Lords' Journals*, vol. iii. p. 134. The house declared in their journals that their proceedings should not be "drawn or used as a precedent," etc. *Parl. Hist.*, vol. v. p. 435.

[4] *Commons' Journals*, pp. 643, 644, 662 ; Lingard, vol. ii. p. 232.

James
claimed the
right to
punish any
man's
misdemean-
ors in par-
liament;

declaration that "we think ourselves very free and able to punish any man's misdemeanors in parliament, as well during their sittings as after; which we mean not to spare hereafter, upon any occasion of any man's insolent behaviour there shall be ministered unto us." [1]   Upon the heels of this controversy as to the imprisonments of Coke and Sandys soon followed another, involving the right of parliament to deliberate upon all matters of national concern, presented by a petition which, after asserting that the pope and the king of Spain were aspiring to universal dominion, protested against the proposed marriage of the infanta and the prince of Wales, who, it was said, should be married to one of his own faith.   Proceeding upon the Tudor theory that there were certain privileged subjects to which the right of parliamentary deliberation did not extend,

also
attempted
to abridge
the right
of delib-
eration;

James directed an angry letter to the speaker, in which, after asserting that the house had trenched upon his "prerogative royal" by debating "publicly in matters far beyond their reach or capacity," he forbade the members to meddle "with mysteries of state," in which were specially included the "match with the daughter of Spain," and "the honour of that king." [2]

protest of
the house;

To this the house answered by protesting against the attempt made in the king's letter "to abridge us of the ancient liberty of parliament for freedom of speech, . . . a liberty which we assure ourselves so wise and just a king will not infringe, the same being our undoubted right and inheritance received from our ancestors, and without which we cannot freely debate nor clearly discern of things in question before us." [3]   Then followed a bitter and sarcastic rejoinder from the king, in the

James
declared
its
privileges
to be a
matter of
favor and
not of
right;

course of which, while promising to be as careful of their lawful liberties and privileges as of his own prerogative, he clearly asserted the belief that such liberties and privileges were not an ancient and undoubted right of inheritance, but a mere boon enjoyed by the grace and permission of his ancestors. [4]

---

[1] *Parl. Hist.*, vol. v. p. 492.

[2] The king to the speaker, December 3, *Proceedings and Debates*, vol. ii. p. 277. It was in this letter that James, after referring to the commitment of Sandys, declared himself in the terms quoted above in the text as to his power to punish any man's misdemeanors in parliament.

[3] *Proceedings and Debates*, vol. ii. pp. 289–300.   It was when the deputation arrived with this protestation that James cried out, "Bring stools for the ambassadors." — *State Papers*, Dom., cxxiv. 40.

[4] King to Calvert, December 16, *Proceedings and Debates*, vol. ii. p. 339.

As a solemn and emphatic dissent from that pernicious doc- the memorable protestation of December, 1621. trine, the commons, before the Christmas recess, entered upon their journal, on the 18th of December, 1621, the following memorable protestation : —

"That the liberties, franchises, privileges, and jurisdictions of parliament are the ancient and undoubted birthright and inheritance of the subjects of England ; and that the arduous and urgent affairs concerning the king, state, and defence of the realm and church of England, and the making and mainte- nance of the laws, and redress of grievances, which daily hap- pen within this realm, are proper subjects and matter of counsel and debate in parliament ; and that in the handling and pro- ceeding of those businesses every member of the house hath, and of right ought to have, freedom of speech, to propound, treat, reason, and bring to conclusion the same : —

"That the commons in parliament have like liberty and freedom to treat of those matters, in such order as in their judgments shall seem fittest, and that every such member of the said house hath like freedom from all impeachment, imprison- ment, and molestation, other than censure of the house itself, for or concerning any bill, speaking, reasoning, or declaring of any matter or matters, touching the parliament or parliament business ; and that, if any of the said members be complained of and questioned for anything said or done in parliament, the same is to be shewed to the king by the advice and assent of all the commons assembled in parliament, before the king give credence to any private information." [1]

On the 30th of December, after the Christmas recess, the king sent for the journals of the house, and in the presence of the council and the judges, tore out with his own hands the page upon which the offensive protestation was written ; [2] and then, after committing Coke, Phelips, and Mallory to the Tower, after banishing Digges, Crewe, Rich, and Perrot to Ireland as royal commissioners, and after confining Pym to his own house in London, [3] he dissolved parliament on the 6th of January, 1622.

8. Before the meeting of James' fourth and last parliament

[1] *Proceedings and Debates*, vol. ii. p. 359.
[2] *Parl. Hist.*, vol. i. p. 1362.
[3] *State Papers*, Dom., cxxvii. 8, 26: *Parl. Hist.*, vol. v. p. 525.

James'
fourth and
last parlia-
ment met
February
19, 1624;

on the 19th of February, 1624, the long and humiliating negotiation for the marriage of the prince with the infanta had
ended in angry disappointment.   In March, 1623, Charles, together with Buckingham, had appeared at Madrid in order to
press the matter to a definite conclusion, and in the following

end of the
Spanish
marriage
negotia-
tions;

October they returned to England without the princess, after
having been informed by Olivares that "we have a maxim of
state, that the king of Spain must never fight against the
emperor.   We cannot employ our forces against the house of
Austria." [1]   Thus disappointed of all hope of Spanish intervention for the restoration of his son-in-law, the elector palatine,
whose electoral dignity had already been transferred by the
emperor to the duke of Bavaria,[2] James at last resolved under
pressure from Buckingham and Charles, by whom the actual
direction of affairs was now assumed, upon an open breach
with Spain and a declaration of war for the recovery of the

James laid
the entire
transac-
tion before
the house
for its con-
sideration
and advice;

Palatinate.   In order to obtain means for carrying on the war,
the houses had been called together,[3] and as a practical confession of his error in contending that they were incompetent to
deal with "mysteries of state," James laid before them the
entire Spanish negotiation for their consideration and advice,
"in the annulling and breaking of those two treaties, both of

subsidies
granted
condition-
ally;

the match and of the Palatinate."   In that happy mood three
subsidies and three fifteenths were cheerfully granted, subject,
however, to the proviso that the money was to be expended
only on the warrant of the council of war, by treasurers responsible to the house for the furtherance of four definite objects,
which were carefully specified in the grant.[4]   Under these
altered conditions the one statesman who seems to have stood
out for the Spanish alliance was the lord treasurer, Cranfield,
the earl of Middlesex, who, while improving the royal exchequer, had not failed to greatly augment his private fortunes.

impeach-
ment of
Middlesex;

Charges of malversation in office were therefore presented
against him by Coke and Sandys at the bar of the lords, where
a heavy sentence, including deprivation of office, was pro-

---

[1] To which Charles replied, "There
is an end of all; for without this, you
may not rely upon either marriage
or friendship."—Buckingham's Relations, *Lords' Journals*, vol. iii. p. 226.

[2] Hurter's *Geschichte Ferdinands II.*,
vol. ix. pp. 152–180.

[3] James "ceased to rule when he issued orders for the convocation of a
parliament.   On that day the reign of
Buckingham began."—Gardiner, vol.
v. p. 160.

[4] *Parl. Hist.*, vol. vi. p. 333.

nounced against him. On account of Cranfield's bitter complaint of the rule which denied him the assistance of counsel, order made the lords made an order that in all future impeachments the by the lords
as to rights accused should upon demand be allowed that privilege, and of accused
in such that he should also be furnished with copies of the depositions cases; for and against him.[1] During a period of fourteen years no new statute had come into existence; and among those now passed the most important was a declaratory "Act concerning an act Monopolies, and Dispensations with Penal Laws and the For- regulating
monopo- feitures thereof,"[2] which, after excepting some of the principal lies; monopolies then in existence, and after providing for the enjoyment for a limited time of monopolies by those who might make new inventions, declared all others utterly void as contrary to the ancient and fundamental laws of the realm. On the 1st of October, 1624, James prorogued his last parliament,[3] James died
March 27, and on March 27, 1625, he died. 1625.

From the statement which has now been made of the pro- An outline gress of the constitutional conflict between the conciliar and of the con-
stitutional parliamentary systems during the reign of James I., it appears conflict that while the drift was in favor of the nation as against the during his
reign; crown, the result was inconclusive. The period was one of the period assertion and not of settlement. James, assuming the divine one of
assertion right of kings, advanced the claims of the conciliar system and not of
settlement. which he had inherited from the Tudors to a point never before known. Not only did he attempt to depress the influence of parliament by dispensing as far as possible with its aid in the administration of government, but also by denying its right to deliberate upon all matters of national concern when its assistance was invoked. Out of that abnormal condition of things arose the necessity for reviving and exaggerating those taxative, legislative, and judicial functions of the council which the growth of the law courts and the parliament were supposed to have paralyzed. In that way it was that James was driven to levy illegal impositions and benevolences, to employ

---

[1] *Lords' Journals*, pp. 307–383, 418.

[2] 21 Jac. I. c. 3. The act declared that its provisions " shall not extend to letters patent & grants of privilege for the term of fourteen years and under, thereafter to be made, of the sole working or making of any manner of new manufactures within this realm, to the true & first inventor or inventors of such manufactures, which others, at the time of making such letters patent and grants, shall not use." Under that exception the crown has since granted letters patent for new inventions.

[3] For the proclamation, see *Fœdera*, vol. xvii. p. 625.

with a fresh severity the inquisitorial powers of the star chamber, to give to proclamations the force of law, to exact every vexatious feudal right annexed to the crown, to call for forced loans, to foster monopolies, and to sell offices and honors. Only by such unconstitutional means could the conciliar system be made to produce the necessary revenue; and in order to make that system more responsive than ever to the king's personal will, James revived the detested influence represented by court favorites. When parliament attempted to counteract these evil tendencies by reasserting its natural and legitimate influence, the privileges which upheld its independence were assailed by the king's contention that such privileges, including the freedom of speech, were matters purely of royal favor and not of right; that the crown was perfectly competent to punish any member, as well during the sitting of parliament as after, for his public conduct, a doctrine often roughly enforced by actual imprisonments. When the law courts in their turn attempted to uphold the rights of the nation against the crown, the judges were threatened and browbeaten before the council; and finally when Chief Justice Coke refused to pledge himself to uniform subserviency, he was punished by dismissal from office. And yet in the face of all such extreme assertions of the royal authority, the undaunted parliament boldly restated its claims to every right which the nation had enjoyed in earlier and better times. It firmly maintained that its privileges were inherent by right of inheritance, that its right to freedom of speech was incontestable, that its right of deliberation extended to all matters of national concern, including the "mysteries of state," that the levy of impositions and benevolences was an incroachment upon its exclusive right to authorize taxation, that the issuance of proclamations was an infringement of its exclusive right of legislation, that it possessed the exclusive right to determine contested election, and that the ancient right of impeachment was to be revived as a weapon of parliamentary warfare not only against private individuals, but also against the king's ministers. Over the vital issues thus made up there was no arbiter, and the result was that the conflict continued with increasing warmth, until in the succeeding reign they were submitted as a last resort to the arbitrament of the sword.

CHAPTER II.

CHARLES I. AND THE CONSTITUTIONAL CONFLICT.

1. THE result of James' "kingcraft" was not only to break down the influence of the trained administrators, who even in the Tudor time had stood as a constitutional check upon the royal prerogative, but also to infuse into a system already too despotic the exaggerated ideas of absolutism embodied in his theory of the divine right of kings. In that extreme and artificial school, in which court favorites were an acknowledged force, both Buckingham and Charles were trained, and from the time the actual direction of affairs passed into their hands they were united by a singleness of purpose that had for its aim the extension of the political system in which they had been reared. While Charles was thus forced by circumstance and education into a continuance of the constitutional conflict which had existed between his father and the popular party for more than twenty years, he intensified of his own accord the religious conflict by the espousal of certain ecclesiastical ideas which the Puritan element in the nation considered as both offensive and reactionary. The statement has heretofore been made that at an early stage of the English Reformation the influence of Luther was forced to yield to that of Calvin, who, about the time of the fall of Cromwell, became the great intellectual light of the protestant world.[1] His triumphant theology it was that inspired that element in the national church which came to be known as Puritan, and which, during the reign of Elizabeth, ventured to attack the religious settlement that she had made by proposing through the mouth of Cartwright, a divinity professor at Cambridge, the abolition of the episcopal in favor of the presbyterian system.[2] The counterblast that came from that division of the national church which rejected the narrow dogmatism of the

The result of James' "kingcraft;"

extreme school in which Charles and Buckingham were trained;

Charles' relation to the religious conflict;

creed of the Puritan element within the church;

[1] See above, p. 168.　　　　　[2] See above, p. 171.

opposing element known as Arminians;

Puritan was embodied in Hooker's "Ecclesiastical Polity,"[1] which finally gave color and form to the opposing elements that grouped themselves loosely under the name of Arminians. While James upheld the tenets of that faction to the extent of maintaining that the episcopal office was inseparable from kingship, he gave support to their opponents by appointing Abbott instead of Andrewes to Canterbury when the primatial see was made vacant by the death of Bancroft in 1611.

Abbott became the leader of the former, Laud of the latter;

During the primacy of Abbott, who became the recognized leader of the Puritan party within the church, the Arminian element gathered under the leadership of Laud, who contended, in opposition to the dominant Calvinism : first, that ordination to the priesthood was absolutely necessary at the hands of the episcopacy, which he regarded as a divine institution; second, that a return to high doctrine concerning the sacraments was indispensable; third, that a strict adherence to the ritualistic system as set forth in the Book of Common Prayer was imperative.[2]

conflict between them;

When in May, 1611, Laud was chosen president of St. John's College, Oxford, Abbott attempted to override the election by reporting to the king that he was "at least a papist in heart, and cordially edicted into popery."[3] But after hearing an exposition of his views, James not only confirmed his election, but made him one of his chaplains; in 1616 he was given the deanery of Gloucester; and in 1621 the bishopric of St. David's.

Laud gained at once the confidence of Charles;

As soon as Charles ascended the throne, Bishop Laud gained his ear and his confidence to such an extent that he was called upon to furnish a list of the clergy worthy of promotion, which resulted in a long catalogue of his own followers, from which the Puritans were severely excluded.[4]

his rapid promotion;

In 1627 Laud was made a privy councillor, and after the departure of Buckingham for Rochelle, chief minister; in 1628 he became bishop of London; and upon Abbott's death in August, 1633, primate of the kingdom. Although Abbott thus lingered on in office until Charles' reign was well advanced, his influence died with its beginning; from Charles' accession Laud became his ecclesiastical guide and councillor. The distrust of the young king which thus arose out of his

[1] See above, p. 172.
[2] Cf. Blount, *Reform. of the Church of Eng.*, vol. ii. p. 489.
[3] See Heylin's *Life of Laud*, pp. 56, 61, 62.
[4] Gardiner, *Hist. Eng.*, vol. v. p. 364.

alliance with those whom the Puritans regarded as papists at heart, as traitors in their own ranks, was greatly heightened by his union with the French princess, Henrietta Maria, with whom he had made a marriage contract at the end of his father's reign, shortly after the failure of the negotiation for the hand of the infanta. Although both James and Charles had assured parliament that there should be no article in that contract in favor of English catholics, Richelieu firmly insisted that the dignity of his sovereign required even greater concessions in their favor than had been made under like circumstances to the king of Spain.[1] The result was a secret agreement,[2] in which James promised to make serious concessions to the recusants, who for the future were not to be molested on account of the private and peaceable exercise of their worship. Subject to that heavy condition, Charles drew to his side the despotic and imperious princess, who at the critical moment spurred him on to his fatal struggle against English liberty, and whose religious influence, fatal at last to the house of Stuart, lived on in the spirit of her sons. To all these adverse circumstances that predestined Charles to continue the conflict with the popular party must be added the dogged obstinacy of his natural temper, upon which neither arguments nor current events seemed to have any influence whatever. Even in his youth the courtiers about him predicted that "if he were in the wrong, he would prove the most wilful king that ever reigned," while of himself he once said, "I cannot defend a bad, nor yield in a good cause."[3] Instead of the power to yield honestly at the critical moment, after the manner of the Tudor princes, Charles possessed only the power to dissemble, a fatal defect, of which at the beginning of his reign the nation seems to have been profoundly ignorant.

Puritan distrust of Charles increased by his marriage with Henrietta Maria;

the secret agreement with France;

obstinacy of Charles' temper;

his duplicity.

2. Despite the presence of the plague then raging in London, there was an unusually large attendance of members at the meeting of Charles' first parliament on the 18th of June. To the expectant assembly, anxious both as to the conduct of

Charles' first parliament met June 18, 1625;

---

[1] Carlisle and Kensington to Conway, August 7, 1624, *State Papers*, France.

[2] This agreement, called a private engagement, was executed apart from

the treaty signed by the ambassadors on November 10. See Gardiner, vol. v. pp. 269-271.

[3] Laud's *Diary*, February 1, 1623.

the war with Spain and as to possible concessions in favor of the English catholics, the king addressed a courteous speech, in which, after declaring his desire to maintain the true religion intact, he asked for subsidies to carry on a conflict which, as it was "begun by your advice and entreaty, what a great dishonor it were both for you and me, if this action so begun should fail for that assistance you are able to give me." The answer made to this reasonable request, put forward at a time when the obligations of the crown amounted to near a million

of pounds, was a petition drawn up by Pym and Sandys, in which the king was asked to execute immediately all existing laws against catholic recusants and missionaries, which was sent to the lords on the 30th of June.[1] Turning then to the question of supply, the commons, after a speech from Phelips deprecating the king's failure to take them into his confidence

as to the conduct of the war, voted two subsidies amounting only to about £140,000. With these preliminaries passed, the Calvinistic or Puritan party, which controlled the house, pro-

ceeded to make a test case against the reactionary or Arminian faction, who were now rejecting alike the doctrines of Rome and Geneva. In 1624 Richard Montague, an Essex rector, in replying to a pamphlet[2] written by a catholic priest, who had denounced the Calvinistic tenets as a part of the doctrine of the state church, repelled the assault by a line of argument[3] which clearly maintained that they could not, after due investigation, be fairly considered as such. When complaint was made of Montague's paper to James' last parliament, the house referred it to Archbishop Abbott, who contented himself with sending for the author, upon whom he bestowed a

mild reprimand. Montague then appealed to the king himself, who permitted him to prepare a second book, entitled "Appello Cæsarem," in which he set forth his original views with even greater intensity. Before the publication of that book, which was duly licensed, James died, and it was issued with a dedication to his successor. These two books of Montague's

---

[1] In addition to the journals, we have for this parliament, Eliot's *Negotium Posterorum*, edited by Dr. Grosart, the *Fawsley MS.*, edited for the Camden Society by Mr. Gardiner, and the volume of *Eliot Notes*.

[2] Entitled *The Gag for the New Gospel*, 1622.

[3] In a paper entitled *A New Gag for an Old Goose*.

were now submitted to a committee of the house, which, while condemning their contents, found it difficult to find a legal basis upon which their author could be punished. Finally, upon the ground that the "Appello Cæsarem" was a contempt of the house, because published while the original question was there pending, Montague was committed to the custody of the sergeant-at-arms,[1] who released him upon a bond for his further appearance. Turning then from the question of religion to that of finance, the house saw fit to ignore the custom that had given tonnage and poundage to the king for life since the time of Henry VI., by limiting the grant of the customs to Charles to the term of one year,[2] with the purpose, no doubt, of reopening the vexed question of impositions, which had been so fiercely contested in the preceding reign. After a further demand for supply had been rejected, the houses, on account of the plague, were adjourned on the 11th of July, to meet again, after a short recess, at Oxford.

held to be a contempt of the house;

grant of the customs limited to one year.

The twelve days' session, which began in that city on the 1st of August, was consumed by a series of angry debates, in the course of which the Puritans reproached the king for his failure to put in force the penal laws against the catholics, while the court faction assailed the popular party in the house for their bad faith in refusing to grant supplies sufficient for the maintenance of a war that had been undertaken at their express invitation. The real difficulty that prevented a settlement of the financial question was the distrust which the house felt of the leadership of Buckingham, a feeling which was intensified by Charles' failure to present for discussion his plans for the conduct of the war. In the course of a memorable debate Phelips made the whole question at issue one of confidence, and Sir Francis Seymour went so far as to name Buckingham, the chief minister, as the man to be held responsible. "Let us lay the fault where it is," he said. "The duke of Buckingham is trusted, and it must needs be in him or his agents;" and to that Phelips added, "It is not fit to

Parliament at Oxford;

house distrusts Buckingham;

---

[1] "The bond was to be given to the sergeant, because it was affirmed by Sir Ed. Coke 'that the house could not take a recognizance.' — *Fawsley Debates*, p. 53. Subsequent practice has decided against Coke. Hatsell's *Pre-*
cedents, vol. iv. p. 276." — Gardiner, vol. v. p. 363, note 1.

[2] The bill was dropped in the lords. For the prior practice as to life-grants, see above, pp. 15, 16.

repose the safety of the kingdom upon those that have not

parts answerable to their places."[1]   In order to save Buckingham from impeachment, and to suspend the conflict thus

unhappily inaugurated between the king and the commons, Charles' first parliament was dissolved on August 12, upon the ostensible ground that the plague had introduced itself into Oxford.[2]   Upon the eve of the dissolution, however, the

house was careful to adopt a protestation, in which its members declared "before God and the world with one heart and voice, that we will ever continue most loyal and obedient subjects to our most gracious sovereign King Charles, and that we will be ready in convenient time, and in a parliamentary way, freely and dutifully to do our utmost endeavor to discover and reform the abuses and grievances of the realm and state, and in the like sort to afford all necessary supply to His Majesty upon his present and all other just occasions and designs." Thus turned adrift with an indefinite promise of supply in the future, Charles and Buckingham were driven to illegal methods of taxation in order to carry on the war.   Under

such circumstances the customs revenue that parliament had failed to grant was levied by royal warrant under an order in council, which declared that it "was now a principal part of the revenue of the crown, and was of necessity to be continued for the support thereof;"[3] and to provide present means for sending out the fleet the council also authorized the issue of

privy seals to raise what was in effect a forced loan.   The failure, however, of the ill-starred expedition against Cadiz, and the increase in the debt which resulted therefrom, forced the king to summon a new parliament, from which he was care-

ful to exclude the opposition leaders, Phelips, Seymour, Coke, Alford, Palmes, and Wentworth, by making them sheriffs of their counties.

3. The clever expedient by which Charles thus removed

---

[1] Gardiner clearly demonstrates that the great speech of Eliot, inserted by Foster, although prepared no doubt for the debate begun on the 10th of August, was never really spoken.   See Preface to *Fawsley Debates.*

[2] The real cause was that "the course which the commons were taking led surely, if indirectly, to the re-

sponsibility of ministers to parliament; and the responsibility of ministers to parliament meant just as surely the transference of sovereignty from the crown to the parliament." — Gardiner, *Hist. Eng.,* vol. v. p. 430.

[3] *Fœdera,* vol. xviii. p. 737 ; vol. xx. p. 118; Dowell, *Hist. of Taxation,* vol. i. p. 192.

from the national arena the popular orators who had sorely harassed him in his first parliament opened the way in the second, which began on the 6th of February, 1626, for a more terrible antagonist, who now assumed the direction of the new struggle for liberty in which he fell as the first martyr. Sir John Eliot, a Devonshire gentleman of high culture and of a lofty and ardent nature, taking up the subject of ministerial responsibility at the point at which Phelips had left it, essayed the mighty task of substituting for the Tudor theory that ministers are responsible to the crown alone, the more ancient doctrine that they are responsible to the nation in parliament, a doctrine finally reëstablished in England through the results of two revolutions. To the mind of Eliot, the cause of all the evils from which the country was then suffering was the maladministration of "that great lord the duke of Buckingham;" and the whole strength of his nature was concentrated into the effort to bring him to justice through the application of the means which had been so successfully applied to the punishment of Bacon and Middlesex. But no sooner was Eliot's attack begun than Charles saw in the assault upon the minister whom he trusted a menace to the crown itself; and he therefore said to the house, "I must let you know that I will not allow any of my servants to be questioned among you, much less such as are of eminent place and near to me;"[1] and at a later day, after a bitter speech from Eliot[2] against Buckingham had moved him to anger, Charles summoned the commons to his presence and told them to "remember that parliaments are altogether in my power for their calling, sitting, and dissolution; therefore, as I find the fruits of them good or evil, they are to be continued or not to be."[3] But in spite of all such menaces the house moved steadily on, and, after voting that they could proceed in such a case upon common fame alone,[4] Buckingham was formally impeached in May at the bar of the lords, where, after a prologue from Sir Dudley Digges, Eliot summed up the charges of incompetency and corruption preferred against him in a speech whose short, incisive sentences, terrible directness, and brilliant invective opened up

Second parliament met February 6, 1626;

Sir John Eliot;

his idea of ministerial responsibility;

his attack upon Buckingham;

Charles' response to the house;

Buckingham impeached in May;

Eliot's great speech;

---

[1] *Parl. or Const. Hist.*, vol. vi. pp. 430, 431.

[2] Foster's *Sir J. Eliot*, vol. i. p. 515, March 27.

[3] March 29, *Parl. Hist.*, vol. ii. p. 56.

[4] *Commons' Journals*, vol. i. pp. 844–848.

a new era in the history of English eloquence by its departure from the cold and stately reasoning of the past.[1]   In the course of his argument Eliot sharply combatted the idea that a minister could claim immunity from punishment by pleading obedience to the commands of his sovereign.   In speaking of the loan made of English ships to serve against the protestant city of Rochelle, he said "that if his majesty himself were pleased to have consented, or to have commanded, which I cannot believe, yet this could no way satisfy for the duke, or make any extenuation of the charge."[2]   The prompt response of Charles to this stirring appeal, into which was concentrated the pent-up wrath of an angered nation, was a declaration that the deeds with which Buckingham was charged were his own, a declaration quickly followed by an assertion of the royal right to imprison members, even during the session, through the arrest of Eliot and Digges, who were seized and hurried off to the Tower for offensive words spoken in the course of the impeachment.[3]   The counterblast of the house to this sudden assault was a refusal to proceed with business until their members should be released, an expedient which, after a short contest, ended in the discharge first of Digges and then of Eliot.[4] Beyond that point Charles refused to go ; in his allegiance to his minister he was immovable ; a fact pointedly emphasized by Buckingham's election on June 1, at the solicitation of his royal master, to the chancellorship of Cambridge University.

In the midst of the conflict in which Charles was thus involved with the commons, he was rash enough to antagonize the house of lords by assailing its privileges, in order to punish two peers who were enemies of Buckingham.   Because the earl of Arundel had permitted his son, Lord Maltravers, to marry clandestinely and without the royal assent Elizabeth Stuart, the sister of the young duke of Lennox, whose hand Charles as the head of her house had intended to bestow in another direction, he was excluded from the council and committed to the Tower during the sitting of parliament.[5]   This

Marginal notes:
denied that a minister can plead obedience to the commands of his sovereign ;

Eliot and Digges imprisoned ;

house refused to proceed with business until they were released.

Charles' conflict with the lords ;

question of privilege involved in case of Arundel ;

---

[1] Foster's *Sir J. Eliot*, vol. i. pp. 324–330.

[2] For the earlier history of that doctrine, see vol. i. pp. 442, 443, 503.

[3] Both houses finally declared that they had heard no such words. *Lords'*

Journals, pp. 592, 627 ; *Commons' Journals,* May 12, 13, 15–17, 19, 20.

[4] The former, May 16, the latter, the 19th.

[5] *Council Register,* March 4.

breach of privilege the lords resented, and after a prolonged contest Charles was forced to release the earl, upon the ground stated in a remonstrance drawn up on April 19, "that no lord of parliament, the parliament sitting, or within the usual times of privilege of parliament, is to be imprisoned or restrained without sanction or order of the house, unless it be for treason or felony, or for refusing to give surety for the peace."[1]

Against a more dangerous enemy of the favorite, the earl of Bristol, who was ambassador to Spain at the time of the visit of Charles and Buckingham to Madrid, and who had thus become possessed of dangerous secrets, the king directed a blow at once novel and revolutionary. Bristol, who had been for two years deprived of his liberty, and who had on two occasions failed to receive a writ of summons, complained of that breach of privilege to the peers,[2] who declared through a committee appointed to investigate the subject that there was no instance of record in which a peer capable of sitting in parliament had been refused his summons.[3] Under the pressure of that report Charles consented to send Bristol his writ, but along with it went a letter from the lord keeper, Coventry, informing him that he could only avail himself of it on pain of the royal displeasure. Ingeniously assuming that a writ under the great seal took precedence of a lord keeper's letter, the earl obeyed the mandate of the former and came to London,[4] in order to lay the correspondence with Coventry before the peers, for which offence he was promptly impeached [5] by the attorney-general, acting under the king's direction, with high treason at the bar of the lords. To that attack Bristol replied by impeaching Buckingham,[6] and on the 1st of May the upper house ordered that the two accusations should be heard together, saving in that way Bristol's right to testify against

case of the earl of Bristol;

denied his writ of summons;

writ finally sent with letter forbidding its use;

Bristol, who was charged with treason, impeached Buckingham.

---

[1] *Lords' Journals*, vol. iii. pp. 558, 564, 566.

[2] By petition Bristol appealed to the peers to obtain from the king his right to a trial or a recognition of his rights as a peer. *Lords' Journals*, vol. iii. p. 537.

[3] Cf. Gardiner, *Hist. Eng.*, vol. vi. p. 94.

[4] *Camden Miscellany*, vol. vi. Pref. p. xxxv, earl of Bristol's defence.

[5] "Twice in the reign of Charles I. attempts were made to break in upon the established theory of impeachment, once in the case of the earl of Bristol, whom the king attempted to accuse of treason in the house of lords without any impeachment by the commons or any indictment found by a grand jury, and once in the famous case of the five members." — Sir J. F. Stephen, *Hist. of the Crim. Law*, vol. i. p. 160.

[6] Such private accusations were known at an earlier day as "appeals." *Ibid.*, pp. 244-247.

Buckingham.[1]   Thus it was that the favorite became the subject of two impeachments : the one presented by an individual peer, the other by the commons acting as the grand inquest of the realm.

Charles demanded passage of supply bill;
While the lower house was thus engaged in pressing the doctrine of ministerial responsibility, on the one hand, and the peers in defending their privileges, on the other, the urgent question of supply which they had been called upon to solve was held in abeyance.   Worn out by the delay, the king demanded on the 9th of June that the subsidy bill should be passed before the end of the following week, at the same time indicating that if it were not, he would be compelled "to use other resolutions."[2]   The commons replied that the question of supply must be preceded[3] by a remonstrance in which, after denying that tonnage and poundage could be lawfully imposed without their consent, they demanded the dismissal of Buckingham, upon the ground "that until this great person be removed from intermeddling with the great affairs of state, we are out of hope of any good success ; and do fear that any money we shall or can give will, through his misemployment, be turned rather to the hurt and prejudice of this your kingdom than otherwise."   Having failed to induce the peers to pronounce judgment against the favorite, the commons thus attempted to use the money power as a means of forcing Charles to concede ministerial responsibility in a form which involved a direct admission of their supremacy over the crown.   The king's response was embodied in a resolve for an immediate dissolution.   In reply to a petition from the peers for a postponement he answered, "No, not a minute ; " and so on the 15th of June his second parliament ended its existence.[4]   And as a manifestation of his contempt for the remonstrance with which the house had closed its labors, a proclamation was issued ordering all copies of it to be destroyed ;[5] and not long after,[6] Sir John Eliot, who was mainly responsible for what had occurred, was declared by the council to be unworthy to hold any longer the office of vice-admiral of Devon.

commons replied by a remonstrance;

attempt to force ministerial responsibility by use of money power;

parliament dissolved June 15; remonstrance ordered to be destroyed.

[1] Elsing's *Notes*, 1624–26, p. 154.
[2] *Lords' Journals*, vol. iii. p. 670.
[3] *Court and Times*, vol. i. p. 110.
[4] *Lords' Journals*, vol. iii. p. 682.
Parl. or Const. Hist., vol. vii. p. 290.
[5] *Fœdera*, vol. xviii. p. 719.
[6] October 26.

The failure of the subsidy bill, the failure to authorize tonnage and poundage, the debts of the crown, the pending war with Spain, created a need for money such as had never before been known, — a need soon increased by the beginning of a war with France, which resulted from the expulsion from the realm of the French attendants of the new queen, through Charles' failure to keep that stipulation of the marriage contract that promised toleration of catholic worship, from the seizure of French ships charged with carrying war materials to the Spaniards, and finally from the king's attempt to act as the champion of the Huguenots in atonement for his past conduct against them. In the vain hope of supplying the exchequer under such circumstances through the unaided resources of the conciliar system, Charles and Buckingham struggled on for a year and a half without a parliament. After imposing tonnage and poundage by an order in council, as had been done after the dissolution of the Oxford parliament,[1] a demand was made upon the counties in July, 1626, for a free gift, which was to be raised by the justices of the peace, who were instructed by letter to exhort their counties to voluntarily supply the amount of the four subsidies provided for in the act that parliament had failed to pass.[2] To this demand, which struck at the very existence of the parliamentary system, sharp resistance came from Westminster and the rest of Middlesex, where the cry was raised of "a parliament! a parliament! else no subsidies;" from Kent, which stood out to a man; and from Bucks, where even the justice neglected to ask for the free aid.[3] The difficulties thus encountered in collecting such an imposition in the very teeth of the statutes against benevolences drove Charles in September of the same year to resort to a forced loan under the name of privy seals, which were of less doubtful legality. The resistance to this new device, however, rapidly developed; the judges themselves signed a paper in which they personally refused to consent to it; and when Chief Justice Crew, who was sent for by the king, refused to yield to pressure, he was promptly dismissed

Marginal notes: Need for money increased by war with France; its causes; fresh attempts to impose royal taxation; a free gift resisted in Westminster and Middlesex; privy seals levied and resisted; the chief justice dismissed for his refusal to pay;

---

[1] Act of council, July 8, *Council Register*. From 1625 to 1641 the port duties were levied without parliamentary sanction. See Dowell, *Hist. of Taxation*, vol. i. pp. 194, 195.

[2] *State Papers*, Dom., xxxi. 30, 31; *Fœdera*, xviii. 764.

[3] See the answers of the counties in the Domestic State Papers for August and September.

on the 10th of November, and his office given to Hyde.[1] But
as the necessities of the crown could brook neither opposition
nor delay, commissioners authorized by the council began a
circuit of the counties in January, 1627, in order to assess the
amounts the landowners were required to lend, and to examine
on oath all that refused. To the widespread opposition offered
to the commissioners by a long list of country gentlemen, including Hampden, Eliot, and Wentworth, the council responded
by imprisoning, by the king's special command, a large number, who were held in confinement, without trial, far from their
homes.[2] And in order to reconcile the royal demands to the
conscience of the nation, that section of the clergy which supported the court was appealed to, and in February and July,
Sibthorpe and Manwaring, following in the servile path that
Laud had marked out for them, preached sermons [3] exalting
the power of the king to absurd heights, and calling upon all
to submit to his mandates on pain of eternal damnation. A
few months later, five of the country gentlemen [4] who were
still in custody appealed to the court of king's bench for a
habeas corpus to test the legality of their imprisonment. On
the 15th of November they were brought to the bar, and on
the 22d the argument was begun on their behalf by eminent
counsel, who contended that they were protected by that clause
of the Great Charter which provides that "no freeman shall
be imprisoned . . . unless by the lawful judgment of his peers,
or by the law of the land." The last clause of that provision,
as interpreted by certain statutes of Edward III., meant, they
said, "due process of law," which a committal by the privy
council, even by *special order of the king*, was not. After the
attorney-general, relying mainly upon the famous dictum contained in Anderson's Reports, had argued that such a commitment, although it assigned no cause, was "due process of
law," — because the judges should so far trust the king as to

Marginal notes: imprisonment of those who resisted the commissioners, 1627; Sibthorpe and Manwaring preached passive obedience; case of the five knights in the king's bench;

[1] *Court and Times*, vol. i. pp. 160, 165; Gardiner, vol. vi. p. 149.
[2] Rushworth, vol. i. p. 426; *Strafford Papers*, vol. i. pp. 36–41; Lingard, vol. vii. p. 310. The poor who resisted were enrolled in the army or navy.
[3] Two of Manwaring's, printed under the title "Religion and Allegiance," are in the Library of Sion College. Gardiner, vol. vi. p. 209, note 1. These were licensed (*State Trials*, vol. iii. p. 351). Abbot, however, refused to license Sibthorpe's, for which he was ordered into confinement.
[4] Sir T. Darnel, Sir J. Corbet, Sir W. Erle, Sir J. Heveningham, and Sir E. Hampden. The return was that they were held under warrant from the privy council by *special command of the king*.

believe that he had good reason for withholding from them for the moment the real cause of the imprisonment, — a judgment was rendered (November 28) by Chief Justice Hyde, refusing bail, but without holding directly that the king could never be required to show cause.[1]

bail refused them.

While well-known devices were thus employed to raise revenue, a new expedient was also put forward, which rested upon a tradition dating back to the beginning of English taxation in pre-Norman times. The statement has heretofore been made that the assessment of 1008, in which is to be found the origin of ship-money, was an extraordinary tax levied by the king and the witan, not only for the purpose of buying off the invader, but also for the raising of fleets by requiring each county to furnish in kind its quota of ships. And according to Earle, who is quoted by Freeman, "this would apply as well to the inland districts as to those on the seaboard." [2] In accordance with the practice existing in the time of the Plantagenets,[3] a part of the fleet which took Cadiz in Elizabeth's reign had been supplied by a levy on the maritime counties, and in June, 1626, Charles had ventured to command such counties to join the port towns in sending out a fleet.[4] When the Dorsetshire magistrates attempted to resist the demand, they were told by the council that "state occasions, and the defence of the kingdom in times of extraordinary danger, do not guide themselves by ordinary precedents;" and when the citizens of London ventured to complain that the twenty ships at which that city was assessed were more than had been formerly demanded, they were told by the same authority "that the precedents of former times were obedience and not direction," an admonition before which the city finally gave way in August.[5] In February, 1628, when all other means had failed him, Charles conceived the idea of levying ship-money as such upon all counties, and letters were accordingly issued, commanding that the sum assessed upon each shire should be paid into the exchequer by the 1st of March.[6] In view, however, of the opposition

Origin of ship-money;

assessment of 1008;

ships as such demanded of the maritime counties in Elizabeth's reign;

Charles conceived the idea in 1628 of demanding money in lieu of ships;

---

[1] *State Trials*, vol. iii. p. 1.
[2] See vol. i. p. 187, note 3.
[3] Extracts from the public records, *State Papers*, Dom., cclxxvi. 65.
[4] For a list of the ports called upon to furnish ships, see *State Papers*, Dom., xxx. 81, June. As to the ships

required from Exeter, see Hamilton, *Quarter Sessions*, p. 119.
[5] See *Proceedings in Council*, July 24, August 11, 15; *Council Register;* Gardiner, vol. vi. p. 132.
[6] For a list of the sums levied upon the counties, amounting for all Eng-

which the unheard-of demand at once provoked, the king promptly revoked the order, and thus suspended the new device until a later day.[1]   In the midst of such desperate efforts to raise revenue, the council did not neglect to issue commissions to compound with recusants for a suspension of the penal laws, while soldiers and sailors whose pay was in arrears were billeted upon counties, where their conduct was often scandalous.[2]   But in spite of all such expedients, Charles was at last forced to give way.   The ignominious failure of Buckingham's expedition for the relief of Rochelle, the broken fragments of which landed at Portsmouth and Plymouth in November,

pressing need for money forced the calling of a new parliament;

1627, and the pressing need for more money to carry on the war with France, compelled the king to yield to the inevitable, and on the 30th of January, 1628, orders were given that writs should issue for a new parliament.   As an attempt at conciliation, seventy-six persons, who had either been imprisoned or banished to counties other than their own for having refused to pay the forced loan, were permitted to return to their homes ; [3] and of that number twenty-seven, including Sir

twenty-seven of those lately imprisoned returned to the house.

Thomas Wentworth, were at once elected to the house, which proved itself to be more determined even than the last to resist all assaults upon the liberties of the nation.

Third parliament met March 17, 1628;

4. Just how pressing was the need which forced Charles to call together his third parliament, which met on March 17, 1628, was clearly disclosed when it was known that the council of war had sent in an estimate of nearly £600,000 for the army and navy during the coming year, besides an immediate demand of nearly £700,000 for munitions and repairs.[4] While the king never dared to ask for the entire sum required,

Charles' threatening speech;

he opened the session with a threatening speech, in which he said, "There is none here but knows that common danger is the cause of this parliament, and that supply at this time is the chief end of it. . . . Every man must do according to his conscience ; wherefore, if you (which God forbid) should not do your duties in contributing what the state at this time needs, I must, in discharge of my conscience, use those other

---

land to £173,000, see *State Papers,* Dom., xcii. 88, 93.

[1] *Court and Times,* vol. i. pp. 322, 324; Gardiner, vol. vi. p. 227.

[2] See *State Papers,* Dom., xcii. 85.

[3] The release of prisoners was ordered on January 2.   Cf. *State Papers,* Dom., xci. 52.

[4] *State Papers,* Dom., xcviii. 1 ; Estimate, March 22.

means, which God hath put into my hands to save that which the follies of some particular men may otherwise hazard to lose." [1] In anticipation of the coming storm the leaders of the popular party had gathered, a few days before parliament met, at the house of Sir Robert Cotton, where it was resolved that before any supplies whatever were granted, the king should be forced to promise, not only to vindicate the rights of his subjects which he had so ruthlessly violated, but also to remedy the maladministration caused by the incompetency and greed of Buckingham.[2] The active work of the session began with expositions, by the popular orators, of the particular grievances for which they demanded immediate and practical redress. The great lawyers of the opposition were Sir Edward Coke and Selden, and the former, in order to deprive the crown of the right of arbitrary imprisonment so lately asserted in the case of the five knights, introduced on March 21 an imprisonment bill, which provided that no person, not under sentence, could be held without trial for more than two months, if he could give bail, or for more than three months if he could not ; [3] and at a later day he made a statement of his view of the law, in which the right of the crown to commit without naming the cause was sharply controverted. In reply Shilton, the solicitor-general, overwhelmed Coke for the moment, not only by referring to the apparently adverse opinion contained in the Reports of Chief Justice Anderson, but also by producing a resolution arrived at in the king's bench, in 1615, in which Coke himself had approved the doctrine that the cause of imprisonment need not be stated when an offender was committed by an order in council.[4] But after Coke had found a means of escape by putting his own construction upon a report of Anderson's opinion, in his own handwriting, brought forward by the heirs of the chief justice during the debate,[5] the house passed three resolutions, in which it was declared that no freeman should be committed without cause shown ; that every one, however committed, had a right to

popular leaders resolved that redress of grievances should precede supply;

Coke's imprisonment bill

attacked by the solicitor-general;

resolutions passed as to the right to habeas corpus;

---

[1] *Lords' Journals*, vol. iii. p. 687 ; *Parl. Hist.*, vol. vii. p. 339.

[2] Foster's *Sir J. Eliot*, vol. ii.

[3] Harl. MSS., 4771, fol. 15.

[4] *State Trials*, vol. iii. p. 81. "Wentworth came to Coke's rescue with a few sarcastic words. 'Mr. Solicitor,' he said, 'hath done that which belongs to his place, but not so ingeniously as he might.'"—Gardiner, vol. vi. p. 243, citing Harl. MSS., 4771, 45 b.

[5] Anderson's *Reports*, vol. i. p. 298. For Hallam's comments on Anderson's judgment, see *Const. Hist.*, vol. i. p. 387.

his habeas corpus, and that, if a legal cause of imprisonment did not appear, he was to be either delivered or bailed. Some days before that conclusion was reached, however, Eliot, after denouncing the whole system of illegal and arbitrary taxation as practised by the crown, had warned the nation against "that false party in religion, which to their Romish idol sacrifice all other interests and respects;"[1] and in order to make a practical application of that statement, Phelips had boldly censured the political sermons recently pronounced by Sibthorpe and Manwaring. Side by side with Eliot, Coke, and Phelips now stood Sir Thomas Wentworth, who did yeoman's service in the popular cause in a great oration in which, after reviewing all the questions in controversy, except those involving the subject of religion, he demanded that there should be no more forced loans, no more illegal imprisonments, no more compulsory employments abroad, no billeting of soldiers without the assent of the householder, — thus outlining the substance of the great statute, afterwards known as the Petition of Right, which derived its form from Coke.[2] In order to give its official sanction to the leading subject of debate, the house on March 26 passed a resolution denouncing all taxation without parliamentary consent, which, together with the three resolutions adopted a week later on the subject of illegal imprisonments, embodied a statement of nearly all the grievances against which the popular party was contending. The commons thus made clear their intention to consider the subject of grievances before that of supply, but at the king's request they consented to consider the two together, and as an evidence of their willingness to be liberal when their petitions should be answered, they voted five subsidies in committee on April 4, which, however, were not reported to the house. This course was taken at the suggestion of Wentworth, who, while desiring above all things to reconcile the nation with the king, was determined that no grant should be actually made to him until he should agree to guarantee the liberties of the subject. The whole difficulty consisted of the unwillingness of Charles to give satisfactory assurances. After a long contention between the

Marginal notes:

Eliot brought forward the religious question;

Wentworth outlined the substance of the Petition of Right;

summing up of grievances by the house;

five subsidies voted in committee;

---

[1] Foster's *Sir J. Eliot*, vol. ii. p. 8.
[2] "If Coke was finally to give to the Petition its form, Wentworth was the originator of its substance." — Gardiner, vol. vi. p. 237.

houses on that subject, the king finally offered to pledge his
royal word that the Great Charter and six other statutes by
which it had been construed in earlier times should be observed; every freeman was to have "a fundamental property
in his goods, and a fundamental liberty of his person," and all
were to enjoy "the just freedom of their persons and safety of
their estates, according to the laws and statutes of the realm." [1]
The house, however, unwilling to accept such a general assurance, resolved to restate in a bill prepared by Coke the substance of the old statutes as then understood; [2] and in order to
make it easier for Charles to consent to such a measure, Wentworth proposed [3] a similar bill of his own, in which the original
proposals were somewhat modified. Not until an earnest effort
to come to terms upon these measures had failed did Coke
remove the difficulty arising out of the apparent refusal to
accept Charles' word by proposing on May 6 a petition of right,
whereby the king could "speak by record and in particulars,
and not in general." Coke said, "Let us put up a Petition of
Right; not that I distrust the King, but that I cannot take
his trust, save in a parliamentary way." [4] The famous document then drawn up by a sub-committee, and which is usually
compared with the Great Charter because it attempted to curb
the power of the Tudor monarchy inherited by the Stuarts,
as the earlier document had attempted to curb the Angevin
monarchy as it existed in the days of John, embraced four
subject matters, which may be summarized as follows : —

1. Addressing itself first to the all-important question involved in the imposition of certain forms of royal taxation,
"not sett by common consent in parliament," the petition —
after referring to the statute *De tallagio non concedendo*,[5]
wherein it was provided "that no tallage or ayde should be
layd or levyed by the king or his heires in this realme" without parliamentary authority; to a statute passed in the 25th
Edw. III.,[6] wherein it was provided "that from thence forth

[Marginal notes:] Charles pledged his word that the Great Charter should be observed; house demanded that he "speak by a record and in particulars, and not in general;" with that end was framed the Petition of Right, which forbade all forms of illegal taxation,

---

[1] The commons were assured that
they would "find as much sincerity in
his royal word and promise as in the
strength of any law they could make."
— *Parl. Hist.*, vol. ii. p. 331.

[2] Brought into the Grand Committee by Coke (April 29), from which it
never emerged. The version of it in

Harl. MSS., 4771, fol. 123, is printed
by Gardiner, vol. vi. p. 264, note 2.

[3] May 1.

[4] *Parl. Hist.*, vol. viii. p. 104.

[5] See vol. i. p. 423, note 2; *Select
Charters*, p. 407.

[6] *Rot. Parl.*, vol. ii. p. 238, No. 11.

no person should be compelled to make any loanes to the king against his will;" and to the famous statute [1] of Richard I. against benevolences — prayed "that no man hereafter be compelled to make or yield any guift, loane, benevolence, taxe,[2] or such like charge, without common consent by act of parliament; and that none be called to make answere or take such oath, or to give attendance, or be confined, or otherwise molested or disquieted concerning the same or for refusall thereof."

arbitrary imprisonments without due process of law,

2. Next, — after referring to the Great Charter wherein it was declared "that no freeman may be taken or imprisoned or be disseised of his freehold or liberties, or his free customes, or be outlawed or exiled or in any manner destroyed, but by the lawfull judgment of his peeres, or by the law of the land;" [3] to the statute of 28 Edw. III. c. 3, wherein it was declared "that no man, of what state or condition that he be, should be put out of his land or tenements, nor taken, nor imprisoned, nor disherited, nor put to death, without being brought to answere by due process of lawe;" and then after reciting the fact that in violation of such statutes, "and other good lawes and statutes of your realme to that end provided,"[4] "divers of your subjects have of late been imprisoned without any cause shewed; and when for their deliverance they were brought before your justices by your Majestie's writts of habeas corpus, there to undergoe and receive as the court should order, and their keepers commaunded to certifie the causes of their detayner, no cause was certified, but that they were deteined by your Majestie's speciall commaund, signified by the lords of your Privie Councell, and yet were returned backe to severall prisons, without being charged with anything to which they might make answere according to the lawe," — the petition prayed "that no freeman, in any such manner as is before mencioned, be imprisoned or deteined."

billeting of soldiers and mariners,

3. Then, — after reciting that "of late great companies of souldiers and marriners have been dispersed into divers counties of the realme, and the inhabitants against their wills have been compelled to receive them into their houses, and

---

[1] 1 Rich. III. c. 2.
[2] No express mention was made of the customs revenue, an omission that afterwards became important.

[3] 9 Hen. III. c. 29.
[4] Cf. 37 Edw. III. c. 18; 38 Edw. III. c. 9; 42 Edw. III. c. 3; 17 Rich. II. c. 6.

there to suffer them to sojourne against the lawes and the customes of this realme, and to the great greivance and vexacion of the people," — the petition prayed "that your Majestie would be pleased to remove the said souldiers and marriners, and that your people may not be soe burthened in tyme to come."

4. And finally, — after reciting at length how many subjects had been tried and put to death in times of peace by commissioners armed "with power and authoritie to proceed within the land, according to the justice of martiall lawe," — the petition prayed "that the aforesaid commissions, for proceeding by martiall lawe, may be revoked and annulled: and that hereafter no commissions of like nature may issue forth to any person or persons whatsoever to be executed as aforesaid, lest by colour of them any of your Majestie's subjects be destroyed or put to death contrary to the lawes and franchise of the land." Thus did the house define its conception of those vital parts of the constitution which were intended to protect the subject against forced loans of every kind, against arbitrary imprisonments, against martial law, and the billeting of soldiers upon the householder without his consent. The petition was brought in by Selden on the 8th of May, and the lords were at once asked to set a day for a conference upon it.[1] Then it was that Charles began the struggle against the new yoke that had been prepared for him, by attempting to save the right of arbitrary imprisonment which it proposed to abolish. In order to aid the king in that design, a new clause was proposed by Arundel,[2] and adopted by the lords on the 17th of May, which ran as follows: "We humbly present this petition to your Majesty, not only with a care of preserving our own liberties, but with due regard to leave entire that *sovereign power* wherewith your Majesty is trusted for the protection, safety, and happiness of your people." To the eagle eye of Pym the purpose of that vague saving clause was obvious, and he was quick to say, " I am not able to speak to this question. I know not what it is. All our petition is for the laws of England, and this power seems to be another distinct power from

and proceedings under martial law.

Petition brought in May 8, and lords asked for a conference;

a saving clause proposed by Arundel;

---

[1] Whereupon the resolution granting the five subsidies was reported to the house. *Commons' Journals*, vol. i. p. 894.

[2] It was brought in by Weston, who claimed its authorship. See Elsing's *Notes*.

the law.   I know how to add sovereign to his person, but not to his power.   Also we cannot leave to him sovereign power, for we never were possessed of it." [1]   After Alford and Coke had spoken to the same effect, the house unanimously rejected the insidious amendment.   In a short time the lords gave way, and on the 28th of May the petition was there adopted in its original form without further discussion.   But Charles' power of resistance was by no means exhausted.   Hoping still to retain his right of arbitrary imprisonment, he submitted a series of questions to the judges in order to elicit from them an indication of the construction which they would put upon the petition in that respect; and, after receiving from them answers more or less satisfactory,[2] it was agreed in council that the king should depart from the usual custom and give a vague and evasive assent to the petition that would be practically worthless.[3]   The house, however, was in no mood to be thwarted by such a device.   It firmly refused to receive such a reply, and after the lords had joined in the contention that there should be a clear answer to the petition, Charles yielded, and on the 7th of June he gave his assent in the terms of the ancient formula, — " Soit droit fait comme est desiré." [4]   As soon as it was known that the petition was to be enrolled like any other statute, the subsidy bill was passed and sent to the lords, and there were such demonstrations of joy "as were never seen but upon his Majesty's return from Spain."

When the commons rejected the lords' amendment to the Petition of Right, whereby they attempted to save "entire that sovereign power wherewith your Majesty is trusted for the protection, safety, and happiness of your people," they intended to set the seal of their disapproval to that pernicious doctrine of unbridled prerogative, which had been asserted in Bate's case, by the barons, Fleming, and Clarke.[5]   And in order to impress the Laudian clergy with the fact that they could not preach from their pulpits the doctrine that the king had a divine right to obedience apart from the laws of the land, the absolutist theory in ecclesiastical form, the commons on the

rejected by the house;

petition then adopted in its original form;

after the house had refused to accept an evasive answer, Charles assented in the usual form;

a subsidy bill then passed.

Condemnation of doctrine asserted in Bate's case;

---

[1] See Foster's *Sir J. Eliot*, vol. ii. p. 55, and note 8.

[2] For original copy of questions and answers, see Hargrave MSS., 27, fol. 97; Ellis, ser. 2, vol. iii. p. 250.

[3] For the form finally agreed upon, see *Lords' Journals*, vol. iii. p. 835.

[4] 3 Car. I. c. I.

[5] See above, p. 226.

9th of June sent articles of impeachment to the lords against
Manwaring, who was there promptly convicted and sentenced
to fine and imprisonment.[1]   Speaking through the mouth of
Pym,[2] to whom the accusation of Manwaring was intrusted,
the house set forth its theory of the constitution, the essence
of which was the responsibility of the crown to the nation
asserted in the preceding parliament in the abortive attempt
to impeach Buckingham.   Returning now under the leadership
of Eliot to that all-important subject, a remonstrance was finally
voted on the 11th of June, which, after demanding the enforcement of the penal laws against the catholics, and denouncing
the Arminian clergy, attributed the maladministration from
which the kingdom was suffering to "the excessive power of
the duke of Buckingham, and the abuse of that power ; and we
humbly submit to your Majesty's excellent wisdom, whether it
be safe for yourself or your kingdoms that so great a power as
rests in him by sea and land should be in the hands of any
one subject whatsoever." [3]   To this resolution, which in modern
times would be called a vote of a want of confidence, Charles
was prompt to reply that under no circumstances would he give
up his chief minister and favorite.   The only thing that the
house had to withhold was tonnage and poundage, which had
not yet been voted.   A second remonstrance was therefore
presented on that subject on June 25, the essence of which
was that these customs duties should not be imposed by the
crown without the assent of parliament,[4] a contention which
they said was supported by the terms of the recent Petition
of Right.   In order to prevent the presentation of "any more
remonstrances to which I must give a harsh answer," Charles
hastened to the house of lords, without taking time to put on
the usual robes, and there, after an emphatic speech [5] explaining "the true intent and meaning of what " had been granted
in the petition, ended the session by prorogation on the 26th
of June.

It was certainly a doubtful question whether the right to

Marginal notes:
Manwaring impeached for preaching such doctrine;

Eliot renewed the attack upon Buckingham;

tonnage and poundage withheld;

parliament prorogued June 26, 1628.

---

[1] The king was also asked to call
in all his books, that they might be
burned. *Parl. Hist.*, vol. ii. pp. 388, 410.
The king instead gave him an additional rectory, and finally made him
bishop of St. David's.

[2] See the interesting extracts printed
in Gardiner, vol. vi. pp. 313, 314.

[3] Rushworth, vol. i. pp. 613–622.

[4] *Parl. Hist.*, vol. ii. p. 431.

[5] *Lords' Journals*, vol. iii. p. 879;
Parl. Hist., vol. ii. p. 434.

Did the
Petition of
Right
embrace the
customs?
impose customs duties was embraced in that portion of the
Petition of Right that provided "that no man hereafter be
compelled to make or yeild any guift, loane, benevolence, taxe,
or such like charge, without common consent by Acte of Parliament," as the word "taxe," which was usually applied to
direct payments only, was the only term sufficiently general
to be made to embrace the customs.[1]   In view of the doubt
thus existing, Charles clearly indicated in the hurried speech
made at the close of the session that he would not yield
the point, but reserve it for the judges to whom "under me,
belongs the interpretation of laws."   As the house in its last

the
merchants
resisted all
such duties
not
imposed by
parliament;
remonstrance had exhorted the merchants to resist the payment
of all duties not imposed by parliament, it was not long before
the question was brought to a practical test.   As soon as the
resistance thus encountered began, the council, after a solemn
declaration from the king that the right to make impositions
was his "by a solemn and legal judgment," issued orders for
the seizure of the goods of all importers who attempted to land
them without paying duties.[2]   When, on September 28, some
of the resisting merchants were brought before the council,

Chambers'
case;
Richard Chambers, who was one of them, ventured to declare
that "merchants are in no part of the world so screwed as
in England.   In Turkey they have more encouragement;"[3]
whereupon he was committed to the Marshalsea for contempt.
After he had sued out his habeas corpus, a return was promptly
made setting forth the cause of his detention, as commanded
by the Petition of Right,[4] and on October 23 he was bailed.[5]

Rolle's
case;
In November another group of merchants, including John
Rolle, a member of the house of commons, attempted to
recover by replevying goods which had been seized for non-
payment of duties.   When that course was resisted by the

---

[1] The house declared in their remonstrance of June 25, "that the receiving of tonnage and poundage and
other impositions not granted by parliament, is a breach of the fundamental liberties of this kingdom, and contrary to your Majesty's answer to their
late Petition of Right."   On the other
hand the king said in his concluding
speech : "But as for tonnage and
poundage, it is a thing I cannot want,
and was never intended by you to ask,
— never meant, I am sure, by me to
grant."

[2] *Council Register*, July 20, August
13; Rushworth, vol. i. p. 639.

[3] Rushworth, vol. i. p. 672.

[4] This was the first case that had
arisen since its adoption.

[5] On November 6, an information
was presented against Chambers, in
the star chamber.   See *Court and
Times*, vol. i. p. 429.

attorney-general, the court of exchequer held on November 27 that replevin was not the proper remedy for taking "goods out of His Majesty's own possession."[1] Upon the great question of substance involved in the proceedings the judges had declined to pass a fortnight before; they then said that it was "only for the parliament now shortly to be reassembled, there to be finally settled, as the desire of His Majesty and the discreeter sort of merchants is it should be." Shortly before the culmination of this vexatious controversy, the dagger of Felton had put an end to the career of Buckingham at Portsmouth on the 23d of August, an event that forced the king to assume for the moment the personal direction of the machinery of government, to every part of which the dead favorite had given inspiration.

[marginal: judges declined to pass upon the real question;]

[marginal: Buckingham assassinated August 23.]

Such was the condition of things when the second session of Charles' third parliament met on January 20, 1629, whose first business it was to complain that the speech in which the king had claimed tonnage and poundage as his due at the close of the last session had been enrolled with the Petition of Right; and that a printed copy of that great statute had been circulated, not only with the final answer and speech in which the king had expounded it, but also with the ambiguous answer which had been rejected as worthless.[2] Passing then to the case of John Rolle, the member whose goods had been seized for his refusal to pay tonnage and poundage, and upon the merits of which the judges had refused to pass because the question involved was "only fit for parliament," the house, ignoring the greater issue involving the right of the king to levy duties without the consent of parliament, proceeded to deal with the matter upon the narrower ground that it was a breach of privilege to seize the goods of a member during his attendance at Westminster. In two out of the three cases that had occurred before the accession of James, the exemption had been limited to such goods only as the member required during his attendance and on his way home, while the exact time before and after each session during which the

[marginal: Parliament reassembled January 20, 1629;]

[marginal: complaint as to enrolment of Petition of Right;]

[marginal: Rolle's case in the house;]

[marginal: the question of privilege involved;]

[1] *Attorney-General* v. *Rolle*, Orders and Decrees in the Exchequer, November 13, 27, 4 Charles I. fol. 254, 262; Gardiner, vol. vii. pp. 3-6.

[2] *State Papers*, Dom., cxxxiii. 4. Such is the statement contained in Nethersole's letter to Elizabeth, queen of Bohemia.

privilege was to last still remained an open question.[1]   Only
by the use of a legal fiction [2] could it be claimed that Rolle's
case came within the rule, as the seizure of his goods had taken
place on the 30th of October, four months after the close
of one session and two months before the actual beginning
of another.   And yet in spite of such difficulties, Lyttelton
demanded that " the parties be sent for that violated the liberties."   In order to compose the controversy, which Phelips
threatened to reopen by moving for a committee upon the

Charles'
offer to
yield the
right of
the crown
to levy
customs;

whole question of the levy of tonnage and poundage, Charles
on January 24 summoned the houses to Whitehall, where he
assured them that he did not intend to levy the customs
by his " hereditary prerogative."   " It ever was," he said,
" and still is my meaning by the gift of my people to enjoy it ;
and my intention in my speech at the end of the last session
was not to challenge tonnage and poundage of right, but for
expedience *de bene esse*, showing you the necessity, not the
right, by which I was to take it until you had granted it into
me ; assuring myself, according to your general profession,
that you wanted time and not good will to give it me." [3]   Instead of meeting the king in the conciliatory spirit thus ex-

the house's
cold
response;

pressed, the house still failed to make the usual life-grant of
the customs by postponing the tonnage and poundage bill in
order to use it as a weapon in the serious religious controversy
yet to come.   At a later day the question of privilege was
resumed when the custom-house officers were called to the bar
to answer for their acts in seizing a member's goods.   At that

Charles
refused to
permit
customs
officers
to be
questioned
for his acts;

point the king intervened for their protection, informing the
house that what had been done " was done by his own direction and commandment of his privy council, . . . and therefore could not in this sever the acts of the officers from his
own act, neither could his officers suffer from it without high
dishonor to His Majesty." [4]   In the face of the mighty problem thus presented by the king's refusal to permit his officers
to be held responsible for his acts, the house, on the 23d of

---

[1] See Hatsell, vol. i. pp. 67, 99.

[2] " It so happened that parliament
had been originally prorogued to October 20, and Rolle was therefore supposed, by a legal fiction, to have been

hindered in the fulfilment of duties,"
etc. — Gardiner, vol. vii. p. 33.

[3] See the extract printed in Lingard,
vol. vii. p. 346.

[4] Rushworth, vol. i. p. 659.

February, adjourned for reflection ; and the next day [1] the sub-committee completed the resolutions which were to be submitted to the house on the subject of recent religious innovations. The real grievance of which the resolutions complained was the departure that had taken place from the Calvinistic theology, dominant in the national church almost from the beginning of the Reformation, in favor of what was now denounced as popery and Arminianism, which commanded that communion tables should give way to altars upon which candlesticks were set, that congregations should stand up at the singing of the *Gloria Patri*, that women coming to be churched should be veiled, that the "setting up of pictures and lights and images in churches, praying towards the east, crossing," and other objectionable gestures should be encouraged, and, last and worst of all, that the Calvinistic clergy should be set aside, when ecclesiastical preferment was in question, in favor of those who, like Neile and Laud, had become apostles of what the Puritan party regarded as a dangerous heresy.[2] In order to arrest discussion and prevent the adoption of these resolutions, the king on the 25th of February sent a command to the house to adjourn until the 2d of March, to the end that "a better and more right understanding might be begotten between him and them." [3] To the first order the house submitted, but when on the 2d of March the speaker, Sir John Finch, declared that it was the king's pleasure that they should adjourn until the 10th, Eliot resolved to resist the power of the crown to force an adjournment, a power which the lords had always admitted, but which the house had refused to recognize by adjourning themselves to prevent the appearance of submission. When the speaker attempted to put the formal question, shouts of No! no! came from every side ; and when Eliot rose to address the house, Finch did his best to check him, saying that he had from the king's own lips an absolute command to leave the chair if any one attempted to speak. In order to prevent the execution of that command, Holles and Valentine seized the speaker by the arms and thrust him back into his seat, and when by the aid of May and Edmondes

Marginal notes:
substance of resolutions concerning religious innovations;
king commanded the house to adjourn;
Eliot resolved to resist the exercise of that power;
the speaker held forcibly in the chair;

---

[1] This is the date accepted by Gardiner (*Hist. Eng.*, vol. vii. p. 65), who has followed Harl. MSS., 4296, fol. 65 b.

[2] *Parl. Hist.*, vol. iii. p. 483.

[3] Ibid., vol. ii. p. 502.

Finch succeeded in breaking away, he was again seized and made to submit to physical force. During the moment of quiet that then ensued, Eliot made an effort to submit to the house some resolutions upon the subjects of taxation and religion, which, after having been burned by their author, who despaired of obtaining a formal vote upon them, were reproduced from memory by Holles in the following form : [1] —

" Whosoever shall bring in innovation in religion, or by favour seek to extend or introduce Popery or Arminianism, or other opinions disagreeing from the true and orthodox church, shall be reputed a capital enemy to this kingdom and the commonwealth.

" Whosoever shall counsel or advise the taking and levying of the subsidies of tonnage and poundage, not being granted by parliament, or shall be an actor or an instrument therein, shall be likewise reputed an innovator in the government, and a capital enemy of this kingdom and commonwealth.

" If any merchant or other person whatsoever shall voluntarily yield or pay the said subsidies of tonnage and poundage, not being granted by parliament, he shall likewise be reputed a betrayer of the liberty of England, and an enemy to the same." [2] Knowing that it would be useless to apply again to the speaker to put the question, Holles put it himself, and after the defiant resolutions had been thus adopted, the commons of their own motion adjourned themselves until the 10th. Thus it was that the career of the house and of its great leader came to an end. Immediately after the adjournment, Eliot and eight [3] of his associates were committed to the Tower or to other prisons, and on the day set for its reassembling, Charles, after making a declaration justifying the act,[4] dissolved the parliament in which Eliot had made his last and Oliver Cromwell his first speech,[5] and whose successor was not to be called until after the lapse of eleven years of personal rule.

[1] For the events of that day, see journals of both houses; Rushworth, vol. i. pp. 655–672 ; Whitelock, pp. 12, 13 ; Nicholas' *Notes ; State Papers*, Dom., cxxxviii. 6, 7. The best restatement of it all is to be found in Gardiner, vol. vii. pp. 67–76.

[2] *Parl. Hist.*, vol. ii. p. 491.

[3] Holles, Valentine, Selden, Strode, Hobart, Long, Coryton, and Heyman.

[4] After referring to the " dissobedient carriage of the lower house," Charles declared that " the vipers among them should meet with their reward." — *Parl. Hist.*, vol. viii. p. 333.

[5] Cf. Carlyle's *Letters and Speeches*, p. 52.

5. Before the close of the reign of Elizabeth, it was esti- Rise of the separatists;
mated that there were in England some 20,000 persons, popu-
larly known as Brownists, who, rejecting the original Puritan
idea [1] of reforming the national church from within, had resolved to break away from it altogether.   Among the several
independent congregations set up by these separatists will
ever be remembered that organized at Gainsborough, Lincoln- the congregations at Gainsborough and Scrooby;
shire, which, under the pressure of persecution, emigrated
under the pastoral care of John Smith [2] to Amsterdam in
1606; and that planted at Scrooby, Nottinghamshire, which,
after an unsuccessful attempt to sail from Boston in 1607,
finally escaped to Amsterdam in the course of the following
year. [3]   In 1609 the Scrooby church removed in a body from the latter went to Leyden, and thence to the New World in 1620;
Amsterdam to Leyden under the leadership of Robinson, [4] and
there remained until the summer of 1620, when a second move
was made to the New World under a patent granted the year
before by the London or South Virginia Company, which
authorized them to make a settlement near the mouth of the
Hudson River. [5]   After resting on the way at Southampton
and Plymouth, the little band of emigrants sailed in the May- Mayflower arrived off Cape Cod November 9;
flower from the port last named on September 6, and arrived
off Cape Cod on the 9th of September.   As they were then
outside the limits of the South Virginia Company, its patent
was useless, and the settlement made at Plymouth after their
landing on the 11th of December would have been without
any control whatever, had not the emigrants agreed before- the famous political compact on shipboard;
hand on shipboard to a political compact under which John
Carver was elected the first governor. [6]   At a later day a license charter granted March 4, 1629, to "Company of the Massachusetts Bay;" [7]
was obtained from the Plymouth or North Virginia Company,
whose domain had thus been invaded without its authority. [7]
On the 4th of March, 1629, two days after the memorable
adjournment of his third parliament, Charles I. granted a royal
charter to "the Governor and Company of the Massachusetts

---

[1] "Such men would find but little sympathy even amongst Puritans." — Gardiner, vol. iv. pp. 144–171.

[2] Hunter, *Founders of Plymouth Colony*, p. 32.

[3] Except at Dover or Plymouth, persons who were neither soldiers nor merchants could not leave the realm without the royal license by reason of 13 Ric. II. s. 1, c. 20.

[4] Bradford, *Hist. of Plymouth Plantation*, p. 16.

[5] Ibid., pp. 27, 41.   The patent itself has not been preserved.

[6] Bradford, *Hist. of Plymouth Plantation*, p. 90.

[7] See vol. i. p. 18.

Bay in New England,"[1] under which gathered the settlements
made at Salem, Boston, and Charlestown by the later Puritan emigrants, who, having been drawn from the professional
and middle classes of Lincolnshire and the eastern counties,
were men of a higher culture than the first comers.   The
only dependence under which the self-governing colony thus
planted suffered at the outset grew out of the fact that it was
subject to the control of a corporation in England composed
of those by whom its organization had been brought about.

colony
became
practically
independ-
ent in
August;
But that tie was severed, and the Massachusetts colony became
practically an independent commonwealth, when in August,
1629, its government was transferred to America by a vote of
the company itself,[2] upon an offer made by Winthrop and eleven
other gentlemen to emigrate upon the happening of that event.[3]
Thus was established upon the soil of the New World the
colony of Massachusetts Bay, into which the Plymouth settlement was finally incorporated in 1691.[4]   With the departure

with
depar-
ture of
Winthrop
migration
began in
earnest;
of Winthrop the migration to New England began in earnest,
and it is estimated that between the sailing of his expedition
and the meeting of the Long Parliament, two hundred emi-
grant ships crossed the Atlantic,[5] bearing to their new homes
in the west twenty thousand Englishmen, whose first thought
was to find in the wilderness freedom from the religious persecution which Laud was relentlessly enforcing against all who
bore the name of Puritan.   The history of the beginnings of

beginnings
of political
organ-
ization;
political organization that thus arose has been summarized
already, from which it appears that the active governing unit
in New England was the township, formed as a general rule
"before the county, the county before the state."   The government of the township was vested in a primary assembly
purely democratic, the principle of representation not coming
into use until the primary plan became inapplicable to the
larger units which arose out of the process of aggregation.[6]
And yet upon this purely democratic substructure the Massachusetts colony did not fail to impose a serious limitation.
In 1631 the general court resolved "that no man shall be

---

[1] See vol. i. p. 19.
[2] See Gardiner, vol. vii. p. 156.
[3] Palfrey, *Hist. of New England*,
vol. i. p. 283; *Life of Winthrop*, vol.
i. p. 305.

[4] Vol. i. p. 19.
[5] Green, *Hist. of the Eng. People*,
vol. iii. p. 171.
[6] Vol. i. pp. 28–31.

admitted to the freedom of this body politic, but such as are members of some of the churches within the limits of the same," [1] and thus it was that the blended church and state passed under the yoke of a democratic theocracy, utterly blind at first to the idea of religious toleration.

the blended church and state.

6. The bitter and determined spirit in which Charles entered upon his new career of personal government was expressed in no uncertain terms in a proclamation against false rumors issued on the 27th of March, just a week after the dissolution, in which, after denouncing Eliot as "an outlawed man, desperate in mind and fortune," he declared, "we shall account it presumption for any to prescribe any time unto us for parliaments, the calling, continuing, and dissolving of which is always in our power, and we shall be more inclinable to meet in parliament again when our people shall see more clearly into our intents and actions, when such as have bred this interruption shall have received their condign punishment, and those who are misled by them, and by such ill reports as are raised in this occasion, shall come to a better understanding of us and themselves." [2]   The great lesson which Charles thus proposed to teach the nation during the period in which parliaments were to be indefinitely suspended was that the king in council was so entirely independent of the king in parliament that adequate revenue could be supplied and the entire machinery of the government carried on by the unaided resources of the conciliar system.   While such a suspension of parliamentary life was in itself a revolution, the king had no intention of employing in the execution of his designs anything but purely legal methods, or such as should be declared so to be by the dependent judiciary which his father and himself had reduced to servility.   Bacon, in one of his essays, had instructed both in the belief that the judges should "be lions, but yet lions under the throne, being circumspect that they do not check or oppose any points of sovereignty," and so faithfully did Charles adhere throughout to that theory that Grimston was able to say in the Long Parliament that "the judges have overthrown the law, and the bishops the gospel."   And yet, in the proceedings which the king now instituted for the "condign pun-

Spirit in which Charles began his personal rule; proclamation of March 27, 1629; no one to suggest the calling of parliament;

government to be carried on by the council only,

with the aid of servile judges;

---

[1] Dexter, *Congregationalism of the Last Three Hundred Years*, p. 420.   [2] *Fœdera*, vol. xix. p. 62.

their reluc-
tance in
the case
of Eliot,
Holles, and
others.
ishment " of Eliot, Holles, Valentine, Selden, and the rest who
had been imprisoned just before the dissolution for their part
in the stormy events that transpired when the speaker was
seized and held in his chair, the judges descended very reluctantly to the servile place their master assigned them,
stimulated as they were by the terms of the Petition of Right,
which were intended to strengthen their hands as arbitrators
between the crown and the nation.

Eliot
refused to
speak of
anything
done in
the house;
When in March the examination of the prisoners began,
Eliot at once presented the mighty issue involved by replying
to every question : " I refuse to answer, because I hold that it
is against the privilege of the house of parliament to speak of
anything which was done in the house." [1]   Alarmed by this
bold assertion of parliamentary privilege, whose extent at that
time had not been distinctly defined, Charles resolved to consult the judges in advance, who were called upon to express
their views in response to a series of questions [2] propounded
to them by the attorney-general, Heath.   While the judges
declined in reply to define the exact extent of parliamentary
privilege prior to full argument, they finally indicated that the
prisoners could be proceeded against in the star chamber, provided they were permitted the help of counsel.   Guided by
that intimation, Heath, on May 7, filed an information against
them in that court, the gravamen of which was that on the
great day in the house upon which Eliot and his associates
had made sweeping charges against privy councillors, they had
been guilty of a conspiracy to publish false rumors in order to
bring the king and government into disrepute.   After pleas
to the jurisdiction [3] had been presented and argued, the star
chamber referred the questions involved to three of its members, — the two chief justices and the chief baron, — who,
habeas
corpus
proceedings
in the
king's
bench;
after withholding their opinions for a long time, advised that
the proceedings should be dropped,[4] as the matter was then
pending in the king's bench upon an application for habeas
corpus there made [5] upon the day before Heath filed his infor-

[1] *State Papers*, Dom., cxxxiv. 7.

[2] *State Trials*, vol. iii. pp. 235, 238 ;
Rushworth, vol. i. p. 662.   Mr. Gardiner expresses the opinion that the two
sets of questions are quite distinct from
each other.   See vol. vii. p. 88, note 1.

[3] *Parl. Hist.*, vol. ii. p. 507 ; *State
Papers*, Dom., cxliii. 4–13.

[4] *State Papers*, Dom., cxliv. 37;
Court and Times, vol. ii. p. 17 ; Gardiner, vol. vii. pp. 90, 92, note 1, 109.

[5] By Selden, Holles, Valentine,

mation in the star chamber.   After the king, in deference to the terms of the Petition of Right, had made a return to the king's bench, in which he stated the ground of the committal to be the commission of notable contempts against himself and his government, and the stirring up of sedition in the state, the counsel for the petitioners undertook to convince the judges that the offence assigned was clearly bailable, for the reason that the contempt and sedition charged did not constitute treason.[1]   When Charles saw that the judges were likely to yield to that contention, instead of producing the prisoners in court on the day set, he conveyed them all to the Tower, where they were to be held "until they were delivered by due course of law."[2]   Finally, in order to solve the question, Heath in October presented an information in the king's bench against the ringleaders, Eliot, Holles, and Valentine, in which they were directly charged with a conspiracy formed in parliament itself to calumniate the ministers, to assault the speaker, and to defeat the king's lawful order of adjournment.[3]   After a plea to the jurisdiction of the court over such acts had been fully argued, the judges held that their jurisdiction was clear, reserving, however, the question whether the prisoners were really guilty of the offence with which they were charged.   When the three still persisted in their refusal to plead in a court whose jurisdiction they denied, a judgment was finally rendered, as upon confession, imposing heavy fines upon them all, and declaring that they should be held in custody until they should acknowledge their offence and give security for their good behavior.[4]   After Eliot's associates had secured their release through the acceptance of these terms which he scornfully rejected, he was left behind prison bars to fight out the great battle single-handed and alone.   Into the proceedings of the parliament which had adopted the Petition of Right he had infused his spirit, and the question now was whether the guarantee which that new charter was intended to give to the personal liberty of every Englishman was to be whispered away

prisoners not produced in court;

the information in the king's bench;

plea to jurisdiction overruled;

defendants fined and imprisoned;

Eliot alone refused to accept his liberty on humiliating terms;

Strode, Hobart, and Long. Eliot did not join.

[1] *State Trials*, vol. iii. pp. 241, 242.
[2] Controlment Roll, King's Bench, 51 Membr. 65. The next day (June 24) the king wrote a letter to the judges, proposing to produce Selden and Valentine. Rushworth, vol. i. p. 680. He then wrote a second letter, saying he had changed his mind. *State Papers*, Dom., cxlv. 40–42. Cf. Gardiner, vol. vii. pp. 95, 96.
[3] *State Trials*, vol. iii. p. 320.
[4] Ibid., p. 309.

by a judgment from servile judges who held, in substance, that while the king might be forced to keep the letter of the Petition by assigning the cause of the commitment, he might defeat its real object by holding the prisoner in custody, no matter what the cause shown might be. Against that ultimate exercise of tyranny Eliot opposed a lofty and unbending spirit of protest, which ended only with his death in the Tower on the 27th of November, 1632. During his long and painful confinement this first martyr in the new struggle for liberty embodied in a political and philosophical treatise, which he called the "Monarchy of Man,"[1] his ideal of government, while in a last letter[2] addressed to Hampden, he unconsciously revealed the fact that in the maintenance of that ideal he was sustained by the spirit of self-abnegation which moved the king of the Greeks, in the Homeric story, to cry out:—

died in the Tower November, 27, 1632;

his "Monarchy of Man;"

his self-abnegation.

> "Let me be deem'd the hateful cause of all,
> And suffer, rather than my people fall."[3]

Charles' last tribute to such a man was recorded upon the petition in which Eliot's son asked permission to take away his father's remains for burial at the Devon home in which he was loved and honored by all: "Let Sir John Eliot," wrote the king, "be buried in the church of that parish where he died."[4]

Charles now insisted upon his right to levy customs;

While Charles was thus trampling upon that part of the Petition of Right which was designed to prevent arbitrary imprisonment, he was also attempting to destroy by like means its opening clause, which was supposed to render impossible all forms of taxation "not sett by common consent in parliament." Whether the royal right to impose the port duties was taken away by the limited terms of the petition was certainly a doubtful question, and Charles frankly stated, shortly after its approval, that it was not his intention that it should "take away my chief profit of tonnage and poundage." As a last word upon the subject, the house in the resolutions heretofore set forth had declared that any merchant who should pay such duties, authorized only by royal authority, would "be reputed a betrayer of the liberty of England, and an enemy to

---

[1] Harl. MSS., 2228. The work has been published by Dr. Grosart.
[2] March 29, 1632.

[3] Pope's translation.
[4] See Gardiner, vol. vii. p. 228.

the same." [1]   Regardless, however, of that anathema, the council on the 7th of March, 1629,[2] promptly ordered that all persons refusing to pay such duties should be held in prison at the king's will, "or that they be delivered by order of law;" and thus by royal warrant only the port duties continued to be levied until 1641,[3] the efforts made first by Chambers [4] and then by Vassall [5] to resist payment by judicial means having proven equally abortive.   How vitally important to Charles was this resource can be well understood when the statement is made that in 1635, the year in which a new book of rates was issued, the port duties, by reason of the great increase in trade, amounted to £328,126, more than half of the average ordinary revenue of the crown, estimated for that year at £618,379.[6] With the port duties as a basis, the council continued to enforce every other financial branch of the prerogative, including some that were dormant, in the hope of supplying the deficit in the exchequer without any open and palpable breach of constitutional law.   In that way large sums were drawn from the landed gentry through compositions accepted for the refusal of knighthood, which was vigorously forced upon them; through a revival of the odious forest laws whereby compositions were drawn from the neighboring landowners who had encroached upon the royal domain; [7] through fines exacted for the curing of defects in title-deeds; through the pitiless enforcement of enormous fines through the star chamber, whose indefinite powers were given the widest extension; [8] through the revival and application of monopolies,[9] abandoned by Elizabeth and abolished by parliament in the preceding reign, to almost every article of ordinary consumption; and finally, through the enforcement against Puritan London of

[marginal notes:]
March 7, 1629, ordered in council that all should be imprisoned who refused to pay them;

importance of this branch of the revenue;

other forms of royal taxation;

---

[1] See above, p. 278.

[2] *Council Register.*

[3] Dowell, *Hist. of Taxation*, vol. i. pp. 193, 195.

[4] Chambers, who refused to submit, was sentenced in the star chamber, May 6, 1629.   See *State Trials*, vol. iii. p. 374.

[5] Vassall, who refused to pay the duties on currants, had his goods sold in June, 1631, by an order made in the exchequer.   *Exchequer Decrees and Orders*, vol. viii. pp. 269, 309 b.; vol. ix. p. 204 b.; xi. p. 466 b.

[6] *State Papers*, Charles I., cccxiv. 84.   The increase in commerce continued to increase the duties until they reached in 1641 nearly half a million. Roberts, *Treasure of Traffic*, published in 1641; Anderson, *Commerce*, vol. ii. p. 391.

[7] Strafford's *Letters*, vol. ii. p. 117.

[8] Cf. Clarendon, *Hist. Rebellion*, vol. i. pp. 16, 67, 68.

[9] Cf. Dowell, *Hist. of Taxation*, vol. i. pp. 204–209.

proclamations prohibiting its extension, by virtue of which the householders in the great suburban districts were forced to pay three years' rental to the crown in order to save their houses from demolition.[1] By the employment of such means as these,

by strict economy ordinary revenue made equal to ordinary budget;

and by the practice of strict economy, the king, who, in 1629–30 had made peace with both France and Spain, was able during the six years' interval without a parliament that ended with the death of Lord Treasurer Portland in March, 1635, to greatly reduce the debt, while the ordinary revenue was made nearly to equal the ordinary budget.[2] It thus appeared that if peace was to continue, the crown could maintain itself without the aid of parliamentary subsidies. It was equally certain, however, that with the breaking out of hostilities, foreign or domestic, an appeal to the nation would become inevitable, unless Charles could find in the arsenal of the prerogative some new or dormant source of supply sufficiently fruitful to

in 1634 Noy suggested that war could be carried on by ship writs only.

satisfy extraordinary demands. When, in 1634, war with the Dutch became imminent, Noy, the attorney-general, suggested that a fleet could be equipped without a resort to parliament by a revival of the precedent through which the maritime counties and port towns had been compelled to provide ships for the war against Spain in 1626,[3] a precedent which dated back to the very beginning of English taxation in pre-Norman times.

The writs of 1626 limited to port towns and maritime counties;

In 1628, as heretofore explained, Charles resolved to widen the precedent of 1626 by levying ship-money as such upon all counties, inland as well as maritime, and the writs for that purpose issued in February of that year were suspended only for the moment in the face of a popular opposition which it was

Noy only proposed to revive that precedent;

not expedient to brave at that time.[4] What Noy really proposed in 1634 was to revive the precedent of 1626, and in accordance therewith writs were issued October 20 of the year first named only to the authorities of the port towns and of

[1] Cf. *Fœdera*, vol. xviii. pp. 33, 97. "The Treasury gained a hundred thousand pounds by this clever stroke, and Charles gained the bitter enmity of the great city whose strength and resources were fatal to him in the coming war." — Green, *Hist. of the Eng. People*, vol. iii. p. 146.

[2] See the comparative statement of revenue and expenditure in the Appendix to Gardiner, vol. x. p. 222, 223.

[3] Ibid., vol. vii. p. 356. Noy died August 10, 1634, before the writs were issued, and Sir Edward Coke died on the 3d of the next month.

[4] See above, p. 265.

places along the coast, commanding them to provide a given number and kind of ships, which were to be brought to Portsmouth by the 1st of March, and authorizing them at the same time to assess the places in question for a sum sufficient to provide for the fitting out and maintenance of the ships and their crews during a period of six months.[1]   The real purpose for which the fleet was to be used was to reassert England's claim of sovereignty over the narrow seas against the growing maritime influence of the Dutch Republic and of France, a monstrous pretension put forward about that time in a book,[2] by Sir John Borough, the keeper of the records of the Tower, who maintained that it had sometimes been acquiesced in by foreign nations at an earlier day.   As reasons of state made it inexpedient to disclose the real purpose for which the ships were intended, the writs vaguely stated that they were needed to defend the realm against "certain thieves, pirates, and robbers of the sea, as well as Turks," who had combined to attack it.   Some of the cities interested complained that the burden had been unequally adjusted, while London, which was called upon to bear one fifth[3] of the whole demand, insisted that it should not have been imposed at all.   But a sharp rebuke from the council to the lord mayor at once broke down the opposition of the capital, and so, as we are told by the Venetian ambassador, "did this most important affair begin and end.   If it does not altogether violate the laws of the realm, as some think it does, it is certainly repugnant to usage and to the forms hitherto observed."[4]

While the ship writs of 1634 were thus confined to the port towns and the maritime counties, they clearly asserted the general principle, first put forward in 1628, that "that charge of defence which concerneth all men ought to be supported by all, as by the laws and customs of the kingdom of England hath been accustomed to be done."   In accordance with that declaration Coventry, the lord keeper, in June of 1635, in a time of profound peace, announced to the judges of assize previous to their going on circuit, the king's intention to extend

the real purpose for which the fleet was to be used;

the purpose stated in the writs;

all opposition rebuked by the council;

in June, 1635, the king announced his intention to extend ship writs to inland counties;

---

[1] For the form of the writ, see Rushworth, vol. ii. p. 257.

[2] His book was entitled *Sovereignty of the Sea.*   See Harl. MSS., 4314.

[3] £20,688 out of £104,252.   *State Papers*, cclxxvi. 8.

[4] Correr's despatch, December 26, 1634.   Ven. MSS., cited in Gardiner, vol. vii. p. 376.

ship-money to the inland counties : " For since that all the kingdom is interested both in the honour, safety, and profit, it is just and reasonable that they should all put to their helping hands." [1] The new writs issued on the 4th of August were therefore directed to the sheriffs of every county in England and Wales, commanding each to provide a warship for the king's service of a given tonnage and equipment; and along with each writ were sent instructions to the sheriff to levy upon his county instead of a ship, a given sum of money, the collection of which he was to enforce, if necessary, by compulsory process, in order that it might be promptly paid to the treasurer of the navy. [2] From the terms of these writs it clearly appeared that they were not intended to meet any sudden emergency, but were to stand as a permanent source of taxation for war purposes; they were to be, as Clarendon tells us, "a spring and magazine that should have no bottom, and for an everlasting supply of all occasions." [3] This startling proposition to set aside the fundamental principle of the constitution, which declared that things for the common good of all must be provided for in parliament, by the common consent of all, was first resisted in the hundred of Bloxham, in Oxfordshire, where the chief constables replied to the sheriff's warrant that they had " no authority to assess or tax any man," nor did the warrant, in their judgment, give " them any power so to do." After similar difficulties had arisen in Essex and Devonshire, the judges were consulted through Finch, in December, and they soon replied, in substance, that where the good and safety of the kingdom in general is concerned, and the whole kingdom in danger, — of which his majesty is the only judge, — there the charge of the defence ought to be borne by all the kingdom in general. [5] Even in the face of such a declaration the indomitable Chambers, who had so resolutely resisted the payment of tonnage and poundage, appealed to the king's bench as a court for a formal judgment. But the judges refused even to permit the question of right to be argued, for the reason assigned by Berkeley, "that there was a rule of law and

the new writs demanded money in lieu of ships of all counties ;

to be enforced by compulsory process ;

"an everlasting supply of all occasions;"

resisted first in Oxfordshire ;

the judges gave answers favorable to the king ;

Chambers presents the matter in the king's bench ;

[1] Rushworth, vol. ii. p. 294.
[2] *Fœdera*, vol. xix. p. 658 *et seq.*
[3] *Hist. Rebellion*, vol. i. p. 68.
[4] *State Papers*, Dom., cccii. 87, 90;
Ibid., ccci. 96.

[5] Rushworth, vol. ii. p. 355; Branston's *Autobiography* (Camden Soc. p. 66. See Gardiner, vol. vii. pp. 92-94.

a rule of government, and that many things which might not be done by the rule of law might be done by the rule of government,"[1]—the *jure divino* doctrine announced in Bate's case. Thus encouraged and sustained by the servile judges, who had before their eyes the fate of Coke and Crew, Charles, as a final indication that ship-money, which produced an annual income of more than £200,000, was to become a permanent tax, issued on October 9, 1636, another set of ship writs to all the realm.[2]   In reply to this fresh demand it was that Danby, an old servant of the crown, boldly advised the king, rather than assert such a claim so opposed to the fundamental laws of the kingdom, to summon a parliament.[3]   The only response was a fresh appeal to the judges, who, in February, 1637, again answered more formally than before, in favor of the crown.[4] The time had now come when the constitution was to find a resolute defender, in the person of John Hampden, a gentleman of the inland county of Buckingham, the bosom friend of Eliot and Pym, and a cousin of Oliver Cromwell, who was determined, no matter what the result should be, that the great question of ship-money should be argued in open court by famous advocates, who could thus be heard by the nation as a whole.   With that end in view, Hampden resisted the payment of the 20 *s.* assessed on his lands at Great Missenden,[5] and when proceedings were instituted against him in the exchequer for his refusal to pay, he appeared and demurred to the writ as insufficient in law.   The issue thus fairly raised was argued in November and December, 1637, for twelve days, before a full bench, by Oliver St. John and Holborne for Hampden, and by the attorney and solicitor-general on behalf of the crown.   The essence of the argument made for Hampden was that the sum in question was a tax imposed for the purpose of raising extraordinary revenue, which could not be levied except by parliament, whose exclusive right so to levy

Margin notes: judges refused to permit the question of right to be argued; the ship writs of 1636; again sustained by the judges in 1637; John Hampden; resisted payment, and demurred to the writs in the exchequer; case argued in November and December; essence of the argument against the writs;

---

[1] Rushworth, vol. ii. p. 323.
[2] *Fœdera*, vol. xx. p. 56.
[3] Correr to the Doge, December 2; Ven. MSS., cited in Gardiner, vol. viii. p. 201.
[4] *State Papers*, Dom., cccxlvi. pp. 11, 14; Rushworth, vol. ii. p. 352. The answer of the judges was then recorded in the star chamber, in chancery, in the king's bench, common pleas, and

exchequer, and an intimation was given by the crown that any lawyer would be very foolish to undertake to oppose ship-money under such circumstances.
[5] He was also assessed 31 *s.* 6 *d.* on his lands in Great Kimble. *Memoirs of Hampden and his Times*, vol. i. p. 230. The suit in the exchequer was, however, as to the assessment at Great Missenden.

their
validity
sustained
in 1638 by
seven
judges
against five;

had been confirmed by many statutes, notably by the Great Charter, *De tallagio non concedendo*, and the recent Petition of Right.   The counter argument made for the crown was sustained by seven of the judges, who delivered their judgments at intervals during the year 1638.   Chief Justice Finch, in summing up the opinions of his brethren, said boldly that "Acts of parliament to take away his [the king's] royal power in the defence of his kingdom are void. . . . They are void acts of parliament to bind the king not to command the subjects, their persons and goods, and I say their money too, for no acts of parliament make any difference."[1]   Of the five judges who sided with Hampden, three based their judgments

only two of
the five
held with
Hampden
on the
merits;

on purely technical grounds, leaving only two who held with him on the merits.   Crooke, speaking in his behalf, said in plain words : "This writ is illegal, not being by authority of parliament.   It is against the common law, as appears by the fact that it is the first since the Conquest sent to any inland town to prepare a ship."[2]   The practical effect of this judicial victory, which Charles won by the smallest majority possible,

Hampden
thus
became a
national
leader.

was to exalt Hampden into a national leader, who dared "on his own charge, to support the liberty and prosperity of the kingdom ;" his case was no longer looked upon, as Clarendon tells us, "as the case of one man, but the case of the kingdom, nor as an imposition laid upon them by the king, but by the judges, which they thought themselves bound in conscience to the public justice not to submit to."[3]   The magistrates whom James and Charles had robbed of their sacred independence possessed no longer the power to convince the nation that their judgments were the law.

Charles'
two great
ministers;

Throughout the eleven years of personal rule during which Charles was driving the conciliar system on to its doom, he was zealously supported by two able ministers, who stood firmly by his side until first one and then the other was stricken down by "that two-handed engine at the door, ready to smite

Wentworth
as a leader
of the
popular
party;

once, and smite no more."[4]   In the parliament of 1614 Sir Thomas Wentworth, a young Yorkshire gentleman of fortune, appeared for the first time as the representative of the great

[1] *R.* v. *Hampden* (case of ship-money), 13 Car. I. 1637, *State Trials*, vol. iii. pp. 825–1316.
[2] See Denman's *Broom's Const. Law*,

pp. 338–355; Thomas' *Leading Cases in Const. Law*, pp. 21, 22.
[3] *Hist. Rebellion*, vol. i. p. 69 *et seq.*
[4] Milton's *Lycidas.*

county of the north, and so zealous did he become in the popular cause that he was put upon the penal list of sheriffs appointed in order to insure their absence from Charles' second parliament, which met in February, 1626.[1] While there is no evidence to prove that he favored the impeachment of Buckingham which then took place, the fact remains that in the following July he was abruptly dismissed as justice of the peace, and the office of *custos rotulorum* bestowed upon his hated rival in the county, Sir John Savile. Aroused by such an insult, he became more resolute than ever in his opposition as a member of the country party, suffering imprisonment in 1627 for his refusal to pay the forced loan demanded in that year.[2] Thus it was that he was able to grasp the leadership in the first session of Charles' third parliament, which began in March, 1628, and whose labors ended in the adoption of the Petition of Right, which drew its substance from Wentworth and its form from Coke.[3] But with that great event ended his connection with the popular cause. On the 26th of June the first session was prorogued, and on July 22 Wentworth was created a peer and entered into the royal favor. And yet the master of the history of that epoch claims that he was neither deserter nor apostate; that having removed through the Petition of Right all abuses which he regarded as prejudicial to good government, he took his place naturally at Charles' side because in his eyes " Presbyterianism in the church and Parliamentarism in the state would seem to be two forms of one disease — of the error which sought to control the government of the wise few by the voice of the ignorant many." As a maintainer of the constitution in its Tudor form, Wentworth is said to have been for a time "with the opposition, but not of it." [4] Whatever his real motives for change may have been, this born administrator was certainly steadfast to the last in the cause of his master, and scornful of all private ends in the desperate struggle which he waged to build up in England, as Richelieu was building up in France, a system of despotism whose organization was to be "thorough." In August, 1628, the dagger of Felton removed Buckingham from his path, and

[marginal notes:] dismissed as justice of the peace; imprisoned in 1627; real author of the Petition of Right; his conversion to the cause of the crown; he is said to have been "with the opposition, but not of it;"

---

1 See above, p. 258.
2 See above, p. 264.
3 See above, p. 268.

4 Gardiner, vol. vi. p. 335; vol. vii. pp. 137, 152.

made president of the Council of the North,

in the following December he was made president of the Council of the North, the first great object of his ambition. Not until November, 1629, was he sworn of the privy council, about the time from which his close alliance with Laud is said to have begun.

then lord deputy for Ireland;

In January, 1632, he was appointed lord deputy for Ireland, but he did not enter Dublin until July of the following year. Before the six years of despotic rule which then began had drawn to a close, Wentworth was able to write to

his correspondence with Laud.

Laud that "the king is as absolute here as any prince in the world can be;"[1] and when in February, 1637, the judges for the second time expressed themselves in favor of the legality of ship-money, he wrote: "This decision of the judges will therefore make the king absolute at home and formidable abroad. Let him only abstain from war a few years, that he may habituate his subjects to the payment of this tax, and in the end he will find himself more powerful and respected than any of his predecessors."[2]

Laud made primate in August, 1633;

It was natural that Wentworth should thus pour his political aspirations into the sympathetic ear of Laud, who, on the 6th of August, 1633, only a few days after the lord deputy's arrival in Ireland, had been raised by Charles to the primacy of the kingdom. A brief statement has already been made as

his career prior to that time;

to Laud's career prior to that time, including a summary of the leading dogmas which he, as the chief of the Arminian element, proposed to substitute for the Calvinistic tenets so firmly engrafted by the Puritan clergy upon the doctrines of the state church.[3] His first serious effort in that direction was made when, as bishop of London, he urged the king in

the Thirty-nine Articles to be accepted "in the literal and grammatical sense;"

December, 1628, to reissue the Thirty-nine Articles, prefaced by a royal Declaration[4] that they should be accepted and expounded by all only "in the literal and grammatical sense," a blow at Puritan interpretation which was fiercely resented by that party in the resolutions adopted by the house in the stormy session which occurred at the close of Charles' third

[1] In the course of this confidential correspondence the word "thorough" or "through" was familiarly used to describe the general policy of which they were both advocates.

[2] *Strafford Papers*, vol. ii. p. 61. For his views upon Hampden's conduct in resisting ship-money, see Ibid., pp. 136, 156.

[3] See above, p. 254.

[4] The Declaration, which every new minister was bound to read, was set as a preface to the edition of the articles of 1628, and is still printed in the Book of Common Prayer.

parliament in March, 1629.[1] Undaunted, however, by that rebuke, Laud moved steadily on with his purpose to force the Puritan element within the church to conform to both creed and ritual as expounded by him, an undertaking that involved the substitution, for that phase of religion dear at the time to the mass of Englishmen, of a more ceremonial system, which as viewed by its adversaries counterfeited the pomp of Rome. Before the close of 1631, Laud gave the Puritan clergy to understand that they must conform to the last tittle or surrender their livings, and when an effort was made to keep them in office by buying up impropriations of livings to be held for their benefit,[2] the feoffees were cited to appear in the exchequer chamber, where in February, 1633, a decree was rendered dissolving the feoffments and declaring that all such patronage should be placed at the king's disposal.[3] And after his appointment as archbishop, which took place in that year, Laud also made it impossible for the Puritan clergy to escape conformity in the rôle of lecturers or chaplains by taking away from the country gentlemen the right to have chaplains at all.[4] The "thorough" system of coercion thus employed within the church was extended with even greater severity to the separatists, who were dragged before the high commission from their hiding-places in the woods, where they vainly sought immunity from mandates by which even private meetings for prayers or preaching were strictly prohibited.[5] Under the pressure of such a ruthless system of persecution, carried on with the aid both of the star chamber and high commission, the tide of Puritan emigration to the New World, which began to rise with the departure of Winthrop, soon reached such a height that in February, 1634, an order in council was adopted prohibiting the sailing of any more vessels.[6] While the church

(marginal notes:) conformity forced upon the Puritan clergy; feoffments for their benefit dissolved; forbidden to act as lecturers or chaplains; persecution of separatists; Puritan emigration to the New World;

---

[1] See above, p. 278. It was as a member of the committee upon that subject that Cromwell made his first speech in parliament. For a statement of the matter from the Arminian point of view, see Blount, *Reform. of the Church of Eng.*, pp. 497–500.

[2] "The originator of this scheme was 'the famous' Dr. Preston, a Puritan College Doctor of immense 'fame' in those and prior years." — Carlyle,

Cromwell's Letters and Speeches, p. 44, citing Heylin's *Life of Laud*.

[3] *Exchequer Decrees*, vol. iv. p. 88.

[4] Ibid., p. 240.

[5] See Laud's letter to Windebank, June 13, 1632. *State Papers, Dom.*, ccxviii. 46.

[6] A week later this order was so modified as to permit emigration under certain conditions. *State Papers, Dom.*, cclx. 17; *Council Register*, February 21, 28. Cf. Gardiner, vol. vii. pp. 317,

was thus being emptied of bishops and ministers, who refused
to accept Laudian standards, the archbishop was careful to
supply their places by a new clergy, whose corporate influence
he attempted to enhance by breathing a fresh life into the
ecclesiastical courts, and by elevating in 1636 Juxon, bishop
of London, to the great post of lord high treasurer, an office
which, as Laud states in his diary, "no churchman" had held
"since Henry the Seventh's time." [1]   At this stage of his career it was that Laud and his system were subjected to bitter
attacks from the unlicensed press, whose Parthian arrows now
pierced him from every side.   Chief among the offenders were
Prynne, Bastwick, and Burton, pamphleteers of the old Martin
Mar-Prelate type,[2] who in June, 1637, were brought before the
star chamber, charged with libels against the bishops in which
were contained denunciations of the entire system of innovation that had been brought about under Laud's direction.
Two of the three were then suffering imprisonment for past
offences.   In 1634 Prynne, a bigoted Puritan lawyer, had been
punished by the star chamber for publishing a ponderous and
stupid book called "Histriomastrix," in which he denounced
with the virulence of that time all innocent human recreations
in general, and female actors in particular.[3]   Bastwick, who
was a physician, had been punished by the high commission
in 1635 for an argument in favor of presbyterianism published
under the name of "Flagellum Pontificis." [4]   Prynne and Bastwick then committed new offences, which brought them before
the star chamber in 1637, with Burton, who the year before
had published two sermons under the title of "For God and the
King," in which he attacked directly or indirectly the entire
episcopal system.   So sharply was Laud assailed that he felt
called upon to defend himself in an elaborate speech [5] before
the star chamber, which rewarded his zeal by a cruel sentence
against all three prisoners, who were condemned to lose their
ears and to suffer heavy fines, in addition to life imprisonment.[6]
But when the time came for the first part of the sentence

Marginal notes:

the new
Laudian
clergy;

Laud and
his system
attacked
by the
unlicensed
press;

Prynne's
"Histrio-
mastrix;"

Bastwick's
"Flagellum
Pontificis;"

Burton's
"For God
and the
King;"

all three
condemned
by the star
chamber;

318, as to the "increase of emigration
to Massachusetts."
  [1] Laud's *Works*, vol. iii. p. 226.
  [2] See above, p. 172.
  [3] It was supposed that this assault
was directed against the queen, who

had taken part in a little play called
The Shepherd's Pastoral.
  [4] *State Papers*, Dom., cclxi. 178.
  [5] See *Works*, vol. vii. p. 355.
  [6] *State Trials*, vol. iii. pp. 711-
770.

to be carried out, the widespread manifestations of sympathy with the prisoners unmistakably revealed the fact that the tide of popular indignation was rising.[1]   The quick response from the government was a star chamber decree, which sharpened the censorship of the press by reducing the number of licensed printers to twenty, and by providing that any one not of that number who should dare to print a book or pamphlet was "to be set in the pillory and whipped through the city of London."[2]

the censorship sharpened.

While Laud, thus aided by the heavy hand of the law, was forcing uniformity upon all within the realm, whether within or without the pale of the state church, he entered upon the more difficult task of subjecting to the same process that turbulent kirk across the northern border which, at the beginning of the Reformation, had adopted not only the dogmatic theology, but the entire system of church government devised by the organizing genius of Calvin.   The attempt has already been made to explain how difficult it was for James to force upon this democratic and aggressive body, with its kirk sessions, presbyteries, and general assembly, the yoke of the episcopal system, which was entirely incompatible with the principles of its organization.[3]   So limited was James' success in building up the rule of bishops in his Scottish kingdom, that when Laud in his earlier days tried to induce him to go a step farther by stripping the kirk of its presbyterian character, in order to drive it into conformity with the English canons and ritual, he waved him away as a foolish man who "knows not the stomach of that people."[4]   Instead of attempting any doctrinal changes, James contented himself with establishing in 1609 a court of high commission,[5] by means of which he forced the kirk to bow in many particulars to the royal authority. But if the mind of Laud was narrow and bigoted, it was firm and persistent in its concentration upon a single object.   The scheme which James contemptuously rejected, Laud was able to put to a practical test in 1636, when upon the sole authority

Laud's attempt to force uniformity upon the Scotch kirk;

James' failure to establish the rule of bishops in Scotland;

contented himself with establishing a court of high commission;

Laud's scheme put to a practical test in 1636;

---

[1] *Strafford Papers*, vol. ii. pp. 99, 114. Cf. also Brodie, *Hist. Brit. Empire*, vol. ii. p. 334.

[2] Rushworth, vol. ii. p. 450, App. 306; *State Papers*, Dom., ccclxiv. 111.

[3] See above, pp. 212, 214.

[4] Green, *Hist. of the Eng. People*, vol. iii. p. 179.

[5] This court, established without any authority from parliament or assembly, was abolished in 1638.

of the crown[1] a book of canons inspired by the archbishop was put in force, by virtue of which the government of the Scotch kirk was placed completely in the hands of the bishops, while the old form of worship contained in Knox's Book of Common Order was by the same authority superseded by a new liturgy based upon the English Book of Common Prayer.[2]   When the Scots attempted to reject the new liturgy upon the ground that it was both popish and English, Charles responded by a proclamation, issued in December, ordering every parish to adopt it and to procure two copies before the next Easter.[3]   Not, however, until the end of July,

resisted by the clergy of Edinburgh in 1637;

1637, was an actual attempt made to force the clergy of Edinburgh to introduce it into their churches, in the hope that its acceptance by the capital would be followed by the rest of the

tumult at St. Giles;

country.   The result was that the tumult at St. Giles was followed by riot after riot, until the tide of opposition, which first gathered the remonstrants around the "Tables" at Ster-

covenant signed at the Grey Friars', March 1, 1638;

ling, finally crystallized into the covenant, signed in the Grey Friars' Church at Edinburgh on the 1st of March, 1638,[4] wherein the subscribers bound themselves "to continue in the profession and obedience of the aforesaid religion, that we shall defend the same and resist all these contrary errors and corruptions, according to our vocation."[5]   When the marquis

abrogation of the Laudian system demanded;

of Hamilton was sent by Charles to end the troubles thus brought about, he was met by a demand for the withdrawal of the obnoxious canons and liturgy, the abolition of the high commission, and for the calling of a free assembly and a free parliament.   After the threat of war with which Charles met this demand had broken down for want of money to execute

swept away by general assembly at Glasgow, in November;

it, a general assembly was summoned by the king's permission, that met at Glasgow in November, in which, despite Hamilton's effort to dissolve it, Laud's whole work was swept away and the episcopal superseded by the presbyterian system.[6]   In the face of such a menace, which the Scots followed up by raising an army under the command of Leslie, Laud stood

---

[1] Burton, *Hist. of Scotland*, vol. vi. p. 397; Laud's *Works*, vol. v. p. 583.
[2] Gardiner, *Hist. Eng.*, vol. viii. pp. 309–312.
[3] The king to the council, October 18, Balfour, vol. ii. p. 224.

[4] Rothes, pp. 71, 79.
[5] *Large Declaration*, p. 57.
[6] Baillie, vol. i. p. 165; Peterkin's *Records*, p. 128; *Hamilton Papers*, p. 62; *Hardwicke Papers*, vol. iii. p. 124.

undaunted.   As a "man to carnage and the Koran given," his voice was for war, and in that resolve he was firmly supported by Wentworth, whose one great aim had been to transform Ireland into an arsenal, from which Charles could draw both money and men in an emergency.   The time had now arrived for action, and when, in February, 1639, the news came that Charles was gathering an army at York, Leslie suddenly assumed the offensive, and, after seizing the strongholds of Edinburgh and Dumbarton, he moved to the border, taking up his position in June near Berwick, almost in sight of the king's camp, some twelve miles distant.   Rather than risk an engagement, Charles there signed, on the 18th of June, the treaty of Berwick,[1] in which the Scots agreed to give up the strongholds, to disband their army, and break up the "Tables" and all unlawful committees, upon Charles' guarantee that they should have both a free assembly and a free parliament, in which were to be settled all matters in dispute as well ecclesiastical as political.   In the assembly opened at Edinburgh on the 12th of August, episcopacy and all its consequences were again abolished as they had been at Glasgow, while in the parliament which met at the end of the same month were proposed serious constitutional changes.[2]   How to undo results such as these, forced upon him by rebellious subjects, became the one subject of Charles' thoughts; and when he was convinced that the end could be attained only through war, he set himself to work to make preparation.   Wentworth, who returned to England in September, now became more emphatically than ever before Charles' chief guide and counsellor. On January 12, 1640, he was made earl of Strafford, and a week later he exchanged the title of lord deputy for that of lord lieutenant of Ireland.   Although the new earl was firmly for war in the last resort, he had already advised the king that he should first call a parliament.   While Charles was hesitating and looking for means by which the dreaded alternative could be avoided, a letter fell into his hands, subscribed by seven of the principal covenanters and directed to Louis XIII., from which he thought he could prove that under the cloak

Side notes: February, 1639, Charles gathered an army at York; treaty of Berwick signed June 18; episcopacy again abolished by general assembly in August; Wentworth now became chief minister; advised the king to call a parliament; letter from the covenanters to Louis XIII.

[1] *State Papers*, Dom., ccccxxiii. 107;   Burnet's *Hamiltons*, pp. 140, 141; Rushworth, vol. iii. p. 94.
[2] Cf. Gardiner, vol. ix. pp. 49, 50.

of religion the Scots were concealing a treasonable conspiracy with a foreign power. In the belief that such a revelation would prompt English loyalty to support him against Scottish treason, he finally accepted Strafford's advice, and in March elections were held, after the lapse of so many years, for a new parliament.

The Short Parliament met April 13, 1640;

7. By the calling of the Short Parliament, which met on the 13th of April, 1640, Charles confessed the impotency of the conciliar system in the face of a great emergency, and that confession was emphasized when Lord Keeper Finch appealed to the houses for an instant grant to pay the army which had been raised to crush rebellion in the north. Finch's proposal was that, after a bill should be passed granting tonnage and poundage from the king's accession, and another granting

subsidies demanded;

extraordinary subsidies, parliament should address itself to the consideration of grievances ; and in the hope of exciting the

intercepted letter exhibited;

zeal of his auditors, the lord keeper then read the intercepted letter [1] which was supposed to prove the treason of the Scots, for whose coercion Strafford had already obtained four subsidies from the Irish commons.[2] To this appeal for aid to destroy the allies who were fighting the battle of English freedom across the border, the house, now led by Pym and Hampden,

ignored by the house, which took up first the question of grievances:

responded by ignoring the intercepted letter, and by resolving on the 23d to reverse Finch's proposal by taking up first the question of grievances : " Till the liberties of the house and kingdom were cleared, they knew not whether they had anything to give or no." [3] Before making a grant the house was determined that redress should be given for the breach of privilege which had arisen out of the prosecution of Eliot,

and resented a suggestion from the lords that "supply should have precedency;"

Holles, and Valentine, and for the unconstitutional exaction of ship-money and the impositions.[4] At this point Charles appealed to the lords, who declared by a great majority [5] that in their judgment "supply should have precedency, and be resolved upon before any other matter whatsoever," a conclu-

---

1 For a full statement, see Lingard, vol. vii. p. 440, and note 3.

2 *Journals of the Commons of Ireland*, vol. i. p. 141. Upon his return to England Strafford left orders for the levy of eight thousand Irish troops. *Fœdera*, vol. xx. p. 359; *Strafford Papers*, pp. 390–404.

3 Harl. MSS., 3, 931, fol. 47 b.

4 *Parl. or Const. Hist.*, vol. viii. p. 441.

5 Sixty-one out of a house of eighty-six voted for the king. *State Papers*, Dom., ccccli. 39.

sion which in conference was expressed to the commons, who promptly resented the suggestion of the lords as a high breach of their exclusive privilege to originate money-bills. The lords, however, maintained their position by a diminished majority,[1] while the king demanded an immediate grant of twelve subsidies, in exchange for which he proposed to give up ship-money. As soon as it was known that the houses would not pay unconditionally so great a sum for the redress of a grievance which should never have existed,[2] parliament was abruptly dissolved on May 5, after a session of three weeks, during which time it sternly expressed by its refusal to do anything the breadth and depth of the national displeasure. " So great a defection in the kingdom," wrote Northumberland, "hath not been known in the memory of man." The failure of parliament to grant supplies released the king, in Strafford's judgment, "from all rule of government," and left him free to return to the "extraordinary means" by which he had filled the exchequer during the last eleven years.[3] Thus it was that the collection of ship-money was quickened, a new imposition called "coat and conduct money" imposed, fresh monopolies created, and forced loans demanded of the city of London, whose aldermen were imprisoned for their refusal to give.[4] And in order to secure a grant from the clergy, convocation was unconstitutionally continued after the dissolution of parliament [5] under a commission authorizing it to sit "during pleasure," [6] and to alter and amend the laws of the church, by virtue of which seventeen "constitutions and canons" [7] were adopted, proclaiming anew the divine right of kings, inculcating passive obedience, imposing a new oath known as the Etcetera Oath,

[marginal notes:] exclusive right of the house to originate money-bills admitted; parliament, after refusing to do anything, dissolved May 5; "coat and conduct money" imposed; convocation continued after dissolution; a new set of canons adopted;

---

[1] Admitting, however, that " the bill of subsidies ought to have its inception in your house ; and that when it comes up to their lordships, and is by them agreed to, it must be returned back to you, and be, by your Speaker, presented."

[2] Cf. Clarendon, *Hist. Rebellion*, vol. i. p. 136.

[3] Rushworth, *Strafford's Trial*, p. 536.

[4] Ibid., vol. iii. pp. 1, 167 ; *State Papers*, ccccliii. 24. Cf. Gardiner, *Hist. Eng.*, vol. ix. p. 130. "Coat and conduct money" was a new imposition levied by the king upon the counties to pay for the clothing and travelling expenses of those who were pressed into service for the war against the Scots.

[5] An opinion was first obtained from Lord Keeper Finch and some of the judges, that convocation could legally sit after the dissolution.

[6] The first commission had authorized it to sit "during the parliament."

[7] Cardwell's *Synodalia*, pp. 380–415 ; Blount, *Reform. of the Church of Eng.*, vol. ii. pp. 528–531.

to prevent innovations in doctrine and government, and subjecting all separatists to the same penalties as catholic recusants.[1] With the inadequate means thus provided Strafford *war with the Scots renewed;* urged upon Charles war against the Scots, which he undertook to conduct with the aid of an army from Ireland. In anticipation of the blow thus aimed against them, the covenanters, encouraged by the refusal of the English parliament to grant supplies, again assumed the aggressive. On the 20th of August they crossed the border, and after occupying Newcastle, offered proposals of peace upon the basis of a redress *Charles forced to buy a truce;* of grievances. As the king dared not hazard a battle with the undisciplined troops under Strafford's command, he sought a truce, which he was forced to buy with the heavy concessions embodied in the treaty of Ripon. Without an effective military force, with an empty treasury to which the city of London refused to lend, with Laud rabbled at Lambeth, and the sittings of the high commission broken up by a mob at St. Paul's, Charles was compelled to accept the inevitable and, *great council of peers held at York in September.* after a vain appeal to a great council of peers [2] which met at York in September, he reluctantly consented, as a last resort, to put himself in the hands of the estates at Westminster.

The death grapple between the conciliar and parliamentary systems: 8. The time had now come for the death grapple between the conciliar system, to which the genius of Strafford had given a fresh inspiration, and the parliamentary system, destined to enter upon a new career under the leadership of Pym, who was the first to put in practice the constitutional principle which has become the basis of the English constitution in its modern form, and which maintains not only that the supreme powers of the state are vested in parliament as against the crown, but that as between the houses themselves the ultimate sovereignty resides in the popular branch of the legislature. Fully conscious of the fact that these mighty issues were bound up in the impending crisis, Pym rode with Hampden through the counties upon the eve of the elections, in order to urge the constituencies to return *the Long Parliament met, November 3, 1640;* men of the right temper to represent them in that famous assembly which met on the 3d of November, 1640, and which was destined to be known for all time as the Long Parliament.

1 Neal, *Hist. Puritans*, vol. ii. p. 302.   seen for centuries. It held its last
2 Such an assembly had not been   meeting October 28.

The response to the joint appeal was such a manifestation of popular support as had not been seen since the days of Simon of Montfort, and the leadership of the great majority which thus gathered at St. Stephen's naturally passed to Pym, who remained as almost the sole survivor of that patriot band which had been led in turn by Coke, Eliot, and Wentworth. If it be true that "Wentworth is the one English statesman of all time who may be said to have had no sense of law, . . . John Pym, the leader of the commons from the first meeting of the new houses at Westminster, stands out for all after-time as the embodiment of law."[1]   According to Pym's conception, the duty of the popular party in the house was to hew away by purely constitutional means the abnormal powers which the conciliar system had taken on during the Tudor period, and which both James and Charles had augmented, in order to restore the parliamentary system to the position of legitimate influence which it had enjoyed in the days of the Lancastrian kings.   The means finally employed for that end consisted, first, of the removal and punishment of the great ministers by whom the conciliar system had been perverted; second, of the correction of the more recent abuses brought about by them; third, of such a diminution of the powers of the council as to render it incapable of serious harm for the future.   Under these three heads may be grouped all of the more important acts of the Long Parliament.

The leadership to which Pym was assigned by the popular party, and which put at his back not only the house of commons but a Scottish army upon English soil, involved him at once in a duel to the death with Strafford, who was supported by all the resources of the council system and by the army of the king.   While the two gladiators thus equipped glared at each other for a moment across the arena, Strafford forced Pym's hand by advising Charles to seize the popular leaders upon a charge of treasonable relations with the Scots.[2]   Only a timely betrayal of the secret[3] enabled Pym to parry the blow by impeaching Strafford so hurriedly at the bar of the lords, on the 11th of November, that he was forced to promise that

Marginal notes: leadership of Pym; his conception of the end to be attained; means employed for its attainment. A duel to the death between Pym and Strafford; Strafford hurriedly impeached on the 11th of November;

---

[1] Green, *Hist. of the Eng. People*, vol. iii. pp. 155, 192.

[2] Rushworth, *Strafford's Trial*, p. 2; Laud's *Works*, vol. iii. p. 295.

[3] Gardiner, *Hist. Eng.*, vol. ix. p. 232.

the house would send up the grounds of the accusation at a later day.[1] The preliminary articles were carried to the lords on the 25th of November,[2] the detailed charges on the 28th and 30th of the following January, and supplementary articles on the 8th of the following April.[3] The real reason for this

difficult to formulate a provable charge of treason against him;

hesitation and delay grew out of the inability of the managers upon the part of the house to formulate a provable charge against Strafford, which clearly constituted treason under the terms of the statute of Edward III. According to Pym's theory the lord lieutenant was guilty of treason, because he was at the head of a conspiracy to overthrow, by force, if necessary, the fundamental laws of the realm, or in other words, the constitution of the country, and that theory was embodied in the first of the preliminary articles, which averred " that Thomas, earl of Strafford, hath traitorously endeavoured to subvert the fundamental laws and government of the realms of England and Ireland, and instead thereof to introduce an arbitrary and tyrannical government against law, which he had declared by traitorous words, counsels, and actions, and by giving His Majesty advice by force of arms to compel his loyal subjects to submit thereto." The reason it was difficult to maintain that the acts alleged came within the terms of the statute

because "the law of England is silent as to conspiracies against itself;"

charged with "levying war against the king;"

was, as Hallam has pithily expressed it, because " the law of England is silent as to conspiracies against itself." [4] That part of the charge which accused Strafford of levying money by his own authority and quartering troops on certain towns of Ireland, in order to compel them to pay, was supposed to make the closest approach to that kind of substantive treason denounced by the English statute as " levying war against the king," and also by two Irish acts, one of the reign of Edward III., and the other of the reign of Henry VI., the last of which provided that " whosoever shall cess men of war against His Majesty's dominions, shall be thought to make war against the King," and be punished as a traitor.[5] In the trial which began March 22, 1641, and lasted until the 19th

---

[1] *Commons' Journals*, vol. ii. p. 26; Clarendon, *Hist. Rebellion*, vol. i. p. 243. See also *Lords' Journals*, vol. iv. p. 88.

[2] Ibid., p. 97.

[3] D'Ewes' *Diary*, Harl. MSS., clxii. fol. 176, 182; Ibid., clxiii. fol. 318.

[4] Hallam, *Const. Hist.*, vol. ii. p. 106.

[5] For a full statement, see Sir J. F. Stephen, *Hist. of the Crim. Law*, vol. i. pp. 360–364.

of April, the turning-point was an unsuccessful attempt to failure in the proof; prove that Strafford proposed at the council board to bring over the Irish army to subdue England.[1]   The consciousness upon the part of the prosecutors that they had failed in the proof led, no doubt, to an abandonment of the impeachment, in order that resort might be had to the surer and swifter means of the bill of attainder, brought in on the 10th of April and approved on the 10th of May,[2] under which Strafford was executed on the 12th.   When the judges were asked by the lords to declare whether or no the charges involved in the attainder amounted to treason, they could only be induced to declare that "they were of opinion, upon all which their lordships had voted to be proven, that the earl of Strafford doth deserve to undergo the pains and forfeiture of high treason by law."[3] Windebank, the secretary of state, who was accused of a corrupt favoring of recusants, fled over sea[4] in the month that followed Strafford's arrest, and Finch, the lord keeper, who was at the same time impeached[5] for high treason, followed his example.

for that reason a bill of attainder brought in April 10;

ambiguous opinion of the judges;

flight of Windebank and Finch.

While the house was thus engaged in the punishment of political offenders, it was not forgetful of the work that had been done by the Arminian clergy in the church, the last phase of which was embodied in the recent canons and the Etcetera Oath.[6]   In the course of the debate on the canons which were annulled, it was suggested that Laud, their "principal solicitor," was guilty of treason, and the commons thereupon secured his imprisonment by impeaching him for that offence on the 18th of December, 1640.[7]   On February 24, 1641, the original articles were voted, and on March 1 he was committed to the Tower.   Not until October, 1643, were the final articles

Impeachment of Laud, December 18, 1640;

articles not presented until October, 1643;

---

[1] "A copy of notes made by the elder Vane of the words used at the Committee of Eight after the dissolution of the short parliament had long been in Pym's hands, and Vane himself was now put into the witness-box." — Gardiner, *Hist. Eng.*, vol. ix. pp. 319, 320. For Strafford's objections to the sufficiency of Vane's testimony, see Ibid.

[2] *Strafford Letters*, vol. ii. p. 432. Charles said as he signed the bill, "My lord of Strafford's condition is better than mine."

[3] The fifty-nine members who voted against the bill in the lower house were placarded as "Straffordians, who, to save a traitor, would destroy their country."   Out of the forty-five peers who attended at the passage of the bill, nineteen voted against it, despite the popular tumult.

[4] Rushworth, vol. iv. p. 91.

[5] December 23, 1640.

[6] See above, p. 299.

[7] *Commons' Journals*, vol. ii. p. 54. He was at once sequestered from parliament and committed to custody.

presented which charged him in substance with attempting to subvert the fundamental laws of the realm in order to introduce arbitrary government, with attempting to subvert true religion in order to introduce popery, and with attempting to subvert the rights of parliament itself, — a part of the charges resting upon his purely ecclesiastical acts, and a part upon his violent proceedings in the courts of high commission and star chamber.   The trial, which did not begin until March 12, 1644, continued until October, when Laud's counsel contended that upon the facts adduced he was not guilty of treason as a matter of law under the statute of Edward III.[1]   The impossibility of answering that argument drove the commons to abandon the impeachment, and to proceed by ordinance of attainder as in Strafford's case.   The ordinance, which was sent to the lords on November 22, there encountered legal difficulties, which were referred to the judges, who answered that "they could deliver no opinion on this case, in point of treason by the law : because they could not deliver any opinion in point of treason but what was particularly expressed to be treason in the statute of 25 Edw. III., and so referred it wholly to the judgment of the house."[2]   The lords, nevertheless, passed the bill under which the then helpless old man was executed on the 10th of January, 1645.

ordinance of attainder finally adopted as in Strafford's case;

opinion of the judges;

executed January 10, 1645;

Two days after the house ordered the impeachment which deprived Strafford of his liberty, it commanded the release of Prynne, Bastwick, Burton, Leighton, and Lilburne, victims of the cruel tyranny of the star chamber, whose return from their island prisons was made the occasion of an ovation by "the common people strewing flowers and herbs in the ways as they passed, making great noise and expressions of joy for their deliverance and return."[3]

release of Prynne, Bastwick, and others;

After the commons had thus disposed of the wrongs inflicted by the council upon private individuals, it proceeded to redress that gigantic evil which had been imposed upon the nation under the name of ship-money by the passage of an act which, after declaring void the late proceedings on that subject, and vacating all records and process concerning the same,

all proceedings concerning ship-money annulled;

---

[1] Cf. Laud's *Works*, vol. vi. p. 416.

[2] *Lords' Journals*, 17th December, 1644. For extracts from the journals relating to the proceedings against Laud, see *Works*, vol. iv. pp. 384–425, and notes.

[3] Clarendon, *Hist. Rebellion*, vol. i. p. 202.

specially annulled the judgment rendered in the exchequer chamber against Hampden as contrary to the liberty of the subject as defined in the laws of the realm in general, and in the Petition of Right in particular.[1] Two months before, an act had been passed for the settlement of the vexed question involving the claim of the crown to impose tonnage and poundage by a mere order in council.   That act, after granting the customs to the king for a very short period, "declared and enacted that it is, and hath been, the ancient right of the subjects of this realm, that no subsidy, custom, impost, or other charge whatsoever, ought or may be laid or imposed upon any merchandise exported or imported by subjects, denizens, or aliens, without common consent in parliament." [2]   By the approval of these two acts the crown finally admitted, after a struggle prolonged through four centuries, that the entire taxing power was vested not in the king in council, but in the king in parliament. _{the entire taxing power declared to be in the king in parliament.}

No less important than the prevention of arbitrary taxation was the revival of the right, guaranteed by two statutes of Edward III., that a parliament should be holden at least once in every year,[3] a provision which Charles and his Tudor predecessors had been able to ignore by reason of the fact that the acts that recognized the right failed to guarantee its execution by providing independent legal machinery in the event of a failure upon the part of the crown to issue the necessary writs.   In order to remedy that defect in the constitution, an Annual Parliament Bill, reciting the old statutes of Edward III., was read a second time in the commons on December 30, 1640, at Cromwell's motion ; but it was shortly afterwards transformed in committee into a Triennial Bill,[4] the essence of which was that if in every third year a parliament was not duly summoned by the crown, the writs should be issued by the lord chancellor or keeper of the great seal ; in case of failure upon his part, by twelve or more peers assembled at West- _{The Triennial Act; machinery provided for its execution;}

---

[1] 16 Car. I. c. 14. Approved August 8, 1641, along with bill limiting the boundaries of the forests. Berkeley, Crawley, Davenport, Trevor, and Weston, five of the judges who had pronounced in favor of ship-money, were impended for their judgments.   See Stephen, *Hist. of the Crim. Law*, vol. i. p. 159.

[2] 16 Car. I. c. 8.

[3] 4 Edw. III. c. 14 ; 36 Edw. III. st. 1, c. 10. Cf. Stubbs, *Const. Hist.*, vol. iii. p. 380.

[4] Cf. Gardiner, *Hist. Eng.*, vol. ix. pp. 253, 282.

minster; in case of failure by the peers, by the sheriffs, mayors, and bailiffs; and finally, in case of their default, the electors themselves were authorized to meet and choose their representatives just as if writs had been regularly issued. It was further provided that no future parliament should be adjourned, prorogued, or dissolved, without its own consent, within fifty days after the time fixed for its meeting. It should be *ipso facto* dissolved, however, at the expiration of three years from the first day of its session, unless it should be actually sitting at that time, in which event the dissolution should be postponed until the first adjournment or prorogation thereafter.[1] As the terms of this statute were prospective, the parliament that passed it, for the ostensible purpose of increasing its capacity to borrow money for the relief of the army of the north, but really to protect itself against a hasty dissolution which was justly apprehended at the time, passed another "Act to prevent inconveniences which may happen by the untimely adjourning, proroguing, or dissolving of the present parliament," without its own consent.[2] The bill for the attainder of Strafford and that against the dissolution of parliament were approved by commission on the same day, the 10th of May, 1641.

In this connection may be conveniently noted the remedial acts[3] by which compulsory knighthood was abolished, the vexatious prerogative of purveyance restrained, and the boundaries of the royal forests reduced to the limits recognized in the twentieth year of James I.

Having thus redressed the more pressing evils which the conciliar system had recently inflicted upon the nation, parliament proceeded to extinguish the powers of the principal agencies through which that system had asserted its inquisitorial interference in all matters whether great or small, whether political or ecclesiastical. By an "Act for the regulating of the privy council, and for taking away the court commonly called the star chamber,"[4] was swept away at a blow all of that abnormal judicial authority which during a century and a half had been exercised by the council to the detriment of the ordinary tribunals. In order to enable such tribunals to reas-

Marginal notes:
dissolution of future parliaments;

present parliament not to be dissolved without its own consent;

acts as to compulsory knighthood, purveyance, and forests;

star chamber abolished;

---

[1] 16 Car. I. c. 1.
[2] 16 Car. I. c. 7.
[3] 16 Car. I. cc. 19, 20, 16.
[4] 16 Car. I. c. 10.

sert their legitimate influence, it was enacted "that neither His Majesty nor his privy council hath, or ought to have, any jurisdiction, power, or authority, by any arbitrary way whatsoever, to examine or draw into question, determine or dispose of the lands or goods of any subjects of this kingdom, but that the same ought to be tried and determined in the ordinary courts of justice, and by the ordinary course of law." And in order to settle the vexed question growing out of the claim of the privy councillors to commit persons charged with crime, it was provided that when any person should be so committed by them, singly or as a body, even by the king's special command, he should be instantly entitled upon application to the proper judge to a writ of habeas corpus, in the return of which the jailer was required to set forth the true cause of the commitment, so that the court hearing the case could promptly determine whether the prisoner should be discharged, bailed, or remanded. The statement is generally made that the act which destroyed the star chamber ended at the same time the existence of the court of the president and council of the north, — a despotic tribunal which the tyrannical conduct of Strafford had made specially odious, — the court of the president and council of Wales and the Welsh marches, together with those of the duchy of Lancaster and county palatine of Chester.[1] How the two courts last named continued their existence down to very modern times is explained in detail in the treatise cited below, in which the history of the Welsh courts is also learnedly expounded.[2] The day upon which Charles signed the bill for the abolition of the star chamber he also assented to another [3] repealing that branch of the statute of 1 Eliz. c. 1, under color of which, as the repealing act recites, "the said commissioners have to the great and insufferable wrong and oppression of the king's subjects, used to fine and imprison them and to exercise other authority not belonging to ecclesiastical jurisdiction." The court of high commission was therefore abolished upon the theory that the

Marginal notes:
council forbidden to encroach upon ordinary judicial tribunals;

right of privy councillors to commit for crime regulated;

habeas corpus;

fate of the council of the north and other irregular tribunals;

court of high commission abolished

upon the theory that it had always been a usurpation;

---

[1] Cf. Hallam, *Const. Hist.*, vol. ii. p. 99, who makes a qualification as to the two courts last named.

[2] Sir J. F. Stephen, *Hist. of the Crim. Law*, vol. i. pp. 133–135, 138–144.

[3] 16 Car. I. c. 11, entitled "A repeal of a branch of a statute *primo Elizabethæ*, concerning commissioners, for causes ecclesiastical."

jurisdiction which it exercised had been throughout a usurpation. This act, which took away the *ex officio* oath, also abolished the minor ecclesiastical courts by providing that no ecclesiastical judge should "award, impose, or inflict any pain, penalty, fine, amerciament, imprisonment, or other corporal punishment upon any of the king's subjects," for anything pertaining to the spiritual jurisdiction. There were therefore no ecclesiastical courts in England from 1641 down to 1661, when by 13 Chas. II. c. 12, s. 1, the entire system was restored, excepting only the *ex officio* oath and the high commission.[1] By the cutting away of the abnormal powers which the extraordinary tribunals had acquired since the accession of the house of Tudor, the path was opened for the reëstablishment of the supremacy of law as now understood. The acts by which that result was accomplished, together with the rest enacted during the ten months preceding the recess, whose tenor and effect have also been recited, constitute the permanent work of the Long Parliament, which, with the exception of the compulsory clauses of the Triennial Act, was accepted at the Restoration as a part of the permanent constitution of the country, while everything enacted after the recess was at the same time rejected as temporary and worthless.[2]

So long as the Long Parliament was able to act as a whole, to strike as one man against abuses that pressed alike upon all, Charles was compelled to yield to an irresistible force, which tore from him not only the star chamber and the high commissions, but Strafford himself. The first check to its triumphal progress occurred when its members failed to agree among themselves as to the disposition which should be made of the episcopal office, — one faction contending for its entire abolition, the other for the retention of the bishops with diminished powers and subject to parliamentary supervision. By the division which occurred on that question on the 8th of February, 1641, the line was first roughly drawn between two political bodies that in the course of time have developed into the two parliamentary parties which, after having been known first as Roundheads and Cavaliers, then as Whigs and Tories, still survive under names so familiar at the pre-

Marginal notes:
no ecclesiastical courts from 1641 to 1661;

permanent work of the Long Parliament accepted at the Restoration.

Long Parliament irresistible while acting as a whole;

its failure to agree as to the fate of the episcopal office;

the origin of political parties;

---

[1] Cf. Sir J. F. Stephen, *Hist. of the Crim. Law*, vol. ii. p. 428.   [2] Gardiner, *Hist. Eng.*, vol. x. p. 34.

sent day.[1]   The first ray of hope which thus came to Charles through the break in the ranks of his adversaries was greatly brightened, when on the 10th of the following August he was able to approve a bill confirming the treaty with the Scots, that promised a large sum as an indemnity and compensation for their brotherly assistance in maintaining upon English soil, as a physical support to parliament, the army which was now to be disbanded.[2]   Immediately upon the consummation of that agreement, Charles hastened to Edinburgh, against the remonstrance of the houses, intent upon the organization of a counter-revolution, which contemplated the pacification of Scotland, and the return of the king at the head of an army, to be composed of Scots as well as of recruits from the English forces in the north, with whose aid he hoped to crush the popular leaders and to reverse the results they had brought about. In furtherance of that design, Charles busied himself at Edinburgh, not only in yielding to all the demands of the assembly and estates, in attending the presbyterian worship, and lavishing favors upon the chiefs of the covenanters,[3] but also in collecting evidences upon which to build up charges of treason against Pym and Hampden.[4]   As a preliminary to such proceeding, the king assented to a design to seize and carry out of the realm Hamilton and Argyle, who were supposed to be intriguing with the English popular leaders, a design which was frustrated only by the sudden withdrawal of both from the Scottish parliament to Kineil castle,[5] a country house of Hamilton's.   Under the apprehension naturally excited by the news of this "Incident," parliament reassembled after the recess, that ended on the 20th of October, the day from which can be traced more distinctly than ever before the beginnings of the two great English parties.   The episcopal party, that had been silently organized by Hyde, the future Lord Clarendon, now became the royalist party, which soon numbered in its

Marginal notes: settlement with the army of the Scots; Charles hastened to Edinburgh to organize a counter-revolution; made important concessions; sought proofs of treason against Pym and Hampden; the "Incident" in parliament after the recess; composition of the royalist party;

---

[1] "Slight as the difference might be between those who took opposite sides on that day, their parting gave the colour to English political life which has distinguished it ever since, and which has distinguished every free government which has followed in the steps of our forefathers."—Gardiner, *Hist. Eng.*, vol. ix. p. 281.

[2] £80,000 was to be paid immedi-

ately, and £220,000 after they should cross the Tweed.

[3] Balfour, vol. iii. pp. 58, 64, 66, 68, 69, 72, 78.

[4] Foster, *Grand Remonstrance*, p. 154.

[5] Baillie, vol. i. p. 392; Balfour, vol. iii. p. 94.   See also Lingard, vol. vii. pp. 499–503.

fold a majority of the nobles and the opulent country gentlemen, with their dependents, the main body of the clergy, all
laymen specially attached to episcopal government and the
Anglican ritual, together with the rank and file of those who,
as men of the world, shrank from the gloom of Puritan auster-
ity.   To this body of men, who had bitterly resented the policy
of Strafford and Laud, it was evident that enough had been
done by the sweeping away of all those abuses of the conciliar
system which had perished under the reforming statutes already enacted.   To men of this class it appeared dangerous to
press further the victory over despotism, lest it should run into
anarchy.   The opposition to this conservative element, which
took its stand close to the throne as now limited, consisted of
a formidable minority of the nobles, followed by the smaller
freeholders of the country and the merchants and shopkeepers of the towns, who numbered in their ranks not only the
whole body of protestant non-conformists, but also most of
those members of the established church who still adhered to
the Calvinistic opinions which Laud had attempted to make
odious.   To this body it was evident, in view of the menacing
attitude which Charles now assumed, that unless they carried
the revolution sufficiently far to obtain more substantial guarantees, a counter-revolution would soon sweep away all that
had been so far accomplished.[1]   This sense of apprehension,
which the two army plots[2] and the Scotch "Incident" had
greatly strengthened, deepened into terror when at the end of
October all England was thrilled by the tales of horror and
outrage that came from the Irish rising, in which the catholic
and Celtic party in the unhappy isle, falsely claiming to act
under the king's commission and in aid of his authority,[3] were
pressing pitiless war upon the English protestant settlers, for
whose benefit they had been plundered without mercy.

The cry of an Irish rebellion which threatened the annihila-
tion of the protestant minority, and which stimulated the belief
in the existence of a vast catholic conspiracy for the extinction

*men who
believed
enough had
been done;*

*composi-
tion of the
Puritan
opposition,*

*who
believed
that the
revolution
must be
carried
farther to
be effective;*

*the Irish
rising.*

*Protest-
antism
menaced;*

---

[1] This has been well put by Macaulay, *Hist. Eng.*, vol. i. pp. 50–52.

[2] As to Pym's resolution concerning
these plots, which contemplated the
bringing up of the army to overawe
the house, see Foster, *Grand Remonstrance*, p. 210.

[3] The forged commission is in Rushworth, vol. iv. p. 400; Lingard (vol. vii.
p. 510, note 1), with his usual frank-
ness, says: "I have no hesitation in
pronouncing it a forgery."

of protestantism in the three kingdoms, carried with it an appeal for aid that the popular leaders of the house could not neglect for a moment. That a new military force must be provided for the suppression of the rebellion was inevitable, and yet to put such a force in the hands of Charles was to create a new danger. This perplexing dilemma Pym boldly met by a revolutionary motion made on the 5th of November, as "an additional instruction," [1] that no attempt would be made to assist the king in Ireland, unless he would dismiss the evil councillors about him, and "take such as might be approved by Parliament." This proposal to lay hold of the executive power through a responsible ministry was passed on the 8th, in a modified form, by a decided majority [2] of the lower house. But the difficulty was that Pym's motion could not pass into law without the sanction of the lords, in which the episcopal-royalist party was in the majority. Thus menaced and baffled on every hand, the popular leaders resolved, under the form of an address to the crown, to appeal for support to the nation; and with that end in view, they now brought forward the historic document known as the Grand Remonstrance, read in the lower house before the close of the sitting of the 8th, in which they set forth in detail the long list of abuses upon the part of Charles' government, that had produced the conflict, the good measures already taken by them for their redress, together with definite and practical suggestions as to what still remained to be done, in order to make their work complete and enduring. The essence of this famous manifesto, with its preamble and two hundred and six numbered clauses, [3] was embodied, however, in those parts of it in which the popular leaders formulated (1) their plan of church reform, and (2) the demand, already made by Pym in his "additional instruction," for a ministry directly responsible to parliament. As to the religious question, the Puritan popular leaders averred that they had been slandered by their opponents, who strove to "infuse into the people that we mean to abolish all church government, and leave every man to his

[marginal notes:]
parliament refused the king an army unless he would accept councillors approved by them;

the appeal to the nation in the Grand Remonstrance;

essence of the demand, church reform and a responsible ministry;

Puritan declarations upon the religious question:

---

[1] To the parliamentary committee in Scotland.

[2] 152 to 110. D'Ewes' *Diary*, Harl. MSS., clxii. fol. 108 b. Two days before, the motion in its original form had been rejected by the house.   Ibid.

[3] For the full text, see Rushworth's *Collections*, pt. iii. vol. i. p. 438. For the best commentaries upon it, see Foster, *Grand Remonstrance*, and Gardiner, *Hist. Eng.*, vol. x. pp. 59–64.

own fancy for the service and worship of God, absolving him from that obedience which he owes under God unto His Majesty, whom we know to be intrusted with the ecclesiastical law as well as with the temporal, to regulate all the members of the Church of England, by such rules of order and discipline as are established by parliament, which is his great council in all affairs both in church and state." In reply to that charge

authority of bishops to be diminished;

they answered that while they did not intend to abolish the bishops, they did intend to greatly reduce their authority; that while they did not "propose or devise to let loose the golden reins of discipline and government in the church, to leave private persons or particular congregations to take up what form of divine service they please; for we hold it requi-

conformity to be upheld and ceremonies to be reformed;

site that there should be throughout the whole realm a conformity to that order, which the laws enjoin according to the words of God," they did propose "to unburden the consciences of men of needless and superstitious ceremonies, suppress innovations, and take away the monuments of idolatry." In a word, the old Puritan party within the church, speaking through the Remonstrance, demanded that the whole Laudian system should be supplanted by their own, to which all should be forced to conform by the law of the land. There was to be

no toleration for Arminians or sectaries;

no toleration either of the Arminian element, which was stigmatized as "the malignant party," or of the sectaries who gathered outside of the state church in separate conventicles.

supplies to be granted only to responsible ministers;

As to the question of ministerial responsibility, the king was given clearly to understand that supplies could not be granted for his support, unless he was willing to appoint such ambassadors and councillors for the management of his affairs, at home and abroad, as parliament could confide in. And with the inadequacy of the right of impeachment clearly in view, as illustrated by the cases of Strafford and Laud, the statement was made, as a reason for ministerial responsibility, in a new

inadequacy of impeachments recognized;

form, that "it may often fall out that the commons may have just cause to take exceptions at some men for being councillors, and yet not charge those men with crimes, for there be grounds of difference which lie not in proof. There are others which, though they may be proved, yet are not legally criminal." The final debate on the Grand Remonstrance which took place on the 22d of November continued until midnight, when it was adopted by a majority of only eleven votes.[1] How bitter and serious this first great parliamentary conflict between the new parties must have been is evidenced by the declaration made by Cromwell when he left the house, that "if the Remonstrance had been rejected, I would have sold all I had next morning, and never have seen England any more; and I know there are many other honest men of this same resolution."[2] The royalists, on the other hand, accepted the result in a spirit of defiance which manifested itself when, upon a motion to print the Remonstrance, Mr. Palmer declared, "I protest for myself and all the rest." At this attempt to thwart the will of the majority by the use of tactics employed in the lords but utterly unknown in the commons,[3] the house broke into flame, and only the sagacity and calmness of Hampden[4] averted a conflict between the excited antagonists, some of whom "took their swords in their scabbards out of their belts and held them by their pommels in their hands, setting the lower part on the ground."[5] As a rebuke to Palmer for having asserted the right of protest he was sent to the Tower, and the Remonstrance, after presentation to Charles on the 1st of December, was on the 15th ordered to be printed by a majority of fifty-two votes.[6]

Through the adoption of that part of the Remonstrance that conceded the retention of the bishops with diminished authority, the moderate element of the Puritan party triumphed over the root-and-branch faction within its ranks, which had demanded the entire abolition of the episcopacy.[7] A bill for the exclusion of the clergy from secular office, and for shutting out the bishops from the upper house, which the moderates had passed through the commons as an evidence of their good intentions, was sent in May, 1641, to the lords, who after conference finally threw it out on the third reading on the 8th of June.[8] As further proof of their sincerity, the moderates reintroduced the exclusion bill in the commons on the 21st of

Sidenotes: Remonstrance adopted by majority of eleven, November 22; Cromwell's memorable declaration; Palmer protested for himself and "all the rest;" sent to the Tower; Remonstrance ordered to be printed. Root-and-branch faction fail to secure abolition of episcopacy; bill excluding clergy from secular office passed by the house and rejected by the lords;

[1] See Foster, *Grand Remonstrance,* p. 316.
[2] Clarendon, vol. iv. p. 52.
[3] Cf. Foster, *Grand Remonstrance,* p. 347.
[4] Hampden coolly asked Palmer, "how he could know other men's minds?"
[5] D'Ewes' *Diary,* Harl. MSS., clxii. fol. 180.
[6] Ibid., *Diary,* Harl. MSS., clxii. fol. 244 b.
[7] In May, 1641, Vane and Cromwell brought in a bill to that end, which was finally dropped.
[8] *Lords' Journals,* vol. iv. pp. 239, 265.

October, where it was passed two days thereafter and sent to the lords.[1]   To get rid of the twenty-six solid episcopal votes that stood in the upper house as an obstacle to all church reform now became a matter of such prime importance as to evoke turbulent expressions of public interest.   On the 27th of December a mob, composed chiefly of London apprentices, who wore the hair closely cropped to the head, gathered at Westminster, where, with cries of "no bishops" no "popish lords," a demonstration was made in which the archbishop was hustled as he passed in and his gown torn.   Whereupon Lunsford, recently in command of the Tower, together with a group of officers from the king's disbanded army which the mob found within, drew their swords and drove the intruders into the street, where the conflict continued amid a shower of stones that finally forced the officers to take refuge in White-hall.   In the midst of conflicts such as these two nicknames came into existence which the opposing parties were destined to wear for a long time to come.   The Puritan popular party were taunted as "Roundheads," because of the mob of closely cropped apprentices by which they were surrounded at West-minster, while the royal-episcopal party were in return dubbed as "Cavaliers," because of the soldiers of fortune who gathered around the king as a guard at Whitehall.[2]   The next day after the affray only two of the bishops were brave enough to take their seats, and eleven of those who thus absented themselves upon the ground that parliament was not free joined Arch-bishop Williams in a protest, to be presented to the king and the lords, that all laws, orders, votes, resolutions, and deter-minations made by the upper house during their absence were null and void.[3]   So incensed were the peers by this indiscreet act that they at once sent the protest to the commons as an assault upon the very existence of parliament,[4] where, after a motion from Pym to call upon the city to send up its trained bands as a guard, the bishops who had signed the protest were impeached for high treason,[5] and before night ten were in the

Marginal notes:

popular demon-stration against the bishops;

origin of the names, "Round-heads" and "Cava-liers;"

bishops protested that all acts done in their absence were void;

impeached for high treason;

---

[1] D'Ewes' *Diary*, Harl. MSS., clxii. fol. 31 b.
[2] Gardiner, *Hist. Eng.*, vol. x. p. 121; Green, *Hist. of the Eng. People*, vol. iii. p. 211.
[3] They asked the king to command

that their protest should be entered in the records of the house. *Lords' Jour-nals*, vol. iv. p. 496.
[4] Ibid., vol. iv. p. 496.
[5] One member said they were stark mad and should be sent to Bedlam.

Tower and two in custody of the Usher of the Black Rod. A few days later Charles was startled by the rumor that the parliamentary leaders would soon strike higher by impeaching the queen herself as an intriguer with the Irish rebels and a conspirator against the public liberties.[1]

impeachment of the queen mooted.

Thus menaced, Henrietta Maria, against whom a serious case could certainly have been made, nerved Charles, who was also urged no doubt by Digby, to the desperate step against her assailants which cost him his crown and his life. On the 3d of January, 1642, the very day upon which the king refused the written request of the commons for a guard,[2] the attorney-general, under an order signed by the king's own hand, impeached at the bar of the lords for high treason Lord Kimbolton, together with Pym, Hampden, Holles, Hazlerigg, and Strode, members of the lower house, who were charged generally with an attempt to subvert the fundamental laws and government, to deprive the king of his royal power, and to place in subjects an arbitrary and tyrannical power over the lives, liberties, and estates of his majesty's loving people, and specially with the authorship of the Remonstrance, with tampering with the army, with inviting an invasion by the Scots, with an attempt " to subvert the rights and very being of parliaments," and finally with actually having "levied war upon the king."[3] As soon as the charge had been made, the attorney-general, who had followed the course pursued without objection in 1626, in the case of the earl of Bristol, asked for the arrest of those whom he had impeached, and for the appointment of a committee to examine into the accusation against them. When the lords in effect refused the request, by simply appointing a committee to inquire whether the attorney-general's procedure had been according to law, Charles took the extraordinary step of himself issuing a warrant commanding a serjeant-at-arms to make the arrest. Before his arrival the house, which had that very day received the king's refusal to furnish them a guard, sent a message to the city

The attempt on the five members;

substance of the articles presented by the attorney-general;

when the lords refused to order their arrest, the king himself issued the warrant;

Commons' Journals, vol. ii. p. 363. See also Clarendon, vol. iv. p. 145.

[1] Clarendon, vol. xv. pp. 154, 280; D'Ewes' *Diary*, Harl. MSS., clxii. fol. 339.

[2] Rushworth, vol. iv. p. 471.

[3] *Lords' Journals*, vol. iv. p. 501. See the copy of the charge, "Articles of treason against Mr. Pym and the rest," taken from the State Papers and printed by Foster, *Arrest of the Five Members*, p. 114.

asking that the trained bands might be made ready for their

house failed
to deliver
them to the
serjeant;

defence. When the serjeant appeared and made his demand, the house answered that as their privilege was involved a committee would be appointed and a reply made after due consideration, and that in the mean time the gentlemen who had been accused would be ready to answer any legal accusation against

Charles
then
resolved to
make the
arrest in
person;

them. Thus baffled in his first attempt, Charles, after conference that night with his intimates, resolved to go to the house the next day[1] in person, and there make the arrest by force, if necessary; and thus, upon a charge based upon his sole authority, and by a warrant for which no minister was responsible, deprive the five members of their legal right to a trial by their peers by dragging them before a tribunal which had no jurisdiction over them. The popular historians have

what
occurred in
the house
January 4,
1642;

all recounted, with more or less dramatic power, what transpired in the afternoon of that fateful 4th of January when Charles set out from Whitehall with the Elector Palatine at his side and a mob of Cavaliers at his back, intent upon the execution of his purpose at Westminster. There, after commanding his retinue to remain without,[2] the king crossed that threshold which none of his predecessors had ever passed, while the earl of Roxburgh leaned against the open door so that the members might see from within what to expect in case of

Charles
took the
speaker's
chair;

resistance. Taking the speaker's chair, Charles, after complaining of the failure of the house to obey his mandate on the day before, said to them: "You must know that in cases of treason no person hath a privilege; and therefore I am come to know if any of those persons that were accused are here." Failing to detect them with his own eyes, he asked the speaker, "Do you see any of them? Where are they?" Whereupon,

Lenthall's
reply to his
demands;

Lenthall made the memorable answer: "I have neither eyes to see, nor tongue to speak in this place but as this house is pleased to direct me, whose servant I am here; and I humbly beg your Majesty's pardon that I cannot give any other answer than this to what your Majesty is pleased to demand of me."

---

[1] For a more elaborate statement, see *Commons' Journals*, January 4; Rushworth, vol. iv. p. 477; Gardiner, *Hist. Eng.*, vol. x. pp. 129–141; Foster, *Arrest of the Five Members*, pp. 184–200.

[2] About eighty, however, followed him into the lobby, and among them, as D'Ewes tells us, were " divers of the late army in the north, and other desperate ruffians."

Before his departure from Whitehall the king's secret was known to the queen, who passed it on to Lady Carlisle, who at once conveyed the news to Essex, by whom the five members had been advised to withdraw. Thus baffled, Charles, after confessing, "I see all the birds are flown. I do expect from you that you shall send them unto me as soon as they return hither," passed out of the house "in a more discontented and angry passion than he came in." The real essence of the charge upon which the house had impeached Strafford was that he had attempted to assert the sovereignty of the crown in such a way as to menace the existence of parliament; the real essence of the charge upon which Charles had impeached the five members was that they had attempted to assert the sovereignty of parliament in such a way as to imperil the existence of the royal authority. As the assertion of these antagonistic views of sovereignty was not within the terms of the statute against treason, and as the conflict which they involved could not be drawn within the jurisdiction of any existing tribunal, the fact was clear that the only arbiter was the sword. So it may be said that "when Charles and his armed attendants passed through the lobby of the house of commons on the 4th of January, the civil war had substantially begun." [1]

Thus conscious of the important part which the sword was destined to play in the settlement of the impending conflict, it was natural that both parties should have been eager to clutch at its possession. The first move in that direction was made in the fall of 1641, when the commons attempted to prevent Charles from raising an army for Ireland by the enactment of an impressment bill, which positively denied the right of the king to force men to perform military service beyond the limits of their own counties, except in the sudden emergency of a foreign invasion. Although it was claimed that that clause, copied verbally from an unrepealed statute of Edward III., heretofore noted,[2] took away a prerogative which the crown had actually enjoyed for more than three centuries, the lords passed the bill without amendment, and the king approved it on the 13th of February, 1642, along with the Bishops' Exclu-

[1] Foster, *Arrest of the Five Members*, pp. 376, 377.   [2] See above, p. 197.

sion Bill.[1]   Before the Impressment Bill, with its negative

clause, thus became a law, a militia bill was brought into the
commons by Hazlerigg, which contained the positive proposal
that the command of the militia or trained bands of the counties should be taken entirely out of the king's hands and
placed in that of a lord general, to be named by parliament,
who should have power to raise men, to levy money to pay

them, and to execute martial law.   While that bill was pending, Charles caused another to be introduced upon the same
subject, by which the command of the militia was to be exercised for one year within the realm under the direction of the
king signified by the two houses, and under the direction of
the parliament alone when the army was employed oversea.[2]
When it was understood that Charles would refuse his assent
to his own bill on account of changes that had been made

in it, the house brought forward a militia ordinance, which
conferred the power upon fifty-five commissioners of array to
name deputy lieutenants with the approval of parliament, to
train the militia for war, to appoint officers, and to suppress
"all rebellions, insurrections, and invasions," according to
directions from the king signified by parliament.   That ordinance, after having passed both houses, was sent to the king
two days after his approval of the Impressment Bill, and on
the 9th of March he refused to accept it absolutely, whereupon the houses early in May ordered it to be put into execution, and it was so enforced to the south of the Humber.[3]

Long before that point was reached, however, Pym, armed
with petitions from every part of England, had been forced to
overcome the opposition of the lords to his policy by declaring
that it would be a sad thing "that the story of this present
parliament should tell posterity that in so great a danger and
extremity the house of commons should be forced to save the

kingdom alone, and that the house of peers should have no
part in the honor of the preserving of it." [4]   Under that spur
the lords joined with the commons early in February, not only
in the enactment of the Bishops' Exclusion Bill,[5] but also in a
petition to the king asking that the fortresses and the militia

---

1 16 Car. I. c. 28.
2 *Lords' Journals*, vol. iv. p. 709.
3 Cf. Gardiner, *Hist. Eng.*, vol. x.
pp. 161, 167, 172, 194, 202.

4 January 25, 1642.
5 *Lords' Journals*, vol. iv. p. 564.

should be put in the hands of persons in whom parliament could confide.[1]   When, on April 23, Charles attempted to enter Hull, the great magazine of the north, its governor, Sir John Hotham, who had secured it by command of the parliament, refused him admission.   So much was the breach widened by that event that before the end of May, Falkland, who had become secretary of state, Culpepper, who had become chancellor of the exchequer, and Hyde, the real leader of the royalist party, who refused to take office, withdrew from their places at Westminster, and with thirty-two peers and sixty members of the commons joined the king at York, Lyttelton, the lord keeper, following with the great seal.[2]   On the 6th of June, parliament distinctly asserted its claim to sovereignty in a resolution which declared that "the king's supreme and royal pleasure is exercised and declared in this high court and council, after a more eminent and obligatory manner than it can be by any personal act or resolution of his own;"[3] and to give force to that declaration, the lords on the 4th of July joined with the commons in appointing a committee "to take into consideration whatsoever may concern the safety of the kingdom, the defence of the parliament, and the present observation of the peace of the kingdom, and opposing any force that may be raised against the parliament."[4]   Only two days before, the houses had won the control of the fleet,[5] and two days later, a vote was passed to raise a special army for active service, of which Essex was appointed commander-in-chief, with whom each member declared his willingness to live and die "in this cause, for the safety of the king's person, the defence of both houses of parliament, and of those who have obeyed their orders and commands, and for the preservation of the true religion, laws, liberties, and peace of the kingdom."[6]   In the mean time Charles had not been idle.   Before the end of February the queen had gone abroad with the crown jewels in order to purchase arms and ammunition and to solicit the aid of foreign powers.   After that it was that the king, who had

Charles refused admission to Hull;

the king's friends withdrew from Westminster;

June 6 parliament claimed to be sovereign;

committee of safety appointed;

houses won control of the fleet;

the army under Essex;

the king not inactive;

[1] *Lords' Journals*, vol. iv. pp. 556, 558.

[2] Green, *Hist. of the Eng. People*, vol. iii. p. 215.

[3] *Lords' Journals*, vol. v. p. 112.

[4] This committee was composed of five lords, Northumberland, Essex, Pembroke, Holland, and Saye; and ten commoners, among whom were Pym, Hampden, Holles, and Marten. *Lords' Journals*, vol. v. p. 178; *Commons' Journals*, vol. ii. p. 681.

[5] Clarendon, vol. v. p. 376.

[6] *Commons' Journals*, vol. v. p. 208.

been asked by parliament to remain near Westminster,[1] withdrew to the north, fixing his residence before the end of March
at York.   In May the lord keeper was ordered to remove the
law courts from Westminster to that city, and there during
that month Charles began the formation of a military force by
calling upon the gentry and the trained bands of Yorkshire to
gather around him in arms.[2]   On the 11th of June more active
measures were taken by the issuance of commissions of array
of the Tudor type, directing the trained bands to place themselves at the disposal of royal officers, a measure whose legality
was sharply challenged by the parliament.[3]   In the midst of
these warlike preparations a final effort to reach an understanding was made by the houses, who submitted to Charles
on the 2d of June nineteen propositions, in which they offered
to be reconciled with him provided he would concede the sovereignty of parliament by placing under their control the entire
executive and judicial machinery of the kingdom, the reformation of the church, together with a certain control over the
selection of all peers to be thereafter created.[4]   On the 18th
these propositions were rejected upon the ground that their
acceptance would deprive the king of all real power and make
him the slave of a faction of his subjects.[5]   On the 22d of
August the royal standard was raised at Nottingham, and a
proclamation read by the herald-at-arms denouncing Essex as
a traitor, a ceremony which was intended as a formal recognition of the fact that the civil war had actually begun.

fixed his
residence
at York;

issued com-
missions
of array;

final
attempt at
reconcili-
ation
June 2;

terms
rejected by
Charles
June 18;

royal
standard
raised
at Not-
tingham
August 22.

[1] *An Exact Collection*, p. 92. For
the king's answer, March 2, see *Lords'
Journals*, vol. iv. p. 641.
[2] Rushworth, vol. iv. pp. 615, 621.
[3] Ibid., vol. iv. p. 655.
[4] *Lords' Journals*, vol. v. p. 97.
[5] Rushworth, vol. iv. pp. 722, 735;

Clarendon, vol. i. pp. 634–647. On the
12th of July the houses made another
offer of an accommodation, which
Charles rejected on the 19th. *Lords'
Journals*, vol. v. p. 235; Clarendon
vol. i. pp. 684–693.

CHAPTER III.

THE GREAT CIVIL WAR.

1. Nothing is more remarkable in the history of the English constitution than the persistent continuity of its development, through which all of the changes and innovations demanded by the wants of a great and growing nationality have been gradually brought about without any open break with the past. The nearest approach to an exception to this general rule is to be found in the revolutionary period, which begins with the meeting of the Long Parliament and ends with the Restoration, the period of upheaval during which the social, political, and religious forces that abide in the England of to-day broke the spell of custom and tradition by which the mediæval church, the mediæval monarchy, and the dying feudalism had so long enthralled the minds of men. True it is that when Puritanism laid down the sword, the republican régime which had been set up in its name gave way to a restoration of the monarchical system, not, however, in the form in which it had been overthrown, but as purified and remodelled by the drastic and enduring legislation enacted during the first ten months of the Long Parliament.[1] And apart from the permanent legal changes thus brought about by positive legislation must also be estimated the ultimate effects of many new ideas then germinated, which, after having been for a time put aside, have ripened at last into some of the most important reforms of modern times. It is thus possible to trace to this period of upheaval, characterized by a freedom of thought never before known, not only the beginnings of the great parties which have ever since dominated the political and religious life of England, but also the germs

Continuity of development of the English constitution

as affected by the revolutionary epoch;

monarchy not restored in the form in which it was overthrown;

ultimate effect of new ideas germinated during period of upheaval;

[1] " Whatever had been done so far by the Long Parliament stood the test of time. The overthrow of the special courts, by which the prerogative had been defended under the Tudors and the first two Stuarts, together with the abandonment by the king of all claim to raise taxes without the consent of parliament, was accepted as the starting-point of the restored monarchical constitution in 1660." — Gardiner, *Hist. Eng.*, vol. x. p. 10.

of religious toleration, of electoral reform, of the cabinet system, of modern taxation, as well as the transition from the ancient to the modern military system. Only the outward forms of the work of Puritanism perished at the moment of its apparent overthrow.[1] While Cromwell and his republic

Puritan spirit lived on as the advancing force in English society;

passed away, the indomitable spirit of civil and religious liberty that culminated in them has lived on as the advancing and reforming force in English society which expressed itself first in the revolution of 1688, and finally in that whose outcome was the Reform Bill of 1832. It is, therefore, from this period of transition from the old to the new, during which the

beginnings of the modern constitution.

continuity of England's political life was for a moment suspended, not broken off, that we can begin to trace the beginnings of the constitution in its modern form.

Conservative basis upon which the war began;

2. At the beginning of the conflict the parliamentary party had no idea either of deposing the king, or of bringing him to justice for his misdeeds. When Essex was appointed commander, each member of the house swore to die "in this cause for the safety of the king's person," and when the new general quitted London, he was commanded to follow the king "and by battle or other way rescue him from his perfidious councillors and restore him to parliament,"[2] and in the covenant with the Scots the houses swore "to uphold the person of the king and his authority." The theory was thus recognized at Westminster that the king was still a factor in the constitution, although separated from his parliament by evil councillors. Out of this anomalous condition of things arose the legal fic-

"the king in parliament waged war against the king in the royalist camp;"

tion that "the king in parliament waged war against the king in the royalist camp." To supply the vacuum thus created by the king's absence, the executive power was for the time being put in the hands of a joint parliamentary Committee of Safety,[3] and in November, 1643, the houses authorized the use of a new great seal, which was intrusted to six commissioners named by themselves.[4] Each party did all in its power to give to its

---

[1] "The history of English progress since the Restoration, on its moral and spiritual sides, has been the history of Puritanism." — Green, *Hist. of the Eng. People*, vol. iii. p. 322.

[2] *Commons' Journals*, vol. v. p. 208 *et seq.*

[3] This committee, appointed July 4,

1642, was composed of five lords and fifteen commons, among whom were Pym, Hampden, Holles, and Marten. *Lords' Journals*, vol. v. p. 178; *Commons' Journals*, vol. ii. p. 651.

[4] *Lords' Journals*, vol. vi. pp. 305, 318. In 1649 the commons, after assuming supreme authority, ordered a new seal.

proceedings constitutional form, in order to prevent anything like social disruption. While the bulk of the nobility and gentry ranged themselves on the side of the king, and the bulk of the townsmen and yeomen on that of the parliament, the exceptions on each side were great enough to prevent a degeneration of the conflict into such a war of classes as distinguished the French Revolution. On December 22, 1643, Charles summoned all the members of either house who had left Westminster, or who were ready to leave it on promise of pardon, to meet him in January at Oxford ; and not until March 9, 1644, did the houses at Westminster refuse to recognize their rivals at Oxford as in any sense members of parliament, in reply to which the Oxford body promptly declared that those who sat at Westminster were guilty of treason.[1]

the war not a war of classes ;

relations of the two parliaments to each other.

As both parties were compelled to equip and maintain armies in the field, the question of ways and means at once became paramount. After the system of voluntary contributions to which both resorted in the beginning broke down, it became necessary for each to employ legal methods of taxation.[2] How to impose such a tax without the royal assent was the troublesome problem at Westminster. At last necessity put aside all constitutional scruples, and taxes were levied by the houses by way of ordinance, after the sums received from the voluntary gifts or loans had been exhausted. In November, 1642, an ordinance directed the assessment of all persons in London and Westminster who had hitherto refused to contribute voluntarily ;[3] on the 8th of December of the same year another extended the demand to the whole country ;[4] and in March, 1645, a still more comprehensive ordinance was passed, providing assessments for the armies, for which the counties were to be responsible.[5] In these parliamentary ordinances, which were departures from the old Tudor subsidy, we find the germs of the fiscal system of modern times. Instead of demanding a yearly or half-yearly tax on the old plan, the houses resorted to monthly assessments, which were apportioned be-

Taxation without the royal assent ;

parliamentary ordinances of 1642 and 1645

contained the germs of the modern fiscal system ;

made with the inscription, "In the first year of freedom, by God's blessing restored, 1648."
[1] Rushworth, vol. v. p. 565.
[2] See Dowell, *Hist. of Taxation*, vol. i. p. 3.
[3] Rushworth, vol. v. p. 71.
[4] D'Ewes' *Diary ; Lords' Journals*, vol. v. p. 482.
[5] *Lords' Journals*, vol. vii. p. 293.

tween the counties and towns named in the ordinance upon the basis of the highest returns ever made by them for a subsidy, — the assessment of the taxpayers, who were more justly rated than ever before, and the collection of the tax being left to the local authorities.[1]   As a supplement to these assessments, a new tax called the excise, which had long existed on the continent, was for the first time introduced into England in the form in which it was employed by the Dutch.[2]   By an ordinance passed in July, 1643,[3] an excise or new impost was imposed upon a variety of articles of consumption, including ale, beer, cider, and strong waters.   While the houses at Westminster thus imposed taxes to carry on war against the king without his consent, he did not hesitate at first to levy them on the country around Oxford[4] without parliamentary sanction. Not until February, 1644, were privy seals for a loan authorized by the Oxford parliament, which afterwards granted an excise upon the Westminster model.[5]

origin of the excise;

the ordinance of 1643;

royal taxation at Oxford.

3.   The constitutional theory that the houses were making war only upon the evil councillors who surrounded the king, in order to rescue him from their hands, for a long time embarrassed military operations by making undesirable a positive triumph which would bring the conservative leaders of the Revolution face to face with a problem they were unprepared to meet. Essex was unwilling to consent to an actual or virtual deposition of the king, and while he held the chief command, he shrank from any decisive stroke which would make such a result inevitable.   His policy seems to have been to force Charles to a peaceful understanding through an exhaustion of his resources.   Under such conditions it is not to be wondered at that the first engagement at Edgehill was indecisive and that throughout the winter the fortunes of war went steadily against the popular cause.   As a stern opponent of Essex vacillating policy, the heroic Hampden passed from the parlia

Constitutional theory of the houses embarrassed military operations;

Essex shrank from a decisive stroke;

first encounter at Edgehill;

energy of Hampden;

---

[1] . . . "The result being not any increase in the amount paid to the treasury, for that was fixed, but the more equitable adjustment of the burden of the tax as regards the various taxpayers in every particular county or town." — Dowell, *Hist. of Taxation*, vol. ii. p. 5.

[2] The proposal was made by Pym, "the father of the excise." His first motion to impose it, however, was rejected, after being denounced as "a unjust, scandalous, and destructiv project."   Cf. D'Ewes' *Diary*.

[3] *Lords' Journals*, vol. vi. p. 145 Ordinance E., 61, 28.

[4] Warburton, vol. ii. p. 69.

[5] Rushworth, vol. v. p. 580; Claren don, vol. vii. p. 396.

ment to a military command, in which he manifested from the beginning his characteristic energy. Largely through his influence, backed by that of his cousin, Oliver Cromwell, were brought into shape the associations of the midland and eastern counties which united in raising an army to be maintained by a common fund, the command of which as a subsidiary force was given by Essex to Lord Manchester as major-general.[1] But in the midst of his usefulness Hampden, while striving to check a raid of Rupert's, was mortally wounded near his own home on the 18th of June, 1643, and a few days thereafter he died. Disaster then followed disaster, until the surrender of Bristol to Rupert gave to Charles the mastery of the west. The first turn in the tide came when Essex, in September, succeeded in raising the siege of Gloucester, which still held out as the only obstacle to communications between the king's forces in Bristol and those in the north. At this stage of the struggle it was that Pym, bereft of Hampden, resolved to turn the fortunes of war through an alliance with the Scots. When the time for negotiation came, the fact appeared, as Baillie wrote, that "the English were for a civil league, we for a religious covenant." The price which the Scots demanded for military aid was "unity of religion," which meant in plain terms the adoption of the presbyterian system by the Church of England. Opposed as Pym was to such a result, he finally acquiesced in it as a political necessity, and after many amendments the Covenant as assented to by the Scots was sworn to by the commons in St. Margaret's church on the 25th of September, and on the 15th of October it was accepted by the little group of peers that still remained at Westminster.[2] The leading purpose of this compact was to "bring the churches of God in the three kingdoms to the nearest conjunction and uniformity of religion, confession of faith, form of church government, direction for worship, and catechizing," and "to extirpate popery, prelacy, superstition, schism, and profaneness." Before the adoption of the Covenant it was submitted for consideration and amendment to the Westminster Assembly of Divines, an ecclesiastical body created by the two houses,

aided in organizing associations of the midland and eastern counties;

died June, 1643;

Pym resolved upon an alliance with the Scots;

who demanded adoption of presbyterian system;

Covenant sworn to by the commons, September 25;

its leading purpose;

submitted to the Westminster Assembly

---

[1] At the request of the houses. *Commons' Journals,* vol. iii. p. 199; *Lords' Journals,* vol. vi. p. 174.

[2] Cf. Gardiner, *Hist. of the Great Civil War,* vol. i. pp. 229, 232, 235, 244.

which had begun its sessions on the 1st of July, and which sat during the five years that followed in order to draw up a confession of faith, to revise the Articles, to prepare a directory of public worship, and to formulate a scheme of church government upon the Scotch model, all of which was finally adopted by the houses and embodied in a series of ordinances designed to maintain the uniformity of belief and worship upon a new basis.[1]

Treaty with the Scots the last work of Pym, who died December 6; "committee of the two kingdoms" contained the germ of the modern cabinet; superseded the old Committee of Safety;

The conclusion of the Covenant between the two kingdoms was the last work of Pym, who died on the 6th of December. But his work lived after him.   In order to execute his plans for the joint conduct of the war, a "committee of the two kingdoms" was formed, in whose organization can be discovered not only the first germ of a political union between England and Scotland, but also the first germ of the modern cabinet system, the English members of the committee taken from the two houses being clothed with general executive powers subject to parliamentary responsibility.[2]   Thus was superseded the original Committee of Safety, which merely conveyed information to the houses and executed their orders.   In compliance with the terms of the coalition the Scots sent an army under Lord Leven, which crossed the border in January, 1644, and a short time thereafter the parliament put in the field three strong forces under the commands of Essex, Fairfax, and Manchester.   On the 2d of July a decisive battle took

Marston Moor, July 2, 1644;

place on Marston Moor, which ended in the "total ruin of the king's affairs in those northern parts."[3]   The results of the victory thus won by Fairfax, Manchester, and Leven, with the aid of Cromwell, were greatly weakened, however, by the

surrender of Essex in September;

forced surrender in September of the greater part of the army of Essex, who had rashly plunged into Cornwall, where the country was specially hostile to the parliamentary cause.   Thus flushed with his triumph over Essex, and further encouraged by the refusal of the Scots to move at that moment from their own country, Charles resolved to march again upon the capital,

---

1 Cf. Blount, *Reform. of the Church of Eng.*, vol. ii. pp. 151, 152.

2 "Though it was not, like a modern cabinet, composed of persons of only one shade of political opinion, the opinion that the war ought to be carried on with vigour was decidedly preponderant in it." — Gardiner, *Hist. of the Great Civil War*, vol. i. p. 307.

3 Carlyle, *Cromwell's Letters and Speeches*, p. 115.

and so it was that on the 27th of October he encountered at battle of Newbury, October 27.
Newbury the victors of Marston Moor under Manchester.
After the battle had gone against the royal forces, Cromwell,
at the head of his now famous "Ironsides," would have made
the ruin of the king complete, had he not been restrained by
Manchester, who, like Essex, was resolved that no such thing
should take place. "They, in fact,"—Manchester and Crom- Cromwell, who quarrelled with Manchester because he was "afraid to conquer,"
well, — "came to a quarrel here. . . . To Cromwell and the
thoroughgoing party it had become very clear that high Es-
sexes and Manchesters, of limited notions and large estates
and anxieties, who besides their fear of being themselves
beaten utterly, and forfeited and 'hanged,' were afraid of beat-
ing the king too well, would never end this cause in a good
way." Under the force of that conviction Cromwell now came now took the lead.
forward and assumed the leadership, which the death of Pym
had left vacant, resolved to relieve the army of commanders
who were "afraid to conquer," and to "bring about a more
speedy, vigorous, and effectual prosecution of the war." [1]

4. Oliver Cromwell, a country gentleman, who came first to Cromwell as a military organizer;
Westminster as a member from Huntington in 1628, and who
was afterwards returned both to the Short and to the Long
Parliament by Cambridge, promptly enlisted at the beginning
of the war as a captain of a troop of cavalry, at the head of
which he appeared at Edgehill. Although without military
training, his practical eye was quick to perceive, as he told his his views as expressed to Hampden;
cousin Hampden, that the "old decayed serving-men and tap-
sters and such kind of fellows," of which his force was composed, would never "be able to encounter gentlemen that have
honour, courage, and resolution in them." [2] Cromwell's remedy for the evil he so graphically described he undertook to
illustrate by the organization, mainly from his own means, of a
regiment for the Association of the Eastern Counties,[3] com-
posed strictly of "godly men," whose religious zeal was to be applied to the organization of the body of "godly men;"
pitted against the chivalry of the Cavaliers. These "men of
religion," drawn largely from the common people, and officered
without regard to social tradition, developed under Cromwell's
organizing hand into the irresistible force that was never
beaten, and which received at Marston Moor the name of

[1] Carlyle, *Cromwell's Letters and Speeches*, pp. 118, 119.

[2] Ibid., Speech XI.

[3] Ibid, p. 98.

"Ironsides." In the light of that successful experiment Crom-

afterwards known as "Iron- sides;"

well, after his quarrel with Manchester at Newbury, in October, 1644, resolved to extend the same principle of organization to the army as a whole, which was to be new-modelled throughout.

resolved to remodel the whole army on the same basis;

While it may be true that the idea of a new national force independent of local contributions was first suggested by Waller,[1] it is equally certain that the move "to consider of a frame or model of the whole militia" received the impulse which made it effective when Cromwell returned to his place in the house

his purpose declared in the house in Novem- ber, 1644;

in November, to give an account of what had transpired at Newbury, and to declare "that the members of both houses have got great places and commands, and the sword into their hands; . . . I hope we have such true English hearts, and zealous affections towards the general weal of our mother country, as no members of either house will scruple to deny themselves, and their own private interests for the public good."[2] Such was Cromwell's preface to the famous Self-

the Self- Denying Ordinance;

Denying Ordinance, which was designed to take the command of the army out of the hands of members of the houses, and to create a New Model whose pay should depend upon the monthly payment of taxes, and not upon the good-will of county communities. The scheme, which took definite form

passed both houses April 3, 1645;

in January, 1645, did not pass both houses in its final shape until the 3d of April,[3] when the work of reorganization was

Fairfax made com- mander-in- chief;

begun by Sir Thomas Fairfax, whom the commons designated as commander-in-chief. The list of officers prepared by him was accepted by the houses,[4] and thus was brought about the retirement of Essex, Manchester, Denbigh, and Waller, who resigned their commands. It appears as if Cromwell also complied with the Self-Denying Ordinance, by renouncing his command according to its direction within forty days after its passage, but at the urgent request of the officers the commons

Cromwell appointed by the house lieutenant- general;

appointed him lieutenant-general on the 10th of June, and commander-in-chief of the horse.[5] Thus it was that he escaped from the personal consequences of the ordinance which

1 "It was from Waller, not from Cromwell, that the first suggestion of the New Model came." — Gardiner, *Hist. of the Great Civil War*, vol. ii. p. 5.

2 *Cromwell's Letters and Speeches*, pp. 119, 120.

3 Ibid., p. 120, note §. This was a second self-denying ordinance.

4 Slight changes were made by the lords. *Journals*, vol. vii. p. 268.

5 *Cromwell's Letters and Speeches*, p. 123; *Lords' Journals*, vol. vii. p. 420.

expelled from the army the commanders he desired to remove. Acting through Fairfax, Cromwell was then able to enforce his principles in the selection of the officers of the New Model, who were chosen regardless of distinctions of rank or diversities of creed. His rule was embodied in his direction to "Be careful what captains of horse you choose, what men be mounted. A few honest men are better than numbers. If you choose godly honest men to be captains of horse, honest men will follow them." "I had rather have a plain russet-coated captain," he once said, "that knows what he fights for and loves what he knows, than what you call a gentleman, and is nothing else." Hewson the cobbler and Pride the drayman were thus accepted as commanders along with the Montagues, Pickerings, Fortesques, Sheffields, and Sidneys. The bulk of those in high command were, however, men of noble or gentle blood, it being estimated "that 'out of the thirty-seven generals and colonels,' who participated in the first great battle, 'twenty-one were commoners of good families, nine were members of noble families, and only seven were not gentlemen by birth.' " [1]

his plan applied to selection of officers of the New Model;

bulk of those in high command of noble or gentle blood.

Cromwell, who thus dared to ignore to a certain extent distinctions of rank in the selection of his officers, was also bold enough to apply to the New Model as a whole principles of religious toleration which were specially offensive to the presbyterian element by which the houses were now controlled. A brief account has already been given of the rise of the separatists, who, rejecting the Puritan idea of reforming the national church from within, resolved before the close of the reign of Elizabeth to break off from it altogether; of the persecutions in the reign of James which drove them to seek a refuge first in Holland and then in America; and finally, of the still sharper measures employed in the reign of Charles by Laud, who, with the aid of the star chamber and the high commission, raised the tide of emigration to the New World to such a height that in February, 1634, an order in council was made prohibiting the sailing of any more vessels.[2] While the independent religious movement, with its various subdivisions, was

Rise of the independents:

beginning of their religious movement;

---

[1] Gardiner, *Hist. of the Great Civil War*, vol. ii. p. 196, citing Markham, *The Great Lord Fairfax*, p. 199.

[2] See above, pp. 279, 293.

its suppression in England caused strongholds to be built upon the Continent and in New England;
thus suppressed for a time in England itself, two great strong-holds were built up on the Continent and in New England, from which its disciples returned in large numbers when the meeting of the Long Parliament gave them the hope of regain-ing a foothold in the land from which they had been so ruth-lessly driven out. In 1641 Hugh Peters, who was the first pastor of the church at Salem, came back, and with him a host of others, who were eager to tell with their tongues and their the "New England way;" pens how the "New England way" of religious liberty had prospered in the wilderness.   From that time the independent or congregationalist body, so called by reason of their mainte-nance of congregational independence,[1] began to attract atten-tion, and four years later a pamphleteer numbered with horror sixteen religious sects as existing in defiance of law.[2]   While the views of the dissenting brethren in their various forms made the greatest progress among the common people; made the greatest progress among the artisans, the small traders, and farmers, they were not without influence in a higher sphere.   Even in the Westminster assembly, Goodwin, Simpson, Nye, Boroughs, and Budge, university men who had been driven for a time to Holland by the Laudian persecutions, were, in spite of their disclaimers, known as independents.[3] no tolera-tion for independ-ents in a reorganized state church; But the parliamentary leaders who charged that assembly with the work of reorganizing the state church upon a presbyterian basis were not prepared to listen for a moment to the idea that that church in its new form should relinquish one tittle of its right to embrace the whole nation within its pale, and to dic-tate to all their faith and form of worship.   Under that theory as inherited from the Tudors and sharpened by Laud, there was no place for liberty of independent sectarian association. Such was the condition of things when Cromwell set himself to gather together an army of "honest," "godly men" from the farmers of the eastern counties, among whom dissident opinions of every kind had taken the deepest root.   As most Cromwell as a medi-ator; of the privates were drawn from that source, it was a mat-ter of absolute necessity that he should stand as a mediator

---

[1] They claimed that neither church nor state possessed the right to inter-fere with the forms of worship, which each congregation might select for it-self. This conception placed them of course in hostility with both Genevan and Anglican ideals.

[2] Green's *Hist. of the Eng. People*, vol. iii. p. 237.

[3] They "had recently come back to England after occupying ministerial po-sitions at Rotterdam and Arnheim." — Gardiner, *The Great Civil War*, vol. i. p. 261.

between them and the parliament, which was not disposed to tolerate their opinions. In answer to remonstrances from the presbyterians, Cromwell, before the battle of Marston Moor, declared that "the state, in choosing men to serve it, takes no notice of these opinions. If they be willing faithfully to serve it, that satisfies." After that event he succeeded in having introduced into the Self-Denying Ordinance a clause "that religious men might serve without taking the Covenant as a first preliminary;"[1] and after the battle of Naseby he declared in a letter to Speaker Lenthall that "honest men served you faithfully in this action. Sir, they are trusty; I beseech you, in the name of God, not to discourage them. . . . He that ventures his life for the liberty of his country, I wish he trust God for the liberty of his conscience, and you for the liberty he fights for."[2] Such were the principles of religious toleration which Cromwell permitted to enter into the organization of the New Model, and yet so little sympathy did they excite in the house that when his letter to Speaker Lenthall was sent to press, the clause in which he had so eloquently expressed them was suppressed.[3] Three months later, however, the independents were able to force the presbyterians to agree to the issuance of writs[4] to fill up the nearly two hundred vacancies which had occurred in the commons by reason of deaths and the expulsion of the royalist members, and in the elections that ensued the independent and republican elements were able greatly to increase their strength.

While Cromwell was thus building up on new lines such a fighting force as England had never seen before, the peace party in the commons, backed by the Scotch commissioners, — jealous of his growing influence and apprehensive as to the results of the alliance between the war party which he led and the independents who were pressing for religious liberty, — resolved upon fresh negotiations with Charles as the only means

Margin notes: declared for toleration before Marston Moor;

his letter to Lenthall after Naseby to the same effect;

coldly received;

independents increased their strength in the house.

Peace party opened a fresh negotiation with Charles;

---

[1] Only the officers were required to take the Covenant. When John Lilburne refused it, he was excluded from his command in the New Model. *Innocency and Truth Justified*, p. 46.

[2] *Cromwell's Letters and Speeches*, pp. 127, 128.

[3] Gardiner, *Hist. of the Great Civil War*, vol. ii. p. 252.

[4] A new writ was first sent to Southwark, and then to a large number of other constituencies. Whitelock, p. 168. Special care was taken, however, to exclude royalist members. A writ was refused to Beverley, where the Yorkshire royalists were specially influential. *Commons' Journals*, vol. iv. p. 249.

by which to cut off the impending revolution in church and
state. In the hope of arriving at a basis of settlement, peace
commissioners from both sides met at Uxbridge on the 29th
of January, 1645, where the representatives of the parliament
at Westminster submitted the three proposals they had been
instructed to make. In the first they demanded that the king
should take the Covenant, and that episcopacy and the prayer-
book should give way to presbyterianism and the directory; in
the second, they demanded that the army and navy for both
kingdoms should be permanently controlled by a mixed commission to be named by the parliaments of the two countries;
while in the third, they demanded that Charles should permit
the English parliament to prosecute the war in Ireland without interference from him.[1] This hopeless negotiation, based
upon proposals made under Scottish influence, dragged on until
the spring, when it was broken off by the king, who in May
reopened the war by a march to the north. The time had now
come for a final trial of strength between the war party still
dominant in the royal councils and that dominant in the parliament of which Cromwell was the real chief. On the 14th
of June the armies met at Naseby, where the New Model demonstrated the irresistible force of its organization through a
victory which virtually ended the war at a blow. By the spring
of 1646, Cromwell and Fairfax had trampled out all formidable military resistance, which finally came to an end when
the last campaign in the west culminated in the surrender at
Stow-on-the-Wold of the royal forces under brave old Astley,
who frankly declared to his captors: "You have now done
your work, and may go to play, unless you fall out amongst
yourselves."[2]

5. While Charles was no longer able to put an army in the
field, he did not regard his cause as by any means hopeless, for
the reason that he believed he could regain through artful
negotiations with his enemies all, or nearly all, that he had lost
through the fortunes of war. Although both political and military power had actually passed from his hands, the theory
remained that he was still a factor in the constitution, a king
separated from his parliament only by differences which he

Marginal notes:

proposals made at Uxbridge in January, 1645;

negotiations broken off in May when Charles marched to the north;

Naseby, June 14, ruined the royal cause at a blow;

last campaign in the west.

Charles attempted to regain by diplomacy what he had lost in war;

---

[1] Rushworth, vol. v. pp. 865, 879, 897.

[2] Ibid., vol. vi. p. 140.

deemed capable of removal through a frank understanding and mutual concessions. But against such a possibility stood the fact that Charles himself was incapable of directness and candor, while the differences which divided him from his adversaries were of such a nature as to render the making of compromises practically unattainable. The parliament at Westminster which had confronted him as such at the beginning of the war was no longer a unit; the contingency which old Astley had indicated had happened: the victors had fallen out among themselves; the parliament was now divided into two hostile camps under the names of presbyterians and independents. The supreme question that divided the king from these factions and the factions from each other was the religious one which overshadowed the political. Charles firmly maintained, as his father had before him, " No bishop no king," and the presbyterian party, which still dominated the parliament upon religious questions, stood pledged by their alliance with the Scots to an abolition of the episcopal in favor of the presbyterian system. As unalterably opposed to both now stood the independents, whose theory of the right of each congregation as a voluntary association to maintain an independent existence under the authority of Christ alone involved them in positive conflict with both the Anglican and Genevan theory. While the presbyterians in the parliament had behind them the Scotch army at Newark, urging the execution of the Covenant and the enforcement, on that basis, of religious uniformity, the independents had behind them the New Model, which, through Cromwell as its spokesman, was growing more and more positive in its demands for religious toleration. After the storm of Bristol Cromwell again wrote to Speaker Lenthall, and told him in no uncertain terms that "presbyterians, independents, all have here the same spirit of faith and prayer; the same presence and answer; they agree here, have no names of difference: pity it is it should be otherwise anywhere! All that believe, have the real unity, which is most glorious; because inward, and spiritual, in the body and to the head. . . . And for the brethren, in things of the mind we look for no compulsion, but that of light and reason." [1] No plainer declaration of war could have been made against the

parliament divided into presbyterians and independents;

the former relying on the Scotch army at Newark, the latter upon the New Model;

Cromwell's new plea for toleration;

----

[1] *Cromwell's Letters and Speeches,* p. 136.

Tudor theory of uniformity, no matter whether enforced under
episcopal or presbyterian forms.   And yet in the face of such
difficulties Charles, during two weary years of intrigue and negotiation, devoted himself to the impossible task of reconciling
the irreconcilable, and while thus engaged he did not shrink
from the unkingly attempt "to piece out the lion's skin with
the fox's."

*two years
of intrigue
and negoti-
ation.*

The diplomatic battle began with a bold assault from Charles,
who, after hearing of the surrender at Stow-on-the-Wold, coolly
asked permission of parliament on the 23d of March, 1646, to
return to Westminster, with the understanding that an act of
oblivion should be passed and his supporters relieved of all
sequestrations.[1]   After brief consideration the commons drew
up a reply, concurred in by the lords and Scotch commissioners, refusing such permission prior to a mutual understanding
as to the constitutional changes to be accepted by both parties
as satisfaction for the past and security for the future.[2]   Thus
baffled in his first attempt, and menaced by the advance of
Fairfax on Oxford, Charles resolved to seek a refuge among
the Scots, whom he hoped through a sense of loyalty to draw
to his side, so as to secure a coign of vantage from which to
deal safely with the two English parties, with the weight of his
northern kingdom behind him.   In execution of this design
he left Oxford late in April, arriving in the Scottish camp on
the 5th of May, where he became virtually a prisoner.[3]   While
thus held captive by the Scots, who were accused of the
intention of employing their army in his cause, Charles early
in June again appealed to parliament for a settlement, ordering
at the same time the commanders of the remaining fortresses
to surrender them at once.[4]   Under such circumstances the
presbyterian party in parliament, who at that moment were
putting their religious system in force in London, promptly
dispatched to Newcastle a commission, which demanded that
the king should not only take the covenant himself, but enforce it upon all his subjects, abolish episcopacy, surrender the
command of the army and the fleet for twenty years, agree to

*Charles
asked leave
to return to
Westmin-
ster, March,
1646;*

*houses
declined to
receive him
prior to
an under-
standing;*

*arrived in
Scottish
camp in
May, where
he was
made a
prisoner;*

*attempt of
presbyte-
rians to
arrive at a
settlement;*

[1] *Lords' Journals*, vol. viii. p. 235.
[2] Such was the answer sent to Oxford on April 1. *Lords' Journals*, vol.
viii. p. 248.
[3] " He fancied himself to be a guest,
but the days of his captivity had in fact
begun." — Gardiner, *Hist. of the Great
Civil War*, vol. iii. p. 102.
[4] *Lords' Journals*, vol. viii. p. 374.

acts for the easier punishment of recusants, and to measures by which many royalists were to be excluded in whole or in part from pardon.[1] But in spite of all the pressure that the Scots and his other friends, including the queen, could put upon him, the king resolved on the 1st of July not to accept such terms, although "a flat denial" was "to be delayed as long as may be."[2] "I am not without hope," he wrote, "that I shall be able to draw either the presbyterians or the independents to side with me for extirpating one another, so that I shall be really king again." Thus baffled in their attempt to force Charles to accept their religious system, the presbyterians did not shrink from the effort to enforce it through parliamentary legislation. On the 2d of September the famous "Ordinance for the suppression of blasphemies and heresies," bristling with death penalties, was brought in,[3] and on October 9 the lords accepted an ordinance for the abolition of episcopacy.[4] The great practical difficulty, however, that lay in the path of the presbyterians grew out of the counter pressure put upon parliament by the New Model, which could not be disbanded so long as a Scottish army remained upon English soil with the king a prisoner in their hands. In order to overcome that embarrassment, the parliament by a clever manœuvre induced the army of the Scots in January, 1647, in consideration of a large payment of money, to surrender the king to a committee of the houses and to retire beyond the border.

The inevitable struggle for the mastery between the presbyterians, who now controlled both houses, and the independents, who controlled the army, was precipitated by the attempt made by the former in February to dissolve the New Model, and to organize a fresh force under presbyterian officers for the suppression of the Irish rebellion. The response that came from the New Model to this attempt upon its existence was embodied in manifestoes made by both officers and men, which were followed in May by a general election of agitators,[5] a name given to elected representatives chosen by each regiment,

their terms rejected;

Charles hoped to extirpate one party with the help of the other;

"Ordinance for the suppression of blasphemies;" abolition of episcopacy;

king surrendered to the houses, January, 1647;

presbyterians and independents struggle for the mastery;

New Model refused to be dissolved;

---

[1] Rushworth, vol. vi. p. 309.
[2] The king to the queen, July 1. *Charles I. in 1646*, p. 51.
[3] It did not pass until May, 1648. *Lords' Journals*, vol. x. p. 240.
[4] Ibid., vol. viii. p. 515.
[5] They were also known as agents

of the army, whose business it was "to do the actual work of [the affairs of] another, to manage, or act as agent." It seems to be clear "that Agitator was the actual title, and Adjutator only a bad spelling of soldiers familiar with Adjutants and the Adjutors of 1642."

who constituted collectively a kind of lower house, whose resolves were moderated by an upper council composed of the
staff officers.[1]   Thus equipped for action under a constitution
of its own, the army was now ready as a corporate entity
to enter upon the enforcement of the peculiar religious and
political ideas which its organization embodied.   The leading
statesman of this strange army and parliament in one was
Ireton, to whom Cromwell had married his daughter a year
before, and who now stood as his representative, since his
exclusion from his command by reason of a vote taken in the
commons on the 8th of March, 1647.   While the army was
thus nominally under the political direction of Ireton, the
fruitless discussion of its rights, which he set forth with great
spirit, was suddenly suspended on the 4th of June by the taking away from the parliamentary commissioners of the king by
Joyce at the head of five hundred troopers, to whom he coolly
pointed when Charles asked his authority for his act.   The
storm of indignation that broke upon Cromwell by reason of
his complicity[2] with this plot at a time when he was assuming
to act as mediator between the parties drove him to seek
a shelter with the New Model, which on June 12 marched
towards London.   Three days later the council of officers put
forth "The Declaration of the Army"[3] as its first deliberate
attempt at a political programme, and that was promptly followed by charges against eleven members of the house, who
were accused of stirring up strife between the parliament and
the army, and of a design to reopen the civil war.[4]   While the
house was bold enough to reject the army's political scheme,
the eleven members were forced to withdraw under pressure
from their accusers.   Turning then from the parliament to
the captive king, the army, under the guidance of Cromwell
and Ireton, opened up a direct negotiation, in the course of
which was submitted to Charles a basis of settlement formulated by Ireton in a skeleton paper entitled, "The Heads of

[side notes]
adopted a
constitu-
tion of its
own;

Ireton its
leading
statesman;

Joyce
seized the
person of
the king
June 4;

army put
forth its
first
political
programme
June 15;

eleven
members
forced to
withdraw
from the
house;

the heads
of the
proposals
submitted
to the king;

— See Dr. Murray in *The New English
Dictionary — Agitators.*
   [1] As to the origin of this council in
the solemn engagement, and its composition, see Gardiner, *Hist. of the
Great Civil War*, vol. iii. p. 81.   In
August, 1647, the council of the army
supported the agitators in their demand for the purging of the house.
   [2] For the evidence on that point, see
Gardiner, *Hist. of the Great Civil War*,
pp. 266, 272, and notes.
   [3] *Lords' Journals*, vol. ix. p. 269.
   [4] Rushworth, vol. vi. p. 570.

the Proposals."[1] This plan of reform demanded that parliament, to be elected every three years, should nominate all the great officers of state, and control the army and navy for a period of ten years; that all coercive power should be withdrawn from the clergy without the abolition of the episcopal office; that all acts enforcing the prayer-book, the Covenant, and attendance at church should be repealed; that belief and worship should be free to all, even to Roman Catholics; that the house of commons should be reformed by a fairer distribution of seats and electoral rights; that taxation should be equalized and legal procedure simplified; that a host of judicial, political, and commercial privileges should be abolished; and finally that an act of oblivion should be passed from which only seven royalist "delinquents" were to be excepted. At this point it was that the alarm excited in London by the prospect of the triumph of this advanced and tolerant programme impelled a mob to burst upon the two houses, and to put them under such coercion that the two speakers, together with eight independent peers and fifty-seven independent members, deemed it necessary to take refuge with the army, where they were enthusiastically received on the 3d of August.[2] As a natural consequence the New Model at once marched upon the city, which they entered in triumph on the 6th, and after restoring the independent members to their places again, insisted upon the expulsion of the eleven who, during the recent excitement, had been recalled. Under the military pressure to which Cromwell now subjected the houses, a sufficient number of the presbyterian members were forced to withdraw to insure for a moment only a bare independent majority. In the midst of these stirring scenes Charles was actively planning for a royalist rising and for a Scotch invasion, and in the hope of giving to them his personal direction, he escaped from his captors on the 11th of November and proceeded to the Isle of Wight, only there to begin a fresh imprisonment. Thus baffled in his effort to lead the second civil war in person, he undertook its direction from his place of confinement, and before the end of the year he finally stipulated with the Scottish commissioners for the establishment of presbyterianism in England,[3] as the

a London mob forced the independents in parliament to fly to the army;

which soon restored them to their places;

Charles escaped November 11, only to begin a fresh imprisonment;

---

[1] *Const. Documents*, p. 232.
[2] Rushworth, vol. vii. pp. 743–751.
[3] See "The Engagement and Additional Articles," December 26, 27, *Const. Documents*, pp. 259, 264.

price of an army which finally crossed the border early in July, 1648. As public evidence of the fact that all hope of recon- ciliation between the independents and the king was now at an end, the New Model, before setting out to meet the threat- ened invasion, gathered in a solemn prayer-meeting, and came " to a very clear and joint resolution on many grounds at large then debated amongst us, that it was our duty, if ever the Lord brought us back again in peace, to call Charles Stuart, that man of blood, to an account for the blood he has shed and mischief he has done to his utmost, against the Lord's cause and people in this poor nation." [1] True to its resolve, the army, when peace was restored, after asserting the doctrine afterwards known as "the sovereignty of the people," de- manded, in "The Remonstrance of the Army" completed by Ireton,[2] "that the capital and grand author of our troubles, the person of the king, . . . may be speedily brought to jus- tice for the treason, blood, and mischief he is therein guilty." On the 20th of November the council of officers presented the remonstrance to the commons; on the 1st of December Charles was sequestered and carried off from the Isle of Wight to Hurst Castle, in Hampshire, and the next day the army entered London. It only remained for the military power which now dominated the city to subject the houses to its complete control, and when they declined to accept the invita- tion presented by the council of officers to dissolve them- selves, a purging process was agreed upon which Colonel Pride, at the head of a troop of soldiers, executed on the 6th of December by forbidding the entrance into the house of those whose names appeared upon a list prepared beforehand. In that way one hundred and forty-three members were removed, forty-seven of whom were subjected to confinement, while ninety-six others who offered no resistance were simply turned away and forbidden to take their places.[3] The "Rump" of a parliament that thus remained as a mere veil for the power of the sword claimed to be sovereign in three resolutions, adopted on the 4th of January, 1649, which declared "That the

---

[1] Allen's Narrative, Somers' *Tracts*, vol. vi. p. 500.

[2] Adopted in the general council of officers held at St. Albans, November 18, 1648.

[3] *A True and Full Relation*, E. pp. 475, 476; *Parl. Hist.*, vol. iii. pt. i. p. 248. The prisoners were promptly released on their parole to make no attempt to return to the house.

people are, under God, the original of all just power : that the commons of England, in parliament assembled, being chosen by and representing the people, have the supreme power in this nation ; that whatsoever is enacted or declared for law by the commons in parliament assembled hath the force of law, and all the people of this nation are concluded thereby, although the consent and concurrence of king or house of peers be not had thereunto." [1]   Two days later this body, which had ceased to be representative, passed the act [2] creating the high court of justice, to consist of one hundred and thirty-five commissioners, [3] who were to exercise the functions of both judge and jury in the trial of the king.   On the 20th Charles appeared before this tribunal, which sat in Westminster Hall under the presidency of John Bradshaw, and challenged its authority by refusing to plead ; [4] on the 27th a formal and final sentence was read declaring that he should be beheaded as a traitor ; on the 29th the signing of his death warrant was completed under pressure ; [5] and on the next day he met his doom robed in a royal dignity which did not bend even at that dreadful door through which he passed into the presence of the Eternal Father.

high court of justice constituted the 6th;

Charles refused to plead the 20th;

executed on the 30th.

---

[1] *Commons' Journals*, vol. vi. pp. 110, 111.

[2] Ibid., vol. vi. p. 113; *State Trials*, vol. iv. p. 1046.   The name of Ordinance had been dropped.

[3] At its first meeting on January 8, only fifty-two members appeared.

[4] *State Trials*, vol. iv. pp. 1069, 1070, 1074.

[5] These are the dates as fixed by Mr. Gardiner, *Hist. of the Great Civil War*, vol. iv. pp. 307–317, and notes.

CHAPTER IV.

THE COMMONWEALTH AND PROTECTORATE.

Results
of the
revolution
unforeseen;

1. THERE is no good reason to believe that a single member of the great popular majority which gathered at St. Stephen's upon the meeting of the Long Parliament imagined for a moment that the revolution then set in motion under legal forms would culminate in the execution of the king, and in the substitution of a republican system for the ancient constitution.

they arose
out of a
great
upheaval,
broken
into four
distinct
stages:

That entirely unforeseen result suddenly arose out of a great religious and political upheaval which is broken into four distinct stages, each one of which was the natural, possibly the inevitable, sequence of the preceding. When Pym, as the leader of the popular party, undertook to settle once and for all the vital principle that the supreme powers of the state are vested in parliament as against the crown, and that as between the houses themselves the ultimate sovereignty resides in the popular branch of the legislature,[1] he contemplated no more than such a readjustment of the constitutional forces as would fix the centre of gravity of the state in the representative chamber.

the first,
embracing
reforms
made
during first
ten months
of Long
Parliament;

The first stage of the revolution consisted of the efforts made in that direction by the popular party while acting as a whole, and striking as one man against abuses which were permanently removed through the measures adopted during the first ten months of the Long Parliament.

the second,
the struggle
that ended
with the
adoption of
the Grand
Remon-
strance;

The second stage began after the first recess, when the triumphant progress of the popular party was checked by a division in its own ranks as to the disposition to be made of the episcopal office, — one faction contending for its entire abolition, the other for the retention of the bishops with diminished powers and subject to parliamentary jurisdiction. The latter claim, maintained by the old Puritan party within the church, triumphed in the memorable struggle over the Grand Remonstrance, whose adoption was accepted as a settlement of the fact that the estab-

[1] See above, p. 300.

lishment, while retaining episcopacy in a modified form, would tolerate neither the Laudian element within its pale, nor the sectaries who gathered without in separate conventicles. The third stage began when the Root-and-branch party, which insisted upon the entire abolition of episcopacy, was able to enforce its ideas through a political alliance with the Scots, who demanded, as the price of military aid to the parliamentary cause, the acceptance of the Covenant, and the substitution of the presbyterian for the episcopal system in the Church of England. That concession, reluctantly made by Pym and his followers as a political necessity, did nothing, however, to advance the cause of religious toleration. The presbyterian party, which thus came into possession of the state church, refused to relinquish one tittle of its right to embrace the whole nation in its fold, and to dictate to all their faith and form of worship. The fourth and last stage of the revolution began when the whole dissenting body of sectaries resolved to band together for the assertion of congregational independence against the scheme of legal uniformity pressed upon them through the state church by the presbyterian majority dominant in parliament. This combined opposition of the sectaries, generally designated as Independents, first assumed a definite and formidable shape when all of its various elements were united by Cromwell and Fairfax in that strange army and parliament in one known as the New Model, whose corner-stones were social and religious toleration. Into the ranks of that organization entered every shade of dissident opinion, not only religious but political. There it was that the religious independent was converted into the political independent; there it was that the levellers appeared as an organized republican association, ready to substitute for the ancient constitution which had developed without design a commonwealth of the saints based on abstract principles. As early as October, 1647, the levellers had embodied their new conception of government in the draft of a constitution, entitled "The Agreement of the People,"[1] which proposed, first, that the constituencies should be "more indifferently proportioned according to the

Margin notes:
the third, the triumph of the presbyterian over the episcopal system;

the fourth, the triumph of the independents over the presbyterians;

all independent elements combined by Cromwell in the New Model;

the levellers as an organized republican association;

"The Agreement of the People;"

---

[1] "An Agreement of the People for a firm and present peace," etc. (E. 412, 21), presented to the council of the army, October 28, 1647, and printed in full in the Appendix to vol. iii. of Gardiner's *Hist. of the Great Civil War.*

number of inhabitants ;" second, that the existing parliament should be dissolved on September 30, 1648 ; third, that all future parliaments should be triennial ; fourth, that a single elected chamber should be supreme in all things not "expressly or impliedly reserved by the represented to themselves." This prototype of all constitutions, state and federal, as they exist to-day in the United States,[1] was to draw its authority from a direct acceptance by the people, who reserved to themselves, by express constitutional limitations upon the powers granted, certain rights, among which the agreement pointedly named the absolute right to religious liberty and due process of law. This republican ideal, destined to such a marvellous expansion, which the levellers, under the lead of Lilburne, persistently pressed upon the leaders of the army, was finally completed in a modified form by the council of officers on the 15th of January, 1649, and by them presented five days later to the house of commons, who agreed to consider it so soon as "the necessity of the present weighty and urgent affairs would permit."[2] It was clearly understood, however, that with that part of this programme which suggested that the Rump should yield to another body elected on more popular principles, its members had no possible sympathy. The army therefore resolved to retain for the moment this fragment of an assembly, which it had purged of its presbyterian elements, as a veil for the power of the sword, and as a link, however weak, with the past. By its voice the sovereignty of the people was proclaimed, and the ancient constitution practically abolished by the resolutions, adopted on the 4th of January, 1649, which declared that the enactments of the commons alone should have the force of law, "although the consent and concurrence of king or house of peers be not had thereunto."[3] Two days later the same assembly, unaided by any precedent in the history of nations, created the tribunal under whose judgment the king passed to his doom.

2. The house of commons, which at the beginning of the Long Parliament consisted of five hundred and six members, had now dwindled to a mere shadow; at the largest division which took place during the month that followed the king's death, only seventy-seven members were present to re-

Marginal notes:

prototype of all American constitutions ;

completed January 15, 1649, and presented to the commons ;

army resolved to retain the Rump,

which proclaimed the sovereignty of the people, speaking through a single chamber.

The Rump cleared the way for the first republican constitution

---

[1] Cf. Bryce's *American Commonw.*, pt. ii. ; Gardiner, vol. iii. p. 387.

[2] *Commons' Journals*, vol. vi. p. 122.

[3] See above, p. 339.

cord their votes.[1] And yet by the sole authority of this Rump of a parliament the monarchy was overthrown, and the first crude and tentative republican constitution that appeared in its stead was set up. In order to clear the ground for the erection of the new structure a vote was taken on the 7th of February, which abolished the monarchy as " unnecessary, burdensome, and dangerous for the freedom, safety, and public interest of the people of this nation," [2] and at the same time the house of peers was swept away as " useless and dangerous." On the same day a council of state was voted " to be henceforth the executive power," [3] and on the 14th, the forty-one members of whom it was composed were elected by a separate vote on each name, and the body thus constituted was charged under " the orders of the house " with the direction of the military and naval forces, the collection of the revenue, the preservation of the internal peace through the police power, the supervision of trade, internal and external, the administration of the colonies, and the negotiation of treaties with foreign nations.[4] The powers of the admiralty vested in this council were delegated to a committee of which Vane was the head, and by its authority the command of the fleet which added so much to the glory of the republic passed to Popham, Dean, and Blake.[5] Upon the threshold of its labors the new executive council, composed in the main of members of the house and of five peers, some of whom put themselves in the category of the former by accepting places as elected representatives,[6] divided against itself when the house demanded of each member an oath approving of the execution of the king and of the abolition of the monarchy and the house of lords.[7] As a settlement of the controversy, Cromwell and his friends, who promptly took the oath, agreed to a compromise, which modified the demand to a promise of adhesion to the existing order of things, and to the future government of the nation " by way of a republic without king or house of peers." [8] The council

by abolishing monarchy and the house of lords February 7;

the executive power vested in a council of state elected by the house; its duties defined;

powers of the admiralty vested in the council;

the oath to support the new régime " by way of a republic without king or house of peers;"

---

[1] *Commons' Journals*, vol. vi. pp. 128, 130, 140, 143, 147; *Old Parliamentary History*, vol. ix. p. 12.

[2] *Commons' Journals*, vol. vi. pp. 132, 133.

[3] Ibid., vol. vi. pp. 133, 138.

[4] Ibid., vol. vi. pp. 139, 140.

[5] Cf. Guizot's *Cromwell*, p. 5; Godwin's *Hist. of the Commonw.*, vol. iii. p. 35.

[6] The earl of Pembroke sat as member for the county of Berks, and his example was followed by Salisbury and Howard of Escrick. Whitelock, *Mem.*, p. 396.

[7] This suggestion came from Ireton.

[8] *Commons' Journals*, vol. vi. p. ?

of state thus constituted and elected for one year was reëlected
without great changes for the years 1650, 1651, 1652, and 1653.
The theory was that all the powers of the state were vested
in the Rump, and that its elected council was a mere agent
in the work of administration.   All writs now ran in the name
of "the keepers of the liberty of England by the authority of
parliament ; " and new commissions were issued to the judges,
sheriffs, and magistrates, who, in lieu of the old oath of allegiance and supremacy, were required to pledge their fidelity
to the commonwealth.   Although ten out of twelve of the
principal judges had been appointed by parliament since the
outbreak of the civil war, six of them refused the required
oath, and the other six refused to serve unless the house would
declare by a formal vote that the common law of the country
should remain as the rule to be enforced by their judgments.[1]
These demands were complied with, and during the following
summer the places of six who resigned were filled with new appointees.   Not, however, until the 19th of May was the act of
parliament passed which formally declared the republic to be
a "commonwealth and a free state ; "[2] and not until the 30th
of that month was the fact formally proclaimed in London,
where in the midst of great popular disapproval some of the
aldermen refused to take part in the ceremony, one of them
declaring at the bar of the house "that his heart did not go
along with the work in that business." [3]   From the very outset the new government was beset with difficulties on every
hand.   Throughout Europe the death of the king was received
with a thrill of horror, which was followed by manifestations of
hostility from nearly all the continental nations.   In Scotland
even the presbyterians, whom Cromwell had restored to power,
joined in proclaiming Charles II. king, and in inviting him to
ascend the throne of that country,[4] while a series of royalist
successes in Ireland had left only Dublin in the hands of the

[marginalia]
theory upon which the new fabric rested;

reorganiza-tion of the judiciary;

the com-mon law un-disturbed;

republic declared to be a "common-wealth and a free state," May 19;

met with hostility everywhere;

Charles II. proclaimed by the Scots;

[1] *Commons' Journals*, vol. vi. pp. 134–136; Guizot's *Cromwell*, p. 6; Gardiner, *Commonw. and Protectorate*, vol. i. p. 10.

[2] To be governed by "the repre-sentatives of the people in parliament . . . without any king or house of lords." — Scobell, vol. ii. p. 30.

[3] *Commons' Journals*, vol. vi. pp. 133, 166, 168, 179, 206, 221; Whitelock, *Mem.*, pp. 393, 394.

[4] The proclamation made at Edin-burgh, February 5, was coupled with the condition that he should rule "ac-cording to the National Covenant and the Solemn League and Covenant." — *Acts of Parl. of Scot.*, vol. vi. pt. ii. p. 157.   Charles was at the time at the Hague, the guest of the prince of Orange.

parliamentary forces. Cromwell was thus called upon to again employ his military genius, and before the close of 1651 his brilliant and bloody campaigns had reduced both Ireland and Scotland to subjection. The great leader then turned his attention to the settlement of internal difficulties, which were at once serious and menacing. In the first place the royal cause had been greatly strengthened by the king's tragic death, which was immediately followed by the publication of the " Eikon Basiliké," the work really of Gauden,[1] but which purported to be a revelation from Charles himself of his inner thoughts and feelings during those last days of suffering and captivity that won for him the name of royal martyr. The task of counteracting the prodigious effect produced at home and abroad by this book, which had an immense circulation, was committed to Milton, already the author of an eloquent pamphlet, " The Tenure of Kings and Magistrates," which maintained " that it is lawful to call to account a tyrant, or wicked king, and after due conviction, to depose and put him to death." [2] Much more serious, however, than the general sympathy thus aroused in behalf of the royal cause was the violent opposition, specially intense in the army, to the continued domination of the Rump, which persistently refused to decree its own dissolution. While it had augmented its numbers somewhat by by-elections, it seemed impossible to compel it to formulate and actually put in force any scheme by which a new and genuine parliament could be elected upon the broad popular basis for which the army had contended from the beginning.[3] On the 17th of November, 1651, a bill for dissolution, though earnestly supported by Cromwell himself, was passed by a majority of only two votes, and even that result had to be purchased by the promise that the house should be permitted to sit for three years more.[4] Then when parliament neglected for a long time to prepare any plan for the new assembly, the army was compelled to force the discussion of " a New Representative " in a petition which demanded not only reform in church and state, but a

[sidenotes:] subjugation of Ireland and Scotland; the "Eikon Basiliké" answered by Milton's "Eikonoklastes;" Rump refused to dissolve itself; the bill passed for that purpose, November, 1651;

---

[1] See Mr. Doble's letters in *The Academy* for May 12, 26, June 9, 30, 1883, which may be accepted as final on that subject.

[2] His reply to the *Basiliké*, entitled *Eikonoklastes*, has been characterized as " barely more than a Miltonic piece of hack work."— Gardiner, *Commonw. and Protectorate*, vol. i. p. 195.

[3] On the 9th of January, 1650, a resolution was adopted that the elected members of future parliaments should number four hundred.

[4] Until November 3, 1654.

positive declaration that the house should bring its labors to a close. When Vane, relying upon the effect of a brilliant victory[1] won by the fleet,[2] to whose organization he had greatly contributed, finally contended that the existing members should not only retain their places, but should act as a committee of revision to pass upon the validity of each election and the fitness of the new members to be chosen, Cromwell resolved to end the discussion by the power of the sword. Therefore, on the 20th of April, 1653, he called in a file of soldiers, and after clearing the chamber he took the mace from the table and then closed and locked the doors. That afternoon he also dissolved the council of state, upon the ground that as the parliament was dissolved, its creature had died with it. Then it was that Bradshaw, president of the council, declared: "But, Sir, you are mistaken to think that the parliament is dissolved. No power under heaven can dissolve them but themselves. Therefore take you notice of that."[3] Thus with the dispersion of what remained of the Long Parliament ended the first attempt made by the army to establish in England a sovereign republic, based upon the theory that the supreme powers of the state were vested in an assembly which in no sense represented the popular will.

3. Having thus torn away the veil by which the power of the sword had been for a time concealed, the military party under the direction of Cromwell, "as captain-general and commander-in-chief of all the armies and forces raised and to be raised within the commonwealth," proceeded to construct a purely military dictatorship, whose executive organ was a self-appointed council of state composed of eight officers of high rank and four civilians, which, with Cromwell at its head, was intended to be symbolic of Christ and his twelve apostles.[4] In order to establish the reign of the saints thus begun upon a parliamentary basis, Cromwell resolved to issue writs in his own name, as "Captain-General," to a hundred and thirty-nine persons chosen on account of the holiness of their lives from

Marginal notes:
Cromwell finally dissolved both the Rump and its council by the sword, April 20, 1653;

Bradshaw's declaration.

The military dictatorship organized by Cromwell "as captain-general,"

who issued writs as such to persons designated by the congregational churches;

---

[1] Blake's victory over Tromp in February, 1653.

[2] This arm of the service was specially devoted to the house, by which the admirals were appointed. See Guizot's *Cromwell*, p. 220.

[3] Cf. Whitelock, p. 554; Ludlow, vol. ii. pp. 19, 23; Leicester's *Journal*, p. 139; Hutchinson, p. 332; *Old Parl. Hist.*, vol. xx. p. 128; Heath's *Chronicle*, p. 628.

[4] *Cromwell's Letters and Speeches*, vol. ii. p. 386; *Old Parl. Hist.*, vol. xx. p. 151.

lists furnished by the congregational churches.   On the 6th of June the writs went out to the chosen, commanding them to meet at Westminster "upon the fourth of July next ensuing the date hereof ; then and there to take upon you the said trust, unto which you are hereby called, and appointed to serve as a member for the county of ———.   And hereof you are not to fail."[1]   Into the hands of this convention, which was intended to act as a constituent assembly, whose authority was to be transferred in fifteen months to another to be elected under its mandate, the provisional councillors of state, with Cromwell at their head, resigned their self-imposed trust in acknowledgment of its supreme authority.   This "Barebones Parliament," so called in derision after a leather-merchant who happened to be a member, after naming a new council, at once boldly undertook the whole work of constitutional reform demanded by church and state.   Specially notable among the commendable yet abortive schemes then proposed are those which were intended to improve the financial administration through an equalization of taxation and the practice of rigid economy, to simplify both the civil and criminal law through the substitution of a single code for the mass of statutes, customs, and precedents that composed the law of the country, — a work which had been undertaken by a committee of the Long Parliament with Sir Matthew Hale at its head, — and to suppress entirely the court of chancery, in which twenty-three thousand cases were then waiting to be heard.[2]   The alarm thus excited among the lawyer class by what they considered a blind and iconoclastic attempt to destroy the law of the land extended itself to the landed proprietors and the clergy when proposals were made to destroy lay patronage, to establish civil marriage, and to abolish tithes through the substitution of voluntary congregational contributions.   At the moment when it was thought that the convention had actually voted

the constituent assembly thus constituted

known as the "Barebones Parliament;"

its abortive attempt at reform

alarmed all classes;

---

[1] *Cromwell's Letters and Speeches,* vol. ii. pp. 386, 387; Guizot's *Cromwell,* p. 219 and note 1; *Commons' Journals,* vol. vii. p. 282; Whitelock, p. 557.

[2] "These measures were prepared by two committees, one of members of parliament, of whom Oliver Cromwell is first named, and the other of persons not in parliament, of whom Matthew Hale, afterwards lord chief justice, is first named.   They are of the highest interest, and have never been noticed as they deserve." — Sir J. F. Stephen, *Hist. of the Crim. Law,* vol. ii. p. 208, citing Somers' *Tracts,* vol. vi. pp. 177–245.

the abolition of tithes, Cromwell himself, alarmed by the tendencies of men who thought of nothing, he said, but "to overturn, overturn," resolved to put an end to its existence, which

dissolved
December
12, 1653;

he accomplished through the adoption, on the 12th of December, of a motion, carried by his friends, "that the continuance
of this parliament, as now constituted, would not be for the
good of the Commonwealth ; and that, therefore, it was requisite that the house, in a body, should repair to the Lord General, to deliver back into his hands the powers which they had
received from him."[1] Four days later, after the members had
signed a formal act of abdication, a pompous cavalcade came
to Westminster, under the lead of Major-General Lambert,
who, in the name of the army and the three nations, prayed
the lord general to accept the office of Protector of the Com-

Cromwell
tendered
the office of
Protector
under a new
constitution
called the
" Instru-
ment of
Govern-
ment ; "

monwealth of England, Scotland, and Ireland. After Cromwell, with apparent reluctance, had announced his acceptance
of the offer, a new constitution, consisting of forty-two articles,
called the " Instrument of Government," was read, whereupon
the new chief of the state signed an oath " to take upon him
the protection and government of these nations, in the manner
expressed in the form of government hereunto annexed." Then

his instal-
lation ;

as a symbol of the change thus wrought, Lambert fell upon
his knees and offered a civic sword in the scabbard, which the
lord protector exchanged for his own as evidence of the fact
that he would thereafter rule by constitutional and not by
military means.[2]

the " Instru-
ment "
vested the
supreme
executive
power in a
protector
and council;

4. The scheme of government embodied in the "Instrument " undertook to impose a twofold limitation upon the
powers of the chief of state, whom it designated as lord protector. The supreme executive power was vested in him, acting
with the advice of a council of state whose members, though
originally appointed by him, were irremovable save by the consent of the rest. With the *advice* of the council the protector
could treat with foreign states, with its *consent* he could make
peace and war, while in it alone was vested the power to choose

---

[1] *Commons' Journals*, vol. vii. p.
363; Ludlow's *Memoirs*, pp. 199, 200;
Somers' *Tracts*, vol. vi. pp. 266–284;
Old Parl. Hist., vol. xx. pp. 239–244;
Whitelock, p. 570.

[2] A proclamation was then issued

with the ceremonies usual upon the
accession of a new monarch. Thurloe,
vol. i. pp. 632, 639, 641, 644; Whitelock, pp. 571–578; Foster's *Statesmen
of the Commonw.*, vol. v. pp. 223–228;
Old Parl. Hist., vol. xx. pp. 246–265.

all future protectors. The supreme legislative power was *the legis-* vested in the protector, and a parliament consisting of a single *lative in a protector* chamber to be composed of four hundred members from Eng- *and single chamber* land, thirty from Scotland, and thirty from Ireland, accord- *parliament,* ing to the plan formulated by Vane at the close of the Long Parliament, but which that body failed to enact into law. No statutes were to be passed nor taxes imposed without the con- sent of this assembly, and all of its enactments were to become law within twenty days even without the protector's consent, unless he could persuade the house of the reasonableness of his objections. It was not to be adjourned, prorogued, or dis- *to be* solved without its own consent within the first five months *assembled triennially;* after its meeting, and a new parliament was to be assembled *the fran-* every three years. Every person possessed of real or personal *chise regu-* property of the value of two hundred pounds had the right to *lated and religious* vote for members, and all were eligible as electors or as mem- *liberty* bers except malignants, delinquents, and Roman Catholics. *guaranteed;* Religious liberty was guaranteed to all Christians except pre- latists, papists, and those who taught licentiousness under the name of religion. As the new chamber thus provided for was not to meet until the 3d of the following September, the protector was authorized in the mean time to raise all money necessary for the public service, and to make ordinances, which *the pro-* should have the force of law until the subjects embraced in *tector's ordaining* them could be provided for by parliamentary enactments. *power;* Under this provision, which gave to the protector a wide scope for the exercise of his administrative genius, he issued before the parliament met sixty-four ordinances, which embraced all *sixty-four* the more important questions then pressing for solution in *ordinances issued.* church and state.

Few assemblies had ever met in England more truly repre- *The parlia-* sentative, or more justly entitled to the name of a "free par- *ment of 1654, in* liament," than the one-chamber body which gathered, in *which* September, 1654, under the mandate of the "Instrument" *represent-* that brought together for the first time representatives from *the three* England, Scotland, and Ireland in the form in which they sit *kingdoms* at the present day.[1] The difficulty was that this parliament, *day;*

---

[1] "It was the first time, for fourteen years, that England had been called upon to elect a parliament, and the electoral system itself was altogether new." — Guizot's *Cromwell*, p. 264.

conscious of its real nature, undertook to revise the protector's acts and to subject his policy to its will. His reply to that affront was a declaration of fundamental principles[1] which were not to be made the subject of discussion; and in order to give effect to his announcement, a file of soldiers was placed at the door of the house with a parchment which all members were required to sign before admission, pledging themselves neither to combat those principles, nor "to alter the government as it is settled in a single person and a parliament."[2] When the conflict thus begun deepened through the determination of the house to revise not only the protector's ordinances but the provisions of the "Instrument" itself, Cromwell resolved to cut it short by a dissolution, declared after a reproachful address on the 22d of January, 1655.[3] Having thus repudiated the constitutional régime which he had sworn to uphold, the protector, menaced by a republican conspiracy and a royalist revolt, fell back upon the power of the sword, and in the hope of more perfectly securing order, he divided the country into twelve military governments, each under the command of a major-general, who was authorized to suppress tumults and insurrections, to collect taxes imposed by the protector's sole authority, to disarm all papists and cavaliers, to inquire into the conduct of schoolmasters and ministers, and to arrest, imprison, or bind over all suspected persons.[4] The ejected clergy, who had been conspicuous in the insurrection, were prohibited from acting as tutors or chaplains, and the press was put under a stricter censorship.

While Cromwell thus subjected the realm to the rule of the major-generals, he pressed on his ambitious foreign policy, which required the organization of fleets whose equipment exhausted the treasury. As his right to collect the ordinary revenue had already been resisted in the courts of law upon the ground that the parliamentary grants had expired,[5] he

(margin notes:) subjected to military coercion;

dissolved in January, 1655;

the major-generals and their powers;

press censorship.

A new parliament met September 17, 1656;

---

[1] Printed by G. Sawbridge, 1654.

[2] *Commons' Journals*, vol. vii. p. 365; Thurloe, vol. ii. p. 606; Whitelock, p. 605; *Old Parl. Hist.*, vol. xx. pp. 370, 371.

[3] *Cromwell's Letters and Speeches*, vol. iii. pp. 89–119; Whitelock, pp. 610–618; *Old Parl. Hist.*, vol. xx. pp. 403–431; Godwin's *Hist. of the Commonw.*, vol. iv. pp. 153–157.

[4] Thurloe, vol. iii. p. 486; Ludlow, p. 559; *Old Parl. Hist.*, vol. xx. p. 433.

[5] Sir Peter Wentworth had refused to pay the assessment in the country, and Coney, a merchant, the duties on imports in London. When the aggrieved persons sued the collectors who had distrained their goods, Cromwell suppressed the proceedings

consented, with the advice of the council, to call a new assembly, which met on the 17th of September, 1657. Forewarned by the antipathy manifested to his government in the elections, the protector resolved to exclude from the new parliament at the outset all who were likely to oppose him. The returns were therefore laid before the council, which, with the aid of reports as to the elected made by the major-generals, prepared a list of the acceptable, to each one of whom was given a certificate that alone could secure admission from the military guard stationed at the door of the house.[1] While this body, from which Cromwell's enemies had been carefully excluded upon the pretext of immorality or delinquency, cheerfully provided for the security of his person and made liberal grants for the support of his war policy, it was so firm in its opposition to the rule of the major-generals that when a bill, introduced for the support of the militia, attempted to invest them with legal authority for the future, it was rejected, thus forcing the protector in obedience to the national will to withdraw their powers.[2] At this juncture it was that the conservative element in the house, which was thus striving to reëstablish the rule of law, gave their influence to a proposal to offer to Cromwell the title of king, in the belief, perhaps, that the prerogative as limited and defined by law was less dangerous to public liberty than the novel powers of a protector, which were unrestrained either by habit or tradition. With that end in view, a new scheme of government was finally adopted by the house on the 25th of March, 1657, that proposed to give to the protector the title of king, provided he would accept it coupled with the new conditions of government which the instrument embodied.[3] There can be but little doubt that Cromwell would have accepted the offer as a whole, had he not been deterred at the critical moment by a protest from the leading officers of the army, who also petitioned parliament

Marginal notes: returns laid before the council, which excluded all who were unacceptable; powers of the major-generals withdrawn; new scheme of government adopted in March, 1657, giving the protector the title of king,

by imprisoning the counsel and intimidating the clients. Rolle, the chief justice, continued the cases when called, and then resigned. Ludlow, vol. ii. pp. 80–82; Carte's *Letters*, vol. ii. pp. 96, 103, 109; Clarendon, *Hist.*, vol. iii. p. 649.

[1] *Old Parl. Hist.*, vol. xxi. p. 24; *Cromwell's Letters and Speeches*, vol.

iii. pp. 240, 241; Thurloe, vol. v. pp. 269, 317, 328.

[2] *Commons' Journals*, January 7, 8, 12, 19, 20, 21, 28, 29; Burton's *Diary*, pp. 310–320.

[3] It was adopted under the amended title of the "Humble Petition and Advice." *Commons' Journals*, vol. vii. pp. 496–514; Thurloe, vol. vi. pp. 74, 78; Whitelock, pp. 665, 666.

to withdraw the offer of the crown which had been made. Thus alarmed by the disaffection of the only power upon which he could really rely, the protector rescued himself from his perilous position by the declaration — "I cannot undertake this government with that title of king, and this is mine answer to this great and weighty business." [1]   The obnoxious title was then expunged from the "humble petition and advice," and after a few more amendments the new scheme became law on the 25th of May, and on the 26th of June a second inauguration of the protector took place in Westminster Hall, during which the speaker, in the name of the commons, invested him with a mantle of state, placed a gold sceptre in his hand, and girt the sword of justice by his side.   After the ceremony the commons adjourned to the 20th of the following January, so that opportunity might be given for the formation of the "other house," for whose creation careful provision had been made. [2]

which was rejected;

new scheme as amended became law May 25;

commons adjourned pending formation of the "other house."

The "act of government" vested the supreme powers in a protector and a two chamber parliament;

5. While the new constitution, which Cromwell himself styled "an act of government," [3] withheld from him the title of king, it indicated an unmistakable purpose to return to the monarchical system [4] by providing for the creation of an upper house, whose members were to be nominated by the protector with the approval of the popular chamber in the first instance, and afterwards with that of the upper house itself.   From the new lords thus to be created the right of voting by proxy was taken, and their judicial powers were materially curtailed. On the other hand, the constitution of the house of commons was strengthened by a restoration of its right to pass upon the qualifications of its members, and by the declaration that no money was to be raised in the future without its consent. The supreme power was still to remain in the protector, who was authorized to name his own successor; but after that event the office was to continue as an elective one.   Restrictions were also imposed upon the protector's right to appoint the members of the council, the great officers of state, and the

protector authorized to name his successor;

---

[1] *Cromwell's Letters and Speeches,* vol. iii. pp. 367, 370; Ludlow, p. 250.

[2] *Commons' Journals,* vol. vii. pp. 577, 578; Whitelock, pp. 662–664; *Old Parl. Hist.,* vol. xxi. pp. 148, 152–159.

[3] *Letters and Speeches,* vol. iii. pp. 367, 370.

[4] "Every constitutional change made by him drew England back to the old forms, and indicated the way which ultimately led to the Restoration." — *Introd. to English Hist.,* Gardiner and Mullinger, p. 150.

chiefs of the army. A fixed revenue was, however, settled upon him, and a liberal sum provided for the maintenance of war and naval forces. While uniformity was to be restored through a confession of faith to be agreed upon between the protector and the new parliament, those who saw fit to reject it were to be secured liberty both of conscience and of worship, unless they rejected the mystery of the trinity, or the inspiration of the Scriptures, or professed prelatic, popish, or blasphemous doctrines. Thus at the height of his power Cromwell pressed on in his career of military glory, entailing upon the treasury as a necessary consequence demands for which only a new parliament could provide. In order to comply with the terms of the new constitution, he issued in De- cember, 1657, writs copied from those formerly used by the sovereign to sixty-two persons, who were to compose the upper house as hereditary peers, subject to certain limitations contained in the " petition and advice." [1] As the ancient peerage shrank from the new dignity, the writs had to be directed to lawyers and officials, to a few dangerous opponents, and to certain gentlemen of fortune who had risen to position through recent events. In order to emphasize the fact that the old parliamentary system was to be revived, the protector met the collective body in the upper chamber on the 20th of January, 1658, where he began his speech with the ancient address : " My lords and gentlemen of the house of commons." [2] The new legislature thus carefully built up was destined, however, soon to suffer the fate already imposed by Cromwell upon three of its predecessors. The moment that a conflict arose out of the contention of the lower house that the new upper chamber had simply judicial and not legislative powers, the protector, who was moved to " rage and passion like unto madness " by this attempt to prevent a return to the older forms of English political life, threw himself into a coach, and with a few guards at his back drove to Westminster, where, on the 4th of February, he pronounced an angry address in which he said, " I think it high time that an end be put to your sitting ; and I do dissolve this parliament ; and let God judge between

---

[1] Thurloe, vol. vi. p. 752. These writs neither granted nor denied an hereditary character to the new peerage.

[2] For a full account, see *Commons' Journals*, vol. vii. pp. 578–587 ; Cromwell's *Letters and Speeches*, vol. iii. pp. 392–399.

me and you." [1]   And yet, in spite of the feverish impatience
which now began to possess him as the result of disease, fortune did not forsake him.   The overthrow of the reactionary
body which he drove out only strengthened his hold on the
army, whose triumph in Flanders, as a part of the allied forces
capitulation of Dunkirk in June; of France and England, was crowned in June by the capitulation and cession of Dunkirk.   But in the midst of all his glory
the fever crept steadily on, until death set its signet seal upon
his face as a sign to those around him that his hour had come.
Cromwell died September 3; On the 3d of September, the great day that had witnessed his
victories at Worcester and Dunbar, he breathed his last, leav-
ing to posterity a mighty name, which has never ceased to be
the subject of blind adulation, on the one hand, and of pas-
conflicting estimates of his character; sionate execration, on the other.   While Thurloe, in announcing his death to the deputy of Ireland, declared, "He is gone
to heaven, embalmed with the tears of his people, and upon
the wings of the prayers of the saints," [2] not "the mourners,"
but dancers "went about the streets" when the news reached
Amsterdam, and "the language at every turn" was, "The Devil
is dead." [3]   In our own time, a great hero-worshipper has attempted to make him tell his own story through a careful collection of extracts from his "Letters and Speeches," which a
consummate critic has declared to be "an invaluable store of
documents, edited with the care of an antiquarian and the
genius of a poet." [4]   As a counterblast to that effort to create
a new conception of Cromwell out of documentary evidence
that could not be questioned, a notable literary man, after great
research, has recently published a book in which he avers that
such evidence has been deliberately garbled and perverted in
order to clothe the Puritan hero in a false glory.   "Carlyle,"
he says, "sought to obscure the 'shot-rubbish' of the protectorate era with 'lurid twilight,' to enhance the whiteness of
his own 'amorphous' creation.   The showman blackened the
the nearest approach to a true portrait. background, to render the phosphorated face of his 'Brave
one' the more conspicuous." [5]   The nearest approach, perhaps,

[1] *Commons' Journals,* vol. vii. p. 592;
Thurloe, vol. vi. pp. 778, 781, 788.

[2] Ludlow, vol. ii. p. 153; Thurloe,
vol. vii. p. 373.

[3] Clarendon, *State Papers,* vol. iii. p.
412.

[4] Green's comment upon the work
of Carlyle in the *Hist. of the Eng. People,* vol. iii. p. 4.

[5] Sir Reginald F. D. Palgrave's *Oliver Cromwell, The Protector,* p. xviii.

to a true portrait has been made by the great historian of that epoch, who, after a calm, judicial review of all the facts, has concluded that Cromwell was "no divinely inspired hero, indeed, or faultless monster, but a brave, honorable man, striving, according to his lights, to lead his countrymen into the paths of peace and godliness." [1]

6. So safely did the fabric of Cromwell's power pass through the ordeal of his death that the council was able to proclaim the peaceful succession of his son Richard, despite the grave doubt that existed as to the fact of his nomination.   A mere verbal statement that he had been designated by his father as his successor a short time before the end [2] was accepted as sufficient, and to the surprise of all the new protector, who was supported neither by personal merit nor public services, promptly summoned a parliament, the popular branch of which was constituted on the old plan, thus reviving the representation of many boroughs disfranchised by the scheme of reform recently employed on several occasions.   In the new assembly that met on the 27th of January, 1659, a strong party that favored the continued existence of the protectorate was at once confronted by a fierce and resolute republican opposition, supported by secret royalists, who, under the leadership of Vane, not only denounced Cromwell's political system, but also the army, which they said had not only "conquered Scotland and Ireland, but rebellious England, too ; and there suppressed a malignant party of magistrates and laws." [3]   Angered by that assault, the army, with Richard's consent, at once established a permanent council of general officers, whose demonstrations were so menacing that the house demanded a cessation of their meetings and a dismissal of all who refused to promise in writing neither to disturb the sittings nor to infringe the freedom of parliament.   Thus in a new form was revived the old struggle between the army and the houses, and Richard, who was forced to choose between them, cast his lot with the former, and at the bidding of the officers dissolved the parliament on the 22d of April. [4]   With that event the authority of the new

Richard Cromwell, protector:

called a new parliament, which

met January 27, 1659;

republicans and royalists combine for his overthrow;

a fresh conflict between the army and the houses; latter dissolved April 22;

---

[1] Gardiner, *Hist. of the Great Civil War,* vol. i. p. x.
[2] Thurloe, vol. vii. p. 372.   See also Ibid., pp. 364, 365.
[3] The declaration of Cooper.

[4] Thurloe, pp. 555, 557, 662 ; Burton's *Diary,* vol. iv. pp. 448–463 ; Whitelock, p. 677 ; Ludlow, vol. ii. pp. 174, 176, 178.

protector really came to an end, and the supreme power again passed to the military chiefs who, in the hope of composing the country, then in a state of anarchy, agreed with the republicans that the protectorate should be set aside in favor of the remnant of the Long Parliament, which had been expelled from St. Stephen's on the 20th of April, 1653.

protecto-rate set aside.

7. On that memorable occasion Bradshaw had warned Cromwell that "no power under heaven can dissolve them but themselves,"[1] and upon that theory forty-two members of the Rump, with Lenthall, the former speaker, at their head, returned to the house on the 7th of May, 1659, to there resume, at the invitation of the army, the direction of affairs which the same power five years before had forcibly taken from their hands.[2] From the republican body thus reconstituted were carefully excluded those members, at once royalist and presbyterian, of whom the house had been purged by Colonel Pride on the 6th of December, 1648.[3] The new coalition thus formed for the defence of republicanism and civil liberty endured, however, only for a moment. Dissensions at once arose out of demands made by the army which the parliament regarded as unbearable, and thus began a new conflict, that culminated on October 13 in a fresh expulsion of the Rump by the officers, who undertook to secure the public peace, and to prepare a new form of government for submission to a new parliament. At this point it was that the army finally divided against itself. The troops in Scotland and Ireland protested against the action of their brethren in England, and General Monk, the commander of the Scottish forces, the moment that he heard of the expulsion of the members, openly appeared as their patron, under the title of "asserter of the ancient laws and liberties of the country." Although Lambert was sent to oppose him, the tide of opposition to the acts of the English army rose so high that before the end of December it was forced to reinstate the Rump in all its former authority.[4] Early in January, 1660, Monk crossed the border, and marched first to York and

Rump returned to power May 7, 1659;

without the members excluded by Colonel Pride December 6, 1648;

Rump expelled in October;

a division in the army;

General Monk, who commanded the Scottish forces,

crossed the border January, 1660;

[1] See above, p. 346.

[2] Ludlow, vol. ii. pp. 179–186; Whitelock, p. 677. By gradual additions the house at last numbered seventy members.

[3] "Of these, one hundred and ninety-four were still alive, eighty of whom actually resided in the capital." — Lingard, vol. viii. p. 573.

[4] *Commons' Journals*, December 26; Ludlow, vol. ii. pp. 268, 276, 282, 290; Whitelock, pp. 689, 690, 691.

IV.] *THE COMMONWEALTH AND PROTECTORATE.*

then to London, where on the 21st of February he agreed to admit the royalist presbyterian members who had been excluded from the house in 1648, upon their promise to settle the arrears of the army, to issue writs for a new parliament to sit at an early day, and to dissolve themselves before that time.[1] Under the terms of that compact a bill was read for the third time on the 16th of March, dissolving "the parliament assembled on the 3d of November, 1640," and convening at the same time a new assembly to be composed of lords, knights, citizens, and burgesses, which was to meet on the 25th of April.   Before its dissolution, however, the Rump had appointed Monk, who was secretly arranging for the return of the king, commander-in-chief of the forces of the three kingdoms, and commander of the fleet jointly with Admiral Montague.   At the appointed time the Convention Parliament, so designated by reason of the fact that it was called without the king's writ, met ; and after the organization of the lower house with the presbyterians in the majority, and with the presence in the upper of the greater part of the peerage,[2] the scheme of restoration was laid bare by the presentation to the two houses of letters directed to them from Breda by the king, who briefly set forth therein the conditions under which he was willing to ascend the throne of his ancestors.   Upon the faith of that declaration,[3] which was accepted as a royal charter, the houses, after declaring that "the government is, and ought to be, by king, lords, and commons," invited Charles to return and continue his reign, which was proclaimed as having commenced from the day of his father's execution.[4]

excluded members admitted;

Long Parliament finally dissolved and the

Convention Parliament met April 25,

and settled the restoration of Charles II.

---

[1] *Commons' Journals*, February 11, 13, 15, 17, 21 ; Price, pp. 768–773 ; Lingard, vol. viii. p. 604.

[2] The peers who sat in the king's parliament at Oxford and those whose patents bore date after the beginning of the civil war did not demand admission for the moment.

[3] *Lords' Journals*, vol. xi. pp. 7, 10.

[4] 1660 is described in the Statute-Book as the twelfth of the reign.

BOOK VI.

THE RESTORATION AND THE REVOLUTION OF 1688.

CHAPTER I.

CHARLES II. AND THE RESTORED CONSTITUTION.

Consti-
tution
restored as
modified
during
first ten
months of
Long Par-
liament;

1. WHEN Cromwell at the height of his power attempted through the "Act of Government"[1] to return as far as possible to the forms of the monarchical system, he clearly manifested his belief in the necessity of restoring the ancient constitution as modified and purified in the crucible of revolution. Animated by the same conservative spirit, the Convention Parliament entered upon its work firmly resolved to restore "government . . . by king, lords, and commons," subject to all the limitations imposed upon the crown by the Long Parliament during the first ten months preceding the recess in which its members were able to strike as one man against abuses that pressed alike upon all. Thus it was that that part of the work of the Long Parliament which embraced the abolition of the star chamber and high commission, the vital declaration that the entire taxing power of the nation was vested exclusively in the king in parliament, and the Triennial Act, minus its compulsory clauses, survived as a part of the permanent constitution of the country,[2] — it being at the same time understood that the commonwealth legislation should be

common-
wealth
legislation
treated as
void;

treated as void, excepting only such parts as were confirmed by express enactments.[3] The presbyterian element dominant in the lower house,[4] which had been elected under ordinances

---

[1] See above, p. 352.
[2] See above, p. 308.
[3] Cf. Sir J. F. Stephen, *Hist. of the Crim. Law*, vol. ii. p. 466.
[4] They put one of their number, Sir

H. Grimstone, in the chair as speaker. The cavaliers complained that this was done before they came into the house. See Mordaunt to Hyde, April 27, *Clarendon State Papers*, p. 734.

that withheld the franchise from royalist "malignants," [1] put forward this general basis of settlement no more persistently than the strong cavalier minority with which they were confronted.   Upon that basis both parties united in the invitation to Charles to return, while he upon his part bound himself in the declaration sent to the houses from Breda (1) to grant a free and general pardon to all, excepting only such as should afterwards be excepted by parliament ; (2) to indemnify the church and the royalists for injuries suffered in their estates ; (3) to make a satisfactory settlement with the army ; (4) and finally to secure "liberty to tender consciences, and that no man shall be disquieted or called in question for differences of opinion in matters of religion which do not disturb the peace of the kingdom." [2]   Before entering upon the task of giving to these guarantees the forms of law, the convention called into being by the Rump declared, while the bishops were still legally excluded from their places in the upper house, that the Long Parliament was dissolved, and that it was in fact "the two houses of parliament, notwithstanding the want of the king's writ of summons, and as if his majesty had been present in person at the commencement thereof," [3] — a declaration which the succeeding parliament indirectly discredited by always describing the convention in its journals as "the last assembly." [4]

Charles invited to return by both parties ;

his declaration from Breda ;

convention declared itself to be "the two houses of parliament."

In addition to the limited promise of pardon given to the regicides in the declaration from Breda, Charles immediately upon landing issued a proclamation, in which he held out inducements to such of his father's judges as should immediately surrender themselves.   After deducting twenty-five who had died and nineteen who had fled beyond sea,[5] twenty-nine finally remained in custody,[6] including those who had surrendered under the proclamation.   After a serious disagreement between the houses the fugitives were attainted, and a bill of indemnity was passed in which was embodied a compromise

Fate of the regicides ;

Bill of Indemnity ;

---

[1] Cf. Green, *Hist. of the Eng. People*, vol. iii. p. 351.
[2] *Lords' Journals*, vol. xi. pp. 7, 10.
[3] 12 Car. II. c. 1.
[4] Hallam, *Const. Hist.*, vol. ii. p. 323, note 2.   The royalist lawyers claimed that as this parliament had been called without the king's writ, its acts could never have any validity until confirmed by a genuine parliament.   Cf. *Life of Clarendon*, p. 74.
[5] For the history of Whaley, Goff, and Dixwell, who fled to New England, see Hutchinson's *Hist. of Massachusetts Bay*.
[6] Lingard, vol. ix. pp. 12, 13.

conceding to the crown the right to try, despite the proclamation, those who had voluntarily surrendered, subject to the proviso that no one of them should be executed without a subsequent act of parliament passed for that purpose.[1]   After trial[2] before a special court composed of thirty-four commissioners, ten of the regicides were immediately executed, and two years afterwards three more, who were surrendered by Holland.[3] Unappeased by vengeance thus taken upon the living, the royalists were permitted by an order of the houses approved by the king to tear the bodies of Cromwell, Bradshaw, and Ireton from their graves, and to draw them on hurdles to Tyburn, on the anniversary of the death of Charles I.[4]   The bill of indemnity which went so far in the attempt to satisfy the passions of those who had suffered in the king's cause did nothing, however, to compensate them for the pecuniary sacrifices which they had made in his behalf.   Parliament refused either to vote a direct moneyed compensation, or to annul such sales as the royalists had voluntarily made.[5]   The only redress actually received was through forcible entries made by the church, the crown, and the dispossessed royalists, upon such of their estates as were held by purchasers[6] who derived their titles under revolutionary proceedings, which were treated as void.

By the making of successive grants the arrears of the army were settled and a large and dangerous body of men disbanded without mutiny or disturbance ; and in a short time after the dissolution of this republican force the militia was reorganized under statutes which placed it more than ever before under the control of the country gentry and rich municipal landowners.[7]

The presbyterians and independents, who in the days of the commonwealth had taken possession of nearly all of the livings

marginal notes:
trial by a special court;

failure to compensate royalists for pecuniary sacrifices ;

their forcible reëntries.

Disbandment of standing army;

reorganization of militia.

[1] 12 Car. II. c. 11 ; Clarendon, *Continuation of Life*, p. 69.

[2] *State Trials*, pp. 947–1364.   See comments upon these trials in Sir J. F. Stephen's *Hist. of the Crim. Law*, vol. i. pp. 370–372.

[3] Corbet, Okey, and Berkstead, thus surrendered, suffered in April, 1662, under the act of attainder.   Ludlow, vol. iii. p. 82; *State Trials*, vol. v. pp. 1301–1335.

[4] *Lords' Journals*, vol. xi. p. 205; Kennet's *Reg.*, p. 367.

[5] For that reason the cavaliers called the bill of indemnity an act for the indemnity of the king's enemies, and of oblivion for his friends.

[6] When they pleaded that they were *bona fide*, the answer was, " You have taken the risk with the benefit."

[7] 13 Car. II. c. 6; 13 & 14 Car. II. c. 3; 15 Car. II. c. 4.

in the reorganized nation church, from which they banished Exclusion of common-wealth clergy from church livings; both the bishops and the prayer-book, were able to derive but little practical consolation from the king's promise to secure "liberty to tender consciences." Immediately after the land-ing of Charles on May 26 the nine surviving bishops returned restoration and election of bishops; to their sees without the aid of legislation, and in a short time the eighteen vacant sees in England and Wales were filled up in the usual way.[1] Not, however, until the next year was the act repealed which prevented the bishops from taking their places in the house of lords.[2] In order to protect the com-monwealth clergy, many of whom had not received episcopal consecration, from attack from the bishops who were thus set over them, Charles attempted to bring about a theological compromise which would enable all to live together in unity within the pale of the state church. While he was not able to secure for the presbyterians the liberal terms embodied in Bishop Usher's model, the only legislation enacted against them by the convention was embodied in an " Act for the " Act for the confirming and restoring of ministers." confirming and restoring of ministers,"[3] a moderate measure mainly for the benefit of the ejected clergy still alive, which was a mere foretaste of the radical policy of wholesale expul-sion soon to be embodied in the new Act of Uniformity.

Among the many delicate and difficult problems which thus Reorgani-zation of the finances: pressed upon parliament for prompt solution no one was more urgent than that which demanded the reorganization of the national finances upon a new basis. As a starting-point the fact was settled that at least £1,200,000 per annum were "necessary to support the king's crown and dignity," that is to say, the crown's ordinary expenses.[4] After appropriating to that object the customs duties,[5] a successful attempt was made to substitute a new source of income in lieu of the sums the crown had so long received as a part of its ordinary revenue from the incidents of feudal tenures, an obnoxious form of incidents of feudal tenures abolished; taxation, which ceased to be enforced during the civil war after the extinction of the court of wards and liveries, which sat for the last time February 24, 1645. In order to prevent

---

[1] Blount, *Reform. of the Church of Eng.*, vol. ii. p. 554.

[2] The "Disabling Act" of 1642 was repealed by 13 Car. II. c. 2.

[3] 12 Car. II. c. 17.

[4] It was admitted that £900,000, the usual revenue in the time of Charles I., was inadequate.

[5] For a full exposition, see Dowell, *Hist. of Taxation*, vol. ii. pp. 15–37.

a revival of that institution an act [1] was passed which abolished the entire obsolete system of military tenures, together with the court in which they were enforced. It was expressly declared that all kinds of tenures held of the king or others be converted into free and common socage, excepting only those in frankalmoign, copyholds, and the honorary services of grand serjeanty.[2] And while the landed gentry were thus relieved of a burden peculiar to themselves, the nation as a whole was freed from the royal rights of purveyance and preëmption. As a compensation for this surrender, it was agreed that £100,000 a year should be settled upon the crown, and that sum was raised by the grant of an hereditary excise upon beer, ale, and other liquors, a form of taxation which had been imported into England in the days of the commonwealth.[3] A supplement was then granted in the form of a temporary excise for life,[4] and in addition to that a new tax, of a French origin, was granted in 1662 known as hearth-money or chimney-money,[5] which, after exciting great resistance, was repealed immediately after the accession of William and Mary. In order to raise sums for extraordinary purposes resort was had during the reign to poll taxes, to the old Tudor subsidy, and to the monthly assessments first employed by the commonwealth. In 1663 four subsidies were granted by the temporality and four by the clergy, which, after being confirmed in the ancient form, produced only £282,000. It was then admitted that the subsidy as a form of taxation was obsolete, and it was never again employed.[6] One important result of its discontinuance was that when the assessment system which took its place was applied to the church, it was agreed between the lord chancellor and the archbishop in 1664 that the clergy should be taxed like the rest of the nation, and as a natural consequence the right of suffrage in parliamentary elections was conceded to them by reason of their freehold tenures.[7]

with a few exceptions all tenures converted into free and common socage;

an hereditary excise;

imposition of hearth-money;

old Tudor subsidy abandoned;

new assessment system applied to both clergy and laity;

---

[1] 12 Car. II. c. 24. See Digby, *Law of Real Property*, pp. 394–398.

[2] The duke of Marlborough holds Woodstock by that tenure (see *Woodstock Manor*, by Rev. E. Marshall, M. A.); and the duke of Wellington, the Strathfieldsaye estate in the same way (see Burke's *Peerage*, s. v. *Wellington*).

[3] First imposed by the Long Parliament in 1643. See above, p. 324.

[4] 12 Car. II. c. 23. This was a duplicate of the hereditary excise granted by 12 Car. II. c. 24.

[5] 13 & 14 Car. II. c. 10. When formed this tax finally produced £170,000 a year.

[6] Dowell, *Hist. of Taxation*, vol. ii. pp. 29, 30.

[7] See vol. i. pp. 481, 482.

Thus while it may be true that the commonwealth failed to bequeath a single permanent organic law to posterity, the fact must not be lost sight of that its legislation worked a revolution in the methods of English taxation.

one effect of common-wealth legislation.

While the question still remained unsettled whether the presbyterians, who had taken the chief part in the restoration, and who were in almost exclusive control of the magistracy as well as of local government in the shires and towns, or the royalists, who stood closest to the king, were to control in the new settlement of the nation, Charles so organized his first ministry as to divide the great offices of state between the chiefs of the two factions, whose influence was nearly equal in the popular branch of the convention. Thus as leaders of the royalist faction Edward Hyde, who had clung to the king in his exile, soon became earl of Clarendon and lord chancellor, and Southampton lord treasurer, while the presbyterian interest was represented by Monk as lord-general, and by Sir Ashley Cooper, afterwards famous as the earl of Shaftesbury, as chancellor of the exchequer. As the chief of that group of constitutional royalists which in 1642 had broken with the Long Parliament under the lead of Falkland, Hyde, whose influence soon became supreme, promptly resolved to break through the system of balance and compromise imposed by the personal disposition of the king and the composition of parliament itself. With that end in view the convention was dissolved in December[1] and new elections ordered, which resulted in the return of a great royalist majority, confronted by a presbyterian opposition now reduced to not more than fifty members. Thus armed, Clarendon boldly entered upon the execution of his policy of reconstruction, which contemplated first the reëstablishment of the national church upon a basis that would enforce uniformity upon all who had escaped from its fold ; second, the restoration to the crown of all its prerogatives, except such as had been extinguished during the first session of the Long Parliament.

Struggle for suprem-acy between royalists and presby-terians ;

Charles' first minis-try com-posed of the leaders of both parties ;

convention dissolved and royalist majority returned ;

Clarendon's scheme of recon-struction.

2. Charles' second parliament, which met on the 8th of May, 1661, and which continued with long adjournments and prorogations for nearly eighteen years, opened its session with an order that every member should take the communion, and that

Charles' second parliament prolonged for nearly eighteen years ;

[1] *Life of Clarendon*, p. 76 ; *Parl. Hist.*, vol. iv. pp. 141, 152.

the Solemn League and Covenant should be burned by the common hangman at Westminster.[1] This condemnation of the creed of the presbyterians was promptly followed by a practical expedient for the suppression of the political influence of that party whose strongholds were the boroughs in which the corporation either actually returned the borough members, or at least exercised a powerful influence upon their *an act for* election. In order to break down that influence by driving *"regulating* presbyterians from municipal offices, an act was passed "for *corpora-* *tions;"* the well-governing and regulating of corporations,"[2] in which a religious test that compelled all office-holders and magistrates to take the sacrament according to the rites of the state church, and to renounce the League and Covenant, was supplemented by a political test that compelled them to subscribe to the royalist doctrine, then current, of non-resistance. But as both test and oath were soon accepted as a mere matter of form by those who regarded them as an insult to their consciences, Clarendon in the following year was prompted by his failure to devise a more drastic measure embodied in an *Act of Uni-* Act of Uniformity,[3] the fourth since the Reformation, which *formity,* *fourth since* proposed to drive from the state church all Puritan minis- *the Re-* ters who would not accept without reservation the whole of *formation;* the prayer-book, repudiate the Covenant and its principles, and submit before the feast of St. Bartholomew to episcopal ordination, in the event that the incumbent had not already received the same. A political test was then added, which required all clergymen to accept the doctrine of non-resistance together with a pledge not "to endeavour any change or alteration of government either in church or state." While Clarendon was driving on this radical measure, the king was striving to render it unnecessary by drawing together the leading di- *fruitless* vines of the two factions in what is known as the Savoy Con- *Savoy Con-* ference, whose deliberations, which began on the 15th of April *ference;* and ended on the 24th of July, were expected to provide a basis of compromise acceptable to both.[4] In May, while this hopeless and fruitless conference was still going on, the bill passed, and on the 24th of August, St. Bartholomew's Day, about two

[1] See *Commons' Journals* of May 17, 1661.
[2] 13 Car. II. st. 2, c. 1.
[3] 13 & 14 Car. II. c. 4.

[4] A clear and brief statement of the proceedings may be found in Blount, *Reform. of the Church of Eng.*, vol. ii. pp. 556–563.

thousand[1] rectors and vicars, at least one fifth of the clergy of the Church of England, were driven out as non-conformists. The religious result of the expulsion of this strong and aggressive element, which ever since the Reformation had been struggling to draw the English church into closer relations with the reformed churches of the Continent, was to end forever that effort, and to fix it in the position of isolation which has continued until the present day; the political result was to infuse new life and vigor into the dissident body outside of the establishment, which under the pressure of a common persecution soon became welded into a fighting force that finally extorted from their adversaries the Act of Toleration.[2] In the moment of his triumph, however, Clarendon, whose sole purpose was to crush by lawful means those who denied his right to make the state church the representative of the whole nation, was thwarted by Charles, who was equally intent upon so using churchmen against non-conformists as to secure toleration for the catholics, to whose belief he was a secret devotee. To promote that object the king, in the midst of the violence and persecution that followed the passage of the Act of Uniformity, issued in December, 1662, his first Declaration of Indulgence, in which he undertook to suspend its operation in favor of "those who living peaceably do not conform themselves thereto through scruple and tenderness of misguided conscience, but modestly and without scandal perform their devotions in their own way." The counterblast of parliament to this attempt to exercise the dispensing power, in a formula that applied to catholics as well as protestants, was an address which forced the king not only to withdraw the indulgence, but to issue a proclamation banishing all catholic priests from the realm.[3] The triumph which Clarendon, with parliament at his back, thus obtained over the king was emphasized by the passage, in 1664, of the Conventicle Act,[4] in which it was provided that every person over sixteen years of age present at a conventicle ("any meeting for religious worship at

expulsion of non-conformist clergy on St. Bartholomew's Day;

the result;

Charles' attempt to secure toleration for catholics;

first Declaration of Indulgence;

parliamentary protest against dispensing power;

Conventicle Act of 1664;

---

[1] Baxter in his *Autobiography*, p. 384, says from 1800 to 2000. See "An account of the ministers, etc., who were ejected or silenced after the Restoration in 1660, by, or before, the Act of Uniformity," by Edmund Calamy, 1713, forming vol. ii. of his *Abridgment of Baxter's Autobiography.*

[2] Green, *Hist. of the Eng. People*, vol. iii. pp. 361-364.

[3] Cf. *Parl. Hist.*, p. 517; Lingard, vol. ix. pp. 84-88.

[4] 16 Car. II. c. 4.

which five persons were present besides the household ") should be subject to three months' imprisonment for the first offence, to six for the second, and to seven years' transportation for the third, after conviction by a jury. In 1665 was passed what is known as the Five-Mile Act,[1] which provided in substance that no dissident minister should " come or be within " five miles of any town represented in parliament, or in any place where he had acted as minister, " unless only in passing upon the road," without swearing to the doctrine that it is not lawful upon any pretence whatever to take up arms against the king, and that the person swearing " will not at any time endeavor any alteration of government in church or state." Then in 1670 the hands of the peace officers were strengthened by the passage of an act [2] for the suppression of seditious conventicles, and thus the law for the repression of protestant dissenters stood down to the revolution of 1688.

Five-Mile Act of 1665;

seditious conventicle act of 1670.

The completeness of Clarendon's success in thwarting the religious policy of the king marked him out as an object of royal vengeance, and the opportunity for its exercise came at the moment when the pressure of taxation and defeat in the naval war with the Dutch deprived him of the support of parliament, the one power upon which he depended. Since the accession of Charles more money had been paid in taxes than in any preceding period of like duration, and yet so unsatisfactory had been its expenditure that in 1665, when a large sum was granted, a proviso was introduced into the act [3] that limited its disbursement to the prosecution of the war, — a form of appropriation which, first occurring in a positive form in 1353,[4] when a subsidy on wool was limited solely to the prosecution of the war then pending, had been last employed in 1624, when parliament granted a supply for the relief of the Palatinate, to be paid into the hands of commissioners of its own selection.[5] In the following year the growing distrust as to the honest expenditure of money appropriated for war purposes induced parliament to revive another ancient precedent, which sanctioned its right to audit public accounts.[6] In order to revive and invigorate that right, a bill was sent up nominating com-

Fall of Clarendon;

parliamentary appropriation of supplies revived;

right to audit public accounts also revived;

1 17 Car. II. c. 2.
2 22 Car. II. c. 1.
3 17 Car. II. c. 1.
4 Vol. i. p. 501.

5 See above, p. 250.
6 For the early history of the right, of audit, see vol. i. p. 502.

missioners, who were to be armed with full power to inspect all public accounts, and to report upon all who had broken their trusts.   Though delayed for one session, this bill was passed at the next,[1] and from that time the ancient rights of parlia- both abide as permanent principles; ment to limit its grants to particular purposes, and then to investigate the method of their expenditure, entered as princi- ples into the restored constitution which the Revolution made permanent.   But this important result was accomplished only in the teeth of violent opposition from Clarendon,[2] who went so far as to appeal to the king to defeat the passage of the bill authorizing the commission of audit by a dissolution, and to support the troops upon the coast by forced contributions to be repaid out of the next supply.   In the midst of the popular resignation and impeachment of Clarendon; excitement aroused against the chancellor by the suggestion of a plan which was said to contemplate the support of a stand- ing army, the king, only too happy to rid himself of a minister who stood as a check upon his policy, ordered him to give up the seals on the 30th of August, 1667 ; and six weeks later the house impeached him of high treason upon seventeen arti- cles, the first of which charged "that the earl of Clarendon the first article; hath designed a standing army to be raised, and to govern the kingdom thereby, and advised the king to dissolve this present parliament, to lay aside all thoughts of parliaments for the future, to govern by a military power, and to maintain the same by free quarters and contributions." [3]   Although the lords lords refused to commit upon a "general charge of treason." refused to commit the accused upon a " general charge " of treason, as in Strafford's case, Clarendon was compelled by a royal order to flee to the continent, and in his absence an act [4] was passed which decreed his banishment for life, provided he should fail to return for trial within a limited time.

The statement has heretofore been made that as the privy Origin and growth of cabinet government; council was gradually developed out of a larger body of which it was once the inner circle, so the inner circle of the privy council itself has been developed into the cabinet of modern times.[5]   The history of the council has already been drawn out

---

[1] 19 & 20 Car. II. c. 1.
[2] He resented this measure as a usurpation, and urged the king never to consent to it (*Life*, p. 368) ; and Burnet says (p. 335) that it was re- garded at the time as a great innova-

tion.   Cf. Hallam, *Const. Hist.*, vol. ii. pp. 358–360 ; vol. iii. p. 117.
[3] *State Trials*, vol. vi. p. 330 ; *Life of Clarendon*, pp. 445, 448, 450 ; *Com- mons' Journals*, November 6, 8, 11.
[4] 19 & 20 Car. II. c. 2.
[5] Vol. i. pp. 541–547.

organiza-tion of Tudor councils;

down to the end of the Tudor epoch, during which, as the great organ of state administration, it was subdivided into commit-tees or departments, at the head of each of which stood a minis-ter responsible primarily for the work specially committed to his charge, but not necessarily responsible for the general policy of the government as a whole.[1] In order to secure the prompt and secret dispatch of great affairs, it was certainly customary

inner circle in the days of Henry VII., Edward VI., and

for the Tudor sovereigns to give their confidence to a limited number of the council, to the exclusion of the rest. Bacon in his "Essays on Councils"[2] tells us that Henry VII., "in his greatest business, imparted himself to none, except it were to Morton and Fox," and we know that Edward VI.'s "com-mittee for the state" was an inner circle of the greater body, not much larger, perhaps, than a modern cabinet.[3] The system of "government by councils" as thus organized passed from the Tudors to the first two Stuarts with its organs and forms of proceeding unimpaired, and in 1640 there was certainly an

Charles I.;

inner circle of eight or nine councillors upon whom Charles I. specially relied. We learn from Clarendon that "these per-sons made up the committee of state (which was reproachfully

origin of the term "cabinet council;"

after called the *Juncto*, and enviously then in court the *Cabinet Council*), who were upon all occasions, when the secretaries received any extraordinary intelligence or were to make any extraordinary dispatch, or as often otherwise as was thought fit, to meet : whereas the body of the council observed set days and hours for their meeting, and came not else together except specially summoned."[4] Such was the condition of

council under pruning-knife of Long Par-liament;

things when the council passed under the pruning-knife of the Long Parliament,[5] whose drastic legislation completely changed its character by taking from it its two great judicial organs known as the star chamber and high commission, and by ex-tinguishing the survivals of its taxing power. The vital change

---

1 See above, p. 215.

2 He also says (XX.) that "The doc-trine of Italy and practice of France, in some kings' times, hath introduced Cabinet Councils — a remedy worse than the disease."

3 Dicey, *The Privy Council*, p. 135.

4 *Hist. Rebellion*, bk. ii. p. 226.

5 In the Grand Remonstrance pre-sented by the commons to Charles I. in 1641, he was told that only such councillors and ministers should be em-ployed as could obtain the confidence of parliament (Foster's *Grand Remon-strance*, pp. 272, 273) ; and in the sec-ond Remonstrance issued in January, 1642, complaint was made of "the managing of the great affairs of the realm in cabinet councils, by men un-known and not publicly trusted." — Clarendon's *Hist. Rebellion*, bk. iv. p. 537.

thus wrought in the constitution of the council constitutes the very essence of the Revolution of 1640, for thereby the whole system of absolutism embodied in the conciliar system was forced to give way to parliamentary government, and to the reign of ordinary law as administered in ordinary tribunals. In this mutilated form Charles II. revived the privy council at the restoration, and following in the footsteps of his predecessors, he continued the practice of selecting out of what was now a purely political and administrative body an inner group of special advisers. His reason for that course he gave in express terms in 1679, when he declared to the whole council that their meetings " might have been more frequent, if the great number of this council had not made it unfit for the secrecy and dispatch that are necessary in many great affairs. This forced him to use a smaller number of you in a foreign committee the [Cabal], and sometimes the advice of some few among them upon such occasions, for many years past." [1] There is positive evidence for the statement that in that way Charles upon his accession organized his first cabinet council, in which Clarendon soon became the dominant and guiding force.[2] Now that Clarendon had fallen, the king resolved to so reorganize the inner circle as to give the first place to Ashley Cooper, who as a representative of the presbyterian interest had stood in the first combination as the opponent of Clarendon's policy, which contemplated the harmonious union of crown, church, and parliament, in an uncompromising system of religious intolerance. As the initials of the names of Clifford, Arlington, Buckingham, Ashley, and Lauderdale, who now composed the inner group, happened to make up the word " Cabal," [3] that term for many years superseded the phrase, " Cabinet Council," which had appeared for the first time in the reign of Charles I. Nothing can better illustrate the impossibility of such a system of government than the utter lack of harmony which existed at this moment not only between the parliament and the Cabal, but between the Cabal itself and the king, who now came to

Marginal notes: essence of the Revolution of 1640; Charles II.'s reasons for employing inner circle of council; after Clarendon's fall first place in council given to Ashley Cooper; the Cabal; lack of harmony between Cabal, parliament, and king;

---

[1] Cf. Todd's *Parl. Govt. in Eng.*, vol. i. p. 226, citing Temple's *Memoirs*, vol. iii. p. 45 n.

[2] The secret committee consisted of Clarendon, Southampton, Ormond, Monk, and two secretaries of state, who "were appointed by the king to consult all his affairs before they came to a public debate." — Continuation of the *Life of Clarendon*, p. 27.

[3] Macaulay, vol. i. p. 104.

the front intent upon giving personal direction to public affairs. The parliament with its great cavalier majority was still wedded to Clarendon's policy of coercing by law all who refused to conform to the state church, while Ashley stood forth as the recognized leader of the growing non-conformist host battling for religious toleration. The king upon his part sympathized with neither, his primary purpose being to so play churchmen and non-conformists against each other as to pave the way for a return to catholicism, to which both his brother James and himself were secretly devoted. Only in the light of these conflicting motives is it possible to unravel the tangled threads of constitutional history, which, during the remainder of this reign, unite the public acts of council and parliament to

relations with France; the personal intrigues of the king, who hoped through a secret alliance with France to render both subservient to his will. The new ministry, which appeared to be presbyterian, intent upon curbing the growing power of that kingdom, menacing at once to the European balance and to English protestantism, sent Sir William Temple to the Hague at the beginning of 1668, to conclude a treaty between England, Holland, and Sweden; and that triple union of the three great protestant

Grand Alliance; powers paved the way for the Grand Alliance,[1] through which, under the masterful leadership of William of Orange, the original purpose was finally carried out. In January of the next year Charles summoned Arlington and Clifford, two members of the council whom he knew to be catholics at heart, to a conference with the duke of York and two others, of whom,

Charles secretly declared himself a catholic; after pledging them to secrecy and declaring himself a catholic, he asked advice as to the best means for the reëstablishment of that faith as the religion of the realm.[2] It was resolved that the only way in which such a result could be brought about was through the "protection" of Louis XIV., with

Treaty of Dover May, 1670; whom the famous secret Treaty of Dover was concluded in May, 1670,[3] under which Louis agreed to furnish both money

---

[1] Temple's *Works*, vol. i. pp. 312–384, 415.

[2] Macpherson, p. 50; Green, *Hist. of the Eng. People*, vol. iv. p. 394.

[3] The full text of this important treaty was kept secret until 1830, when Lord Clifford permitted Dr. Lingard to publish it for the first time from the original in his possession. See Note B. to vol. ix. of his *History of England*. The substance of the treaty had been actually brought to light fifty years before by Dalrymple (vol. ii. p. 80), who gave a rough draft drawn by Sir Richard Bealing for the French court. It is said that Louis XIV. him-

and men at the proper moment in exchange for Charles' promise that he would declare his conversion and bring England to the side of France in a war with the Dutch. In order to win the consent of Ashley and his protestant colleagues to an unpopular war with Holland, in violation of the Triple Alliance, Charles was forced to make them a promise of religious toleration, which was embodied in a second Declaration of Indulgence, issued upon the beginning of hostilities in March, 1672, in which, after claiming "supreme power in ecclesiastical matters," the king declared that "all manner of penal laws in matters ecclesiastical, against whatsoever sort of non-conformists or recusants, should be from that day suspended." A promise then followed that a certain number of conventicles would be licensed, with the express proviso, however, that the right of public worship was not to be enjoyed by catholics who should confine themselves to private houses.[1] In attempting thus to conciliate the Cabal, Charles so offended the parliament that immediately after its assembling in February, 1673, it not only declared that "penal statutes in matters ecclesiastical cannot be suspended but by an act of parliament,"[2] but the houses also refused to make a large grant of supply available, until the king should withdraw his recent proclamation. After a bitter controversy, during which Charles attempted to array one house against the other, he was not only forced to give way, but also to declare that "what had been done with respect to the suspension of the penal laws should never be drawn into consequence."[3] Unsatisfied with such a victory, the houses, full of suspicion and dread of a movement in favor of catholicism, proceeded to pass without opposition the famous Test Act,[4] "for preventing dangers which may happen from popish recusants," which provided that before any person could be admitted to the king's or duke of York's households, or into any other office or place of trust or profit, civil or mili-

second Declaration of Indulgence;

parliament again resisted exercise of the dispensing power;

Test Act, 1673;

---

self permitted the publication of the treaty by the Abbé Primi in a book that was immediately suppressed, extracts from which were published, however, in London, just after the French Revolution. Cf. Hallam, *Const. Hist.,* vol. ii. p. 382, note q. The first volume of Dalrymple's work, which drew largely from despatches preserved in

the "*Dépôt des Affaires Etrangers,*" at Versailles, was published in 1771 ; the second in 1773.

[1] *Parl. Hist.,* vol. iv. p. 515.
[2] *Commons' Journals,* February 10.
[3] As to the happy conclusion of the matter, see Dalrymple, vol. ii. pp. 93–96; *Lords' Journals,* vol. xii. p. 549.
[4] 25 Car. II. c. 2.

tary, he should take the oath of supremacy, subscribe a declaration against transubstantiation, and publicly receive the
disqualified sacrament according to the rites of the state church. This
protestant act, which likewise disqualified nearly every class of protestant
dissenters dissenters,[1] at once forced the duke of York to resign as lord
as well as
catholics; high admiral, Clifford as lord treasurer, together with hundreds
of other catholics in the civil and military service of the crown.
By this time Ashley, who had learned of the Treaty of Dover
and of the secret of the king's religion, resolved to be his dupe
no longer, and in the parliament which assembled in October
Ashley he united himself with the opponents of the court, now known
joined op- as the country party, and with them not only opposed the mar-
ponents of
court now riage of James with the catholic princess, Mary of Modena,
known as but also attempted to bring about an end of the war by a
the country
party; parliamentary declaration that no further supplies would be
granted until guarantees, in addition to those contained in the
Test Act, should be given against the influence of catholic
councillors.   In order to put an end to such demonstrations,
Charles, on the 4th of November, suddenly prorogued the
ordered to houses, and five days thereafter the chancellor was ordered to
give up
the seals. give up the seals as the penalty of his desertion.[2]

Shaftesbury When the bold, the versatile, the self-reliant Shaftesbury[3]
becomes
the leader retired from the service of the crown, he openly avowed him-
of the coun- self an adversary of the court and a champion of the liberties
try party;
of the people, and as such he at once put himself at the head
of the country party, a political organization which had been
formed a short time before by Lord Russell, Lord Cavendish,
and Sir William Coventry as a means of resisting the political
its objects; and religious designs of the king, and for advancing at the
same time the cause of religious toleration.[4]   So strong did
this organization become under the leadership of its new chief,
address who fanned into flame the growing belief of the nation that
presented
upon the high offices of state were in the hands of men catholic at
meeting of heart, that upon the reassembling of the houses in January,
parliament
in January, 1674, they proceeded to vote the removal of all ministers
1674;

---

[1] By compelling them to conform by
taking oath and sacrament as prescribed by law.
[2] The whole story is well told by
Green, *Hist. of the Eng. People,* vol. iii.
pp. 405–410.

[3] In 1672 Ashley had been raised to
the earldom of Shaftesbury and made
lord chancellor.
[4] Macaulay, vol. i. pp. 100, 108.

"popishly affected, or otherwise obnoxious or dangerous;" and under the pressure thus applied Arlington and Buckingham were forced to resign office.[1]   Thus menaced by the hostility of the lower house, in which cavalier churchmen still predominated, Charles resolved to parry Shaftesbury's thrust by giving the direction of affairs in the cabinet to Sir Thomas Osborne, already earl of Danby and lord treasurer, because he was known to represent in every material particular that policy of union between crown, church, and parliament under which the house had been so firmly held at the side of the king in the days of Clarendon.   In order to enable Danby to rescue the popular chamber from the hands of the country party, it was necessary to allay the popular excitement which grew out of the dread that the childless king would be followed by a catholic successor.   With that end in view, Mary, James' eldest child and presumptive heir, was by a royal order confirmed as a protestant, and before the close of 1674 a secret negotiation was opened for her marriage with the prince of Orange, who,[2] as the grandson of Charles I., stood next to the throne in the event that James and his house should be excluded from the succession.   The reunion thus consummated between the crown and the state church was cemented by a fresh persecution of catholics and by a renewed assault upon conventicles, which followed as the result of a council held at Lambeth in January, 1675, composed of several of the bishops and certain members of the cabinet;[3] and when parliament met in the following April, it was assured that the law would be rigorously enforced against all dissidents.   To means such as these Danby[4] at this time added a grosser kind of persuasion in the form of the direct and systematic bribery of members, an art practised by ministers since the days of James I., and which for nearly a century remained as a recognized agency in the manipulation of English politics.   When the country party, thus assailed on every hand, attempted to retaliate by refusing to grant supplies, a

Danby becomes the leader of the court party;

secret negotiation opened for marriage of Mary with prince of Orange;

bribery as a means of political influence;

---

[1] For the details of the proceedings against Lauderdale, Buckingham, and Arlington, see Lingard, vol. ix. pp. 243–245.

[2] James gave a reluctant consent to the proposal, and William received it coldly. *Life of James*, p. 501; Temple's *Memoirs*, p. 397.

[3] Wilkins, *Conc.*, vol. iv. p. 595; Kennet, p. 301; Lingard, vol. ix. pp. 259, 260.

[4] "With him began that system of direct bribery which was to culminate in the parliamentary corruption of the Pelhams." — Green, *Hist. of the Eng. People*, vol. iii. p. 414.

prorogation was ordered in November, which lasted for the unprecedented period of fifteen months. During that interval it was that Charles, in the hope of freeing himself from parliamentary coercion through the money power, entered early in 1676 into a secret treaty with Louis XIV., who agreed to grant him a yearly pension upon condition that neither sovereign should enter into any engagement with other powers without mutual consent.[1] Thus matters stood upon the reassembling

of the houses in February, 1677, when Buckingham, supported by Shaftesbury, Salisbury, and Wharton, was unwary enough to contend, despite the terms of the Triennial Act,[2] that as the statutes of Edward III.[3] provided that parliaments should be held "once a year, or oftener if need be," the present parliament had no legal existence because prorogued for longer than that time. Seizing upon the opportunity thus offered to strike a blow at his adversaries, Danby persuaded the lords that the motion was a contempt of the house, which forthwith

ordered the commitment of Buckingham and his supporters to the Tower. At this moment it was that the victorious progress of the army of France in Flanders and the defeat of the prince of Orange at Cassel caused an outcry for war against that country, which prompted Danby to revive the project for the marriage of Mary with that prince, an event celebrated shortly after William's arrival in England in October.[4] Aroused by that affront, Louis at once rejected the pending overtures for peace, and put a new army in the field, a move which compelled Danby to obtain a grant of supplies for the war, whose actual declaration was delayed by a series of base and mysterious negotiations. Foremost among them stands the memorable transaction which took place in May, 1678, when Danby,

only five days after the grant of supplies for war, addressed at the king's command a letter to Montagu, the English minister at Versailles, authorizing him to make an offer to sell England's neutrality for the price of six million livres. To satisfy Danby's scruples the king with his own hand wrote as a postscript,

"This letter is writ by my order, C. R."[5] Disheartened by

---

[1] *Danby Letters*, pp. 2, 5; Dalrymple, vol. ii. pp. 99, 102.

[2] 16 Car. I. c. 1.

[3] 4 Edw. III. c. 14; 36 Edw. III. s. 1, c. 10.

[4] Bailey, *Succession to the English Crown*, p. 217.

[5] See Danby defence, *Memoirs relating to the Impeachment of the Earl of Danby, 1710*, pp. 151, 227.

England's desertion, the hostile powers one after another yielded to the demands of France, and in July was concluded the peace of Nimeguen, which dissolved the confederacy against Louis, who thus became as never before the arbiter of the destinies of Europe. *[margin: peace of Nimeguen.]*

For Danby's part in this transaction he was impeached in December of high treason and other high crimes and misdemeanors,[1] and his case is memorable for the reason that five grave questions of constitutional law were involved in its discussion. On the 24th of January, 1679, the parliament of 1661, after a longer unbroken life than any other in English history, was at last dissolved, and the impeachment which it had begun against Danby was revived in Charles' third parliament, which began on the 6th of the following March. Thus at once arose (1) the momentous question whether an impeachment abated on the dissolution of parliament as distinguished from a prorogation from session to session ; in answer to which the lords declared "that the dissolution of the last parliament did not alter the state of the impeachments brought up by the commons in that parliament." [2]   (2) By impeaching a minister who had acted under the express command of his sovereign the commons greatly strengthened a doctrine firmly settled in modern times, that no minister can shelter himself behind the throne by pleading obedience to such commands.[3]   (3) When Danby was called upon to give a written answer to the charges which the commons had presented against him, he pleaded a pardon secretly obtained from the king absolving him of all the offences of which he was accused, whereupon the commons replied "that there was no precedent that ever any pardon was granted to any person impeached by the commons of high treason, or other high crimes, depending the impeachment," and resolved that the pardon so pleaded "ought not to be allowed in bar of the impeachment of the commons of England." [4]   The question was not settled at the time, as the *[margin: Danby's impeachment involving five grave questions: Does an impeachment abate upon a prorogation or dissolution? Can a minister plead his sovereign's command? Can a pardon be pleaded in bar of an impeachment?]*

---

[1] The house also ordered that his letters should be entered on the journals. *Commons' Journals*, December 19; *Parl. Hist.*, vol. iv. p. 1054.

[2] *Lords' Journals*, March 18, 19, 1679, vol. xiii. pp. 464, 466. In 1673 a committee of the lords had made a report, confirmed by the house, that

judicial proceedings brought up by "appeals" remained *in statu quo* from session to session.

[3] Hallam, *Const. Hist.*, vol. ii. p. 411 ; Sir T. Erskine May, *Const. Hist.*, vol. i. p. 115.

[4] *Commons' Journals*, April 28 and May 5, 1679.

parliament was prorogued and the impeachment never after revived; and thus it remained until it was put at rest by the Act of Settlement [1] expressly declared, that "no pardon under the Great Seal of England shall be pleadable to an impeachment by the commons in parliament."   (4) When the preliminary question concerning the plea was under discussion, the

Can bishops sit on the trial of peers in capital cases?

commons challenged the right of the bishops to sit and vote on the trial of peers in capital cases, upon the ground that such questions often determined the final judgment.   The lords replied by a resolution afterwards adhered to, "that the lords spiritual have a right to stay and sit in court in capital cases till the court proceeds to the vote of guilty or not guilty." [2]

Can a commitment be ordered on a "general charge" of treason?

(5) During the first parliament the lords refused, as in the case of Clarendon, to commit Danby on the "general charge" in the absence of a specific allegation of some overt act of treason, but in the second they committed him, as in the case of Strafford, upon their own motion. [3]   Under that order he remained in the Tower until February, 1684, when, together with the earl of Powis and the lords Arundel and Belasyse, he was admitted to bail by the king's bench. [4]   In the next year, in order to secure the discharge of the "popish lords" still under impeachment, the upper house reversed and annulled the resolution of March 19, 1679, in which they had declared that an impeachment did not abate upon the prorogation or dissolution of parliament. [5]   Danby's commitment in April of that year at

Danby resigned, April, 1679.

once brought about the appointment of a new lord treasurer and the fall of the ministry to which he belonged.

The popish plot:

3. At the time when Danby was writing his fatal letter to Montagu, in the course of a transaction that revived the well-grounded suspicion that Louis, then at the height of his power, was intriguing with Charles against English liberty and English religion, Titus Oates was busy with the fabrication of his cruel story, which pretended that the catholics were engaged in a

Titus Oates;

---

[1] 12 & 13 Will. c. 2.

[2] "It was in conformity with the eleventh of the constitutions of Clarendon that the bishops, in virtue of their baronies, are bound to be present till 'sentence is about to be pronounced of life or limb.'" — Lingard, vol. ix. p. 422, note 1.

[3] Then it was that he put in his answer denying the charges against him, and pleading the king's pardon in discharge of all offences of which he was accused. *Lord's Journals*, pp. 476, 479, 481, 496, 505–537.

[4] Luttrell in *State Trials*, vol. ix. p. 1019; Shower's *Reports*, vol. ii. p. 335; Reresby, p. 177.

[5] *Lords' Journals*, May 22, 1685.

mighty plot, whereby the king was to be assassinated and the protestant population of the country massacred by a great army to be brought into England from abroad.   The principal parties to the scheme were said to be the Jesuits in France and Spain, who were supposed to be in close correspondence with their confederates in England, chief among whom was Coleman, secretary to the duchess of York. The assumption was that upon the death of Charles, James as his successor would attempt with foreign aid to wipe out the work of the English Reformation.[1]   On the 29th of September, 1678, Oates told his tale to the council, after having made an affidavit of its truth to Sir Edmondbury Godfrey, a London magistrate, whose mysterious murder on the 12th of October aroused popular passion almost to frenzy.[2]   At this moment it was that the last session of Charles II.'s Long Parliament began, when Shaftesbury, now released from imprisonment, undertook to fan into flame the passions which Oates had excited, by making his disclosures the basis of parliamentary action to which he gave direction and force.   As a result of that movement, apart from the trial of private individuals, five popish lords, as they were called, were at once impeached and sent to the Tower,[3] and an act[4] was passed "for the more effectual preserving the king's person and government, by disabling papists from sitting in either house of parliament," which provided that no one should sit in either house who would not take the oaths of allegiance and supremacy, and make a declaration repudiating the vital doctrines of the Catholic Church.   Only upon his personal application was an exception made in favor of the duke of York.   Thus flushed with success, Shaftesbury pressed for the impeachment of Danby and for the dissolution of parliament, in the hope that new men might be brought to Westminster more in harmony with the national will.   In order to influence the elections which took place immediately, Danby, still in power, extended his system for the bribery of members to the bribing or "treat-

alleged scope and purpose of the plot;

murder of Godfrey, October, 1678;

impeachment of five "popish lords;"

bill disabling catholics from sitting in parliament;

"treating" of constituencies.

---

[1] See the excellent epitome of Sir J. F. Stephen, *Hist. of the Crim. Law*, vol. i. pp. 384–404.

[2] Cf. *State Trials*, vol. vi. p. 1408; vol. vii. pp. 33, 189, etc.

[3] Powis, Viscount Stafford, Lords Petre, Arundel, and Belasyse. The articles of impeachment were not sent to the lords until April, 1679. Cf. *Commons' Journals*, April 3, p. 23; *Lords' Journals*, pp. 500, 517, 521, 535.

[4] 30 Car. II. st. 2, c. 1.

ing " of the constituents themselves ; [1] and to counteract the effects of the new scheme of corruption thus inaugurated, it is said that the leaders of the country party did not scorn to freely employ money furnished by foreign hands.

A new ministry formed from the chiefs of the country party, 1679;

The elections thus held resulted in the defeat of the friends of the ministers of the crown, and when Charles' third parliament met on the 6th of March, 1679, it was with the determined purpose to overthrow an administration which they believed was secretly friendly to the catholic cause.   The impeachments against the popish lords and Danby were therefore revived and pressed so vigorously against the latter, that his imprisonment in April forced upon the crown the necessity of forming a new ministry from the chiefs of the country party now dominant in the lower house.   At this moment it was that

Temple's scheme for reorganizing the council;

the king called upon Sir William Temple, the most philosophic statesman of the age, to devise a plan for the reorganization of the privy council, whose inner circle, the Cabal, after absorbing the powers of the greater body, had become a sham as a

its essence;

check upon the royal will.   The essence of Temple's scheme as described by himself embodied an attempt to combine the old system of government by councils, of the Tudor time, with the modern idea of a cabinet composed of the great parliamentary leaders of the day.   Upon that basis a new council composed of thirty persons was organized, embracing representatives of the church and the law along with influential members of parliament, whose collective wealth "in revenues of land and offices was found to amount to about £300,000 a year, whereas those of a house of commons are seldom found to have excelled

the new body too small for a parliament and too large for a cabinet;

£400,000." [2]   But this artificial scheme, constituting upon inconsistent principles a body too small for a parliament and too large for a cabinet, utterly failed, and Temple himself, whose cardinal idea was that the whole council should always be consulted, consented as secretary of state to become a member

Shaftesbury its first president.

of an inner circle of his own creation.   Shaftesbury became the president of this new council, which also included the lords

---

[1] " I am told," writes the Venetian ambassador, Sarotti, " that in the more conspicuous and populous places their election will cost some of the candidates five thousand scuti (about a thousand pounds) each." — Green,

Hist. of the Eng. People, vol. iii. pp. 424, 425.

[2] Temple's *Memoirs*, by T. P. Courtney, vol. ii. pp. 34-74; Dicey, *The Privy Council*, pp. 139-142.

Russell, Cavendish, Holles, and Roberts, who stood with him as leaders of the opposition by which Danby had been overthrown. The new spirit of liberty thus infused into parliament and council promptly manifested itself in two memorable acts, that have widened English freedom in two of its vital forms.

An account has already been given of the control asserted over the press by the star chamber, which limited the right of printing to certain presses that were subject to regulations issued by virtue of the royal authority.[1] Alongside of these original restrictions, which seem to have been inadequate, there grew up a system of licensing which constituted a political censorship in the full sense of that term.[2] The right to set the bounds to human thought and knowledge first assumed by the church passed after the Reformation in England to the crown as a part of the ecclesiastical supremacy, and thus the right to appoint a licenser, without whose *imprimatur* no writing could be lawfully published, became during the Tudor epoch a recognized part of the prerogative, which was also asserted through the issuance of patents and monopolies limiting the right of printing to certain individuals and corporations. Such was the nature of the censorship at the accession of the Stuarts; and during the reigns of James I. and Charles I. the star chamber employed without mercy mutilation, the dungeon, the pillory, in the vain effort to suppress religious and political discussion, which during that period exchanged the heavy folio for the newspaper, the pamphlet, the flying-sheets that multiplied themselves without number.[3] When the Long Parliament in 1641 abolished the star chamber, it continued the censorship, and in order the more effectually to enforce it against its royalist and theological adversaries, it promulgated a set of tyrannical ordinances which prompted Milton[4] to cry out in his "Areopagitica" that the suppression of truth by the licenser was an attempt to slay "an immortality rather than a life." After the restoration the censorship was revived and given a strictly legal foundation by the Licensing Act of 1662,

Marginal notes: Censorship of the press; first assumed by the church, then passed to the crown; as administered by the star chamber; continued by Long Parliament; outcry of Milton; revived at Restoration by a statute renewed down to 1679;

---

[1] See above, pp. 181, 182.

[2] Odgers, *Libel and Slander*, pp. 10, 11; Dicey, *The Law of the Constitution*, p. 247.

[3] Cf. Sir T. Erskine May, *Const. Hist. of Eng.*, vol. ii. pp. 238–243. "The first example of a newspaper is to be found late in the reign of James I., . . . *The Weekly Newes*, May 23rd, 1622, printed for Nicholas Bourne and Thomas Archer."—Ibid., p. 240, and note 2.

[4] *Works*, vol. iv. p. 400, ed. 1851.

a temporary statute kept in force by renewals down to the meeting of parliament which began in March, 1679. By that parliament, dominated by Shaftesbury at the head of the country party, the yoke was first broken by a refusal to renew the act. Then it was that the twelve judges, with Chief Justice Scroggs at their head, declared it to be a crime by virtue of the common law, regardless of the act of parliament, to publish any public news, whether true or false, without a royal license.[1]   In the midst of the reaction that followed the accession of James II. in 1685, the Licensing Act was continued for a period of seven years, which extended it beyond the Revolution, when it was once more renewed in 1692 for one year and until the end of the following session of parliament. When in 1695 the period thus fixed came to a close, parliament permitted the censorship as a system of political control to expire simply by refusing to renew the act.[2]   But the press was only thus emancipated from the control of the licenser to pass under the judicial censorship embodied in the law of libel as enforced in the courts of common law. How that system of judicial control was gradually transformed into the moderate restrictions that exist at the present day is a vitally important subject, to be reserved for subsequent consideration.

first refusal to renew the act;

declaration of Scroggs;

Licensing Act renewed in 1685;

permitted to finally expire in 1695;

judicial censorship embodied in law of libel.

The parliament that first attempted to secure freedom of discussion by refusing to renew the censorship of the press passed the famous "act for the better securing the liberty of the subject, and for prevention of imprisonments beyond seas," generally known as the Habeas Corpus Act,[3] a remedial measure intended to destroy all the devices then employed to deny to imprisoned persons the right to an immediate examination by a court of law into the legality of their imprisonments. The right to personal freedom, inherent in the law of the land, was supposed to be specially guarded by that clause of the Great Charter which provides that "no freeman shall be taken, or imprisoned, or disseized, or outlawed, or exiled, or anywise destroyed; nor will we go upon him, nor send upon him, but by

Habeas Corpus Act;

right to personal freedom inherent in law of the land;

---

[1] Carr's case, 1680, *State Trials*, vol. vii. p. 929. Not until 1765 was this monstrous doctrine judicially condemned by Lord Camden, chief justice of the common pleas, in the case of *Entick* v. *Carrington, State Trials*, vol.

xix. p. 1030. See also Broom's *Const. Law*, by Denman, p. 555.

[2] See Macaulay's brilliant exposition of the "effect of the emancipation of the English press," vol. ii. pp. 532–535.

[3] 31 Car. II. c. 2.

the lawful judgment of his peers or by the law of the land." [1]
By that formula was intended the common law as administered
in the ordinary tribunals.   In order to give practical security
to the right thus recognized and defined, the common law,
in addition to the writs *de odio et atiâ* and *de homine reple-*
giando, applicable only to particular cases, offered as a matter
of right, *ex debito justitiæ,* to all imprisoned persons a writ of
habeas corpus, or *corpus cum causâ,* which issued from the
king's bench to the keeper of the prison, commanding him to
bring up the body of the prisoner with the cause of his detention so that the court, after examination, could either discharge,
bail, or remand him, according to the facts. [2]   This remedy, theoretically complete, was embarrassed in practice by many inconveniences. [3]   In the first place, it was doubtful whether any
court other than the king's bench could issue the writ at all,
and it was also claimed that it could not be issued by a single
judge of that court.   In the second place, the gaoler was not
bound to make an immediate return ; he could wait until a
second and a third writ was issued, and the delay thus occasioned was also prolonged by removing the prisoner from
prison to prison.   Upon these lesser difficulties a greater was
superimposed when the star chamber arose out of the council
as a supreme and extraordinary court, which undertook whenever it saw fit to suspend the ordinary law of the land as administered in the ordinary tribunals.   In order to give greater
efficiency to that usurpation, it was claimed that whenever a
person was committed by the "special command of the king,"
that is by the king in council, a return to that effect deprived
the ordinary law courts of the power to deliver him.   Against
that monstrous doctrine a legal battle was waged in the king's
bench in 1627 in the case of the Five Knights to whom the
chief justice refused bail, without holding directly, however,
that the king could never be required to show cause.   With
that case specially in view, the framers of the Petition of Right
introduced a clause into it which was intended to put imprisonments by order of the king in council upon a footing with
all others.   But when upon the dissolution of the parliament

Margin notes: securities guaranteed by the common law; their inadequacy; means by which they were often defeated; commitments by "special command of the king;" case of the Five Knights;

---

[1] Cf. vol. i. p. 389.
[2] Blackstone's *Com.*, vol. iii. pp. 123, 124.
[3] Dicey, *The Law of the Constitu-tion,* pp. 205–207.

cases of
Eliot and
others;

that enacted the Petition, Eliot, Valentine, Selden, and others were imprisoned in the old form by a royal order, an attempt to deliver them by habeas corpus was defeated by a subterfuge which consisted in setting forth a colorable case of commitment.   Thus it was that Eliot, forsaken by his companions, after suffering years of imprisonment, finally died in the Tower rather than make humiliating concessions contrary to his convictions.[1]   With his fate, no doubt, specially in view, parliament in the act which abolished the star chamber expressly provided that any person imprisoned by a privy councillor, or by the council as a whole, or even by the king's special command, should be instantly entitled to his habeas corpus as in other cases.[2]   Despite all such provisions, however, difficulties were still opposed after the Restoration to the execution of the writ; and in the impeachment against Clarendon, it was specially charged that he "advised and procured divers of His Majesty's subjects to be imprisoned against law, in remote islands, garrisons, and other places, thereby to prevent them from the benefits of the law."[3]   Nine years later the case[4] of Francis Jenkes, who was committed by the privy council for having delivered a speech urging a petition to the king to call a new parliament, emphasized the fact that all kinds of vexatious delays were still employed within the realm to prevent the discharge by habeas corpus of those who were held for political offences.   To put an end forever to every device, plea, or excuse by which the right to the actual benefits of the writ had been formerly made abortive, was finally passed the Habeas Corpus Act of 1679, the essence of which is that the chancellor and all of the judges are charged with the duty upon a proper application to direct the writ even to the privileged places, including the islands of Jersey and Guernsey, requiring any person who is imprisoned to be actually and speedily brought before the court, together with the cause of the imprisonment, to the end that such court may either set him free, bail him, or remand him for a speedy trial, as justice may require.[5]   As the act failed to fix any limit to the bail that might

provisions
of act abol-
ishing star
chamber;

charge
against
Clarendon;

Jenkes'
case;

scope and
purpose
of the act
of 1679;

1 See above, pp. 282, 283.
2 See above, p. 307.
3 Life of Clarendon, pp. 424, 445–448; State Trials, vol. vi. p. 330.
4 State Trials, vol. vi. p. 1189.

5 James Sommersett, the negro slave actually confined in irons on board a ship lying in the Thames and bound for Jamaica, was delivered by the king's bench in 1772, by habeas corpus. State

be demanded, the Bill of Rights declared "that excessive bail ought not to be required." Thus matters stood until the reign of George III., when an important addition was made by the provision[1] that the terms of the original act which was limited to persons committed on criminal charges should be extended to all persons deprived of their liberty otherwise than on a criminal accusation. In that act the judges were empowered to examine into and determine the facts set forth in the return, and in a doubtful case to discharge the prisoner. After the court of queen's bench had gone so far as to send the writ into upper Canada,[2] legislation on the subject was brought to an end by an act[3] which provides that no writ of habeas corpus shall be sent from England into any colony or foreign dominion of the crown where there are courts of justice competent to issue and enforce it.

provision of the Bill of Rights as to bail;

act extended to persons committed on other than criminal charges;

writ not to be sent to colonies having competent courts.

While the Short Parliament of 1679 was thus paving the way for freedom of discussion and fixing upon a new basis the right to personal freedom, its leaders were absorbed in the discussion of a still more urgent question which, after stirring the nation to its depths during the remainder of this and the whole of the succeeding reign, finally culminated in the Revolution of 1688. The duke of York, who had years before declared himself a catholic, was the heir to the throne, and through the terror and rage excited by the "popish plot" the protestant population had been made to believe that his accession would be followed by their certain overthrow and possible extermination through the aid of a foreign power. With this great wave of popular excitement and apprehension behind him, Shaftesbury advocated in the council and his followers introduced into the house a bill to exclude James, then absent from the realm, from his right to the crown, which was to pass upon the death of Charles to the next protestant in the line of succession. In order to save the doctrine of indefeasible hereditary right from this assault, the king proposed in the council and then sent to the houses a bill of securities so framed as

Question of the succession that culminated in the Revolution of 1688;

first exclusion bill

Trials, vol. xx. p. 1. Reported as *Somerset* v. *Stewart*, Lofft. 1.

[1] 56 Geo. III. c. 100. "The effect of 56 Geo. III. c. 100 was in substance to apply to non-criminal cases the machinery of the great Habeas Corpus Act, 31 Car. II. c. 2."—Dicey, *The Law of the Constitution*, p. 208.

[2] See Anderson's case, *Law Journ. Rep.*, xxx. 2 B., 129.

[3] 25 & 26 Vict. c. 20.

to permit James to succeed shorn of all real power in church and state, which was to be vested in the two houses.[1]   But this visionary scheme was set aside as impracticable, and the commons, after listening to exciting extracts tending to show James' complicity with the plot, passed the exclusion bill in May by a large majority.[2]   To prevent further agitation of the subject in the lords, Charles suddenly prorogued parliament May 27, and finally dissolved it on the 10th of July.[3]

passed the house in May; parliament prorogued July 10.

Division in country party as to settlement of succession;

4. Before the dissolution took place, the leaders of the country party unfortunately disagreed among themselves as to the disposition to be made of the throne in the event of James' exclusion from it.   While Temple, Sunderland, Essex, and Halifax were resolved to deal as gently as possible with the hereditary theory, by simply setting James aside in favor of his protestant daughter Mary, Shaftesbury was equally determined upon a revolutionary programme involving the succession of the duke of Monmouth, one of Charles' bastards by Lucy Waters, who promptly declared himself "against popery and tyranny."   Under these circumstances Shaftesbury was dismissed from his post of president of the council [4] on the 15th of October, 1679, just as the new parliament, called at the time of the dissolution of the last, was about to meet after elections which had resulted so unfavorably to the court as to promise him an easy victory over his adversaries.   To prevent such a result, the king, on the day appointed for the opening of the session, prorogued parliament for a few weeks, then by repeated commissions for a whole year.[5]   In order to force Charles to untie his hands by calling the houses together, Shaftesbury, before the end of the year, organized a formidable agitation throughout the kingdom, that consisted of the signing of petitions in every district, which demanded that parliament should be permitted to sit for the suppression of popery and despotism.   In order to assist the crown in resisting this revolutionary pressure which revived the memories of 1641, the cavaliers and churchmen suddenly came forward with addresses

Shaftesbury dismissed in October;

conducted an agitation by means of petitions;

---

1 Temple, vol. ii. p. 501; James (*Memoirs*), p. 548; *Commons' Journals*, April 30.

2 207 against 128.   *Commons' Journals*, May 21.

3 Temple, vol. ii. pp. 509–512.

4 Charles said that "Shaftesbury began to play the devil, and could no longer be suffered." — James (*Memoirs*), vol. i. p. 563.

5 Temple, vol. ii. p. 521; *Lords' Journals*, vol. xiii. pp. 597, 609.

to the king full of the strongest expressions of confidence in him and of "abhorrence" of the practices of those who were petitioning against him.   At this time it was that the country party, who were the "petitioners," came to be known as Whigs, and the cavalier or court party, who were the "abhorrers," came to be known as Tories,[1] — the former a term of reproach originally applied to the extreme covenanters of the west of Scotland, and the latter a term then employed to describe a native Irish outlaw or "bogtrotter."   At this moment it was that Russell, Essex, and Cavendish resigned from the council to join Shaftesbury, leaving the direction of the king's affairs in the hands of Sunderland, Halifax, Hyde, and Godolphin. Thus strengthened, the great earl ventured to present the duke of York, who had been recently recalled to court,[2] to the grand jury of Middlesex as a popish recusant,[3] while Monmouth paraded himself through the country, winning adherents to his cause.   Thus matters stood upon the meeting of parliament in October, 1680, when the house, after declaring its purpose "effectually to suppress popery, and prevent a popish successor,"[4] finally resolved "that a bill should be introduced to disable the duke of York from succeeding to the imperial crown of England,"[5] which was promptly passed without a division in the midst of great enthusiasm.[6]   But the house of lords still stood firmly by the king, and the bill was there rejected by a decisive vote of sixty-three to thirty voices.[7]   In the midst of the anger and disappointment excited by a second defeat, the popular leaders resolved to reinflame the passions of the nation by a great public trial, in which all the details of the plot could receive a fresh rehearsal.   With that end in view the proceedings against the "popish lords" in the Tower, who had been impeached a year and a half before, were revived by the trial of Lord Stafford[8] which, beginning at the end of November,

marginal notes: "petitioners" and "abhorrers" came to be known as Whigs and Tories; reorganization of the council; fate of second exclusion bill; trial and conviction of Lord Stafford;

---

[1] "Hence the *abhorrers* branded the *petitioners* with the name of Whigs; and the petitioners in revenge bestowed on their opponents the name of Tories." — Lingard, vol. ix. p. 461.

[2] He had been sent away to Brussels early in 1679.

[3] He was presented at the Old Bailey, but the case was removed by *certiorari* into the court of king's bench. *State Trials*, vol. viii. p. 179; James (*Memoirs*), vol. i. p. 666.

[4] *Commons' Journals*, October 26.

[5] It was further resolved "that the exclusion in the said bill do extend to the person of James, duke of York, only." — Cf. Bailey, *Succession to the Eng. Crown*, p. 218.

[6] *Commons' Journals*, November 11.

[7] *Lords' Journals*, p. 666.

[8] *Trial of Lord Stafford*, fol. 1680; *State Trials*, vol. vii.

ended, after a fresh performance by Oates, in his conviction and death before the close of December. Upon the heels of that event followed the attempt of Halifax, acting in the interest of the prince of Orange, to pass through the lords a bill for "the security of the protestant religion," based upon the old idea of securing the crown to James, shorn of its prerogatives, which were to be exercised during his life by parliament.[1] That scheme met, however, with no response from the commons, who forced the king to dissolve the houses on the 18th of January, 1681, by the adoption of a set of violent resolutions, declaring, among other things, that until the duke of York was excluded they could not conscientiously vote any supply to his majesty.

parliament dissolved January 18, 1681.

5. When the dissolution was ordered, a new parliament was called[2] to meet at Oxford, on account of the supposed disloyalty of the capital; and upon its assembling in March, the memories of the civil war were revived by the coming of the king at the head of a troop of horse-guards, and by the coming of Shaftesbury, the leader of the popular party, at the head of a group of armed men wearing around their hats a ribbon with the inscription, "No popery, no slavery." Under these circumstances Charles again attempted to satisfy the demands of his adversaries by offering a new bill of securities, which proposed to banish James from the realm during his natural life, and to vest the actual administration of affairs while he held the title of king in the prince and princess of Orange as regents.[3] But after a two days' debate the house rejected even that concession, and ordered a bill to be brought in disabling the duke of York from inheriting the crowns of England and Ireland and the dominions thereunto belonging.[4] In order to aid the passage of that bill, the house resolved to impeach Edward Fitzharris of high treason, in the hope of bringing to light disclosures of a pretended "popish plot" with which he was supposed to have been connected. As the crown had already instructed the attorney-general to proceed against Fitz-

New parliament met at Oxford March 21;

another failure to settle the succession;

impeachment of Fitzharris;

---

[1] James urgently combatted the scheme. James (*Memoirs*), vol. i. p. 635; *Lords' Journals*, vol. xiii. pp. 684, 740.
[2] Temple, vol. ii. p. 536.

[3] *Life of James*, vol. ii. London, 1703 App. p. 44; Reresby, p. 117.
[4] *Commons' Journals*, March 24, 26 *Parl. Hist.*, vol. iv. pp. 1308, 1317-1332.

harris in the king's bench for a treasonable libel,[1] an interesting question of constitutional law arose as to the right of the house to impeach a commoner for a capital offence, and thus deprive him of his common-law right of trial by his peers. The lords who sided with the king declared that "Fitzharris should be proceeded with according to the course of common law, and not by the way of impeachment,"[2] relying upon the supposed authority of the case of Sir Simon de Beresford, which had occurred in the reign of Edward III.; while the commons, relying upon precedents of the reigns of Richard II. and Charles I., voted "that if any inferior court should proceed to the trial of Fitzharris, it would be guilty of a high breach of the privilege of the house of commons."[3] Before the controversy could be fought out,[4] the king, on the 28th of March, suddenly dissolved his fifth parliament, which, despite the provisions of the Triennial Act, proved to be the last of the reign. In order to justify himself in the eyes of the nation, Charles promptly published a declaration[5] of the motives that had induced him to dissolve the last two parliaments, which were charged with the commission of a long list of offences, including, of course, the rejection of all "expedients" offered in the hope of rendering the exclusion of James unnecessary. Thus indicted in the forum of public opinion, the leaders of the popular party made a stirring reply,[6] in which they undertook to refute every accusation that the king had made against them. But deprived as they were of the support of the houses, the contest became an unequal one, and the king, backed by the tide of reaction that now set in in his favor, turned fiercely upon the Whig chiefs, who had tried in vain to bend him to their will.

Marginal notes: right of lower house to deprive a commoner of trial by jury; Charles dissolved his fifth and last parliament March 28; his attack upon the leaders of the popular party;

[1] *The True Englishman speaking plain English* was the joint product of Fitzharris and Everand. Cf. *State Trials*, vol. viii. p. 357; *Parl. Hist.*, vol. iv. pp. 1313–1317.

[2] *Lords' Journals*, p. 755. This untenable theory the lords rejected in 1689 in the case of Sir Adam Blair and four other commoners impeached of high treason for having published a proclamation of James II. After an examination of all the precedents, including the cases of Simon de Beresford and Fitzharris, the house resolved to proceed with the impeachments. *Lords'*

Journals, vol. xiv. p. 260; May, *Parl. Practice*, p. 626, 10th ed.

[3] *Commons' Journals*, March 26.

[4] The case against Fitzharris in the king's bench was then pressed, and when he pleaded the pending impeachment in abatement the plea was overruled. He was then found guilty and executed. *State Trials*, vol. viii. pp. 243, 330.

[5] It was read in the churches, and sympathetic addresses came in reply from every quarter. Kennet, p. 398.

[6] A joint production of Somers, Sidney, and Jones. *Parl. Hist.*, vol. iv. App. No. 15.

As the *facile princeps* of the constitutional opposition, Shaftesbury was marked out as a victim, and in July he was committed to the Tower upon the charge of having suborned witnesses to give false testimony implicating the queen and the duke of York with the popish plot. And yet, despite the pressure which the crown applied, the grand jury of Middlesex ignored the bill,[1] and the indomitable agitator thus released returned in triumph to the capital, where his intrigues and conspiracies culminated at last in an abortive appeal to his comrades to rise in arms. Thus forced by failure to seek safety in flight, he found a refuge at Amsterdam, where he died in January, 1683. Undaunted by his loss, Monmouth, backed by Lord Russell, Lord Essex, Lord Howard of Ettrick, Hampden, and Algernon Sidney, pressed on the agitation to a point which seems to have warranted the charge of an intention to levy war against the king ; while certain of their more desperate subordinates went so far as to devise, without their participation, a plot for the assassination of Charles and James as they passed the Rye-house on the road by which the king usually returned from Newmarket to London. Despite the lack of evidence that they were privy to that plot, which was improperly blended with the other charge, Lord Russell and Algernon Sidney were convicted ;[2] and to escape the fate which they suffered, Essex sought death by his own hand in the Tower, while Monmouth fled in terror over-sea. On the very day upon which Russell perished in vindication of the lawfulness of resistance, the University of Oxford published its famous decree declaring passive obedience to be a religious duty, "clear, absolute, and without exception of any state or order of men."[3]

Having thus trampled the leaders of the country party in the dust by means of the judicial power, Charles proceeded to make his victory complete by directing the same engine against their strongholds, the towns, which were now called upon by writs of *quo warranto* to show cause why their charters should not be forfeited by reason of abuse of their privileges. The

---

[1] *State Trials*, vol. viii. pp. 759–842 ; James (*Memoirs*), vol. i. pp. 687, 714.

[2] *State Trials*, vol. ix. pp. 577, 823. For a concise statement of the legal questions involved, see Sir J. F. Stephen's *Hist. of the Crim. Law*, vol. i. pp. 408–412.

[3] July 21, 1683. Wilkins, *Cônc.*, vol. iv. p. 610; Somers' *Tracts*, vol. viii. pp. 420, 424. The decree was publicly burned by order of the house of lords in 1709.

infamous Jeffreys, who had risen to a bad eminence in the Jeffreys' part in the work; preceding political trials of individuals, was specially charged with the task of subduing the corporations ; and while on the northern circuit in 1684, he is said to have "made all the charters, like the walls of Jericho, fall down before him, and returned laden with surrenders, the spoils of towns." [1] In the forfeiture of the charter of London; course of these unprecedented proceedings to take away corporate privileges the disloyal capital, in which the administration of justice was largely influenced by elected sheriffs by whom all juries were chosen, was made the subject of an information, *quo warranto*, in the king's bench, where it was alleged that its charter had been forfeited, (1) by reason of the imposition of certain tolls through an ordinance of its own, and (2) by reason of the publication of a petition presented to the king in 1679 through its common council calling upon him to order a meeting of parliament. By reason of these two acts a judgment of forfeiture was rendered against the corporation,[2] which was used as a lever to compel it to submit to certain regulations permitting the enjoyment of its franchises under conditions that really involved a surrender to the crown of its municipal independence. With the principle of law thus settled that a misuser of corporate powers was a basis for a judgment of forfeiture, the position of every town in the realm became precarious ; and many of them, to prevent attack, made many voluntary surrenders; voluntary surrenders, followed, during the remainder of this and a greater part of the next reign, by renewals of their char- character of the new charters; ters,[3] under which the exercise of all municipal powers was generally vested in a mayor and town council, nominated by the crown in the first instance and then perpetuated by self-election. Thus was finally consummated the process of reac- consummation of the process of disfranchisement; tion which, before the close of the Middle Ages, had brought about the disfranchisement of the landless freeman and lesser freeholders within the shires, and a still more sweeping restriction of the franchise in the cities and towns. In the effort heretofore made to ascertain who were the electors of borough representatives, the general conclusion was reached that the electors in a city were the citizens; in a borough, the bur-

[1] North's *Examen*, p. 626; Hallam, *Const. Hist.*, vol. ii. p. 455.
[2] *State Trials*, vol. viii. pp. 1039–1340.
[3] North, pp. 624–627; Bulstrode, p. 388.

gesses.   Who were citizens and who were burgesses seems to
have depended everywhere upon local custom, and such custom was uniform only in its tendency to take away the suffrage
from the main body of the townsmen and vest it either in a
self-elected governing body, — generally known as the mayor
and common council, — or in a still smaller circle of "select-
men" nominated and controlled by them.   Thus through the
silent operation of local custom, which finally received legal
sanction, the rights of the many were usurped by the few;
the self-elected governing bodies of the towns finally assumed
the exercise of the electoral rights that had originally belonged
to the whole community.   In the charters of incorporation
which began to be issued to the municipalities after the accession of the house of Tudor, the right of electing representatives in parliament was usually vested in the governing body
styled the mayor and common council.   When the fact is
remembered that these governing bodies were as a rule nominated by the crown in the first instance, and then perpetuated
by self-election, it is quite possible to understand how those
boroughs, which were not already under the dominion of the
great landed proprietors, became subject to royal control, or
rather to that of the local magnates known as the high stewards, by whom, in many instances, the royal and aristocratic
influence was directly exercised.   Through the results of this
disfranchising process the county constituencies were finally
overshadowed by the paramount influence of the greater landowners, while the borough constituencies became, in the main,
the property of the crown and the aristocracy.   The Tudor
kings, whose policy it was not to abolish parliaments, but to
convert them into convenient tools for the advancement of
their own interests, systematically pursued a policy of creating
petty parliamentary boroughs, especially in localities where the
crown had the greatest influence, for the express purpose of
packing the lower house with members amenable to royal dic-
tation.   The policy thus inaugurated by the Tudors "was pursued by the Stuarts; and the last two of that race violated the
liberties of the few corporations which still retained popular
constitutions after the encroachments of centuries." [1]

Marginal notes: tendency to take away suffrage from main body of townsmen and vest it; in self-elected governing bodies; the high stewards as local magnates; policy of creating petty boroughs as a means of packing lower house.

[1] May, *Const. Hist.*, vol. iii. p. 280,
citing the case of *Quo Warranto*, 1683.
See his entire statement of the loss of
popular rights by English municipal
corporations.   Ibid., pp. 275–283.

While Charles was thus striving to stifle the voice of the Charles strengthened the guards, the nucleus of present standing army; English democracy in those cities and towns in which it was still able to express itself, he was careful to provide against the might of the people in another form by strengthening the guards, a standing military force retained in the royal service when the army of the Commonwealth was disbanded after the Restoration, and consisting of Monk's Foot Regiment known as the Coldstream, and another of horse, to which was added still another formed from troops brought from Dunkirk. The body thus made up, amounting in 1662 to five thousand men, was swelled by the addition of the garrison of Tangier, recalled to England in 1684, to about seven thousand foot and seventeen hundred cavalry and dragoons, — the nucleus of the regular army of the present day. When in the midst of such prosperous conditions, with his enemies cowering at his feet, Charles was called upon to meet the inevitable, he gave the clue to his mysterious dealings with France, which began in 1670 with the making of the secret treaty of Dover, by a died in communion with Rome February 6, 1685. profession of the faith of the Church of Rome, in communion with which he died February 6, 1685.[1]

[1] See the accounts in Lingard, vol. x. pp. 107–110; and in Green, *Hist. of the Eng. People*, vol. iv. pp. 65, 66.

CHAPTER II.

JAMES II. AND THE ATTEMPT AT REACTION.

Origin of the social contract theory;

1. In the midst of the great upheaval that overturned the monarchy and established the Commonwealth, the modern school of English political theory begins with the speculations of Hobbes, who developed in his "Leviathan"[1] the then novel idea that civil society had its origin in an original contract between its members, by virtue of which each, in order to

its essence as stated by Hobbes;

secure the boon of living in peace with all the rest, agreed to give up so much of his natural rights as was inconsistent with such a state. Then, for the purpose of constituting "a common power to keep them in awe, and to direct their actions to the common benefit," a further surrender was supposed to have been made upon the part of all of the right of governing the whole in favor of some person or body, "and he that car-

sovereign and subject;

rieth this person is called *sovereign,* and hath sovereign power ; and every one besides, his *subject.*" "The sovereign, which is the person of the commonwealth," commands his subjects through civil law, defined to be "those rules which the commonwealth hath commanded him by word, writing, or other sufficient sign of the will, to make use of for the distinction of

right and wrong in the legal sense;

right and wrong ; that is to say, of what is contrary and what is not contrary to the rule." And thus the important conclusion is reached that right and wrong, in the legal sense, is nothing more than that which the law of the state allows and forbids. As Aristotle accomplished the separation of ethics

separation of policy from legality;

from politics, so Hobbes worked out the further separation of policy from legality, of that which is wise and expedient from that which is allowed by positive law. At that point he fell

[1] In 1651 appeared the "*Leviathan, or the Matter, Form, and Power of a Commonwealth, Ecclesiastical and Civil,* with a quaint frontispiece . . . of a crowned giant, made up of tiny figures of human beings and bearing sword and crozier in the two hands." Not until the theory of the *Contrat Social* had passed through the hands of Locke did Rousseau make it "one of the most successful and fatal of political impostures." — Sir F. Pollock, *Hist. of the Science of Politics,* p. 75.

into confusion by attempting to swallow up policy, and to a great extent even morality, in positive law, an error that made it necessary for Austin and Holland to carry the process of division further by a fresh analysis, which rigidly separates the general science of law from the ethical part of politics.[1] When after the Revolution of 1688 it became necessary for Locke to justify what had been done, he, adopting with many reservations Hobbes' social contract theory as a starting-point, rested his defence[2] of the proceedings of the convention upon the assumption that the people, even after the delegation of the supreme power to the state, always reserve to themselves the right to withdraw it whenever it has been used for purposes inconsistent with the end for which society was formed. In that event he claimed that the people had a right to resist the prince, and, acting through their supreme legislative assembly,[3] to visit upon him the consequences of an abuse of their trust. In order to counteract the effect of such doctrines so dangerous to monarchy, it became necessary after the Restoration to revive and intensify the political theory of the indefeasible hereditary right of kings,[4] which was supposed to flow from the divine institution of the royal office, an assumption that lifted the succession to the crown above the supremacy of the legislature. And in order to give still greater security to kingship, that doctrine was supplemented by the obligation of passive obedience even to the worst of sovereigns, which, first taught as a religious duty, finally passed from the homilies to the statute-book. When the University of Oxford, on the day of Russell's execution, published its famous decree[5] in support of passive obedience, it was at the same time careful to consign to everlasting reprobation the doctrine that all civil authority was originally derived from the people through a compact, express or implied, between the prince and his subjects, whereby the former might forfeit his right to govern by

[margin notes:] process of division as extended by Austin and Holland; Locke's assumption in defence of the Revolution; inalienable right of the people; counter theory of indefeasible hereditary right supplemented, after the Restoration, by that of passive obedience; social contract theory condemned at Oxford;

[1] "It would not be too much to say that Professor Holland's *Elements of Jurisprudence* is the first work of pure scientific jurisprudence which has appeared in England." — Pollock, p. 63.

[2] That defence or apology is embodied in his *Essay on Civil Government*, published in 1689.

[3] Locke's fundamental principle is that the real sovereignty resides in the legislature and is forfeitable by misuse : "While the government subsists, the legislature is the supreme power," and yet not indefeasible, "being only a fiduciary power to act for certain ends."

[4] See above, p. 383.

[5] See above, p. 388.

antagonistic political theories involved in the Revolution.

virtue of misconduct.[1] Without a clear comprehension of these two opposing theories, the one claiming the supreme political authority for the crown, the other for the legislature, it is impossible to perfectly understand the full significance of the acts which culminated in the fall of the house of Stuart through what is generally known as the glorious Revolution.

James concealed his real designs at the outset;

2. The fact that James, an avowed catholic, held higher notions of the prerogative perhaps than any of his predecessors, coupled with events which transpired when his reign was well advanced, has given rise to the not improbable assumption that he ascended the throne with the fixed purpose of making himself absolute, and of overthrowing the established church in favor of that of Rome. If such was his design at the outset, his first declaration was artfully devised to conceal his real intentions. Passing from the death-chamber of his brother to the room in which the council was assembled, after expressing

his declaration to the council;

the wish to follow in Charles' footsteps he said, " I shall make it my endeavor to preserve this government, both in church and state, as it is now by law established. I know the principles of the Church of England are for monarchy, and the members of it have shown themselves good and lawful subjects, therefore I shall always take care to defend and support it. I know, too, that the laws of England are sufficient to make the king as great a monarch as I can wish ; and, as I shall never depart from the just rights and prerogatives of the

Charles' ministers continued in office under leadership of Rochester;

crown, so I shall never invade any man's property." [2] The new king then requested the ministers who were in office to retain their places, and the direction of affairs thus continued in the hands of Hyde, now earl of Rochester, Sunderland, Halifax, and Godolphin, with the first named at the head of

parliament met May 19, 1685;

the board as lord high treasurer. A parliament was immediately called to meet on the 19th of May, 1685, after an interval of five years ; and we have the authority of Barillon for the

James renewed his brother's secret treaty with France.

statement that James at once revived the humiliating relations with Louis which the dead king had so long maintained, by apologizing for the calling of the houses without the French

---

1 Twenty-four propositions, including the social contract theory, taken from the works of Hobbes, Milton, Buchanan, Baxter, Cartwright, Knox, and others, were denounced by the

decree as "false, seditious, and impious, . . . and destructive of all government in church and state."

2 James II., 3; Fox, *App.*, 16.

king's consent, an explanation at once followed by a request for a fresh pension from that source.[1] But as Barillon persisted in withholding the money, although actually in his possession, until the happening of future events, it became necessary to provide present means for pressing necessities.

As the legal grant of the whole of the port duties and one half of the excise had expired with the life of Charles, James undertook, by a proclamation alleging state necessity as the cause,[2] to continue such duties until they could be regularly settled upon him by parliament, which, in view of the fact that the king had not claimed it by virtue of the prerogative, promptly granted him for life the revenue enjoyed by his predecessor.[3] And as that was insufficient as a whole to meet the expenses of the crown, certain selected articles of commerce were subjected to additional burdens.[4] No change was made, however, during the reign in the system of direct taxation, "and, as the general result of the arrangements connected with the revenue made under the later Stuarts, we have (1) the continuation of the old system of port duties on merchandise imported and exported, with additional taxes on wine, sugar, tobacco, and French and India linens and silk, and brandy; (2) the substitution, in lieu of the revenue from the feudal tenures and in supplement to the revenue from demesne, of certain items of the commonwealth excise; (3) the imposition of hearth-money; and (4) the suppression of the old subsidy in favor of the commonwealth rate or assessment, as a tax for extraordinary purposes."[5]

Settlement of the revenue;

summary of the fiscal system as it existed under the later Stuarts.

To his first parliament, which met on the day appointed, James renewed the vows he had made at his accession to the council; and then, in order to hasten the grants already described, he announced the fact that the protestant earl of Argyle had raised the standard of rebellion in Scotland in the hope of ending his rule in that kingdom.[6] Upon the heels of

James renewed his vows to his first parliament; standard of rebellion raised by Argyle and Monmouth;

[1] As to the value of Barillon's statements, see Lingard, vol. x. pp. 128–131.

[2] As the language of the proclamation admitted by implication that the duties could not be legally levied without authority of parliament, addresses were presented from the barristers of the Middle Temple and from many companies of merchants, thanking the king for his action. Burnet, vol. iii. p. 9; Lord Lonsdale, *Memoirs*, p. 4; Fox, *App.*, pp. 18, 39; Kennet, vol. iii. p. 427.

[3] 1 Jac. II. c. 1.

[4] 1 Jac. II. cc. 4, 5.

[5] Dowell, *Hist. of Taxation*, vol. ii. p. 33.

[6] *Lords' Journals*, vol. xiv. p. 9; Evelyn, vol. iii. p. 159.

that attempt in the north soon followed the invasion of the duke of Monmouth, who on the 11th of June landed in the west at the head of an armed force, whose purpose was declared to be "the defence and vindication of the protestant religion, and the laws, rights, and privileges of England."[1]   But the two expeditions thus organized in concert by the Scotch and English exiles who in the later years of Charles had found a refuge in Holland soon collapsed, and their unfortunate leaders were sent to the block after proceedings at once prompt and summary.   Argyle was beheaded on the 30th of June; and Monmouth, after a crushing defeat at Sedgemoor on the 6th of July, shared the same fate on the 15th of that month. While the royal bastard thus suffered at London, his followers in the west were given the first instalment of James' vengeance through the execution of martial law at the hands of Colonel Kirk, whose brutal proceedings were suspended only in order to make place for the "bloody circuit" of Chief Justice Jeffreys, who, with a strong military escort which he conducted with the temporary rank of lieutenant-general,[2] set out at the head of a judicial commission, opened with the trial of Lady Lisle[3] at Winchester on the 27th of August.   She was sentenced to be burned alive for harboring two rebels for a night; and before the terrible inquisition ended, about three hundred and thirty persons were executed as traitors and felons; many were whipped and imprisoned, while more than eight hundred were sold into slavery to persons who were authorized to transport them for ten years to the West Indies.[4]   Then taking advantage of the opportunity furnished by the revolt, which had found the crown unprepared to repel invasion, James ventured to make a great increase in the standing army, and thus a way was opened for the commissioning of many catholic officers, in defiance of the terms of the Test Act expressly forbidding it.   The king therefore resolved to bring about the repeal of that act, as well as a modification of the Habeas Corpus Act, whose provisions had greatly hampered the crown

Margin notes: both leaders sent to the block;

Colonel Kirk and martial law; Jeffreys and the "bloody circuit;"

over three hundred executed as traitors and felons, and eight hundred sold into slavery;

James resolved to secure the repeal of the Test Act;

---

[1] In this declaration the whole career of James is bitterly denounced and the purposes of Monmouth fully set forth. Somers' *Tracts*, vol. iv.; *Collect.*, tom. iii. p. 190; *State Trials*, vol. xi. pp. 1032.

[2] Not only the writs but James himself spoke of "Jeffrey's campaign."— Dalrymple, p. 165.

[3] See comments of Sir J. F. Stephen on this case, *Hist. of the Crim. Law*, vol. i. p. 413; vol. ii. p. 234.

[4] Lingard, vol. x. p. 181.

in commitments made in connection with the recent rebellion. When Halifax ventured to oppose his plans, James dismissed him from the council ; and when the parliament, which had made prompt and generous grants as well as dangerous innovations in the law of treason for the protection of the king's person and succession, manifested the same spirit of resistance, it was rebuked by a prorogation from the 2d of July to the 9th of November.   Upon the opening of the second session, which began at the time appointed, the contest was renewed by a demand from the king that a grant should be made for the support of the new troops which he had raised, and by an assurance that he would neither disgrace nor dismiss the officers of his own faith who had stood by him in the hour of danger.[1]   The commons responded with a grant of £700,000, but they coupled with it the condition that the king should recall the illegal commissions issued in defiance of the Test Act, lest the continuance of the catholic officers in the army should " be taken to be a dispensing with that law without act of parliament."   As a counterblast to the resolute opposition of the lower house, earnestly seconded and accentuated by the lords, to any modification of a statute which both regarded as the bulwark of the protestant cause, James suddenly prorogued parliament to the 10th of February, 1686 ; and although it was continued in existence by further prorogations for about eighteen months, it was never again permitted to meet during the remainder of his reign.[2] *commons demanded recall of commissions issued in defiance of the act;*

parliament never permitted to meet after prorogation in November, 1685.

3. Thus baffled in his attempt to induce the houses to repeal a fundamental law fatal to his designs, the king resolved to accomplish the same end through the exercise of an ancient prerogative of the crown generally known as the dispensing power, which had been immemorially employed either for the exemption of particular persons for special reasons from the operation of penal laws, or for the suspension of an entire statute or set of statutes in conflict with the royal will.   This exempting and suspending power, which is said to have been borrowed from the papal practice of issuing bulls " *non obstante* any law to the contrary," seems to have had its beginning in England in the reign of Henry III., who, when he attempted *James' use of the dispensing power;*

its origin and character;

said to have been borrowed from papal practice of issuing bulls non obstante;

---

[1] *Commons' Journals*, November 9.   [2] It was finally dissolved in July, 1687.

to justify its use by a reference to the papal precedents, was sharply rebuked by the grand prior of the Hospitallers for having made a graceless and absurd speech.   As long as you observe justice, he said, you will be king ; but as soon as you infringe it, you will cease to be one.[1]   The protest thus made against the *non obstante* clause at the outset was repeated in 1391, when the commons — after assenting that the king, by the advice and assent of the said lords, might make such sufferance respecting the Statute of Provisors as should seem reasonable and profitable to him until the next parliament — declared that such assent, which was a novelty and had never been given before, should not be considered as a precedent for the future.   Such limited power of suspension, despite such advice, was renewed in the parliaments of Henry IV.[2]   The full power seems to have been first asserted without protest and without parliamentary authority by Henry V., who, when he granted the request of the commons that the statute for the expulsion of aliens should be executed, made the express proviso that he would suspend the same at his pleasure.   In the next reign, however, parliament, after passing a statute declaring void all patents for the holding of the office of sheriff for more than one year, as emphatically repudiated such power by a proviso that the king should neither dispense with the requirements of the law, nor grant pardons or remissions to those who might violate it.[3]   The dispensing power which thus grew up in the midst of a continuous conflict between the crown and the legislature as to its existence and extent was reduced to something like definite form in the reign of Charles II., when in the case of Thomas *v.* Sorrel [4] — wherein the jury returned a special verdict, on the ground that they found a patent of 9 Jas. I. incorporating the Vintners' Company, with leave to sell wine *non obstante* the statute of 7 Edw. VI. — it was held that "*malum per se* cannot be dispensed with ; and as to *mala prohibita*, those statutes only may be dispensed with which were made for the king's profit, but not where they are for the general good, or the good of a third party.

Marginal notes:
early protests against its exercise ;

full power first exercised without protest by Henry V.;

repudiated in the next reign ;

defined in the case of Thomas *v.* Sorrel ;

---

[1] Matthew Paris, *Hist. Major*, p. 854. See the "Note to the Seven Bishops' Case," in Broom's *Const. Law*, Denman's ed., pp. 495–506.
[2] *Rot. Parl.*, vol. iii. pp. 285, 301.
[3] 23 Hen. VI. c. 8.
[4] Vaughan, pp. 330–339 (25 Car. II. 1674). Such was the law laid down by Coke, 1 Inst. 120 a ; 3 Inst. 154 (Cox, *Inst. Eng. Govt.*, p. 24, note b).

He may dispense with nuisances and penal laws by which no third party has a particular cause of action."

James first consulted the judges privately;
So the law stood at the time that James resolved to appeal to the courts to sanction his suspension of a general statute which his protestant subjects regarded as a bulwark of the national church.   In order to make sure, he first consulted the judges privately, and when it appeared that the chief justice of the common pleas, the chief baron of the exchequer, and two puisne judges were refractory, they were all dismissed, and their places supplied by others who were known to be subservient to the royal will.[1]   With the tribunal thus prepared, James issued patents under the great seal to the catholic officers of the army, relieving them of all penalties to which they were liable by virtue of the Test Act,[2] and authorizing them to hold their commissions, "any clause in any act of parliament notwithstanding."   A collusive action was then brought by Godden, a coachman to Sir Edward Hales,[3] against his master for a heavy penalty to which he was liable for holding a commission in the army without having previously complied with the conditions which the Test Act imposed.   The question was then presented whether the pardon and dispensation from the king contained in the letters patent were a bar to the action; and after the case had been heard in the king's bench in June, " eleven judges out of twelve concurred in holding that they were.   It is a question of little difficulty.   There is no law whatever but may be dispensed with by the supreme law-giver ; it is his inseparable prerogative to dispense with penal laws, in particular cases and upon particular reasons ; and of these reasons the king himself is sole judge."   Thus it was that the judges, plausibly supported by both parliamentary and judicial precedents, attempted to reverse the results of the Revolution of 1640, by declaring that the supreme power of the state was vested not in the king in parliament, but in the king in council.

and then issued patents to catholic officers exempting them from the Test Act ; collusive action of Godden v. Hales ;

judgment sustaining the dispensing power ;

attempt to reverse the results of the Revolution of 1640.

Armed with that fateful weapon, James now threw off the

---

[1] "I am determined," said the king, "to have twelve judges who will be all of my mind as to this matter." " Your Majesty," answered Jones (C. J.), " may find twelve judges of your mind, but hardly twelve lawyers."— See Macaulay, vol. i. p. 368, citing Reresby's *Memoirs ;* Echard, vol. iii. p. 797 ; Kennet, vol. iii. p. 451.

[2] 25 Car. II. c. 2.

[3] *Godden* v. *Hales*, 2 Shower, 475 ; *State Trials*, vol. xi. p. 1165.

James' attack upon the state church;

mask, in order to vigorously begin his attack upon the established church, utterly regardless of the promise made at his accession to both council and parliament "to preserve this government, both in church and state, as it is now established by law." Prior to the rendition of the judgment in the case

archbishops ordered to admonish the clergy;

of Hales, orders had been issued to the two archbishops by virtue of the ecclesiastical supremacy, commanding them to admonish the clergy to abstain from controversy detrimental

resistance of Dr. Sharp;

to "the king's religion," in defiance of which Dr. Sharp, dean of Norwich, had preached a sermon impugning with severity the motives of the many whose conversions to catholicism had

bishop of London refused to suspend him;

followed the "dragonnades." When Compton, bishop of London, was called upon to suspend Dr. Sharp, he declined to do more than advise him to keep silent, as his case had never come judicially before him. In order to provide an engine for the coercion of all ecclesiastics who might dare to oppose his plans,

practical reëstablishment of the court of high commission;

James resolved upon the practical reëstablishment of the court of high commission, which had been swept away by the act of the Long Parliament, abolishing the entire system of spiritual tribunals. As heretofore explained by the act of 13 Chas. II.

theory of its existence;

c. 12, s. 1, that system was restored, excepting only the *ex officio* oath and the high commission.[1] Upon the theory that only the *extraordinary* powers of the spiritual courts had thus perished, the king, after consultation with the judges, issued a commission in July to a new "Court of Commissioners for Ecclesiastical Causes," with Jeffreys, now lord chancellor, at its head, which as a permanent court was endowed with *ordinary* powers to hear ecclesiastical causes, and to pronounce ecclesiastical censures. When to the jurisdiction of this court, which was called in derision the *Congregatio de Propaganda*

Compton's plea to its jurisdiction treated with contempt;

Fide transferred from Rome to London, Compton filed a plea, it was treated with contempt; and after he had made every offer of reparation he was suspended, and the administration of his diocese handed over to three of his brethren.[2] In April the king had thrown open the old chapel at St. James for the public exercise of his religion; in May an army of about sixteen thousand men was encamped on Hounslow Heath, as a menace to the capital; and a few days after the high commis-

[1] See above, pp. 307, 308.   *Hist. of King James' Eccl. Commis.*,
[2] *State Trials*, vol. xi. pp. 1156–1166;   p. 2.

sion was constituted, four catholic lords [1] were sworn of the privy council in order to strengthen the royal hands against those tory councillors who opposed the repeal of the Test Act, which they regarded as the bulwark of the state church as then constituted.   At the head of that formidable opposition stood Laurence, earl of Rochester, the king's brother-in-law, and lord treasurer, who was dismissed from office early in January, 1687, as evidence of the fact that no one opposed to the king's ecclesiastical policy could hope to participate in the administration of government.   Thus bereft of the support of tory churchmen, James was driven as his brother had been driven before him to seek popular support by an appeal to protestant non-conformists, whom he hoped to placate by granting to them a freedom of worship which could at the same time be extended to his catholic brethren.   With that twofold purpose in view, a declaration of indulgence was issued on the 4th of April, in which the king contented himself for the moment "with suspending the execution of all penal laws for religious offences, and with forbidding the imposition of religious oaths or tests as qualifications for office," at the same time clearly intimating the belief that both measures would at the next meeting of parliament meet with its approval.[2]   To obtain such a compliant parliament as would lend itself to the execution of his designs now became the primary object of James' policy, and encouraged as he was by the outburst of gratitude which came from the independents, the presbyterians, the quakers, the anabaptists, and the catholics, for the boon of religious liberty, regardless of the means by which it had been obtained,[3] he dissolved the refractory body then in existence in the hope that new elections would vindicate his boast that by his liberality he had made his subjects a united people.

Two months prior to the Declaration of Indulgence the king had attempted to strengthen the catholic cause by seizing upon the universities, the strongholds held by the clergy of the establishment as training-schools for the youths of the higher classes destined to control in church and state.   The first step

Marginal notes: four catholic lords sworn of the privy council; Rochester and others dismissed from office, January, 1687; James' appeal to protestant non-conformists; Declaration of Indulgence issued April 4. parliament dissolved and new elections ordered. James' attack upon the universities;

---

[1] Powis, Arundel, Belasyse, and Dover.

[2] *Gazette*, 2231.

[3] Echard, 1084; Kennet, pp. 463– 465; *Ellis Correspondence*, pp. 260, 269, 274; *Gazette*, 2234, 2238, 2243; Marshall's *Early Hist. of Woodstock Manor*, p. 245.

a royal let-
ter sent to
Cambridge;
in that direction was taken by the sending of a royal letter to
the vice-chancellor of the University of Cambridge, commanding him to admit to the degree of master of arts without exacting from him the usual oaths, Francis, a Benedictine monk
and catholic missionary who lived in that neighborhood. When
its vice-
chancellor
deprived of
office by the
high com-
missioners;
the vice-chancellor refused to obey, unless Francis would
qualify according to law, he was summoned to appear before
the high commissioners, who deprived him of his office upon
the ground that a literary body could not be permitted to dispute the dispensing power which had been solemnly confirmed
by the judges.[1]   While that dispute was still pending, a more
serious attack was made upon the University of Oxford, where
the death of Dr. Clarke had made vacant the presidency of
Magdalen College, one of the richest foundations in Europe.
When mandatory letters were sent to the Fellows recommend-
ing them to choose Anthony Farmer, who was said to have
conformed to the Church of Rome, they replied that apart from
his bad moral character, he was not even qualified by statute
for the office.   After presenting these facts to the king and
asking for another nomination, the Fellows, before such nomination was received, met and elected Mr. Hough, one of their
controversy
submitted
to high
commis-
sion — its
finding;
number, president.   The claims of the opposing parties were
then submitted by royal order to the ecclesiastical commission,
who held that Hough's election was void, because a mandate to
choose one person prohibited by implication the right to choose
any other.   When the king next ordered the Fellows to elect
Dr. Parker, the bishop of Oxford, who is said to have been a
catholic at heart and the meanest of his courtiers, they resisted upon the ground that there was no vacancy in the office,
of which Hough was in actual possession.   To settle the controversy a special commission of visitors was sent to Oxford,
who pronounced Hough an intruder and installed Parker in
his place by force ; and the Fellows who resisted were not only
deprived of their fellowships, but declared incapable of holding
ecclesiastical preferments, or, if laymen, of being admitted to
holy orders.[2]   Upon the death of Parker, which quickly followed his installation, James by mandatory letters ordered the

---

[1] *Hist. of Eccl. Commis.*, p. 25;
State Trials, vol. xi. pp. 1315–1340;
James, vol. ii. pp. 125–127.
[2] *Hist. of Eccl. Commis.*, pp. 30, 32;

James, vol. ii. pp. 119, 124; Burnet, vol.
iii. pp. 143, 150; *State Trials*, vol. xii.
pp. 1, 112.

presidency to be given to Dr. Clifford, a catholic bishop *in partibus;* and thus Magdalen College, the majority of whose Fellows were already catholics, was taken from protestant hands and placed under the control of those who professed the king's faith.   The bitterness which arose out of these proceedings was intensified as they advanced by the introduction of Father Petre into the council, and by the public reception at Windsor of the papal nuncio, despite a statute expressly forbidding all diplomatic relations with the court of Rome.

Magdalen finally placed in catholic hands;

Father Petre admitted to the council.

The dogged opposition which met every attempt to set aside the Test Act by means of the dispensing power convinced James that the only effective way of removing that obstacle to his designs was through its repeal by parliament, and with that end in view he began in August, 1687, a royal progress, in the hope of convincing by argument those who opposed his political views.[1]   As an adjunct to that design he at the same time appointed a board called "regulators," who, under the pretext of reforming the corporations, were directed to so remould those bodies as to bring them in harmony with the court,[2] and orders were likewise given to the lord-lieutenants to so manipulate the political machinery of their counties as to produce the same result.   And in order to apply pressure to every individual, the three following questions were asked: Will you vote for the repeal of the Test Act and the penal laws if you are chosen to the next parliament? Will you promise to aid those candidates who pledge themselves to such repeal? Are you willing to live peacefully with men of different religious principles under the liberty of conscience which the crown has already proclaimed? But all such attempts utterly failed. The refusal of half of the lord-lieutenants and many of the justices to comply was followed by a wholesale dismissal of both, while despite the "regulations" it was found impossible to bend the corporations to the royal will.[3]   Under such discouraging conditions it was found necessary to adjourn the elections that had been fixed for February, 1688, until a further effort could be made to win popular support.   With that end in view a fresh appeal was made to the nation in

A royal progress made in August to influence the elections;

"regulators" directed to manage the corporations, the lord-lieutenants the counties;

failure of the scheme and dismissals from office;

[1] James, *Memoirs*, vol. ii. p. 134.
[2] *Life of James*, p. 139; Ralph, p. 965 *et seq.*
[3] For all details, see Lingard, vol. x. p. 264; Green, *Hist. of the Eng. People*, vol. iv. p. 22.

April by a republication of the Declaration of Indulgence, to which was now added the statement that as merit and not oaths should henceforth be the one qualification for office, all subjects of the crown would be secured "freedom of conscience forever." A new parliament was then promised for the following November, and all were exhorted to vote for representatives who would carry out therein the good work so happily begun.[1] And in order to give the greatest publicity

and solemnity to the document, the clergy of the established church, embittered as they were by jealousy and resentment, were commanded by an order in council to read it during divine service on two successive Sundays.[2] The almost universal refusal of the clergy to perform what they regarded as

an act of humiliation was sanctioned by Archbishop Sancroft, who, together with six of his suffragans, ventured to present a respectful petition to the king, in which they asked that the clergy might be excused from reading the Declaration, not from any lack of reverence for the sovereign or of tenderness for dissenters, but because it was founded on the dispensing power, "often declared illegal in parliament, and particularly in the years 1662 and 1672, and the beginning of your majesty's reign."[3] Despite the respectful form of the petition, its substance was accepted as "a standard of rebellion," and the

first answer to its prayer was an order to the "high commissioners" commanding them to deprive the seven subscribing bishops of their sees. In the presence of that proposal even Jeffreys faltered, and by his advice a prosecution was begun for seditious libel, upon which the seven, after their refusal to give bail, were committed to the Tower on the 8th of June.

In the course of the trial, which began in Westminster Hall on the 29th of that month in the presence of a vast and excited auditory, the counsel for the bishops contended (1) that they had simply exercised the right of petition touching an

[1] Wilkins, *Conc.*, vol. iv. p. 616.

[2] On the 20th and 27th of May at London and Westminster, and on the 3d and 10th of June in all other places.

[3] *State Trials*, vol. xii. p. 183. The first and second Declarations of Indulgence (4th and 27th of April), the order in council (May 4), and the petition of the bishops presented on May 18, are all printed in full in the case of the *Seven Bishops*, in Broom's *Const. Law*, Denman's ed., pp. 406-519. As to this important trial, see also Burnet, vol. iii. pp. 222-226; Macpherson, vol. i. p. 266; *Hist. of Eccl. Commis.*, pp. 53-60; Macaulay, vol. i. pp. 499, 500, 504, 513-517, 518.

ecclesiastical question with which they were specially charged; (2) that the dispensing power which the petition challenged had no legal existence. After argument the judges held that only two questions remained for the jury; the first involving the fact of the publication of the petition, the second, the character of its contents. Upon the last point two of the judges, Wright and Allybone, instructed the jury that the petition was libellous, while the other two, Holloway and Powell, declared that it was not. After a night passed in stormy debate the jury rendered a verdict of not guilty, which was received with an enthusiastic shout, that swelled through the capital and adjoining hamlets until it reached the king himself at Hounslow Heath, where in the midst of his standing army he thus received the first warning of the mighty change that was soon to come.[1]

two questions submitted to the jury;

verdict of not guilty.

4. Two days after the bishops were committed to the Tower, an event occurred which precipitated the Revolution. From the time of James' conversion to catholicism the nation had been pacified by the assurance that, although temporary evils might flow from his accession, the crown at his death would pass first to Mary and then to Anne, the two surviving children of his first marriage with Anne Hyde, the daughter of Clarendon. In order to strengthen that hope, Mary as presumptive heir was confirmed a protestant by royal order in 1674; and to make assurance doubly sure she was married on November 4, 1677, to her cousin, the great protestant prince, William of Orange. When the first Exclusion Bill was read in the commons on the 5th of November, 1680, Mary was still her father's presumptive heir,[2] and thus it was that William came to be looked upon, not only by the protestant chiefs but by James himself, as a person to be reckoned with in every crisis which involved the future of the succession. Thus it was that, when in May, 1687, the month following the Declaration of Indulgence, the king appealed to William and Mary to declare in favor of the abolition of the penal laws and of the Test, many of the great nobles, together with the bishop of

Birth of a male heir to James precipitated the Revolution;

until then Mary the presumptive heir;

[1] Barillon, in his letter to Louis July 12), said : " La joie et les acclamations ont été fort grandes à Westminster, quand on a su la décision. Il y a eu des boites tirées sur la rivière. On fit des feux de joie. La populace brula une représentation du pape."

[2] Bailey, *Succession to the English Crown*, pp. 217, 218.

London, hastened to offer the prince either assurances of support, or counsel against compliance with the king's demand.

William's firm response that "I cannot concur in what your majesty desires of me," left no room for doubt as to his position upon the vital question by which the nation was then convulsed.[1]   In the following December a proclamation appeared in the "Gazette" that Mary of Modena, the catholic princess whom James had married two years after Anne

Hyde's death, was again pregnant; and on the 10th of June, 1688, in the midst of the indignation excited by the committal of the bishops to the Tower, the queen, then only thirty years old, gave birth to a son, the ill-fated prince generally known in history as James III., or the old Pretender.   Thus it was that the prospect, so long assured, of a protestant succession was suddenly blasted by the advent of a catholic heir, just at the moment when James' fierce and persistent attack upon the established church he had promised to defend was fast driving

the nation to open resistance.   In the presence of the emergency thus presented the leaders of the protestant cause resolved, in the teeth of facts no longer disputed, to assume that the birth of a male heir to James was a deliberate invention, and then to invite William to come in arms not only for the defence of English liberty and religion, but also for the restoration of the reign of law which had broken down under the king's attempts to coerce the church and remodel the magistracy in open defiance of existing statutes.   Under the pressure of this common danger tories and whigs, high churchmen and nonconformists, putting aside for the moment all differences, drew

together; and on the 30th of June, the very day on which the verdict in favor of the bishops was rendered, the leaders of the coalition subscribed in cipher an invitation to William to come at once at the head of an army strong enough to justify his friends in rising to sustain him.[2]   Danby signed as the chief of the tories, Devonshire as the leader of the general body of whigs and non-conformists, Compton, bishop of London, as the representative of the high churchmen; and to their names were added those of the earl of Shrewsbury, of Lord Lumley, of Edward the cousin of Lord Russell, and of Henry the

---

[1] Green, *Hist. of the Eng. People*,   [2] See Burnet, vol. iii. p. 265.
vol. iv. p. 22.

brother of Algernon Sidney. Tempted less, perhaps, by the prospect of securing the English crown for his wife than by the hope of ending with England's aid the supremacy of France in Europe, the ruling passion of his life, William resolved to accept the invitation ; and as soon as the assent of those in Holland who opposed his plans could be obtained, he began to gather a fleet with forces sufficient for the enterprise. Thus menaced, James suddenly gave way ; and in the hope of winning back the confidence he had lost, he began before the end of September to reverse all of his recent acts by appealing for aid and counsel to the bishops whom he had so lately prosecuted ; by sending back in state its forfeited charter to the city of London, and by restoring to other cities and towns their ancient privileges ; by the dissolution of the ecclesiastical commission ; and by the restoration of Dr. Hough and the Fellows to their places in Magdalen College, and the removed deputy lieutenants and magistrates to their offices in the counties. When Sunderland pressed James to go a step further by calling a parliament, the king, suspicious of a treacherous design to place him absolutely in William's hands, drew back ; and before the end of October he dismissed Sunderland from office. At that moment it was that William's declaration reached England, promising freedom of conscience to catholics and toleration to protestant non-conformists, and demanding the calling of a free parliament for the settlement of the succession, and for the reëstablishment of English freedom and religion upon a secure basis.[1] On the 5th of November the prince landed at Torbay at the head of a force including representatives from every part of the protestant world, which, after a momentary hesitation, was so swelled by adherents from every quarter as to make its advance a peaceful and triumphal progress. In the midst of the panic that ensued, Grafton and Churchill deserted the king and went over to the enemy's camp, where they were soon joined by Prince George and Princess Anne ; while the royal army, broken by dissensions and distrust, after shrinking from an engagement with William's forces, was disbanded. Thus abandoned, James re-

his acceptance;

James' attempt to win back the nation by concessions;

arrival of William's declaration;

he landed at Torbay November 5;

[1] Burnet, vol. iii. p. 286; Dumont, vol. vii. pt. ii. pp. 198, 205. He was "called in to vindicate practically those maxims of liberty for which, in good and evil days, England had contended through so many centuries." — Taylor, *Book of Rights*, p. 211.

flight of
James.

solved upon flight, and, after sending the queen and the young prince away before him, he left the palace in disguise by night only to be captured and brought back the next day in safety to London. When upon the entry of the Dutch troops into the capital he was ordered to quit Whitehall, he withdrew to Rochester, whence, after writing a declaration[1] of his motives for quitting the kingdom, he embarked for France on the 23d of December.

[1] Echard, 1134; James, *Memoirs*, vol. ii. 273.

CHAPTER III.

WILLIAM AND MARY AND THE REVOLUTION-SETTLEMENT.

1. WILLIAM had already declared that his purpose in coming into England at the head of an army was to make possible the calling of a free parliament for the settlement of the succession, and for the reëstablishment of English freedom and religion upon a firm basis. As there was no parliament in existence when James' first flight suspended for a time all regular government, it was a difficult matter to determine how to assemble the estates without the king's writ, from which, according to the immemorial legal theory, parliament derives its being and its powers. For the third time since the Conquest the English people were now called upon to set aside that theory in favor of the earlier doctrine that parliament really derives its existence and authority from the call of the nation from which its life is drawn. The Revolution of 1399, wherein Richard II. was deposed and Henry IV. elected in his stead, was worked out by an assembly which, though summoned by the king's writ, was not opened by his commission, an irregularity aggravated by the legal assumption that the assembly ceased to exist when Richard ceased to be king. To meet the last difficulty the same assembly, shrinking from the name of parliament and assuming to act only by the name of the estates of the realm, was by a legal fiction summoned again under writs issued by Henry, which were not and could not be followed by any real election. To further obscure the true nature of the transaction, the deposition of Richard was veiled by a pretended resignation, and the election of Henry justified by a claim of the crown as a matter of right.[1] But despite all such legal subtilties, the fact remained that in the presence of a great emergency the national assembly, continued without the royal writ in the traditional form, deposed one king and elected

Marginal notes:
Second Convention Parliament and its work;

theory that parliament cannot be legally constituted without the king's writ;

parliament of 1399, wherein Richard II. was deposed and Henry IV. elected;

legal subtilties employed to conceal defects in its organization.

[1] Lingard, vol. iii. pp. 394–398; Hallam, *Middle Ages*, vol. ii. p. 214; Freeman, *Growth of the Eng. Const.*, pp. 133 and 134, and note 15.

another, whose right to reign was thus made to rest upon a parliamentary title.[1]   As heretofore explained, the assembly known as the first Convention Parliament, that secured to Charles II. the right to reign, was called not by a royal writ, but by the authority of the Long Parliament, which had protected itself by positive law against either a prorogation or dissolution without its own consent.   And yet in order to remove the doubt that existed as to the validity of its organization, the convention felt called upon to declare that it was in fact "the two houses of parliament, notwithstanding the want of the king's writ of summons;"[2] and as an additional assurance its acts were confirmed by its successor summoned in the traditional manner.   In the light of these precedents, William was called upon to convene the estates of the realm without the aid either of the king's writ or the mandate of a preceding parliament.   In the presence of such difficulties he resolved, by virtue of his own *de facto* authority, to call together representatives who had in time past been honored with the confidence of the nation, in the hope that they would convoke such an assembly as would be able to authoritatively express the national will.   Thus it was that the prince attempted, on the 21st of December, 1688, to constitute an upper house by summoning to St. James the lords spiritual and temporal who were then in London;[3] and two days thereafter he invited to attend him on the morning of the 26th all gentlemen who had sat in the lower house during the reign of Charles II., together with the lord mayor of London, the aldermen, and fifty citizens, as representatives of the common council, to the end that they, as representatives of the whole nation, might advise him "as to the best manner how to pursue the ends of his declaration."[4]   On the 25th the lords, without waiting for the action of the popular body, presented an address requesting the prince (1) to take upon himself provisionally the administration of government; (2) to issue circular letters to all the constituent

Margin notes:

first Convention Parliament called without the king's writ;

declared itself "the two houses of parliament;"

expedients employed by William in calling second Convention Parliament

to advise him "how to pursue the ends of his declaration;"

---

[1] Vol. i. pp. 513, 514.

[2] See above, p. 359.

[3] On the 11th of December about thirty temporal and spiritual peers had joined the mayor and aldermen at the Guildhall, in the formation of a council that assumed for the moment the supreme authority, and presented to the prince a declaration of their willingness to aid him in calling a free parliament.   Clarendon, *Diary*, p. 224; Barillon, December 22.

[4] Kennet, p. 505; Clarendon's *Diary*, December 21, 1688; Burnet, vol. i. p. 803, and Onslow's note.

bodies of the kingdom inviting them to send up in the usual way persons to represent them in a convention of estates to be held at Westminster on the 22d of January, 1689.[1] Not, however, until the representatives of the counties and towns had concurred in the recommendation of the lords [2] did the prince reply to each assembly separately, assuring them that he would accept the advice they had given him.[3] The elections which began on the 9th of January were rapidly and peacefully concluded, and at the appointed time the peers, about a hundred in number, met under the presidency of Halifax, while the commons organized themselves by calling Powle to the chair. In the course of its proceedings the assembly proclaimed itself to be "the two houses of parliament, and so shall be and are hereby declared enacted and adjudged to be to all intents, constructions, and purposes whatsoever, . . . as if they had been summoned according to the usual form." [4] However, notwithstanding that declaration, the succeeding parliament deemed it necessary to pass an act declaring the acts and proceedings of its predecessor valid.[5]

elections began January 9, 1689;

second convention declared itself to be "the two houses of parliament."

The assembly which thus set aside the legal theory that a valid parliament can only be convened by the king's writ became entangled at the very outset of its labors in the meshes of another that proved more difficult to overcome. The high function the convention was first called upon to perform involved no less than the deposition of James, who had declared that he had left the realm only because his life was in danger, and the election of William and Mary to the vacant throne, — a proceeding that would have been at once natural and easy had the mind of the nation been swayed by the obsolete and forgotten precedents of pre-Norman times which tell us, among other things, how the witan of Wessex once deposed Sigeberht

Deposition of James and election of William and Mary;

pre-Norman precedents;

[1] Clarendon's *Diary*, December 24, 1688; *Parl. Hist.*, vol. v. p. 26; *London Gazette*, December 31.

[2] Van Citters, $\frac{\text{December 25,}}{\text{January 4,}}$ 168$\frac{8}{9}$.

[3] Ibid., $\frac{\text{December 28,}}{\text{January 7,}}$ 168$\frac{8}{9}$; *Life of William*, 1703; Macaulay, vol. i. pp. 616–620.

[4] 1 Will. & Mar. sess. 1, c. 1.

[5] The bill, which originated in the lords, passed the commons after a sharp debate in which Somers took part. See *Commons' Journals*, April 8 and 9,

1690. By some strange oversight, although Macaulay comments at length upon the passage of the confirming act (vol. ii. p. 160), Mr. Freeman says that no such act was passed. "The acts of the Convention of 1688 were not deemed to need any such confirmation." — *Growth of the Eng. Const.*, p. 137. Taswell-Langmead, in quoting Mr. Freeman, has fallen into the same error. *Eng. Const. Hist.*, p. 766, and note 4.

from the royal dignity and elected his relative, Cynewulf, in his stead.[1]   The fact was, however, that this early conception of an elective and deposable king had been supplanted ages before by the hereditary theory, which, under the influence of feudal ideas, gave birth to the doctrine that the throne can never be vacant because the king never dies; that there can be no such thing as an interregnum because the reign of the heir begins the moment that of his predecessor is ended.[2]   To that doctrine, which, according to the claim of Edward IV., constituted such an indefeasible hereditary title as parliament could neither ignore nor set aside,[3] James I. added the claim of divine right,[4] supplemented in the reign of Charles II. by the religious dogma of non-resistance or passive obedience,[5] invented by servile churchmen who were the first to repudiate it.   Such was the nature of the kingship with which James claimed to be clothed when he and his infant heir were forcibly driven from the palace of their ancestors to seek shelter in a foreign land.   How to dispose of the king and heir thus circumstanced was the problem with which the convention was confronted, and the attempt to solve it divided the assembly into groups, each distinguishable from the other by the possession of its own political expedient.   After deducting the few blind adherents of James who desired his unconditional recall, and a handful of republicans who dreamed of reviving the Commonwealth, the main body of the convention was divided, as was the nation itself, into two parties, Tories and Whigs, the former being in the majority in the upper, the latter in the lower house.   When on the 28th of January the battle began in the commons, the Whigs, who were there charged with the responsibility of power, attempted to solve all theoretical difficulties, not by appealing to the simple yet obsolete precedents of the earliest times, but by boldly employing the new-fangled political philosophy of Hobbes,[6] which rested upon the unhistorical assumption of an original contract between the nation and the king, under which the latter might forfeit his rights by misconduct.   By the aid of that theory the popular party was able to unite every element of opposition to

conception of an elective and deposable king superseded by hereditary theory;

supplemented by doctrine of divine right and passive obedience;

the problem to be solved;

division of parties;

commons appealed to political philosophy of Hobbes;

---

[1] Cf. vol. i. pp. 189, 190.
[2] Ibid., pp. 241, 405.
[3] Ibid., p. 577.
[4] See above, p. 212.
[5] See above, p. 393.
[6] See above, p. 392.

James, in passing without a division the famous resolution which declared "That King James II., having endeavoured to subvert the constitution of the kingdom by breaking *the original contract between king and people*, and having, by the advice of Jesuits and other wicked persons, violated the fundamental laws, and withdrawn himself out of the kingdom, has abdicated the government, and that the throne is thereby vacant." On the next day it was further resolved unanimously, "that it hath been found by experience inconsistent with the safety and welfare of this protestant kingdom to be governed by a popish prince."[1] When these resolutions were sent to the upper house, the lords, after giving their unanimous assent to the latter, entered upon a critical discussion of the former, which disclosed how hard it was to reconcile the fact of a vacant throne with the royalist theory of indefeasible hereditary right that assumed such a fact to be legally impossible. In the presence of that difficulty the Tories had already broken into three groups, each of which had its own way of meeting it. The extreme wing, led by Sherlock, and specially strong among the clergy, proposed to negotiate for the return of James upon the basis of satisfactory civil and ecclesiastical guarantees; another group, headed by Sancroft, proposed to continue the title in James, while taking from him, upon the assumption of his unfitness, all control over the administration, which was to be vested in a regency; while a third, headed by Danby, contended that James had by his flight abdicated the royal power and dignity, which had already devolved upon the next heir, the princess of Orange, for the reason that the throne could not be for one moment vacant.[2] The fact that James' infant son and not the princess of Orange was his next and lawful heir, if he had really abdicated, was disposed of by the convenient legal fiction that there was really no such heir in existence.[3] After full debate, in which these various schemes were duly considered, that one which proposed a regency, with the regal title still in James, was lost by only a

Margin notes: theory of the social contract as embodied in its resolution; a vacant throne impossible under the indefeasible theory; tory expedients for meeting the difficulty; legal fiction that James had no male heir; proposal of a regency defeated by only one vote;

---

[1] *Commons' Journals*, January 28 and 29; *Parl. Hist.*, vol. v. pp. 150, 152; Van Citters, January 29, February 8.

[2] For a detailed statement of the plans of Sherlock, Sancroft, and Danby, see Macaulay, vol. i. pp. 628–630.

[3] "It seemed to be tacitly understood by both sides that the infant child was to be presumed spurious." — Hallam, *Const. Hist.*, vol. iii. p. 95.

single vote.[1]   Passing then to verbal criticism, the lords, after admitting that there was an original contract between king and people,[2] substituted the word " deserted " for " abdicated," and rejected entirely the final and vital clause, " that the throne is thereby vacant." [3]   At this point it was that William, alarmed by the heavy vote in favor of a regency, felt it his duty to declare that he would not only decline to be regent with the regal title in James, but that he would also decline to carry on the administration with the regal title in his wife alone.   He said that if the estates saw fit to confer upon him the crown for life he would accept it, otherwise he would return to his own country.   He was willing, however, that Anne and her descendants should be put in the succession before any children that he might have by any other wife than Mary, who upon her part declined to accept the crown save in conjunction with her husband.[4]   In order to remove all such differences, two conferences [5] were held between the houses, after which the lords agreed to adopt the original resolution of the commons without amendment ; and that action was followed by a resolution in which the upper house declared that the prince and princess of Orange should be proclaimed king and queen of England, and of all dominions thereunto belonging.[6]   The commons refused, however, to concur in such a hasty settlement of the crown until a formal document could be drawn up, setting forth in a clear and solemn form the fundamental principles of the constitution in accordance with which the new dynasty was expected to govern.[7]   That duty was intrusted to a committee whose chairman was John Somers, a young barrister, who had distinguished himself in the trial of the bishops ; and after some unimportant amendments by the lords, the Declaration of Right, which thus came into being, was approved by both houses on the 12th of February.[8]   On the

Marginal notes:
William's refusal to be regent;

Mary refused to accept the crown alone;

lords finally agreed to adopt commons' resolution without amendment;

commons then insisted upon a declaration of principles;

John Somers;

Declaration of Right approved February 12;

---

[1] 51 votes against 49. *Lords' Journals*, vol. xiv. p. 110; Clarendon's *Diary*, January 29 ; Burnet, pp. 810, 811.

[2] 53 votes against 46.

[3] 55 votes against 41. Thereupon thirty-six peers entered their dissent in the journals (pp. 112, 113) ; Kennet, p. 510; Clarendon's *Diary*, January 31.

[4] Burnet, p. 820 ; Macaulay, vol. i. p. 645.

[5] For the discussions, see *Parl.*

Hist., vol. v. pp. 64, 108 ; *Life of James*, p. 11.

[6] The first proposition was carried by a majority of four; the second, by a majority of about twenty. *Lords' Journals*, pp. 118, 119 ; Clarendon's *Diary*, February 6 ; Dalrymple, App. 340. See Lingard, vol. x. p. 400, and note 1.

[7] *Parl. Hist.*, vol. v. pp. 52, 58 ; Burnet, p. 822.

[8] *Commons' Journals*, February 4, 8,

next day the convention met the prince and princess of Orange at Whitehall, where, after the clerk of the house of lords had read his declaration in a loud voice, Halifax, speaking in the name of the estates, requested them to accept the crown upon that basis. Whereupon William, speaking in his own name and in that of his wife, said : " We thankfully accept what you have offered us," declaring at the same time the resolve of both to uphold the laws and to govern with the advice of parliament.[1]

crown tendered and accepted on that basis.

The Declaration of Right thus put forth was a summing up in a dogmatic form of that code of positive law regulating the prerogatives of the crown, the privileges of parliament, and the liberty of the subject now generally known as " the Law of the Constitution,"[2] as distinguished from that body of political maxims, of silent understandings, undefined either by common or statute law, which have been invented since the beginning of the reign of William III., as the most convenient means of regulating the changed relations of the two houses to each other and of the crown to both, necessarily resulting from the transfer through the Revolution of the sovereignty of the state from the crown to the legislature. In that practical temper which has always characterized Englishmen on such occasions, the declaration entered directly upon the question of recent grievances by asserting that King James II., misled by evil counsellors, did endeavor to subvert and extirpate the protestant religion and the laws and liberties of the kingdom by an abuse of the dispensing power ; by erecting the court of commissioners for ecclesiastical causes ; by denying parliament's exclusive right of taxation ; by maintaining without its consent a standing army in time of peace, and by quartering soldiers contrary to law ; by disarming good protestants when papists were armed and employed contrary to the law ; by violating the freedom of election of members to serve in parliament ; by prosecutions in the king's bench for matters cognizable only in the houses ; by the return of partial and corrupt juries, especially in trials for high treason ; by the exaction of ex-

The Declaration a summing up of the law of the constitution

as distinguished from the conventional constitution;

recent grievances, religious and political, clearly defined;

11, 12 ; *Lords' Journals,* February 9, 11, 12, 1688–89. On the 12th of February Mary arrived in England.

[1] " Parliament thus conferred the crown, but **William soon found that**

they meant to retain the sceptre."— Torrens, *Hist. of Cabinets,* vol. i. p. 3.

[2] See Mr. Dicey's *Introduction to the Study of the Law of the Constitution,* 1893.

cessive bail; by the imposition of excessive fines and the infliction of cruel and illegal punishments; and finally by promising away estates as forfeited prior to the conviction of the in order to remove them, new sovereigns called upon to join estates in declaring illegal persons to whom they belonged.   In order to put an end to these mighty evils, the prince of Orange had come as "the glorious instrument of delivering this kingdom from popery and arbitrary power."   Therefore in order to make that deliverance perpetual, the new sovereigns were called upon to join the estates in declaring : —

the suspending "1. That the pretended power of suspending of laws, or the execution of laws, by regall authoritie, without consent of Parlyament, . . . is illegall.

and dispensing powers; "2. That the pretended power of dispensing with laws, or the execution of laws, by regall authoritie, as it hath beene assumed and exercised of late, is illegall.

the commission for ecclesiastical causes; "3. That the commission for erecting the late Court of Commissioners for Ecclesiasticall causes, and all other Commissions and courts of like nature, are illegall and pernicious.

all forms of conciliar taxation; "4. That levying money for or to the use of the Crowne by pretence of prerogative, without grant of Parlyament, for longer time or in other manner than the same is or shall be granted, is illegall.

all attempts to deny the right of petition; "5. That it is the right of the subject to petition the king, and all commitments and prosecutions for such petition are illegall.

a standing army in time of peace; "6. That the raising or keeping a standing army within the Kingdome in time of peace, unless it be with consent of Parlyament, is against law.

denial of the right to bear arms; "7. That the subjects which are Protestants may have arms for their defence suitable to their conditions, and as allowed by law.

denial of free elections; "8. That elections of members of Parlyament ought to be free.

denial of freedom of speech; "9. That the freedome of speech, and debates or proceedings in Parlyament, ought not to be impeached or questioned in any court or place out of Parlyament.

excessive bail and cruel punishments; "10. That excessive baile ought not to be required nor excessive fines imposed; nor cruell and unusuall punishment inflicted.

juries improperly chosen; "11. That jurors ought to be duely impannelled and returned, and jurors which passe upon men in trialls for high treason ought to be freeholders.

"12. That all grants and promises of fines and forfeitures of particular persons before conviction, are illegall and void.

"13. And that for the redresse of all grievances, and for the amending, strengthening, and preserveing of the lawes, Parlyament ought to be held frequently.

"And they doe claime, demand, and insist upon all and singular the premisses, as their undoubted rights and liberties; and that noe declarations, judgments, doeings or proceedings, to the prejudice of the people in any of the said premisses, ought in anywise to be drawn hereafter into consequence or example." Then, — after declaring that "the said late King James the Second haveing abdicated the government, and the throne being thereby vacant;" and further that the Prince of Orange will "preserve them from the violation of their rights, which they have here asserted, and from all other attempts upon their religion, rights and liberties," — the declaration proceeds upon that basis to "resolve, that William and Mary, Prince and Princesse of Orange, be, and be declared, King and Quenne of England, France and Ireland, and the dominions thereunto belonging, to hold the Crowne and royall dignity of the said kingdomes and dominions to them the said Prince and Princesse dureing their lives and the life of the survivour of them; and that the sole and full exercise of the regall power be onely in, and executed by the said Prince of Orange, in the names of the said Prince and Princesse, during their joynt lives; and after their deceases, the said Crowne and royall dignitie of the said kingdomes and dominions, to be to the heires of the body of the said Princesse; and for default of such issue to the Princesse Anne of Denmarke; and the heires of her body; and for default of such issue to the heires of the body of the said Prince of Orange."[1] Through this parliamentary deposition of one sovereign and election of another the preposterous doctrine of a divine and indefeasable hereditary right independent of law, which claimed that the throne could not be for one moment vacant, was destroyed, first by the assumption that there was no legal sovereign from the abdication of James on the 23d of December to the election of

Marginal notes: promises of forfeitures before conviction; denial of frequent parliaments: all insisted upon as "undoubted rights and liberties;" throne declared to be vacant through James' abdication; election of William and Mary; limited settlement of the succession; Princess Anne; destruction of the indefeasible hereditary theory.

[1] See *Lords' Journals*, vol. v. p. 125.

William and Mary on the 13th of February ; second by the settlement of the principle that "an English monarch is now as much the creature of an act of parliament as the pettiest tax-gatherer in his realm." [1]

Convention, after declaring itself a parliament, took a recess until October 19.

Ten days after the accession of William and Mary, the royal assent was given to a bill which declared the convention a parliament, "notwithstanding any fault of writ or writs of summons ;" [2] and on the 20th of August, after seven months of active work, it took a recess until the 19th of October. Then

Declaration turned into a Bill of Rights;

it was that the act [3] was passed which turned the Declaration of Right into a formal Bill of Rights, whereby two somewhat important additions were made to the original instrument. In

new barriers against a possible catholic sovereign,

order to make more effectual the barriers against a possible catholic sovereign, it was now enacted that every king or queen hereafter succeeding to the crown should repeat and subscribe in full parliament the Declaration against Transubstantiation ; that no person who should marry a papist should be capable of reigning in England ; and that if an actual sovereign should contract such a marriage, the subject should be thereby ab-

and against the dispensing power;

solved from allegiance. And in order to remove all doubts upon the subject of the dispensing power, which the declaration had simply declared illegal "as it hath beene assumed and exercised of late," the dreaded and anomalous prerogative was at last entirely taken away. [4] But while deficiencies in the

no attempt to secure freedom of discussion;

declaration were thus being supplied, no attempt was made to secure freedom of speech and of the press to the nation as a whole. The original instrument, which entirely ignored the right last named, only guaranteed the former so far as pro-

regulation of commerce.

ceedings in parliament were concerned. [5] In like manner the right of regulating English commerce, which the houses shortly afterwards silently claimed and obtained, in the discussions on the charter granted to the East India Company, was left as of old to the control of the crown. [6]

2. In order to give the highest possible security to the sovereignty with which the Revolution had crowned them, the

---

1 Green, *Hist. of the Eng. People*, vol. iv. p. 44.

2 1 Will. and Mar. sess. 1, c. 1.

3 1 Will. and Mar. sess. 2, c. 2.

4 " Except in such cases as shall be specially provided for by one or more

bill or bills to be passed dureing this present session of Parlyament." No such bill or bills were passed.

5 § 9.

6 Cf. Green, *Hist. of the Eng. People,* vol. iv. p. 46.

houses resolved to assume more perfectly than ever before the control of both the purse and the sword. When the time came for the parliament of 1690[1] to make a permanent settlement of the revenue, it kept steadily in view the all-important fact that the life-grants made to the last two kings had rendered both largely independent of the coercion incident to the power of withholding supplies. Thus warned, the lower house began by agreeing that £1,200,000[2] should be the ordinary annual revenue of the crown in time of peace, to be provided from two distinct sources, — the first consisting of hereditary dues derived from fees and fines, from the royal domain, from wine licenses, from firstfruits and tenths, from the receipts of the post-office, and from that part of the excise which had been granted forever to Charles II. and his successors, in lieu of the fruits of feudal tenures surrendered upon those terms.[3] To all these sources, which produced an annual income estimated at between four and five hundred thousand pounds,[4] parliament added a grant of the excise, in addition to that which was hereditary, for the lives of William and Mary and that of the survivor.[5] Still there was a great deficit. The mainspring of government, the second great source of revenue, was the customs, the port duties, settled for life upon Charles and James successively, without which the state machinery could not be kept in motion, and with which a despotic king could rule without parliaments. Upon that vital resource therefore the house, when in grand committee on the supply, resolved to seize, and after several members had pressed for a life-grant to William of the customs or port duties, it was resolved to grant them only for a limited term of four years,[6] it being "taken for a general maxim, that the revenue for a certain and short term was the best security that the nation could have for frequent parliaments, and the question was settled on that ground."

Legislation supplementary to Bill of Rights:

power to withhold supplies;

revenue derived from hereditary dues

and the excise;

mainspring of government the customs;

granted only for a short term to secure frequent parliaments;

---

[1] It met March 20, under writs issued upon the dissolution of its predecessors in the month before.

[2] *Parl. Hist.*, vol. v. p. 193. It had been fixed at that sum at Restoration. See above, p. 361.

[3] Macaulay, vol. ii. p. 155; Dowell, *Hist. of Taxation*, pp. 41, 42.

[4] *Commons' Journals*, March 28, 1690, and March 1 and 20, 1688-89.

[5] 2 Will. and Mar. c. 3. Contin-

ued by 1 Anne, st. 1, c. 7, and 1 Geo. I. st. 1, c. 1; and perpetuated by 1 Geo. I. st. 2, c. 12, §8. Estimated at the accession of William at £300,000.

[6] *Parl. Hist.*, vol. v. p. 561; 2 Will. and Mar. c. 4. As to William's reluctance to accept the gift in that form, see Burnet, vol. iv. pp. 76, 77. The bishop explained to him that the jealousy was of those who might succeed him.

The important principle thus settled as to the raising of the revenue was at the same time coupled with an equally important legal rule as to the manner of its expenditure. The principle imperfectly recognized in the reign of Charles II., that *appropriation of supplies;* money voted by parliament could be appropriated only by its direction to certain specific heads of expenditure, has since the Revolution become the settled usage. Thus came into being *origin of the "Civil List;"* at that time what is known as the "Civil List," a term originally used to designate the sources of revenue appropriated to produce a fund out of which was to be defrayed the expenses of the royal household and of certain civil officers, such as judges, ambassadors, and the like, of which a list had been laid before the house.[1] The necessary result of this arrangement *necessity for annual appropriation bills;* was annual appropriation bills, into which were introduced clauses forbidding the lords of the treasury under heavy penalties to order by their warrants the payment of any moneys in the exchequer except such as were specially appropriated. In that way the old idea that taxes once raised were in fact a gift from the houses to the crown was forced to give way to the rigid legal rule of the modern constitution, which provides that *not a penny to be spent without parliamentary authority;* not a penny of the national revenue can be expended without the authority of some act of parliament.[2] The grant of the *vote of supplies an annual one;* port duties to William for four years was soon followed by the resolve to make the vote of supplies an annual one, and so it came to pass that parliament must meet at least once a year in order to keep the machinery of the state in motion. As an addition to the perfect control over the executive power thus practically vested in the house of commons, those who were mindful of the fact that Charles II. had continued his second

---

[1] Dowell, *Hist. of Taxation*, vol. ii. pp. 43, 44. The amount of the civil list was fixed in 1689 at £600,000, and to that purpose was applied the hereditary excise, the other hereditary revenues, and the ordinary excise, what remained being set apart for other public expense and contingent expenditure. *Parl. Hist.*, p. 193. "The expenses of the royal household are now entirely separated from the expenses of civil government; but, by a whimsical perversion, the name of Civil List has remained attached to that portion of the revenue which is appropriated to the expenses of the royal household."— Macaulay, vol. ii. p. 155.

[2] "This authority may be given by a permanent Act, as for example by the Civil List Act, 1 & 2 Vict. c. 2, or by the National Debt and Local Loans Act, 1887; or it may be given by the Appropriation Act, that is, the annual Act by which Parliament 'appropriates' or fixes the sums payable to objects (the chief of which is the support of the army and navy) which are not provided for, as is the payment of the National Debt, by permanent Acts of Parliament."— Dicey, *The Law of the Constitution*, p. 295.

parliament for seventeen years resolved to prevent in future such a divorce between the people and their representatives, and the corruption incident thereto, by the enactment of a law forbidding the existence of a parliament for a longer period than three years. Such a measure, after having passed both houses early in 1693, was destroyed by the royal veto; and then, after reënactment, received the royal assent in November of the following year.[1]

Triennial Bill of 1694.

The statesmen of the Revolution, imbued with the hatred of a standing army which began in the days of the Commonwealth, resolved, after providing that no such thing should exist in time of peace, without the consent of parliament,[2] to make its support and discipline at all times dependent absolutely upon the will of that body. With that end in view was passed the first Mutiny Act of 1689,[3] whose object and principles are the same as the Army Act, 1881,[4] under which the regular army of the land is now substantially governed. The two vital principles underlying that system of government are these: first, that no pay can be issued to the troops without a previous appropriation by parliament; second, that no officer or soldier can be punished for disobedience, nor any court-martial held, save through an annual reënactment of the Mutiny Bill, without which "no man may be forejudged of life or limb, or subjected to any kind of punishment by martial law, or in any other manner than by the judgment of his peers."[5] By English law a soldier, although a member of a standing army, is still a subject endowed with all the rights and duties of an ordinary citizen, and as such is amenable to "the ordinary process of law."[6] It is therefore only in his military capacity, which is simply superimposed upon his civil, that he can be tried and punished by court-martial. The civil courts, however, reserve the right to determine what persons are subject to military law; and in the event that either an officer or a court-martial exercises authority over a soldier not authorized by that law, such courts also reserve the right of supervision,

Control of the army.

first Mutiny Act of 1689;

without its annual reenactment army can neither be paid nor disciplined;

every soldier still a citizen;

only in his military capacity can he be tried by court-martial,

subject to review by civil tribunals

---

1 6 Will. and Mar. c. 2.
2 Bill of Rights, s. 6.
3 1 Will. & Mar. c. 5.
4 44 & 45 Vict. c. 58.
5 Preamble to first Mutiny Act.
6 The first Mutiny Act so provided

expressly. 1 Will. & Mar. c. 5, s. 6. Cf. Clode, *Military Forces of the Crown*, vol. i. pp. 499, 500. A soldier is also subject to the same criminal liability as a civilian.

through
habeas
corpus
proceed-
ings.

which may be enforced by prohibition, certiorari, or habeas corpus, according to the facts of the particular case.[1]   Thus by simply refusing to pass the Mutiny Act, which like the grant of supplies has been an annual measure since the Revolution,[2] parliament can at a blow destroy the standing army, not only by withholding its supplies, but by dissolving the code of military law by which its discipline is maintained.

Act of
Settlement
constitu-
tional cap-
stone of
Revolution,

Despite the supplementary legislation which has now been mentioned, the deficiencies of the Bill of Rights, made obvious by time and change of circumstances, were never fully remedied until the passage in 1701 of the famous Act of Settlement,[3] the constitutional capstone of the Revolution.   In December, 1694, Queen Mary had been carried off by small-pox, and in July, 1700, the duke of Gloucester had died, leaving Anne, then only in her thirty-sixth year, childless.   Ignoring James' son, the next in line, according to the ordinary rules, were the descendants of Henrietta of Orleans, the daughter of Charles I., whose daughter, Anna Maria, had married the catholic duke of Savoy, in April, 1694.[4]   Under that condition of things parliament resolved to cling to the Stuart blood, and

and source
of title of
the house of
Hanover ;

yet secure a protestant succession, by vesting the crown in Sophia, wife of the late and mother of the then elector of Hanover, who was nearly the youngest of the thirteen children of Elizabeth, queen of Bohemia, and daughter of James I.[5]   At the time of the making of the Declaration of Right, William, anxious to unite the house of Hanover to the Grand Alliance, suggested that the reversion to the crown should be settled on Sophia,[6] but the commons rejected the amendment as unnecessary in view of the fact that Anne was then pregnant.[7]   But as the death of the duke of Gloucester had left Anne as well as William childless, the Act of Settlement provided "That the

[1] *Manual of Military Law*, pp. 177, 178.   "It should, however, be noted that the courts of law will not, in general at any rate, deal with rights dependent on military status and military regulations." — Dicey, *The Law of the Constitution*, p. 287, note 1.

[2] Green, *Hist. of the Eng. People*, vol. iv. p. 45.

[3] 12 & 13 Will. III. c. 2.

[4] "The duchess of Savoy entered an unavailing protest against the new settlement.   She lived to see it take effect, dying on the 26th of August, 1728." — Bailey, p. 233.

[5] As to her marriage, see above, p. 243.

[6] It has also been said that William, after the death of the duke of Gloucester, wished to set aside Anne in favor of Sophia.

[7] Cf. *Succession to the English Crown*, Bailey, pp. 227–237.

Most Excellent Princess Sophia, Electress and Dutchess Dow-ager of Hanover, daughter of the most excellent Princess Eliza-beth, late Queen of Bohemia, daughter of our late sovereign Lord King James the First, of happy memory, be and is hereby declared to be the next in succession in the Protestant line to the Imperiall Crown and Dignity of said Realms of England, France, and Ireland, . . . and continue to the said most ex-cellent Princess Sophia and the heirs of her body, being Pro-estants," after the deaths of William and Anne, and in case of failure of their issue. And in order to more perfectly secure the " religion, laws, and liberties " of the realm after the acces-sion of the new dynasty which the Act of Settlement thus created, it was deemed necessary to embody in the act itself eight additional articles or clauses, that were to take effect only after the happening of that event. The first, second, seventh, and eight, which have remained as permanent elements in the constitution, are as follows : —

crown set-tled upon Princess Sophia and her de-scendants.

eight additional articles for security of "religion, laws, and liberties;"

four of which became permanent;

(1.) "That whosoever shall hereafter come to the posses-ion of this crown shall joyn in communion with the Church of England as by law established."

necessity of communion with state church;

(2.) "That in case the crown and imperiall dignity of this realm shall hereafter come to any person, not being a native of this kingdom of England, this nation be not obliged to en-gage in any warr for the defence of any dominions or terri-ories which do not belong to the crown of England, without the consent of parliament."

no war to be under-taken for dominions not belong-ing to Brit-ish crown;

(7.) "That after the said limitations shall take effect as foresaid, judges' commissions be made *quamdiu se bene ges-erint*, and their salaries ascertained and established ; but upon the address of both houses of parliament, it may be lawfull to remove them."

tenure and salaries of the judges;

(8.) "That no pardon under the Great Seal of England be pleadable to an impeachment by the Commons in Parliament."

no pardon to be pleaded to an impeach-ment;

The third article, which forbade the sovereign to go beyond the realm without the consent of the houses, was repealed by George I. st. 2, c. 51, in order to make more easy the frequent visits of that monarch to Hanover. The fourth — which at-tempted to revive the ancient authority of the privy council by the provision that matters properly cognizable in it " shall be transacted there, and all resolutions taken thereupon shall

repeal of the third and fourth articles;

be signed by such of the privy councill as shall advise and consent to the same " — was repealed by 4 Anne, c. 8, s. 24, as a confession of the fact that the results of the Revolution had made a return to the ancient system impossible.   The fifth —

article fifth repealed so far as it conflicted with Mr. Hutt's Naturalization Act of 1844;

which provided that no person (although he be naturalized or made a denizen) born without the British dominions, " except such as are born of English parents, shall be capable to be of the Privy Councill, or a member of either House of Parliament, or to enjoy any office or place of trust, either civill or military, or to have any grant of lands, tenements or hereditaments from the crown to himself, or to any other or others in trust for him " — was repealed by 7 & 8 Vict. c. 66 (Mr. Hutt's Naturalization Act of 1844), as to those provisions that conflicted with the terms of that act enabling naturalized aliens who had obtained certificates from the home secretary and taken the oath of allegiance, to acquire all the rights and capacities of native born British subjects, except the right of becoming a member of the privy council or of the nether house of parliament, or except such as were specially excepted by the terms of the certificate itself.   In 1870, Mr. Hutt's act was super-

that act superseded by Naturalization Act of 1870; its essence;

seded by the Naturalization Act (33 & 34 Vict. c. 14),[1] which virtually repealed the whole of the fifth clause of the Act of Settlement as to all persons obtaining a certificate of naturalization, which now endows the holder, in the United Kingdom, with all the political and other rights and privileges, and subjects him to all the obligations and duties of a native-born subject.   It also provides that British subjects may be naturalized in foreign states ; and then that they may reacquire their nationality by permission of a secretary of state ; and that citizens who are not naturalized may acquire and hold and dispose

abrogation of ancient doctrine of allegiance to be deduced from Calvin's case;

of real and personal property in the United Kingdom (except British ships) in all respects as a native-born citizen.   Thus by recent legislation has been practically abrogated the common law maxims that no man can rid himself of his nationality (*nemo patriam in quâ natus est exuere aut ligeantiæ debitum*

---

[1] " But the last mentioned act (Mr. Hutt's Act) is now repealed by the Naturalization Act, 1870, which, together with the Naturalization Act, 1872 (35 & 36 Vict. c. 39), now provides a simple and inexpensive method whereby aliens desirous of settling in the United Kingdom can obtain the advantages of naturalization without the necessity of a private Act of Parliament." — Broom's *Const. Law*, Denman's ed. p. 45.

ejurare potest), nor abjure the allegiance due from him (*jus originis nemo mutare potest*),[1] — maxims upon which was founded the doctrine of allegiance to be deduced from Calvin's case. The sixth — which provided "that no person who has an office or place of profit under the King, or receives a pension from the Crown, shall be capable of serving as a member of the House of Commons" — was repealed by 4 Anne, c. 8, s. 25, passed in order to prevent the cutting off of all direct connection between the representative chamber and the cabinet, a connection rendered more necessary than ever before by the transfer of the real sovereignty from the crown to that chamber.

unconditional repeal of article sixth.

3. While the parliaments of William and Mary were thus engaged in a genuine attempt to secure by adequate legislation the political liberty he had promised to reëstablish, they undertook in a narrow and jealous spirit to guarantee religious toleration to the great body of non-conformists who had united with churchmen in the common struggle against catholicism. The union thus brought about lasted, however, no longer than the common danger. The old strife, reopened by insults to the episcopal clergy in Scotland, prompted convocation to set aside the latitudinarian scheme for a modification of the prayer-book, while a Comprehension Bill designed to enlarge the basis of the established church failed to pass, despite the support of the king,[2] whose attempt to secure to dissenters a measure of civil equality through the repeal of the Corporation Act proved equally abortive.[3] The only concession actually made was embodied in the Toleration Act[4] of 1689, which, while failing to repeal any of the prior acts exacting conformity, practically established freedom of worship in separate conventicles in favor of such protestants as would take the oaths of allegiance and supremacy, and subscribe the declaration against transubstantiation; and in favor of such dissident ministers as would, in addition to the administration of the sacrament and preaching in meeting, sign the Thirty-nine Articles with certain exceptions. When these requisites were complied with, all registered

Toleration Act and slow growth of religious liberty:

William failed to secure passage of Comprehension Bill or repeal of Corporation Act; Toleration Act for benefit of protestant dissenters only;

---

[1] Brown's *Const. Law*, Denman's ed., Note to Calvin's case, p. 27, citing *Leg. Max.*, 6th ed. p. 71; Foster, *Disc. High Treason*, p. 184; Arg. Duke of Hamilton's case, *State Trials*, vol. iv. p. 1163.

[2] Cf. Kennet's *Complete Hist. Eng.*, pp. 557, 558, etc.

[3] Green, *Hist. of the Eng. People*, vol. iv. p. 46.

[4] 1 Will. & Mar. c. 18.

meeting-houses, whose doors were neither "locked, bolted, nor barred," were to be protected from molestation. Not until the middle of the nineteenth century was concluded that series of acts, whose contents will be briefly epitomized, through which the stingy instalment thus granted to protestant non-conformists as the result of the Revolution was widened into the perfect freedom of religious worship enjoyed at the present day. During the period of Tory reaction that closed the reign of Anne, the scope of the Toleration Act was narrowed (1) by the passage in 1711 of the Occasional Conformity Act,[1] designed to thwart the attempt of dissenters, who, while clinging to their own forms of worship, attempted to evade the Test Act by occasionally receiving the sacrament at the hands of the state church; (2) by the passage in 1713 of the Schism Act,[2] designed to suppress non-conformists' schools, — proscriptive measures happily repealed early in the reign of George I.[3] The more liberal tendency thus manifested was advanced in the reign of his successor by the Annual Indemnity Acts,[4] whereby the civil offices were really opened to such dissenters as had failed to qualify themselves under the Test and Corporation Acts. It was not, however, until the reign of George III. that a genuine spirit of toleration was stimulated by the preaching of Wesley and Whitefield, who proclaimed the broad principles judicially affirmed by the house of lords in the case of the City of London and the Dissenters,[5] — a case specially memorable by reason of the noble utterances of Lord Mansfield, who, in moving the judgment of the house, declared that "it is now no crime for a man to say he is a dissenter;" that nothing could be "more iniquitous and unjust, more impolitic than persecution."[6] In 1799 it was that the Dissenting Ministers' Act relieved all preachers and schoolmasters who came under that head from the limited subscription to the Thirty-nine Articles still imposed by the Toleration Act; and in 1812 the Five-mile Act and the Conventicle Act were repealed by 52 Geo. III. c. 155, which contained a section (s. 4) extending

---

[1] 10 Anne, c. 2.

[2] 12 Anne, c. 7.

[3] 5 Geo. I. c. 14, 1718.

[4] The first of these acts was passed in 1727, and after that time they were enacted annually with a few exceptions,

down to the repeal of the Test and Corporation Acts in 1828.

[5] *Chamberlain of London* v. *Allen Evans.*

[6] Cobbett's *Parl. Hist.*, vol. xvi. pp. 313-327.

in effect to unitarians the advantages of the Toleration Act, toleration of unitarians; from which they had been excluded by virtue of the clause that withheld its benefits from all who denied the doctrine of the Trinity.[1]   Not, however, until 1828, was Lord John Russell, undaunted by the failures of four predecessors,[2] able to bring about at last the civil enfranchisement of dissenters through the repeal of the Test and Corporation Acts, by vir- repeal of Test and Corporation Acts in 1828; tue of which civil disabilities were still imposed.[3]   Two acts of Elizabeth — one of 1581, the other of 1593 — that continued nominally in force, subject to the provisions of the Toleration Act, were repealed in 1844;[4] and that section of her Act of repealing acts of 1844 and 1846, Uniformity which imposed a penalty of a shilling for non-attendance at church was repealed in 1846.[5]

In 1833, Mr. Pease, the first Quaker who had been elected Quakers, Moravians, and separatists; to the house of commons for nearly a century and a half, was permitted to take his seat after making an affirmation instead of an oath;[6] and in the same year that privilege was guaranteed to all Quakers, Moravians, and separatists by statute.[7]   In May, 1880, Mr. Bradlaugh, member-elect from Northampton, Bradlaugh's case; who did not claim to belong to either class, offered to make an affirmation by virtue of the Evidence Amendment Acts, 1869–70.   After careful examination by a select committee it was held that those acts applied to courts of justice and not to the house of commons, and that ruling was sustained by the high court of justice, whose judgment was affirmed by the court of appeal. Being returned a second time, Mr. Bradlaugh offered to take the oath, but the house refused to permit him to take either affirmation or oath, upon the grounds that the first was illegal, and that the second, owing to his special belief, would have no binding effect upon his conscience.   He then insisted upon taking the oath upon his own initiative without the consent of the house, and without being called upon by the Speaker, and in February, 1884, he voted twice during the proceedings caused by the course he had taken.   In an action brought by the crown to recover the penalty consequent upon the vote of

---

[1] Sir J. F. Stephen, *Hist. of the Crim. Law*, vol. ii. p. 483.

[2] Lord Stanhope in 1718; Mr. Plumer in 1736; Mr. Beaufoy in 1787; and Mr. Fox in 1790.

[3] 9 Geo. IV. c. 17.

[4] 7 & 8 Vict. c. 102.

[5] 9 & 10 Vict. c. 59.

[6] Several statutes had been previously passed upon the subject. See Report of select committee on his case, 1833 (b).

[7] 3 & 4 Will. IV. cc. 49, 82.

judgment
of the court
of appeal;

an unsworn member, the court of appeal held that the parliamentary "oath must be taken by a member, with the assent of the house, according to the requirements of the standing orders, and after he has been called upon by the Speaker to be sworn." The court also held that a member of parliament who does not believe in the existence of a Supreme Being, and upon whom an oath has no binding effect as such, is, owing to his want of religious belief, incapable by law of subscribing the parliamentary oath.[1] However, upon the opening of the new parliament in January, 1886, Mr. Bradlaugh took the oath, the speaker holding that he knew nothing of the resolutions of the past upon the subject, and that he had no independent authority to forbid a member returned to the house from coming to the table and taking the oath prescribed by statute.[2] And to prevent such controversies in future, sec. 1 of the

Oaths Act,
1888.

Oaths Act, 1888, provides that a solemn affirmation may be made in lieu of an oath by every person who states that the taking of an oath is objectionable, either because it is contrary to his religious belief, or because he has no religious belief whatever.

Emancipation of the
Jews,

The declaration " upon the true faith of a Christian " at the end of the oath of abjuration imposed by 9 Geo. IV. c. 17 not only hindered the entry of Jews into municipal offices, into which they had been occasionally admitted along with protestant dissenters by virtue of the Annual Indemnity Acts, but it also denied them the right of sitting and voting in parliament. So far as the corporations were concerned, the disability was taken away by a statute passed in 1845 ; but not until thirteen years later was it removed so far as the parliamentary oath

cases of
Rothschild
and Salomans.

was concerned. Not until the cases of Baron Rothschild and Mr. Salomans[3] had pressed the matter upon the house of commons was the act of 1858 passed, providing that either house could resolve that any person professing the Jewish religion may omit the words "and I make this declaration upon the true faith of a Christian ;" and a few years later 28 & 30 Vict. c. 19 entirely removed the phrase from the form of oath prescribed for members of the lower house.

[1] *Law Reports*, 1885, pt. v. p. 667;
14 Q. B. D. 101.

[2] Cf. May, *Parl. Practice*, pp. 160, 162, 163, 198.
[3] Ibid., p. 158.

The Toleration Act expressly provided that its terms should not be so construed as "to give any ease, benefit, or advantage to any papist or popish recusant whatever;" and in 1700, when the intolerant spirit thus manifested was fanned into flame by the presence of many priests who came over after the Peace of Ryswick, a very severe penal law was passed making it a crime for any "popish bishop, priest, or Jesuit" to exercise any of his functions, and offering a large reward to any one who should detect and prosecute to conviction such as should attempt to violate the act. Every catholic was to take the oaths of allegiance and supremacy six months after becoming eighteen, and to make the declaration in the act excluding that sect from parliament. Any one who failed to comply, but not his heirs, was to be disabled from inheriting land; and during his life until the oaths should be taken, "the next of his kindred, which shall be a Protestant, shall have and enjoy the said lands, tenements, and hereditaments." To that humane provision was added another, by which papists, who were prohibited from sending their children abroad to be educated, were made incapable of purchasing land after a certain date, and uses and trusts for their benefit created after that time were declared void.[1] That act, which thus openly attempted to strip the Roman Catholic gentry of their landed property, was the last of the penal laws against that sect; and it remained in force down to 1778, when it was practically repealed by Sir George Saville's Roman Catholic Relief Act,[2] as against all persons who, disclaiming the Stuarts, and certain catholic doctrines including the deposing power of the pope, would take an oath of allegiance to George III. During the trial of Lord George Gordon, who headed the "no popery" riots of the following year, the attorney-general, speaking of the operation of the laws against the catholics, especially of the act of William III., said: "The penalties and punishments appeared to everybody so extremely hard and severe that very few prosecutions were carried on upon this act: in my own time I only remember one, which was against a person for saying mass in a house

Margin notes: Roman Catholics expressly excepted from Toleration Act; subjected to severe penalties by act passed in 1700; disabled from inheriting and purchasing land; last of the penal laws against them; Relief Act of 1778; act of 1700 too severe for enforcement;

---

[1] 11 & 12 Will. III. c. 4. For a commentary upon the act and its objects, see Burnet, vol. iii. p. 253.

[2] 18 Geo. III. c. 60. "This act, for the first time for nearly two hundred years, allowed mass to be said in England without the risk of perpetual imprisonment." — Stephen, *Hist. of the Crim. Law*, vol. ii. p. 492.

somewhere about Wapping; he was committed, and of course doomed by the provisions of this act to perpetual imprisonment."[1]   Despite a still more liberal act than that of 1778,

Relief Act of 1791;

enacted for the emancipation of catholics in 1791,[2] they continued subject to many disabilities, which deprived them not only of the right of holding office, but also of sitting in parlia-

Emancipation Act of 1829;

ment down to the year 1829, when, under pressure from the "Catholic Association" formed by Daniel O'Connell, a tory ministry, headed by the duke of Wellington, passed, with the aid of the whigs and in order to prevent civil war, the Catholic Emancipation Act[3] of that year, by which all such disabili-

process completed by repealing acts of 1844 and 1846;

ties were swept away.   Whatever obsolete statutes still remained were removed either by the act of 1844[4] "to repeal certain penal enactments made against her Majesty's Roman Catholic subjects," or by the act of 1846[5] "to relieve her Majesty's subjects from certain penalties and disabilities in regard to religious opinions."   The history of the process through which religious liberty was thus gradually established in England by the repeal of the disabling acts directed against all non-conformists, whether catholic or protestants, has been sen-

summary of Sir J. F. Stephen.

tentiously epitomized as follows : "The Revolution of 1688 produced a narrowly limited toleration, in the strict sense of the word, for Protestant Dissenters.   'You are a set of narrow-minded bigots, but we will not punish you for it,' was the language of the legislature towards them.   The Roman Catholics, on the other hand, were treated as men who would be rebels if they dared, and were placed under laws nominally harsher than any which had been in force before.   The laws, however, were not executed, and, after being practically repealed in 1791 and 1829, were formally repealed in 1844 and 1846."[6]

The non-jurors;

The Convention Parliament, bitter as it was to Roman Catholics, stingy as it was to protestant non-conformists, failed to satisfy a large section of the clergy of the state church, who, as teachers of the doctrines of divine right and passive obedi-

---

[1] *State Trials*, vol. vi. p. 501.

[2] 31 Geo. III. c. 32.

[3] 10 Geo. IV. c. 7.   In 1832 the act of 2 & 3 Will. IV. c. 115 extended to catholic schools, places of worship, charities, and to persons employed about them the same privileges secured by law to protestant dissenters in like cases.

[4] 7 & 8 Vict. c. 102.

[5] 9 & 10 Vict. c. 59.

[6] Stephen, *Hist. of the Crim. Law*, vol. ii. p. 496.

ence, were unable to admit without confusion the new theory
that the houses could depose one king and set up another at
will.   Passive obedience, it is true, had come to be regarded as
a dead heresy, since the clergy themselves had been forced to
resist the persecution to which they were subjected by James ;
but to the doctrine of divine right a large number of the higher
dignitaries, with Sancroft, the primate, at their head, resolved
to be faithful when the time came for them to take the new
oath of allegiance to William and Mary, imposed by an act [1] of
parliament upon all public functionaries in church and state.
An amendment made by the lords exempting the clergy from
the oath was rejected by the commons,[2] and so the act as
passed provided not only for the expulsion from office of all
civil officers who should refuse it, but also for the suspension
and finally for the deprivation of all priests and bishops who
after a certain time should persist in declining it.   When the
final test came, while about twenty-nine thirtieths of the profession reluctantly complied, eight bishops, including Sancroft,
and about four hundred clergymen, some of them highly distinguished, resolved to give up their sees and their livings
rather than admit that the sovereign parliament could not only
depose a king, but deprive a bishop and expel a priest.   Those
refusing to take the oath, and their adherents, came to be known
as non-jurors, who claimed to be the only true members of the
Church of England.   The sees thus made vacant were promptly
filled, however, by the appointment of new incumbents, who
were for the most part latitudinarians, Tillotson, the new archbishop of Canterbury, being then at the head of that school.[3]

4. In order to defend more perfectly the new dynasty against
the Jacobites, including the non-juring clergy, who persisted
in regarding the exiled king as their real sovereign, and who
propagated their opinions through secret printing-presses of
their own, it was deemed necessary to so enlarge the law of
treason as to cover every contingency that might arise out of
such circumstances.   Thus, in 1698, it was made in substance
treason for those who had followed James into France to re-

Marginal notes:

many of the greater ec-clesiastics, including Sancroft, refused the new oath of allegiance ;

suspension and depri-vation the penalty of disobedi-ence ;

Sancroft and his followers accepted both rather than submit ;

their places filled by latitudina-rians.

Legislation concerning treason :

law enlarged by acts passed from 1698 to 1709 ;

[1] 1 Will. & Mar. c. 8.
[2] *Lords' Journals*, April 17, 1689 ;
Parl. Hist., p. 218.
[3] Macaulay, vol. i. pp. 704–711 ; vol.
ii. pp. 99, 100, 102–110, 256. " It was
indeed only among Whigs and Latitudinarians that William and William's
successors could find friends in the
ranks of the clergy." — Green, *Hist. of
the Eng. People*, vol. iv. p. 48.

turn to England without a license ; [1] in 1701, it was made treason to correspond with "the pretended prince of Wales ;" [2] and after the accession of Anne such precautions were made still more stringent by an act passed in 1702, making it treason to attempt to prevent the succession as established by the Act of Settlement.[3]   In 1705, two more acts were passed, the first making it treason to return without license into England after going without license into France ; [4] the second making it treason to maintain, by writings, the title of the Prince of Wales or others ; [5] and in 1709 still another was enacted making it treason for officers to hold correspondence with rebels or enemies.[6]

remedial statute for protection of those tried for treason;

Nevertheless, before the substantive law of treason was thus extended, parliament had been careful to enact a highly remedial statute, which protected more perfectly than ever before the rights of those who were subject to trial for the highest of all offences.   It seems that the all-important act of 5 & 6 Edw. VI. c. 11, whose terms have been heretofore set forth,[7] had been for a century after its passage practically ignored in criminal trials by the judges, some of whom went so far as to contend that as a rule of evidence it had been repealed by 1 & 2 Phil. & Mar. c. 10, which provided that "all trials for treason shall be according to the due order and course of the common law and not otherwise." [8]   And yet it was frankly admitted upon the trial of the regicides that the law required two witnesses, and upon Lord Stafford's trial in 1680 that fact was "treated as a point beyond all doubt, . . . his lordship insisting that there ought to be two to *each overt act.* . . . One witness to one overt act, and another to another overt act of *the same species of treason*, are two sufficient witnesses within the statutes."   In order to put that construction beyond all doubt, it was confirmed by 7 & 8 Will. III. c. 3,[9] which also provided that a copy of the indictment against a prisoner charged with high treason should be delivered to him at least five days

act of 5 & 6 Edw. VI. for a long time ignored;

said to have been repealed by 1 & 2 Phil. & Mar. c. 10;

its existence admitted in trials of regicides and of Stafford;

confirmed by 7 Will. III. c. 3;

---

[1] 9 Will. III. c. 1.
[2] 12 & 13 Will. III. c. 3.
[3] 1 Anne, c. 17.
[4] 3 & 4 Anne, c. 14.
[5] 4 Anne, c. 8.
[6] 7 Anne, c. 4.
[7] See above, p. 117, note 4.
[8] That clause, Sir Michael Foster says, " was intended in favour of the subject, not in the least to his preju-

dice." — *Crown Law*, p. 237, 2d ed., 1791.
[9] Speaking of that act, Sir Michael says, " though it requireth two witnesses to each treason, yet a collateral fact, not tending to the proof of the overt acts, may be proved by one." — *Crown Law*, p. 240.   Ch. iii. is a commentary upon the act.

before the trial,[1] and a copy of the panel of jurors two days before the trial; that he should be entitled to process to compel the attendance of witnesses to be examined on oath, and throughout the trial to the assistance of counsel. Then to remedy the evil arising out of the power of the high steward to constitute his court for the trial of a peer by summoning only such members of the peerage as he might see fit to select, it was enacted that all peers having the right to vote in parliament shall be summoned on the trial of any peer for treason, and that upon such trial every peer so summoned and appearing shall vote.[2] *{power of high steward limited on trial of peers.}*

5. A brief reference must here be made to certain measures of national taxation and finance originating in this reign whose influence has been permanent. An explanation has already been attempted of the manner in which the old Tudor subsidy was superseded during the great civil war, by a system of monthly assessments under which a fixed sum to be raised was partitioned between the several counties and towns wherein the taxpayers were rated by the local authorities at what they were really worth.[3] But that method, which was employed in 1688, became inequitable by reason of the "exorbitant inequality of the old proportions of charge, both between county and county, division and division, and parish and parish."[4] Therefore, in 1689, a new plan was adopted, which consisted of a rate of so many shillings in the pound in respect to incomes derived from personal property, offices, and employment, and lands; and in 1692, a rate then imposed of 4 *s.* in the pound produced about £1,922,000. When that sum began to decline through imperfect assessments, parliament "abandoned the principle of a rate by *fixing what a rate should produce.* . . . Henceforth the assessment of 1692 was to determine the quota of the district towards making up the sum charged in the Act upon the particular county or town of which it formed an integral part. . . . So now after the Revolution, when a *{Taxation and finance: old Tudor subsidy superseded by assessments, which also became inequitable; in 1689 a rate imposed of so many shillings in the pound; parliament abandoned the "rate by fixing what a rate should produce;"}*

---

[1] By 7 Anne, c. 21, the time was extended to ten days, and at the same time a list of the witnesses, and of the jury, with their professions and places of abode, was to be delivered to the accused.

[2] See Stephen, *Hist. of the Crim. Law,* vol. i. p. 165.

[3] See above, pp. 323, 324.

[4] And thus the assessment became "as unpolitic and unreasonable a method of raising great sums of money as ever was introduced in any nation." — Halifax, *Essay ;* Somers, *Tracts,* vol. iv. p. 63.

character of
the rate
after the
Revolu-
tion;

how appor-
tioned;

rate had again been tried, it fell into the same groove as the subsidy and the fifteenth and tenth ; and, though still nominally a rate of 1 s. or 2 s. or 3 s. or 4 s. in the pound, was, in effect, but a sum of about half a million, a million, a million and a half, or two millions, charged in specific amounts on particular counties and towns, and within those counties and towns portioned out between particular parishes or districts, according to the assessment of 1692." [1]   Such was the origin

William's
land tax
continued
down to
1798;

tax on
hackney
coaches;

first impo-
sition of
stamp
duties.

and character of the land tax of William's reign, which continued in force down to 1798, when Mr. Pitt, prior to the introduction of his income tax, made it perpetual at 4 s. in the form of a redeemable rent charged on the several districts.   In 1694 a tax was imposed on the hackney coach business of London, which was a mere extension of the licensing system introduced in the reign of Charles I. ; and in the same year stamp duties were first introduced into England, modelled after those of Holland, where it was necessary to use for legal documents paper impressed with the greater or lesser seal of the states, according to the nature of the transaction. [2]

Origin of
the national
debt;

At the moment when the nation began to rebel against this alarming growth of taxation made necessary by the prolonged struggle with France, Charles Montague, afterwards Lord Halifax, [3] who as a commissioner of the treasury had developed skill as a financier, proposed in December, 1692, that England should adopt the Continental plan of lightening the annual burden resulting from war by contracting a national debt.   And in order to improve upon the old method of borrowing from the London goldsmiths, whose credit with capitalists had been seriously shaken through the closing of the exchequer by the

Montague's
scheme of
a national
bank;

Bank of
England
incorpo-
rated in
1694

Cabal, Montague resolved to utilize a plan of a national bank, such as already existed in Holland and in Genoa, previously suggested by a Scotchman, William Patterson.   Thus it was that in the spring of 1694, when another great loan became necessary for the sustenance of the war, Montague introduced a bill for the incorporation of the Bank of England. [4]   A loan

---

[1] Dowell, *Hist. of Taxation*, vol. ii. pp. 49, 50, and 51.

[2] 5 & 6 Will. & Mar. c. 21 ; 9 & 10 Will. III. c. 25. Cf. Dowell, pp. 52, 60.

[3] His " Life " is embraced in his *Poetical Works*, published in 1716. His *Miscellaneous Works* were published in

1704 ; and his *Life and Miscellaneous Works* in 1715, London.

[4] The bill, which originated in the commons as a money bill, passed the lords without amendment in April. See *Lords' Journals*, 23d, 24th, and 25th of April, 1694.

of £1,200,000 had already been proposed and accepted at _{for commercial purposes, and as financial agent of the state;} eight per cent., and the subscribers were then organized under the act as a chartered company,[1] which became not only an ordinary commercial bank, but also the financial agent of the state in procuring loans from the people in exchange for its obligations.   The complete success of the enterprise was followed by Montague's appointment as chancellor of the exchequer ; and in the next year, when it became necessary in the execution of his scheme for the reform of the currency, reduced far below its nominal value by clipping, to provide for the temporary absence of coin, he issued for the first time exchequer bills.

6. A brief account of the inner circle of the privy council — first reproachfully termed in the reign of Charles I. "the Juncto" or "Cabinet Council," and in that of Charles II. "the Cabal" — has been carried down to Temple's fruitless attempt to establish such a reform as would revest in the council as a whole those vital functions silently usurped by the favored few who were for the moment specially endowed with the sovereign's confidence.[2]   The utter failure of Temple's inpracticable scheme was made complete by his consent to become, as secretary of state, a member of the inner circle of his own creation, after which event the executive power was again committed to cabinets, which, as secret committees of the king's personal advisers, directed the royal administration down to the Revolution of 1688.   Thus it was that William and Mary inherited the system of government by cabinets composed of ministers, each one of whom could be appointed and removed by the king without the consent of the rest, and each one of whom as a mere servant of the crown was directly responsible for the performance of his special duties to it alone.   While such ministers were members of parliament, they could not unite among themselves in carrying out any joint scheme of government because there was no internal cohesion growing out of the possession of common political principles.   "The truth was that

---

[1] A royal charter was issued under the great seal to "The Governor and Company of the Bank of England," subject to the terms prescribed by parliament. The charter was granted for only eleven years certain, parliament reserving the right to end its existence by paying the debt at any time after 1705, upon a year's notice. The result has been, however, a continual increase of the debt and of renewals of the charter down to the present day.

[2] See above, pp. 367, 368.

the change which the revolution had made in the house of commons had made another change necessary ; and that other change had not yet taken place. There was parliamentary

parliamentary government but no ministry ;

government ; but there was no ministry." [1]   There were only ministers "distributed not unequally between the two great parties," who as political opponents "were perpetually caballing against each other, haranguing against each other, moving votes of censure on each other ; and, as a natural consequence, the temper of the house of commons was wild, ungovernable, and uncertain." [2]   How to remove this fatal evil arising out of

statesmen of the Revolution failed to meet the difficulty ;

the lack of power upon the part of the cabinet to act as a unit with the majority of the popular chamber, in which the real sovereignty was vested, was the question of questions whose answer the statesmen of the Revolution left to those who came after them.   In the course of time the mighty problem, incapable, no doubt, of an instantaneous and dogmatic solution, was finally worked out through the establishment of the two

finally solved through establishment of two fundamental principles ;

fundamental principles upon which the executive government of the British empire now reposes : first, that the select committee of the privy council known as the cabinet shall be composed only of ministers bound together by party ties for the support of a definite political programme in which they must all agree ; second, that the ministers who compose this compact political unit shall hold office no longer than they can control a majority of the house of commons.   The remarkable fact is, that this complete transformation in the character and functions of the cabinet, which involved a revolution in the internal mechanism of the constitution, has been brought about

change brought about, without enactment of any positive law,

without any change in its outward forms, and without the enactment of any positive law whatever.   As it is all-important to clearly indicate the means by which this marvellous change was effected, the attempt will be made to unfold the subtile process actually employed in a separate paragraph.

through a set of tacit understandings which the Revolution made necessary ;

From what has now been said, the fact appears that the modern ministerial system, through whose silent growth the sovereignty of the British empire has been transferred from the king to the house of commons, is the fruit of the final triumph won by parliament over the monarchy in the Revolution of 1688.[3]   The Revolution settled the principles which

[1] Macaulay, vol. ii. p. 451.
[2] Ibid., vol. ii. p. 453.

[3] See above, pp. 417, 418.

made the great change inevitable, and then left it to time
to press them to their ultimate conclusion, through a set of things of
tacit understandings of which the positive law knows nothing, which the
positive
and of which there is no written memorial.   No such body as law knows
nothing;
the cabinet is known to English law ; no such office as that of
prime minister is recognized by any statute ; there is no legal
provision which requires the king to appoint ministers of whom
the house of commons approves, or to dismiss ministers of
whom it does not approve ; the law knows nothing of the collective responsibility of ministers ; it knows nothing of their
duty to resign, or to appeal to the country, when they are rebuked by an adverse vote of the popular chamber.   Of the the cabinet,
existence of the privy council the law is aware, but of the inner which has
no legal
circle of the privy council, called the cabinet, it knows abso- existence,
lutely nothing.   The meetings of this inner circle are secret,
and its proceedings, which are highly confidential, are not even
recorded.   From a strictly legal standpoint the cabinet is
a mere phantom which passes between the parliament and
the crown, impressing the irresistible will of the one upon the
other.   And yet, from a political and practical standpoint, the the main-
cabinet is the mainspring of the modern constitutional system. spring of
the modern
So long, and only so long, as the royal authority is wielded in constitu-
tion;
obedience to the will of the majority of the house of commons
does the machinery of government continue in motion.   The
unwritten and conventional code of tacit understandings — conven-
out of which the ministerial system has been slowly evolved, tional con-
stitution as
and from which it derives moral and political as distinguished distin-
guished
from legal authority — has, within the last two centuries, grown from writ-
ten code
up by the side of the older code of written constitutional law
from which it must be sharply distinguished.[1]   At the end of
the Revolution of 1688 the written code had reached its com- embodied
pletion ; at that time the Great Charter, the Petition of Right, in certain
documents;
the Bill of Rights, and the Act of Settlement, when taken to-
gether, defined the prerogatives of the crown, the privileges of
parliament, and the rights of the subject with about as much

---

[1] " We now have a whole system of
political morality, a whole code of pre-
cepts for the guidance of public men,
which will not be found in any page of
either the Statute or the Common Law,
but which are in practice hardly less
sacred than any principle embodied in
the Great Charter or in the Petition of
Right.   In short, by the side of our
written Law there has grown up an
unwritten or conventional constitution." — Freeman, *Growth of the Eng.
Const.*, p. 114.

precision as an American constitution now defines the relative rights and duties of the governors and the governed. The

written code contained in these four documents, like an American constitution contained in one document, did not pretend to be complete within itself, — for details and definitions it depended, as an American constitution now depends, upon that strange mixture of tradition and precedent generally known as the English customary law. Down to the Revolution of 1688 the written code thus supplemented and explained by the cus-

tomary law was the constitution. No distinction had yet been drawn between the constitution and the law. Any act which failed to offend against some provision or principle either of the written code or of the customary law could be in no sense illegal. With that fact clearly in view it becomes easier to explain the nature of the conventional and extra-legal constitution which has grown up alongside of the written code, and which, without altering its outward form, has completely

changed its practical working.[1] By the Bill of Rights the legal character of the kingship was fully recognized and reëstablished with all the prerogatives inherent in the crown prior to the usurpations introduced by the Tudor and Stuart kings. After the Revolution settlement, as before, the king still possessed the absolute legal right to assemble, prorogue, and dissolve parliament, and to refuse his assent, as a coördinate branch of the legislature, to any bill the two houses might enact. As the supreme executive he retained the control of foreign affairs through the sending and receiving of ambassadors, the contracting of treaties and alliances, and the making of war and peace. In the same capacity he acted at home as the general conservator of the peace, the guardian of the public health, the arbiter of commerce, and as the supreme head of the army and the fleet. As the fountain of justice he still appointed the judges, and prosecuted offenders whose crimes he alone could pardon after conviction. As the fountain of honor he could create peers, bestow titles, offices, and pensions, and erect corporations. As the head of the national church he could ap-

---

[1] "The code of our unwritten constitution has, like all other things, grown up bit by bit, and for the most part, silently and without any acknowledged author. . . . The beginning may be placed in the reign of William the Third, the first time when we find anything like a *ministry* in the modern sense." — Freeman, *Growth of the Eng. Const.*, p. 122.

point prelates, and prorogue, regulate, and dissolve all ecclesiastical synods and convocations, whose canons were valueless unless made by his leave and with his approval. And last and most of all he still possessed the legal right, after the Revolution as before, to appoint his own ministers and to dismiss them at his pleasure. But under the unwritten conventional constitution which has grown up alongside of the written code since that time, it is understood that the crown can neither appoint ministers of whom the house of commons does not approve, nor dismiss ministers of whom it does approve. And it is also understood that while such ministers are in office all the legal prerogatives of which the crown is possessed by virtue of the written law shall be entirely subject to their direction and control. By virtue of such understandings the king reigns and the ministers govern; and "the king can do no wrong," because all unwise and improper acts are those of his ministers, who can be promptly and sufficiently punished simply by a dismissal from office. Thus it is that the sovereign powers of the state are exercised by virtue of positive law through a political body whose existence that law does not recognize, and whose highest duties and responsibilities are neither defined in it nor punished by it. Out of that condition of things has grown the distinction, now well understood by English lawyers and statesmen, between the conventional constitution and the law, — between acts which may be unconstitutional and yet not illegal. The cabinet ministers may, individually or collectively, commit some breach of the written law which may be in the strictest sense of the term an illegal act, for which they may be punished in the ordinary tribunals, or by the extraordinary process of impeachment in the high court of parliament. At the same time such ministers may commit a grossly unconstitutional act which in no sense of the term can be called illegal, and of which no cognizance can be taken in any court whatsoever. Such an offence would be committed should the ministers refuse to resign office after a vote of censure had been passed upon them in the house of commons. No court could compel them to resign, and yet their act would constitute the most highly penal offence that could be committed against the modern constitution. The best possible reason which can be given for the absence of any

Marginal notes:

under conventional constitution royal prerogatives subject to ministerial control;

acts may be unconstitutional and yet not illegal;

no court can compel ministers to resign after a vote of censure;

political
method
of coercion
vested in
house of
commons;

legal method of punishment for such an act is that the house of commons holds in its own hands a political method of coercion which is at once summary and irresistible. When the ministers under proper circumstances refuse to resign, the house can compel obedience by simply refusing to keep the machinery of government in motion.

How far
did the
process of
change
actually
advance
during the
reigns of
William
and Anne?

Having now defined : first, the nature of the ministerial system as it existed prior to the Revolution of 1688 ; second, the new character which it has assumed since that time ; third, the means by which the change was gradually brought about through the readjustment of the vital parts of the constitutional machinery under a set of tacit understandings of which the written law knows nothing, the attempt will be made to indicate, in view of the disposition to exaggerate it, just how far this process of change actually advanced during the reigns of William and Anne. Certain it is that the personal disposition of the Stadtholder king was to continue the old system of ministers without collective authority, for the reason that he considered himself more capable than any one around him not only of directing all matters relating to war, but also of conducting foreign affairs, always regarded as the personal function of the sovereign as the thinking head of the state.[1]

William
disposed to
continue
the old
system:

bitterly
opposed to
party
govern-
ment;

Besides, he was bitterly opposed to party government, which offered the only practical means by which ministers could be bound together as a political unit. Active and influential as the Whigs had been in securing him the crown, he was adverse to the idea of committing to them the exclusive control of the executive power ; and for that reason he acted for years as his own first minister, taking his colleagues in about equal proportions from the leaders of both parties. Not until 1693 did William, under pressure arising out of the utter lack of power upon the part of his ministers to direct and control the house of commons, agree to accept the advice of Sunderland, who induced him to abandon his position of neutrality between

acted for
years as his
own first
minister;
not until
1693 did he
consent to
accept Sun-
derland's
advice to
form a
cabinet of
Whigs
alone;

[1] " Though mainly occupied with military and foreign affairs, William's superior energy of character led him to meddle personally in the administration of various departments. When complaints reached him of delays in paying the troops, he would ride down to the Treasury and inquire into the cause, and wait until he saw the order issued which the public service required." — *Hist. of Cabinets*, Torrens, vol. i. p. 7. " William negotiated and concluded the Partition Treaty without the knowledge of the majority of his ministers." — *Ibid.*, p. 20.

the two opposing parties, and to reconstitute the cabinet of Whigs, at that time the dominant party in parliament. So slowly was the suggestion carried out that a year elapsed before the new ministry thus formed upon a party basis was substantially complete ; and not until the end of two years more was the last Tory removed from the council board. When that point was reached the Whigs, by the frequent assembling of their supporters in the house of commons, originated that system of party organization which in its matured form has been adopted by all like bodies in the state.[1] While the party vested with the control of the executive power was thus providing for its discipline as a whole, those members of it who formed the new ministry made it a rule to repel as a unit all attacks upon any of its members, — a circumstance which led to their being known as the "Juncto," a term of reproach first employed in the time of Charles I.[2] *origin of system of party organization;*

why the new ministry was called a "Juncto."

During the year that preceded William's attempt to establish cabinet government in its modern form by the appointment of his advisers from the party dominant in the house of commons, that house passed a bill, which, if it had become law, would have rendered the entire scheme abortive by preventing a fusion between the executive and legislative powers. In the days when the great ministers of state were taken almost exclusively from the nobles, who as the leaders of the nation were regarded as the hereditary councillors of the crown, nothing seemed more natural than they should sit with their brethren in the upper house and join with them in their legislative and judicial functions. But when the council through the decline in the influence of the nobles was gradually transformed from an independent body that stood as a bridle upon the royal authority into a corps of trained officials subject to the king's will and direction, its active duties passed, during the reigns of Henry VIII. and Elizabeth, more and more into the hands of such commoners as "the Cromwells, the Sadlers, the Petres, and the Cecils, who constitute the glory of the Tudor's rule." [3] Out of the introduction thus brought about of numerous commoners into the council, the question arose whether the great

Right of placemen to sit in the houses;

great nobles as ministers in the house of lords;

when the great offices passed to commoners, question arose as to their right to sit in the lower house;

[1] Macaulay, vol. ii. pp. 453–457; Todd's *Parl. Government*, vol. i. pp. 232, 248, 249.

[2] See above, p. 368.

[3] See above, p. 177.

officers of state and other privy councillors had the right to sit in the house of commons. Perhaps the earliest complaint against the practice is embodied in the statement that "in Henry VII.'s time, and Henry VIII.'s, ministers of state, officers of the revenue, and other courtiers found an account in creeping, through boroughs, into the house of commons;"[1] and in a debate on placemen in parliament that took place in 1680 the statement was made that a certain act to relieve Henry VIII. of certain sums he had borrowed, though much opposed, passed "because the house was mostly the king's servants."[2] While it is impossible to determine precisely when the great officers of state and other privy councillors were first permitted to sit in the lower house, it is clear that the practice was tolerated during the reigns of Edward VI., Mary, and Elizabeth; and when in 1614 the matter was made the subject of debate in the house, no disposition was shown to disturb such as were then in possession of seats in that body.[3] From that time down to the Revolution of 1688 it was the custom to permit those members of the house who were appointed to the great offices of state or to places of profit under the crown to retain their seats unless their employments required prolonged residence abroad, in which event new writs were sometimes issued to fill their places;[4] and after the restoration of Charles II. the statement is expressly made that writs were issued to fill the places of such members of the house as were appointed to the bench.[5] In 1614 it was resolved that "Mr. Attorney-General Bacon [who had been appointed prior to his election] remain in the house for this parliament, but never any attorney-general to serve in the lower house in future," a rule of exclusion that remained in force until 1670, when it was abolished in favor of Sir H. Finch,[6] who had been promoted from the office of solicitor-general — the right of whose incumbent to sit had always been admitted[7] — to that of attorney-general.

Marginal notes: earliest complaints against the practice; great officials permitted to sit in commons in reigns of Edward VI., Mary, and Elizabeth; practice continued down to Revolution, except in cases of long residence abroad; rule excluding attorney-general abolished; solicitor-general always admitted;

[1] Gurdon, *Hist. of Parls.*, vol. ii. p. 355.
[2] *Parl. Hist.*, vol. iv. p. 1269.
[3] Todd's *Parl. Government*, vol. i. p. 234, *et seq.*
[4] Ibid., p. 235. In the case of a member appointed in 1609 governor of a colony in America, a new writ was issued. *Commons' Journals*, vol. i. p. 393.
[5] Ibid., vol. viii. pp. 80, 104, 187, 510, 535.
[6] Campbell, *Lives of the Chancellors*, vol. iii. p. 390.
[7] *Parl. Hist.*, vol. i. p. 1163; General Index, *Commons' Journals*, vol. i.–xvii. p. 425.

And yet, so strong was the prejudice against the practice of permitting royal officials to sit in the house that that body in 1680 resolved that no one of its members, without its leave, should accept any office or place of profit from the crown, or any promise of the same, while he held a seat, under the pain of expulsion.[1] After the Revolution, in order to give legal validity to the principle which that impotent[2] resolution embodied, a bill whose purpose was to deny to all office-holders of the crown the right to sit in the commons was passed by that body in 1692 ; and upon its rejection by the lords[3] another, prospective in character, was passed by the lower house in 1693. After the lords had accepted the measure, subject to the important proviso that all office-holders who should be unseated by the act might " be afterwards chosen again to serve in the same parliament," William, who regarded the proposal even in that form an encroachment upon the prerogative, interposed the veto by formally laying aside the bill, January 25, 1694 ;[4] whereupon the lower house resolved that "whoever advised the king not to give the royal assent was an enemy to their majesties and the kingdom."[5] Thus defeated in their main purpose, the house succeeded during the same year in securing a more limited exclusion through an addition made to the Bill of Supply,[6] which provided "that no member of the house of commons shall be concerned, directly or indirectly, in the farming, collecting, or managing of the duties to be collected by this bill, or any other aid to be granted to their majesties, other than the present commissioners for managing the customs and excises." This, the first statutory prohibition against office-holders sitting and voting as members of the lower house, after being extended by other similar acts, was followed in 1700 by that clause of the Act of Settlement,[7] which provided "that no person who has an office or place of profit under the king, or receives a pension from the crown, shall be capable of serving as a member of the house of commons." That prohibition, designed to take effect only after

house resolution of 1680;

bill denying to all office-holders right to sit in commons passed in 1693;

destroyed by veto;

limited exclusion incorporated in Supply Bill of same year;

first statutory prohibition;

exclusion contained in Act of Settlement;

[1] *Parl. Hist.*, vol. iv. p. 1270.
[2] Impotent because the house alone had not the power to exclude a member without the concurrence of the other branches of the law-making power.
[3] *Parl. Hist.*, vol. v. p. 745 n.

[4] Macaulay, vol. ii. pp. 473-475.
[5] *Commons' Journals*, vol. ii. pp. 71, 74, 75; Torrens, *Hist. of Cabinets*, vol. i. p. 16.
[6] 5 & 6 Will. III. c. 7, s. 57.
[7] 12 & 13 Will. III. c. 2.

the accession of the house of Hanover, was repealed as before stated in 1705,[1] when the Act of Settlement was revised; and act of 1707 providing for new election after appointment. in 1707 a new act [2] was passed, which has since afforded an effectual security against the undue influence exerted by the crown through placemen in the lower house by the provisions, first, that every member of the house shall vacate his seat by accepting an office of profit from the crown, other than a high commission in the army; second, that the member thus ousted shall be capable of reëlection, unless the office accepted has been created since October 25, 1705, or has been otherwise declared to disqualify for a seat in parliament.

William's first parliamentary ministry and its work. Such was the condition of things when William, under the advice of Sunderland, attempted to bring the lower house into harmony with the crown through an arrangement which, for the first time in English history, enabled the executive to be represented in that body by a politically united group of its members, who, as the representatives of the dominant party, constituted at the same moment the inner circle of the privy council. The Whig ministry thus formed, under the lead of Russell, Somers, Montague, Wharton, and Shrewsbury, was able to sustain the king during the trial that followed the death of the queen at the end of 1694, and to hold the parliament at his side in the prosecution of the war until the Alliance succeeded in winning in 1695 its first great triumph over France through the capture of Namur.[3]

Committee of Privy Council known as Board of Trade; In that year it was that the "Committee of Privy Council for Trade," generally known as the Board of Trade, was revived after having been for a long time abolished. Not until Cromwell found it wise to give to trade and the colonies a stable administration was any attempt made to establish a permanent department for that purpose; and after the Restoration a committee of the privy council appointed in 1660 was charged with the duty of looking out for the general interests of trade and the plantations. That committee, which had been dissolved since 1675, William and his advisers reconstituted; and its secretary, John Locke, was not slow to make it the organ of more enlightened opinions upon commercial subjects.

---

[1] See above, p. 425.

[2] 6 Anne, c. 7, ss. 25, 26; *Parl. Hist.*, vol. vi. p. 474. For a more detailed statement of the whole subject, see

Todd's *Parl. Government*, vol. i. pp. 233–248.

[3] Green, *Hist. of the Eng. People*, vol. iv. p. 63

By an order in council made in 1786, the legal constitution of the Board of Trade was perfected, and since that time its president has become practically the secretary of state for trade, usually with a seat in the cabinet.[1] legally constituted in 1786.

The quickness of perception that enabled the Junto to grasp the first principle of the new ministerial system by repelling as a unit all attacks upon any of its members was fully equalled by their inability to comprehend the second, involving their duty to resign office when, through the elections that took place at the close of 1698, their political opponents won a majority in the house of commons.   In the face of adverse votes the ministers failed to resign, thus illustrating that "to the evil of having a house of commons permanently at war with the executive government, there is absolutely no limit.   This was signally proven in 1699 and 1700.   Had the statesmen of the Junto, as soon as they had ascertained the temper of the new parliament, acted as statesmen similarly situated would now act, great calamities would have been averted.   The chiefs of the opposition must then have been called upon to form a government. . . . But these lessons, the fruits of the experience of five generations, had never been taught to the politicians of the seventeenth century.   Notions imbibed before the Revolution still kept possession of the public mind.   Not even Somers, the foremost man of his age in civil wisdom, thought it strange that one party should be in possession of the executive administration while the other predominated in the legislature.   Thus, at the beginning of 1699, there ceased to be a ministry; and years elapsed before the servants of the crown and the representatives of the people were again joined in a union as harmonious as that which had existed from the general election of 1695 to the general election of 1698.   The anarchy lasted, with some short intervals of composedness, till the general election of 1705."[2]   During that period of ministerial anarchy it was that the attempt was again made to revest the executive power in the whole council by that clause of the Act of Settlement which provided that, after the acces-

Refusal of the Junto to yield to a hostile majority in the commons;

that principle not understood at the time;

not even by Somers;

long disunion between servants of the crown and representatives of the people;

attempt made in Act of Settlement to revive old system;

---

[1] In addition to the president, the parliamentary secretary, and a permanent secretary, there are six assistant secretaries, each at the head of a department named as follows: the Commercial, the Railway, the Marine, the Harbor, the Finance, the Fisheries. Cf. *Enc. Brit.*, vol. xxiii. pp. 497, 498.

[2] Macaulay, vol. ii. pp. 709, 710.

sion of the house of Hanover, all matters cognizable in the privy council " shall be transacted there, and all resolutions taken thereupon shall be signed by such of the privy council as shall advise and consent to the same," — a provision happily repealed years before it could come into operation.[1] Upon the heels of that final attempt to check by positive law the growth of the new ministerial system an event occurred which clearly indicates the fact that the idea that offending ministers could be sufficiently punished for purely political offences by merely depriving them of office had not then sufficiently advanced to render obsolete the ancient procedure by impeachment, under which angry parliaments had so recently consigned Clarendon to exile and Danby to a long imprisonment in the Tower.   In

impeach-
ment still
used as a
weapon to
punish
ministers.

1701, a Tory house of commons impeached of high treason Bentick, Russell, Montague, and Somers, the great Whig leaders, who were then peers, for their share in the making of the then recent Partition Treaties, and for other alleged offences.[2] This " disgraceful instance of party spirit " [3] failed, however, of its purpose, as a quarrel between the two houses culminated in a refusal upon the part of the commons to appear with their evidence upon the day appointed, and in the consequent acquittal of the respondents.

Death of
William,
March 8,
1702;

In the midst of this uproar of contending parties, William, whose personal idea from beginning to end had been to combine under his own leadership as the thinking head of the state " abilities in the public service without identity of aim, unison of expression, or the pretense of mutual trust," [4] ended his great career on the 8th of March, 1702, after having commended Marlborough to Anne as the man most fit to command

Marl-
borough
becomes
"himself
the Govern-
ment;"
formed at
first
coalition
ministries;

her armies and to guide her counsels.   The new chief, who in a few years grew so great as to become " himself the Government," [5] did not venture at the outset to do more than so reorganize the ministry as to give a decided preponderance to the Tories, with a respectable recognition of the Whigs, — an arrangement that continued down to 1705, when his great

---

[1] See above, p. 423.

[2] *State Trials*, vol. xiv. p. 233. Somers rested his defence upon the unwarrantable doctrine that he had acted under the king's commands, thus ignoring the true principle of responsible government.

[3] Hallam, *Const. Hist.*, vol. iii. p. 147.

[4] Torrens, *Hist. of Cabinets*, vol. i. p. 35.

[5] Ibid., p. 44, quoting from a letter of the duke of Wellington to Lord Mahon.

triumph at Blenheim enabled him through a dissolution and new elections to obtain a majority in favor of the continuance of the war.   Under these conditions, with the extreme Tories and Jacobites threatening him with ruin, Marlborough formed a coalition ministry of moderate Tories and such Whigs as sustained his foreign policy, and that system of political balance continued until the duke was forced in the following year to drive most of the moderate Tories from office, and to set up a party administration upon a purely Whig basis, under the lead of Sunderland as secretary of state.   When Anne, who hated party government in every form as an enslavement of the crown, — whose personal influence she attempted to uphold by presiding to the last at every weekly meeting of the cabinet council,[1] and by exercising for the last time the veto power,[2] — was thus forced to bow to the Whigs, whom she regarded as but little better than republicans, she declared in her letters to Godolphin, when the entry of Sunderland into the ministry had become inevitable, that "the appointment would be equivalent to throwing herself entirely into the hands of a party ; that it was the object of her life to retain the faculty of appointing to her service honorable and useful men on either side ; that if she placed the direction of affairs exclusively in the hands either of Whigs or Tories, she would be entirely their slave, the quiet of her life would be at an end, and her sovereignty would be no more than a name." [3]

first Whig ministry under Sunderland;

last exercise of the veto power;

Anne's outcry against party government.

The ministry to which Anne thus committed the direction of affairs with this prophetic warning consummated the most important domestic transaction by which her reign is distinguished.   William's last act was a message to the houses advising them to complete without delay a union of the three kingdoms, a measure made specially urgent so far as Scotland was concerned by reason of an Act of Settlement passed in the parliament of that kingdom in 1703, which, by omitting the name of the Princess Sophia, clearly pointed to a recognition upon the death of Anne of the claims of the Pretender.   Ever since the honest attempt made by Cromwell to establish a legis-

Union of England and Scotland;

threat contained in Scotch Act of Settlement of 1703;

---

[1] Campbell, *Chancellors*, vol. iv. p. 287.

[2] In 1707, when she rejected a Scotch militia bill.   In 1693 and 1694 William III. had refused to assent to the

Triennial Bill and the Place Bill.   See above, pp. 421, 443.

[3] See Lecky, *Hist. of Eng. in the Eighteenth Century*, vol. i. p. 224.

lative union [1] had come to nothing, thinking men had been

trying to devise some plan that would overcome the serious obstacles to such a result arising out of conflicting commercial interests, and political and religious jealousies. And so when the design came to be discussed, "some wished an entire union, some a federal one, and these latter seemed to make the greater party." Somers brought the question to an issue by insisting

upon a legislative union against the Scotch proposal of a federative one, while Godolphin braved English prejudice by offering as a compensation free trade to Scotland. Upon that basis was completed in 1706 the scheme of union under which the two

kingdoms were to be united under the name of Great Britain, the whole to be governed by a fusion parliament under a single crown, the right to which was to depend upon the English Act

of Settlement. Thus it was that forty-five Scotch members were added to the English house of commons, and sixteen representative peers to the English house of lords, through an incorporation which, while guaranteeing to Scotland both her law and her religion, has secured uniform systems of coinage and taxation and equal rights of trade to both nations. When

in 1707 the Treaty of Union was converted into an Act of Union, passed in that year by the parliaments of both kingdoms, the queen gave a prompt assent, expressing at the same

time the hope and expectation to her "subjects of both nations that from henceforth they act with all possible respect and kindness to one another, that so it may appear to all the world they have hearts disposed to become one people."

In the year that followed the consummation of the union, Marlborough, hard pressed by fresh demands from the Whigs, was compelled to present a fresh cup of bitterness to the lips of Anne by demanding the dismissal from office of the whole of the moderate Tories, including Harley and St. John, — a Whig triumph crowned by the recall of Somers to office as lord president of the council. Thus matters continued until 1710, when the smouldering discontent at the prolongation of the war, from which it was supposed that the great duke was deriving disgraceful pecuniary profits, was fanned into flame

[1] Torrens, *Hist. of Cabinets*, vol. i. p. 46, quoting Marchmont to the queen, 29th of December, 1705. " But the veteran official preferred the scheme of incorporation, as likely to bring about what he termed the ' mainest and greatest benefits.' " — *Ibid.*

by two sermons preached in that year by Dr. Sacheverell, one at Derby the other at St. Paul's, in which that high church divine, while admitting the necessity of the Revolution, boldly assailed the only principles upon which it could be defended through his advocacy of the doctrine of unconditional and unlimited passive obedience.   Thus challenged, the Whig leaders unwisely resolved to impeach Sacheverell [1] for a stupid performance that grew into a mighty forensic struggle between the two political parties, in the course of which the advocates of the popular cause went so far as to assert, even in the queen's presence, that if the title to the crown was really hereditary and indefeasible, the right to wear it belonged to the Pretender beyond the sea, and not to one who derived her only claim from the popular election in which the Revolution culminated. While the lords by a small majority inflicted a light sentence upon the militant champion of non-resistance,[2] he had the satisfaction of seeing the Whig ministers swept from office by the storm he had raised, and their places taken by the Tories under the lead of Harley and St. John, — bitter rivals, who put aside their personal differences for a moment in order to crush Marlborough, and to end the war by the treaty concluded between England, France, and the Dutch at Utrecht in April, 1713.   From that time onward the failing health of the queen made the question of the succession supreme, the Whigs, to whose policy Harley, now Lord Oxford, strongly inclined, zealously advocating the rights of the house of Hanover, while St. John, now Lord Bolingbroke, plotted for the return of the Pretender.   The popular story,[3] discredited by some, is that on the 30th of July, 1714, when Anne was prostrated by a stroke of apoplexy, the privy council was at once assembled, and thereupon the Whig dukes of Somerset and Argyle, members of the council but not of the cabinet, suddenly appeared, though not specially summoned,[4] and took their places at the board, at

Dr. Sacheverell preached passive obedience in 1710;

his impeachment grew into a great party struggle,

resulting in his conviction, and in the expulsion of Whigs from office;

question of the succession raised by the queen's failing health;

popular story of the final struggle for party supremacy;

[1] *State Trials*, vol. xv. p. 1 ; *Parl. Hist.*, vol. vi. p. 805 ; Coxe's *Life of Marlborough*, vol. iii. p. 141 ; *Lockhart Papers*, vol. ii. p. 312.

[2] By a vote of 67 to 59 he was suspended from preaching for three years, and his sermons ordered to be burned by the common hangman.   As a consolation the queen afterwards rewarded him with the rich living of St. Andrew's, Holborn.

[3] See the graphic account given by Lord Mahon, *Hist. Eng.*, vol. i. pp. 133, 144.

[4] "One may be sure that none appeared masked, and that the dramatic tale of startling intrusion rests on mere misconception or on imagination." — Torrens, *Hist. of Cabinets*, vol. i. p. 50.

whose head sat Shrewsbury, a rival of Bolingbroke, who, although the president of the council, was at heart a Whig. Then, while the Jacobites sat helpless and dispirited, Argyle and Somerset carried without opposition the proposal that the post of lord treasurer should be given to Shrewsbury by the

rights of
the house
of Hanover
said to have
been se-
cured by a
kind of
coup d'état;

dying queen. Thus by a kind of *coup d'état* it is said that the rights of the house of Hanover were secured, and the way paved for the peaceful proclamation of Elector George upon the death of Anne on the 10th of August. No matter which version of this tragic scene is accepted, the fact is certain that at the critical moment there were bitter internal dissensions and divisions in that inner circle of the privy council which should have been capable of firm and united action. Therefore, after a careful review of all the facts, it is not difficult to accept with certain reservations the following statement, into which the last special inquirer has condensed his conclusions as to the advance actually made towards cabinet government

summing-
up of re-
sults at the
end of
period in
question.

during the period in question : " Government by cabinet was not a cunning device aforethought, or announced as a discovery on or about a particular day in the almanac. No group or body of advisers deserving that distinct appellation is recognizable in the reign of William or of Anne. Neither during the interregnum, when the transfer of the crown was pending, was there any effective combination of influential men in office capable of exercising the duties and responsibilities of executive rule." [1] And yet, despite the internal disorganization thus existing in the embryonic ministerial system, we find before the close of the reign of Anne, in a discussion that took place in the house of lords in 1711, the first positive declaration that the sovereign should not be held responsible for the acts of his servants, but that, " according to the fundamental constitution of this kingdom, the ministers are accountable for all ; " [2] and that no prerogative of the crown may be exempt from parliamentary advice and criticism. On this occasion it was that an objection was made to the propriety of using the term " cabinet council " in an address to the throne, upon the ground that it was " a word unknown to the law ; " whereupon Lord Peter-

[1] Torrens, *Hist. of Cabinets*, vol. i. p. 2.

[2] *Parl. Hist.* vol. vi. p. 972 ; Hern *Eng. Government*, p. 135.

borough observed that he had heard the privy council defined
as a body "who were thought to know everything and knew
nothing," and the cabinet as those " who thought nobody knew
anything but themselves." [1]

[1] *Parl. Hist.*, vol. vi. p. 974; Knight, *Hist. Eng.*, vol. v. p. 168; Todd's *Parl.*
Government, vol. i. pp. 251, 252.

BOOK VII.

GROWTH OF THE MODERN MINISTERIAL SYSTEM.

—◆—

CHAPTER I.

ITS PROGRESS DURING THE REIGNS OF GEORGE I. AND GEORGE II.

Sovereignty now really vested in the house of commons;

1. In the English constitutional system as it now exists the supreme powers of the state are vested, not in the theory but in fact, in the representative branch of the imperial parliament, whose members under the provisions of recent reform bills are chosen by an electorate so broad as to embrace every element necessary for the full and free expression of the will of the people as a whole. The commands thus given by the nation to its rulers through the medium of this electoral system are executed by a committee chosen by the crown from the ranks of that party which for the moment commands a majority of the house of commons. In order to secure perfect concord between the supreme legislative and executive powers the committee that acts as the agent of the representative chamber is also made the agent of the crown by being intrusted with the offices that pertain to those who constitute the inner circle of the privy council known as the cabinet. The primary object of this delicate and complex mechanism is to secure a perpetual accord between those who wield the executive power in the name of the crown and the electorate by which the members of the representative chamber are chosen. As a means to that end three fundamental principles have been gradually established in practice upon which parli-

concord between crown and legislature secured by the employment of a common agent;

1 "A cabinet is a combining committee — a *hyphen* which joins, a *buckle* which fastens, the legislative part of the state to the executive part of the state. In its origin it belongs to the one, in its functions it belongs to the other." — Bagehot, *The Eng. Cons.* p. 14.

mentary government in England now reposes. The first of these demands that the cabinet council shall be bound together as a unit through the possession of identical political principles held in common with a majority of the house of commons; the second, that the moment that condition of things ceases to exist the cabinet shall resign as a whole; the third, that for the more convenient execution of the policy approved by the representative chamber, the headship of the cabinet shall be vested in a single person known as prime minister. If the several parts that enter into the structure of this subtile mechanism had been created by the conscious action of the state embodied in charters, orders in council, or parliamentary statutes, the method to be pursued by those who attempt to draw out its history would be at once obvious and easy. But the fact is that the cabinet system as it now exists is the gradual and unpremeditated outcome of the progressive history of the nation as it has unfolded itself since the Revolution of 1688; it is the product of the growth of that set of tacit understandings generally known as the conventional constitution, which has developed alongside of the written code since that time.[1] As it is true, then, that the wonderful thing to be described was not made but grew, nothing more can be attempted than a detailed statement of the successive stages through which it grew. For convenience the entire period of growth, which began with the Revolution and paused rather than ended with the last Reform Bill, may be broken into two distinct epochs, that should be clearly distinguished from each other. As a matter of historical fact, the three fundamental principles already defined regulating the relations of the cabinet to the crown, on the one hand, and to the house of commons, on the other, came into being long before the house itself was made a really representative body and as such a true exponent of the national will. The first epoch, therefore, in the growth of the modern ministerial system — coextensive with the reigns of George I. and George II. — is that during which the three vital principles defining the functions of the cabinet were so firmly settled in practice as to enable them to resist all subsequent efforts to overthrow them. If at the end of this first epoch the house of commons had been really

three principles upon which parliamentary government now reposes;

modern cabinet system the unpremeditated outcome of progressive history;

two distinct epochs of growth;

during the first, the three vital principles defining the functions of the cabinet were firmly settled;

[1] See above, pp. 436–438.

an independent and representative body, parliamentary government as now understood in England would have been substantially complete. In theory the lower house was at that time both representative and independent, — in fact it was both dependent and corrupt. The unreformed mediæval representative system, which the nation had outgrown, had through the restriction of the franchise been made dependent upon an absurdly small number of electors who were in the main subject to the control of the crown and the aristocracy. The prolonged and bitter struggle through which the nation has so reconstructed the popular chamber as to make it a truly representative body, dependent upon the will of the people alone, rounds out the second epoch in the history of modern cabinet government, which, beginning with the reign of George III., ends for the moment with the last Reform Bill. Through the exercise of the right of public discussion as embodied in the freedom of the press, the right of petition, and the right of public meeting, each one of which was sharpened and defined as the struggle progressed, the nation, after going to the very verge of civil war, was able to emancipate the representative branch of parliament, and to reconstitute it upon its present basis. By the reformed parliaments that followed the victory have been enacted the great schemes of recent legislation which have remodelled in a conserving spirit every branch of administration, central, local, and colonial. The development therefore, of the existing ministerial system, which began in earnest with the accession of the house of Hanover, has drawn after it not only every organic but every important administrative change that has taken place since that time. The effort to unfold that development in such a natural and orderly sequence as will show the historical as well as the logical connection of each part with the other will be embodied in this and the following chapters.

during the second, the house of commons was made a really representative body;

organic and administrative changes that have followed the growth of the ministerial system.

Growth of cabinet government stimulated by accession of George I.;

2. The growth of cabinet government in its modern form, retarded by unpropitious surroundings during the reigns of William and Anne, was suddenly stimulated at the accession of George I. by the advent of new conditions specially favorable to its development. Foremost among those conditions was the impersonality of the new sovereign, resulting from willingness upon his part to surrender his right to rule into the

hands of his constitutional advisers.   So bitterly opposed was William III. to that idea that for a long time after his accession he acted as his own first minister, while he struggled to the end to break down the system of party organization out of which it arose.[1]   The personal characteristics of George I., coupled with the circumstances surrounding his accession, brought about a diametrically opposite result.   As heretofore explained, the fact that he was to succeed peacefully to the throne at all was the fruit of the triumph of the Whigs in the council at the moment of Anne's demise ; and their loyalty he rewarded by placing the executive power entirely in their hands.   Nothing could have been more natural, therefore, than that this foreign king, who could not speak the English language,[2] and who always regarded his English kingdom only as an appendage to his Hanoverian electorate, should have been content to leave its entire management to an English cabinet while he devoted his personal energies to the promotion of his electoral interests.   Thus from George's accession it became the custom for ministers to hold cabinet meetings by themselves, and to report the result to the sovereign through some particular minister ; and by the end of the reign of his successor it had become " unusual " for the sovereign to be present at such meetings ;[3] and since the death of Anne no sovereign has ventured to refuse his or her assent to an act of parliament.[4]   George II., who was also born and bred in a foreign country, was almost as incapable as his father of taking a leading part in English affairs, and the result was that he submitted, although to a less extent, perhaps, to the absolutism of cabinet rule.   It is certainly true, so far as the reign of George I. is concerned, that " the personal authority of the sovereign seems to have been at the lowest point it has ever reached ; "[5] while it may be equally true, from what we learn through Chancellor Hardwicke, that George II. — who was fond of the

[margin notes:]
his personal characteristics ;

as he could not speak English, entire control given to his Whig ministers,

who held meetings by themselves ;

it became "unusual" for the sovereign to be present ;

---

[1] See above, p. 440.

[2] As Walpole, his chief minister, could not speak French, the story goes that they conversed with each other in Latin.   Coxe's *Walpole*, vol. i. p. 266 ; H. Walpole's *Works*, vol. iv. p. 426 ; Hallam, *Const. Hist.*, vol. iii. p. 293.

[3] An instance of the practice occurs, however, shortly after the accession of George III.   Waldegrave's *Memoirs*, p. 66 ; Harris, *Life of Hardwicke*, vol. iii. p. 231 ; Todd, *Parl. Government*, vol. i. p. 262.

[4] In 1707 Queen Anne rejected a Scotch Militia Bill.   Since then the royal veto has not been exercised.

[5] Hallam, *Const. Hist.*, vol. iii. p. 296.

George II.
struggled in
vain against
the new
system;
arbitrary exercise of power, and who " seems to have entered fully, even to the very details," into every important transaction — attempted to revive the prestige of the crown by refusing to put his prerogatives absolutely into the hands of his advisers.   We have his own words as authority for the statement that his resistance was unavailing.   When the chancellor told him, " Your ministers, sire, are your only instruments of " Ministers," he
said, " are
the kings in
this coun-
try." government," the king replied with a smile, " Ministers are the kings in this country." [1]   Under such conditions it was that the cabinet government made its great advance during the reigns of the first two Georges, whose personal insignificance contributed largely to the result.

At the ac-
cession of
George I.
there was
for the first
time simul-
taneous
change of
a whole
ministry;
At the accession of the house of Hanover there was, for the first time since the Revolution, a simultaneous change of a whole ministry, and their replacement by another whose members took charge of all the principal offices of state.[2]   The Whig party, which thus came into power under the leadership in the cabinet of Townshend, Stanhope, and Walpole, was able, by virtue of its excellent organization, to perpetuate its rule Whigs
remained in
power for
more than
thirty
years; for more than thirty years, supported as it was by a group of noble families, at whose head stood the Benticks, the Manners, the Cavendishes, the Russells, and the Grenvilles.   It had also the sympathy and support of the commercial classes and the larger towns, won over by its maintenance of the public credit and by its interest in all questions of trade and finance.   In feebleness
of Tory
opposition; the presence of such a force the Tory opposition, weakened by the Jacobite secession to the cause of the Pretender, dwindled in the first parliament called by the new king to about fifty members.[3]   When in 1715 the Jacobites attempted to rise in the north under the earl of Mar, the government promptly impeachment of
Oxford, Bo-
lingbroke,
and
Ormond; crushed the revolt ; and in that year it was that the triumphant Whigs impeached Oxford, Bolingbroke, and Ormond, the Tory ministers who had taken part two years before in negotiating the Peace of Utrecht.[4]   While Bolingbroke and Ormond fled to

[1] Harris, *Life of Hardwicke*, vol. ii. pp. 106–109; vol. iii. p. 222; Todd, *Parl. Government*, vol. i. p. 89.

[2] See Torrens' *Hist. of Cabinets*, vol. i. ch. i., entitled " The First Cabinet."

[3] Green, *Hist. of the Eng. People*, vol. iv. p. 119.

[4] As to the proceedings of the secret committee appointed to inquire into the means whereby the treaty had been brought about, see Torrens' *Hist. of Cabinets*, vol. i. pp. 100, 101.   The precise charge was that the Tory peers in negotiating for peace had endeavored to secure the city of Tournay for the king of France, which was claimed to

France, and were attainted in their absence, Oxford, who was committed to the Tower, ventured to combat the new theory of ministerial responsibility by pleading in justification of his acts, as Danby had before him, the personal commands of his sovereign.[1] After suffering two years' imprisonment, Oxford was set at liberty because the commons, unable to agree with the lords as to the mode of procedure, declined to continue the prosecution.[2] Thus ended the last purely political impeachment. "The last hundred years present but two cases of impeachment, — the one against Mr. Warren Hastings, on charges of misgovernment in India, — the other against Lord Melville (in 1804) for alleged malversation in his office. The former was not a minister of the crown, and he was accused of offences beyond the reach of parliamentary control ; and the offences charged against the latter had no relation to his political duties as a responsible minister."[3] In that way it is possible to mark the triumph of the new idea that a minister whose political conduct has displeased the house of commons can be sufficiently punished by simply depriving him of power.

While the country was still in a state of unrest by reason of the Jacobite rebellion of 1715, the Whigs resolved to prevent a general election that might affect the stability of the new dynasty, and at the same time to render more secure their hold upon the house of commons, then the supreme power in the state, by the enactment of a Septennial Act, making possible the duration of a parliament for the period of seven years. Prior to the passage of the Triennial Act,[4] in the reign of William and Mary, a parliament once elected, unless sooner dissolved by the crown, continued to exist until the demise of the reigning sovereign.[5] In order to abrogate that act which had been in force twenty-two years, the Whigs introduced in the house of lords, and carried through the commons in 1716 the Septennial Act,[6] which not only provided for the future, but also extended the duration of the then existing house of commons for a period of four years beyond the time for which it

Margin notes: Oxford's plea; the last purely political impeachment; ministers now punished by expulsion from office. The Septennial Act; Triennial Act repealed;

---

constitute an adhering to the queen's enemies under the statute of Edward III.

[1] *Parl. Hist.*, vol. vii. p. 105.
[2] *State Trials*, vol. xiv. p. 233.
[3] May, *Const. Hist.*, vol. iii. p. 93.

[4] 6 Will. & Mar. c. 2. See above, p. 421.
[5] One of the parliaments of Charles II. sat for eighteen years.
[6] 1 Geo. I. c. 38.

had been elected.   The effect of the act was so to strengthen ministers by increasing the stability of the chamber to which they were primarily responsible, that Speaker Onslow declared that its passage marks " the era of the emancipation of the British house of commons from its former dependence on the crown and the house of lords." [1]   And yet so strong and persistent were its adversaries that from 1734 down to 1849 a series of determined efforts was made to repeal it by such statesmen as Lord Chatham, Mr. Grey, Mr. Brougham, Sir Samuel Romilly, and Mr. Tennyson.   But such efforts were all unavailing ; and since the last unsuccessful attempt made by Mr. Tennyson D'Eyncourt in 1849, the question of its repeal has passed from the domain of practical politics to that of abstract speculation. [2]

Speaker Onslow's declaration as to effect of Septennial Act ;

unavailing efforts to repeal it.

During the year that followed the successful attempt of the Whig ministry to secure by means of the Septennial Act their hold upon the house of commons, they gave convocation to understand that they would not tolerate for a moment any attempt upon the part of the clergy to promote discussion even indirectly hostile to the house of Hanover.   As heretofore explained, the clergy in 1664 gave up their immemorial right of taxing themselves in their own convocation ; and thus in becoming subject to the general law of the land in that particular they gained in return the right to vote for members of the house of commons. [3]   Thus deprived of its most vital function, convocation lingered on until an attempt was made about the time of the Revolution to revive it, specially by Atterbury, [4] afterwards bishop of Rochester, who published a book upon its " Rights and Privileges."   When in 1717 the withering ecclesiastical parliament again came into view through the denunciation directed by its lower house against the bishop of Bangor for having preached a sermon in favor of religious liberty, the ministry suddenly prorogued it ; and from that time onward, for a period of a hundred and thirty-five years, though regularly summoned, convocation was as regularly prorogued immediately after its assembling. [5]   Not until 1850 was it per-

The Whig ministry and convocation ;

how the clergy became subject to the general system of taxation ;

Atterbury's attempt to revive convocation ;

for a hundred and thirty-five years prorogued immediately after assembling.

---

[1] Coxe's *Life of Walpole*, vol. i. p. 75.

[2] May, *Const. Hist.*, vol. i. pp. 441, 442.

[3] Vol. i. pp. 481, 482.

[4] Macaulay's estimate of Atterbury has been reprinted in the collected Biographies published by Messrs. Longmans.

[5] Tindal's *Continuation*, p. 539.

mitted to renew the discussion of church business, from which time its vigor has been feebly increasing.   In 1865 it was permitted by royal license, after an interval of two hundred and sixty-two years, to make new canons ; [1] and in 1872 it received authority from the same source to frame resolutions concerning public worship which were afterwards incorporated in an act of parliament.[2]

Not content with silencing convocation and tightening their hold upon the house of commons, the Whigs resolved in 1720 to intrench themselves more securely in the house of lords.   The creation of twelve Tory peers in 1712, to insure the assent of the upper house to the Peace of Utrecht, had recently demonstrated the power of the crown to swamp a majority of that body.[3]   As the Whigs were in control of the hereditary chamber, they resolved to put an end to the new creations that were then exciting its jealousy, and at the same time to perpetuate their political hold upon it by introducing a bill whose ostensible purpose was to secure the liberty of the upper house by limiting the power of the crown to add to its membership.   By this measure the crown was to be restrained from creating more than six peerages beyond the then existing number of one hundred and seventy-eight, — the power being reserved of course to fill vacancies whenever a peerage became extinct.   Twenty-five hereditary Scotch peers were to be substituted for the sixteen elected peers then sitting for that kingdom.   This bill, after having passed the lords, was sent down to the commons, where — after the unconstitutional attempt embodied in it to destroy the new ministerial system by depriving the crown of the ultimate power to force the upper house to bow to the will of the lower had been fully exposed by Sir Richard Steele and Sir Robert Walpole — it was rejected by a decided majority.[4]

Attempt of the Whigs to limit the creation of peers;

a bill with that end in view passed the lords;

rejected in the commons by a decided majority.

3. Three years prior to that event both Townshend and

---

[1] New ones were made in the place of the 36th, 37th, 38th, and 40th, every formality as to license and publication prescribed by the " Act of Submission " (25 Hen. VIII. c. 19) being strictly observed. Blount, *Reform. of the Church of Eng.*, vol. ii. p. 372.

[2] Act of Uniformity Amendment Act, 35 & 36 Vict. c. 35.

[3] Green, *Hist. of the Eng. People*, vol. iv. p. 100.

[4] 269 against 176.   See *Parl. Hist.*, vol. vii. pp. 606–627 ; Coxe's *Life of Walpole*, vol. i. pp. 117–125 ; vol. ii. p. 551 ; Mahon, *Hist. Eng.*, vol. i. pp. 530–546.

Walpole, who had refused to go to extremes in carrying out a Hanoverian policy, had been forced to resign office; and in the reconstructed cabinet the chief direction of affairs had passed to Sunderland and Stanhope, who introduced the Peerage Bill as a ministerial measure. Walpole's defeat of that scheme, suggested, as was believed, by Sunderland, forced his rivals to permit his return along with Townshend to subordinate places in the government, — a condition of things that continued until 1721, when the breaking of the South Sea Bubble, which Walpole had steadily opposed, gave him the leadership as first lord of the treasury, with Townshend at his side as secretary of state.[1] The world was soon made to know, however, that henceforth "the firm should be Walpole and Townshend, and not Townshend and Walpole;" and during the twenty years that followed, the new leader so dominated the action of the cabinet and so impressed his personal will upon his party as to become the first prime minister, in the modern sense of that term, as distinguished from those royal favorites under the prerogative system of government whose rise and fall depended upon the personal will of the king alone. Walpole's robust common sense, seizing at once upon the fact that peace abroad and prosperity at home were the two conditions necessary for fixing the new dynasty firmly upon the throne, and for maturing the new system of cabinet government then under his control, resolutely refused to meddle with any matter that threatened to disturb either. As Carlyle[2] has told us, "He had one rule, that stood in place of many: To keep out of every business which it was possible for human wisdom to stave aside. 'What good will you get out of going into that? Parliamentary criticism, argument, and botheration! Leave well alone.'" When for once he attempted to depart from that rule by proposing, in 1733, an Excise Bill, designed to prevent the enormous frauds to which that branch of the revenue was then subject, he was confirmed in his philosophy by popular demonstrations and riots so violent as to force him to drop it.[3] "I will not be

Marginal notes: Return of Walpole to power; assumes the leadership with Townshend at his side; first prime minister in the modern sense of that term; his one rule of action as stated by Carlyle; his Excise Bill;

---

[1] Torrens, *History of Cabinets*, vol. i. pp. 298, 299.

[2] *Life of Frederick of Prussia*, vol. iii. pp. 373, 374; Todd, *Parl. Government*, vol. i. p. 267.

[3] *Parl. Hist.*, vol. viii. p. 1306; vol. ix. p. 7; Coxe's *Life of Walpole*, vol. i. p. 372.

the minister," he said, "to enforce taxes at the expense of blood."[1]   Despite that reverse, however, his supremacy in parliament was maintained down to 1742.   The struggle for his overthrow began in February of the year preceding, with a motion made in the lords for an address praying the king "to dismiss Sir Robert Walpole from his presence and councils forever."   Although defeated by a large majority, the motive for the assault was revealed by a protest entered on the journals by thirty-one peers, who declared that as "a sole, or even a first minister, is an officer unknown to the law of Britain, inconsistent with the constitution of this country, and destructive of liberty in any government whatsoever;" and that "it plainly appearing to us that Sir Robert Walpole has for many years acted as such, by taking on himself the chief, if not sole direction of affairs, in the different branches of the administration, we could not but esteem it to be our indispensable duty, to offer our most humble advice to his Majesty for the removal of a minister so dangerous to the king and the kingdom."[2]   At the same time a like motion was introduced in the commons, which assailed him because he had "grasped in his own hands every branch of government; had attained the sole direction of affairs; monopolized all the favors of the crown; compassed the disposal of all places, pensions, titles, and rewards."   While the house rejected the motion by a large majority,[3] a dissolution followed, and in the new body then chosen the fact was soon revealed that Walpole's rule was over by an adverse vote on a mere election petition.   Thus that member of the cabinet who was the first to appear in the rôle of a modern prime minister was the first as such to resign office,[4] not because he had lost the personal confidence of his sovereign, but because he could no longer control a majority of the house of commons.   But in order not to exaggerate the advance actually made by the cabinet system in Walpole's time, three important considerations must be kept steadily in view : first, that the control he managed to establish as the leader of the cabinet perished with him, and that

(marginal notes) struggle for his overthrow; a first minister declared to be an officer unknown to the law; because Walpole had acted as such, the peers asked the crown to discharge him; like motion defeated in the lower house; finally forced to resign by an adverse vote of that body;

---

[1] Green, *Hist. of the Eng. People*, vol. iv. p. 144.

[2] *Parl. Hist.*, vol. ii. pp. 1083, 1126, 1215.

[3] Mahon, *Hist. Eng.*, vol. iii. pp. 101–155.

[4] He resigned all his offices and retired to the house of lords as the earl of Oxford.

when it became the rule for a prime minister to dominate the cabinet, old system of independent departments disappeared;

not until the time of the younger Pitt did it become a settled rule of government for the cabinet to contain a prime minister with paramount authority over his colleagues ; second, that down to that time the old system of government by departments of state, each independent of the other,[1] and subject only to the general supervision of the crown, refused to yield to the new system resting upon a union of sentiment and responsibility directed and borne by an acknowledged and responsible chief ; third, that when Walpole as prime minister gave up his office in obedience to the will of the representative chamber, the rest of the cabinet did not retire with him, — not until the fall of Lord North in 1782 was there a simultaneous change of the whole cabinet resulting from a conviction upon the part of that minister that his failure to resign would be followed by a vote of a want of confidence in the lower house.[2] Since that time it has been the custom for ministries thus discredited to resign as a whole.

not until the fall of Lord North did it become the rule to change the whole ministry simultaneously.

A minister must resign when in conflict with a majority of his colleagues;

During the period that intervened between the retirement of Walpole to the house of lords as earl of Oxford and the end of the reign of George II., the most important incident that occurs illustrative of the growth of cabinet government is that which resulted in 1744 in the resignation of Lord Granville, because of a political difference between that minister and the Pelhams, who were supported by a majority of their colleagues.   When the controversy reached an acute stage the king was forced to interfere, and by the advice of Oxford he took part with the majority and indicated to Granville his wish that he should resign office.[3]   The "broad-bottom" administration, so called because it represented a coalition of all elements, then constituted under the lead of Pelham, continued down to his death in 1754, when he was succeeded by his brother, the duke of Newcastle, who was momentarily driven from office in 1756 by the disastrous beginning of the Seven Years' War.   In the hope of turning the tide, the elder Pitt was then called to office as secretary of state, and in the

the "broad-bottom" administration;

---

[1] Macaulay, *Hist. Eng.*, vol. iii. p. 14 ; *Quar. Rev.*, vol. 138, p. 418.

[2] "The first instance on record of the resignation of a prime minister in deference to an adverse vote of the house of commons, is that of Sir Robert Walpole." — Todd, *Parl. Government*, vol. i. p. 260, citing Cox, *Inst. Eng. Government*, pp. 249, 251 ; Knight, *Hist. Eng.*, vol. vi. p. 435.

[3] *Bedford Corresp.*, vol. i. pp. 25–35.

course of the year Newcastle returned to the treasury.   After a brief struggle for supreme control, the rivals agreed to am- icably divide the powers of the cabinet between them, — Pitt assuming the general direction of affairs, and Newcastle the management of parliament, the distribution of patronage,[1] and the work of corruption.   Upon that strange basis of a union of all that was highest and noble with all that was selfish and ignoble was constructed the most brilliant and the last of the purely Whig administrations.

division of power between Pitt and Newcastle;

last of the purely Whig administrations.

4. In view of the preceding statement that the modern par- liamentary system would have been substantially complete before the end of the reign of George II., if the house of com- mons had been at that time both representative and inde- pendent, the effort must now be made to explain somewhat in detail why it was neither the one nor the other.   In the first chapter devoted to the origin and growth of parliament a care- ful examination was made, first, of the internal mechanism of the shire and town communities, with special emphasis upon their peculiar methods of election and representation ; second, of the process through which their elected representatives were drawn together in one house, — a process that reached its completion with the assembling of Edward's model parliament of 1295, whose representative chamber embraced seventy-four knights of the shire and two hundred citizens and burgesses.[2] Of the two elements that entered into the representative sys- tem, as thus constituted, one was elastic by reason of the fact that under the writ directing the sheriff to return members from every city and borough in his county, he possessed the power not only to extend the right of representation to any town he saw fit to recognize, but also to ignore others equally worthy, or even such as had once enjoyed the right of electing members.[3]   The immense power thus vested in the crown to control the composition of the house of commons does not seem to have been abused, however, until a motive was given for such abuse by its increasing importance.   Then it was that efforts began to be made by courtiers to influence the elec- tions by recommendations in favor of particular candidates ;

Why the house of commons was neither representa- tive nor independ- ent;

internal mechanism of shire and town com- munities;

the elastic element in the system;

abuse by the crown of its power to control the lower house;

[1] Jesse, *Life of George III.*, vol. i. p. 123; Earl of Shelburne's *Life*, vol. i. pp. 85, 91; Todd, *Parl. Government*, vol. i. p. 271.

[2] Vol. i. pp. 445–466.

[3] *Ibid.*, p. 470.

and, as we learn from "The Paston Letters," when it was doubted whether such means would be efficacious to secure the return of a particular candidate, the suggestion was made that "there were many decayed boroughs in England which ought to return members to parliament, but did not ; and that from one of those he might be returned." In the reign preceding that in which this suggestion was made, the crown had inaugurated a new policy for the control of the borough communities that was momentous in its consequences. In 1438

first charter of incorporation to a municipal body ; (18th of Henry VI.) the first charter of incorporation to a municipal body was granted to Kingston-upon-Hull. The effect of like grants that followed was greatly to accelerate the process, already advancing by virtue of natural causes, through which the right of the burgesses — that is, "the inhabitant householders resident, paying scot and lot" — to govern the communities without the aid of town councils or other representative bodies was being gradually usurped by such bodies, whose members, originally elected, perpetuated themselves in power by self-election. Thus the tendency was for the more wealthy inhabitants to take away from the inferior townsmen

municipal authority gradually taken away from the many and vested in the self-elected few; all municipal authority by vesting it in governing bodies whose composition was not controlled by the suffrages of burgesses and freemen. In order to give legal sanction to this process through which the self-elected few were drawing to themselves the power to govern the borough communities, the crown inaugurated the policy of incorporation, whereby each community was given its own constitution, in which was confirmed the right of the selected few not only to carry on the

who were often authorized to return the borough members to parliament; local government, but also, in many instances, to return the borough members to parliament. "By the doctrines from time to time applied to the artificial creation of corporations, the control of the select bodies and the capricious election of corporators and non-residents were gradually introduced. Those abuses arose from slight beginnings in the reign of Elizabeth, — increased in the reigns of James and Charles I., — were carried to the greatest extent by the violent acts perpetrated in the reigns of Charles II. and James II., and were finally confirmed in the time of William III. and Queen Anne."[1]

1 For the best exposition of the whole subject, see Merewether and Stephens' *Hist. of Boroughs*, Introd.

In the charters of incorporation, which began to be issued to municipalities after the accession of the house of Tudor, the right of electing representatives in parliament was usually vested in the governing body styled the mayor and common council, nominated by the crown in the first instance, and then perpetuated by self-election.   Thus those boroughs not already under the control of the great landed proprietors became subject to the control of the crown, acting through the local magnates known as high stewards, by whom, in many instances, the royal and aristocratic influence was directly exercised.[1] With such an instrument in their hands, it is not strange that the sovereigns of the houses of Tudor and Stuart should have systematically pursued a policy of creating petty parliamentary boroughs, in localities where the crown had the greatest influence, for the express purpose of packing the lower house with members obedient to the royal will.   Thus between the reigns of Henry VIII. and Charles II. a hundred and eighty members were added to the house of commons by royal charter,[2] the last being that granted to Newark in 1673, which declared it to be "a borough town, with power to elect and send two burgesses to serve in parliament, who should be chosen by the mayor and aldermen, or the major part of them."   From that time down to the Reform Bill of 1832 no new boroughs were created in England or Wales, for the reason that the house of commons then took the issuance of writs into its own hands. The house also undertook to determine, in the case of the borough of Newark, that while the crown had the undoubted right to create boroughs, "upon which creation would follow all the legal consequence," it did not have the right to say "who should be the voters for members of parliament."   Upon that basis it held that the right of election in Newark, despite the terms of its charter, was vested in the mayor and aldermen, and "all the inhabitants who pay, or ought to pay scot and lot."   And finally, in the hope of doing something to settle the endless conflicts arising out of the uncertain and confused rights of election claimed in the different boroughs, the house, "in the reign of William III., passed the act (7 Will. III. c. 7) compelling the sheriffs to make returns from the elections

right to return such members usually vested in mayor and council, after the accession of the house of Tudor;

last royal charter that granted to Newark in 1673;

determination of the lower house as to right of election in that case;

rule that last determination of commons should govern in all cases;

[1] Cf. May, *Const. Hist.*, vol. iii. p. 279.

[2] Glanville's *Reports*, cii.; May, *Const. Hist.*, vol. i. p. 329, note 2.

according *to the rights which had last been determined by the house of commons*. By which means the varying and anomalous *usages* of the different boroughs, and the contradictory decisions of committees, were sanctioned and confirmed."[1]

contracting tendency of such decisions;

Contradictory and capricious as such determinations were, their general tendency was. to still further restrict the ancient franchise, and to vest it in a still more limited number of persons. In some of the corporate towns the right to vote was vested exclusively in the governing body of the corporation, while in others, the inhabitants paying scot and lot, and freemen, or the freemen only, were permitted to vote.

unjust distribution of borough representation;

The short-sighted and selfish spirit which guided the crown in multiplying borough members precluded the possibility of that high prerogative being used for correcting deficiencies existing from the beginning in the representative system, or for adjusting the disproportion that necessarily arose as time advanced out of the unequal distribution of wealth and population. In order to make the control of the crown and nobles more complete, the rule was to give the right of sending members to parliament to inconsiderable places, afterwards notorious as nomination boroughs, without any importance of their own, and dependent for patronage and protection upon the

great manufacturing centres overlooked and insignificant hamlets favored;

great adjacent landowners, while cities like Manchester, Leeds, and Birmingham, that rose into importance with the growth of trade and manufactures, were left entirely outside of the representative system. Thus places like Old Sarum, not larger than an ordinary hamlet, unblushingly returned the nominees of their proprietors, while many of the growing commercial cities were obliged to submit to taxation without representa-

Cromwell's attempt at reform.

tion. The bold and statesmanlike attempt made by Cromwell in 1653[2] to remedy such conditions by disfranchising many of the smaller boroughs, by increasing the number of the county members, and by enfranchising Manchester, Leeds, and Halifax, died with him, and thus the whole wretched scheme of inequality lingered on until it was finally corrected in the main by the Reform Bill of 1832.

However great may have been the evils arising out of the

---

[1] Merewether and Stephens' *Hist. of Boroughs*, Introd.

[2] Act for the Settlement of the Government of the Commonwealth, December 16, 1653.

failure to allot representatives to the counties, cities, and towns, according to their wealth and population, they shrink into insignificance when compared with the enormous abuses incident to an organized system of bribery and corruption, applied not only to those by whom the representatives were chosen in the local communities, but also to the representatives themselves after their arrival at Westminster.   In dealing with the first branch of the subject some one has divided the constituencies into two classes : first, those who were sold by others ; second, those who sold themselves.   The first class embraced, of course, the small nomination boroughs, in which certain lords and other wealthy patrons were able to dictate the choice of their nominees, over whose political conduct their control was unquestioned.   In that way the peers not only had a voice in their own house, but they were represented by their nominees in the lower.   At one time the duke of Norfolk was thus represented by eleven members ; Lord Lonsdale by nine ; Lord Darlington by seven ;[1] and in 1821 Sydney Smith[2] writes : "The county belongs to the duke of Rutland, Lord Lonsdale, the duke of Newcastle, and about twenty other holders of boroughs.   They are our masters."   The control of such patrons dates back to the fifteenth century, and in Elizabeth's time the commons were warned lest "lords' letters shall from henceforth bear all the sway."   The right of the patron was regarded as a part of his estate, which he could dispose of as he pleased, but he was supposed to sell the nomination, as a general rule, to one of his own political faith ;[3] if he sold to an opponent, a greater price had to be given as a compensation for the sacrifice.   While the price of boroughs ranged from £2500 to £5000, George Selwyn, the owner of the representation of Ludgershall, sold it for £9000.[4]   In the case of Westbury, the property of Lord Abingdon, the two seats valued at £10,000 were even put in the hands of trustees for the benefit of creditors.[5]   The one feature which is supposed to have somewhat redeemed this part of the system consists of the fact that a generous patron, instead of selling the nomination, would sometimes give it to a worthy and rising man

Margin notes:

An organized system of corruption applied both to electors and elected;

corruption in small nomination boroughs belonging to wealthy patrons,

whose control dates back to the fifteenth century; regarded as a property interest;

prices at which certain boroughs were sold;

a generous patron sometimes gave the nomination to a rising young man;

[1] Oldfield's *Rep. Hist.*, vol. vi. p. 286.
[2] *Mem.*, vol. ii. p. 215 ; May's *Const. Hist.*, vol. i. pp. 333, 361.
[3] Romilly's *Life*, vol. ii. p. 202.

[4] *Letters of Lord Chesterfield to his Son* (1767, 1768), vol. iv. pp. 269, 274.
[5] Romilly's *Life*, vol. ii. pp. 200, 201.

who would not otherwise find a seat in the house.[1]   Such

nominees, whether through friendship or purchase, were not supposed to have any personal connection with their constituents ; and we learn from the diary of Lord Palmerston that when he came into parliament from a borough belonging to Sir Leonard Holmes, "one condition required was, that I would never, even for the election, set foot in the place." [2]

Methods of
corpora-
tions that
sold them-
selves :
the case of
Oxford;
As illustrations of the methods of those constituencies or corporations that enjoyed the privilege of selling themselves and of applying the proceeds to their own uses, reference may be made to the notorious case of the corporation of Oxford, which, availing itself of the general election of 1768, offered to return its members, upon condition that they would pay off its bonded debt of £5670.   When the matter was brought before the house of commons by those to whom the offer had been made, the mayor and ten of the aldermen were committed to Newgate ; but while they were there they actually sold the representation of the city to the duke of Marlborough and the earl of Abingdon ; and in the hope of concealing the facts the clerk of the corporation carried off the books containing the evidence of the bargain.[3]   More shameless still, however,

was the conduct of the notoriously corrupt borough of Sudbury, which, without any attempt at disguise, shamelessly advertised itself for sale to the highest bidder.[4]   While the nomination boroughs of patrons and boroughs under control of close corporations could be thus disposed of, there were more populous places, such as the few great cities, the ports, and the thriving manufacturing towns, where the franchise was sufficiently extended to insure a genuine expression of popular opinion, had the voters been permitted to act without the pres-

sure of corruption and undue influence.   In order to secure the representation of such places for the crown, the government candidates not only resorted to money bribes, but to the zealous support of the army of government officials employed in the collection of the customs and excise, who were appointed with

[1] The younger Pitt was given a place in the house in 1781 by Sir James Lowther, who controlled the pocket borough of Appleby.

[2] Bulwer's *Life*, vol. i. p. 23.

[3] *Parl. Hist.*, vol. xvi. p. 397; Walpole's *Mem.*, vol. iii. p. 153; May, *Const. Hist.*, vol. i. pp. 338, 339, 344, 346.

[4] Walpole's *Mem.*, vol. i. p. 42. Sudbury was ultimately disfranchised by 7 & 8 Vict. c. 58.

a view to such work.   If an opposition candidate by virtue of his personal popularity seemed likely to triumph despite such obstacles, the government was ready to destroy his hopes through a fraudulent return, or by keeping open the poll for forty days,[1] during which time he was permitted to accept either defeat, or the financial ruin that such prolonged contests involved.   The habit of corrupting electors by money bribes — the giving of money bribes; which had become a recognized abuse in the reign of Charles II., and which the fresh importance given to the lower house by the Revolution had greatly advanced — was still farther stimulated by the advent of the "nabobs,"[2] as those success- stimulated by the "nabobs;" ful adventurers were called who returned from the East and West Indies, laden with spoils they were willing to divide with those who were ready to help them to places in parliament. Surrounded by such conditions, elections finally gave rise to a regular stock-jobbing traffic, in which "for many boroughs there stock-jobbing traffic in elections; was a fixed price."[3]   Rather to prevent the intrusion of the nabobs into the political preserves of the great landed proprie- tors than to suppress bribery, already recognized as an offence by the common law,[4] was passed the act of 7 Will. III. c. 4. Not until 1729 was that act followed by the first statute[5] aimed statutes enacted against bribery. directly against bribery in parliamentary elections, which, after an interval of eighty years, was reinforced by 49 Geo. III. c. 118.   To cover cases not embraced in that act was enacted, in 1842, 5 & 6 Vict. c. 102, s. 20 ; and, in 1852, the Corrupt Practices Act (17 & 18 Vict. c. 102), now in force.

The backbone of the representative system as thus organ- Backbone of the repre- sentative system, the county con- stituencies; ized was the county constituencies, in which all forty-shillings freeholders, including the country gentlemen and independent yeomanry, were entitled to vote.   Under so liberal a franchise it was certainly to be expected that the independent class in whom it was vested would give forth a clear and bold expres-

---

[1] "During this period, the public houses were thrown open ; and drunk- enness and disorder prevailed in the streets, and at the hustings." — May, *Const. Hist.*, vol. i. p. 350.

[2] For Lord Chatham's denunciation of them, see *Parl. Hist.*, vol. xvi. p. 752.

[3] Davenant's *Works*, vol. iii. pp. 326, 328, "Essay on the Balance of Power."

[4] Burrow, vol. iii. pp. 1235, 1388 ; Douglas, vol. iv. p. 294 ; Male's *Election Law*, pp. 339–345, cited by May, *Const. Hist.*, vol. i. p. 334.   Sir J. F. Stephen, however, rather discredits the assump- tion.   *Hist. of the Crim. Law*, vol. iii. p. 252.

[5] 2 Geo. II. c. 24.   Stephen, *Hist. of the Crim. Law*, vol. iii. pp. 253, 254.

sion of the popular will, unfettered by the ignoble influences that prevailed in the cities and towns. The difficulty, however, was that the county voters as a class were slaves of that social custom which recognized the nobles and other great landowners as local potentates, authorized by virtue of their status to direct the political affairs of their counties either in person, or through dependents over whom they exercised a kind of feudal sway.[1] The political control in many counties thus remained permanently in the hands of certain great families, whose battles for supremacy often rivaled in bitterness the feuds of the Montagues and Capulets, while the expenditures incident to electoral struggles often overtaxed even princely fortunes. In contesting Westmoreland and Cumberland with Sir James Lowther in 1768, the duke of Portland is said to have expended over £40,000, and in comparatively recent times an election for the county of York is known to have cost upwards of £150,000.[2] When all of the influences, tending as well in the shires as in the towns to take away the franchise from the main body of freemen and to vest it in a comparatively few individuals, have been carefully estimated, it is certain that the actual number of persons who returned the five hundred and fifty-eight members composing the house of commons after the union with Scotland was comparatively small. While such evidence as exists upon the subject is open to suspicion, we may accept as substantially correct the statement contained in the petition presented in 1793 by the Society of the Friends of the People, from which it appears that three hundred and fifty-seven members — more than a majority of the house as then constituted — were returned to parliament by one hundred and fifty-four patrons, of whom forty were peers.[3] Then in corroboration of that estimate we have, after the union with Ireland, the statistics contained in Dr. Oldfield's " Representative History " (1816), from which we learn that of the six hundred and fifty-eight members then composing the lower house, four hundred and eighty-seven were returned by nomination of the government, and two hundred and sixty-seven private patrons, of whom one hundred

Marginal notes:

control of nobles and other great landowners over county politics;

enormous expenditures incident to electoral contests;

actual number of independent voters comparatively small;

a majority of the lower house in 1793 nominated by 154 patrons;

Dr. Oldfield's estimate made in 1816;

---

[1] Oldfield's *Representative Hist.*, vol. vi. p. 285.

[2] Walpole's *Mem.*, vol. iii. p. 197; Speech of Lord J. Russell, March 1, 1831, in *Hans. Deb.*, 3d ser. vol. ii. p. 1074; May, *Const. Hist.*, vol. i. pp. 354, 355.

[3] *Parl. Hist.*, vol. xxx. p. 787.

and forty-four were peers.   Thus only a hundred and seventy-one — less than a third of the house — remained as the free choice of such independent constituencies as were possessed of the limited franchise then existing.[1]

less than a third of the house the free choice of independent constituencies.

It would have been strange indeed if the members of the representative chamber, chosen in the local communities as a general rule through an organized system of corruption and undue influence, should have been insensible to all the blandishments of power to which they were subjected after their arrival at Westminster.   From the accession of William III. it was necessary for the cabinet to control a majority of the house of commons, and from that time dates the lavish use of everything at the disposal of the crown to secure that end. Noblest among the bribes thus parcelled out were the coveted distinctions that flowed from the crown as the fountain of honor.   During the administration of Lord North he either created or promoted about thirty British peers ; the younger Pitt, more lavish still, created during the first five years of his administration nearly fifty peers ; while between 1761 and 1821 the extraordinary number of four hundred and ninety-four baronetcies was added to the hereditary knighthood of the realm.[2]   While the crown thus pandered to the pride of the rich, the poor and necessitous were consoled by places, pensions, and money bribes, paid either in hard cash, or realized through shares in lotteries and loans, or through lucrative government contracts.   As heretofore explained, William III., who was first called upon to manipulate the new ministerial system, attempted to do so to a great extent by a multiplication of offices, which were so lavishly bestowed upon members of the lower house that parliament, at the instance of that body, was forced to enact a series of statutes against placemen whose history has been drawn out already.[3]   The grosser expedient of using direct pecuniary bribes, begun under Charles II. and continued under William III., after having been systematized by Sir Robert Walpole, reached its highest point under Henry Pelham and his wretched brother the duke of Newcastle.   Lord

Bribery as employed at Westminster ;

gifts of peerages and baronetcies ;

gifts of places, pensions, and money bribes ;

systematized by Walpole and perfected by Pelham and Newcastle ;

---

[1] Oldfield's *Representative Hist.*, vol. vi. pp. 285–300.

[2] Beatson's *Political Index*, vol. i. pp. 137, 140; *Parl. Hist.*, vol. xxvii. p. 967 *et seq.*; May, *Const. Hist.*, vol. i.

pp. 277, 279, 323, citing as to the baronetcies a paper by the late Mr. Pulman, Clarencieux King-at-Arms.

[3] See above, pp. 441–444.

Bute, who was no unworthy pupil of such masters, intrusted Mr. Henry Fox[1] with "the management of the house of commons," and in 1762 Horace Walpole tells us that when voters were needed to support the preliminaries of the Peace of Paris,

a shop opened at the Pay Office;

"a shop was publicly opened at the Pay Office, whither the members flocked, and received the wages of their venality in bank bills, even to so low a sum as £200 for their votes on

loans and lotteries;

the treaty."[2] In the next year it was that Lord Bute invented the new method of bribery by means of shares in loans and lotteries.[3]

abuse of the right to decide contested elections;

Political parties that succeeded by means of such expedients in securing majorities in the house of commons soon learned how to take away from hostile voters the right to chose representatives by an abuse of the sacred judicial function involved in the determination of contested elections. An account has heretofore been given of the process through which not only the right to pass upon the legality of returns and the conduct of returning officers, but also upon the qualifications of the electors themselves, became the exclusive possession of the lower house, and of the manner in which it was recognized and affirmed in turn by the peers, the courts of law, and by the act of 7 Will. III. c. 7.[4] Originally the house exercised the right thus acquired by means of a select committee specially chosen for that purpose; and afterwards by that formally

Committee of Privileges and Elections;

designated as the Committee of Privileges and Elections, into whose composition for a long time entered such privy councillors and eminent lawyers as were qualified to perform the delicate judicial duties required of them.[5] But in the course of time, specially during the reigns of George II. and George III., the power to seat a party friend and to oust a party rival

superseded by committee organized under Mr. Grenville's Act of 1770;

was so grossly abused that in 1770 Mr. Grenville introduced his famous measure that passed into law, by virtue of which the right to try election petitions was transferred from the house itself to a committee of thirteen, armed with the right to decide without appeal, and selected by the petitioners and the

---

[1] Rockingham, *Mem.*, vol. i. p. 127.
[2] Walpole, *Mem. George III.*, vol. i. p. 199.
[3] *Parl. Hist.*, vol. xv. p. 1305; Lord Mahon's *Hist.*, vol. v. p. 20; May, *Const. Hist.*, vol. i. p. 382; Lecky, *Hist. Eng.*, vol. i. p. 368.

[4] Vol. i. pp. 528–531.
[5] As to the trial of controverted elections prior to 1770, see May, *Parl. Practice*, p. 613; *Const. Hist.*, vol. i. pp. 363–369.

sitting members from a list of forty-nine chosen by ballot, to which each party was entitled to add a representative of his own interests.[1]   That act, at first limited to one year and afterwards made perpetual,[2] continued to regulate the proceedings in election cases down to 1839, when Sir Robert Peel secured the passage of a new measure designed to remove its admitted deficiencies.   Under the Peel Act the trial committee, first reduced to six members and then to five,[3] was selected by what was called an impartial body, — the general committee of elections, in whose nomination one party or the other had necessarily a majority of one.   In order to remove the lingering suspicion of partiality which that fact involved, the trial of contested elections was finally transferred in 1868 to the judges of superior courts of law,[4] in accordance with a notable precedent [5] drawn from the history of earlier time.

renewed down to 1839, when it was superseded by the Peel Act;

trial of all contested elections transferred to the courts in 1868.

No attempt to explain why the house of commons was not, at the accession of George III., a free and representative organ through which the nation as a whole could impress its will upon its rulers, would be at all complete, if no mention was made of the secrecy of its proceedings, resulting from its right to exclude strangers and to prohibit the publication of its proceedings and debates.   The first named, and the most ancient of these rights, grew, no doubt, out of the necessity felt by members to protect their consultations from the intrusion of emissaries who might come to report their doings and sayings either to the king himself, or to the courts of law.   The privilege thus originating in a desire to protect the house against the arbitrary action of the crown was perverted, however, as time advanced, to the sinister purpose of concealing what occurred behind closed doors from the gaze of the constituencies. From the beginning the intrusion of strangers was punishable

Right of the lower house to exclude strangers and to prohibit the publication of its proceedings;

motives for its exercise;

---

[1] The design was thus to constitute a tribunal composed of members of the house, and yet independent of it. Cf. *Parl. Hist.*, vol. xvi. pp. 904–923.

[2] *Parl. Hist.*, vol. xvii. p. 1071.

[3] 2 & 3 Vict. c. 38; 4 & 5 Vict. c. 58; 11 & 12 Vict. c. 98.

[4] 31 & 32 Vict. c. 125. By that act, supplemented by the Parliamentary Elections and Corrupt Practices Act of 1879, and by 44 & 45 Vict. c. 68, the trial of controverted elections is con-

fided, as regards England, to two judges selected from the queen's bench division of the high court of justice; for Irish cases the judges are taken from the court of common pleas at Dublin; for Scotch cases, from the court of session.

[5] By 11 Hen. IV. c. 1 the justices of assize were authorized to inquire into the returns, and to fine the sheriffs for returning persons not duly elected. See vol. i. p. 528.

by their immediate commitment or reprimand;[1] and when the interest excited by the debates finally induced a relaxation of that rule in favor of such as desired to attend, the right was reserved to dismiss them instantly whenever any member saw fit to call upon the speaker to enforce the orders of the house.

Thus it became easy to cut off any orator who endeavored to make his influence felt beyond the walls of the chamber simply by a motion from his opponents to close the doors.[2]   When the press, as an organ of public opinion, attempted to invade the secrecy of parliament, the right to publish its proceedings and debates, without its consent, was strenuously resisted. Thus, in 1641, the Long Parliament, while permitting the publication of its proceedings under the title of "Diurnal Occurrences in Parliament," for the first time expressly prohibited the printing of speeches without leave of the house.[3]   Sometimes when a speech was acceptable to the dominant party its publication was permitted, but when it was not the offender was liable to suffer the fate of Mr. Dering, who, for printing a collection of his speeches, was expelled from the house and committed to the Tower, while his book was ordered to be burned by the common hangman.[4]   The entire restriction was continued in full force after the Restoration down to 1680, when the house, to insure a correct report of its transactions, ordered its "votes and proceedings"[5] to be printed under the direction of the speaker.   In order to avoid the prohibition still resting upon the publication of debates, resort was had down to the Revolution to news-letters and pamphlets as circulating mediums, which were supplemented by private memorandums and reports kept by members and published a long time thereafter.   Notwithstanding frequent resolutions passed after the Revolution to prevent news-letter writers from "giving any account or minute of the debates," imperfect reports of the more important ones were published by the aid of notes taken by members, in Boyer's "Political State of Great Britain," the "London Magazine," and the "Gentleman's Magazine," with the names of the speakers omitted.   How

---

[1] *Commons' Journals*, vol. xxxiii. pp. 118, 417; Ibid., vol. ii. pp. 74, 433.

[2] For the standing order that now regulates the withdrawal of strangers, see May's *Parl. Practice*, p. 201.

[3] *Commons' Journals*, vol. ii. pp. 209, 220.

[4] February 2, 1641; Ibid., vol. ii. p. 411.

[5] Ibid., vol. ix. p. 74.

accurate and impartial such clandestine reports were we may infer not only from the humorous complaint made by Sir Robert Walpole, of the ridiculous account published of a debate that took place in 1738, but also from the confession of Dr. Johnson, who was then engaged in the manufacture of such reports, that "he took care that the Whig dogs should not have the best of it." [1] complaint of Sir R. Walpole; confession of Dr. Johnson.

During the period in which the various causes which have now been briefly reviewed were making the house of commons "the representative of nominal boroughs, of ruined and exterminated towns, of noble families, of wealthy individuals, of foreign potentates," a new political force was being rapidly evolved out of the moral consciousness of the people that was destined after a prolonged and bitter struggle to abolish alike the antiquated customs and the modern corruptions that rendered it impossible for the representative chamber to be, as Burke expressed it, "the express image of the feelings of the nation." While Whitefield and the Wesleys were bringing about by their asceticism and their stirring eloquence a revival of religious enthusiasm, William Pitt, the grandson of a wealthy governor of Madras, and the fiery spokesman of that younger group of public men generally known as "the patriots," [2] undertook to break the political torpor, the studied indifference to all nobler political aims, so long and so carefully nourished by the cold cynicism of Walpole. Pitt was the first to see that out of the progress of English commerce and industry there had been born a great middle class that was fast becoming the dominant force in the nation, and yet without adequate representation in the legislature. It was from that growing element that Pitt had sprung, and it was by virtue of its power and sympathy that he hoped to rule. When he attempted to save Byng by appealing to the sentiment of parliament, George II. taunted him with the reminder: "You have taught me to look for the voice of my people in other places than within the house of commons;" [3] and when upon the acces- Public opinion as a factor in politics; influence of Whitefield and the Wesleys; William Pitt born of the growing middle class inadequately represented in the legislature;

---

[1] Upon the whole subject, see Prefaces to Cobbett's *Parl. Hist.*, vols. ix.–xiii.; Walpole's *Mem.*, vol. iv. p. 278; *Parl. Hist.*, vol. x. pp. 300, 800; Cavendish, *Deb.*, vol. ii. pp. 244, 257; May, *Const. Hist.*, vol. ii. pp. 34–60.

[2] These were reinforced by the younger Whigs, whom Walpole called the "boys."

[3] Green, *Hist. of the Eng. People*, vol. iv. p. 180.

sion of George III. his purpose to declare war against Spain was successfully resisted by his colleagues, he resigned office, declaring to the cabinet council that he had been called to power by the voice of the people, to whom he considered himself accountable for his conduct. It was as the leader of this new political force embodied in the corporate person of the people, whose aggregate voice made up what was called public opinion, that Pitt won his highest title of "the great commoner." In the hope of establishing harmony between the political machinery of the state and the new force by which it was destined to be impelled, Pitt was the first to advocate such a reform of the representative system as would enable the sovereign people to speak through the sovereign parliament. Thus before the end of the reign of George II., England, in the words of Frederick of Prussia, after having been "for a long time in labor at last brought forth a man," and that man it was who, after widening the limits of the British empire in two hemispheres, was the first to give direction and force to the new-born power of public opinion which, with the rude weapons at its command, finally broke the hold of the crown and the aristocracy upon the legislature, and thus made possible the completion of the ministerial system in the form in which it exists to-day. The progress made during the reigns of George III. and George IV. by the liberalizing movement thus begun will be drawn out in the following chapter.

first to advocate a reform of the representative system;

Frederick declared that England had "at last brought forth a man."

CHAPTER II.

ITS PROGRESS DURING THE REIGNS OF GEORGE III. AND GEORGE IV.

1. JUST as the new ministerial system under the leadership of Pitt, who was the first to arouse the nation to a sense of its new and higher destiny, had made England the first maritime and colonial power in the world, its growth was suddenly checked by the accession of George III., who was the first and the last of the Hanoverian kings who aspired not only to reign but to rule. Defective as the education of the young king was, it had been so directed as to imbue him with a love for arbitrary principles of government, and the tendency thus begun was stimulated and encouraged by his mother's continual precept of "George, be king." [1] Unlike his two immediate predecessors he was native born, and in order the more perfectly to play the part of "a patriot king," as Bolingbroke [2] had conceived it for him, he added with his own hand to his first speech to parliament the stirring declaration, "Born and educated in this country, I glory in the name of Briton." [3] In the review already made of the growth of cabinet government during the reigns of George I. and George II., the fact was emphasized that their foreign birth and personal incompetency, coupled with a consequent willingness to surrender their personal right to rule into the hands of their constitutional advisers, had gone far to develop the idea of the impersonality of the sovereign, the cornerstone of the existing system. Under such conditions it was that the Whig ministry that came into power as a whole, upon the accession of George I., were able to meet apart from the king under the presidency of one of their own number; and so before the end of the

Growth of ministerial system checked by accession of George III.;

his mother's precept, "George, be king;"

he gloried "in the name of Briton;"

impersonality of the sovereign developed under his foreign predecessors;

---

[1] Rockingham's *Memoirs*, vol. i. p. 3.
[2] *Works*, vol. iv. p. 274, "The Idea of a Patriot King;" May, *Const. Hist.*, vol. i. pp. 9–12.
[3] Rose's *Corr.*, vol. ii. p. 189. As to the composition of the speech and the manner in which it was forced upon the ministry, see Harris, *Life of Harwicke*, vol. iii. p. 231.

reign of George II. the sovereign's right to preside at cabinet councils had not only become obsolete, but the new office of prime minister, which Walpole was the first to fill, had arisen as a necessary substitute for that headship which the king himself had before supplied. The first member of the cabinet who thus arose to the post of premier still further advanced the growth of the new system by resigning office after a long period of power, not because he had lost the confidence of his sovereign, but because he could no longer control a majority of the house of commons. Then followed the settlement of the principle in the case of Lord Granville, that it is the duty of a minister to resign when he is no longer in political harmony with the majority of his colleagues.[1] In the light of these facts it is possible to say that at the death of George II. "cabinet rule had been upon its trial for nearly half a century; and, despite many blemishes and errors, its superiority to the systems of government that had preceded it was tacitly accepted by the nation."[2] Such was the condition of things when George III. came upon the scene, firmly resolved to restore the crown to its ancient position by becoming his own first minister, and by breaking up the system of party organization and control, without which cabinet government in its modern form is impossible. His design thus to strike at the roots of an institution whose growth was fast overshadowing the royal office was greatly facilitated by the internal disorganization of the Whigs, who, since their cohesion had been broken by the fall of Walpole, had become divided into cliques and factions. In order to remove the weakness arising from that cause, and at the same time to perpetuate the rule of the great Whig families that filled all the higher offices of state, a coalition had been formed between Pitt and Newcastle, which, during the three years preceding the accession of George III., had crystallized into a political power that seemed well-nigh impregnable. As a means of dissolving that coalition, and of revesting the entire executive power in the crown, the king called to his aid his personal friend, the earl of Bute, and along with him a set of secret counsellors, the greater part of whom were Tories, with a Jacobite conception of the preroga-

Marginal notes:

Walpole, the first prime minister,

resigned because he could no longer control the commons;

Granville, because no longer in harmony with his colleagues;

George's design to undo what had been done promoted by dissensions of the Whigs;

---

[1] See above, p. 462.   [2] Torrens, *Hist. of Cabinets*, vol. ii. p. 566.

tive, who soon came to be known as "the king's men," or "the king's friends."[1] Then, instead of advising with his responsible ministers, the king counselled with this secret and irresponsible coterie behind the throne,[2] to strengthen whose hands he dissolved parliament, after he had prepared with Bute's aid a list of court candidates whose return was urged by the whole power of the crown, even against the ministers themselves when they were known to be opposed to the king's designs. Bute, who had been immediately sworn of the privy council, was, in March, 1761, made one of the secretaries of state. When, therefore, in October of that year Pitt insisted upon an instant declaration of war with Spain,[3] the new favorite, as the mouthpiece of his master, joined forces with Newcastle and the rest of the Whigs, who were jealous of his supremacy, and thus by rejecting Pitt's proposal drove him from power.[4] The disruption of the Whig ministry thus begun was completed in May, 1762, when the miserable duke of Newcastle, with the more powerful of his colleagues, was driven out[5] in order to give a free hand to Lord Bute, who at once became the nominal head of the government as first lord of the treasury. The king's plans were now complete. The ministerial system which the Whigs had been constructing for nearly fifty years was broken down, and its place supplied by a coterie of "the king's friends" under the leadership of Bute, who was not prime minister in the sense in which Walpole had been, but a mere court favorite or grand vizier, whose rise and fall depended solely upon the will of his master, and not upon that of the house of commons. In order to render himself more independent of that body and more secure from the attacks of the Whig leaders, who had been forced by his revolutionary proceedings into an organized opposition, the king resolved upon the making of a peace, whose preliminaries were approved in December, 1762, by a majority of five to one, obtained through means so shameful as to constitute a notable

Margin notes: "the king's friends;" a secret and irresponsible coterie; Bute made a secretary of state; joined Newcastle in driving Pitt from power; ministerial system superseded by a body of court favorites under nominal leadership of Bute;

---

[1] Burke's "Present Discontents," *Works*, vol. ii. pp. 240–242; May, *Const. Hist.*, vol. i. p. 13.

[2] Called by Burke the "double" or "interior cabinet."

[3] That country had made a secret treaty with France, then at war with England. *Grenville Papers*, vol. i. p. 386.

[4] *Chatham Corr.*, vol. ii. p. 159; *Grenville Papers*, vol. i. pp. 391, 405.

[5] As to the king's conduct to the duke, see his letter to Lord Rockingham, May 19. *Memoirs*, vol. i. p. 111; May, *Const. Hist.*, vol. i. p. 21.

outburst of popular opinion against the change soon drove Bute from power;

episode in the history of parliamentary corruption.[1]   Against this new system of absolutism which thus enslaved the house of commons, while it committed the greatest ministerial office to a court favorite, public opinion protested in such a burst of popular indignation as had not fallen upon the throne since the days of the Stuart kings.   So intense did the riot and uproar become that Bute, fearful lest he should involve "his royal master in his ruin," was forced in the spring of 1763 to withdraw from the perilous office he had enjoyed for less than

succeeded by George Grenville.

eleven months.   Before disappearing from the scene, however, Bute arranged for the appointment of George Grenville as the head of a cabinet composed of his more courtly colleagues, whose policy he proposed to direct from his hiding-place in the royal closet.[2]

The freedom of the press;

2. In the course of the tumult that caused the fall of Bute, the new-born force of public opinion, which could find expression neither in the councils of the king nor in the halls of parliament, invoked the aid of the organ destined to grow into

John Wilkes and

the great political power now known as the fourth estate.   John Wilkes, who was the first to establish the right of the press to freely discuss public affairs, had come upon the scene as a bitter opponent of Bute, and in order to make his opposition

the "North Briton;"

the more effective he had founded a paper called "The North Briton," which had assailed the obnoxious Scot without mercy. When he resigned, the issue of the paper was suspended; but when the king's speech, framed by the Grenville ministry, revealed the fact that there had been a mere change of men and not of measures, a supplemental number of "The North

No. 45, of April 23, 1763;

Briton," No. 45, was issued on the 23d of April, 1763, containing an offensive criticism not only of the cabinet and the unpopular Peace of Paris, but also of the terms of the king's speech at the prorogation.[3]   Three days before he received any evidence that Wilkes was the author of "The North Briton," Lord Halifax, the leading secretary of state, issued

a general warrant issued by a secretary of state;

as such a general warrant "to search for authors, printers, and publishers," who were to be brought before him for examination.   The messengers who held this roving commission

---

[1] See above, p. 472.

[2] *Grenville Papers*, vol. ii. pp. 32, 33, 85.

[3] *Parl. Hist.*, vol. xv. p. 1331, n.; Lord Mahon's *Hist.*, vol. v. p. 45; Adolphus' *Hist.*, vol. i. p. 116.

arrested in the course of three days not less than forty-nine persons, on mere suspicion, and among them Dryden Leach, a printer, and Wilkes himself, who was committed to the Tower.   After he had been removed from his house the messengers returned, and after ransacking his drawers carried off all his private papers.   The right of a secretary of state, claiming to act as a conservator of the peace, to issue general warrants without previous evidence of guilt, and without identification of the person of the accused, rested only upon a usage that had prevailed in the days of high prerogative.   "It is said that the usage has been so; and that many such warrants have been issued, since the Revolution, down to this time."   In order to test the legality of such warrants, Dryden Leach brought an action of trespass in the king's bench against the messengers, and after full argument it was held that such warrants were illegal because the usage of a particular office upon which the right to issue them was based, not being a general usage, had never grown into law.   The court also declared that the usage was a bad one, and that "no degree of antiquity can give sanction to a usage bad in itself."[1]   In the warrant under which Wilkes and Leach were arrested, the messengers were authorized not only to search for "printers and publishers," but "to apprehend and seize, *together with their papers*," such as they might suspect.   The right to issue a general search warrant of that character was said to rest upon a practice of the star chamber which, after its abolition, had been revived and revested in the secretary of state by the Licensing Act of Charles II.   In order to test the validity of that special part of the writ, Wilkes brought an action against Wood, the under-secretary of state, who had personally superintended the search of his house and the carrying away of his papers.   The result was a judgment against Wood, in which the chief justice declared it to be his opinion that "the office precedents, which have been produced since the Revolution, are no justification of a practice in itself illegal, and contrary

Marginal notes: forty-nine persons arrested on suspicion; right to issue such writs rested only on usage; in Leach's case it was held that they were illegal, because "usage bad in itself;" right to issue a general search warrant said to rest upon practice of star chamber; declared illegal in Wilkes v. Wood;

---

[1] *Leach* v. *Money, State Trials*, vol. xix. p. 1000; Burrow's *Rep.*, vol. iii. pp. 1692, 1742; Sir W. Blackstone's *Rep.*, p. 555.   The principle announced was that "A general warrant issued by a secretary of state to search for and seize the author (not named) of a seditious libel is illegal;" but the case actually went off on the ground "that the warrant in question had not been pursued." — Cf. Broom's *Const. Law*, p. 543, note (c.).

to the fundamental principles of the constitution." [1] Two years later the same question was again presented in the case of Entick v. Carrington, when the illegality of a general search warrant issued by a secretary of state to seize the papers of the author of a seditious libel, even when the author was named, was finally put at rest by a judgment in which Lord Camden declared that if such writs were upheld, "the secret cabinets and bureaus of every subject in the kingdom will be thrown open to search and inspection of a messenger, whenever the secretary of state shall think fit to charge, or even suspect, a person to be the author, printer, or publisher, of a seditious libel." [2]

and in Entick v. Carrington;

Lord Camden's judgment.

Wilkes, at the time of his arrest, was a member of the house of commons, and he therefore applied, on a writ of habeas corpus, for his release, which was granted by reason of his privilege. [3] It being then known that he was the author of "The North Briton," an information charging him with criminal libel was filed against him in the court of king's bench, where he refused to put in an appearance, also upon the ground of privilege. [4] The arch offender was thus in the hands of two great courts, each of which claimed the right to punish him for the way in which he had seen fit to exercise the right of freedom of discussion; and the struggle which he then inaugurated against the right of either to punish a citizen for the exercise of that privilege finally resulted in its establishment in the form in which it is now understood. The high court of parliament itself, whose summary jurisdiction must first be considered, claimed the right not only to punish its own members guilty of libellous publications, but also to censure or commit any other person who might print anything that could be construed into a contempt against itself. As illustrations, refer-

Wilkes claimed his privilege as a member of the commons;

refused to plead in king's bench on that ground;

power of parliament to punish authors of libellous publications;

[1] *State Trials*, vol. xix. p. 1153; Lofft's *Rep.*, p. 1. It was thus settled that, "A general warrant issued by a secretary of state to search for and seize the papers of the author (not named) of a seditious libel is illegal." — Cf. Broom's *Const. Law*, p. 544.

[2] *State Trials*, vol. xix. p. 1030. "A warrant issued by a secretary of state, to seize the papers of an author (named) of a seditious libel, is illegal." — Cf. Broom, p. 555.

[3] *Rex* v. *Wilkes*, Wilson's *Reports*, vol. ii. p. 151; *State Trials*, vol. xix. p. 539.

[4] He declared, however, upon the meeting of parliament in November, 1763, that if his privilege should be affirmed he would waive it, and "put himself upon a jury of his countrymen." — Cobbett's *Parl. Hist.*, vol. xv. p. 1359, *et seq.*

ence may be made to the case of Sir Richard Steele, who was case of Sir Richard Steele;
expelled from the lower house in 1714 for writing "a seditious
and scandalous libel" hostile to the house of Hanover, published in a pamphlet called "The Crisis;" [1] and to that of
Mr. Gale Jones, who was committed to Newgate in 1810 for of Mr. Gale Jones;
publishing an offensive placard announcing the conduct of two
members of the commons as a subject for discussion in a de-
bating society.[2] When the house was called upon to deal action of the commons in Wilkes' case;
with the case of Wilkes, it began, as a mark of sympathy to
the king, by voting No. 45 of "The North Briton" to be "a
false, scandalous, and malicious libel," which it ordered to be denounced his publication;
burned by the common hangman. And then in defiance of its
former decisions that the only exceptions to the privilege of
freedom from arrest were in cases of "treason, felony, and
breach of the peace," "or refusing to give surety of the peace,"
it resolved "that the privilege of parliament does not extend delivered him to the courts of law;
to the case of writing and publishing seditious libels, nor ought
to be allowed to obstruct the ordinary course of law, in the
speedy and effectual prosecution of so heinous and dangerous
offence." [3] Having thus delivered Wilkes to the tender mer-
cies of the ordinary courts of law, after prejudging his case,
the house, in 1764, proceeded to expel him as the author of expelled him twice;
a seditious libel. In the next parliament he was accused of
another, and on February 3, 1769, he was again expelled on
the same ground; and when a new writ was ordered for the
county of Middlesex, which he represented, he was returned
without a contest. Then it was resolved on February 17 that, and then declared him incapable of re-election;
Wilkes "having been in this session of parliament expelled
this house, he was and is incapable of being elected a member
to serve in this present parliament." [4] Despite that attempt
at disqualification, Wilkes was again elected, and after his election had been declared void, a new expedient was resorted to

---

[1] *Parl. Hist.*, vol. vi. p. 1265.
[2] Sir F. Burdett denied the authority of the house so to act, and denounced its conduct in a published address to his constituents, for which he
was sent to the Tower on a warrant of
the speaker. Burdett then brought an
action against the speaker and serjeant-
at-arms, who submitted to the jurisdiction of the court of king's bench. That
court sustained the authority of the

house, and its judgment was sustained
on appeal by the exchequer chamber
and the house of lords. For a full
statement of the famous case of *Burdett* v. *Abbot*, see East, vol. xiv. pp. 1–
163; Broom's *Const. Law*, p. 968, *et
seq.*
[3] *Commons' Journals*, vol. xxix. p.
689; *Parl. Hist.*, vol. xv. pp. 1362–
1378.
[4] Cf. May, *Parl. Practice*, p. 53.

as a sure means of disposing of him.   Mr. Luttrell was put up
to oppose him, and when he was defeated by an overwhelming
majority, he petitioned against the return of his opponent,
whereupon the house held that while a majority of the electors
had voted for Wilkes, Luttrell ought to have been returned.[1]
Although the petition of the Middlesex electors in Wilkes'
favor was put aside for the moment, the proceedings against

him were finally declared to be illegal ; and in May, 1782, the
disqualifying resolution of February 17, 1769, was ordered
to be expunged from the journals, as "subversive of the rights
of the whole body of electors of this kingdom." [2]   So firmly
did that action settle the fact that an expulsion does not create
a disability, that upon the immediate return in 1882 of Mr.

in Brad-
laugh's case
it was held
that expul-
sion does
not create a
disability. Bradlaugh, after his expulsion in that year, no question was
raised as to the legality of the proceeding.[3]   The right of the
commons to punish with their own hands those who commit
contempts by publishing libels either upon the house itself or
its member is gradually yielding to the more recent practice
of remitting such cases to the attorney-general for prosecution
in the king's bench.[4]

In this connection it will be convenient to explain how the
serious restrictions upon the publication of debates existing at
the accession of George III. have been so relaxed as to make
possible the liberal system of reporting existing at the present
day.   From the statement heretofore made upon that subject

it appears that the fruit of the system of clandestine reporting
in which the real names of the speakers were omitted was
gross inaccuracy and unfairness,[5] and to that was added as an
irritating adjunct the habit of using nicknames, designed to
render those to whom they were applied either ridiculous or

contemptible.   In 1771, when for the first time the real names
of the speakers began to be used, Colonel Onslow, member
for Guildford, who had been aroused by an attack from some
of the reporters, made a complaint against two newspapers,
printed for Thompson and Wheble, because they were "mis-
representing the speeches, and reflecting on several of the

1 *Cavendish Deb.*, vol. i. pp. 360–
386.   April 14, 1769.
2 *Parl. Hist.*, vol. xxii. p. 1407.
3 May, *Parl. Practice*, p. 54.
4 "In some cases, it orders the attorney-general to prosecute of its own
authority, and in other cases addresses
the crown to direct such prosecutions."
— Ibid., p. 74.
5 See above, pp. 473–475.

members of this house." [1]   Despite sharp opposition from the minority,[2] the commons, upon a further complaint of Onslow against six other printers, made an order requiring the accused to appear at the bar, where some of them submitted to a repri- mand on their knees for their misconduct.   But three of them, Miller, Wheble, and Thompson, resolved to resist the power of the house to take them into custody for what they claimed was no crime under the laws of the land, and in order to give dignity and force to their contest they adroitly called to their aid the popular magistracy of London, at whose head stood Mr. Brass Crosby, the lord mayor, backed by the irrepressible John Wilkes, who had been recently vested with aldermanic honors, and who was no doubt the prime mover and director of the whole controversy.   When Miller was seized by a mes- senger of the house under the speaker's warrant, instead of submitting, he sent for a constable and, after accusing the messenger of assaulting him in his own house, gave him into custody.   Both were then taken to the Mansion House, where the case was heard by the lord mayor, Alderman Oliver, and Alderman Wilkes.   When the legality of the speaker's warrant came in question, the lord mayor stated that under the charters of the city no warrant, process, or attachment could be exe- cuted within its limits but by its own magistrates, and as the messenger of the house was not such, and as his warrant was not backed by a civil magistrate, Miller was discharged out of custody.   The result was that the conflict between the house and the press precipitated by Colonel Onslow was thus suddenly converted into a contest between that body and the magistrates of London, who with the mob at their backs defied its authority.   The lord mayor, as well as Oliver, was a mem- ber of the house, and when the two [3] were there accused of a breach of privilege, they were so defiant that they were com- mitted to the Tower, whither they were followed by crowds, that made their progress a popular ovation.   While they failed to obtain their release on habeas corpus, on the 8th of May they were set at liberty by the prorogation of parliament, after

Miller and other printers deny the right of the house to commit them;

adroitly transfer the controversy to the Mansion House;

a conflict between the commons and London magis- trates;

lord mayor and Oliver sent to the Tower;

---

[1] Colonel Onslow had been called "little cocking George," and "the lit- tle scoundrel." — *Cavendish Deb.*, vol. ii. pp. 257, 258, 379.

[2] During the contest there were twenty - three divisions.   *Cavendish Deb.*, vol. ii. p. 377.

[3] Wilkes was eliminated from the proceedings by a subterfuge.

six weeks of confinement.[1] With that virtual triumph of the popular magistrates over the house, all real opposition to the publication of parliamentary debates passed forever away. And yet with that disposition to cling to ancient forms after the spirit has departed, the house made no modification of its principles ; in theory reporting still remains, as before, a breach of privilege, and as such it may still be punished whenever any wilful misrepresentation occurs.[2]

right to publish debates the practical outcome ;

no change of theory.

After the fire that destroyed both houses of parliament in 1834, a commendable disposition was shown to encourage reporting, always carried on under great physical difficulties, by the construction of separate galleries for reporters ; and in 1836 the house took the final step necessary to secure the complete publicity of its proceedings and responsibility of its members by recording their votes, and publishing daily the division lists, a custom not adopted by the lords until 1857.[3] The only practical difficulty that still remained grew out of the power of every member to employ, when he pleased, the ancient usage of "spying" strangers, through which the speaker could be compelled to order the withdrawal without putting the question. After the exercise of that power in 1849, in 1870, and in 1872 had resulted in considerable inconvenience, a modification of the rule was finally made in May, 1875, by a resolution which, while leaving the personal discretion of the speaker untouched, directs him, wherever the presence of strangers is brought to his attention, to put the question of their withdrawal, without debate or amendment, to the vote of all the members present.[4] That resolution, now standing order No. 93, has been acted on in every case that has arisen since its adoption.

Separate galleries for reporters provided after fire of 1834 ;

since 1836 division lists published daily ;

resolution of 1875 as to withdrawal of strangers.

Having now attempted to explain how it was that the once serious restraints imposed upon the freedom of the press through the privileges of parliament gradually dwindled into insignificance, an effort must be made to draw out the process through which the law of libel, as administered in the ordinary tribunals, has, through the joint action of the courts and the

Growth of the law of libel ;

---

1 *Parl. Hist.*, vol. xvii. pp. 59–163 ; *Chatham Corresp.*, vol. iv. p. 533 ; *Grenville Papers*, vol. iv. p. 533 ; May, *Const. Hist.*, vol. ii. pp. 39–48.

2 Cf. May, *Parl. Practice*, pp. 70–73.

3 Ibid., pp. 339, 349.

4 Ibid., p. 201.

legislature, been reduced to its present form. After the extinction of the censorship "the law of England" became, in the language of Lord Ellensborough, "a law of liberty, and consistently with this liberty we have not what is called an *imprimatur;* there is no such preliminary license necessary; but if a man publish a paper, he is exposed to the penal consequences, as he is in every other act, if it be illegal." [1] Or, as Lord Mansfield has expressed it, "The liberty of the press consists in printing without any previous license, subject to the consequences of law." [2] The law to which reference was thus made was the law of libel through which the star chamber had enforced its control over the press, and which had become a highly important branch of jurisprudence in the days of the Tudors and Charles I. Hudson,[3] in his treatise on the star chamber, tells us that "in all ages libels have been severely punished in this court, but most especially they began to be frequent about 42 & 43 Elizabeth (1600), when Sir Edward Coke was her attorney-general," in whose reports are to be found the earliest important authorities upon the subject.[4] And here let the fact be emphasized that the star chamber, in which the law of libel was first administered, possessed the power to decide both the law and the fact. Influenced by that tradition, the courts of common law for a long time persisted in the effort to retain in the hands of their judges substantially the same power, when in the latter part of the seventeenth century the expiration of the Licensing Acts put the enforcement of the law of libel entirely under their control.[5] That result was accomplished by withholding from juries the right to pass upon the vital question which every prosecution for libel involved, — they were permitted only to pass upon the fact of publication, seldom disputed, and upon the truth of what were called innuendoes. As an illustration, reference may be made to the case of Francklin, the publisher of the "Craftsman," who was prosecuted in 1731

[marginal notes:] only restraint upon the press, after the extinction of the censorship;

has its origin in the procedure of the star chamber,

that passed on both the law and the fact;

effort of the law courts to retain the same power;

juries denied the right to pass upon the real issue;

in Francklin's case it was held that

---

[1] *Rex* v. *Cobbett, State Trials,* vol. xxix. p. 49; Odgers, *Libel and Slander,* p. 10.

[2] *Rex* v. *Dean of St. Asaph, Term Reports,* vol. iii. p. 431 (note); Dicey, *The Law of the Const.,* p. 235.

[3] Pp. 100–104.

[4] "The cases relating to libel in Coke's *Reports* are the case *de famosis libellis,* and Lamb's case. These are the earliest authorities upon the law of libel of any importance." — Sir J. F. Stephen, *Hist. of the Crim. Law,* vol. ii. p. 304, citing Coke's *Reports,* vol. iii. p. 254; vol. iv. p. 108.

[5] See above, p. 380.

for an article in which the ministers were accused of incapacity and bad faith in concluding a treaty with Spain. After counsel had argued that the expression "certain ministers" meant the king's ministers, the judges declared that the only questions for the jury were the fact of publication and the truth of the innuendoes, questions about which there was really *the court alone could determine what constituted a libel;* no doubt whatever. They then declared, "There is a third thing, to wit, whether these defamatory expressions amount to a libel or not? This does not belong to the office of the jury, but to the office of the court." [1] It was also clearly settled *truth of libel not to be given in evidence;* by the judges that the truth of a libel could not be in any way given in evidence, not even in mitigation of punishment. The greater the truth the greater the libel passed into a proverb. The only means juries could employ to break through these rigid rules, by which the real question at issue — the character and truth of the subject-matter of the publication — *juries forced to resort to general verdicts;* was withheld from them, was through the rendition of general verdicts of acquittal, despite the instructions of the court that the substance of the publication in question was libellous as a matter of law. But such means were illegitimate; and whenever such a verdict was rendered, the judges, while forced to *their legal right to do so admitted;* admit the jury's legal power so to act, sternly denied their moral right to do so.[2] Such was the state of the law of libel, inherited by the courts of common law from the star chamber, at the moment the information was filed in the king's bench against Wilkes, as the author of No. 45 of "The North Briton." *Wilkes fled to France rather than trust the king's bench.* So little was that fearless agitator inclined to regard that law as "a law of liberty" that he fled to France, and during his absence he was found guilty in February, 1764, of reprinting No. 45, and of publishing the "Essay on Woman."

The great forensic contest between Mansfield and Erskine; The transformation of the law of libel from the despotic form in which it existed at the time when Wilkes began the struggle for the freedom of the press, to the mild and rational form in which it exists to-day, is the result of a great forensic contest carried on for many years in the courts of common law, in which the most prominent actors were Lord Mansfield, who, on the one hand, put forth his whole power in the effort

[1] *State Trials*, vol. xvii. p. 672.

[2] For a full history of the development of the law of political or seditious libel from the Revolution to 1783, see the judgment of Lord Mansfield in the case of the dean of St. Asaph (Shipley), *State Trials*, vol. xxi. pp. 847-1046.

to uphold the old doctrine, and Erskine, the famous advocate, the former battling for the old doctrine, the latter, for the new; who, on the other, employed all the resources of his genius to convince not only the judges, but the nation, that the law should be so modified as to give to juries in trial for libels the same scope as in all other cases. The contest may be said to have fairly begun in 1770, with the trials of Almon, Miller, trials of Almon, Miller, and Woodfall, 1770; and Woodfall,[1] against whom informations were filed for the printing and publishing in the year before of Junius' celebrated letter to the king.[2] Upon the trials of the printers of "The North Briton," his lordship, following the well-established doctrine, had declared that it was the province of the court alone to pass upon the criminality of the libel, and in the case of Woodfall he simply emphasized that doctrine by judgment in Woodfall's case as to the rights of juries; adding that "as for the intention, the malice, the sedition, or any other harder words which might be given in informations for libels, public or private, they were merely formal words, mere words of course, mere inferences of law — with which the juries were not to concern themselves." In the hope of evading the instruction thus put upon them, the jury hit upon the expedient of returning a verdict against Woodfall of "guilty of printing and publishing only."[3] Almond[4] was found guilty in the usual form, after the court had announced some very extreme doctrines as to the criminal liability of a criminal liability of publisher for acts of his servants as settled in Almond's case; publisher for the acts of his servants,[5] which continued in force until 1843, when they were annulled by Lord Campbell's Libel Act, to be considered hereafter. Miller was acquitted. Such was the prelude to the more memorable struggle which took place in the case of the dean of St. Asaph (Shipley), who dean of St. Asaph's case, 1778; was prosecuted for publishing a pamphlet entitled "A Dialogue between a Gentleman and a Farmer." At the trial, at the Shrewsbury assizes, the defendant was represented by

---

[1] *State Trials*, vol. xx. pp. 803, 870, and 895.

[2] It appeared in the *Morning Advertiser* of the 19th of December, 1769, Letter No. XXV.; Woodfall's ed., vol. ii. p. 62.

[3] Upon that verdict a new trial was granted, but the proceedings were dropped. Sir J. F. Stephen, *Hist. of the Crim. Law*, vol. ii. p. 324.

[4] He was tried for selling the *London Museum*, in which the letter was reprinted. *Parl. Hist.*, vol. xvi. pp.

1153, *et seq.;* Walpole, *Memoirs*, vol. iv. p. 160.

[5] It appearing that the paper had been sold in Almond's shop without his knowledge or authority, Mansfield said that "was sufficient evidence to convict the master of the house or shop, though there was no privity or concurrence in him, unless he proves the contrary, or that there was some trick or collusion." — Note to *State Trials*, vol. xxi. p. 971.

Erskine, and after Justice Buller had told the jury that the only question for them was the fact of publication and the truth of the innuendoes, a verdict was rendered of "guilty of publishing only." Upon a motion for a new trial made at the next term, Erskine was brought face to face with Mansfield, and then it was that he made what Fox declared to be "the finest argument in the English language," — an argument embodying "five propositions most logically framed and connected, which, if true, completely established his case, and he supported them with a depth of learning which would have done honor to Selden or Hale." [1] The essence of those propositions, as restated by a master of the criminal law, is "that the case of a libel forms no legal exception to the general principles which govern the trial of all other crimes, . . . that it is a question of fact and not of law whether a libel is or is not seditious." [2] So little did Mansfield appreciate Erskine's argument, that he not only refused the new trial, but sneered at the "jealousy of leaving the law to the court" as "puerile rant and declamation." And in speaking of this judgment some years afterwards, in his defence of Paine,[3] Erskine said, Lord Mansfield "treated me not with contempt indeed, for of that his nature was incapable, but he put me aside with indulgence, as you do a child when it is lisping its prattle out of season." But the argument of Erskine, in the dean of St. Asaph's case, forced Mansfield into the first solemn judicial exposition of the old law of political libels, and in that way its whole history was set forth from the Revolution down to that time. The result was a declaration from the chief justice that Buller, in his summing up, had simply followed the practice of all his predecessors since the Revolution, and that "such a judicial practice . . . is not to be shaken by arguments of general theory or popular declamation." Undaunted by such rebuffs, Erskine persevered in his contention, and in the trial of Stockdale [4] in 1789, upon an information filed against him for publishing a defence of Warren Hastings, which was taken to be a seditious

Marginal notes:
Erskine's famous speech upon the motion for a new trial;

his five propositions;

"it is a question of fact and not of law whether a libel is or is not seditious;"

Mansfield overruled Erskine's motion,

but was forced to defend himself by a judicial exposition;

trial of Stockdale in 1789;

---

[1] Campbell, *Lives of the Chancellors,* vol. viii. p. 277, *et seq.*
[2] Sir J. F. Stephen, *Hist. of the Crim. Law,* vol. ii. pp. 337, 338.
[3] Paine was found guilty. *State Trials,* vol. xxii. p. 357.

[4] *State Trials,* vol. xxii. p. 237; Erskine's *Speeches,* vol. ii. p. 205. He was prosecuted by the attorney-general at the instance of the house of commons. *Parl. Hist.,* vol. xxvii. pp. 1, 7.

libel intended to vilify the house of commons, he was able to win from Lord Kenyon, who tried the case, something like a concession. He contended that in applying the innuendoes the jury, in order to ascertain whether or no the publication in question was really intended as an aspersion upon the house of commons, should look not only to the isolated passages selected and put together in the information by the attorney-general, but to the entire context of the publication for its true meaning. After obtaining an instruction sustaining that contention,[1] a verdict of not guilty was rendered, based no doubt upon the idea that the innuendo, as to the house of commons, was not made out. But upon the main question, Erskine was never able to win from the judges any concession whatever. The law of libel, as they had found it, was judge-made law, and that was for them an unanswerable reason why it should never be altered.

Lord Kenyon's concession on a minor question;

no concession upon the main question.

Fortunately, however, for the cause of public liberty, the English people took a different view of the matter, and their outcry against the judges became so loud as to be heard even in the halls of parliament itself. The moment that Lord Mansfield, in the trials of Woodfall and Almond, emphasized the fact that trial by jury, the only security for the freedom of the press, really had no place in the law of the land, his doctrines were sharply questioned in both houses. In December, 1770, a motion was made in the commons for an inquiry into the administration of criminal justice and into the constitutional powers of juries, specially in cases touching the liberty of the press;[2] and in reply to an assault made upon him in the upper house by Lords Chatham and Camden, Lord Mansfield considered it necessary to leave a copy of his judgment in Woodfall's case for the consideration of that body.[3] And in the next year Mr. Dowdeswell, anticipating Mr. Fox by twenty years, moved for a bill to settle all questions of doubt as to

Rights of juries in libel cases discussed in parliament;

motion made in the commons in 1770;

Mansfield attacked in the lords;

defeat of Dowdeswell's bill;

[1] Lord Kenyon said to the jury: "In forming your opinion you are not bound to confine your inquiry to those detached passages which the attorney-general has selected as offensive matter, and the subject of prosecution."

[2] *Parl. Hist.*, vol. xvi. p. 1211; *Cavendish Deb.*, vol. ii. p. 80; Campbell, *Chief Justices*, pp. 480–490.

[3] Lord Camden then submitted a series of questions, based upon the judgment deposited with the clerk of the house of lords, which Lord Mansfield refused to answer; "he said he would not answer interrogations." See Sir J. F. Stephen, *Hist. of the Crim. Law*, vol. ii. p. 325; *Parl. Hist.*, vol. xvi. p. 1321.

the rights of juries in libel cases.[1]   Although that motion was supported by Sir G. Savile and Mr. Burke, and encouraged by Lord Rockingham, it was defeated,[2] and the old law of libel continued to be administered with all its severity down to the trial of Stockdale in 1789.[3]   Then it was that Mr. Fox, aroused from his original indifference by the eloquence of Erskine, undertook to induce parliament to abolish the doctrines as announced by Mansfield, and to establish in their stead the more liberal principles for which the peerless advocate had so long and so brilliantly contended.   With that end in view he introduced in May, 1791, his famous act,[4] "to remove doubts respecting the functions of juries in cases of libel," in which it was "declared and enacted . . . that on every such trial the jury sworn to try the issue may give a general verdict of guilty or not guilty upon the whole matter put in issue upon such indictment and information; and shall not be required or directed by the court or judge before whom such indictment or information shall be tried to find the defendant or defendants guilty, merely on the proof of the publication by such defendant or defendants of the paper charged to be a libel, and of the sense ascribed to the same in such indictment or information."   When the bill reached the upper house, Lord Thurlow succeeded in delaying it until the end of the session;[5] and when it was again sent up from the commons he again insisted that it should await the answers of the judges to seven questions submitted to them as to the existing state of the law.[6]   Their unanimous responses,[7] reiterating and even expanding the dangerous principles against which Erskine had contended, emphasized the necessity for the act, which was rapidly passed, despite the protest of Thurlow and five other lords that it would bring about "the confusion and destruction of the law of England."[8]   The growth of freedom of discussion thus fixed upon a secure legal basis was soon checked, however, by the reactionary spirit excited in England

Mr. Fox's libel act of 1791;

Thurlow delayed it in the lords until the judges could answer seven questions;

passed despite their adverse responses;

[1] Rockingham, *Memoirs*, vol. ii. p. 198, *seq.*

[2] *Parl. Hist.*, vol. xvii. p. 43; Burke's *Works*, vol. x. p. 109; May, *Const. Hist.*, vol. ii. p. 257.

[3] *State Trials*, vol. xxii. p. 237.

[4] 32 Geo. III. c. 60.

[5] *Parl. Hist.*, vol. xxix. pp. 726–742.

[6] Ibid., p. 1293; *State Trials*, vol. xxii. pp. 296–304.

[7] For their substance, see Sir J. F. Stephen, *Hist. of the Crim. Law*, vol. ii. pp. 343, 344.

[8] *Parl. Hist.*, vol. xix. pp. 1404, 1534–1538; Campbell, *Lives of the Chancellors*, vol. v. p. 346.

by the excesses of the French Revolution, which prompted the government during a long period of time to subject the press to a series of political prosecutions that did not entirely cease until the passing of the Reform Bill in 1832.[1] Not, however, until 1843 was the legislative work, begun by Mr. Fox, completed by the passage of Lord Campbell's Libel Act [2] of that year, which abolished (1) the old rule that the truth was no defence to a criminal prosecution for libel, by providing that defendants in such cases could plead the truth of the matters charged, and that "it was for the public benefit that the said matters charged should be published;" (2) the hard rule laid down in Almond's case, as to the criminal liability of publishers for the acts of their servants, by allowing them to prove that the publication in question was made without their knowledge, consent, or authority, and without the lack of due care or caution upon their part. The English law of libel, as thus finally settled, has been summed up by two competent authorities as follows: "Our present law permits any one to say, write, and publish what he pleases; but if he make a bad use of this liberty, he must be punished. If he unjustly attack an individual, the person defamed may sue for damages; if, on the other hand, the words be written or printed, or if treason or immorality be thereby inculcated, the offender can be tried for the misdemeanor either by information or indictment." [3] "Freedom of discussion is, then, in England little else than the right to write or say anything which a jury, consisting of twelve shopkeepers, think it expedient should be said or written." [4] From a constitutional point of view the all-important fact to be borne in mind is that the right to consider and pass upon the character of any writing charged to be a criminal libel belongs neither to the crown nor to the legislature. The right to pass upon such questions pertains exclusively to the courts of law; and there the right of judgment is vested not in the judges, but in juries alone.

Side notes:

Lord Campbell's Libel Act of 1843, providing that the truth could be pleaded; and that publishers could free themselves of the acts of their servants;

the law of libel as it now exists;

"the right to write or say anything which a jury, consisting of twelve shopkeepers, think it expedient should be said or written."

---

[1] Not until then was fully recognized the truth of Lord Bacon's maxim, that "the punishing of wits enhances their authority; and a forbidden writing is thought to be a certain spark of truth, that flies up in the faces of them that seek to tread it out."

[2] 6 & 7 Vict. c. 96; *Hans. Deb.*, 3d ser. vol. lvi. p. 395, *et seq*. As to the legal difficulties that grew out of the act, see Sir J. F. Stephen, *Hist. of the Crim. Law*, vol. ii. p. 383.

[3] Odgers, *Libel and Slander*, Introd. (1st ed.), p. 12.

[4] Dicey, *The Law of the Const.*, p. 234, citing *Rex* v. *Cutbill*, State Trials, vol. xxxii. pp. 642, 675.

Freedom of the press as restrained by taxation;

The only restraints upon the freedom of the press that have not so far been noticed are those that arose out of the imposition of stamp, advertisement, and paper duties, the first two of which originated in the reign of Anne, rather as a means of restraining the circulation of the press than as a fiscal expedient.[1]   The stamp duty thus imposed was finally raised to four pence, and by one of the Six Acts[2] it was extended to tracts and other unstamped periodicals filled with political news and discussions that had freely circulated among the poor upon the ground that they were not newspapers.   Cheap publications were thus forced into an attempt to evade the law, and the contraband traffic then carried on by unstamped newspapers continued in full force until the stamp was reduced in 1836 to one penny, and then abolished altogether in 1855. Two years before, the advertisement duty, that had been reduced in 1833, was swept away as one of the results of a movement directed by Mr. Gibson, whose watchword was the repeal of all "taxes on knowledge."   As a fitting consummation of that movement the duty on paper, for a long time a stumbling-block in the path of popular education, fell after a memorable parliamentary contest recorded in the debates of 1861.[3]

stamp duty, imposed in the reign of Anne,

first reduced and then abolished in 1855; advertisement and

paper duties also removed.

Right of public meeting;

3. Wilkes, who by his publication of the famous No. 45 of "The North Briton" began the contest that ended at last in the freedom of the press, organized and developed during his electoral struggle with the house of commons a still more imperious influence, through which parliament and the crown could be forced to bow to the mandates of public opinion. The right of Englishmen to assemble in public meetings is not the creation of positive law; it is the result of the immemorial natural right of each individual to meet with his fellows in the open air for a lawful purpose.[4]   It is one of the forms

not the creation of positive law;

---

[1] 10 Anne, c. 19, §§ 101, 118; *Parl. Hist.*, vol. vi. p. 1141.   As such legislation limited the circulation of cheap papers, it was extended in the two following reigns.   11 Geo. I. c. 8; 30 Geo. II. c. 19.

[2] 60 Geo. III. and 1 Geo. IV. cc. 1, 2, 4, 6, 8, 9, — a group of repressive measures passed by the government in 1819, on account of the disturbed state of the country.   The sixth extended the newspaper stamp duty to cheap political literature.

[3] For all details, see May, *Const. Hist.*, vol. ii. pp. 108, 245, 327, 380–383.

[4] "The right of assembling is nothing more than a result of the view taken by the courts as to individual liberty of person and individual liberty of speech."— Dicey, *The Law of the Const.*, p. 258.

in which may be exercised the right of freedom of discussion without previous license, but subject to the consequences of law. The common law, while recognizing the right of any number of persons to hold a lawful assembly, made it a crime to hold an unlawful one;[1] and the penalty was extended to those who, lawfully assembled, so conducted themselves thereafter with a common purpose as to render their meeting unlawful.[2] By an act passed in the reign of Edward VI.[3] against unlawful assemblies, it was declared to be treason for twelve or more persons to meet together on any matter of state, and felony if the purpose of the meeting was to destroy inclosures. Despite, however, such limitations imposed by the common and statute law upon political "agitation," the government of Sir Robert Walpole, when, in 1733, it proposed an obnoxious Excise Bill, was forced by popular demonstrations and riots to abandon it.[4] More violent and more extensive still was the demonstration made by the Spitalfields silk-weavers, who in 1765 ventured to parade in front of St. James Palace, to surround the houses at Westminster, and to question the peers as they came forth as to the votes by which a bill for the protection of their trade had been rejected by the upper house. Although this riotous attempt to overawe the deliberations of parliament had to be dispersed by the military,[5] it was nevertheless successful, inasmuch as a bill was passed in the following year conceding what the rioters had demanded.[6] But it is from the persistent and organized agitation of the Middlesex electors in 1769 that can be dated distinctly the beginnings of such public meetings as have since been recognized as a legitimate means of constitutional influence in the institutions of the country. The attempt then made by the lower house to take away by means of its disqualifying resolution[7] the right of the populous county of Middlesex, itself a great organ of public opinion, to choose representatives struck at the very root of the representative system; and the result was such an

[marginal notes:] common law made it a crime to hold an unlawful assembly; act of Edward VI. against such assemblies; meetings of opponents of Excise Bill in 1733; of Spitalfields silk-weavers in 1765; agitation of Middlesex electors in 1769;

---

[1] For the earliest definition of an unlawful assembly, see Year-Book, 21 Hen. VII. 29.

[2] Sir J. F. Stephen, *Hist. of the Crim. Law*, vol. ii. p. 386.

[3] 3 & 4 Edw. VI. c. 10. See above, p. 125.

[4] See above, p. 460.

[5] *Grenville Papers*, vol. iii. pp. 168–172; Walpole's *Memoirs*, vol. ii. p. 155, *et seq.*; Lord Mahon's *Hist.*, vol. v. p. 152.

[6] A bill restraining the importation of foreign silks. 6 Geo. III. c. 28.

[7] See above, p. 483.

outburst as had never been seen before of popular resentment expressed through public meetings held in no less than seventeen counties,[1] in support of what was regarded as the cause of all.   The new-born power of public opinion embodied in this movement was followed by the creation of a " Society for supporting the Bill of Rights ; " and that was the prelude of the more definite and extensive form of political association, developed ten years later, through which large and organized bodies of men were able to bring their special views more urgently to bear upon the conduct of government, by combining public discussion with imposing and menacing displays of physical force.

4. Closely allied with the right of public meeting is the right of petitioning, which, originating in earlier times as a means of redress for private and local grievances,[2] finally grew into one of the favorite forms in which political associations submitted their demands to the crown and to parliament as to matters of national concern.   The practice of petitioning in its later and wider form was first employed during the Revolution of 1640 by large bodies of people, who thus undertook to present their grievances to Charles I. and to the Long Parliament, an intolerant body that did not hesitate to punish their political opponents as delinquents whenever they attempted to address them in that manner.[3]   The memory of the tumults and intimidations that thus arose during the revolutionary epoch prompted, no doubt, the enactment shortly after the Restoration of the statute[4] of Charles II., which provided that no petition to the king or to either house of parliament for the alteration of matters established by law in church or state should be signed by more than twenty or presented by more than ten persons without the previous authorization of certain designated local magistrates.   Despite, however, that restraining statute, Shaftesbury, when in 1679[5] he resolved to force the king to call the houses together, organized a formida-

Marginal notes: extended to seventeen counties; "Society for supporting the Bill of Rights;" organized political association.

Right of petitioning; first applied to redress of private and local grievances; employed in a wider form during the Revolution of 1640; restraining statute of Charles II.; Shaftesbury's use of petitions in 1679;

---

[1] *Ann. Reg.*, 1770, p. 58.

[2] " Such as courts of equity and private acts of parliament have since been accustomed to provide." — May, *Const. Hist.*, vol. ii. p. 61.

[3] Clarendon, *Hist.*, vol. i. p. 357; vol. ii. pp. 166, 206, 222; vol. v. p. 460; *Commons' Journals*, vol. v. pp. 354, 367.

[4] 13 Car. II. c. 5.

[5] In December of that year, petitions to the king for the calling of parliament were discontinued by proclamation.

ble agitation throughout the kingdom by means of petitions signed in every district demanding that parliament should be permitted to sit for the suppression of popery and despotism. Then it was, as heretofore explained, that the country party, who were the "petitioners," came to be known as Whigs, and the cavalier or court party, who were the "abhorrers," as Tories.[1] Although the Bill of Rights expressly recognized the right of every subject to petition the king, and denounced as illegal all prosecutions for such petitioning,[2] after the Revolution as before, parliament manifested no disposition to listen patiently to popular appeals in that form. In 1701 the commons imprisoned five of the Kentish petitioners until the end of the season, for praying the house to listen to the people and to turn their loyal addresses into bills of supply;[3] and from that time onward through the reigns of Anne and the first two Georges petitions seemed to have been directed rather to the old subjects of private and local relief than to matters of general concern. Not in fact until the first nineteen turbulent years of the reign of George III. had passed by was the right of petitioning added to the other means of popular agitations employed during that time. Petitioning in its modern form is now generally dated from 1779,[4] when the freeholders of Yorkshire,[5] supported by many other important counties, and by the principal cities and towns, headed a movement which attempted to promote by that means economic and parliamentary reform. The plan then devised contemplated the signing of petitions in every part of the country through the agency of corresponding committees, the result of whose combined action was to be submitted to parliament as the basis of motions in favor of the common object. Thus was formally introduced into the English political system that method of

[margin notes:] right recognized by Bill of Rights; five Kentish petitioners imprisoned in 1701; petitioning in its modern form dates from 1779; plan then devised the basis of existing system of correspondence and association.

---

[1] See above, pp. 384, 385.

[2] "That it is the right of the subject to petition the king, and all commitments and prosecutions for such petitioning are illegall." That clause, however, did not conflict with 13 Car. II. c. 5, as to *tumultuous* petitioning. *Rex v. Lord George Gordon, State Trials,* vol. xxi. p. 650.

[3] *Parl. Hist.,* vol. v. p. 1255; Somers' *Tracts,* vol. xi. p. 242.

[4] That is the date as fixed by May, *Const. Hist.,* vol. ii. p. 63. Hallam says, however, that "the great multiplication of petitions wholly unconnected with particular interests, cannot, I believe, be traced higher than those for the abolition of the slave trade in 1787." — *Const. Hist.,* vol. ii. p. 434, note.

[5] Their petition was signed by upwards of eight thousand; the Westminster petition, by five thousand electors. *Parl. Hist.,* vol. xx. p. 1374; Ibid., vol. xxi. p. 287.

correspondence and association, devised to give greater force and effect to the right of petitioning, that has been so often employed, generally for good but often for evil, since that time.

The Gordon riots of 1780;

No sooner was the new form of petitioning thus developed than it was seized upon by a dangerous fanatic, whose hysterical zeal soon demonstrated the fact that it might be so employed as to drive the nation to the very verge of civil war.

Catholic Relief Act of 1778;

Through the Roman Catholic Relief Act of 1778, to which reference has already been made,[1] the members of that faith were relieved of some of the more oppressive of their disabilities upon condition that they would renounce certain catholic doctrines and swear allegiance to George III.   Aroused by

resisted by extreme protestants of Scotland;

that concession, the extreme protestants of Scotland began to organize an association, by means of correspondence committees, to resist the extension of the limited emancipation to that country ; and so formidable did the movement become that the Scotch catholics, menaced by mobs, were forced for the

the association there organized extended to England;

sake of peace to forego their rights.[2]   The protestant associations thus organized soon spread beyond the border into England, where a great federation of local committees was formed that undertook upon a vast scale the preparation of petitions, to one of which as many as a hundred and twenty thousand signatures were annexed.   Of the combined associations of

Lord George Gordon chosen president ; headed a mob that marched to Westminster to present petition ; terrific riot ensued ;

Scotland and England, Lord George Gordon, who had won some notoriety in parliament, was chosen president ; and on the 2d of June, 1780, he headed a mob that marched to Westminster, where they took possession before the two houses met in order to present a monster petition against the Catholic Relief Acts.   In the midst of the tumult the petition was presented ; and then after the commons adjourned a terrific riot ensued that continued for several days, during which time numberless outrages were committed against Roman Catholics, the Bank of England was threatened, and a conflagration started that at one time threatened the destruction of the metropolis itself.   Before it was extinguished the home of the aged Mansfield, who was to bring the rioters to justice, was consumed with his priceless books and manuscripts.   Finally, the mili-

---

[1] See above, p. 429.
[2] *Parl. Hist.*, vol. xx. p. 280.   Much of their property was destroyed, for which they were promised compensation.   Ibid., p. 322.

tary, in the absence of the helpless magistracy, dispersed the mobs after killing and wounding hundreds.[1] The event has a permanent constitutional interest by reason of the legal definitions that ensued as to the right, on the one hand, of the people peaceably to assemble for a lawful purpose, and of the state, on the other, to punish those who, transcending that right, violate its laws. Lord George Gordon, as the leader of the movement, was charged with high treason upon the ground that he had levied war against the king; and his trial came on in the king's bench before Mansfield, C. J., and Willes, Ashurst, and Buller, JJ., who were fully imbued with the strained and technical interpretation that had been put by Coke, Hale, and Foster [2] upon those clauses of the statute of Edward III. that related to imagining the king's death, and to levying war against him. The charge was that by virtue of all that had happened the defendant was guilty of constructive treason; his defence was that as far as he was concerned he had no connection with those treasonable acts of the mob that amounted to the levy of war; that such acts were the unexpected consequences of his highly imprudent, perhaps criminal, conduct in putting himself at the head of a mob for the purpose of tumultuous petitioning.[3] In summing up the authorities construing the statute, the chief justice said : " I tell you the joint opinion of us all, that if this multitude assembled with intent, by acts of force and violence, to compel the legislature to repeal a law, it is high treason." And then in leaving that question to the jury he added : " If there was no such intention either in the mob or the prisoner, he ought to be acquitted ; but if you think there was such an intent in the multitude, incited, prompted, or encouraged by the prisoner, then you ought to find him guilty." [4] The failure of the government to obtain a conviction in this case, also in the like cases against Hardy [5] and others in 1794, has given rise to the popular and sound idea that, for practical purposes, the law of constructive trea-

Marginal notes: mobs dispersed by the military; trial of Lord George in the king's bench; his defence against charge of constructive treason; summing up of the chief justice; since the failure to obtain conviction in that and like cases, constructive treason a dead letter;

[1] For a statement of the well-known facts, see *State Trials*, vol. xxi. pp. 485–652; *Parl. Hist.*, vol. xxi. pp. 654–686; *Ann. Reg.*, 1780, p. 265, *et seq.* Nearly five hundred were killed and wounded.

[2] As to their views, see Sir J. F. Stephen, *Hist. of the Crim. Law*, vol. ii. pp. 266–268, 278.

[3] See his defence as explained in Erskine's celebrated speech, *State Trials*, vol. xxi. pp. 589–591.

[4] Ibid., p. 644.

[5] *State Trials*, vol. xxiv. p. 19. For case of Horne Tooke, acquitted about the same time, see Ibid., vol. xxv. p. 725.

son has been a dead letter since that time.   The difficulty was the unwillingness of juries to transform tumultuous political agitations into forcible political revolutions through artificial legal constructions.   From a scientific point of view, however, modern statutes regulating the law of treason. the old law was not altered until the passage in 1795 of 36 Geo. III. c. 7, which put the law of treason on a new basis that remained unchanged until 1848, when the continental revolutions of that year made necessary the further modifications embodied in the Treason Felony Act of 11 & 12 Vict. c. 12.[1]

When the military may be lawfully employed; As to the use of the military, Lord Mansfield said in the Gordon case that as the insurgents were engaged in the commission of overt acts of treason, felony, and riot, it was the duty of all citizens, whether soldiers or not, to resist them ; and in 1832, Chief Justice Tindall, in charging the grand jury as to the Bristol riots of the preceding year, said : " But where the danger is pressing and immediate, where a felony has actually been committed or cannot otherwise be prevented, and from the circumstances of the case no opportunity is offered of obtaining a requisition from the proper authorities, the military subjects of the king, like his civil subjects, not only may but are bound to do their utmost of their own authority to prevent the perpetration of outrage, to put down riot and tumult, and to preserve the lives and liberty of the people." [2] Riot Act of George I. st. 2, c. 5, still in force; The undertone of that judgment is the famous act of 1 Geo. I. st. 2, c. 5, known as the Riot Act, still in force, which makes it a felony for twelve rioters to continue together an hour after a proclamation of a magistrate ordering them to disperse.   The effect of the act is that a failure to disperse after such proclamation authorizes the magistrate to order the troops to fire upon the rioters or charge them sword in hand ; and if any of when magistrates ordering troops to fire will be indemnified; them " happen to be killed, maimed, or hurt in dispersing, seizing, or apprehending, or endeavoring to disperse, seize, or apprehend them," the magistrate and those who act under his orders shall be indemnified.   Whenever, therefore, there is in England a public meeting for a political or other purpose, the

---

1 Cf. Sir J. F. Stephen, *Hist. of the Crim. Law*, vol. ii. pp. 279–281.
2 *C. and P. Reports*, vol. v. p. 261, *seq.*   As to the duty of officers and soldiers, under the Mutiny Act, that subjects them to discipline, to fire, see Dicey, *The Law of the Constitution*, p. 282.

first question that arises is this : Is it a lawful assembly ? If delicate questions always involved.
so, what are the rights and remedies of its members when such
a meeting is interfered with or dispersed by force ? On the
other hand, if it is an unlawful assembly, the question is as to
the rights and duties of the crown and its servants in dealing
with it as such.[1]

5. The attempt of George III. to break down the power of George III.'s temporary success in breaking down the ministerial system;
the great Whig families, and with it the rapidly developing
ministerial system which they had controlled since the Revolution, has been traced down to the fall of Lord Bute, and the
substitution in his place, at his instance, of George Grenville,
who was expected to be entirely subservient, as he had been, to
the royal will.[2] As an answer to that expectation, Grenville, Grenville's futile attempt to resist the king's will;
an imperious, self-willed man, who refused to be the tool of any-
body, attempted to force not only the king, but the nation to
yield everything to him. The result was that his short-lived
administration, which Macaulay has declared to be " on the
whole the worst which has governed England since the Revolution," by reason of its "outrages on the liberty of the people,
and outrages on the dignity of the crown," was ungraciously
dismissed in 1765.[3] Then it was that the marquis of Rock- succeeded by Rockingham in 1765;
ingham, as first lord of the treasury, took the direction of
affairs, backed by a weak combination of that part of the Whig
aristocracy who had not followed the lead of Grenville. In
the next year, when the gathering storm in America demanded
that a stronger hand should hold the helm, the king was forced
to recall Pitt, who returned to power with a seat in the house recall of Pitt in 1766;
of lords as the earl of Chatham, taking for himself the office
of privy seal, while the duke of Grafton as the first lord of the
treasury acquiesced in his supremacy.[4] No change was made
in that arrangement until 1768, when Chatham, overwhelmed Chatham succeeded by Grafton in 1768;
for a time by physical and mental infirmity, was forced to re-
tire,[5] leaving Grafton as the nominal head of a divided and distracted administration, entirely subject to the king's personal
direction and control. Such was the pitiful condition to which

---

[1] See Mr. Dicey's exhaustive statement of the whole matter in Appendix
to *The Law of the Constitution*, Note
V., pp. 429–442.

[2] See above, p. 480.

[3] Cf. Todd, *Parl. Government*, vol. i.
p. 273.

[4] As to Pitt's paramount influence
at that time, see Mahon's *Hist.*, vol. v.
p. 271 ; Jesse, *Life of George III.*, vol.
i. p. 389.

[5] See his letter to the king, of October 14. *Chatham Corr.*, vol. iii. p.
318.

result of
the king's
personal
policy at
the end of
his first ten
years;
accession of
North as
chief of
new Tory
party in
1770;

George III.'s personal policy had reduced the new ministerial system at the end of the first ten years of his reign, when, after having had already six prime ministers, he tendered in February, 1770, the first place in the cabinet to Lord North, who accepted it as the chief of the new Tory party that gathered around the throne, without any distinctive ecclesiastical policy such as they had professed in the reign of Queen Anne, but with the definite understanding that the king could nominate his own ministers and give personal direction to their conduct. In working out that result, the youthful monarch never for a moment lost sight of the fact that, to exalt the kingly office, it

king's
resolve to
crush all
great party
leaders,

was absolutely necessary to crush the great party leaders who had enslaved it; and thus it was that he determined "never upon any account to suffer those ministers of the late reign, who had attempted to fetter and enslave him, to come into his service, while he lived to hold the sceptre." [1] In the estimation of the king the one trait that redeemed the greatest of the ministers to whom he thus referred was his willingness to aid him in his cherished purpose of breaking up all party connections. In a letter addressed to that minister in July of 1766,

and to
destroy all
party or-
ganization;

he said: "I know the earl of Chatham will zealously give his aid toward destroying all party distinctions, and restoring that subordination to government which can alone preserve that inestimable blessing, liberty, from degenerating into licentiousness." [2] And in December of the same year he again wrote to the earl of Chatham: "To rout out the present method of parties banding together can only be obtained by withstanding their unjust demands, as well as the engaging able men, be

with that
accom-
plished, he
hoped to
dominate
proceed-
ings in par-
liament;

their private connections where they will." [3] With all organized party opposition in parliament broken down, the king hoped to be able so far to disregard its privileges as to watch its debates and divisions, and then to mete out rewards and punishments to his friends and his enemies according to their deserts. When the duke of Devonshire attempted to with-

Devonshire
insulted;

hold his support from the preliminaries of the Peace of Paris, he was not only insulted by the king and forced to resign as lord chamberlain,[4] but his name was by the sovereign's own

[1] Lord Bute to the duke of Bedford, April 2, 1763. *Bedford Corr.*, vol. iii. p. 224.
[2] *Chatham Corr.*, vol. iii. p. 21.
[3] Ibid., vol. iii. p. 137.
[4] Walpole, *Memoirs*, vol. i. p. 201; Rockingham, *Memoirs*, vol. i. pp. 135, 155.

hand stricken from the list of privy councillors ; and in the same way, when General Conway attempted in the proceedings against Wilkes to oppose the court, he was not only dismissed from his office as groom of the bedchamber, but also from the command of his regiment of dragoons.[1]   Having thus paved the way, the king, upon the accession of Lord North, fully developed his policy, by becoming in fact his own first minister, to such an extent that he assumed the personal direction of all important political business, including the management of debates in parliament,[2] while the amiable and indolent chief of the cabinet, surrendering his own judgment, became a mere passive instrument in the hands of his master.[3]   The most memorable outcome of those twelve miserable years during which, as Fox [4] expressed it, "his Majesty was his own unadvised minister," was the loss of England's American colonies : it was the surrender at Yorktown in 1782 that finally drove Lord North to resign office,[5] after a tenure of eleven years. Such disastrous consequences, however, do not at all weaken the fact that in his main purpose the king was entirely successful.   So completely did he succeed in erasing from the mind of Englishmen the idea that the immature system of cabinet government upon which he trampled was a permanent part of the constitution of their country, that the great contemporary expounder of the laws of England gives it no place in his Commentaries, which were first published in an authoritative form in 1765.   Blackstone in his great work, which has so profoundly influenced all thought upon the subject of English institutions since that time, does not mention the name "cabinet " at all ; and the same thing may be said of the work of De Lolme, " *La Constitution de l'Angleterre*," first published at Amsterdam in 1771.   Both of these famous writers, who put forth their views just before George III.'s destructive work had reached its consummation,[6] perfectly comprehended

Marginal notes: Conway dismissed; although George, as his own first minister, lost his American colonies, he succeeded in his main purpose; the idea of cabinet government was so completely erased that it is not mentioned either by Blackstone or De Lolme;

---

[1] *Grenville Papers*, vol. ii. p. 296. Cf. May, *Const. Hist.*, vol. i. pp. 23, 27, 29, 40, 46.

[2] Brougham's *Works*, vol. iii. pp. 71, 88, 106; *Corr. of George III. with Lord North*, vol. i. p. 96, *et seq.*

[3] Lord North, however, in 1783, thus expressed his ideas as to the kingly office : " The king ought to be treated with all sort of respect and attention, but the appearance of power is all that a king of this country can have."— Russell, *Corr. of Fox*, vol. ii. p. 38.

[4] *Memoirs*, vol. i. p. 203.

[5] There were first repeated motions of want of confidence.

[6] In 1780 it was that Mr. Dunning carried through the house of commons

they knew only the privy council; the history and structure of the privy council, but of its mysterious inner circle, unknown to the law, called the "cabinet," the mainspring of the constitution in its modern form, they framers of the constitution of the United States modelled their executive after George III., and not after Queen Victoria. seem to have known absolutely nothing. On the other side of the Atlantic the practical statesmen who met at Philadelphia in 1787 to frame the present constitution of the United States, with the English original as their avowed model, manifested throughout their marvellous work the same unconsciousness of the existence of the cabinet system that characterized their scientific European contemporaries. The fact has been heretofore explained that the framers of the American constitution, when constructing the presidential office, had no conception of the shadowy kingship of to-day, which reigns but does not govern ; "the figure they had before them was not a generalized English king, nor an abstract constitutional monarch ; it was no anticipation of Queen Victoria, but George III. himself, whom they took for their model."[1]

At the fall of North the Whig opposition consisted of two factions; the greater led by Rockingham, 6. When Lord North and his Tory followers were forced by the fortunes of war to give up against the king's will their long lease of power, the parliamentary opposition consisted of two factions, which for the moment seemed to be cordially coöperating with each other. The greater, embracing the main body of the Whig aristocracy, acknowledged as their leader the marquis of Rockingham, who was represented in the house of commons by Fox and Burke ; the lesser by Shelburne, the lesser, composed of the old followers of Chatham, was led by the earl of Shelburne, to whom were united Lord Camden, famous for his constitutional knowledge, Barré, a fiery debater, and Dunning, one of the with whom was allied the younger Pitt; foremost lawyers of that time. With this smaller group, composed of his father's political friends, the younger Pitt naturally allied himself, when, shortly after reaching his majority, entered parliament in January, 1781; he was enabled by the aid of Sir James Lowther to find a place in parliament in January, 1781, as a member from the pocket borough of Appleby. By his first speech made in the next month in support of Burke's bill for economic reform, he as viewed by Burke and Fox; lifted himself so high in the estimation of the house that Burke himself exclaimed, with tears in his eyes, "It is not a chip of

his famous resolution affirming "that the influence of the crown has increased, is increasing, and ought to be diminished."—Cobbett's *Parl. Hist.*, vol. xxi. p. 347.

[1] Vol. i. p. 69.

the old block, it is the old block itself ;" while Fox declared to a member of the opposition, who suggested that " Pitt will be one of the first men in parliament," that "he is so already." [1] Such was the position to which the youthful orator had suddenly lifted himself just before the king sullenly acquiesced in the formation by Rockingham of a ministry with Fox and Shelburne as secretaries of state, and with Thurlow as the king's special retainer, in possession of the great seal.   When this new combination, consisting, as Fox [2] expressed it, " of two parts, one belonging to the king, the other to the public," offered Pitt, who had but three hundred a year, the office of vice-treasurer of Ireland, with five thousand a year, he coolly declined, because of his resolve not to accept any place that would not entitle him to a seat in the cabinet.   Presumptuous as his claim then seemed to be, it was soon to be justified. No sooner was a treaty of peace set on foot acknowledging the independence of the United States of America, than Rockingham died, at the end of March, 1782, leaving his ministry broken into two factions : the one composed of his personal followers united through aristocratic connections and influence, under the lead of Fox ; the other reaching out for popular support through active reforms, under the lead of Shelburne. When the king, compelled to choose between the two, made Shelburne the first lord of the treasury, Fox, Cavendish, and Burke at once resigned ; [3] and thus it was that the new prime minister, forced to find some one who could confront the brilliant orators of the opposition in the lower house, gave to Pitt in July the great post of chancellor of the exchequer.[4]   Parliament was soon prorogued, and the preliminary treaty of peace with the United States, which Rockingham had begun, was concluded on the 30th of November.   Not, however, until February, 1783, were the preliminary treaties taken into consideration by the house of commons, when the rumor began to circulate that the parties led by Fox and North, so long and

Marginal notes: declined a place in Rockingham's ministry, because it did not carry with it a seat in the cabinet; upon Rockingham's death in 1782, Shelburne became prime minister, and Pitt chancellor of the exchequer; coalition of Fox and North in February, 1783;

---

[1] Macaulay's " William Pitt," *Essays*, vol. iii. p. 323.

[2] *Memoirs*, vol. i. p. 292; Russell's *Life of Fox*, vol. i. p. 284, *et seq.*

[3] Burke tells us how his friend Fox realized " the utter impossibility of his acting for any length of time as a clerk in Lord Shelburne's administration."

— Russell's *Corr. of Fox*, vol. i. p. 457; Jesse, *Life of George III.*, vol. ii. p. 380.

[4] Macaulay's " William Pitt," *Essays*, vol. iii. p. 326.   He was then only a little more than twenty-three years old. See Tomline's *Life of Pitt*, vol. i. p. 86. Mr. Pitt was born May 28, 1759.

so bitterly hostile to each other, had coalesced in order to overthrow the king's party headed by Shelburne and Pitt. When the test came, the rumor was confirmed by the rejection of the address presented by the supporters of the government by a

when Shelburne resigned in March, Pitt declined to become premier;

majority of sixteen.[1]   Thus left in the minority, Shelburne resigned on the 31st of March; and then followed a bitter struggle, during which the king, in the hope of breaking up the coalition, appealed in vain to Pitt to become his first minister.   Counselled by the intuition of genius, he firmly declined, and thus forced the crown to accept a ministry presided

Portland became such in name;

over by the duke of Portland as the nominal head, but with all real power divided between Fox and North as secretaries of state.[2]   When parliament met in November, this unnatural and scandalous alliance, which drove at once the ultra-Tories from North and the ultra-Whigs from Fox, was soon hurried

Fox, the real chief, attacked the East India Company by adopting a bill drawn by Burke;

to its doom through the adoption by the latter, who was the real prime minister, of a bill drawn up by Burke embodying a bold and startling project that proposed to take away from the East India Company the authority it had previously exercised, and to vest it in seven commissioners, to be appointed by parliament and to be irremovable by the crown.   Revolutionary as the proposition was, the coalition, eager to possess the power and patronage that would pass to its nominees, hurried it through with great majorities, and sent it up to the house of

the king, after defeating the bill of his own ministers in the lords,

lords.   Then it was that the king undertook to oppose his own ministers by authorizing Temple, Pitt's cousin, "to say that whoever voted for the India Bill was not only not his friend, but would be considered by him an enemy."[3]   Under that pressure the bill was first postponed and then finally rejected

dismissed them from office;

by the upper house.[4]   To the humiliation thus put upon Fox and North, their implacable sovereign added by sending them an order to return their seals by their under-secretaries, as a personal audience with them would be disagreeable to him.[5]

---

[1] Lord Auckland's *Corr.*, vol. i. pp. 9, 41.

[2] Fox was the real head. See Russell's *Life of Fox*, vol. ii. p. 4; *Corr. of Fox*, vol. ii. p. 95.

[3] And to make his meaning still more clear, the king added, "And if these words are not strong enough, Earl Temple might use whatever words

he might deem stronger, and more to the purpose." — *Court and Cabinets of George III.*, vol. i. pp. 288, 289; Fox's *Memoirs*, vol. ii. p. 253; May, *Const. Hist.*, vol. i. p. 68.

[4] December 17, 1783. *Parl. Hist.*, vol. xxiv. p. 196.

[5] Tomline's *Life of Pitt*, vol. i. p. 230.

The time had now come for the king to commit the power thus wrested from his adversaries to the keeping of some one who could unite fidelity to the crown with the trust of the nation.   Under such circumstances it was that Pitt became in December first lord of the treasury and chancellor of the exchequer.   In outward seeming he was only the king's minister, as Bute had been ; and his position as such he at once emphasized by refusing to bow to the will of the house of commons during a contest that lasted from the 17th of December, 1783, to the 8th of March, 1784.   During that time the opposition, led by Fox, North, and Sheridan, carried sixteen divisions against him, but with dwindling majorities.[1]   In thus apparently defying the fundamental principle of parliamentary government, Pitt was sustained by the consciousness that he had not only the king, but the nation behind him ; and as a proof of his faith in that fact, he did what no other minister of a Hanoverian king had ever dared to do, — after the supplies and the Mutiny Bill were voted, he appealed from the representatives in parliament to their constituents.   In thus appealing to the people, Pitt relied, as his father had before him, upon that great and growing middle class, composed of merchants and manufacturers, whose mighty force was working a revolution in English society and in English politics, and yet without any adequate representation in the legislature.   Since the middle of the century a large part of the population had applied its thought to the practical problems affecting industry, and thus was set in motion the revolution that was fast bringing about the transfer of wealth and population from southern to northern England, and from the country to the town, while the kingdom as a whole was becoming the great workshop of the world.   As a result of the progress thus set in motion, population more than doubled during the eighteenth century, and the increase in wealth was even greater than in population.[2]   In 1776, at the moment when such a work was sorely needed, appeared Adam Smith's epoch-making book upon the

Pitt became the king's minister in December, 1783;

as such he refused to bow to the commons ;

sixteen divisions carried against him ;

conscious that the nation was behind him ;

his appeal to the constituencies ;

the growing middle class ;

effects of the industrial revolution ;

growth in wealth and population ;

[1] Macaulay's "William Pitt," *Essays*, vol. iii. p. 333.

[2] "Under these conditions the growth of English commerce was very rapid. . . . The expansion had been so rapid that merchants strained their credit to engage in vast speculations, and when the war broke out in 1803, the consequences were very serious." — Cunningham, *Growth of Eng. Ind. and Com.*, vol. ii. pp. 508, 514.   See also Green, *Hist. of the Eng. People*, vol. iv. p. 283, 291.

"Wealth of Nations," and Pitt, then an undergraduate at
Cambridge, whose mental temper was mathematical and financial, became at once a disciple of the new master, whose principles soon became the groundwork of his policy.[1]   Nothing
could have been more natural than the instinct that led the
manufacturing and trading classes, in the midst of the political confusion by which every interest was clouded, to turn to
Pitt as a deliverer.   To the support that thus came to him
from the most aggressive element in the nation was added the
influence of the potential body surrounding the throne, who
saw in him the only man who could rescue the king from his
peril.   By the combined force of these two great currents, the
will of the nation was able to break through the corrupt influences that ordinarily dominated the representative system,
and the result was that the new government was so enthusiastically sustained by the constituent bodies that upwards of a
hundred and sixty of the coalition that had opposed Pitt lost
their seats,[2] he coming in at the head of the list from the University of Cambridge,[3] where a few years before he was at the
bottom of the poll.   Thus the prime minister of twenty-five,
who had entered public life as a Whig, was lifted through the
wreck of that party to a height of political authority which no
other statesman had been able to reach since the Revolution.
As the favorite of the king, the parliament, and the nation,
Pitt was able to consolidate the power he had gained, and to
retain it unbroken down to 1801, while the Tory ascendency
thus established continued in name, at least, almost without
interruption, down to the era of the Reform Bill of 1832.

The importance of Pitt's ascendency to the history of the
constitution is embodied in the fact that through the combined
strength of his personal character and political position he was
able to neutralize to a great extent the efforts that George III.
had made to destroy the new ministerial system, whose recon-
stitution was absolutely necessary for the execution of Pitt's
political ideas.   In a conversation with Lord Melville in 1803

---

[1] "He had learned from Adam
Smith the first principles of political
economy, and the commercial treaty
with France was the first visible result
of the new science." — Gardiner and
Mullinger, *Introd. to Eng. Hist.*, p.
189.

[2] Tomline's *Life of Pitt*, vol. i. p.
469; Stanhope's *Life of Pitt*, vol. i. p.
204, *et seq.*

[3] Macaulay's "William Pitt," *Essays*,
vol. iii. p. 334.

he, when out of office, gave expression to those ideas "pointedly and decidedly," in explaining "the absolute necessity there is in the conduct of the affairs of this country that there should be an avowed and real minister, possessing the chief weight in the council, and the principal place in the confidence of the king. In that respect (he contended) there can be no rivalry or division of power. That power must rest in the person generally called the first minister, and that minister ought (he thought) to be the person at the head of the finances. . . . If it should unfortunately come to such a radical difference of opinion that no spirit of conciliation or concession can reconcile, the sentiments of the minister must be allowed and understood to prevail, leaving the other members of administration to act as they may conceive themselves conscientiously called upon to act under such circumstances." [1] While such ideas were directly in conflict with the aggressive position the king had assumed from his accession, his perfect confidence in the integrity and ability of Pitt, coupled with the fact that his principles were entirely in accordance with his own, made it possible for him so far to yield to the superior intelligence of his first minister as to approximately establish the constitutional relations between the sovereign and his advisers that had existed in the two preceding reigns. And yet it would be a grave error to suppose that the surrender upon the part of the king was either sudden or absolute. George III. persevered to the end in having all matters of government, both great and small, submitted to his judgment and approval, while he jealously held on to the distribution of patronage in church and state.[2] But if Pitt was thus forced to veil his absolutism as prime minister by an outward show of submission to the royal will, within the cabinet itself he so asserted his authority as to put beyond all question the fact that he was the real chief of state. It is said to have been his custom to briefly discuss at cabinet meetings with Dundas such matters as they had not previously arranged, and then after communicating his decision to his colleagues they were told that they might go.[3] By thus firmly establishing the paramount influence of the prime min-

he avowed that a real first minister was a necessity;

and that his will should always prevail;

how the king was able to reconcile Pitt's ideas with his own;

his submission only partial;

while Pitt made an outward show of submission to the sovereign, he was autocratic with his colleagues;

[1] Stanhope's *Life of Pitt*, vol. iv. p. 24.
[2] Cf. *Parl. Hist.*, vol. xxiv. p. 294;

May, *Const. Hist.*, vol. i. pp. 75, 86–88.
[3] Fitzmaurice, *Life of Lord Shelburne*, vol. iii. p. 411.

broke down
the system
of independ-
ent depart-
ments;
ister over his associates, Pitt was able to break down at last the bad system of government by means of separate and independent departments of state that had existed since the Revolution simply because the ministers had never been forced to accept the supremacy of a common chief.[1]   The foundations of such a supremacy laid down by Walpole ripened under Pitt into a rule of government which, with perhaps two exceptions, has never been disputed since that time.   The statement may therefore be made that, from the moment that Pitt entered into office as first lord of the treasury and chancellor of the exchequer, the right of the sovereign not only to reign but to rule began again to sink into the background, in order to make place for the supremacy of the prime minister as now understood.   Before the reign of George III. drew to a close the principles were firmly settled, (1) that the prime minister was the personal choice of the king, and as such the depository of his constitutional confidence; (2) that the trust thus assumed was to be discharged with the aid of colleagues selected by the first minister [2] himself, subject of course to the sovereign's approval.

with the
rise of Pitt
the personal
influence
of the
sovereign
began to
wane;

two great
principles
settled
before the
end of the
reign of
George III.

Pitt as
legislator
and finan-
cier;
7. Apart from the inestimable service rendered by Pitt in removing the obstruction that forced for a time the new system of government by cabinets into eclipse, he was the author of two far-reaching schemes of legislation which have become permanent parts of the constitution.   As the responsible head of the national finances he was immediately called upon to provide for increased taxation, made necessary by the expenses of the War of American Independence, that added a hundred and twenty-one millions to the permanent debt.[3]   The rapid increase of wealth and prosperity during the eight years of peace with which his administration opened made that task a comparatively easy one; and the result was that, at the end of the

increased
taxation
made neces-
sary by
American
war;

[1] "It was not until the accession to office of the younger Pitt, in 1783, that the paramount authority of a prime minister over his associates in the government was unreservedly confessed, and that as a natural consequence government by departments came to an end." — Todd, *Parl. Government*, vol. i. pp. 264, 265. See also pp. 277, 278.

[2] "As the cabinet stands between the sovereign and the parliament, and is bound to be loyal to both, so he stands between his colleagues and the sovereign, and is bound to be loyal to both." — Gladstone, *Gleanings*, vol. i. p. 242.

[3] "At the time of the revolt of the American colonies, it was under one hundred and thirty millions, an amount which frightened all the political economists of that day." — *Whitaker's Almanack*, 1896, p. 183.

year 1792, the total debt of the nation was not more than £237,400,000; and the public credit, which when he entered office was at the lowest ebb, had become so strong that the English funds were looked upon as the safest of all investments. Such was the prosperous condition of things when the declaration of war from France in February, 1793, drew England into the great continental struggle which cost her £831,000,000, of which sum about £622,000,000 were added to the permanent debt. As the war progressed, enormous loans were contracted, while the current expenses of government were met by credits on the Bank of England, which was finally ordered by the privy council in 1797 to suspend cash payments. Down to that time the extraordinary demand thus made necessary had been raised by indirect taxes on consumption, and sometimes on production, but not by direct taxes on property. Driven at last by necessity to resort to that method of taxation, Pitt in his budget of November, 1797, introduced his scheme for the "Triple assessment for 1798,"[1] which he prefaced with a splendid appeal to the patriotism of the nation. This triple assessment, which trebled all the assessed taxes imposed on individuals, with the limitation that it should not exceed a tenth of the taxpayer's income, was not only unpopular, but disappointing in its practical results;[2] and for such reasons it was permitted to expire at the end of the year. As a substitute Pitt then suggested "that a general tax should be imposed upon all the leading branches of income," estimated by him to amount at that time, after liberal deductions, to £102,000,000. His famous income tax, first levied in 1798, consisted of the imposition of a tax of 10 per cent. upon all incomes arising from annual rent and profits. Though levied as a war tax which was to cease at the declaration of peace, it was immediately pledged to a loan, and thus after being repealed and reimposed, it has become like the land tax a permanent element in the national revenue.[3]

While Pitt was thus straining every nerve of the financial system in order to raise the vast quotas contributed by Eng-

national debt in 1792;

vast increase resulting from continental wars;

the extraordinary demand first met by indirect taxes;

then by direct,— "Triple assessment for 1798;"

superseded by a temporary income tax,

which became permanent.

Pitt and Ireland;

---

[1] Passed January 12, 1798, 38 Geo. III. c. 16.

[2] Pitt said that the measure was destroyed by "shameful evasion or rather scandalous fraud."— *Speeches*, vol. iii. p. 372.

[3] Upon the whole subject, see Dowell, *Hist. of Taxation*, vol. ii. pp. 182–228, 230, 332.

land for the maintenance of the war upon the continent, he was called upon to deal with a complex problem nearer home for which no English statesman has yet been able to find a satisfactory solution.   Although at the accession of George III. Ireland, with her separate parliament, army, and magistracy, preserved all the outward seeming of national life, in her relations with the English government and people she was nothing more in fact than a conquered province.   By one of

her dependent condition under Poynings' Act;

"Poynings' Acts,"[1] existing since the reign of Henry VII., the Irish parliament was deprived of all initiative in legislation; it could only answer "aye" or "no" to such bills, including even money bills,[2] as were submitted to it by the English privy council.   And even in the deliberations of that impotent assembly the mass of the Irish people had no voice.   The Irish

proscription of Irish catholics and

catholics, that numbered five to every Irish protestant, were not only excluded from membership in parliament, but also from the right of voting for the representatives who composed it, as well as from all offices civil, military, and municipal, — a disqualification likewise extended to about one half of the

protestant dissenters;

protestant population.   The presbyterian dissenters, who formed the bulk of the Ulster settlements, were as severely proscribed as their catholic brethren.   The result was that

country governed by about a twelfth of the population; composition of the Irish parliament;

the entire administration of the country was vested in such protestants as belonged to the established church, numbering all together about a twelfth of the population of the island. The Irish house of lords was composed of protestant bishops and peers of the same faith, while the house of commons, that assumed to represent the country, was made up of members returned either by rotten boroughs, or close corporations under the control of the great protestant landowners, into whose hands had been concentrated the bulk of the soil through the vast confiscations that had followed successive revolts.[3]   And

how far subject to the supremacy of the English;

in order to make the supremacy of the ruling race still more secure, the English parliament passed an act[4] in the reign of George I. affirming its right "to bind the people and kingdom

---

1 10 Hen. VII. c. 4 (Irish).

2 Grattan's *Life*, vol. i. p. 57.

3 The whole matter is well summed up by Green, *Hist. of the Eng. People*, vol. iv. pp. 262–266. See also Tor-

rens, *Hist. of Cabinets*, vol. i. pp. 206–222.

4 6 Geo. I. c. 5, affirming 10 Hen. VII. c. 22. "The legislature of Ireland was that of a British dependency." — May, *Const. Hist.*, vol. iii. pp. 305, 306.

of Ireland" by its enactments, and transferring the appellate jurisdiction of the Irish peers to the English house of lords.[1] The main body of the Irish people, thus made, so far as the administration of government and law was concerned, mere hewers of wood and drawers of water for their protestant masters, were still further crippled by a set of commercial restrictions dating back to the reign of Charles II.,[2] and so designed as to interdict almost entirely the export of Irish products and manufactures into England, and to prohibit entirely all direct trade between Ireland and foreign countries, including the British possessions. It is not strange, therefore, that the Irish, thus crushed down by a cruel system of political, economic, and social oppression, which the English themselves now denounce with unmeasured severity, should have embraced the first opportunity that promised emancipation. That opportunity came in 1779, when the threat of the French invasion and the lack of any other means of resistance forced the English government to call upon the protestant oligarchy in Ireland to defend the country. In response to that call an army of more than forty thousand protestant volunteers gathered under protestant officers, not simply to repel the invasion, but to unite with the rest of the population, headed by Grattan and Flood, in a common struggle for the redress of Irish grievances.[3] As the best means to that end, the volunteers in 1780 demanded with one voice the legislative and judicial independence of the Irish parliament;[4] and under that pressure the English legislature in 1782 repealed all the acts that obstructed that result.[5] After that severance, the only tie that bound the two countries to each other was the possession of a common sovereign; and for nearly twenty years English statesmen were baffled in their efforts to bring about anything like harmonious concert between the two independent legislatures. When in 1785 Pitt, in a just and generous spirit of conciliation, attempted to remove all unreasonable restrictions from Irish commerce, he was forced to finally abandon the effort in dis-

Marginal notes: commercial restrictions upon Irish commerce; in 1779 the protestant oligarchy called upon to defend the country; the volunteers demanded redress of Irish grievances; independence of Irish parliament the result; countries bound together only by a common sovereign; Pitt's unsuccessful attempt to emancipate Irish commerce;

[1] *Parl. Hist.*, vol. vii. p. 642; Lord Mountmorres' *Hist.*, vol. i. pp. 339, 360.

[2] See 32 Car. II. c. 2; 10 & 11 Will. III. c. 10; *Parl. Hist.*, vol. xix. p. 1100, *et seq.*

[3] Plowden's *Hist.*, vol. i. p. 493.

[4] Ibid., p. 513; Grattan's *Life*, vol. ii. pp. 39–55.

[5] *Parl. Hist.*, vol. xxiii. pp. 16–48; Rockingham's *Memoirs*, vol. ii. pp. 469–476; Grattan's *Life*, vol. ii. p. 289, *et seq.*; May, *Const. Hist.*, vol. iii. pp. 314–317, 320, 328.

gust because the British parliament could not be induced to ratify the eleven resolutions embodying the scheme which the Irish had gratefully accepted.[1]   The dangers of the situation

conflict as to the Regency Bill of 1789;

were further emphasized by the conflict that arose as to the Regency Bill in 1789, when the Irish legislature admitted and the English repelled the claims of the prince of Wales to the regency as a matter of right.[2]   In order to put an end to what

Pitt resolved to incorporate the Irish parliament in that of the United Kingdom;

he considered an impossible condition of things, Pitt, who "resented and spurned the bigoted fury of Irish protestants," [3] resolved after the suppression of the dreadful rebellion of 1798 to establish a more tolerant and equitable rule by uniting the two countries, not by federal bonds, but by the incorporation of the Irish parliament into that of the United Kingdom.   The

details of the scheme of union

scheme of union proposed by Pitt at the opening of 1799 contemplated the admission into the house of commons at Westminster of a hundred Irish members, and of twenty-eight temporal peers, elected for life by the Irish peerage, and four spiritual peers, sitting by rotation of sessions in the house of

to be carried out by acts approved by both legislatures;

lords.   In order to give legal sanction to that scheme, it was necessary that it should be embodied in separate acts,[4] to be adopted by the legislatures of the two countries, which could become effective only when ratified by both.   By the employ-

shameless bribery of Irish parliament; Grattan's protest;

ment of wholesale and shameless corruption,[5] the Irish parliament, despite the indignant protest of Grattan [6] and a few other patriots against the sale of the free constitution of their country, was induced to extinguish itself.   The immediate

restrictions upon Irish commerce removed;

compensation to Ireland was the removal of all restrictions upon the commerce of the two countries, and the extension of every trading privilege enjoyed by the one to the other,[7] a boon which could not have been attained in any other manner.

Pitt's plan to abolish all religious tests;

Pitt's whole plan contemplated, however, a far higher and nobler compensation through such a removal of all religious

[1] *Irish Deb.*, vol. iv. p. 116; Plowden's *Hist.*, vol. ii. p. 113, n.; *Parl. Hist.*, vol. xxv. pp. 311, 575.

[2] For a list of the Irish statutes defining the relations of that kingdom to the English crown, see Bailey, *Succession to the Eng. Crown*, pp. 263–266.

[3] Wilberforce's *Diary*, July 16, 1798.

[4] 39 & 40 Geo. III. c. 67; 40 Geo. III. c. 38 (Irish).

[5] The total cost was about a million and a half pounds.   As to its application, see *Castlereagh Corr.*, vol. ii. p. 151; *Cornwallis Corr.*, vol. iii. pp. 81, 110.

[6] *Life*, vol. iii. pp. 17, *et seq.*, 75–80.

[7] 39 & 40 Geo. III. c. 67; Cunningham, *Growth of Eng. Ind. and Com.*, vol. ii. pp. 522, 658.

tests as would have conferred alike upon the Irish catholics and the Irish dissenters a perfect equality of civil rights.[1] When his intention to follow up the union with such a measure, to which he had clearly committed himself, was disclosed to the king, his opposition, upon the absurd ground that his coronation oath would be violated should he assent to any bill relieving Roman Catholics of civil disabilities,[2] was so strong that Pitt, rather than forfeit his word, resigned office in February, 1801.[3]

opposed by the king;

resigned February, 1781.

8. The review heretofore made of the history of regencies ended with an account of the arrangements made under 28 Hen. VIII. c. 7, for the minority of Edward VI., the earliest regency resting upon an express statute.[4] No other example of a statutory provision for a regency occurs until 1751, when the regency act[5] of that year, passed after the death of Frederick, prince of Wales, constituted the princess dowager of Wales regent of the kingdom in the event that any of her children should succeed to the throne before attaining the age of eighteen years. A council of regency was nominated by the act, to which the king was permitted to add four members by instrument under the sign manual, to be opened after his death. It was declared unlawful for the regent to make war or peace, or to ratify any treaty with a foreign power, or to prorogue, adjourn, or dissolve parliament, or to give her assent to any bill repealing or varying the Act of Settlement, the Act of Uniformity, or the act of the Scottish parliament for securing the protestant religion and presbyterian church government in Scotland, without the consent of a majority of the council of regency. Such was the nature of the last precedent when the severe illness of George III. in 1765, the first of his attacks, made it necessary for him to provide for a regency in the event of his death. With his usual jealousy of the power of parliament he insisted, at first, that he should be

History of regencies resumed;

regency act of 1751 the first since 28 Hen. VIII. c. 7;

contents of the act first named;

the last precedent prior to first illness of George III. in 1765;

---

[1] *Cornwallis Corr.*, vol. i. p. 440; Lord Stanhope's *Life of Pitt*, vol. iii. p. 160; Lord Sidmouth's *Life*, vol. i. p. 289; May, *Const. Hist.*, vol. iii. pp. 118, 333.

[2] He had consulted Lord Kenyon on that subject as far back as 1795.

[3] The king in reply to his communication declined to discuss "any proposition tending to destroy the groundwork of our happy constitution." Cf. Pellew's *Life of Lord Sidmouth*, vol. i. p. 291. See also the pamphlet published by Dr. Phillpot in 1827, containing all the correspondence between the king and Mr. Pitt.

[4] See above, pp. 109–112.

[5] 24 Geo. II. c. 24.

vested unconditionally with the right of appointing any person he might choose as regent;[1] but in the bill as finally passed,[2] his right of nomination under his sign manual was limited to the queen, the princess of Wales, or to any descendant of George II. resident in the kingdom, — the nominee to be guardian of his successor while under eighteen years of age, and "regent of the kingdom." A council of regency was then appointed, and the relative powers of regent and council defined upon the basis of the act of George II. The question of a regency next arose in 1788–89, when the king's illness so completely deprived him of his reason that he had to be placed under restraint. The question was how to provide for the administration of the powers of an insane king under a constitution that contained no method for his removal. The bill then introduced brought on a discussion memorable for the extreme views expressed, on the one hand, by Fox as to the rights of the prince of Wales, and, on the other, by Pitt as to the right of parliament to name a regent under such circumstances. Fox, blinded by prejudice and self-interest, went so far as to declare that during the king's incapacity the prince of Wales had as much right to exercise the powers of the sovereign as if he were actually dead; and that parliament possessed only the right to declare the exact time when the exercise of such powers by the prince should begin. Pitt, on the other hand, while correctly assuming that the whole power of providing for a regency rested in parliament alone, overstated the case by declaring that "unless by their decision, the prince of Wales had no more right — speaking of strict right — to assume the government than any other individual subject of the country."[3] When the question came on for discussion in the house of lords, the duke of York disavowed any claim of right upon the part of the prince, who "understood," he said, "too well the sacred principles which seated the house of Brunswick on the throne, ever to assume or exercise any power, be his claim what it might, not derived from the will of the people, expressed by their representatives and their lordships in parliament assembled."[4] That declaration

[1] Walpole's *Memoirs*, vol. ii. p. 98.
[2] 5 Geo. III. c. 27.
[3] *Parl. Hist.*, vol. xxvii. pp. 707–709. For Lord John Russell's judicious criticism of both extremes, see his *Memoir of Fox*, vol. ii. p. 263.
[4] *Parl. Hist.*, vol. xxvii. pp. 678, 684 May, *Const. Hist.*, vol. i. pp. 177–188.

was the only practical outcome of the controversy, cut short controversy cut short by king's recovery in April, 1789; by the king's sudden recovery in April, 1789, except the settlement of the principle that, in the event of the mental incapacity of the sovereign, the lord chancellor can be empowered when the lord chancellor can give the royal assent; by a vote of the two houses to affix the great seal even to commissions [1] for opening parliament, and for giving to a regency bill the royal assent. Passing over the ministerial embarrassments, caused by the king's third illness in 1801,[2] we come to the proceedings that took place in 1810–11, when regency act of 1810–11; the poor demented old man, after reigning for fifty years, passed into the custody of keepers, while the royal authority was assumed under the regency act of that year by the prince of Wales. In the enactment of that statute parliament followed substantially the same course that had been laid down constructed on lines laid down in 1788; in 1788,[3] the royal assent being given by commission authorized by resolution of both houses. By the terms of the act the prince of Wales was appointed regent during the king's prince of Wales regent without a council; incapacity without the aid of a council of regency; and while his power to grant peerages, offices, and pensions was restrained, there was no limitation upon his authority, as in previous acts, to make war and peace, treaties with foreign nations, and to adjourn or dissolve parliament. At the accession of William IV. the duchess of Kent was appointed guardian and regent in the event the present queen should come arrangements for a regency at accession of William IV.; to the throne before attaining eighteen years.[4] In that event the regent was to carry on the government, with the aid of the responsible ministers of the crown, without any special council of regency. At Queen Victoria's accession, when the at the accession of Queen Victoria; king of Hanover became the presumptive heir, an act [5] was passed providing that, in the event of the queen's death while her successor was out of the realm, the government should be carried on in his name and until his arrival by lords justices acting as a kind of regency council. After the present queen's marriage the last statute [6] upon the subject was enacted, in

---

[1] For the form of the commission used to open parliament in February, 1789, see *Lords' Journals*, vol. xxxviii. p. 344. On the 23d of April the king, attended by the houses and the court, gave thanks for his recovery at St. Paul's.

[2] Mr. Addington, who was then prime minister, resolved to follow, if neces-

sary, the precedent established in 1788. Pellew's *Life of Sidmouth*, vol. i. p. 347.

[3] Walpole's *Life of Perceval*, vol. ii. chs. v. and vi.; Lewis, *Adminis.*, p. 325.

[4] 1 Will. IV. c. 2.

[5] 1 Vict. c. 72.

[6] 3 & 4 Vict. c. 52.

last act
upon the
subject
passed
after her
marriage
with Prince
Albert.

which her husband, Prince Albert, was appointed regent without a council of regency, in the event that any child of her majesty should succeed to the throne before arriving at the age of eighteen years.   The only limitation upon the authority of the regent was embodied in the usual prohibition to assent to the certain acts specially named in the regency act of George II.

Regency
and reign
of George
IV.;

From 1811 to 1820 the royal authority was exercised by the prince regent as such ; from 1820 to 1830 he exercised it in his own right as George IV.   As the bosom friend of Fox and Sheridan, it was supposed upon his accession as regent that he would force the Tory ministry then in power, with Perceval at its head, to give way to a new one to be composed of the Whigs.   When, however, the opportunity for change was offered by the assassination of Perceval in May,

after a
feeble effort
to install
the Whigs,
Tories
continued
in power
under
Liverpool ;
succeeded
by Well-
ington in
1828 ;

1812, the faint-hearted effort of the regent to install the Whigs was foiled by mutual distrust ; and the result was the restoration of the old ministry under Lord Liverpool, who continued in office down to 1827, when, after two short administrations under Canning and Viscount Goderich, the direction of affairs passed in 1828 to the duke of Wellington, who was in office at the king's death.   During the twenty years occupied by the regency and reign of George IV., the ministerial system was thus in the hands of the Tories, who managed the affairs of the

affairs
managed
with but
little royal
interfer-
ence ;

nation with little interference from the king, except when his personal interests or those of the royal family were directly involved.[1]   And yet, even in matters of that character, he was not always permitted to dominate.   Immediately after his

conflict
arising out
of the
divorce ;

accession as king he was brought into collision [2] with his ministers through his desire not only to procure a divorce from Queen Caroline, who, like himself, had no doubt been guilty of serious misconduct, but also to proceed against her for high

ministers
finally
assented
to a bill of
pains and
penalties ;

treason.   Finally, upon her imprudent return to England, in July, 1820, all the ministers, except Canning,[3] were induced to consent to the introduction in the house of lords of a bill of

---

[1] He could then be very determined. Campbell's *Lives of the Chancellors*, vol. vii. pp. 345, 346; Todd, *Parl. Government*, vol. i. pp. 67, 68, 92.

[2] Their original objections were embodied in minutes of the cabinet of the 10th and 14th of February, 1820. Stapleton's *Life of Canning*, pp. 266, 279, 299.

[3] Ibid., pp. 290–295, 315–323; May, *Const. Hist.*, vol. iii. pp. 129–133.

pains and penalties, providing for the dissolution of her marriage with the king upon the ground of adultery and for her degradation. When the charges contained in the preamble came on to be heard, Brougham and Denman, by their bold and brilliant defence of the queen, so aroused popular sympathy in her favor, by holding her up as a deserted and persecuted woman, that the ministry deemed it wise to drop the bill after the majority in its favor in the lords had dwindled to nine. The personal humiliation thus put upon the king at the beginning of his reign was repeated at its close, when his ministers, headed by Wellington and Peel, extorted from him by tendering their resignations his assent to the measure of 1829 in favor of catholic emancipation.[1] "It may, therefore, be said that, from the beginning of his regency in 1811 to the close of his reign in 1830, the regal influence was limited to the strict exercise of the prerogative. George IV. had no personal influence; instead of his popularity supporting the ministry, the difficulty was for the ministry to support his unpopularity, and to uphold the respect for the crown when it encircled the head of such a sovereign."[2] Thus it was that the short-lived yet desperate struggle inaugurated by George III. for the reëstablishment of the mediæval supremacy of the royal office ended under his less resolute successor in the complete triumph of the existing ministerial system.

brilliantly assailed by Brougham and Denman;

dropped after majority in the lords had dwindled to nine;

catholic emancipation;

final triumph of the ministerial system.

9. The attempt which has now been made to indicate the progress of cabinet government during the reigns of George III. and George IV. was prefaced by a summary of the causes whose combined influence at the beginning of that period took away from the house of commons its character as a free and representative organ, through which the nation as a whole could impress its will upon its rulers.[3] By reason of the existence of such conditions the elder Pitt was impelled to counsel George II. to look for the voice of his "people in other places than within the house of commons;" and in the same way the great unrepresented body outside of the legislature was forced to employ with a fresh vigor the press, the right of public meeting, and the right of petition, as substitutes for the normal means of expression, which the constitution failed to supply.

Struggle to reform the representative system;

Pitt counselled George II. not to seek the voice of his people "within the house of commons;" channels through which public opinion expressed itself,

---

[1] See above, p. 430.
[2] Lewis, *Adminis.*, p. 421.
[3] See above, p. 463 *et seq.*

Such were the weapons that began to be actively employed during the stormy period of agitation that followed the accession of George III.; and during the seventy years that elapsed between that time and the death of George IV. the imperious demand never ceased to be heard in parliament and without, that the house of commons should be so reformed as to make it the representative not of the crown and the aristocracy, but "the express image of the feelings of the nation." Pitt, who was the first to advocate reform, boldly denounced in the lower house in 1766 the borough representation as "the rotten part of our constitution. It cannot continue the century; if it does not drop, it must be amputated;"[1] and in 1770 he proposed that a third member should be added to every county, "in order to counterbalance the weight of corrupt and venal boroughs."[2] In 1774 appeared Lord Stanhope's pamphlets, which seem to have been the earliest publications in favor of reform; and in 1776 they were followed by the work of John Cartwright, whose second edition was entitled "The Legislative Rights of the Commonalty vindicated." In that year it was that John Wilkes introduced a comprehensive scheme of reform, which embodied substantially all the principles that have been successfully advocated since that time. He moved for a bill, which was negatived without a division,[3] to give additional members to Middlesex, Yorkshire, and other large counties, as well as to the metropolis; to disfranchise the rotten boroughs, and to add the electors to the county constituencies; and, finally, to enfranchise "rich populous trading towns" like Manchester, Leeds, Sheffield, and Birmingham. In 1780, when the duke of Richmond, in the midst of the Lord George Gordon riots, presented a bill for the establishment of annual parliaments, equal electoral districts, and universal suffrage, the upper house likewise set aside, without a division, a scheme then considered unworthy of serious consideration.[4]

Such was the prelude to the efforts in favor of reform made by the younger Pitt, who introduced in May, 1782, while Rockingham was in power, a motion for a committee to inquire into

Marginal notes:

during seventy years of agitation that followed accession of George III.

Pitt's denunciation of the borough representation in 1766;

Stanhope's pamphlets in 1774; work of Cartwright in 1776;

scheme of reform then introduced by Wilkes;

fate of duke of Richmond's scheme in 1780.

Younger Pitt undertook work of reform in 1782;

---

[1] Debates on the Address, January, 1766, Cobbett's *Parl. Hist.*, vol. xvi. p. 100; vol. xvii. p. 223.

[2] Walpole, *Memoirs*, vol iv. p. 58.
[3] *Parl. Hist.*, vol. xvii. p. 223, n.
[4] Ibid., vol. xxi. p. 686.

the state of the representation, prefaced by a speech in which
he denounced without mercy the nomination boroughs as "the
strongholds of that corruption to which he attributed all the
calamities of the nation," — an abuse that "had grown with
the growth of England and strengthened with her strength,
but had not diminished with her diminution or decayed with
her decay." [1]   While the speech was wise and judicious, it was
at the same time in harmony with the political ideas of that
ultra-Whig faction which the persecution of Wilkes had developed and whose favor Pitt was then courting.   The motion,
which was supported by Fox, was lost by only twenty votes [2]
in a house of more than three hundred, a division more favorable to reform than any other that occurred prior to the year
1831.   In May, 1783, after the Shelburne ministry had yielded
to the coalition headed by Fox and North, Pitt, whose position had been strengthened by numerously signed petitions,
renewed his efforts in a more vigorous form by bringing forward three resolutions, which contemplated, (1) an addition to
the house of a hundred county members and several for the
metropolis ; (2) the prevention of bribery and expense at elections.   In supporting his resolutions he did not hesitate to
visit the disastrous results of the American war upon the corruption of the house of commons and the secret influence of
the crown, which he said "was sapping the very foundation of
liberty, by corruption."   That within the year the cause had
lost ground is manifest from the fact that the resolutions were
rejected by a vote of nearly two to one. [3]   Pitt's third and last
effort in favor of reform was made as prime minister, after his
triumph over the coalition in the elections of 1784 had secured
him the control of the house of commons by a great majority.
In April, 1785, in the second session of the new parliament,
he moved for leave to introduce a bill "to amend the representation of the people of England, in parliament," which
contemplated the gradual extinction of all decayed boroughs
and the distribution of their members among the counties and
the metropolis.   Seventy-two members were to be obtained
through the disfranchisement of thirty-six decayed boroughs ;

(marginal notes:) his denunciation of nomination boroughs; although supported by Fox, his attempt failed; in 1783 renewed his efforts by presenting three resolutions, rejected by a vote of two to one; in April, 1785, he introduced his third and last scheme; its main features;

---

[1] Macaulay's "William Pitt," *Essays*, vol. iii. p. 325.

[2] *Parl. Hist.*, vol. xxii. p. 1416; Stan-hope's *Life of Pitt*, vol. i. pp. 72–75; Fox, *Memoirs*, vol. i. p. 321.

[3] *Parl. Hist.*, vol. xxiii. p. 827 ; Stan-hope's *Life of Pitt*, vol. i. p. 118.

and that number was to be swelled to a hundred through the purchase of the exclusive rights of ten close corporations, and of the rights of four small boroughs, whose members were to be transferred to certain populous towns. The notable feature of the scheme was the formal recognition of the right of a borough to representation as salable property, which the state could not justly take away without compensation. Proceeding upon that idea, the bill provided that no borough was to be disfranchised without the consent of its proprietors, and as a means of obtaining such consent a million pounds was to be immediately set aside to accumulate at compound interest.[1] Pitt, while frankly admitting this to be "a tender part" of the scheme, assumed it to be "a necessary evil, if any reform was to take place." As an additional inducement to the counties, he proposed to enlarge their constituencies by the addition of copyholders to the freeholders. But the time was not ripe for such sweeping changes. The king was hostile,[2] the house itself unsympathetic, and the nation indifferent; and the result was the rejection of the motion to bring in the bill by a majority of seventy-four.[3] When in 1790 Flood moved for a bill to amend the representation of the people, embodying substantially the plan rejected five years before, Pitt, while expressing unabated interest in the subject, refused to assent to the motion, which was superseded by the adjournment of the house.[4] The next attempt to advance the cause was made in 1792–93 by Grey and Erskine as the leaders of a popular movement promoted by several associations, chief of which was that known as the "Friends of the People." Thus supported, Grey brought on a debate in May, 1793, upon a motion to inquire into the system of representation, just at the moment when the disruption of the Whig party, and the disinclination "to make hazardous experiments" consequent upon the horrors of the French Revolution, foredoomed this effort to failure. After a two nights' debate the motion was supported by only forty-one votes.[5] Thus discouraged, Grey permitted the matter to rest until 1797, when he moved for leave to bring

Margin notes:

right of a borough to representation recognized as salable property;

a great sum to be appropriated to such purchases;

copyholders to be added to county constituencies;

scheme rejected by a decided majority; failure of Flood's effort in 1790;

attempt of Grey and Erskine in 1792–93;

motion supported by only forty-one votes;

---

[1] *Ann. Reg.*, 1784, 1785, p. 189.
[2] As to the correspondence of Pitt with the king on this subject, see Tomline's *Life of Pitt*, vol. ii. p. 40.
[3] *Parl. Hist.*, vol. xxv. pp. 432–475; Stanhope's *Life of Pitt*, vol. i. p. 256.
[4] Ibid., vol. xxviii. p. 452.
[5] Ibid., vol. xxx. pp. 787–925.

in a bill to increase the number of the county members, and to admit to the county franchise along with the freeholders not only copyholders, but leaseholders for terms of years.   In the boroughs he proposed to substitute a uniform household franchise for the anomalous and complicated systems resting on local custom.   And in order to diminish the expense of elections, he proposed that the poll should be taken throughout the kingdom at the same time.   Although this scheme, which embodied the outline of the great measure finally passed in 1832, was ably supported by Erskine and Fox, the motion was defeated by a large majority,[1] in the midst of the reactionary sentiments then existing, which postponed all further efforts in favor of reform for a period of thirteen years.

fate of a more comprehensive measure introduced by Grey in 1797.

Not until 1809 was the subject revived by Sir Francis Burdett, who entered the field made vacant by the deaths of Pitt and Fox, and by the removal of Grey and Erskine to the upper house.   The cause was, however, rather retarded than advanced by the new champion, who so alarmed all moderate reformers by his radical proposal to divide the counties into electoral districts, each to return a member, and to vest the franchise in the male taxed population, that his project was supported by only fifteen votes.[2]   And in the next year, when Bland moved for a committee of inquiry into parliamentary reform, his proposal was defeated by a majority of two to one.[3]   In the midst of such discouragements Earl Grey and Lord Erskine did not venture to do more than promise their aid to any temperate and feasible plan that might be proposed in the future for the improvement of the representation.   Such qualities were certainly not attributed at the time to the next proposal brought forward in 1818–19 by Sir F. Burdett in resolutions favoring annual parliaments, equal electoral districts, universal male suffrage, and vote by ballot.[4]   The only significant circumstance connected with the discussion thus renewed was the expression of opinion made during the debate by Lord John Russell, not many years before elected to parliament before he was of age, in favor of the disfranchisement of such boroughs as were notoriously corrupt.

Sir F. Burdett entered the field in 1809;

his radical proposals;

Bland's efforts in the next year;

Burdett's resolutions renewed in 1818–19;

appearance of Lord John Russell.

[1] *Parl. Hist.*, vol. xxxiii. p. 644.
[2] *Hans. Deb.*, 1st ser. vol. xiv. p. 1041.
[3] Ibid., vol. xvii. p. 123.

[4] The motion was superseded by the order of the day. Ibid., vol. xi. p. 1440.

In 1820
Lord John
undertook
the work of
reform in a
temperate
spirit;

In 1820 Lord John, who was destined to shape the great reform bill of 1832, began to deal in a wise and temperate spirit with the crying evils of the representative system at a time when the task was rendered more difficult by reason of the extreme demands made, on the one hand, for universal suffrage, and by the unreasoning denials, on the other, of the

to provide
middle
ground he
introduced
three
resolutions;

necessity for any change whatever. In the hope of providing middle ground for views so wide apart, he moved resolutions proposing, (1) that the borough of Grampound, whose scandalous proceedings he had denounced in the preceding session, should be disfranchised; (2) that boroughs convicted of notorious bribery and corruption should be deprived of the right to return members; (3) that the representation thus taken away from corrupt boroughs should be given to some of the larger counties and to certain towns with not less than fifteen thousand population, — the innocent borough electors to be permitted to vote for the county.   As the govern-

withdrawn
in favor
of a bill to
disfran-
chise Gram-
pound;

ment was willing to concur in the disfranchisement of Grampound, the resolutions were withdrawn and a bill offered for that purpose.[1]   But when the bill reached the lords for the second time in 1821, two additional members were assigned to the county of York,[2] and in that form it was finally agreed

Lord John's
unsuccess-
ful efforts
in 1821,

to.[3]   In that year, — after a sweeping scheme of reform offered by Lambton and based on the idea of equal electoral districts had been defeated by a majority of only twelve,[4] — Lord John again introduced resolutions looking to the disfranchisement of corrupt boroughs and the distribution of their representation, which were superseded by the previous ques-

1822, 1823,
1826,

tion carried by a majority of thirty-one.[5]   In 1822, 1823, and 1826 he again presented similar proposals, which were each time rejected by steadily increasing majorities.   Passing over

and 1828;

his unsuccessful effort made in 1828 to enfranchise Manchester and Birmingham through the disfranchisement of Penryn and East Retford,[6] whose corruptions had been given special prominence in the disclosures that followed the general election of

---

[1] *Hans. Deb.*, 1st ser. vol. xli. pp. 1091–1122.

[2] The commons had given them to the town of Leeds.

[3] 1 & 2 Geo. IV. c. 47.

[4] *Hans. Deb.*, 2d ser. vol. v. pp. 356–453.

[5] Ibid., p. 603.

[6] Ibid., vol. xviii. p. 83.

1826, we come to the motion made by Lord John in 1830, in which he proposed to immediately enfranchise Birmingham, Leeds, and Manchester, and to disfranchise the next three places found guilty of corruption,[1] — a moderate programme that so conflicted with the unreasoning dread of innovation then existing as to cause its rejection by a majority of forty-eight.   When during the same session O'Connell, who a year before had secured the tardy yet complete triumph of catholic emancipation, attempted to go further by moving resolutions in favor of triennial parliaments, universal suffrage, and vote by ballot, Lord John at once attempted to guard the cause of reform against the effects of such radical proposals by moving as a substitute other resolutions, in which he reiterated his own moderate ideas in favor of such a disfranchisement of the smaller boroughs as would make possible the enfranchisement of the great commercial towns, and the grant of additional representation to the more populous counties, without any increase in the total membership of the house of commons.[2] The ministry of the duke of Wellington, which had so recently been forced to bow to the demands of O'Connell, who had offered the alternatives of concession or civil war, now firmly resolved to yield no further; and as an expression of that conclusion Sir Robert Peel, home secretary and government leader in the lower house, declared in the course of the debate that "they had to consider whether there was not, on the whole, a general representation of the people in that house; and whether the voice of the people was not sufficiently heard. For himself he thought it was."[3]   Under that blow both the resolutions of O'Connell and the amendment of Lord John went down; and thus the last word spoken at the close of the reign of George IV. seemed to settle the fact that the seventy years of agitation in favor of reform that had actively begun at his father's accession had ended at last in failure and disappointment.   While the direct bribery of members had visibly declined, no change whatever had taken place for the better in the constitution of the popular chamber, excepting only the

defeat of his motion made in 1830 to enfranchise Birmingham, Leeds, and Manchester;

O'Connell's radical resolutions;

Lord John's substitute;

Wellington's ministry resolved to defeat both;

Peel's declaration that no reform was needed;

at the close of George IV.'s reign, cause of reform seemed to be lost;

[1] *Hans. Deb.*, 2d ser. vol. xxii. p. 859.
[2] *Ibid.*, vol. xxiv. p. 1204.
[3] Upon the whole subject see May, *Const. Hist.*, vol. i. pp. 393–417, where the most complete exposition is to be found.

summary. results brought about through catholic emancipation. The system of rotten boroughs had neither "dropped" nor been "amputated;" the electoral basis had not been widened; and not a step had been taken to insure the redistribution of seats, so imperatively demanded by the shiftings of wealth and population.

CHAPTER III.

ITS PROGRESS DURING THE REIGNS OF WILLIAM IV. AND VICTORIA.[1]

1. THE dissolution[2] made necessary by the death of George IV. on the 26th of June, 1830, opened the way for new elections, that were held just at the moment when the revolution that overthrew Charles X. in France, followed immediately as it was by another in Belgium, gave a fresh impulse to the liberal tendencies in England, which only a year before had enforced catholic emancipation despite the obstinate resistance of the high Tories. When the new parliament, elected under such circumstances, met in October, Wellington, upon the first reference made by Earl Grey to the subject of reform, attempted to stem the tide by pronouncing an ill-tempered and ill-advised panegyric upon the then existing system of representation, that ended with the declaration that " he was not prepared to bring forward any measure of the description alluded to by the noble lord. He was not only not prepared to bring forward any measure of this nature, but he would at once declare that, as far as he was concerned, as long as he held any station in the government of the country, he should always feel it his duty to resist such measures when proposed by others." [3] The inevitable result of such a statement at such a time was a storm of opposition, that rose so fast that within a fortnight the duke was forced to resign office, — thus ending the Tory ascendency that had lasted for sixty years. Earl Grey, who now assumed office, with Brougham at his side as lord chancellor, introduced the ministerial programme by

[marginal notes:] William IV. and the reform bill of 1832:

Wellington's declaration against reform in October, 1830;

driven from office, accession of Earl Grey;

---

[1] After a careful perusal of this chapter, my good friend, Sir Henry Drummond Wolff, the British ambassador at Madrid, made many valuable suggestions for which I am very grateful. He is not only a charming gentleman and an accomplished diplomat, but a statesman rich in practical experience. And I must at the same time express my thanks to another Englishman, Arthur Houghton, Esq., many years representative of the London *Standard* at Madrid, for much judicious advice in connection with this volume, and for unfailing personal kindness. They are an honor to their nation.

[2] Parliament was dissolved July 24.

[3] *Hans. Deb.*, 3d ser. vol. i. p. 52.

who at once declared in favor of reform;

the announcement that the government would "take into immediate consideration the state of the representation, with a view to the correction of those defects which had been occasioned in it by the operation of time." [1]   To Lord John Russell, who was not in the cabinet, was assigned the honorable duty of drafting the new measure by reason of his mastery of the subject; [2] and when he presented it to the house on March 1, 1831, it was brought in without a division after a debate that lasted for seven nights.   The first trial of strength came upon the second reading of the bill, which was carried by a majority of one only, in a house of six hundred and eight. Thus warned, the ministry, when defeated upon a resolution that the number of members returned for England should not be diminished, resolved not to proceed with the bill; and on April 22 parliament was prorogued "with a view to its immediate dissolution." [3]   So triumphant were the reformers in the appeal soon made to the nation, that the second reading of the second reform bill was agreed to on July 6, by a vote of 367 to 231.   Not, however, until September 21 did it finally pass the house by a vote of 345 to 239. [4]   Then came the first struggle in the upper house, where, on October 7, that body ventured to resist the national will by rejecting the bill on the second reading by a majority of 41. [5]   Undaunted by that rebuff, the ministry, sustained by a vote of confidence from the popular chamber, persisted in their purpose, and on December 18 the second reading of the third reform bill was carried in the house of commons by a majority of 162. [6]   Not, however, until March 23, 1832, did it finally pass that body; and on April 13 the second reading was agreed to in the upper house by the slender majority of nine. [7]   The supreme moment had now arrived; the lords, who did not dare in the face of the intense popular excitement then existing to reject the bill, resolved to emasculate and delay it by amendments.   As a counterblast to that attempt, the people gathered in political

new measure drafted by Lord Russell presented March 1, 1831;

ministry defeated and parliament dissolved;

after an appeal to the nation second reform bill passed the commons September 21;

rejected by the lords;

third reform bill passed the commons March 23, 1832;

attempt of the lords to defeat the bill aroused intense popular feeling;

---

[1] *Hans. Deb.*, 3d ser. vol. i. p. 606.
[2] For the draft of the original plan, as submitted by Lord John in December, 1830, see his *Essay on the Hist. of the Eng. Govt. and Const.*, pp. 226, 227.

[3] *Hans. Deb.*, 3d ser. vol. iii. p. 1810.
[4] Ibid., vol. iv. p. 906; vol. vii. p. 464.
[5] Ibid., vol. viii. p. 340.
[6] Ibid., vol. ix. p. 546.
[7] Ibid., vol. xii. p. 454.

unions and excited meetings, resulting in personal insults to peers and other acts of mob violence, which brought the country to the very verge of civil war. As a constitutional method of coercion, the ministry proposed that the king should overcome the majority against the bill by the creation of new peers; and when he shrank from that radical proposal, they resigned office. Not until the Tory opposition, under the lead of Wellington, had utterly failed to form a government did the king consent at last to make the necessary creations; and then, in order to render the performance of his promise unnecessary, he sent a circular letter to the opposition peers, appealing to them to declare "that in consequence of the present state of affairs, they have come to the resolution of dropping their further opposition to the reform bill, so that it may pass without delay, and as nearly as possible in its present shape." [1] Thus admonished, the lords resolved to accept the inevitable and to withdraw their opposition, and thus the bill finally passed by a vote of 106 to 22.[2]

mob violence, ministry resigned when the king refused to create new peers; to render such creations unnecessary, the king appealed to the lords to pass the bill; his suggestion accepted.

The primary object of the measure that thus became law was to equalize the representation by the withdrawal of a large number of seats from the rotten or nomination boroughs, which were distributed among the greater districts that had hitherto been either imperfectly represented or not represented at all. Thus were completely disfranchised fifty-six boroughs, including Old Sarum, Winchelsea, and Fowey, which had returned two members each, while thirty more, including Petersfield, Calne, and Rye, were reduced to one member only. The one hundred and forty-three seats thus obtained were redistributed as follows: twenty-two large towns, including Manchester, Birmingham, and Leeds, were for the first time permitted to return two members; twenty more, including

Transfer of seats from rotten boroughs to larger districts; a hundred and forty-three seats thus redistributed;

[1] Roebuck's *Hist. of the Whig Ministry*, vol. ii. p. 334; Earl Grey's *Corr.*, vol. ii. pp. 420, 444; May, *Const. Hist.*, vol. i. pp. 144, 419–427. Sixteen peers were actually created to aid the measure, and it was understood that the king had consented to a further increase if necessary.

[2] It received the royal assent, and became 2 & 3 Will. IV. c. 45. "In the house of lords the obstinate resistance of the majority, marshalled under the authority of the duke of Wellington, and guided by the powerful ability of Lord Lyndhurst, was at last overcome by the perspicuous wisdom and consistent integrity of Lord Grey, supported by the wonderful eloquence and vigor of Lord Brougham, and borne along to triumph by the invincible energy and enthusiasm of the people." — Lord John Russell, *Essay on the Hist. of the Eng. Govt. and Const.*, p. 231.

Cheltenham, Salford, and Whitby, were for the first time permitted to return one member; while certain places in Wales,
such as Tenby, Swansea, and Neath, were permitted to share
in electing members with the shire towns. The increase in
the county representation from ninety-four to one hundred
and fifty-nine was readjusted by the division of twenty-five
great counties into two districts, to each of which was given
two members; while seven other English counties obtained
three members instead of two, and three Welsh counties two
instead of one. Having thus rearranged the electoral areas,
the act worked a greater revolution still in the qualification of
electors by extending the right of voting in counties, immemorially possessed by freeholders alone, not only to leaseholders holding at a rent of £10, if the lease were for sixty,
and at a rent of £50 if the lease were for twenty years, but
also, by the clause termed the Chandos clause, to tenant occupiers holding at a rent of £50. And in order to prevent a
multiplication of votes by the parcelling of estates, it was
enacted that, if the freehold should be for life only, either the
voter should be required to be in actual occupation, or the
freehold itself should be required to be of the annual value of
£10. In the boroughs, in order to extend the franchise to the
whole of the municipal middle class, the right of voting was
given as a uniform rule to all occupiers of houses, shops, or
buildings of any kind, of the annual value of £10. The receipt,
however, of parochial relief constituted a disqualification of the
borough electors. Electoral procedure was also greatly im-
proved by the introduction from France of the system of registration of electors, which was made a condition precedent to
the right of voting. Comprehensive registers of electors were
finally established in every county and borough under the
supervision and control of revising barristers, with the right
of appeal to the higher courts of justice. It was further provided that the polls, which under the old system could be kept
open for an indefinite time, should be closed after two days, a
limit finally reduced to one day only.[1]

As the legislatures of Scotland and Ireland had long before

Marginal notes:
county representation increased from ninety-four to one hundred and fifty-nine;

county franchise extended to leaseholders and tenant occupiers;

Chandos clause;

borough franchise extended to all £10 occupiers;

introduction of registration;

polls to be closed after two days.

---

[1] See the excellent summary contained in Lely and Foulkes' *Parl. Elec. and Reg. Acts*, pp. xvi–xviii.

been incorporated with that of England, and as their repre- Reform bills for Scotland and Ireland;
sentative systems were subject even in greater degree than
the English to prevailing infirmities, it was absolutely necessary that Earl Grey should extend his reform by two separate
bills to those kingdoms.   By the Act of Union (6 Anne, c. 7),
the English house of commons, which then contained 513
members, was increased by the addition of 45 Scotch representatives; and by the Act of Union with Ireland (39 & 40
Geo. III. c. 67), the 100 new Irish members raised the total to
658. By the Scotch Reform Act of 1832, the 45 members eight new members given to the former;
assigned to Scotland at the union were increased to 53,[1] of
whom 31 were allotted to the counties, and 23 to the cities
and boroughs.   The main task, however, was to regulate the
franchise which, in the Scotch boroughs, was vested in self-
elected corporations, and in the counties, in the owners of
feudal "superiorities," who were not necessarily either land-
owners or residents in their counties. In order to correct that Scotch franchise extended;
condition of things, the borough franchise was extended to all
£10 householders, while the county franchise was extended
to all owners of "lands, houses, feu duties, or other heritable
subjects" of the yearly value of £10, and to certain classes
of leaseholders.[2] Disfranchisement in Irish boroughs formed
no part of the Irish Reform Act of 1832,[3] for the reason that
several rotten and nomination boroughs had been disfranchised
at the time of the union. The new act, after adding five to five new members given to Ireland, and franchise extended;
the representation as fixed at that time, dealt only with the
franchise which, in the boroughs, was taken away from the
corporations and vested in £10 householders, while great
additions were made to the county constituencies by the in-
clusion of certain classes of leaseholders and of £10 copyholders.   By extensions of the franchise it has been estimated
that the total number of electors, reckoned at the passing of total number of electors about doubled.
the Reform Bill of 1832 at 400,000, was about doubled;[4] and
down to 1868, prior to the operation of the Reform Acts of
1867–68, that total, for all the counties and boroughs of the
United Kingdom, had not, according to the parliamentary

---

[1] In 1867 seven members more were
added for Scotland. No further
changes were made until 1885.
[2] 2 & 3 Will. IV. c. 65.

[3] 2 & 3 Will. IV. c. 88.
[4] See the estimate of Dr. Gneist,
Hist. of the Eng. Constitution, p. 722.

returns, grown beyond 1,370,793. To that extent, and only to that extent, did the reform measures of 1832 rescue the representation from an oligarchy of peers and landowners and vest it in the hands of the middle classes.

The result thus attained by the old Whigs in their constitutional charter of 1832 was looked on for a long time as a finality. Despite several efforts made by Lord John Russell himself, and also by the earl of Derby,[1] to further revise the representative system, all such efforts failed to pass into law down to the time when the conservative ministry of the latter, mainly through the energy and tact of Mr. Disraeli, succeeded in passing the Representation of the People Act of 1867.[2] During the intervening period of thirty-five years several acts were passed, however, developing and perfecting the original measure, which are worthy of special mention. By the Parlia-

mentary Registration Act of 1843[3] the incomplete provisions of the act of 1832 upon that subject were perfected in many particulars, it being provided among other things that the register should be conclusive against the claim of any person

to vote who was not registered. More important still were the acts passed for the prevention of bribery at elections, for which the Reform Act of 1832 had made no direct provision, and which continued to a disgraceful extent after its passage. The first effort to protect the new electorate against the tendency of the rich to traffic within its tempting ranks was

embodied in Lord John Russell's Bribery Act of 1841;[4] and when that proved insufficient, other acts of the same character were passed in 1842 and 1852,[5] which were consolidated in the more comprehensive measure known as the Corrupt Practices Act of 1854,[6] a temporary law continued from time to time, and so amended in 1858 as to render legal the payment of a voter's travelling expenses.[7] The policy of excluding from the lower house all except the proprietors of land, adopted in

---

[1] Special reference is made to Lord John's measures of 1852, 1854, 1860, and 1866, and to the earl of Derby's measure of 1859, referred to below.

[2] 30 & 33 Vict. c. 102.

[3] 6 Vict. c. 8. Cf. Lely and Foulkes' *Parl. Elec. and Reg. Acts*, p. xviii; and for a table of all acts on that subject, p. 74.

[4] 4 & 5 Vict. c. 57.

[5] 5 & 6 Vict. c. 102; 15 & 16 Vict. c. 57.

[6] 17 & 18 Vict. c. 102. In 1872 the provisions of this act were extended to municipal elections by 35 & 36 Vict. c. 60. Cf. Sir J. F. Stephen, *Hist. of the Crim. Law*, vol. iii. pp. 253–255.

[7] 21 & 22 Vict. c. 87.

the reign of Anne,[1] was continued down to 1838, when a new qualification of the same amount was substituted which could be made up either in real or personal property, or in both.[2] In 1858 such property qualification was entirely abolished by a statute[3] repealing all acts upon the subject from 9 Anne, c. 5, to 41 Geo. III. c. 101.

land qualification for members abolished.

2. Just as the revolution that occurred in France in July, 1830, revived the agitation that precipitated the enactment of the first reform bill of 1832, so that which occurred in Paris in 1848 seems to have rekindled the drooping interest in the subject that brought about the enactment of the second of 1867. The support given to the efforts made by Locke King and Mr. Baines in 1851 to lower both the county and borough franchises was sufficient to make Lord John Russell admit that his original scheme was neither perfect nor final ; and in the next year he brought in a new reform bill, designed to cure defects in that measure which had been emphasized by the great increase that had taken place in twenty years in the wealth, population, and industry of the country. And yet, so absorbed was the nation at that time in more pressing events that the measure of 1852, designed not only to extend existing franchises but to create a new one, together with another more comprehensive still introduced by Lord John in 1854, was postponed without action.[4] When in 1859 the earl of Derby as the leader of the conservative party made the next move by bringing forward a bill whose central idea was not to reduce the borough franchise but to establish an identity of franchise between county and town, he was met with opposition not only in his own ranks but by Lord John himself, whose main objection rested upon the apprehension that such a principle would lead in the end to electoral districts. That objection, together with two others, he embodied in an amendment, which after a long debate was carried by a majority of thirty-nine, a result that led at once to a dissolution of parliament and an appeal to the people.[5] By the hostile verdict then rendered Lord Palmerston was inducted into office, and on March 1, 1860, Lord John as a member of his administration brought forward a

Reform bill of 1867–68 :

measures proposed by Lord Russell in 1852 and 1854 ;

Lord Derby's proposal in 1859 to establish an identity of franchise ;

---

[1] 9 Anne, c. 5; 33 Geo. II. c. 15.
[2] 1 & 2 Vict. c. 48.
[3] 21 & 22 Vict. c. 26.
[4] *Hans. Deb.*, 3d ser. vol. cxix. pp.

252, 971 ; Ibid., vol. cxxx. p. 49; Ibid., vol. cxxxi. p. 277.
[5] *Hans. Deb.*, 3d ser. vol. cliii. pp 389–1157, 1301.

reform measure which proposed to lower both the county and borough franchises, avowedly in the latter case for the benefit of the working classes, and to increase the representation of the counties and large cities without entirely disfranchising any of the smaller boroughs. But the measure failed to excite either enthusiasm or interest in or out of parliament, and under the pressure of more urgent affairs the bill was withdrawn,[1] and thus further action was postponed until the death of Lord Palmerston in October, 1865, cast the premiership upon Earl Russell as the leader of the whigs and the champion of reform.   Thus circumstanced, Lord John, with Mr. Gladstone at his side, resumed the task imposed both by honor and conscience; and in order to satisfy the long-deferred

hopes of the more advanced members of the liberal party, he introduced early in the session of 1866 a reform bill, which contemplated only a reduction of the franchise, so designed as to add at least 400,000 voters to the registers, one half of whom were to be workingmen. The failure of the measure to embrace any provision for the redistribution of seats provoked, however, serious opposition, and upon an amendment designed to cure that defect the government escaped defeat by only five votes.[2] In the face of an opposition made up not only of conservatives but of a strong body of the liberals themselves, who pretended to regard even this moderate measure as revolutionary, Earl Russell, with his party broken and disorganized, was forced to resign office, in order to make way for

the opponents of further reform under the lead of the earl of Derby, whose government found itself in a minority of seventy in the house of commons. Not until that anomalous condition of things had been reached did the awakened spirit of democracy resolve through public agitation to force its opponents to grant what it had refused to aid its friends to secure. The

Hyde Park riot of July 23, 1866, consequent upon the meeting organized by the Reform League as a demonstration in favor of an extension of the suffrage, clearly indicated the presence of the new impulse in favor of reform, and in response thereto the Derby ministry promptly indicated its pur-

---

[1] *Hans. Deb.*, 3d ser. vol. clix. p. 226.
[2] On May 7 a bill for the redistribution of seats and reform bills for Scotland and Ireland were introduced, but even that expedient did not save the original measure from defeat.

pose to offer a satisfactory scheme not as a party measure, but as a compromise that could be accepted by all. That dexterous expedient, first outlined in vague resolutions introduced by Mr. Disraeli, was on March 18 introduced in the concrete form of a bill that finally passed into law, with the aid of liberal votes, as the Representation of the People Act, 1867.[1]

Disraeli's Representation of the People Act, 1867.

While parties were thus being played off one against the other, the advanced reformers, who gave fresh emphasis to their demands by a second memorable meeting held in Hyde Park in May during the discussion upon the bill in question, were able to press upon the more conservative element claims that could not otherwise have been enforced. Thus it was that by the Representation of the People Act the electoral basis was greatly widened by an extension of the franchise to a large section of the working classes. In the counties, while no existing qualification was abolished, the qualification for a vote of owners for a life and of leaseholders was cut down from £10 to £5, and a £12 occupation qualification added. In the boroughs two most important qualifications were introduced by extending (1) what is commonly called "household suffrage" to the occupier of a dwelling-house of any value; (2) to the occupier of lodgings of £10 yearly value (unfurnished). As the dwelling-house qualification in boroughs and the £12 occupation qualification in counties were both made strictly dependent upon rating and the payment of rates, it was provided that the habit of permitting owners to be rated instead of occupiers, which had grown up under the Small Tenements Act and other acts, should cease. That part of the bill relating to electoral areas was less important. Although no borough was deprived altogether of direct representation, from thirty-eight, having less than 10,000 population, one member each was taken. The seats thus gained were redistributed by giving an additional member to Liverpool, Manchester, Birmingham, and Leeds, a member each to ten new boroughs including Chelsea, that gained two, and the remainder to thirteen counties that were further divided. A novel and peculiar feature was then introduced, providing that

Parties played off one against the other in the interest of reform;

concessions made in favor of working classes both as to county and

borough franchises;

owners not to be rated;

change in electoral areas less important;

an experiment in favor of minority elections;

---

[1] For a more complete statement of the political history see May, *Const.* *Hist.*, vol. i. pp. 450, 452, 456; vol. iii. pp. 431–440.

at a contested election for any county or borough represented by three members no person should vote for more than three candidates,[1] — an experiment in favor of minority elections.

act of 1867 extended to Scotland and Ireland;

In 1868 the Representation of the People Act was extended to Scotland by 31 and 32 Vict. c. 48 ; and to Ireland by 31 and 32 Vict. c. 49. After the acts thus extended were fully developed, they finally raised the electorate for the three kingdoms, including the universities, to a grand total of 3,183,552[2] (1885), as against 1,370,793, the highest product (1868) of the reform measures of 1832.

great increase in the electorate.

Introduction of voting by ballot;

While the second reform bill made no direct change in electoral procedure, the widening of the electorate effected by it hastened the adoption of a measure that for forty years had been the subject of discussion as a political theory. From the earliest times nominations had been made at the "hustings" in public speeches of the supporters of each candidate, and the choice of the electors was manifested in the first instance by show of hands, from which the apparently defeated candidate could appeal by demanding a poll, by means of which each elector was required to openly state his name together with that of his candidate to a poll-clerk, who recorded the result in the poll-books.[3] In order to reduce the expense, and to restrain the bribery and intimidation incident to that method of voting, — evils which tended to increase as the electoral system widened, — the advanced liberals demanded the substitution of a new system of secret voting by ballot, a proposal for a long time resisted by Lord Palmerston and the more conservative element that followed after him. In 1870, however, a ballot bill was introduced in the house of commons as a government measure ; and in the next year another was brought in and passed by that body, after prolonged discussion. As the bill reached the lords too late in the session for consideration, it was not until 1872 that the act was passed, generally known as the Ballot Act,[4] "to amend the Law relating to Procedure

the old system

involved expense, bribery, and intimidation;

a ballot bill passed the commons in 1871;

Ballot Act of 1872;

[1] "A provision which has ceased to operate by virtue of the Redistribution of Seats Act, 1885, although it has not been expressly repealed." — Lely and Foulkes, *Parl. Elec. and Reg. Acts*, p. xix.

[2] Borough electors, 1,651,732; county electors, 966,719; 310,441 electors for

Scotland; 224,018 electors for Ireland, and 30,642 electors for the universities.

[3] "Commonly afterwards printed at the cost of one or other of the parties." — Lely and Foulkes, *Parl. Elec. and Reg. Acts*, p. xx.

[4] 35 & 36 Vict. c. 33.

at Parliamentary and Municipal Elections," by virtue of which the old method of voting at such elections was superseded, except as to the universities,[1] by the new system requiring nominations in writing by ten registered electors, and a poll by secret voting taken by means of a ballot-paper, to be marked by a single X by each elector. Originally passed as a temporary measure to expire at the end of 1880, the Ballot Act has been continued by annual reënactments. *annually reënacted.*

3. The moment that the second reform bill was thus rounded out and completed by the Ballot Act of 1872, a fresh demand for a still further extension of the electoral system arose whose war-cry was "equalization," — equalization of the franchise in county and borough ; equalization of the electoral areas by such a redistribution of seats as would place the county and borough voter upon an equal plane as to representation. Not, however, until 1884 was the political understanding reached which finally transformed that demand into law. Then it was that the house of lords agreed to pass the Representation of the People Act, 1884,[2] upon the understanding that a Redistribution of Seats Act should be introduced in the lower house in 1885.[3] Thus the subject of electoral qualifications and that of electoral areas were dealt with in separate bills, and not jointly as in the acts of 1832 and 1867. By the terms of the first act, — which embraces not only England but the United Kingdom, and whose main object was to assimilate the qualification for the county vote with that already established for the borough vote,[4] — it was provided that exactly the same dwelling-house and lodgings qualification as that established in the boroughs by the act of 1867 should confer the franchise in the counties. And in order to further extend the uniformity, the county occupation qualification was reduced from £12 to £10, subject, however, to the diverse conditions of the qualifications which had been annexed in the case of boroughs by the act of 1832, and in the case of counties *Reform bills of 1884–85 : cry for "equalization ;" Representation of the People Act, 1884 ; Redistribution of Seats Act, 1885 ; county and borough franchises assimilated*

[1] As to their methods of voting, see Lely and Foulkes, *Parl. Elec. and Reg. Acts*, pp. 394, 411, 419, 424, 440.
[2] 48 Vict. c. 3.
[3] 48 & 49 Vict. c. 23.
[4] Mention should here be made of the Registration Act, 1885 (48 Vict. c. 15), which is "a corollary of the Representation of the People Act, 1884, assimilating the procedure for registration in counties to that for boroughs, in like manner as the qualification of electors had already been assimilated." — Lely and Foulkes, *Parl. Elec. and Reg. Acts*, p. xxi.

by the act of 1867. All former rights to the suffrage were reserved, subject to the same conditions as to rating, length of residence, and the like; and some electoral privileges were added in favor of service occupiers, whose tenure, not being in law a tenancy, did not cover the right to register and vote.

Effort to create equal electoral divisions to be represented by one member only; the "single-seat system" applied both to counties

By the terms of the Redistribution of Seats Act, 1885, — which became law on June 25 of that year,[1] and which deals with the electoral areas of Scotland and Ireland, as well as with those of England, — the effort was made to so reconstruct the electoral districts as to arrange them in divisions with substantially equal populations, each division to return one member only. In order to attain that result, known as the " single-seat system " of division, seventy-nine boroughs, of less than 15,000 inhabitants, were entirely disfranchised, while thirty-six, of less than 50,000 inhabitants, were reduced to one member instead of two. A redistribution was then made by splitting up all the counties into electoral districts, nearly equal in population, to each of which was given one member. Fourteen boroughs, such as Birmingham, Manchester, and Leeds, gained additional members, and thirty-five new boroughs, such

and boroughs;

as Croydon and St. Helen's, were created. The " single-seat system " was then applied as far as it could be to the larger boroughs, twenty-six of them being divided on the same plan.

the net result;

Liverpool, for instance, was split up into as many as nine divisions. " The net result is that the Act gives the [English and Welsh] counties 253 members instead of 187, and the [English and Welsh] boroughs 237 instead of 297, the proportion to population being one to 52,800 in counties instead of one to 70,800, and one to 52,700 in boroughs instead of one to 41,200, the increased representation of the counties being necessitated by the increase in the number of county electors caused by the act of 1884." [2]

number of electors and estimate of population in 1896;

In the following table [3] appears the total number of electors in the United Kingdom upon the register in 1896, together with the registrar-general's estimate of the population in the middle of the year.

---

[1] The act first named became law on December 6, 1884.

[2] Lely and Foulkes, *Parl. Elec. and Reg. Acts*, p. xxii.

[3] For parliamentary returns I am indebted to Sir Reginald Palgrave, clerk of the house of commons.

	England and Wales.	Scotland.	Ireland.	United Kingdom.
Electors . . .	5,038,818	647,178	729,473	6,415,469
Population . .	30,717,092	4,186,849	4,547,756	39,457,697

It thus appears that England and Wales are represented by one member for every 10,180 electors, Scotland by one member for every 8,988 electors, and Ireland by one member for every 7,082.

The representation in the house of commons, which has stood at 670 since 1885, is distributed as follows :— number of representatives and their distribution.

	Counties.	Boroughs.	Universities.	Total Members.
England	234	226	5	465
Wales	19	11	–	30
Scotland	39	31	2	72
Ireland	85	16	2	103
United Kingdom .	377	284	9	670

4. It is a notable fact in the history of the revolution, carried on under constitutional forms, by which the electorate of the house of commons was widened from about 400,000 voters in 1832 to 6,415,469 in 1896, that the membership of that house remained throughout substantially unchanged. Before the passing of the first reform bill, the representative chamber contained 658[1] members, and now it contains only 670. On the other hand, the notable fact in the history of the process through which the house of lords has been developed into its present form is that its membership, which at the accession of the house of Tudor numbered only 52 lay peers,[2] has been so extended as to now embrace, all told, 567.[3] Only once

Present constitution of the house of lords; trifling increase in membership of the lower house,— vast increase in that of the upper;

[1] See above, p. 541.
[2] See above, p. 28.
[3] 5 princes of the blood, 26 archbishops and bishops, 21 dukes, 22 marquesses, 117 earls, 27 viscounts, 305 barons, 16 Scottish and 28 Irish representative peers, exclusive of 15 minors. See the list in *Whitaker's Almanack* for 1897.

under the
Tudors,
about sixty
temporal
peers, who
were
under the Tudors, who restricted their creations almost exclusively to the old knightly families, did the aggregate of the
temporal peers reach the number of sixty. Before the destruction of the greater monasteries by Henry VIII. in 1539, and
the consequent withdrawal of the abbots and priors, who sat
by virtue of their baronial status as lords of parliament, the
generally
exceeded in
number by
the spirit-
ual lords,
prior to
their reduc-
tion to
twenty-six
through
destruction
of greater
monas-
teries;
lavish
creations
made by
the Stuarts;
lords spiritual generally exceeded the temporal lords in number, and even after that event the twenty-one archbishops and
bishops remaining constituted more than a third of the house.
To the twenty-one old bishoprics that thus survived Henry
VIII. added six, one of which was soon after suppressed.[1]
To the number of spiritual peers, thus finally reduced to twenty-
six, no subsequent additions have ever been made, while the
lay peers have been multiplied many-fold. Through the somewhat lavish creations made by the Stuarts, the peerage numbered at the Revolution about one hundred and fifty, — a total
raised by William III. and Queen Anne to one hundred and
sixty-eight.[2] In Anne's reign it was that by the Act of Union
Act of
Union
added six-
teen Scotch
peers;
with Scotland the upper house was further increased by the
addition, in 1707, of sixteen representative peers for that kingdom, elected at the beginning of each parliament. While no
Scotch
peerage per-
petuated to
elect them;
new Scotch peers were to be created after the union, the
Scotch peerage, which then numbered one hundred and fifty-
four, was perpetuated in its integrity as an aristocratic body
endowed with the right to chose from their own ranks the
requisite number to speak for them at Westminster. An account has already been given of the unconstitutional attempt
made by the whigs in 1720 to secure their hold upon the
upper house by limiting the power of the crown to add to its
membership.[3] After the failure of that audacious effort to
make the hereditary chamber a close aristocratic body, inde-
at the end
of reign of
George II.
peerage
numbered
about one
hundred
and sev-
enty-four.
pendent of the crown and irresponsible to the nation, George
I. and George II. continued to add to its ranks by so moderate
an exercise of the peer-creating power vested in the crown
that at the end of the reign of the latter the peerage numbered
only one hundred and seventy-four, of which thirteen minors
and twelve Roman Catholics were incapable of sitting and
voting in parliament.[4]

---

[1] See above, p. 90, and notes 3, 6.

[2] Macaulay, *Hist. Eng.*, vol. iv. p.
753; May, *Const. Hist.*, vol. i. p. 274.

[3] See above, p. 459.

[4] *Court and City Register* for 1760.

During the long reign of George III. it was that the peer-creating power was employed on such a gigantic scale that the total number of actual creations during a period of sixty years, including the promotions of certain peers to a higher grade, amounted to three hundred and eighty-eight,[1] a number slightly greater than the total number of the hereditary peers of the United Kingdom in 1860, exclusive of the peers of the blood-royal. While this new policy of wholesale creations was inaugurated by the king himself as a means of drawing around him the personal coterie with whose aid he hoped to break down the then existing system of party government, the plan was enlarged and developed by Pitt, who, in order to consolidate his own political authority, created or promoted during the seventeen years of his first administration about one hundred and forty peers, sitting by hereditary right.[2] That fact does not, however, preclude the idea that the ambitious minister who scorned all such honors for himself was also animated by nobler ends. Certain it is that a great change for the better was thus wrought in the constitution of a body which up to that time "had been a small assembly of great nobles, bound together by family or party ties into a distinct power in the state. By pouring into it members of the middle and commercial class, who formed the basis of his political power, small landowners, bankers, merchants, nabobs, army contractors, lawyers, soldiers, and seamen, Pitt revolutionized the upper house. It became the stronghold, not of blood, but of property, the representative of the great estates and great fortunes which the vast increase of English wealth was building up. For the first time, too, in our history, it became the distinctively conservative element in our constitution."[3] But apart from the hereditary creations which Pitt promoted and which his successors continued, must be considered the twenty-eight representative peers which he added to the parliament of the United Kingdom through the union with Ireland in 1801. Under that arrangement the Irish peerage, which at that time

Increase of the peerage under George III.:

policy inaugurated by the king,

and expanded by Pitt;

a great change for the better wrought by the addition of new elements;

twenty-eight Irish peers added in 1801;

---

[1] Between 1761 and 1821 were created 11 dukes, 19 marquesses, 75 earls, 66 viscounts, 217 barons, according to a table prepared by Mr. Pulman, Clarencieux King of Arms, and printed by May, *Const. Hist.*, vol. i. p. 283. See also p. 279.

[2] Beatson's *Political Index*, vol. i. p. 149, *et seq.*

[3] Green, *Hist. of the Eng. People*, vol. iv. p. 322.

numbered two hundred and thirty-four members, was permitted to elect twenty-eight representatives, not as in Scotland for the parliament only, but for life; while the Irish episcopate, then consisting of twenty bishops and archbishops,[1] was authorized to send to the upper house four of their number,[2] to sit by rotation of sessions. It was further provided that Irish peers should be eligible for the house of commons for any place in Great Britain. On the other hand, in order to gradually reduce the Irish peerage, which was admitted to be too large, it was provided that one Irish peer only can be created, when three such peerages in existence at the time of the union have become extinct. And that process is to be kept up until the total number shall be reduced to one hundred, at which figure it shall be maintained by the creation of one Irish peerage for every one that shall become extinct, or as often as an Irish peer shall become entitled, by descent or creation, to a peerage of the United Kingdom.

to sit for life;

four spiritual peers to sit by rotation;

scheme to reduce Irish peerage

to one hundred members.

Fusion of Scotch and Irish peerages with English;

While the Scotch and Irish peerages are thus permitted to survive under different conditions as distinct bodies, both are gradually losing their identity through a process of fusion naturally resulting from the principle of incorporation upon which the legislatures of the lesser kingdoms were merged into the imperial parliament. In 1711 the English lords attempted to resist that tendency by denying the right of the duke of Hamilton, who was a peer of Scotland at the time of the union, to sit and vote in their house by virtue of a patent raising him to the peerage of Great Britain as the duke of Brandon.[3] While the determination barred for many years the direct admission of any other Scottish peers, it was first evaded by a clever device,[4] and then in 1782 entirely set aside by a decision of the judges, who held as a matter of law that the Act of Union did not prevent the promotion of Scottish peers to the peerage of the United Kingdom.[5] Not long after

English lords resisted the tendency in duke of Hamilton's case;

precedent set aside by the judges in 1782;

---

[1] By 3 & 4 Will. IV. c. 37, Schedule B, provision was made for the reduction of that number to ten.

[2] When the Church of Ireland was disestablished in 1869, these bishops lost their seats.

[3] *Lords' Journals*, vol. xix. p. 346; Peere Williams, vol. i. p. 582.

[4] Their eldest sons were created peers, and then upon the death of their fathers, they were permitted to succeed to their Scotch peerages. Walpole's *Memoirs of George III.*, vol. ii. p. 412.

[5] The lords thereupon reversed their decision made in 1711. *Lords' Journals*, vol. xxxvi. p. 517.

that point had been settled, the earl of Abercorn and the duke of Queensbury, who were then sitting as representative peers of Scotland, were raised to the peerage of Great Britain, whereupon the house decided in 1787 that they thereby lost not only their representative character, but also the right to vote as Scottish peers for their successors, under a resolution of the house passed in 1708.[1] In 1793 that resolution was superseded, and since then all Scotch peers have been permitted to vote for their representatives.[2] The existence of that right cannot, however, change the fact that through the admission of Scottish peers to hereditary seats in the British house of lords the ancient peerage of Scotland will soon be absorbed into that of the United Kingdom, except the sixteen, who may in the end find it more convenient to be disposed of in that way than to perpetuate themselves by self-election. So rapidly has the process already advanced that "there are now no less than 45 peers of Scotland with such hereditary seats, and by this process of absorption, as well as by extinctions and dormancies, the number of peers of Scotland who have not hereditary seats in the house of lords has been diminished from 154 in 1707 to 34 in 1875. Out of these 34 Scottish peers 16 have seats as representative peers, leaving only 18 without seats in the house of lords. Of the 45 absorptions, 39 have taken place since the beginning of the present century. At that rate, and without taking into account possible extinctions, the 18 peers may be absorbed in about 35 years' time. . . . The peerage of Ireland, which in 1801 numbered 234, has been reduced by extinctions, and notwithstanding the creation of 19 post-union peers, to 185. Of these, no less than 81 are now peers of the United Kingdom. Of the remaining 104, who are solely peers of Ireland, 28 are representative peers, thus leaving 76 without seats in the house of lords. Since the union there have been 66 extinctions, in addition to 81 absorptions into the peerage of the United Kingdom. If the same average rates of extinction and absorption should continue, the 76 peerages now without seats may be expected to be extinguished or absorbed in about 39 years."[3]

marginal notes: cases of Abercorn and Queensbury; since 1793 all Scotch peers have been permitted to vote for representatives; Scotch peerage will soon be absorbed; rapid advance of the process; extinction and absorption of Irish peerage;

[1] *Lords' Journals*, vol. xxxvii. p. 594; *Parl. Hist.*, vol. xxvi. p. 596.
[2] Ibid., vol. xxxix. p. 726; May, *Const. Hist.*, vol. i. pp. 286–290.
[3] *Law Magazine and Review*, No. ccxx., May, 1876, art. "The Representative Peerage of Scotland and Ireland," by the late T. P. Taswell-Langmead.

nationaliz-
ing effect of
the process.
Through this process of absorption, which is continually destroying one of the great landmarks dividing the three peoples, the house of lords is growing more national and more representative of the idea of indivisible sovereignty which it is intended to embody.

Political
status of
the upper
house since
reform bill
of 1832;
The greatest event in the history of the peerage of the United Kingdom occurred when the resistance interposed by the upper house to the passage of the reform bill of 1832 put in issue the fact whether or no that body is still a coördinate branch of the legislature in the full sense of that term. As heretofore pointed out, the growth of the modern ministerial system, as the agent of the supreme power vested in the

effect of
Revolution
of 1688
upon
literary
theory of
the consti-
tution;
house of commons by the Revolution of 1688, entirely destroyed the old literary theory that the English constitution embodies three balanced and coördinate powers, legislative, executive, and judicial.[1] From the time when the representative chamber, through its great committee known as the cabinet, possessed itself of the right to exercise the royal prerogatives in the name of the crown, a condition of things was

fusion of
the execu-
tive and
legislative
powers;
brought about which "is not an absorption of the executive power by the legislative power; it is a fusion of the two. Either the cabinet legislates and acts, or else it can dissolve. It is a creature, but it has the power of destroying its creators. It is an executive which can annihilate the legislature, as well as an executive which is the nominee of the legislature."[2] The

difficulty
growing
out of this
new con-
ception of
sover-
eignty;
only difficulty that stood in the path of this new and complex conception of sovereignty vested in the popular chamber was the peculiar constitution of the house of lords, whose composition could not be affected by a dissolution. Only by the exercise of the peer-creating power of the crown could the political complexion of the hereditary chamber be changed, and that might require, if exercised in the usual way, half a century. When, therefore, the time came to overcome the opposition of the lords to the fixed resolve of the nation to emancipate the

lower house
can coerce
upper
through
peer-creat-
ing power.
representative system from their control, the lower house seized upon the one possible expedient that could insure that result without the destruction of the outward forms of the constitution itself. That expedient consisted of the creation by

---

[1] See above, pp. 435–440. See below, p. 593.

[2] Bagehot, *The English Constitution*, p. 15.

the representative chamber through its agent the crown of a sufficient number of peers to overcome the opposition to its sovereign will.　When the creation of sixteen peers failed to produce the desired result, the ministry demanded of the king a promise to make such wholesale creations as would if necessary "swamp the house of lords," and upon his refusal they resigned office.　Under that pressure the crown was forced to give way, and the upper house, as heretofore explained, bowed to the national will without further resistance, and thus abdicated its claims as a coördinate branch of the legislature.[1]　The duke of Wellington may have been right in declaring the threatened exercise of this extraordinary peer-creating power to be revolutionary, but as such it was only the inevitable consequence of the greater revolution of which it was a mere corollary.　As Earl Grey well said in reply, "If a majority of this house is to have the power, whenever they please, of opposing the declared and decided wishes both of the crown and the people, without any means of modifying that power, then this country is placed entirely under the influence of an uncontrollable oligarchy."[2]　The practical outcome of the conflict was that the house of lords should continue to exist under the tacit understanding that it would always bow to the will of the nation in the last resort, after that will has been clearly and finally expressed by the popular branch of the legislature.　"Since the Reform Act, the house of lords has become a revising and suspending house.　It can alter bills; it can reject bills on which the house of commons is not yet thoroughly in earnest, — upon which the nation is not yet determined.　Their veto is a sort of hypothetical veto.　They say, We reject your bill for this once or these twice, or even these thrice; but if you keep on sending it up, at last we won't reject it."[3]

When in 1856 a fresh assault was made upon the constitution of the upper house through the efforts of the crown to reëstablish at that time its right to create life peerages, it was successfully resisted.　That such a right had once existed during the period between the reigns of Richard II. and Henry VI. could not be doubted,[4] but against that fact the argument

Marginal notes: ministry resigned when crown refused to "swamp the house of lords;" lords ceased to be a coördinate branch of the legislature; Earl Grey's statement; house of lords as a revising and suspending chamber. Creation of life peerages successfully resisted;

[1] See above, p. 539.
[2] *Hans. Deb.*, 3d ser. vol. xii. pp. 995, 1006.
[3] Bagehot, *The English Constitution*, p. 100.
[4] See the cases collected in the Re-

right not
exercised
for four
centuries,
with certain
exceptions; was opposed that it had not been exercised during a period of four hundred years, except in the cases of certain ladies endowed in the mean time with life peerages, as mere titles of honor, without the right to sit in parliament. While the constitutional lawyers admitted that the position of the crown could not be strengthened by cases of that character, they, relying upon the maxim *Nullum tempus occurrit regi*, contended that the immemorial right of the crown to create life peerages, although long suspended, had not been lost. They
Coke's
claim that
the crown
could create
peerages
"for life, in
tail or in
fee;" said that Coke had often declared that the crown could create peerages "for life, in tail or in fee," and that doctrine had been accepted as unquestionable law not only by Comyns, Cruise, and Blackstone, but by Lord Redesdale's famous committee "On the Dignity of a Peer."[1] Thus armed, the ministers of the crown, in the hope of improving the appellate jurisdiction of the upper house, which for a long time had been
patent to
Baron
Wensley-
dale, "for
and during
the term of
his natural
life;" sadly deficient in judicial learning, resolved to make a beginning by creating Sir James Parke, lately an eminent baron of the exchequer, Baron Wensleydale, "for and during the term of his natural life." As all temporal peers, whether English, Scotch, or Irish, and whether sitting by hereditary right or by election, claimed that they, having been ennobled in blood, possessed the right to transmit their dignities to their heirs, a majority of them resolved to resist this unusual creation as an assault upon the constitution of the house as a whole. Therefore, after a great speech from Lord Lyndhurst, the patent of
referred to
committee
of privi-
leges;
adverse
report
confirmed
by the
lords; Baron Wensleydale was in February, 1856, referred to the committee of privileges by a decided majority; and after a careful examination of the precedents, that committee reported and the house agreed "that neither the letters patent, nor the letters patent with the usual writ of summons issued in pursuance thereof, can entitle the grantee to sit and vote in parliament."[2] As a bill passed shortly after by the lords themselves authorizing the crown to confer life peerages upon two persons who had served for five years as judges miscarried in the lower house, the judgment of the upper that such creations cannot properly be made without the supreme authority of the

port of the Committee on Privileges, 1856.

[1] Steph. Blackstone, vol. ii.; May, *Const. Hist.*, vol. i. p. 294.

[2] *Hans. Deb.*, 3d ser. vol. cxl. pp. 263, 1152, *et seq.*; Clark's *House of Lords Cases*, vol. v. p. 958.

legislature has since been accepted as a sound exposition of constitutional law. Upon that basis an act [1] was passed twenty years later constituting two lords of appeal in ordinary, who were intended to aid the upper house, as law lords with the rank of baron for life, but with the right of sitting and voting only during their tenure of office.

accepted as a settlement of the question; such creations only made by statutory authority.

Such in short is the present status of that ancient assembly whose identity can be traced for a period of a thousand years through the great councils of the Norman and Angevin reigns back to the witenagemots of the earliest times. While during that marvellous process of unbroken development the elements composing it have been constantly changing, the assembly itself has been able to preserve throughout its corporate character. With that truth clearly in view the statement should surprise no one, that of the 507 [2] hereditary peerages of the United Kingdom at present existing, 111 were created during the reign of George III.; 32 in the reign of George IV.; 30 in the reign of William IV.; and 242 in the reign of Queen Victoria. Thus of the existing peerages only 92 are older than the accession of George III., — an imperfect criterion of the antiquity of the peerage, which should be qualified by the fact that, "when the possessor of an ancient dignity is promoted to a higher grade in the peerage, his lesser dignity becomes merged in the greater, but more recent title." [3] Although the ancient rule of procedure, which authorized the peers to vote by proxy, was voluntarily surrendered in 1868, they still uphold the right of any three members to constitute a quorum, any two of whom are competent to pass or reject a law so long as their unanimity conceals the defect in their organization. While the "indifference to business" — which has often induced the lords to commit their ordinary powers of legislation to a number so small as to appear merely as a select committee of the whole — has subjected them to well-merited reproach, no one who has witnessed their proceedings

Corporate identity of upper house traceable through a thousand years; its elements constantly changing;

creations during the last four reigns;

only 92 of the existing peerages older than the accession of George III.;

peers no longer vote by proxy, but three still constitute a quorum, any two of whom may pass or reject a law;

---

[1] 39 & 40 Vict. 59. For a definition of lords of appeal under the Appellate Jurisdiction Act, 1876, see Lely and Foulkes, *Judicature Acts*, pp. 99, 100.

[2] Including 15 minors not sitting. Total number of upper house 567. Excluding 5 princes of the blood, 26 archbishops and bishops, 16 Scottish and 28 Irish representative peers, the number of hereditary peers sitting is 492. That is for the year 1897, according to the data contained in the list of the peerage in *Whitaker's Almanack* for that year.

[3] May, *Const. Hist.*, vol. i. p. 282.

spirited
proceedings
on great
occasions. upon great occasions when their best orators are stirred by the spirit of high debate can fail to admit, despite any prejudices that may possess him, that he is in the presence of a real senate, "whose years are awful and whose words are wise."

The cabinet, and its relations to the crown and the legislature; 5. From the beginning of its history to the present time the inner circle of the privy council, conventionally known as the "cabinet," has been the agent of the supreme executive power, discharging its functions through the exercise of those attributes known to the law as the royal prerogatives.[1] When that supreme authority was in fact vested in the sovereign himself, the ministers composing the cabinet were his personal appointees, responsible to him alone for the discharge of their duties, and dismissable at his pleasure.   When the Revolution transfer of sovereignty to commons worked no outward change in the constitution; of 1688 transferred the supreme executive power from the person of the sovereign to the majority in the house of commons, there was no change made whatever in the outward forms of the existing system.   The new sovereign thus created cabinet continued as agent of the new sovereign; simply continued the cabinet as its agent, with the understanding that it should exercise the royal prerogatives as before in the name of the old sovereign, but only in such manner as it should direct.   Out of that anomalous condition of things in which the ostensible sovereignty is vested in the crown and the real sovereignty in the majority of a popular assembly, does any real authority still reside in the old? the question has arisen whether or no there still resides in the ostensible sovereign any personal authority whatever.   A striking illustration of the extreme views entertained upon that subject by the house of commons can be found in the incident Bedchamber question of 1839; known as the "Bedchamber question," raised by Sir Robert Peel when he was called upon to form a government upon the resignation of the Melbourne ministry in 1839.   As nearly all the ladies of the household were related to the outgoing ministers, or to their dependents, Sir Robert, unwilling to be embarrassed by difficulties incident to the nearness of his political Peel's demand of the queen; adversaries to the person of the sovereign, informed the queen that the ministerial changes would necessarily embrace some of the higher offices of her court held by ladies, including the ladies of the bedchamber.   After consultation with Lord John

---

[1] For an enumeration of the royal prerogatives and a legal definition of them, see Kerr's *Blackstone*, vol. i. pp. 213–254.

Russell and Lord Melbourne, the queen embodied her refusal to comply with such a demand in a letter to Sir Robert Peel, in which she informed him that she could not "consent to adopt a course which she conceived to be contrary to usage, and which was repugnant to her feelings." [1] Sir Robert thereupon refused to accept office on any other terms, and thus the Melbourne ministry was for more than two years continued in power. When, however, a subsequent resignation in 1841 forced the sovereign to again call upon Sir Robert to form a government, the principle for which he contended was admitted, and an arrangement was then made "which has now long prevailed. The Mistress of the Robes, who is not periodically resident at the Court, but only an attendant on great occasions, changes with the Ministry; the Ladies in Waiting, who enjoy much more of personal contact by virtue of their office with the Sovereign, are appointed, and continue in their appointments, without regard to the political connections of their husbands." [2]

her refusal to comply and its result;

Peel's victory in 1841;

understanding that has since governed.

A much more important incident of the same general character arose in 1850 out of an attempt made by Lord Palmerston, as minister for foreign affairs, to resist not only the personal right of the sovereign, but of the prime minister and the rest of his colleagues, to supervise and control the details of the department over which he presided. In order to reduce the controversy to a definite issue, the queen directed Lord John Russell to deliver to Lord Palmerston the following memorandum: "The queen requires, first, that Lord Palmerston will distinctly state what he proposes in a given case, in order that the queen may know as distinctly to what she gives her royal sanction. Secondly, having once giving her sanction to a measure, that it be not arbitrarily altered or modified by the Minister. Such an act she must consider as failing in sincerity towards the crown, and justly to be visited by the exercise of her constitutional right of dismissing that minister.

What is due to the sovereign and prime minister from the minister of foreign affairs;

memorandum delivered to Lord Palmerston in 1850;

[1] *Hans. Deb.*, 3d ser. vol. xlvii. p. 985. "The queen, in her letter, mentions, and refuses, the proposal of Sir Robert Peel 'to remove the ladies of her Bedchamber.' Sir Robert Peel, in his answer, speaks only of his desire to remove a portion of them. . . . She declined to remove them as a body;

he resigns his charge, because he is not allowed to remove a few among them." — Gladstone, *Gleanings of Past Years*, vol. i. p. 40. The record of the transaction in Hansard rests in the main upon these two letters.

[2] *Ibid.*, vol. i. p. 40.

She expects to be kept informed of what passes between him and the foreign ministers before important decisions are taken, based upon that intercourse ; to receive the foreign despatches in good time ; and to have the drafts for her approval sent to her in sufficient time to make herself acquainted with their contents before they must be sent off.   The queen thinks it best that Lord John Russell should show this letter to Lord Palmerston." [1]   Although the latter, upon receiving this warning, promised "that he would punctually obey the directions contained in it," he sent shortly after to the representative of Austria a note containing a paragraph which both the queen and the prime minister considered as "derogatory to the honor of England, as well as discourteous to Austria."   When the premier insisted that the note should be recalled and another substituted without the offensive paragraph, Lord Palmerston, after threatening to resign, submitted.   But after the French *coup d'état* of the 2d of December, 1851, he again fell from grace by stating upon his own responsibility to the French ambassador "his entire approbation of the act of the President, and his conviction that he could not have acted otherwise than he had done," despite the fact that the cabinet as a whole had agreed upon a policy of non-intervention.   Lord Palmerston was thereupon removed from office, not only because he had exceeded his authority as secretary of state, but also because he had taken upon himself alone the right to speak for the whole government.   Thus the doctrine was clearly settled that the prime minister, with the consent of the crown, controls all state affairs as the recognized medium of communication between the sovereign and the heads of the several departments ; and that the prime minister and the cabinet can exercise through the crown the right to dismiss any minister who does not accept the will of the government as a whole.[2]   To prevent such conflicts in the conduct of foreign affairs, the practice now is for the drafts of despatches to be agreed upon between the prime minister and the for-

his offer to comply ;

his second submission ;

his conflict with the cabinet in 1851 by reason of statement to French ambassador ;

removed from office for exceeding his authority ;

premier, with consent of the crown, controls all state affairs ;

right of dismissal ;

present practice as to drafts of despatches.

---

[1] *Hans. Deb.*, 3d ser. vol. cxix. p. 90 ; Martin, *Pr. Consort*, vol. ii. pp. 302-310.

[2] The position of the prime minister has been thus defined : "As the cabinet stands between the sovereign and the parliament, and is bound to be loyal to both, so he stands between his colleagues and the sovereign, and is bound to be loyal to both." — Gladstone, *Gleanings of Past Years*, vol. i. p. 243.

eign secretary before they are submitted for the sovereign's approval; [1] and if the former sees fit to rewrite the whole despatch, the latter has no right to be offended. [2]

While thus considering the vestiges of political authority still inherent in the person of the sovereign, it will be convenient to briefly epitomize the financial arrangements made by parliament since the Revolution for the maintenance of the royal dignity and household. An account has heretofore been given of the nearly absolute control established by the legislature at the accession of William and Mary over the revenue, involving both the appropriation of supplies and the direction of their expenditure, — a system out of which arose what is known as the "civil list," a term originally used to designate the sources of revenue appropriated to produce a fund to be devoted to the king's personal expenses, the support of the royal household, and to the payment of certain civil officers and pensions embraced in a list that was laid before the house. The principle was thus settled that out of the annual revenue voted for the support of the crown in time of peace a certain portion should be appropriated to those objects, and that portion embraced the hereditary revenues and a certain part of the excise heretofore specially defined. [3] During the reigns of Queen Anne and George I. their expenditures far exceeded the sums thus appropriated, and parliament was called upon to pay the loans made to cover such deficits. [4] When the hereditary revenues were passed on to George II., it was expressly agreed that if they should fall below £800,000 a year parliament should pay the deficit, and that if they exceeded that sum the king should have the surplus. [5] As that arrangement proved unsatisfactory, parliament upon the accession of George III. induced him to accept a fixed amount "for the support of his household and the honour and dignity of the crown," [6] in consideration of which he relinquished his

Margin notes:
Maintenance of royal dignity and household;

parliamentary control over the revenue since the Revolution;

"civil list" defined;

principle of appropriation settled;

during the reigns of Anne and George I. expenditures exceeded appropriations;

contingent arrangement upon accession of George II.;

George III., for a fixed sum, surrendered all claim to hereditary revenue;

---

[1] Gladstone, *Ch. Quar. Rev.*, vol. iii. p. 481.

[2] Lord Russell testified that when Lord Palmerston was premier and he minister of foreign affairs (1859 to 1865), "according to the uniform practice of the foreign office, the despatches which I wrote were submitted to him as prime minister; frequently he would write the whole despatch over again, and I was always ready to accept his draft." — *Hans. Deb.*, 3d ser. vol. ccvi. p. 1833. Cf. Todd's *Parl. Government*, vol. ii. pp. 18, 19.

[3] See above, pp. 419, 420.

[4] 1 Geo. I. c. 1; Burke's *Works*, vol. ii. p. 309.

[5] 1 Geo. II. c. 1.

[6] *Commons' Journals*, vol. xxviii. p. 28.

life interest in the hereditary revenues, and all claim to the surplus.[1] A further arrangement was necessary, however, to make the control of parliament complete, for the reason that the king still enjoyed considerable sums independent of its grants in the form of droits of the crown and admiralty and other casual sources of revenue in England, in addition to certain hereditary revenues in Scotland and a separate civil list for Ireland.[2] Not until the accession of William IV. did the crown surrender all of these independent sources of revenue in consideration of a civil list of £510,000, which represented a reduction by reason of the fact that it was then relieved of nearly all of the charges that properly belonged to the ordinary expenses of civil government.[3] Upon that basis of absolute parliamentary control was settled the civil list [4] of Queen Victoria, the first sovereign of her house to be deprived of the revenue of the kingdom of Hanover, detached at her accession from the crown of England.

William IV. surrendered all independent sources of revenue for a civil list of £510,000; parliament's absolute control over civil list of present sovereign.

In the account heretofore given of the royal revenue as it existed in the days of the Old-English commonwealth, the fact was emphasized that it was not contingent upon legislative grants.   In addition to the private estates (*propria hereditas*) which he possessed as an individual and which he could dispose of by will, the king enjoyed the use of the royal demesne, which belonged to him as king, and which he could neither burden nor alienate without the consent of the witan, and also certain dues in the nature of rent which finally became compulsory charges, certainly upon all holders of folkland.   The distinction thus clearly drawn between the king's private estates and the folkland, the land of the people, gradually dis-

Royal revenue originally independent of legislative grants; of what it originally consisted; how the distinction between king's private estate and folkland disappeared;

---

1 1 Geo. III. c. 1. He surrendered "the hereditary revenues, which were carried to the Fund termed 'the Aggregate Fund,' receiving a grant of 800,000 *l.* per annum secured on the Fund." — Dowell, *Hist. of Taxation*, vol. ii. p. 507. When that amount was found to be inadequate, it was increased to £900,000.   17 Geo. III. c. 21.

2 For the history of these sources, see May, *Const. Hist.*, vol. i. pp. 235–245.

3 Report on Civil Government Charges, 1831, 1 Geo. IV. c. 1.   The £510,000 was appropriated to their

majesties' privy purse, salaries of the household, expenses of the household, special and secret service, and pensions.   "The term civil list was retained as a convenient short term to designate this expenditure, though the civil list, properly so termed, no longer was included therein." — Dowell, *Hist. of Taxation*, vol. ii. p. 511.

4 Its amount was then fixed at £385,000, with the item of £75,000 for pensions omitted. Pensions granted under the Civil List Act, 1 Vict. c. 2, had increased the original amount to £409,000 in 1884–85.

appeared, however, as the idea gained ground that the king of the whole nation was the lord of the whole people, and as such was possessed of their land as *terra regis.* With the full development of feudalism after the conquest, the artificial conception gained ground that all land was originally held of the crown by feudal tenures; and the revenue thus flowing from the national domain, considered as the private patrimony of the king, was swelled by the feudal incidents into great proportions.[1] Not until the accession of Queen Anne was the process through which the land revenues of the crown had been wasted for centuries by improvident alienations checked by an act of parliament, in which the confession was made that such revenues had already been so reduced that they "could then afford very little towards the support of her government."[2] By that act all absolute alienations were positively prohibited, and stringent limitations imposed upon the making of all future leases, which were to be granted for a term not longer than thirty-one years, or three lives.[3] As a final settlement of the whole matter, parliament, in the arrangement made with George III. for the support of his household and of the royal dignity, stipulated that the crown should surrender to the nation all that remained of its land revenues in exchange for the civil list then secured to him.[4] Thus were the royal demesnes "handed over to be dealt with like the other revenues of the state, to be disposed of by parliament for the public service. That is to say, the people have won back their own; . . . the *terra regis* of the Norman has once more become the folkland of our earliest freedom."[5] And in accordance with the precedents of those early times, the sovereign was again endowed by law with the right to acquire and dispose of private property like any other individual.[6] As an exception to the arrangement thus made, the crown has been permitted to retain the revenues of the duchies of Lancaster

[marginal notes:] feudal theory that all land was originally held of the crown; in Queen Anne's reign waste of land revenues of the crown checked by statute; limitations then imposed on royal grants; complete surrender finally made by George III.; terra regis converted into folkland; sovereign now empowered to deal with property like any other individual.

---

[1] Vol. i. pp. 178, 182, 233, 236, 383.

[2] 1 Anne, c. 7, s. 5.

[3] And even in that event a reasonable rent was to be reserved.

[4] See above, p. 551.

[5] Freeman, *Growth of the Eng. Const.*, p. 140.

[6] Cf. 39 & 40 Geo. III. c. 88; 4 Geo. IV. c. 18; 25 & 26 Vict. c. 37. "As our present sovereign in so many other respects holds the place of Ælfred rather than the place of the Richards and Henries of later times, so she again holds the right which Ælfred held, of acquiring and disposing of private property, like any other member of the nation." — Freeman, *Growth of the Eng. Const.*, p. 143. See, also, Allen, *Royal Prerogative*, pp. 154, 155.

and Cornwall, — the former the property of the reigning sovereign, the latter the independent inheritance of the prince of Wales, as duke of Cornwall.

Origin of cabinet officers and method of their distribution;

Before attempting to explain the delicate relations that bind the cabinet to the legislature, it may be well to indicate briefly the origin of the offices usually allotted to its members, and the manner in which such offices are distributed by the crown through the prime minister as its immediate representative.

in theory, sovereign personally chooses premier, and he his colleagues; in fact, sovereign's right to choose premier very limited;

The theory is that the sovereign personally chooses the prime minister, and that he selects his colleagues subject to the crown's approval. The fact is that the crown can choose only one of the few great leaders of the two historic parties as prime minister, and he in turn is limited in his choice to the under chiefs in his own ranks who stand next to him in the public confidence. "Between the compulsory list, whom he must take, and the impossible list, whom he cannot take, a prime minister's independent choice in the formation of the cabinet is not very large; it extends rather to the division of the cabinet offices than to the choice of cabinet ministers." [1]

number of cabinet settled by premier;

The number of the cabinet, which is variable, is determined by the prime minister himself with the consent of the sovereign. [2] The first of George III. consisted of fourteen members, of whom only one was a commoner; [3] and in 1785 that number was reduced by Mr. Pitt to seven, all of whom had seats in the house of lords except himself. [4] After his time it became customary for the cabinet to consist of from ten to sixteen members, — a number "as large as it ought to be, and it seems to be generally adopted as such by both parties." [5] The officers of state who according to modern usage generally compose the cabinet are the lord chancellor, the president of the council, the privy seal, the first lord of the treasury, the chancellor of the exchequer, the five principal secretaries of state for the home, foreign, colonial, war, and Indian departments, the first lord of the admiralty, the president of the

officers of state who usually compose the cabinet;

1 Bagehot, *The Eng. Const.*, p. 12.
2 Mahon, *Hist. of Eng.*, vol. i. p. 153.
3 There were eight of ducal rank, and five earls. Jesse, *Life of George III.*, vol. i. p. 59.
4 Stanhope's *Life of Pitt*, vol. i. pp. 71, 165.

5 Lord Granville, Rep. Com. on Education, *Com. Pap.*, 1865, vol. vi.; Evid. 1883; Todd, *Parl. Government*, vol. i. p. 283. The number is, however, increasing. The present cabinet of Lord Salisbury consists of twenty members. See the list in *Whitaker's Almanack* for 1897, p. 150.

Board of Trade, the chancellor of the duchy of Lancaster, and the president of the Local Government Board.[1] It is hardly necessary to add that some of these offices are very ancient, some of the while others are of quite modern creation. The attempt has offices very ancient; heretofore been made to show how it was that the council, through the decline in the influence of the nobles as leaders of the nation, was gradually transformed from an independent body that stood as a bridle upon the will of the king into a mere corps of trained officials subject to his direction. While the nobles still retained the hereditary offices with ever dimin- hereditary ishing duties, the council was continually reinforced by com- offices with diminishing moners, who during the days of Henry VIII. and Elizabeth duties; began to assume the more active duties of administration.[2] In the course of the transition from that state of things to the modern ministerial system a few of the ancient great offices a few have have been retained; others have been dissolved and their survived, while others duties distributed; while in order to meet the requirements of have been dissolved; new conditions, others have been very recently created. Four four officers officers of state of the first class who usually form a part of who usually enter into all modern cabinets are the lord chancellor, whose duties are all cabinets. political as well as judicial; the president of the council, who serves without a portfolio in order to perpetuate an honorary political station whose importance has dwindled with that of the council as a whole: the lord privy seal, who seals warrants for the great seal and as such is at the head of a ministerial as distinguished from an administrative department; and the chancellor of the duchy of Lancaster.[3]

The vast income and expenditure of the British Empire, an British estimate of which is annually laid before the house of com- finances managed by mons in a balance sheet called "The Budget," is managed by a a depart- ment that department of finance which has grown out of the dissolution arose out of of the ancient office of lord treasurer, who in the seventeenth dissolution of the century frequently appears as the leading minister of state. office of lord During that century the administration of the office was car- treasurer; ried on at intervals by a commissioner;[4] and since the reign

[1] The lord lieutenant and the lord chancellor of Ireland are sometimes members.

[2] See above, p. 177.

[3] The lord chamberlain is an hered-itary officer without administration.

The lord high constable, whose office became extinct as an hereditary office in 1521, is created only for one day at the coronation.

[4] As in 1612, 1635, 1641, 1658, and 1679.

since the
accession of
George I.,
its duties
have been
vested in
a board
consisting
of a first
and junior
lords, and
chancellor
of the
exchequer;

Bank of
England
the de-
pository;

sources of
the annual
income
known as
"consol-
idated
fund;"

nearly four
fifths of it
derived
from per-
manent
acts;

only one
fifth derived
from annual
acts;

comp-
troller and
auditor-
general;

of George I. its powers and duties have been vested in a board consisting of a first lord commissioner, who has a general control of the department without any special connection with the details of finance ; of three or four junior lords selected from parliament to aid in administrative work ; and of the chancellor of the exchequer, who as the maker of budgets is the real head of the treasury and the moulder of its policy.[1]   The actual guardian of the national revenue is the Bank of England, into which it is paid to the "account of Her Majesty's Exchequer"[2] mainly through the Inland Revenue Office, a place where the bulk of the taxes are collected in the first instance. The total annual income known as the "consolidated fund," amounting now to about £100,000,000, which thus finds its way into the bank is the product (1) of the hereditary or "ordinary" revenue, surrendered absolutely to the state by William IV. in exchange for a definite civil list as heretofore explained, and (2) of the "extraordinary" revenue, levied by acts of parliament either temporary or permanent.   And here the fact should be emphasized that nearly four fifths of the entire annual revenue is derived from the proceeds of such taxes as the land tax, the excise, the stamp duties, and the like, which are levied by permanent acts that would remain in force though parliament should not be convened for years.   Only the remaining one fifth, composed in the main of the income tax and the tea duties, is derived from taxes imposed by annual acts.[3] Not a penny of the vast sums thus collected under the authority of statute law can be expended except under the authority of some act of parliament, either annual or permanent.   In order to secure the faithful enforcement of such acts regulating the disbursement of the public revenue, the Exchequer and Audit Department has been created, at whose head stands the comptroller and auditor-general, who is a non-partisan, independent officer, whose tenure is good behavior, and who can-

---

[1] Upon the recommendation of a commission of inquiry into the public accounts in 1831 (*Com. Pap.*, 1857, sess. 2, vol. ix. p. 569) was passed 4 & 5 Will. IV. c. 15, s. 2, whereby the ancient office of the exchequer was reformed and its functions more clearly defined. Several subordinate offices were abolished, and all prescriptive powers and duties transferred to the comptroller-general.

[2] Exchequer and Audit Dept. Act, 1866 (29 & 30 Vict. c. 39), s. 10.

[3] "The receipts of these taxes for the year 1887–88 amounted, in round numbers, to about £18,000,000." — Dicey, *The Law of the Constitution*, p. 293, note 1.

not be a member of either house of parliament.[1] Leaving out of view his duties as comptroller of the issue of public money, it is his duty as auditor of the public accounts to see that the entire revenue for the year deposited in the Bank of England is paid out according to law. It is his business to submit the result of his work at the beginning of every session of parliament to the Public Accounts Committee of the house of commons, whose habit it is to subject every apparently irregular item to a searching scrutiny.[2] According to the regulations, "All unexpended balances of the grants of a year are surrendered to the exchequer, as also are all extra receipts and the amount of appropriations-in-aid received in excess of the sum estimated to be taken in aid of the vote;" while "any excess of expenditure over the amount voted by parliament for any service must receive legislative sanction."[3]

his duty to see that revenue is paid out according to law;

his report to Public Accounts Committee;

all unexpended balances surrendered to exchequer.

We know already that in the reign of Henry VIII. the increasing pressure of business made necessary the appointment of two secretaries, to both of whom, as mere clerks, was given a signet for the sealing of all warrants and cabinet letters. When by the Statute of Precedence passed before the close of that reign they were made members of the council *ex officio*, it required but one more step for them to pass from mere secretaries into secretaries of state, and that was taken when in 1601 Robert Cecil was endowed for the first time with the formal title of "our principal secretary of state,"[4] while his coadjutor, John Herbert, was described as one of "our secretaries of state." Soon after the Revolution the office was divided between a first and second secretary, and after the union with Scotland a third was appointed for the affairs of that kingdom, whose office was finally abolished in January, 1746.[5] The office of a third secretary of state, created in 1768 for the American or colonial department, was likewise abolished in 1782.[6] In March of that year it was that the two chief secretaries concurred in the important resolve to super-

Two secretaries appointed in reign of Henry VIII.;

pass into secretaries of state;

Robert Cecil first to receive the title;

a first and second secretary after the Revolution:

in 1782 office as a whole finally divided

---

[1] See The Exchequer and Audit Dept. Act, 1866 (29 & 30 Vict. c. 39), s. 3.

[2] May, *Parl. Practice*, p. 563.

[3] *Control and Audit of Public Receipts and Expenditures, 1885*, pp. 24, 25.

[4] See above, p. 178.

[5] The office was first abolished in 1725, when the duke of Roxburghe was removed. It was then restored in 1731 and continued until 1746, the marquis of Tweeddale being the last incumbent. Smith's *Secretary for Scotland*, p. 10.

[6] 22 Geo. III. c. 82.

sede the then existing system, — under which the business had been for a time apportioned between a northern and southern district,[1] — by a definite and final division of the secretary-
into a home and foreign department. ship of state as a whole into a home department and a foreign department, to the last of which was assigned the direction of all diplomatic and consular business, while the affairs of Ireland and the colonies remained to the older or home secretary.   In 1794, pending hostilities with France, a third principal secretary of state for war was appointed,[2] and in March, 1801, the business of the colonies was transferred to that secretary from the home department.[3]   In June, 1854, a fourth principal secretary of state for war was appointed, and in that way the third principal secretary was left in charge of colonial affairs only.   In September, 1858, upon the abolition of the charter of the East India Company, a fifth principal secretary of state was appointed for the affairs of India.

Out of the office of lord high admiral has grown the court of admiralty and department for government of the navy; Out of the office of lord high admiral has grown the court of admiralty, to which his judicial functions were assigned,[4] and the admiralty department for the government of the navy, whose control is vested in seven lords represented in the cabinet by their chief, who is known as the First Lord of the Admiralty.[5]   As the origin of the office of president of the Board of Trade has already been given,[6] reference need
president of the Local Government Board; only be made to the president of the Local Government Board, whose office was created in 1871.[7]   Such then is the origin and character of the offices usually assigned by a prime minister to those who together with himself constitute the inner
every member of the cabinet must be a privy councillor; circle of the privy council known as the cabinet.   It is, therefore, absolutely necessary that every member of the cabinet should be a privy councillor ; and if he is not such already, he

---

1 " The northern department, or province, included the Low Countries, Germany, Denmark, Sweden, Poland, Russia, etc. ; and the southern department, or province, France, Switzerland, Italy, Spain, Portugal, Turkey, etc." See *The Foreign Office List,* 1897, pp. 1 and 2, in which a list is given of the officials assigned to the two departments from 1761 to 1782.

2 Sir Thomas Erskine May (*Const. Hist.,* vol. iii. p. 360) therefore errs in stating that the secretaryship of state for the colonies was revived in 1794.

8 " The Department of Secretary for the Colonies and War was so constituted that sometimes the colonies were the chief and the war administration the secondary department, and sometimes *vice versa.*" — Gneist, *Hist. of the Eng. Constitution,* p. 692, note 7.

4 See vol. i. pp. 547–551.

5 In 1755 the admiralty department consisted of seven lords commissioners.

6 See above, p. 445.

7 See Local Government Board Act of that year, 34 & 35 Vict. c. 70.

is made so immediately after his appointment.[1]   And here the fact should be emphasized that the terms "cabinet" and "ministry" are not synonymous.   The last and broader term properly includes all the ministers, while the former comprises only that smaller circle ranging from thirteen to nineteen, who undertake to carry on the government,[2] and who are required, certainly by the spirit of the constitution, to have seats in one or other of the houses of parliament.[3]   For the distribution of cabinet ministers between the two houses the prime minister is responsible ; and the proportion to be assigned to each must of course vary with circumstances.   As the office of prime minister, like the cabinet itself, over which he presides, is utterly unknown to the law, it is necessary for its incumbent, who may be either a peer or a commoner, to acquire a legal status by taking to himself some post that the law does recognize.   From the fall of Lord Bute in 1762 down to the formation of Lord Salisbury's first administration, it was the settled custom for the prime minister to hold the office of first lord of the treasury, either alone or in connection with the chancellorship of the exchequer.   The elder Pitt was, however, for four years (1757 to 1761) secretary of state ; so was Lord Bute during his short administration ; and so has been Lord Salisbury during his three administrations.[4]

The cabinet in its relations with the legislature may be defined to be a corporate entity, with a definite policy and an acknowledged chief, which, certainly since the reform bill of 1832, has been charged (1) with the duty of initiating and carrying through parliament all great and important acts of national legislation ; (2) with the control of measures of general interest introduced by private members ; and (3) with such a direction of the entire mass of business submitted to the two houses as will best secure and maintain the privileges

Marginal notes: "cabinet" and "ministry" not synonymous ; distribution of cabinet ministers between the houses ; prime minister must take some post recognized by law ; usually that of first lord of the treasury ; sometimes that of secretary of state. Relations of the cabinet with the legislature ; its cardinal duties ;

---

[1] When a cabinet has been formed, "the *London Gazette* announces that the queen has been pleased to appoint certain privy councillors to fill certain high offices of state." — Todd, *Parl. Government*, vol. ii. p. 3.

[2] For the best practical illustration of the relation of the terms to each other, see the list of the present ministry of Lord Salisbury in *Whitaker's Almanack*, 1897.   Those who form the cabinet are specially distinguished from the other ministers, who outnumber them nearly two to one.

[3] It is well settled, however, that a person may be admitted to the cabinet without being required to assume the labor and responsibility of any departmental office.   For the precedents, see Todd, *Parl. Government*, vol. i. p. 284.

[4] Ibid., p. 280.

necessity
for unity
among its
members;

of both.   An indispensable condition to success in such a difficult and complex undertaking is unity and coöperation among the ministers themselves in the execution of the policy agreed upon by all, and for which all are equally responsible.   Except

excepting
an "open
question,"
every member bound
by every
act or
declaration
of his
colleagues;

in the case of an admitted "open question," the cabinet as a whole is presumed to have assented to every act or declaration made by any member speaking in its behalf ; and it is, therefore, expected that the cabinet collectively and individually will support every government measure, whether proposed as such in their joint names or by any member in favor of his particular department.[1]   The programme or policy thus undertaken

as the
production
of the
cabinet, the
speech from
the throne
is subject
to liberties
of debate;

by cabinet ministers in the name of the crown is first outlined in the speech from the throne for which they are responsible, and which as their production is subject to all the liberties and licenses of debate.[2]   Until a very recent period it was always the custom for the sovereign himself to be present at the opening of his great council in order to address to them personally words of congratulation or advice, in addition to the more formal " opening of the cause of the summons," which was assigned to one of the principal ministers, generally the

since the
Revolution
there has
been but
one address
from the
throne.

lord chancellor.   Since the Revolution, however, there has been but one address from the throne at the opening of parliament, which is uttered by the king himself when present, or by the lord chancellor by his express command, or in his absence by commissioners appointed by royal authority.[3]   No matter by whom uttered, it is now the settled practice to consider such speech as a declaration for which the then existing cabinet is responsible.

Demand of
aid and
supply for
fiscal year;

Generally the most important matter contained in the speech from the throne is the demand presented to the commons by the crown for grants of aid and supply for the service of the

---

[1] For Mr. Gladstone's views, quoted and indorsed by Lord Grey, see *Hans. Deb.*, 3d ser. vol. cxvii. p. 2057.   See also Ibid., vol. clxviii. pp. 176, 276, 280, for further views of Mr. Gladstone and Lord Grey, and Todd, *Parl. Government*, vol. ii. p. 78.

[2] Massey, *Reign of George III.*, vol. i. p. 156 ; *Parl. Hist.*, vol. xxiii. p. 266. The same freedom is also allowed in the debate upon the address.   Todd, *Parl. Hist.*, vol. ii. p. 54, and note 5.

[3] May's *Parl. Practice*, pp. 41, 168, 170.   As George I. could not speak English, he directed the lord chancellor to read the speech, when he opened parliament in person.   Campbell's *Lives of the Chancellors*, vol. iv. p. 600.   On every occasion since 1866, when the present queen has met parliament in person, she has directed the lord chancellor to read the speech for her.

fiscal year, which is invariably attended by the promise that in due time estimates will be laid before them of the amount required for that period.   It is settled constitutional doctrine that no money can be voted by parliament for any purpose except upon the demand and upon the responsibility of cabinet ministers.   " Thus the crown demands money, the commons grant it, and the lords assent to the grant : but the commons do not vote money unless they be required by the crown ; nor do they impose or augment taxes, unless such taxation be necessary for the public service, as declared by the crown through its constitutional advisers." [1]   As soon as the speech from the throne is read, an address in answer thereto is moved in each house at the instance of the administration, which, since the session of 1890–91, has taken the form of a single resolution expressing the thanks of each house to the sovereign for the gracious speech addressed to both.   Amendments to the address are immediately in order, and public business is carried on while such proceedings are still undisposed of.   To hasten the progress of financial measures the commons have adopted a standing order, " That this house will, in future, appoint the committees of supply, and ways and means, at the commencement of every session, so soon as an address has been agreed to in answer to Her Majesty's speech."   The ordinary sessional estimates are presented in three parts, comprising the three branches of the public service, — the army, navy, and civil services ; and, under the resolution agreed to by the house on February 19, 1821, " whenever parliament shall assemble before Christmas, the estimates for the navy, army, and ordinance departments should be presented before January 15, then next following, if parliament be then sitting ; and that such estimates should be presented within ten days after the opening of the committee of supply, when parliament shall not be assembled until after Christmas."   Upon these and all other estimates of expenditure for the current year, it is the duty of the committee of supply to pass in the first instance, and in the hope that the vote of that committee would be taken upon the bulk of them in the earlier part of each session, the financial year was made to close on the 31st of March, and to begin on the 1st of April.   But as that hope is seldom realized,

promise of estimates;

no money can be voted, except upon proper demand;

how the speech from the throne is answered.

amendments to the address immediately in order;

when committees of supply, and ways and means appointed;

ordinary sessional estimates presented in three parts;

when they should be presented;

these and all other estimates passed on by committee of supply;

financial year ends 31st of March;

---

[1] May, *Parl. Practice*, p. 515.

it is continually necessary to demand a vote on account during the first quarter of each year, in order to keep the machinery of government in motion.   It is the duty of the committee of ways and means to provide by taxation the income necessary to meet the expenditures approved by the committee of supply, and to vote the resolutions that authorize the payment out of the Consolidated Fund of the grants thus made.   As the consideration of the taxes for the current year thus devolves upon the committee of ways and means, it is to that committee that the chancellor of the exchequer generally addresses the financial statement called "The Budget," "when the minister has completed his estimate of the probable income and expenditure for the ensuing financial year, and usually after some progress has been obtained in voting the grants for the army and navy and other public services.   In that statement the chancellor of the exchequer develops his views of the resources of the country, communicates his calculations of probable income and expenditure, and declares whether the burdens upon the people are to be increased or diminished." [1]   The proceeds of the various duties and taxes thus imposed, which originally constituted separate funds, have been concentrated by law into a single fund, called the "Consolidated Fund," that finds its way into the Bank of England as explained already.   Not a penny of the money thus concentrated in the national depository can be legally disbursed except under the authority of appropriation acts, either permanent or annual.   By virtue of permanent acts are paid out the sums necessary for interest on the national debt ; the civil list ; annuities to the royal family and pensions ; courts of justice ; salaries and allowances of certain independent officers, and for certain other miscellaneous services.   The Annual Appropriation Act, which is not brought in until all the supply grants have been voted, is therefore limited in its operation to those supplies not otherwise appropriated by the permanent acts.   It is the last word spoken by the committee of ways and means, that concludes the financial arrangements of the year through the authorization given for the payment of the remaining sums due from the Consolidated Fund.

To the general rule that forbids the imposition of taxes,

duty of the committee of ways and means;

to which chancellor of exchequer addresses financial statement called "The Budget;"

origin of the "Consolidated Fund;"

all moneys disbursed through

permanent appropriation acts, or through an

annual appropriation act

that closes the financial business of the year.

[1] May, *Parl. Practice*, p. 555.   See also, pp. 170, 171, 516, 517, 560, 563, 588.

except when demanded by ministers of the crown upon their responsibility, there is a notable exception : "No private member is permitted to propose an imperial tax upon the people ; it must proceed from a minister of the crown, or be in some other form declared to be necessary for the public service. But any member may bring in a bill to impose heavy local burdens." [1] Cabinet ministers are relieved also of all responsibility as to private bills. For the reason no doubt that in the majority of such cases parliament is called upon to exercise quasi-judicial functions, it was declared by the chancellor of the exchequer in 1840 to be "contrary to all established practice for ministers of the crown to give an opinion on a private bill." [2] They are, therefore, excused from service on private bill committees. [3]

No private member can propose an imperial tax, but can propose any bill for a local purpose, upon which no minister should give an opinion.

Having now defined in general terms the positive responsibilities of cabinet ministers as initiators and directors of legislation, a word must be said as to their negative duties when called upon in the houses to answer questions. The usage that permits such questions to be addressed, not only to ministers but to other members, was first formally recognized and limited in the house of commons by the following rule, formulated in 1854 and embodying the existing practice, which provides that "before the public business is entered upon, questions are permitted to be put to ministers of the crown, relating to public affairs ; and to other members, relating to any bill, motion, or other public matter connected with the business of the house, in which such members may be concerned." [4] "Within these lines an explanation can be sought regarding the intentions of the government, but not for an expression of their opinion upon matters of policy. An answer to a question cannot be insisted upon, if the answer be refused by a minister on the ground of public interest ; nor can the question be replaced upon the notice paper. Questions may be asked of the ministers who are the confidential advisers of the crown, regarding matters relating to those public duties for which the sovereign is responsible ; but no question can be

When questions can be put to ministers and other members ; the rule adopted in 1854 ; government can be asked as to its intentions ; answer may be refused upon ground of public interest ;

---

[1] Sir T. E. May's evidence before Joint Committee on Despatch of Business, *Com. Pap.*, 1868–69, vol. vii. p. 185 ; *Hans. Deb.*, vol. ccxv. p. 1676.
[2] *Mir. of Parl.*, 1840, p. 4657.

[3] *Hans. Deb.*, vol. ccxii. p. 627 ; Todd, *Parl. Government*, pp. 67, 68, 194.
[4] See Rule 152, Revised Rule, ed. of 1859.

put which brings the name of the sovereign or the influence
of the crown directly before parliament, or which casts reflec-
tions upon the sovereign." [1]   Questions to members outside
of the cabinet are usually addressed to the leader of the opposition, to ex-ministers, to the archbishop of Canterbury, to
members placed on royal commissions, to the trustees of the
National Gallery, to the parliamentary representative of the
British Museum, and to the lord chamberlain; and are limited
under the terms of the rule to matters " relating to any bill,
motion, or other public matter connected with the business of
the house, in which such members may be concerned." [2]

When in 1877 the house of commons was called upon to
deal with an offence of which the speaker said any member
was guilty who " wilfully and persistently obstructed public
business, without just and reasonable cause," [3] the fact was
admitted that its then existing rules contained no adequate
provision for the closure of debate under such circumstances.
As temporary expedients to facilitate the consideration of several important bills then pending were adopted the urgency
resolutions of the sessions of 1881 and 1882; and in the sessions
of 1887 and 1888 were passed the standing orders now governing the subject, which provide, (25) " That, after a question
has been proposed, a member rising in his place may claim
to move, ' That the question be now put,' and, unless it shall
appear to the chair that such motion is an abuse of the rules
of the house, or an infringement of the rights of the minority,
the question, ' That the question be now put,' shall be put
forthwith, and decided without amendment or debate;" (26)
" That questions for the closure of debate under standing
order No. 25 shall be decided in the affirmative, if, when a
division be taken, it appears by the numbers declared from the
chair, that no less than one hundred members voted in the
majority in support of the motion." [4]

6. While the inner circle of the privy council known as the
cabinet — whose members in legal contemplation derive their
authority and responsibility from the fact that they have been

---

[1] May, *Parl. Practice*, p. 237, 10th
ed.
[2] Ibid., p. 338.
[3] *Commons' Journals*, vol. cxxxii. p.
375.

[4] For the text of the orders of the
18th of March, 1887, and 7th of March,
1888, see May, *Parl. Practice*, Appendix, p. 828. See, also, pp. 211, 212,
324.

sworn of it — has been absorbing all the real powers of government, the outer circle, which now embraces a membership of about two hundred, has since the Revolution of 1688 sunk into comparative insignificance. Its once mighty judicial authority has dwindled in criminal matters down to the right of taking examinations and issuing commitments for high treason, while in civil it retains only an appellate jurisdiction over the colonial and ecclesiastical tribunals. These vestiges of its ancient jurisdiction do not belong, however, to the council as a whole, but to the judicial committee, connected with the main body by little more than its name, to which they were transferred by 3 & 4 Will. IV. c. 41. Among the administrative functions still exercised by the crown, nominally at least, through the privy council, are such as those of proclaiming ports or fairs, and deciding when a given act shall be put into effect, — functions whose very insignificance best illustrates how the council has fallen from its high estate. "Through privy councillors, and through them alone, can the monarch act; and hence the powers of the crown are in a sense the powers of the council. They have risen, they have flourished, they have declined, together." [1] This shadowy body, which thus exists as a mere survival of the past, is unlimited in number, and its members, who are appointed without patent or grant at the discretion of the crown, may be dismissed by it at any time, individually or as a whole. Subject to that contingency the ancient rule was for the privy council to continue during the life of the sovereign; but that rule was changed by 6 Anne, c. 7, that continues its existence for six months longer, subject of course to the right of the new monarch to dissolve it at will. The only necessary qualification for a privy councillor is that he should be born a British subject; and the nature of his duties, including the obligation of secrecy, is clearly epitomized, not only in the oath of office anciently imposed, but in the modern one now in use. [2]

remains of its judicial authority as exercised by

its judicial committee;

its administrative functions;

powers of crown and council have flourished and declined together;

its numbers unlimited;

tenure of a privy councillor,

6 Anne, c. 7

qualification and duties;

oath of office.

7. The same general longing for a wider freedom that forced the aristocracy, through the reform bill of 1832, to relinquish

---

[1] Dicey, *The Privy Council*, pp. 144, 145.

[2] For the ancient oath, see Coke, *Inst.*, vol. iv. p. 54; for the present oath, see Report of Oaths Commission, *Com.*

Pap., 1867, vol. xxxi. p. 84; Ibid., 1876, vol. lxi. p. 275. The oath of allegiance prescribed by 31 & 32 Vict. c. 72 must also be taken.

Great acts
of the
reformed
parlia-
ments:their hold upon the house of commons also brought about the
enactment of that series of statutes through which the ancient
system of local self-government has been emancipated from
the control of the few and reëstablished upon a popular basis.
The attempt has heretofore been made to draw out the process
through which the simple primitive system of local administration embodied in the township, the borough, the hundred,
and the shire, upon which the central government pressed very

how the
franchise
was with-
drawn from
the main
body of the
people;

lightly, was gradually undermined by a series of encroachments that finally resulted in withdrawing the franchise from
the main body of the people and vesting it in local magnates,
or in close corporations.   Thus it was that in many parishes
the powers of the vestry, — anciently the assembly of the
township for ecclesiastical matters only, — in which all rated
parishioners had the common law right to assemble for the
regulation of all parish affairs, were usurped by a few of the

self-elected
vestries;

inhabitants, who assumed not only to act for all, but to perpetuate their existence by self-election.[1]   In the boroughs,

self-elected
municipal
councils;

where the municipal councils were generally self-elected and
for life, the tendency was still stronger upon the part of the
favored few to exclude the main body of the townspeople from

condition of
things at
Plymouth,
Ports-
mouth, and
Ipswich;

any share in the town government.   From the report of the
royal commission appointed in 1833 to make a searching inquiry into the whole subject, we learn that at Plymouth, in a
population of 75,000, there were only 437 freemen, of whom
145 were non-resident ; at Portsmouth, in a population of
45,000, there were only 102 freemen ; while at Ipswich, less
than two per cent., many of whom were paupers, enjoyed
corporate privileges. . Passing over the obsolete subdivisions
known as hundreds, we also find a notable exception to the

govern-
ment of
counties by
justices
appointed
by the
crown;
system of
local self-
govern-
ment ceased
to be either
popular or
adequate;

general rule of representation in local affairs in the county
governments, whose administrative control finally passed from
the local parliaments known as the county courts to the quarter
sessions, composed of the justices of the peace appointed by
the crown, generally upon the recommendation of the lord lieutenant.[2]   As time went on, the strong and simple system of local
self-government, once sufficient for all the wants of primitive
communities, not only ceased to be popular, but became en-

[1] See above, p. 192; vol. i. p. 37, and notes.   [2] See above, pp. 192, 193; vol. i. p. 453, *et seq.*

tirely inadequate to the ever increasing requirements of a progressive society. As the state thus outgrew its immemorial system of local administration an attempt was made to supply the more glaring deficiencies, not only by general legislation relating to local affairs, but also by thousands of local and special acts which apply to particular towns and districts.[1] When, therefore, the work of reformation and reorganization began, those who were brave enough to undertake it were called upon to keep three objects steadily in view : firstly, to reëstablish local self-government upon a popular basis ; secondly, to supersede the endless local exceptions and anomalies by something like a uniform system ; thirdly, to make such additions to the ancient machinery as were peremptorily demanded by the complex wants of modern civilization. *its reformers called upon to keep three things steadily in view.*

It was admitted on all hands that the most vicious and corrupt part of the local system was that embodied in the municipal organization of the boroughs, whose charters from a very early period generally granted or confirmed to each the right of sending one or more burgesses to parliament to represent it.[2] Thus "a great number of corporations have been preserved solely as political engines, and the towns to which they belong derive no benefit, but often much injury, from their existence. To maintain the political ascendancy of a party, or the political influence of a family, has been the one end and object for which the powers entrusted to those bodies have been exercised."[3] After the reform bill of 1832 had taken away these exclusive political privileges from the few and revested them in the many so far as the right to elect parliamentary representatives was concerned, steps were immediately taken to abolish such oligarchies entirely, and to reorganize the borough system upon a broad popular basis by vesting the municipal franchise in the rate-paying residents. As a prelude to that undertaking parliament in 1833 appointed a Royal Commission which, after a thorough investigation of the whole subject, reported in 1835 ; and in the same year was *Reform of the municipal system ; corporations preserved as political engines ; after reform bill of 1832 borough system reorganized on a broad popular basis ; Royal Commission of 1833 ;*

---

[1] "Our local legislation begins with the statute *De Officio Coronatoris*, passed in 1275, and ends for the present with the Divided Parish Act of 1882. Between these terminal marks the various Acts are scattered up and down in wild confusion." — M. D. Chalmers, *Local Government*, Citizen Ser. Preface.

[2] See above, p. 390.

[3] *Rep. Mun. Corp.*, 1835, p. 34.

Municipal Corporations Act, 1835; its leading features;

passed the first Municipal Corporations Act,[1] justly regarded as the basis of English municipal freedom in its modern form. By the terms of that act the franchise was given to all inhabitant ratepayers; magisterial powers were taken away from the aldermen, and the tenure of elective officers shortened; provision was made for the honest administration of corporate funds and for an efficient discharge of municipal duties; and all exemptions, restrictions, and trading monopolies were abolished. So imperfect, however, was this tentative measure that

after forty-two amendments, whole subject recast and condensed into Municipal Corporations Act, 1882;

after forty-two amendments in subsequent enactments it was deemed necessary to recast and condense the whole subject into the complete municipal code embodied in the Municipal Corporations Act,[2] 1882, said to be one of the best drafted acts upon the statute-book. There the titles of municipal corporations are fixed, the franchise for both men and women defined, the rights and duties of burgesses, the duties of mayors, the general powers of the governing body known as the council, the manner in which borough justice shall be administered, and the manner in which new municipalities may be created clearly set forth.

Municipal Corporations Acts not extended to the City of London; it retains its ancient constitution and boundaries;

And here the fact must be emphasized that these Municipal Corporations Acts have never been extended to the City of London, which still retains its ancient constitution embodied in one hundred and twenty charters, supplemented by about fifty general and a mass of local acts. The ancient city thus constituted occupies, however, within municipal and parliamentary boundaries only 671 statute acres, with a population estimated in 1896 at 31,148.[3] The corporation, which within these narrow limits exercises nearly all local authority, performs its

governed by three assemblies

functions through three assemblies, — the court of aldermen, the court of common council, and the court of common hall, — over each of which the lord mayor presides. The charter[4]

charter granted by William the Norman;

granted to the city by William the Norman was addressed to William the bishop, Gosfrith the portreeve, and all the burgesses, French and English; but the portreeve in due time received the Norman title of bailiff, which in 1189 was changed

---

[1] 5 & 6 Will. IV. c. 76.
[2] 45 & 46 Vict. c. 50.
[3] See article on London in *Whitaker's Almanack*, 1897.
[4] "And I do you to wit that I will

that ye two be worthy of all the laws that ye were worthy of in King Edward's day."—Stubbs, *Select Charters*, p. 83.

into that of mayor.[1] In the charter granted by King John in 1215[2] a direction was contained that the mayor should be chosen annually, a precept which has since been carefully observed. The chief legislative and executive organ of the corporation is the court of common council, the successor of the popular assembly of early times known as the folkmoot, which consists of 26 aldermen chosen in as many wards for life, and of 240 common councilmen elected annually in the several wards in different proportions.[3] With this statement clearly in view, it will be more easy to distinguish the ancient City of London from that great and growing surrounding district of which it is the heart, called in statutes the Metropolis, whose boundaries are difficult to define because they vary for different purposes. If, however, we limit the term "Metropolis" to the vast settlement that has agglomerated itself outside of the city walls within the limits of what is known as the Metropolitan Police District, we have an area extending over a radius of fifteen miles from Charing Cross which, exclusive of the City of London, contained in 1891 a population of 5,596,101, with a ratable value in 1895–96 of £38,716,378.[4]

charter granted by John; chief legislative and executive organ, court of common council; City of London must be distinguished from vast surrounding district known as the "Metropolis;" its area and population.

Between 1805 and 1855 the population of greater London swelled from a million to two millions and a half;[5] and between 1855 and 1891 that aggregate grew into the five millions and a half ascertained by the census of 1891. The rising tide of humanity that thus spread beyond the walls of the ancient city into the disorderly mass of townships, manors, parishes, and extra-parochial places surrounding it found therein only such forms of organization as their antiquated and disconnected systems of local self-government provided. The only common head to which this outlying population could look was crown and parliament, from which it derived a metropolitan police force that kept fairly good order, and a government commission of sewers which provided an imperfect system of drainage, that emptied its pollution into the Thames in such a way as at times to obstruct navigation. To remedy

Growth of greater London; lack of municipal organization in outlying districts;

[1] In the mean time, however, was granted the charter of Henry I. *Fœdera*, vol. i. p. 11. As to the status of London under that charter, see vol. i. p. 458.

[2] Stubbs, *Select Charters*, p. 314.

[3] See Shaw, *Municipal Government in Great Britain*, p. 229.

[4] See article on London in *Whitaker's Almanack*, 1897.

[5] Shaw, *Municipal Government in Great Britain*, p. 235.

selfishness
of the old
corpora-
tion;

this wretched condition of things, the corporation of London offered to do nothing, for fear that an extension of its system of government beyond its ancient limits would result in depriving it of its monopoly of exclusive privileges. The task of giving municipal organization to the new creation devolved, therefore, upon the central government, which in 1838 first recognized the fact that London embraced the outlying dis-

registry
of vital
statistics
in 1838;
Metropolis
Manage-
ment Act,
1855;

tricts by the provisions then made for the registry of vital statistics.[1] The first rudiments, however, of a municipal constitution were contained in the Metropolis Management Act of 1855,[2] which created within an area practically identical with that of the Registrar-General's District as extended a central authority called the Metropolitan Board of Works. At that date local affairs within the area thus organized were managed by seventy-eight parishes, twenty-three of which were considered large and populous enough to continue under the control of single vestries, while the remaining fifty-five were grouped in fifteen districts, governed by boards elected by the vestries

functions of
vestries
and district
boards;

of the combined parishes. To these vestries and district boards were confided under a somewhat uniform system the local functions that the parishes had immemorially exercised, including street-making, local sewerage, sanitary administration, watering and paving streets, and the removal of nuisances,

Metropoli-
tan Board
of Works;

— functions that have never been taken away.[3] The Metropolitan Board of Works, consisting of one representative from each district board or vestry and three from the corporation of the City of London, was charged primarily with the task of constructing a system of trunk sewers, an enterprise too vast of course for the petty boards and vestries to undertake with any hope of success. From that time onward effort after effort was made by leading English statesmen to develop the germ embodied in the act of 1855 into a great and complete municipal system. Foremost among such attempts stands that

Sir William
Harcourt's
measure of
1884;

of Sir William Harcourt, who as Home Secretary in Mr. Gladstone's cabinet introduced in 1884 a measure that proposed to create a sort of federalized municipal government for greater London, which was to be divided into thirty-nine administra-

---

[1] "In 1838 the wider area came to be definitely known as the Registrar-General's District." — Ibid., p. 233.

[2] 18 & 19 Vict. c. 120.

[3] M. D. Chalmers, *Local Government*, Citizen Ser. p. 144.

tive areas under the control of a great central council, to be composed of two hundred and forty members. The ancient City of London was to be considered only as one of the thirty-nine areas, to which a large representation was to be given in recognition of its historical importance and great property interests. Nothing, however, was actually done until 1888, when parliament, in enacting the Local Government Act[1] of that year, found it convenient to treat all the great urban communities of England as separate counties for administrative purposes. In that way the area embraced within the jurisdiction of the superseded Metropolitan Board of Works was transferred to the administrative county of London, whose governing body is an elected county council, endowed with functions analogous in many respects to those exercised by the governing bodies of other great towns. The measure is, however, a very imperfect one. As the most recent writer upon the subject has tersely expressed it : "Thus the City of London and its functions remained practically untouched, and the parish vestries and district boards continued to exercise their accustomed jurisdiction in minor affairs."[2] In order to place such vestries and boards upon a broad popular basis, by restoring the right of local self-government to the main body of townsmen, by whom it was no doubt exercised in earlier times, Mr. Henry Fowler, as president of the Local Government Board in Mr. Gladstone's last cabinet, introduced the "Local Government Bill, England and Wales," which became law in 1894.[3] By that act, which does for the townships or civil parishes of England what the Municipal Corporations Act of 1835 did for the larger towns, the election of London vestries is regulated through provisions that make all resident citizens, men and women, eligible for election by an electorate composed of all whose names appear on the parliamentary or county council rolls.[4]

Local Government Act, 1888;

London county council and its functions;

act of 1888 an imperfect one;

Local Government Bill, 1894.

A somewhat detailed account has already been given of the township as the modern parish, and of the manner in which

Decline of the parish;

---

[1] 51 & 52 Vict. c. 41.
[2] Shaw, *Municipal Government in Great Britain*, p. 242. See the scheme for a complete unification of the Metropolis described in Appendix III. of that work.

[3] 56 & 57 Vict. c. 73.
[4] For the latest and best commentary, see *The Local Government Act, 1894*, by Macmorran and Dill, 3d ed. 1896.

its composite machinery has been applied, first to church and then to state purposes. In that connection reference was the parish as the agent of the state under the great act of Elizabeth (1601); made to the special functions the parish was thus called upon to perform as the agent chosen by the state for the execution of the great act of Elizabeth (1601),[1] upon which the English system of poor relief rested until it was superseded by the Poor Law Amendment Act, 1834.[2] A special student of the results of that act as they appeared in 1834; subject has declared that "this was the state of things down to the reform of 1834. The public funds were regarded as a regular part of the maintenance of the labouring people engaged in agriculture, and were administered by more than 2000 justices, 15,000 sets of overseers, and 15,000 vestries, acting always independently of each other, and very commonly in opposition, quite uncontrolled, and ignorant of the very rudi- system remodelled by the act of 1834; ments of political economy."[3] In the hope of improving that unfortunate condition of things, the reformed parliament passed the act of 1834, whereby the poor law administration was remodelled and its control vested in a central commission, the Poor Law Board; made permanent in 1847 as the Poor Law Board, which, under the presidency of a responsible minister eligible to a seat in the house of commons,[4] possessed among its other ample powers the right of grouping parishes for poor law purposes into boards of guardians; how the parish as such was affected by the new statutory system; a central bureau at London; unions,[5] subject to the control of boards of guardians. Thus was the individual parish as such stripped of its most impor- tant function by the creation of a new statutory system, em- bodying the vitally important principle that a leading branch of local administration was thereafter to be moulded and directed after the French fashion by a central bureau at London, whose powers over the local unions embraced not only their creation but their dissolution. Then through two sets of causes, — one how the civil parish was sepa- rated from the ecclesi- astical; lay, the other ecclesiastical, — what is known as the civil parish was in many localities separated from the ecclesiastical; and "since the abolition of compulsory church rates by the act of 1868, the ecclesiastical parish has ceased to be of much prac- tical importance for purposes of local government. It is almost

---

[1] See above, p. 189, *et seq.*
[2] 4 & 5 Will. IV. c. 76. Cf. Nicholl's *Hist. of the Eng. Poor Law ;* Report of the Poor Law Commissioners in 1834; and the Sixth Report of the Poor Law Commission in 1839.

[3] T. W. Fowle, *The Poor Law*, Citi- zen Ser. pp. 73, 74.
[4] Traill, *Central Government*, Citi- zen Ser. p. 134.
[5] See chap. iv., "The Union," in Chalmers, *Local Government*, Citizen Ser. pp. 51–60.

entirely a permissive institution." [1] As a part of the police system, the importance of the parish practically ended when the act of 1856 — the first law for the whole of England requiring that there should be paid policeman — rendered unnecessary the old parish constables, whose offices were permissively abolished by an act of 1872, as those of the high constables, old officers of the hundred, were in 1869. *effect of the new police system upon parish constables.*

In 1831, in the midst of the movement for parliamentary reform, and four years prior to the passage of the first Municipal Corporations Act, Sir John Hobhouse secured the enactment of his Vestry Act,[2] which attempted to restore to the parish its ancient popular constitution through provisions that revived the common law right of every rated parishioner to vote for members of the vestry ; that directed that the votes of the electors should be taken by ballot ; that every ten-pound householder, with certain exceptions, should be eligible as a vestryman ; that no one so chosen should have more than a single vote ; that due publication should be made of the accounts of the parish charities ; and that the auditors to audit the accounts should be elected. The act was, however, permissive ; it could be adopted only by parishes having more than eight hundred ratepaying inhabitants, and that only after due notice and by a two thirds vote. As the act has been repealed as regards the Metropolis, to whose populous parishes it had been extensively applied, it is supposed to have had a very limited operation.[3] Not even such a legislative stimulant as the Hobhouse Act could check the tendency of the parish to become obsolete as an active unit of local administration ; it is mainly important at the present day "as the unit for taxation and electoral purposes. All rates included in the poor rate are collected parochially, and the lists of voters for parliamentary and municipal elections are made out parochially." [4] *Sir J. Hobhouse's Vestry Act, 1831 ; attempt to restore ancient popular constitution of the parish ; act permissive ; repealed as to the Metropolis ; has failed to check tendency of parish to become obsolete ; still a unit for taxation and electoral purposes.*

While the causes just enumerated were dragging down the ancient parishes and their vestries from their once high estate, others were at work which, in the same general way, have *Declining importance of county government ;*

[1] Chalmers, *Local Government*, Citizen Ser. p. 45. "There are now (1883) about 15,000 civil and 13,000 ecclesiastical parishes. Out of the 15,000 civil parishes, there were in 1871 not more than 10,000 whose boundaries coincided with the ecclesiastical parishes of the same name." — *Ibid.*, pp. 38–40.

[2] 1 & 2 Will. IV. c. 6.

[3] See Toulmin Smith, *The Parish*, pp. 240–243.

[4] Chalmers, *Local Government*, Citizen Ser. p. 40.

reduced the counties and their governments to the attenuated form in which they now appear. During the period that followed the Conquest, the shire organization reached no doubt its highest point of influence in the county parliaments, called together by the sheriffs to meet the itinerant justices, in order to participate with them in the administration of justice, and in the transaction of other public business. The process has already been drawn out through which the bodies thus constituted have been transformed into the modern courts of assize, in which the itinerant justices still preside, but in which the great assemblies of the shire are now represented only by the grand and petty jurors summoned for the trial of civil and criminal cases. One of the notable consequences of the development of this itinerant system was a steady decline in the judicial powers of the sheriff, who finally became simply the executive head of the shire, whose duty it was to convene the ancient county court that lingered on after its more important powers had been absorbed by the royal tribunals. That court met once a month, probably at the county town, for general purposes, military, judicial, and fiscal, and twice a year in every hundred as the great court-leet of the county for criminal trials, under the name of the sheriff's *tourn* or circuit.[1] What thus remained of administrative and judicial work to the ancient assembly of the shire, with the sheriff at its head, was subjected to a second process of diminution with the rise of the royal officers known as justices of the peace, who in their courts of quarter sessions acquired not only the right to try all minor criminal cases once tried in the courts-leet, but also the sheriff's ancient control over the county constabulary. All administrative functions of the county were then conferred upon the justices assembled, either in quarter or special sessions, by a series of statutes extending from Tudor and Stuart times down to the present day.[2] Thus it was that the ancient county courts were gradually reduced through a process of centralization to the shadowy theoretical existence which they still maintain. The decline and fall of the sheriff himself has gone on hand in hand with that of the

Marginal notes: period of its greatest influence: ; great assemblies of the shire gave way to the courts of assize; decline in the judicial powers of the sheriff; ancient county court and its functions; how decline was advanced by the rise of justices of the peace; administrative work cast on quarter sessions by statute; result of the process of centralization;

---

[1] Vol. i. pp. 319, 320. See, also, Sir J. F. Stephen, *Hist. of the Crim. Law*, vol. i. pp. 67, 81.

[2] Vol. i. pp. 192, 193.

ancient district in which he was once a viceroy.   One by one his functions have been taken from him until he now appears simply as a country gentleman, who, may be against his will, has been called upon to perform for a single year a set of disconnected duties, many of which are purely formal, and nearly all of which may be performed by an under-sheriff of his appointment.   He acts as returning officer in parliamentary elections, he receives the judges on their circuits, he summons jurors, and sees to the execution of judgments, both civil and criminal.   In theory only it is still his duty to proclaim in the obsolete county court all the new acts of parliament ; and he still has the immemorial right to quell sudden disturbances by calling out the *posse comitatus*, a proceeding which the justices of the peace and the police constables have long since rendered unnecessary.[1]

present functions of sheriff largely formal.

On its military side, the importance of the sheriff's office was entirely obscured by the rise of that of lord lieutenant, which gradually came into being in the Tudor time, as it became evident that, in order to render the county force more efficient, the sheriff appointed for only a year should be superseded by a permanent commander.   Thus as a revival of the ancient local earldom the lord-lieutenancy was bestowed by a special commission from the crown, usually upon a peer or other great landowner, who, once appointed, generally continues in office for life.[2]   But with the growth of a standing army the county militia became less and less important, and with it dwindled the importance of its permanent commander, until by an act[3] passed in 1871 his military jurisdiction was restored to the source from which it had emanated.   In the mean time, however, he had become the honorary head of the county magistracy, and as such he was appointed by the commission of the peace the keeper of their records, *custos rotulorum*.   In that capacity he still appoints the clerk of the peace, who acts as clerk of the sessions ; and it is usually upon his recommendation that the chancellor, acting in the name of the crown, appoints the justices themselves.

As military head of the county sheriff superseded by lord lieutenant;

revival of the ancient local earldom;

effect of the growth of a standing army on county militia;

lord lieutenant as honorary head of county magistracy;

how the chancellor usually appoints justices of the peace.

[1] "For purposes of county government, therefore, his office is now but of little practical account.   Its interest is historical rather than practical."— Chalmers, *Local Government*, Citizen Ser. p. 95.

[2] See above, p. 198.

[3] By the Army Regulation Act, 34 & 35 Vict., the authority of the lord lieutenant over the county militia has been revested in the crown, to be exercised by the secretary of state for war through officers appointed by his advice.

Coroners still elected in the ancient form ;

office conferred for life, subject to removal ;

a coroner's limited functions.

The right of the counties to elect their own coroners, confirmed by 3 Edw. I. c. 10, still survives ; and when a vacancy occurs the sheriff is commanded by a writ of *De coronatore eligendo* to hold an election in full county court, in which every freeholder has a vote, the result of which proceeding confers the office for life, subject to removal for misconduct by the lord chancellor. But the coroner no longer holds pleas of the crown,[1] and his ancient right to make inquisitions concerning wrecks, treasure-trove, and deodands has become obsolete. He must now content himself with holding inquests in cases of violent or sudden deaths, and in discharging the functions of the sheriff in the event of the disability of that officer.

Decline of the ancient police system ;

liability of every man to serve as constable practically without compensation ;

ancient system superseded by that of paid policemen ;

Peel's act of 1829 creating Metropolitan Police Force ;

An explanation has heretofore been made of the manner in which the high constables, originally chosen at the courts-leet of the hundred or franchise, came to be appointed by the justices at their quarter sessions, a practice afterwards extended to the petty constables as well. From the right of appointment naturally followed the right of dismissal, and in that way the quarter sessions finally acquired full control over the local constabulary, including even the control of the coroners themselves.[2] Thus every man in the township became liable to serve his turn as constable without compensation, excepting certain lawful fees, and to discharge under the orders of the justices a variety of duties, common law and statutory, chief among which was that of arresting offenders. It is not strange, therefore, that two efforts made by statute in 1831 and 1842 to compel the discharge of such unattractive duties so completely failed to put life into the primitive and worn-out institution that it was found necessary to entirely supersede it by the modern system of paid and trained policemen.[3] The new system developed within the last sixty years has its origin in Sir Robert Peel's act[4] of 1829, which brought into being the Metropolitan Police Force, which in 1830 superseded the "Night Watchmen," and which now has under its control a district extending over a radius of fifteen miles from Charing Cross, exclusive of the ancient City of London, with a popula-

---

[1] Vol. i. p. 319.
[2] Ibid., pp. 192, 193. For the most complete history of the English constabulary, see Gneist, *Self-Government*, §§ 77–82.

[3] F. W. Maitland, *Justice and Police*, Citizen Ser. pp. 103–107.
[4] Hence a policeman is called a *bobby* and a *peeler*.

tion of between six and seven millions, and embracing fourteen police courts. This force, organized on the military plan,
which consisted in 1896 of more than 15,000 men, is under
the direct command of a commissioner and two assistant commissioners, who hold office at the pleasure of the crown, subject to the supreme supervision and control of the Home
Secretary.[1] In 1839 an act was passed authorizing the City
of London to create a similar force, and in the same year the
justices of quarter sessions were permitted to create a paid
county constabulary. The boroughs in the mean time had
acquired through the great scheme of municipal reform inaugurated in 1835 the right to have a body of paid constables
under the control of the town council. The failure, however,
of many counties to adopt the permissive act of 1839 resulted
in such confusion that a new compulsory statute was passed
in 1856 forcing the new system upon them, — the first law for
all England requiring that there should be paid policemen.
Although the county force thus organized is subject to the
general control of the Home Secretary, who asserts his authority through royal commissioners upon whose favorable report
only can be obtained a treasury subvention, still the justices
of quarter sessions are permitted to appoint and dismiss the
chief constable with the permission of the Home Secretary,
and in the same way to increase or diminish the number of
constables to be employed, fixed by them in the first instance.
In the City of London, as in the rest of the boroughs, the police
is virtually under the control of the civic corporation.[2]

The justices in quarter sessions who were thus stripped of
their supreme control over the county police force have also
been deprived of their right to regulate the administrative
affairs of their counties by the Local Government Act, 1888,[3]
vesting such right in elective county councils. The system of
county government by quarter sessions, which was strictly
non-representative, was carried on by justices of the peace
appointed by the crown, generally from the landlord class, who

[sidenotes:] subject to supreme control of the Home Secretary; acts of 1839 creating like force for City of London, and paid county constabulary; paid constables for the towns; act of 1856 requiring paid police-men for all England; control of Home Secretary over the county force. City of London police. Quarter sessions superseded in part by county councils; Local Government Act, 1888;

---

[1] See the article on the subject in
Whitaker's Almanack, 1897.

[2] "Thus the police forces of England are (1) the metropolitan force, (2)
county forces, (3) borough forces, (4)
the city of London force. . . . In 1882–

83, the numbers of the men in these
several forces were: . . . total, 34,488.
Population (last census) 25,974,439."
— F. W. Maitland, *Justice and Police*,
Citizen Ser. p. 110, note 2.

[3] 51 & 52 Vict. c. 41.

met four times a year, not only to attend to the minor judicial work of the county, but also to perform all local legislative and administrative work, including the levying of the county tax, the management of roads and bridges, and the grant of liquor licenses.   As all the greater towns within the counties had won through the Municipal Corporations Acts the right to reg-

motive for its enactment;

ulate their local affairs through representative municipal councils chosen by their own citizens, it was considered no more than just that those who dwelt outside of the towns should be endowed with the same privilege.   In order to accomplish that end was enacted the Ritchie Act, 1888, which has given to the English counties elective councils organized on the same general plan as those of the municipalities.[1]   The first effort at

its great defect;

local government reform thus made was, however, very incomplete, because the formation of subordinate district councils for subdivisions of the county contemplated by the act was never carried out.   In order to complete the scheme by supplying that deficiency Mr. Fowler introduced his measure,

Local Government Act, 1894;

which passed as the Local Government Act,[2] 1894, whose primary purpose was to transform the vestries into district councils, and thus to restore local autonomy under a purely democratic system, similar in many respects to the township

its leading provisions;

system of the United States.[3]   By that act "A parish council was, at the appointed day in the year 1894, called into existence in every parish situate in a rural sanitary district which had a population of three hundred or upwards at the census of 1891. Where the population amounts to one hundred but is less than three hundred, a parish council is to be established by means of an order of the county council, if the parish meeting so resolves ; while in parishes where the population is less than one hundred, the county council may establish a parish council with the consent of the parish meeting.   Parishes may also be grouped under a common parish council by an order of the county council, but not without the consent of each member

"the hierarchy of local authorities is complete;"

of the group."[4]   Thus "the hierarchy of local authorities is complete by the creation of parish councils for rural parishes. . . .   The system of Local Government which is established by

---

[1] Shaw, *Municipal Government in Great Britain*, p. 240.
[2] 56 & 57 Vict. c. 73.

[3] Shaw, *Municipal Government in Great Britain*, pp. 254, 255, 257.
[4] *The Local Govt. Act, 1894*, Macmorran and Dill, Introd. p. xxxv.

this Act is founded upon the principle of the direct popular representation of parishes. For this purpose an electorate is formed by taking the registers of parliamentary and of local government (county council) electors which relate to a parish so as to form a list of 'parochial electors,' and the right of a person to vote at an election under this Act, whether of parish or district councillors or guardians, will depend upon whether his name is or is not inserted upon the list of parochial electors for the parish or ward which forms or is included in the area for which the election is held. . . . For the purposes of *enfranchisement of married women.* this Act, a married woman who would be qualified to be an elector, but for the disability of coverture, will be entitled to have her name inserted on any local government register and to vote at the election of any of the authorities whose election is governed by this Act." [1]

While the ancient courts and magistrates of the county have *Subdivision of counties for judicial and parliamentary purposes;* thus been forced to yield to new institutions, the county itself as a local division for judicial and parliamentary purposes has not escaped the reorganization and dividing hand of modern innovation. Through a construction given to a statute of 1278, the contentious jurisdiction of the ancient county courts, *jurisdiction of ancient county courts limited to forty shillings;* which had long ago ceased to do much business, was confined to forty shillings, a limit that became narrower and narrower as that sum sank in relative value.[2] Thus this inadequate provision for local justice in small matters lingered on until 1846,[3] *new system of county courts organized under act of 1846;* when a new system of county courts was provided by statute whose jurisdiction, fixed first at £20, was soon raised to £50 in ordinary actions for debt or damage, with the right to enforce certain contracts even when as much as £500 is at stake. Under the simple procedure that prevails in these courts an *their simple procedure;* intelligent suitor can conduct his own cause, which is usually heard by a judge alone, who decides both law and fact. With his leave in any case, and without it in any claim that exceeds

---

[1] *The Local Govt. Act, 1894*, Macmorran and Dill, Introd. pp. xxxi, xxxii.

[2] "The discovery of Mexico and Peru altered the meaning of several rules of English law, the letter of which remains unchanged; it extended the county franchise and the sphere of capital crimes; it also made

our petty tribunals very petty indeed." — Maitland, *Justice and Police*, Citizen Ser. p. 22.

[3] County Court Act, 1846, 9 & 10 Vict. c. 95. For the several amendments to this act, see Lely and Foulkes, *Judicature Acts*, pp. 608–612. The most important amendments are those made in 1850, 1856, 1867, 1868, 1875.

trial by
jury ;

£5, a trial by a jury, to be composed of only five jurors, may be demanded. The connection between these statutory creations and the ancient county courts in which the freeholders, under the presidency of the sheriff, were the judges is, however, little more than in name. The new county courts differ from the old not only as to procedure and limit of jurisdiction,

geographi-
cal areas ;

but also as to the geographical areas over which such jurisdiction extends. The ancient county court was a court for the whole county; the new is a court for an arbitrary subdivision

all England
divided,
regardless
of county
lines, into
491
districts ;
which are
grouped in
circuits ;

of a county. By the original act all England, except the City of London, was subdivided regardless of county lines into 491 county court districts, which by orders in council have been somewhat increased. The districts are grouped in circuits, to each of which is usually assigned a single judge. Each district has generally but one place at which its court is held; and the rule is that any one may be sued in the court of that district

county cut
up into
divisions
for electoral
purposes ;

in which he dwells or carries on business.[1] As heretofore explained, the counties have also been cut up into divisions for electoral purposes. The immemorial right of each county to have two parliamentary representatives has been forced to give

"single-seat
system."

way to the new "single-seat system," under which the counties have been broken into divisions in proportion to their population, each division being entitled to return one member.[2]

Origin of
the system
of national
education :

The feeble tentative effort that has grown into the existing system of national education in England was made in the very year in which the reform bill of 1832 passed into law. Then it was that the state recognized for the first time its duty to aid at least in the work of instructing those by whom it was to

annual
grant first
applied
through two
religious
societies ;

be governed. The beginning consisted of an annual grant of £20,000, made at the instance of the executive government for public education, which for six years was applied by the treasury through two great religious societies, upon certain conditions, in aid of local efforts for the building of school-

how Educa-
tion De-
partment
of privy
council
was con-
stituted;

houses for the poor. In order to give harmonious direction to the work, by an order in council made in 1839 a special committee of that body was charged with its control, and a special staff of officers and inspectors engaged to aid in its execution.

[1] For a good commentary on the act, see Maitland, *Justice and Police*, Citizen Ser. pp. 20–30.

[2] See above, p. 548.

Thus the Education Department of the privy council was constituted. Not, however, until 1870 did this primary effort, which only assumed to aid the work of national education, develop into the wider scheme under which the state then undertook to "complete the voluntary system, and to fill up the gaps" that might be found to exist in it in any community. Such Mr. Forster declared to be the object of his Elementary Education Act,[1] that became law in August of that year, founding a system which has prevailed without fundamental change down to the present time. By that act England and Wales were mapped out into school districts, based as a general rule upon the principle that every borough under the Municipal Corporations Acts constitutes a district, every parish not in a borough a district, — the Education Department being authorized at the same time to combine two or more of such districts into a new whole. Every school district must be under the control of a local authority known either as a School Board or as a School Attendance Committee. Whenever the local authorities fail to supply sufficient public school accommodation, it becomes the duty of the Education Department, after due notice, to cause such a board to be elected for the district, and at such election every ratepayer has the right to vote. A board thus constituted becomes a corporation, and its members hold office for three years. The school fund administered by such boards at first consisted (1) of parliamentary grants in aid of permanent improvements; (2) of fees paid by children; (3) of the proceeds of a compulsory local rate, which the board can collect with the aid of the proper rating authority. In boroughs such rate is levied as a part of the borough rate; in parishes outside of boroughs as a part of the poor rate. As a settlement of the religious difficulty that had long been a stumbling-block in the way of a uniform and compulsory system of education, a compromise was embodied in the act in the form of a "conscience clause," that permitted children to come for secular instruction, although they were withdrawn from all religious teaching. With that understanding the school boards were permitted to try the experi-

Elementary Education Act of 1870;

scheme embodied in it;

duty of Education Department when local authorities fail;

sources of the school fund;

how the rate is levied in boroughs and parish; settlement of the religious difficulty; a "conscience clause;"

---

[1] 33 & 34 Vict. c. 75, called "the charter of national education. That act has been several times amended by subsequent statutes, but only for the purpose of supplementing and working out the details of the original scheme." — Chalmers, *Local Government,* Citizen Ser. p. 124.

how far
the system
is com-
pulsory;

ment, new in England, of compelling children of certain ages to attend school, under certain conditions, through by-laws made with the consent of the Education Department. But under the act of 1870 a school board could be established in a district only in the event that adequate school accommodation was not supplied by voluntary effort ; and in the event that the vote of those who would be electors went in favor of such a

act of 1876
providing
for School
Attendance
Com-
mittees;

board. To meet such contingencies a supplementary act was passed in 1876, providing that where no school board exists a School Attendance Committee shall be constituted for the purpose, among other things, of enforcing school attendance. Still another act was necessary, however, to make compulsory attendance, under strictly defined rules, the general law for the whole country. "To do this was the object of the short

Mr. Mun-
della's act
of 1880;

but comprehensive act passed by Mr. Mundella in 1880. That act made the framing of bye-laws, which had before been op-tional in the case of School Boards, an imperative duty for every Board which had not already framed them ; and in the case of School Attendance Committees, not only was the necessity for the previous requisition of the ratepayers done away with, but it became the duty of these Committees — and not merely a matter of choice — that they should frame bye-laws forth-

act of 1891
providing
for "free
education."

with." [1] The most important act upon the general subject since that time is perhaps that of 1891, introducing what is called the system of "free education," under which the parent has been relieved of the obligation to pay fees.

Creation of
Boards of
Health
under the
act of
1848;

The advance of the science of public hygiene led to the enactment of the Public Health Act of 1848, which authorized the crown to appoint a General Board of Health, with power to create through orders in council local boards, — in some cases upon its own motion, and in others on the petition of

how created
in munici-
pal bor-
oughs, ex-
cepting the
Metropolis;
Public
Health Act
of 1875,
the present
sanitary
code;

the ratepayers. In municipal boroughs the town council was constituted the local board, while the Metropolis was excepted from the terms of the act altogether. After the original scheme had been amended and extended piecemeal by many subsequent enactments, it was repealed by the Public Health Act of 1875, which embodied at that date the entire English sanitary code. The two facts to be specially noted in connec-

[1] Craik, *The State in its Relation to Education*, Citizen Ser. p. 117. See, also, Owen's *Education Acts Manual*, 15th ed. Introd.

tion with this new creation are : first, that when the original board of health was permitted to expire, its functions, which were for a time divided between the home office and the privy council, were finally vested in 1871 in the Local Government Board then created ; second, that by the Public Health Act of 1872 through which the whole of England, except the Metropolis, was divided for sanitary purposes into districts, either urban or rural, the boundaries not of the parishes but of the poor law unions were adopted as the boundaries of the rural sanitary districts, while the guardians of such unions and not the parish vestry were made the rural sanitary authority. Thus the confession was again made that the ancient unit of the constitutional machinery was not equal to the requirements of the new department of public hygiene, whose local administration was intrusted to a statutory creation, while its general direction and control was vested in a central bureau dominated by experts who can apply their authority to the sanitary affairs of every locality not only in the form of advice, but in the way of administrative and financial control.

functions of original Board of Health finally vested in Local Government Board;

how the boundaries of rural sanitary districts are defined;

inadequacy of parish organization to demands of modern sanitary science.

From the brief review which has now been made of the legislation enacted since the reform bill of 1832 for the purpose of remodelling and elaborating the entire system of local self-government as originally embodied in the counties, towns, and parishes of England, it clearly appears that the necessity for the sweeping changes thus made grew out of the fact that the primitive local machinery that was perfectly adapted to the simple wants of earlier times had ceased to be adequate to the complex and ever-increasing demands of a progressive and enlightened modern society. The plain fact was that modern England had outgrown the local institutions of ancient England, and out of that condition of things arose the necessity for the creation of new statutory agencies in the form of local boards that could be specially commissioned to execute each new demand as it arose. As a result the country has been enveloped in a network of local jurisdictions, each with its own boundaries, its own staff of officials, and its own power to levy rates. As a special student of the subject has lately expressed it : "Local government in this country may be fitly described as consisting of a chaos of areas, a chaos of authorities, and a chaos of rates. Mr. Rathbone stated in the house of com-

The Local Government Board:

inadequacy of ancient local machinery forced creation of new statutory agencies;

their vast and complex organization

mons that in the place where he lived there were no less than thirty-five different local authorities. The local government areas into which England and Wales are divided may be enumerated as follows: There are 52 counties, — 40 in England and 12 in Wales, — 239 municipal boroughs, 70 Improvement Act districts, 1006 urban sanitary districts, 41 port sanitary authorities, and 577 rural sanitary districts; 2051 school-board districts, 424 highway districts, 853 burial-board districts, 649 unions, 194 lighting and watching districts, 14,946 poor-law parishes, 5064 highway parishes not included in urban or highway districts, and about 13,000 ecclesiastical parishes. The total number of local authorities who tax the English ratepayer is 27,069, and they tax him by means of 18 different kinds of rates." [1]   In the effort to remedy the confusion and uncertainty that arose out of the isolated action of such a vast number of almost independent local bodies, the necessity was recognized for the existence of some central authority that could officially correspond with the local agencies, keep them in motion, supervise and direct their action, and supply them with a higher skill and information — so indispensable for the proper exercise of their numerous and delicate functions — than they could possibly obtain through their own unaided efforts. The great truth was thus recognized that "Power may be localized, but knowledge to be most useful must be centralized. There must be somewhere a focus at which all its scattered rays are collected, that the broken and coloured lights which exist elsewhere may find there what is necessary to complete and purify them. The central authority ought to keep open a perpetual communication with the localities, informing itself by their experience, and them by its own, giving advice freely when asked, and volunteering it when it seems to be required." [2]   The ideal so beautifully portrayed by the great English philosopher was approached in that cautious, tentative, sure way by which English statesmen usually solve great problems, by gradually widening an imperfect beginning into a well-rounded and complete system. When in 1834 the poor-law system was remodelled, its direction and control was vested in a temporary central commission made permanent in

Marginal notes:
forced creation of a controlling central authority;

"power may be localized, but knowledge to be most useful must be centralized;"

---

[1] Chalmers, *Local Government*, Citizen Ser. pp. 17, 18. See, also, p. 158.

[2] J. S. Mill, *Representative Government*, ch. xv.

1847 as the Poor Law Board, whose presidency was then con- Poor Law Board, 1847; ferred upon a responsible minister with a seat in the house of commons.[1]   In the same way a central control was exercised by the privy council over vaccination and the prevention of disease, while the home office was charged with certain powers and duties touching the public health and sanitation, local taxation and local government, including local returns, public and town improvements, and artisans' and laborers' dwellings.[2] In order to concentrate this divided authority in a single central body was passed the Local Government Board Act,[3] 1871, Local Government Board, 1871; which recites that "it is expedient to concentrate in one department of the Government the supervision of the laws relating to public health, the relief of the poor, and local government."   For the execution of those duties the act created a Local Government Board, consisting of "a president to be appointed by her majesty, and to hold office during the pleasure of her majesty," and of the lord president of the council, of all the secretaries of state, of the lord privy seal, and of the chancellor of the exchequer as *ex officio* members.   The body thus constituted not only superseded the Poor Law Board, but it also became the depository of the powers and duties touching the public health and local government exercised at that time by the privy council and home office.   Since 1871 the Local Government Board, whose powers and duties have been greatly expanded by subsequent statutes, has developed into a central force, whose influence is exercised through its adminis- general scope of its powers and duties. trative, financial, and advisory control over the entire system of local administration.   Only by an examination of one of its voluminous annual reports to parliament,[4] including among other things exhaustive returns as to local taxation and expenditures, loans and debts, can the wide range of its jurisdiction be at all clearly understood.   It is authorized of its own motion to *initiate* a variety of acts in various localities without reference to the local authorities ; it can likewise *remedy* many of the omissions of such authorities by its own immediate action ; and can also *supervise* through its inspectors their proceedings

[1] See above, p. 572.
[2] Traill, *Central Government*, Citizen Ser. pp. 134, 135; Chalmers, *Local Government*, Citizen Ser. pp. 150, 151.
[3] 34 & 35 Vict. c. 70.

[4] See the Twenty-fifth Annual Report of the Local Government Board, 1895–96, presented to both houses of parliament by command of Her Majesty, embracing 689 pages.

in many important particulars. Under this last head should be noted the duty of the board to audit the accounts of most of the local authorities, excepting the municipal boroughs and counties, and to pass upon the making of local loans not authorized by special acts.[1]

Transfer of personal obligations of citizenship to paid officials;

There can be no doubt that this reorganized and business-like system of local self-government directed by a central bureau at London does differ in several material particulars from the ancient régime it has superseded, — one of the greatest of such differences consisting of the transfer of the personal obligation and responsibility of every member of a local community to perform public functions to paid officials, who

the case as stated by Dr. R. Gneist;

assume their exercise for a definite compensation. Dr. Rudolph Gneist, notable for his researches into the history of self-government in England, ventured not long ago to prophesy that the apparently vital change thus made at the very foundation of the English constitution would produce gravely disastrous consequences throughout the entire superstructure. He declared that "With this fatal step, that of *doing away with every personal obligation and responsibility* within the *communa*, the roots of the whole structure have been eradicated, and this change, but little noticed, will be productive of more momentous consequences for England than the abolition of universal military service would for modern Germany. Here is *the organic fault in the political system of modern England*, a fault productive of even acuter symptoms. With this abolition of the personal duties of citizenship, the community actually passes into a *limited company* system, which quite erroneously goes by the name of self-government. . . . Thus arose the modern system of internal government by 'boards,' which, in its centralization and '*tutelle administrative*,' is very similar to the French. But, together with the responsibility, the essential part of the official *influence* passed to the paid officials, and left only inferior functions to the remaining local commissions and honorary officers, so much so that the inclination of the upper classes to take part in it disappears more and more, and more still that of the justices of the peace to share in such a

---

[1] As to the powers of the board, see Shaw, *Municipal Government in Great Britain*, p. 68; Chalmers, *Local Government*, pp. 151–160; Traill, *Central Government*, pp. 133–139.

piece of business, where they are even made *ex officio* members." This desire to escape from personal responsibility, the author declares, has given rise to the "demand for a ballot, by which the elector completely isolates himself, and declines all moral responsibility, just as the representative of the parish refuses all legal responsibility. The bureaucracy humored public opinion here also, by the invention of nomination papers, sparing the electors all trouble of meeting, deliberating, consulting, and counting; thus reducing the act of electing to a few strokes of the pen, which the elector puts upon his voting paper. This is the last residuum of self-government, the sole trouble with which the industrial society of these days believes itself capable of exercising and asserting the 'sovereignty of the people.'"[1] Nothing has transpired during the sixteen years that have elapsed since that rashly premature prophecy was made to indicate that it rests upon any substantial foundation whatever. The fundamental error upon which it proceeds is the assumption that as a society progresses along a line of development that continually demands changes in the methods in which political duties must be performed, such changes cannot be safely made even when there is no departure from the essential principles upon which the constitutional fabric is founded. That no such departure has actually taken place during the statutory process through which the ancient system of local self-government in England has been remodelled and adapted to changed conditions would no doubt have been clear to Dr. Gneist if he had been one of the English people, with conceptions of English law imbedded in his mind as a natural instinct. In that event he would no doubt have perceived that in the recent sweeping reform of the system of local self-government, as in all other English reforms, "The new building has been raised upon the old groundwork; the institutions of one age have always been modelled and formed from those of the preceding and their lineal descent has never been interrupted or disturbed."[2]

his predictions based upon an unfounded assumption;

the new building raised upon the old groundwork.

While the reformed parliaments were thus absorbed in the

[1] Gneist, *Hist. of the Eng. Const.* (Ashworth trans.), pp. 733, 734. The author's preface is dated Berlin, 1882.

[2] Sir Francis Palgrave. See title-page. It is appalling to think what the burdens of English citizenship would now be, if the intricate mass of existing local duties had to be performed personally and not by paid and trained officials.

Reform of the judicial system:

mighty task of reorganizing and systematizing the entire scheme of political administration, central and local, they were not unmindful of the many defects existing in the antiquated judicial machinery of the kingdom that had remained practically unaltered for centuries. As heretofore pointed out, the

creation of new county courts;

inability of the ancient county courts to provide for local justice in small matters prompted the creation in 1846 of a system of statutory county courts, differing from the old not only as to procedure and limit of jurisdiction, but also as to the geographical areas over which such jurisdiction extends.[1] The

how the *curia regis* was subdivided;

drastic hand of innovation that thus began at the roots of the judicial fabric reached in due time the great central courts at Westminster, which have been consolidated into a single tribunal, whose procedure has been placed upon a strictly modern basis. An account has already been given of the process through which the *curia regis* of Norman and Angevin times

three courts of common law;

was finally divided into the three distinct courts of exchequer, common pleas, and king's bench, whose severance from each other was completed when during the reign of Henry III. each received a distinct staff of judges, whose last connecting link was broken by the abolition of the office of justiciar in the reign of Edward I.[2] After that event the only remaining trace of their former unity was represented by the court of exchequer chamber, which sat as a court of mere debate for the hearing of causes of great moment,[3] and also as a court in which judgments of each of the superior courts of common law were subject to review by the judges of the other two

courts of chancery, admiralty, probate, and divorce;

courts sitting collectively as a court of error and appeal.[4] Alongside of the three law courts sat the court of the chancellor, administering equity as distinct from common law; the court of admiralty, with jurisdiction over maritime cases;[5]

---

[1] See above, pp. 579, 580.
[2] Vol. i. pp. 248, 249, 398.
[3] In that capacity it heard Calvin's case, the chancellor and all the judges being present. See above, pp. 228, 229.
[4] By 31 Edw. III. c. 12 was created the first court of exchequer chamber, with power to determine errors from the common law side of the court of exchequer. By 27 Eliz. c. 8 a second court of exchequer chamber was created to pass upon writs of error from the king's bench. By 11 Geo. IV.

and 1 Will. IV. c. 70, s. 8, both were abolished and a new court constituted, in which judgments of each of the superior courts of common law were subject to review by judges of the other two courts sitting collectively as a court of error in the exchequer chamber. Cf. Stephen, *Commentaries*, vol. iii. p. 428. By the Judicature Act of 1873 (s. 18) the jurisdiction of that court was merged in that of the new court of appeals.
[5] Vol. i. pp. 250, 547–551.

the court of probate, substituted by statute[1] in 1857 for the ecclesiastical courts of each diocese that formerly exercised jurisdiction over wills and intestacies, in respect of personal property; and the court of divorce, established at the same time by a statute[2] that vested in it the jurisdiction over matrimonial causes previously exercised by the ecclesiastical courts, together with the power to decree the dissolution of a marriage, until then exercised by parliament alone. The chief difficulty that arose in practice out of this complex system of tribunals administering different codes of law through widely different methods of procedure was that embodied in the conflict between law and equity, whose divergencies were so great that it was often said that a litigant might be pronounced clearly right on one side of Westminster Hall and clearly wrong on the other. To prevent the confusion that thus arose, a feeble and partial effort was first made to declare by statute whether the rules of law or equity were to be followed in particular instances, — the rule of law always being favored by such statutes against that of equity.[3] Not, however, until 1850 did parliament make the first decided attempt to end the conflict by providing for the administration of law and equity in a single tribunal. Then it was that a royal commission appointed to consider the reform of the law courts finally reported that "a consolidation of the elements of a complete remedy in the same court was obviously desirable, not to say imperatively necessary, to the establishment of a consistent and rational system of procedure;" and in the next year the chancery commissioners, looking at the matter from the other point of view, made a report to the same effect. After the Common Law Procedure Acts of 1852 and 1854 and Lord Cairn's Equity Procedure Act of 1859 had failed to attain the end in view by conferring upon each of the conflicting tribunals some of the powers of the other, the Judicature Commission, appointed in 1867 to inquire into the working of all the courts, reported in 1869 that "the first step towards meeting and surmounting the evils complained of would be the consolidation of all the courts of law and equity into one court, in which could be vested all the jurisdiction exercisable by each and all

the conflict between law and equity;

first effort made in 1850 to blend the two systems in one court;

Report of Judicature Commission, 1869;

---

[1] 20 & 21 Vict. c. 77.
[2] 20 & 21 Vict. c. 85.

[3] 11 Geo. IV. and 1 Will. IV. c. 46; 30 & 31 Vict. c. 48, and 31 Vict. c. 4.

the courts so consolidated."[1]   As the result of that report was enacted the Supreme Court of Judicature Act,[2] 1873, which provided that "the High Court of Chancery of England, the Court of Queen's Bench, the Court of Common Pleas at Westminster, the Court of Exchequer, the High Court of Admiralty, the Court of Probate, the Court for Divorce and Matrimonial Causes, *and the London Court of Bankruptcy*,[3] shall be united and consolidated together, and shall constitute, under and subject to the provisions of this act, one Supreme Court of Judicature in England."   The one Supreme Court thus constituted consists of two parts, — "Her Majesty's High Court of Justice," and "Her Majesty's Court of Appeal." The first part, which possesses original jurisdiction, was at first organized in five divisions, called the Chancery Division, the Queen's Bench Division, the Common Pleas Division, the Exchequer Division, and the Probate, Divorce, and Admiralty Division.   But by an order in council made under the authority of the act, the five divisions were reduced to three " by the consolidation and union in one division of all the judges now attached respectively to the Queen's Bench Division, the Common Pleas Division, and the Exchequer Division."[4]   The High Court of Justice is constituted of the lord chancellor, the three chiefs of the former common law courts, the master of the rolls, the three vice-chancellors, twelve of the puisne justices and junior barons of the former courts of common law, the judge of the probate and divorce courts, and the judge of the high court of admiralty.   Thus the old courts were not abolished but consolidated in a single tribunal, that administers in its several divisions law and equity concurrently under a system of rules that favor the principles of equity in cases of conflict.   The second part, which possesses appellate jurisdiction, was originally intended to be a court of last resort, and as such the depository of the appellate jurisdiction of the house of lords and of the privy council ; but in 1876 it was

Margin notes:
Judicature Act of 1873;

Supreme Court of Judicature; the High Court of Justice ;

how constituted ;

the court of appeal;

appellate jurisdiction of lords,

---

[1] Lely and Foulkes, *Judicature Acts*, Introd. pp. xlvii–li.

[2] 36 & 37 Vict. c. 66.

[3] That clause was repealed by the Judicature Act of 1875, s. 9, which provides that "The London Court of Bankruptcy shall not be united or consolidated with the Supreme Court of

Judicature." As to the constitution of that court, see Bankruptcy Act, 1869 (32 & 33 Vict. c. 71).

[4] For the full text of the consolidating order of December 16, 1880, see Lely and Foulkes, *Judicature Acts*, pp. 561–565.

finally decided to retain the appellate jurisdiction of the former. It was provided, however, that no appeal should be entertained in the upper house unless there shall be present at least three "lords of appeal," that is, peers who have held high judicial office.[1] The court of appeal as now constituted is therefore an intermediate court between the high court and the house of lords, and as such it is composed of five *ex officio* judges, of "ordinary" judges, whose number depends upon the will of the crown, and of "three additional ordinary judges," —at present nine in all. *judges composing court of appeal.*

It was originally intended that the act of 1873 should come into operation in November, 1874; but it was found necessary to amend it twice, and in that way the second amending act, the Supreme Court of Judicature Act of 1875,[2] together with the principal act of 1873, did not take effect until the 1st of November, 1875. As early as 1865 parliament had authorized the construction of the splendid pile known as the "Royal Courts of Justice," for the express purpose of "bringing together into one place or neighborhood all the Superior Courts of Law and Equity, the Probate and Divorce Court, and the Court of Admiralty."[3] In 1882 the new structure was dedicated by the queen, and at the beginning of the Hilary sittings, 1883, the consolidated court, moving from its old habitations in Lincoln's Inn and from the quarters adjoining Westminster Hall, took up its abode in one place, where it can the more conveniently execute its mission of administering law and equity concurrently. The entire code of procedure of the Supreme Court of Judicature was originally embodied as a whole in the schedule to the act of 1875; and as such it was divided into orders, each order being subdivided into rules. The power to alter such rules is vested in the "Rule Committee" of the judges, who are directed to present all changes to each house of parliament; and upon the address of either house the crown may be required to annul the same by an order in council.[4] *When Judicature Acts of 1873 and 1875 took effect; consolidated court took possession of its new home in 1883; its code of procedure.*

8. Such in brief is the present condition of the vital organs

[1] The Appellate Jurisdiction Act, 1876, s. 5.
[2] 38 & 39 Vict. c. 77.
[3] Preamble to the Courts of Justice Concentration Act, 1865, 28 & 29 Vict. c. 49.
[4] Upon the whole subject, see the excellent treatise of Lely and Foulkes, *Judicature Acts*, 4th ed.

of the English constitution, and such their relations to each other at the end of ten centuries of unbroken development, which has adapted the primitive institutions of the Old English commonwealth, without any break in their continuity, to the ever-increasing wants of one of the most progressive and powerful of modern societies.   As heretofore explained, the result of the Revolution of 1688 was to shift the centre of gravity of the state from the crown to the popular branch of the legislature.   The statesmen of the Revolution did little more, however, than establish irrevocably a political theory which their posterity have been able to press only in our time to its ultimate and logical conclusion, — a conclusion which was not fully reached until the reform bills of the last sixty years widened the electorate of the house of commons from about 400,000 in 1832 to nearly six millions and a half in 1897.   From that electorate the popular chamber, that embodies and enforces the new principle of sovereignty to which the Revolution gave birth, draws its authority.   The mighty transformation thus brought about in the internal mechanism of the constitution has been effected with the least possible change in its outward forms.   As Bagehot has happily expressed it, this "ancient and ever-altering constitution is like an old man who still wears with attached fondness clothes in the fashion of his youth; what you see of him is still the same; what you do not see is wholly altered." [1]   That profound change thus concealed beneath ancient forms is embodied in the practical effect finally given to the results of the Revolution, by virtue of the arrangement under which the representative chamber now administers the royal authority through a committee of its own members called the cabinet. The outcome of the first efforts made to establish such an arrangement during the reigns of William III., Anne, and the first two Georges was so unsubstantial that George III., during the first ten years of his reign, was able to eliminate it almost entirely.   So completely was he successful that when the mem- bers of the federal convention that met at Philadelphia in 1787 took the English constitution for their model, the modern cabinet system was found to have no place in it either in theory or in fact.   That it did not then exist in theory is put beyond

[1] *The Eng. Const.*, p. 2.

all question by the contemporary works of Blackstone, De Lolme, Paley, and others, who, without even referring to the existence of the cabinet,[1] formulated a doctrine of "checks and balances" absolutely incompatible with it; that it did not then exist in fact is equally certain because at that time the king himself and not the prime minister was the real executive.[2] It was, therefore, held by the doctrinaires at that moment that the supreme sovereignty was vested in a balanced union of three elements, — democratic, aristocratic, and monarchical; that without the concurrence on equal terms of king, lords, and commons, sovereignty could not be properly exercised. The cornerstones of the theory as thus expounded were, first, that the king had the exclusive right to exercise the entire executive authority through ministers appointed by himself and responsible to him alone; second, that the legislative authority was divided between king, lords, and commons as coördinate powers. Only by contrasting that conception of the constitution with that which exists to-day can we estimate the immense change that has actually taken place during the intervening period. The modern ministerial system was so completely in eclipse a century ago that it could not be perceived even by the most acute observers; to-day it is the central figure in the picture, the great driving-wheel that moves the entire constitutional machinery. The indirect source of its power is the electorate; the direct, the house of commons, which is no longer looked upon as a coördinate department, but as a corporate entity in which the supreme sovereignty is vested. Upon the one hand stands the crown, with all its prerogatives vested in a committee of its members; on the other, the house of lords as a mere revising chamber to counsel against the making of rash and ill-advised decrees, to which it must always bow in the last instance. Thus the old literary theory of "checks and balances," based upon the idea of a coördination between separate and coequal powers, has completely broken down in the presence of the incontestable fact that the English constitution now embodies "the close union, the nearly complete fusion, of the executive and legislative powers. No doubt, by the traditional theory as it exists in all the books, the goodness of our constitution consists in

the conception of sovereignty that then prevailed;

only by contrasting that conception with existing conditions can we perceive what has actually taken place;

old literary theory of coördination has yielded to the fact that executive and legislative powers are now blended;

---

[1] See above, p. 503, 504.   [2] Vol. i. p. 69, note 3.

the entire separation of the legislative and executive authority, but in truth its merit consists in their singular approximation. The connecting link is *the cabinet*. By that new word we mean a committee of the legislative body selected to be the executive body." [1]   As that committee draws its authority from an electorate so broad as to be removed only by a single step from manhood suffrage, it may now be safely assumed

mediæval monarchy transformed into an hereditary republic.

that the cycle has come round; that the gradual and silent process of change has been fully worked out through which the mediæval monarchy has been finally transformed into the hereditary republic, in which, under the ancient and still useful forms of the throne and the regalia, the English people is king.

[1] Bagehot, pp. 10, 11.

INDEX.

INDEX.

---

ish a person not a member, 203; claims the right to release a member by authority of the mace, 203, 204; claims the right to determine contested elections, 203; claims the right to punish its members, 203; claims the right to punish bribery at elections, 204; defends its exclusive right to originate money bills, 204; discusses the marriage of Elizabeth, 205; first links the question of succession with that of supply, 205; Elizabeth assaults the right of deliberation in, 205, 206; attempts to assume the initiative in regard to church affairs, 206, 207; growth of privileges under Elizabeth, 208, 209; attacks monopolies, 208, 209; reasserts the right to try contested elections, 220; freedom of arrest of members vindicated, 220; introduces bills against purveyance and wardship, 211; refuses to confer with convocation as to religious question, 221; on the union of England and Scotland, 221; protestation entitled "A Form of Apology and Satisfaction to be delivered to His Majesty," 222; refuse to grant a supply, 223; debate over commissioners' scheme of union between England and Scotland, 227; expels Pigott, 227; discussion of Scottish naturalization in, 227–229; all legislation hostile to Scotland conditionally repealed, 228; discussion of the Great Contract, 230; debate over king's right to levy impositions, 230; discusses purveyance and wardship, 231; discusses the abuse of the ordaining power, 231; asks for the exemption of four Welsh counties from the jurisdiction of the president and council of Wales, 232; fails to secure a redress of ecclesiastical grievances, 232, 233; revives the subject of impositions, 237; impeachment of Mompesson, Mitchell, and Yelverton, 245, 246; impeaches the king's minister, Bacon, 246; attempts to act as a court in Floyd's case, 246; resists the effort of James I. to punish parliamentary misdemeanors, 247, 248; protests against the attempt of James I. to abridge right of deliberation, 248; its privileges and liberties declared a matter of kingly favor, 248; the protestation of December, 1621, 249; grants conditional subsidies to James I., 250; requests Charles I. to enforce laws against catholics, 256; votes two small subsidies, 256; prosecutes Richard Montague, 256; distrusts Buckingham, 257; protests its loyalty to Charles I., 258; lectured by Charles I., 259; impeaches Buckingham, 259; refuses to transact business until Eliot and Digges released, 260; its remonstrance ordered destroyed by Charles I., 262; numerous persons imprisoned by Charles returned as members, 266; resolution denouncing taxation without parliamentary consent,

268; subsidies voted in committee, pending redress of grievances, 268; preparation and adoption of the Petition of Right, 269–273; impeaches Manwaring, 273; withholds subsidy while Charles I. refuses to listen to remonstrances, 273; claims a breach of privilege in the Rolle case, 275, 276; calls customs officers to the bar, 276; resolutions introduced against Arminianism, 277; Charles I.'s efforts to adjourn resisted, 277, 278; Eliot's resolutions on taxation and religion, 278; refuses to discuss subsidies before the question of grievances, 298, 299; secures the execution of Wentworth and Laud, 302–304; all proceedings concerning ship-money annulled, 304, 305; secures acknowledgment that the taxing power is vested in the king in parliament, 305; the Triennial Act, 305, 306; redresses grievances resulting from the conciliar system, 306–308; proposal for a responsible ministry, 311; the Grand Remonstrance, conflict of parties over, 311, 313; case of the five members, 315–317; struggle with king over control of the militia, 317, 318; swears loyalty to Charles I., 322; swears to the Scottish Covenant, 325; appoints Cromwell lieutenant-general, 328; efforts of the peace party in, to come to an understanding with Charles I., 331, 332; the remonstrance of the army presented to, 338; Pride's purge of, 338; declared sovereign by the Rump, 338, 339; as constituted by William of Orange, 410, 411; employs the philosophy of Hobbes in the deposition of James II., 412, 413; regulation of membership by the Act of Settlement, 425; method of coercing refractory ministers, 440; system of party organization in, adopted, 441; question of the right of ministers to sit in, 441–444; new election of members required after appointment to office by crown, 443, 444; attempt to impeach ministers in 1701, 446; addition of Scotch members, 448; becomes a real representative body, 453, 454; increase in membership under Henry VIII. and Charles II., 465; reasons why representation in, was not representative, 463–470; number of persons choosing members small, 470, 471; bribery in, 471, 472; abuse of the trial of contested elections, 472; secrecy in, 473, 474; press forbidden to publish its proceedings without permission, 474; votes and proceedings printed under direction of speaker, 1680, 474; rise of a public opinion destined to make commons independent and representative, 475; right to commit for publication of parliamentary debates lost, 485, 486; publication of division lists, 1836, 486; action on the withdrawal of strangers, 486; efforts for the reform of representation, 519–

The Riverside Press
PRINTED BY H. O. HOUGHTON & CO.
CAMBRIDGE, MASS.
U. S. A.